The Fortunes of Apuleius and the *Golden Ass*

MARTIN CLASSICAL LECTURES

The Martin Classical Lectures are delivered annually at Oberlin College through a foundation established by his many friends in honor of Charles Beebe Martin, for forty-five years a teacher of classical literature and classical art at Oberlin.

John Peradotto, *Man in the Middle Voice: Name and Narration in the Odyssey*

Martha C. Nussbaum, *The Therapy of Desire: Theory and Practice in Hellenistic Ethics*

Josiah Ober, *Political Dissent in Democratic Athens: Intellectual Critics of Popular Rule*

Anne Carson, *Economy of the Unlost (Reading Simonides of Keos with Paul Celan)*

Helene P. Foley, *Female Acts in Greek Tragedy*

Mark W. Edwards, *Sound, Sense, and Rhythm: Listening to Greek and Latin Poetry*

Michael C. J. Putnam, *Poetic Interplay: Catullus and Horace*

Julia Haig Gaisser, *The Fortunes of Apuleius and the Golden Ass: A Study in Transmission and Reception*

The Fortunes of Apuleius and the *Golden Ass*

A STUDY IN TRANSMISSION
AND RECEPTION

Julia Haig Gaisser

PRINCETON UNIVERSITY PRESS
PRINCETON AND OXFORD

Copyright © 2008 by the trustees of Oberlin College

Requests for permission to reproduce material from this work should be sent to
Permissions, Princeton University Press

Published by Princeton University Press, 41 William Street, Princeton, New Jersey 08540
In the United Kingdom: Princeton University Press, 3 Market Place, Woodstock,
Oxfordshire OX20 1SY

All Rights Reserved

Library of Congress Cataloging-in-Publication Data

Gaisser, Julia Haig.
  The fortunes of Apuleius and the Golden Ass: a study in transmission and
reception / Julia Haig Gaisser.
     p. cm. — (Martin classical lectures)
  Includes bibliographical references and index.
  ISBN: 978-0-691-13136-8 (hardback: alk. paper)
  1. Apuleius. Metamorphoses. 2. Latin fiction—History and criticism. 3. Latin wit
and humor—History and criticism. I. Title.
  PA6217.G35 2008
  873.009—dc22   2007020949

British Library Cataloging-in-Publication Data is available

This book has been composed in Sabon

Printed on acid-free paper. ∞

press.princeton.edu

Printed in the United States of America

10 9 8 7 6 5 4 3 2 1

For T. K. G.

Contents

List of Illustrations	ix
Preface	xi
CHAPTER 1 Apuleius: A Celebrity and His Image	1
CHAPTER 2 Exemplary Behavior: The *Golden Ass* from Late Antiquity to the Prehumanists	40
CHAPTER 3 A Mixed Reception: Interpreting and Illuminating the *Golden Ass* in the Fourteenth Century	76
CHAPTER 4 Making an Impression: From Florence to Rome and from Manuscript to Print	129
CHAPTER 5 Telling Tales: The *Golden Ass* in Ferrara and Mantua	173
CHAPTER 6 Apuleius Redux: Filippo Beroaldo Comments on the *Golden Ass*	197
CHAPTER 7 Speaking in Tongues: Translations of the *Golden Ass*	243
CONCLUSION The Fortunes of Apuleius and the *Golden Ass*	296
APPENDIX 1 Ancient Readers of Apuleius (ca. 350 to ca. 550 AD)	300
APPENDIX 2 Manuscripts of Apuleius' *Metamorphoses*	302
APPENDIX 3 Extant Manuscripts of the *Metamorphoses* Written before 1400	309

APPENDIX 4
The Florentine Connection   311

APPENDIX 5
Adlington and His Sources for *Met.* 11.1   315

Bibliography   319

Index of Manuscripts   355

General Index   357

Illustrations

PLATES

1. Constantinische Deckenmalerei. Bischöfliches Dom- und Diözesanmuseum, Trier.
2. Cupid and Psyche. Constantinische Deckenmalerei, Detail. Bischöfliches Dom- und Diözesanmuseum, Trier.
3. Apuleius. Constantinische Deckenmalerei, Detail. Bischöfliches Dom- und Diözesanmuseum, Trier.
4. Apuleius on a Roman contorniate. Cabinet des Médailles, Paris 17163. Bibliothéque Nationale de France.
5. Apuleius as a philosopher. Biblioteca Apostolica Vaticana, Vat. lat. 2193, fol. 1.
6. Apuleius as a writer. Biblioteca Apostolica Vaticana, Vat. lat. 2193, fol. 19v.
7. Apuleius as a magician or scholar. Biblioteca Apostolica Vaticana, Vat. lat. 2193, fol. 27r.
8. Apuleius as the Ass. Biblioteca Apostolica Vaticana, Vat. lat. 2193, fol. 43r.
9. The Theological Virtues in the initial *A* of the *Golden Ass*. Biblioteca Apostolica Vaticana, Vat. lat. 2194, fol. 1r.
10. Lucius in bed. Biblioteca Apostolica Vaticana, Vat. lat. 2194, fol. 5v.
11. Psyche in Cupid's garden. Biblioteca Apostolica Vaticana, Vat. lat. 2194, fol. 24r.
12. Psyche in Ceres' temple. Biblioteca Apostolica Vaticana, Vat. lat. 2194, fol. 30r.
13. The Ass and the bucket of water. Biblioteca Apostolica Vaticana, Vat. lat. 2194, fol. 48v.
14. Lucius bathing by moonlight. Biblioteca Apostolica Vaticana, Vat. lat. 2194, fol. 65v.
15. The story of Psyche from her conception to the flight of Cupid. Cassone panel by the Argonaut Master. Staatliche Museen zu Berlin: Gemäldegalerie (cat. 1823). Photo: Jörg Peter Anders.
16. The story of Psyche from her wanderings to her marriage with Cupid. Cassone panel by the Argonaut Master. Staatliche Museen zu Berlin: Gemäldegalerie (cat. 1824). Photo: Jörg Peter Anders.

x • List of Illustrations

17. Apuleius in a Byzantine cap. Firenze, Biblioteca Laurenziana, ms. Laur. Plut. 54.13, fol. 1r. Su concessione del Ministero per i Beni e le Attività Culturali. È vietata ogni ulteriore riproduzione con qualsiasi mezzo.
18. Apuleius' works in a Platonic context. Firenze, Biblioteca Laurenziana, ms. Laur. Plut. 84.24, fol. 1v. Su concessione del Ministero per i Beni e le Attività Culturali. È vietata ogni ulteriore riproduzione con qualsiasi mezzo.
19. Transformation of Lucius in Niklas von Wyle's *Der goldene Esel* (Strassburg, ca. 1478, reprint of the Augsburg edition of ca. 1477). Wolfenbüttel, Herzog August Bibliothek, 130 Quodl. 2°(3).
20. Frontispiece of *Lucii Apuleii fabulosa enarratio de nuptiis Psyche* by Andreas Ernnst [Erfurt, ca. 1515]. Wolfenbüttel, Herzog August Bibliothek, G 507.4° Helmst. (10).

FIGURES

1. Filippo Beroaldo, *Commentarii in Asinum aureum Lucii Apuleii* (Bologna, 1500), fol. 3r. Rare Book and Manuscript Library, Van-Pelt-Dietrich Library, University of Pennsylvania, Folio Inc. A-938. 204
2. The Ass and the amorous matron in Pseudo-Lucian's *Asinus Aureus* (Augsburg, 1477).The Pierpont Morgan Library, New York. PML 145. Photographic credit: The Pierpont Morgan Library, New York. 246
3. Title page of Johann Sieder's *Ain schön lieblich auch kurtzweylig gedichte Lucii Apuleii von ainem gulden Esel.* (Augsburg, 1538). Wolfenbüttel, Herzog August Bibliothek. Lh4° 7. 254
4. *Baptesel*. Martin Luther and Phillip Melanchthon, *Deuttung der czwo grewliche[n] Figuren: Bapstesels czu Rom. und Munchkalbs zu Freyberg ynn Meysszen funden* (Wittenberg, 1523). Division of Rare and Manuscript Collections, Carl A. Kroch Library, Cornell University, BR336 D4 1523. 255
5. Title page of Guillaume Michel's *Lucius apuleius de Lasne dore* (Paris, 1518). The Pierpont Morgan Library, New York. Purchase; 1949. NNPM PML 41001. Photographic credit: The Pierpont Morgan Library, New York. 263
6. Title page of Diego López de Cortegana's *Lucio Apuleyo del asno de oro* (Medina del Campo, 1543). Hispanic Society of America. 276

Preface

Apuleius' *Metamorphoses* (often called the *Golden Ass*) is the only complete Latin novel to have come down to us. This book examines the causes and mechanisms of its survival and the ways in which it was read and interpreted from antiquity through the sixteenth century. The history of these intersecting and interrelated themes of transmission and reception is not unlike the plot of the *Golden Ass*—full of adventures, chance meetings, mistaken identity, opportunism, and narrow escapes. It is inextricably linked with the reception of Apuleius himself; his reputation as a philosopher, together with perceptions of the personality or "image" he projected in his works, shaped later interpretations of the *Golden Ass* and contributed to its survival.

I began to think about the *Golden Ass* quite by chance over twenty years ago when I came upon a little manuscript bound into a Renaissance edition of Catullus. Its text, irresistibly entitled *Lepida fabula de adulterio* (A Charming Tale of Adultery), turned out to be an obscene sixteenth-century pastiche of the adultery stories in book 9 of the *Golden Ass*. Unaccountably inspired by this deplorable work (which will not appear elsewhere in this volume), I agreed to write the article on Apuleius for the *Catalogus Translationum et Commentariorum* and started to collect material on Apuleius' manuscripts and interpretations. But other projects intervened, and I made little progress. An invitation from the Department of Classics at Oberlin College to deliver the Martin Classical Lectures provided me with the stimulus and opportunity to work on Apuleius in earnest. I thought that it might be fun to talk about the reception of the *Golden Ass*. And indeed it was.

Following the fortunes of Apuleius and his novel has turned out to be even more rewarding than I imagined. The reception of the *Golden Ass* is wonderfully diverse, including literary, critical, and artistic interpretation in a variety of periods and genres. Its fortunes both intersect with and illuminate each of the major events in the transmission of classical literature, providing us with the opportunity to observe the novel at each step in the series: the transition from roll to codex, transcription in a monastic scriptorium, rediscovery at the beginning of the Renaissance, the transition from manuscript to print, university teaching, and finally the appearance of the translated book as a commercial product.

This book is based on the four Charles Beebe Martin Classical Lectures I presented at Oberlin College in the spring of 2000. I called the lectures

"Transformations of Apuleius," but my present title is intended to be more descriptive and at least slightly more precise. I have expanded the original four lectures to seven chapters to fill in lacunae in the original presentation. I have also devoted even more attention to the visual reception of Apuleius and the *Golden Ass* than I did in the lectures, since the numerous artistic representations in paintings, manuscripts, and printed books have much to say about the interpretations and mind-set of their makers. Without them the story of the fortunes of Apuleius and his novel would be one-sided and incomplete. All quotations from Latin and other languages have been translated; the translations, unless otherwise noted, are my own.

Some portions of my discussions of Fulgentius, Boccaccio, and Beroaldo have appeared in earlier versions: "Teaching Classics in the Renaissance: Two Case Histories" (Presidential Address to the American Philological Association: *TAPA*, 2001); "Allegorizing Apuleius: Fulgentius, Boccaccio, Beroaldo, and the Chain of Receptions" (*Acta Conventus Neo-Latini Cantabrigiensis*, 2003); "Reading Apuleius with Filippo Beroaldo" (in *Being There Together: Essays in Honor of Michael C. J. Putnam on the Occasion of His Seventieth Birthday*, 2003); "Filippo Beroaldo on Apuleius: Bringing Antiquity to Life" (in *On Renaissance Commentaries*, 2005); "Apuleius in Florence: From Boccaccio to Lorenzo de' Medici" (in *Classica et Beneventana: Essays Presented to Virginia Brown on the Occasion of Her 65th Birthday*, 2007).

The happiest part of completing any long project is the opportunity to thank all those who made it possible. My greatest thanks must go to the Charles Beebe Martin Lecture Fund and to the Department of Classics at Oberlin College for their invitation, their hospitality, their splendid collegiality, and their patience in waiting for this book. More than they know, Nate Greenberg, Jim Helm, and Tom Van Nortwick influenced this final product. I am also grateful both to the National Endowment for the Humanities and to Bryn Mawr College for their support.

Anyone who ventures into the waters of reception is soon out of her depth and needs the help of friends who know the shoals and currents of foreign times and places. I have benefited from the generosity of many who helped me navigate strange waters from late antiquity to sixteenth-century Germany and France and places in between. They include Oliver Nicholson, Benjamin Todd Lee, Carol Kaske, James John, Frank Coulson, Danuta Shanzer, Greg Hays, Ann Kuttner, Erika Simon, Francis Newton, Michael Maas, John Duffy, Marianne Pade, Bruce Swann, Patricia Osmond, Craig Kallendorf, Stella Revard, David Marsh, Lawrence Buck, Anna Grotans, Walther Ludwig, Philip Ford, and Ann Moss. My Bryn Mawr colleagues have assisted me in countless ways; in particular

I want to thank Pat McPherson, Alice Donohue, Dale Kinney, Darby Scott, David Cast, Nancy Dersofi, Peter Koelle, and Roberta Ricci. I have been helped time and again by many librarians, but especially Robert Babcock of the Beinecke Library and John Pollack of the Van Pelt-Dietrich Library of the University of Pennsylvania, as well as Anne Slater, Andrew Patterson, Charles Burke, Eric Pumroy, Marianne Hansen, Camilla MacKay, and Elliott Shore of the Bryn Mawr College Library. And finally, I owe special thanks to Helen North, Nico and Kezia Knauer, James O'Donnell, Virginia Brown, and James Hankins for the gift of their learning and friendship.

Bryn Mawr, Pennsylvania
December 2006

The Fortunes of Apuleius and the *Golden Ass*

CHAPTER 1

Apuleius: A Celebrity and His Image

> Don't you know that there is nothing a man would rather look at than his own form?
> —*Apuleius,* Apology

Apuleius is best known today for his racy novel, the *Golden Ass (Asinus Aureus)*, or *Metamorphoses* (both titles were current in antiquity); but he also gained celebrity and fortune in his own time as a Platonic philosopher and skillful rhetorician. He claimed to cultivate both philosophy and the nine Muses (*Fl.* 20.6), and the diversity of his writings is so great that one can almost believe him.[1]

Most of what we know about his life comes from Apuleius himself, particularly from comments in the *Florida* (excerpts from his epideictic orations) and the *Apology*, or *De Magia* (On Magic), in which he defends himself against a charge of practicing magic.[2] He was born in North Africa, probably in Madauros (modern Mdaourouch in Algeria), in the mid-120s AD. After his early education in Carthage, he spent several years studying in Athens, drinking deeply, as he says, of the cups of the Muses: "the cup of poetry, made with artifice, the clear cup of geometry, the sweet cup of music, the dry one of dialectic, and the one of which a person can never have enough—the nectarlike cup of all philosophy."[3] In this period he probably traveled elsewhere in the Greek east, almost surely to Samos and perhaps to Phrygia as well.[4] He then moved on to

---

[1] In addition to the *Golden Ass*, Apuleius' extant works include erotic poetry, forensic and epideictic oratory, and philosophical orations and treatises. For detailed accounts of his oeuvre, including fragmentary and lost works, see Hijmans, "Apuleius, Philosophus Platonicus," 398, 408–12; Harrison, *Apuleius*, 10–38. For the title of the novel, see n. 130 below. For Apuleius as a Platonist, see Gersh, *Middle Platonism and Neoplatonism* 1: 215–328.

[2] For Apuleius' biography, see especially Harrison, *Apuleius*, 1–10. I cite the *Apology* and *Florida* from the text of Vallette: *Apulée: Apologie, Florides*. For the *Apology*, see also Hunink, *Apuleius: Pro se de magia*. For the *Florida*, see La Rocca, *Il filosofo e la città*; Lee, *Apuleius' Florida*. For translations, see Harrison, ed., *Apuleius' Rhetorical Works*.

[3] "[Ego et alias creterras Athenis bibi:] poeticae commentam, geometriae limpidam, musicae dulcem, dialecticae austerulam, iam vero universae philosophiae inexplebilem scilicet <et> nectaream." *Fl.* 20.4.

[4] He reports having seen a statue of Bathyllus on Samos (*Fl.* 15.6) and a mountain in Phrygia that emitted poisonous gases (*Mun.* 327). For the latter, see Hijmans, "Apuleius,

Rome.⁵ We find him back in North Africa in the mid-150s, and well into the best-known and most notorious event in his life: the marriage and subsequent charge of magic documented in the *Apology*.

According to the *Apology*, around 155 or 156 Apuleius came to the town of Oea (modern Tripoli) and married a wealthy widow named Pudentilla, the mother of Sicinius Pontianus, an old friend from his student days in Athens. He did so at his friend's request, to save her estate from the relatives of her late husband. The marriage did not sit well with Pudentilla's former in-laws, and in late 158 or early 159 Apuleius was brought to trial on a charge of magic. Specifically, it seems, he was accused of using magic to induce Pudentilla to fall in love with him. The charge was serious, since sorcery was potentially a capital offense.⁶ Apuleius spoke in his own defense and with evident success, for a few years later he was giving orations in Carthage, where—by his own account, at least—he was a prominent and popular figure. We hear nothing of him after the late 160s.⁷

Apuleius was a quintessential product of his time, for both were bicultural, prosperous, nostalgic for the classical past, and enamored of display. The predominant cultural phenomenon of the age was the movement called the Second Sophistic, whose distinguishing feature was what we might describe as oratory for entertainment.⁸ Its practitioners,

---

Philosophus Platonicus," 429–30. On the basis of two inscriptions from the late second or early third century discovered at Petri, near Corinth, Kritzas has suggested that he might also have visited Corinth ("Δύο επιγράμματα από το Πετρί Νεμέας"; and see the discussion by Jennifer Tobin in *Bryn Mawr Classical Review* 97.5.10). The inscriptions celebrate a woman named Salvia, a Thessalian married to a Corinthian, and Kritzas speculates that Apuleius perhaps became acquainted with Salvia and her family on a visit to Corinth and used her name and history in describing the background of Lucius in the *Golden Ass*: Lucius was from Corinth (*Met.* 1.22.4; 2.12.3), and his mother, Salvia, was from Thessaly (*Met.* 2.2). But Salvia was not an unusual name, and the parallel between the historical and fictional Thessalian women may well be only a coincidence.

⁵ *Fl.* 17.4. In an interesting and speculative discussion, Coarelli ("Apuleio a Ostia?") argues that Apuleius spent several years (ca. 145–52) in Rome and was the proprietor of the "House of Apuleius" in Ostia. The house is so called from the name "L. Apulei Marcelli" found on two water pipes near the house (p. 27 n. 2). See also Beck, "Apuleius the Novelist." Harrison calls the identification "interesting but ultimately unconvincing" (*Apuleius*, 1).

⁶ See Bradley, "Law, Magic, and Culture," 207.

⁷ But Harrison would date the *Metamorphoses* in the 170s (*Apuleius*, 250–51). Arguments have also been made for dating *De Mundo* and *De Platone* after 177; for discussion and earlier bibliography, see Lee, *Apuleius' Florida*, 9–11.

⁸ See Sandy, *The Greek World of Apuleius*, and Anderson, *The Second Sophistic*, both with further bibliography. For "the cult of learning" and the craze for classical culture, see also Zanker, *The Mask of Socrates*, esp. 198–266.

the sophists, were—or aspired to be—celebrities. The more successful ones were highly paid, achieved fame well beyond their native cities, and attracted large numbers of followers. Sometimes they attained public office or positions of high status and influence.[9] Their activities included displaying and purveying classical (but primarily Greek) culture, self-promotion, and playing to the local pride of the cities and regions they spoke in. Above all, however, they professed an attachment to philosophy—or rather to their own brand of philosophy, which Apuleius defines as "a royal science devised to promote the art of speaking as much as the art of living."[10]

The sophistic movement grew out of the ancient educational system, which was largely based on rhetorical training. Many of the sophists were teachers of the rhetorical art, and many in their audiences had been brought up in it. Listeners who had spent their school days practicing rhetorical exercises enjoyed and savored virtuoso oratorical performances. They could recognize a speaker's techniques and tricks and many of his themes, and they could criticize the fine points of his strategy and delivery. But the sophists' orations were also entertaining and accessible enough to appeal to those with little education, who would have been in the vast majority in every audience.[11] The extent and success of the movement were fostered by the relative ease of travel throughout the Greco-Roman world and by the bilingualism—or at least biculturism—of its educated inhabitants. Sophists practiced their ostentatious art all over the empire; and although the cultural basis of the movement was Greek, it also had room for Hellenized Romans like Apuleius.[12]

The chief subject of every sophist was himself—or rather his ostensible self, the self that he wished his public to see. (I say "he" advisedly, for the sophists were all male.) The sophist's self-presentation extended to every aspect of his appearance: both on- and offstage he suited his clothes, coiffure, gestures, mannerisms, voice, and possessions to his role.[13]

---

[9] But rhetoric seems to have provided prominence and reputation rather than social mobility, since most sophists came from elite families; see Bowie, "The Importance of Sophists."

[10] "Disciplinam regalem tam ad bene dicendum quam ad bene vivendum repertam." *Fl.* 7.10.

[11] For the mixed nature of Apuleius' audience, see Bradley, "Apuleius and Carthage." Bradley points out that the theater in Carthage Apuleius describes in *Fl.* 18.3–5 had a capacity of about eleven thousand, of whom only a small portion would have been highly educated (19). See also Sandy, *The Greek World of Apuleius*, 83.

[12] For Apuleius as a sophist, see Sandy, *The Greek World of Apuleius*. For Apuleius as a Roman or Latin sophist, see Harrison, *Apuleius*.

[13] For the self-presentation of both philosophers and sophists, see Hahn, *Der Philosoph und die Gesellschaft*, 33–53. See also Gleason, *Making Men*; Zanker, *The Mask of Socrates*, 217–47.

He created the role, however, with words, in the first-person utterance of his orations.

This verbal image of the sophist is best seen as a special case of what happens when any writer uses the first person. By using the word *I* the author creates a persona, a mask or character whose identity, emotions, and experiences are presented as autobiographical, whether they are real or imaginary. Whatever its degree of reality, the first person invites us to elide the persona with the writer, to identify the mask with the man or woman behind it, or—to put it another way—to conflate the puppet with the person pulling the strings. The effect is necessarily increased when authors read or perform their own works before an audience, as they did so often in antiquity. When orators spoke in law courts or declaimed in theaters or poets gave readings to audiences large or small, they brought to life the characters of their own creation, making the "I," or "ego," of their scripts into credible likenesses of themselves.

Ancient writers fully exploited the persona—sometimes hiding behind it completely, sometimes lifting it for a moment to create a play between their real and fictional selves. Orators and politicians tended to stay in character, holding up to the world the self they had so carefully fashioned.[14] Poets were more willing both to acknowledge the existence of the mask and to advertise its distance from reality, as Catullus does in the notorious lines from poem 16.[15]

> Nam castum esse decet pium poetam
> ipsum, versiculos nihil necesse est,
> . . .
> vos, quod milia multa basiorum
> legistis, male me marem putastis?
>   (Cat. 16.5–6, 12–13)

> It's fitting for the upright poet himself to be free of filth,
> but there's no need for his verses to be so.
> . . .
> Because you read about many thousands of kisses,
> Did you think I wasn't much of a man?

[14] For self-fashioning as a field of inquiry, see Greenblatt, *Renaissance Self-Fashioning*. For Roman self-fashioning, see the following, all with earlier bibliography: Leach, "The Politics of Self-Presentation"; Gleason, *Making Men*; Dugan, "How to Make (and Break) a Cicero."

[15] Apuleius himself quotes Cat. 16.5–6 as a defense of his own erotic verses (*Apol.* 11.1–2). Catullus' words are less transparent than they appear. He does not say "My verses may be naughty, but I am chaste." Rather, by abandoning the first person and using the slippery *decet* ("it's fitting") instead of an indicative, he presents only a general statement of propriety that leaves his own character unrevealed. See Gaisser, *Catullus and His Renaissance Readers*, 210–11.

The sophists, like the poets, liked to play with the mask. They did so ostentatiously, in full view of their audience, for their personae were—quite literally—their stock in trade, the material of their celebrity. Apuleius, sophist par excellence, teases his public with two principal personae: the "I" of his orations and philosophical works and the "I" of his novel the *Golden Ass*. Like Catullus and other poets, he sometimes takes off his mask (or pretends to), hinting that the persona he has displayed might not be his "real" self; but he can also replace one mask with another, confusing and blurring the identities he has placed before us.

This chapter is concerned with Apuleius and his fortunes in antiquity, especially with the creation and development of his "image"—a term that I will be using in all of its possible senses, including the one we have in mind when we talk about the carefully constructed image of a public figure or a commercial product. We will consider how Apuleius professes to see himself, the image or persona he presents to his public, and the images (both literary and artistic) made of him by others.

Creating an Image

Like his fellow sophists, Apuleius presented his image chiefly through his orations. We see his constructed self most extensively in the *Apology* and *Florida*, but it also peeks out tantalizingly from time to time in the *Golden Ass*.

The *Apology* presents itself as the speech that Apuleius actually delivered before the court, but it seems likely that he revised and perhaps even rewrote it after the fact. This point is controversial, but the speech in its present form would be a risky defense: it shows too much detailed knowledge of magic and magical terminology, is too arrogant, and treats the charges too lightly.[16] It has been argued that the presiding judge, Claudius Maximus, was highly educated and philosophically minded, and thus could be relied on to be sympathetic to a fellow intellectual facing a trumped-up charge.[17] Nonetheless, there was still a chance that Apuleius' cleverness could backfire, and that even a sympathetic judge could find the levity he displays in the *Apology* offensive and impertinent enough to convict him. Matters would have been quite different,

---

[16] The point is well made by Gaide, "Apulée de Madaure." For the arguments on both sides with earlier bibliography, see Hijmans, "Apuleius Orator," 1715–19; Hunink, ed., *Apuleius of Madauros, Pro se de magia* 1:25–7.

[17] Bradley ("Law, Magic, and Culture," 215–19) emphasizes his affinities with Apuleius. But the serious Maximus described by Bradley, with his moral virtues and "qualities of consistency and balanced character" (216), seems to have little in common with the persona of Apuleius in the *Apology*.

however, after the trial and its successful conclusion. Then the triumphant Apuleius would have been free to indulge himself, rewriting his speech as a brilliant and wickedly funny pseudodefense.[18] If this assessment is correct, the persona that Apuleius presents in the *Apology* is one step removed from the one he revealed at his trial—a fiction of a fiction. At the same time, however, it is consistent with the persona he presents in the various excerpts from epideictic orations preserved in the *Florida*: self-absorbed, confident, intellectual, and constantly on display.

In both the *Florida* and the *Apology* we see Apuleius as a man who likes to talk about himself but does not do so carelessly or merely to impart autobiographical detail. Almost every word is designed to present him to his hearers (or perhaps readers, in the case of the *Apology*) in a particular, and highly flattering, light. Like a spotlight in a modern theater, the beam he directs on himself changes its color and intensity and direction, but it always shows the persona of Apuleius center stage—and from his best side. That does not mean, however, that it always shows him clearly, for Apuleius manipulates light and shadow so adroitly that sometimes we cannot be sure of what we have seen, or even of what we were supposed to see. These doubtful or ambiguous aspects of Apuleius' identity are important, for they are precisely the ones that posterity would find most intriguing. We shall consider them presently, but first let us look at the parts of his image that are clearly revealed.

The figure onstage is above all a philosopher, specifically "Apuleius the Platonic philosopher of Madauros," as he was known both in antiquity and to posterity.[19] But it is important to note that Apuleius uses the word *philosopher* with a special meaning, one he has given it himself.

---

[18] Cf. Gaide, "Apulée de Madaure," 231: "Apulée aura considérablement revu et augmenté son discours, pour se venger à fond de toutes les médisances dont il avait été l'objet, pour transformer insolemment son apologie en un *De Magia* qui est souvent un 'Pro Magia', et pour se faire applaudir."

[19] The second- or third-century base of a lost statue, almost certainly of Apuleius, is inscribed "to the Platonic philosopher"; see p. 13. The author of *Peri Hermeneias* treats the phrase as a synonym for Apuleius: "Licet autem eadem vi manente utramvis partem in plura verba protendere, ut si pro Apuleio dicas philosophum Platonicum Madaurensem, item pro disserendo dicas eum uti oratione" (*Peri Hermeneias* 267). (The work, although ascribed to Apuleius very early in the tradition, should probably not be attributed to him; for the arguments, see Hijmans, "Apuleius, Philosophus Platonicus," 408–11; Klibansky and Regen, *Die Handschriften*, 18–23.) Augustine calls him "Apuleius Afer Platonicus nobilis" (*Civ.* 8.12), "Apuleius Platonicus Madaurensis" (*Civ.* 8.14), and "philosophus Platonicus" (*Civ.* 8.19); see Hagendahl, *Augustine and the Latin Classics* 1:18–19.

The title also appears in the oldest manuscripts of both branches of the manuscript tradition. In the eleventh-century manuscript Florence, Biblioteca Laurenziana 68.2 (called F), the phrase "Apulei Platonici Madaurensis" appears in the explicit of the *Apology* (fols. 125v–126r). (The folio is illustrated in Pecere, "Esemplari con *subscriptiones* e tradizione dei testi latini," plates 3a–b.) In the early ninth-century manuscript Brussels, Bibliothèque Royale Albert Ier 10054–10056, "Apulei Platonici Madaurensis" appears in the incipit of

Like an artist making a self-portrait by looking into a mirror, he has redrawn the image of the philosopher to match his own features and activities. In this new usage it is not so much that Apuleius is described by the word *philosopher* as that the word *philosopher* is defined as "Apuleius."

This new philosopher is a celebrity. Crowds flock to his performances—in greater numbers than have ever assembled to hear a philosopher, as we learn in *Florida* 9. "Indeed, even my talent, however small," he says in *Florida* 17, "has long been so well known to the public for what it is that it requires no new commendation."[20] In *Florida* 9 he asserts that his extraordinary fame has created almost impossibly high expectations in his audience: "Who among you would forgive me a single solecism? Who would grant me one syllable barbarously pronounced? . . . And yet you pardon these things in others easily and very justly."[21] Naturally his works are equally famous. In the *Apology* he reminds the court of his celebrated speech praising the god Aesculapius and calls on his hearers to recite its opening lines. "Do you hear all the people supplying them?" he asks the judge. Someone in the audience even has a copy of the book, which Apuleius asks to have read out in evidence.[22]

But fame is not all he has to offer. Our philosopher claims other merits, which appear to their best advantage in comparison with the qualities of others—whether beasts, men, other philosophers, or even gods. Birdsong, for example, as he tells his audience in *Florida* 13, is limited in both time and repertoire, for each species sings a particular strain and only at a single time of day. "Philosophy did not bestow utterance like that on me. . . . Rather, the thought and utterance of the philosopher are continual—august to hear, useful to understand, and tuneful in every key."[23] In *Florida* 9 Apuleius compares himself in versatility to the old Athenian sophist Hippias. Hippias, he says, was famous for having made every item of his apparel—including not only his clothes and sandals but even his ring, oil bottle, and strigil. Apuleius, by contrast, boasts of versatility not as a craftsman but as a writer,

---

De deo Socratis (fol. 2r), and "Apulei Platonici Philosophi Madaurensis" in the explicit (fol. 16v). See Munk Olsen, *L'Étude des auteurs classiques latins aux Xi^e et Xii^e siècles* 1:13; Klibansky and Regen, *Die Handschriften*, 60–62.

[20] "Nam et quantulumcumque ingenium meum iam pridem pro captu suo hominibus notius est, quam ut indigeat novae commendationis." *Fl.* 17.2.

[21] "Quis enim vestrum mihi unum soloecismum ignoverit? quis vel unam syllabam barbare pronuntiatam donaverit? . . . Quae tamen aliis facile et sane meritissimo ignoscitis." *Fl.* 9.7.

[22] "Audisne, Maxime, multos suggerentis? Immo, ecce etiam liber offertur." *Apol.* 55.12.

[23] "Non enim mihi philosophia id genus orationem largita est. . . . Sed enim philosophi ratio et oratio tempore iugis est et auditu venerabilis et intellectu utilis et modo omnicana." *Fl.* 13.1 and 3.

claiming to have composed not only poetry of every kind but also riddles, histories, orations, and dialogues—and all in both Greek and Latin (*Fl.* 9.15–29). In *Florida* 20 he claims to have surpassed even the great philosophers of the past in the variety if not in the quality of his compositions.[24]

In appearance, too, he compares himself with others, aligning physical beauty and philosophic sophistication on one side against ugliness and boorish ignorance on the other. In such matching of outer and inner qualities Apuleius is very much a man of his age, for although even Homer practiced the art of physiognomy (which we might define as believing that one *can* tell a book by its cover), the association of physical features with qualities of character reached its height as a full-blown pseudoscience under the Second Sophistic.[25]

In the *Apology* Apuleius uses the argument from physiognomy to overturn the prevailing picture of the philosopher and reshape it in his own image. He claims that his adversaries opened their case by describing him pejoratively as " 'a handsome philosopher' (and horror of horrors!) 'eloquent in both Greek and Latin.' "[26] A strange criticism, we might think. Their argument, however, was that his speaking ability and appearance identified him as a sophist and belied his claim to be a philosopher. Philosophy and oratory were traditionally deemed incompatible; and although the distinction between them in practice had largely broken down by this time, the "rhetoric of rivalry"[27] between the two callings remained. Sophists could and did profess philosophy, and philosophers orated; but they cultivated separate images—the philosopher as a bearded sage, the sophist as a smartly dressed dandy.[28] Apuleius' accusers had the traditional distinctions firmly in mind, evidently claiming that as a

---

[24] "Canit enim Empedocles carmina, Plato dialogos, Socrates hymnos, Epicharmus modos, Xenophon historias, Crates satiras: Apuleius vester haec omnia novemque Musas pari studio colit, maiore scilicet voluntate quam facultate." *Fl.* 20.5–6.

[25] For Homer's association of appearance and character, see especially *Il.* 2.211–64, where the ugliness of Thersites reflects his low social class and tendency to quarrel with his betters. For physiognomy in the Second Sophistic, see Evans, "The Study of Physiognomy in the Second Century A.D."; Gleason, *Making Men*, esp. 55–81. For Apuleius, see Opeku, "Physiognomy in Apuleius."

[26] " 'Accusamus apud te philosophum formonsum et tam Graece quam Latine' pro nefas! 'disertissimum.' " *Apol.* 4.1.

[27] The expression is Gleason's (*Making Men*, 131).

[28] See the important discussion of Hahn, *Der Philosoph und die Gesellschaft*, 46–53. For the sophist's appearance, see also Zanker, *The Mask of Socrates*, 243. Both Hahn (51) and Zanker (235) cite Philostratus' account of the philosopher Aristokles (*VS* 567), whose conversion to rhetoric as a follower of Herodes Atticus was accompanied by changes in his grooming, friends, and recreations. But Hahn places Apuleius, along with Favorinus and Maximus of Tyre, in a gray area of sophistic/philosophical polymathy and performance (53).

sophist (for that is the point of the word *eloquent*) Apuleius was ipso facto not a philosopher. Their argument about appearance is more interesting. The epithet "handsome philosopher" is intended as a contradiction in terms exposing Apuleius as a hypocrite. For in this period, as Zanker observes, "if a man wanted to be acknowledged publicly as a philosopher, . . . the one thing he could not appear was handsome."[29] Contemporary busts and statues of philosophers show them as men well past their first youth, wrinkled in thought, with careless or disordered hair and the distinguishing feature of the so-called philosopher's beard.[30] Literary accounts present the same picture.[31]

Apuleius responds to his opponents by trying, with transparent insincerity, to convince the court that he is *not* good-looking—long hours of study have worn him down, and his hair is a mess.[32] But his real argument lies elsewhere. He implicitly rejects the contemporary picture of the philosopher and refutes the charge of hypocrisy, using the physiognomical connection between appearance and character to make the phrase "handsome philosopher" not a contradiction in terms but rather a self-evident proposition. Both Pythagoras and Zeno were good-looking, he tells the court, and so were many other philosophers, "who enhanced the grace of their bodies with the integrity of their character."[33] By contrast, Apuleius' accuser Sicinius Aemilianus embodies the opposite qualities. According to Apuleius, he is an ignorant rustic—uncouth, wicked, and correspondingly hideous to look at, for he is as ugly as the tragic mask of Thyestes or the hideous boatman Charon.[34] He no doubt also had a

---

[29] Zanker, *The Mask of Socrates*, 235.

[30] For the description, see ibid., 217–47 and figs. 129, 133, 143. For the "philosopher's beard," see 220, 229.

[31] See Hahn, *Der Philosoph und die Gesellschaft*, 33–45.

[32] *Apol.* 4.10. Apuleius' protestations are intentionally unconvincing. I do not agree with Zanker's argument (*The Mask of Socrates*, 234) that he tried to present an unkempt or disheveled appearance in court. At *Apol.* 92.5 he casually describes himself as "iuvenem neque corpore neque animo neque fortuna paenitendum."

[33] "Itemque multos philosophos ab ore honestissimos memoriae prodi, qui gratiam corporis morum honestamentis ornaverint." *Apol.* 4.9. Most of the philosophers in Apuleius are good looking. The hunchback Cynic Crates of *Florida* 14 is a notable exception.

[34] *Rustic and uncouth*: "Agrestis quidem semper et barbarus" (*Apol.* 10.6). *Wicked*: "At ego non mirer, si boni consulis me de isto distortissimo vultu tuo dicere, de moribus tuis multo truculentioribus reticere" (*Apol.* 16.8). *Like Thyestes*: "Quamquam teterrimum os tuum minimum a Thyesta tragico demutet" (*Apol.* 16.7). Hunink (*Apuleius . . . de Magia*) observes ad loc.: "The ugly mask of the horrified Thyestes is a theatrical element with clearly negative associations; it is firmly put on Aemilianus' face." *Like Charon*: The nickname not only attacks Aemilianus' ugliness ("ob oris et animi diritatem"; *Apol.* 56.7) but insinuates that he is a murderer: "Neque enim diu est, cum te crebrae mortes propinquorum immeritis hereditatibus fulserunt, unde tibi potius quam ob istam teterrimam faciem Charon nomen est" (*Apol.* 23.7).

beard, if not a philosophical one, if the comparisons with Thyestes and Charon are anything to go by. The mask of Thyestes was probably bearded, and Apuleius could have counted on his audience to remember Vergil's famous description of Charon in *Aeneid* 6:

> . . . appallingly filthy he is, with a bush of unkempt
> White beard upon his chin, with eyes like jets of fire;
> And a dirty cloak draggles down, knotted about his shoulders.[35]

In *Florida* 3 Apuleius transposes the alliance of beauty and wisdom against ugliness and ignorance into the world of myth, using as his protagonists Apollo and Marsyas. He tells how the rustic Marsyas entered into a musical competition with Apollo: "a monster [contending] with a beautiful youth, a rustic personage with a learned one, an animal with a god."[36] Minerva and the Muses stood by, ostensibly as judges, but they had really come to mock Marsyas' lack of culture and punish his stupidity. Marsyas, unaware that he was an object of derision, began not by playing his flute (his sole talent) but by babbling foolishly like the barbarian he was. He first praised himself, as Apuleius says, "because his hair was pulled back and he had a ragged beard and shaggy chest, because his art was flute playing and he was lacking in wealth."[37] Then he went on to attack Apollo for the opposite qualities—for his beautiful long hair, fair beardless cheeks and smooth body, and for his manifold talents and opulent wealth. The Muses laughed at his accusations and left the defeated Marsyas flayed alive and with his naked flesh torn to pieces. The selection ends: "But Apollo was ashamed of such a paltry victory."[38]

The contest of Apollo and Marsyas is an unmistakable allusion to the dispute between Apuleius and his accusers in the *Apology*.[39] Neither the date nor the audience of *Florida* 3 is known, but the excerpts in the *Florida* whose dates and audiences can be determined all belong to the

---

[35] *Aen.* 6.299–301. The translation is by C. Day Lewis. Apuleius also compares Aemilianus to Mezentius, another bearded character from Vergil (*Apol.* 56.7; cf. *Aen.* 10.838).

[36] "Teter cum decoro, agrestis cum erudito, belua cum deo." *Fl.* 3.6.

[37] "Quod erat et coma relicinus et barba squalidus et pectore hirsutus et arte tibicen et fortuna egenus." *Fl.* 3.8. For the argument that Apuleius is applying the rules of physiognomy in his description of Marsyas, see Opeku, "Physiognomy in Apuleius," 472–73.

[38] "Enimvero Apollinem tam humilis victoriae puditum est." *Fl.* 3.14.

[39] Hunink calls the similarity between the two contests "a fascinating parallel" (*Apuleius . . . de Magia*, 21). The parallel was noted as early as 1820 in Bayle's *Dictionary*: "Au reste, il me semble (je n'ose néanmoins l'affirmer) qu'Apulée avait en vue son procès, lorsqu'il décrivit dans l'une de ses harangues celui d'Apollon et de Marsyas." *Dictionnaire historique et critique* (Paris, 1820), 2:212. For a different view, see La Rocca, *Il filosofo e la città*, 144–52, who also identifies Apollo with Apuleius but sees Marsyas as one of Apuleius' philosophical rivals.

period 160–69 and were delivered to the Carthaginians.⁴⁰ That is, they were delivered both several years after Apuleius' trial for magic and in the cultural capital of North Africa. *Florida* 3 no doubt has the same date and place. It refers, not very subtly, to the success of the *Apology*, for the story of Apollo and Marsyas as Apuleius presents it is a virtual allegory of his triumph over his boorish small-town opponents. Marsyas' ugliness and ignorance are like those of Apuleius' accusers, and his complaints of Apollo's beauty and talent certainly recall their accusation that Apuleius was "a handsome philosopher and eloquent in both Greek and Latin." Minerva and the Muses have their counterpart in the learned and distinguished judge Claudius Maximus, whom Apuleius compliments so often in the *Apology*. The parallels are clear enough, and Apuleius need not labor them. He does not spell out the likeness between himself and Apollo but leaves the audience to infer that he, like the god, was a little embarrassed by his easy victory.

In *Florida* 3, then, Apuleius is keeping his victory alive in the minds of his audience and making sure that they remember it in a particular way—as the virtually foreordained triumph of divine beauty and talent over subhuman barbarity. To put it another way, Apuleius is promoting and controlling his image. But an image is not always an intangible abstraction. Physical likenesses and portraits are equally important— both to keep a sophist's features in the public eye and to reflect them back to his own.

SELF-REFLECTION

Apuleius treats this second purpose—that of seeing his own image—in a famous passage in the *Apology*. His enemies have charged that he possesses a mirror, no doubt both to accuse him of vanity and to hint that he has used it in nefarious magical practices, but primarily to suggest that the possession of a mirror, like being good-looking, is incompatible with philosophy.⁴¹ This charge, like that of being a handsome philosopher, is phrased as an obvious oxymoron: "The philosopher has a mirror. The philosopher possesses a mirror."⁴²

---

⁴⁰ For the dating, which is based on internal evidence in *Fl.* 9, 16, and 17, see Vallette, *Apulée: Apologie, Florides*, xxvi–xxviii; Hijmans, "Apuleius Orator," 1723–25. Harrison suggests that *Fl.* 16 might be dated as late as the early 170s (*Apuleius*, 116). *Fl.* 9, 16, 17, 18, and 20 are explicitly addressed to the Carthaginians.

⁴¹ Mirrors were associated primarily with women, and their use by men was suspect; see McCarty, "The Shape of the Mirror," 167–168. For mirrors in magic, see Hunink, *Apuleius . . . de Magia*, 57–58.

⁴² "Habet speculum philosophus, possidet speculum philosophus." *Apol.* 13.5.

Apuleius handily refutes the contradiction; indeed, to hear him tell it, every philosopher needs a mirror for both ethical and scientific purposes. But he directs most of his argument in a different direction, praising the power of the mirror to reflect the features of its owner, and comparing mirror images with likenesses presented by statues or paintings. "Don't you know that there is nothing a man would rather look at than his own form?"[43] he asks the court. Statues can certainly fulfill this function, and that is one reason that a city rewards a deserving man with a statue of himself to look at (*Apol.* 14.2). But for his own contemplation Apuleius prefers a mirror. The image in a mirror is portable and can be gazed at whenever one likes. The reflection has the color and motion and vitality lacking in artificial likenesses and shows a man exactly as he is at a given moment, reflecting every movement and change in expression. The image in a painting or statue, by contrast, is fixed in time and space and conveys but a single expression, so that from the moment of its completion it is unlike its subject.

Apuleius has no objection to statues—on the contrary.[44] But he does like to look into the mirror, not only for the immediacy and accuracy and availability of its image but because he creates and controls it. He can create or dissolve the image at will simply by bringing the mirror to his face or moving it away. He can change it with a smile or a frown or twist of the head. But his connection with it is even more intimate than we might expect. From his survey of scientific and philosophical explanations of the mirror we learn that a reflection may be a thin mask of atoms emanating from the subject's body and bounced back to his eyes from the mirror's surface, or perhaps a creation of the fiery effluence from his eyes as it mingles with air or light.[45] That is, in whatever explanation one chooses, a person's reflection is, quite literally, a part of himself.

Thus, the image in the mirror is doubly appealing, both for its symbiotic relation with its subject and because it is under his control to an extent inconceivable with other likenesses. (Only Alexander the Great, Apuleius observes, was able to ensure that his image came down to posterity as he wished. He did so by allowing only the three greatest artists of his age to portray him and deterring the others with the fear of death.)[46] But if artificial likenesses have the disadvantage of being

---

[43] "An tu ignoras nihil esse aspectabilius homini nato quam formam suam?" *Apol.* 14.2.

[44] *Pace* Lee Too, "Statues, Mirrors, Gods." Her argument is correctly dismissed by Hunink (*Apuleius . . . de Magia,* 59 n. 3).

[45] *Apol.* 15.11–15. See ad loc. Hunink, *Apuleius . . . de Magia,* and Butler and Owen, *Apulei Apologia.*

[46] *Fl.* 7.5–8. The story perhaps orginated in Plutarch (*Alex.* 4 and *Mor.* 335A–C); versions of it appear in Cicero, *Ep. fam.* 5.12.7, Horace, *Ep.* 2.1.239–41, and Pliny, *HN* 7.125. See Brink, *Horace on Poetry,* 247–48. But Apuleius is apparently the first to have Alexander threaten unauthorized portrait makers with death.

outside their subject's control, the mirror image has two fatal limitations of its own: it is impermanent, and only its subject can see it. The philosopher who wants to keep his face and fame before the public needs something more substantial and permanent. He wants statues, and preferably as many as possible.

Many statues and busts of philosophers survive from antiquity.[47] Cities erected statues to honor and lay claim to famous men; philosophers and sophists in turn sought and desired them. The practice was so common that philosophers had a standard form of giving thanks to the cities that erected statues in their honor, as Apuleius tells us (*Fl.* 16.29). The presence or absence or (heaven forbid!) the removal of a statue measured a sophist's current reputation as well as his chances of future fame or oblivion. In Hadrian's reign the famous sophist Favorinus made a passionate speech to the Corinthians when they took down his statue.[48] A generation later Apuleius delivered and published an oration lobbying for a statue in Oea over the objections of his detractors, who were no doubt still angry over his marriage and victory in the *Apology*. We have the story from Augustine; unfortunately the speech itself is no longer extant.[49]

Did Apuleius persuade the citizens of Oea? We will probably never know. But there is evidence that other statues were erected to him. A statue base found in Madauros (without the statue) is dedicated by his fellow citizens "To the Platonic Philosopher."[50] Although the name is lacking, Apuleius is the obvious candidate. In *Florida* 16 Apuleius thanks the citizens of Carthage for voting him one statue, hints that they should put up a second, and states that he had statues in other cities as well.[51]

---

[47] See Richter, *The Portraits of the Greeks* 3:282–89; Schefold, *Die Bildnisse der antiken Dichter, Redner und Denker*. But Zanker argues that many of the statues are portraits of laymen subscribing to "the cult of learning" who have had themselves depicted as philosophers (*The Mask of Socrates*, 210–66).

[48] Favorinus' statues were pulled down in both Corinth and Athens—perhaps because he had fallen out of favor with Hadrian. His speech to the Corinthians is discussed by Gleason, *Making Men*, 3–20.

[49] "An forte ista [i.e., the trappings of worldly success] ut philosophus voluntate contempsit, qui sacerdos provinciae pro magno fuit, ut munera ederet venatoresque vestiret et pro statua sibi apud Oenses locanda, ex qua civitate habebat uxorem, adversus contradictionem quorundam civium litigaret? Quod posteros ne lateret, eiusdem litis orationem scriptam memoriae commendavit." Augustine, *Ep.* 138.19.

[50] "[Ph]ilosopho [Pl]atonico [Ma]daurenses cives ornament[o] suo. D(ecreto) d(ecurionum), p(ecunia) [p(ublica)]." Gsell, ed., *Inscriptions latines de l'Algerie* 1:2115. But this statue seems not to have been a lasting memorial, for the base was reused in the middle of the fourth century for a dedication to one of the sons of Constantine. Its reverse is inscribed "D(omino) n(ostro), divi C[ons]tanti[ni] Maxim[i fil(io)] . . ." (Gsell, 1:4010).

[51] See Lee, *Apuleius' Florida*, 145–48; *Fl.* 16.1 and 36–48 with Lee's commentary ad loc. It was not uncommon for a philosopher to have several statues in one city: there were at least seventeen statues of Herodes Atticus in Athens. See Richter, *The Portraits of the Greeks* 3:286.

One statue even found its way to Constantinople, for Christodorus, writing in the fifth century AD, tells us that there was a statue of Apuleius in the Baths of Zeuxippos.[52] Here is how he describes it: "And Apuleius was reverent as he considered the ineffable rites of the intellectual Latin Muse. He was a man whom the Italian Siren brought up to be an initiate of arcane wisdom."[53]

In keeping with good physiognomical principles, statues and other portraits were judged for their ability to convey their subject's inner nature and not merely his physical appearance. The images of Alexander the Great, Apuleius tells us, all revealed "the same fierce warrior's vigor, the same noble nature, the same youthful beauty, and the same attractive high forehead."[54] We can guess some of the qualities that Apuleius would have wanted posterity to see in his own statues: for example, beauty, eloquence, and, above all, philosophical wisdom. Christodorus adds another that he surely would have welcomed, for he characterizes the Apuleius in Constantinople as "an initiate of arcane wisdom." His language recalls Apuleius' claim in the *Apology* to have been initiated in several mystery cults; but it is also metaphorical, since literary education was frequently described as a "mystery," into which only the elect were "initiated."[55]

ROLE-PLAYING

So far we have been looking at Apuleius' persona as a handsome celebrity philosopher, a character that he has clearly revealed—or perhaps one should say unambiguously advertised. But there are also places where the picture is less clear, and where Apuleius has deliberately created doubt about who and what he is, raising and leaving open two separate but intersecting questions about his identity. First, is he a magician? Second, what is his relation to Lucius, the hero of the *Golden Ass*?

---

[52] For a good discussion, see Scarcia, *Latina Siren*, 13–18.

[53] καὶ νοερῆς ἀφθεγκτα Λατινίδος ὄργια Μούσης / ἄζετο παπταίνων Ἀπολήϊος, ὄντινα μύστην / Αὐσονὶς ἀρρήτου σοφίης ἐθρέψατο Σειρήν. *Anth. Pal* 2.303–5.

[54] "Eo igitur omnium metu factum, solus Alexander ut ubique imaginum simillimus esset, utique omnibus statuis et tabulis et toreumatis idem vigor acerrimi bellatoris, idem ingenium maximi honoris, eadem forma viridis iuventae, eadem gratia relicinae frontis cerneretur." *Fl.* 7.8. See also Plutarch, who points out that merely duplicating physical features cannot produce a successful portrait. *De Alex. M. Fortuna aut Virtute Or.* 2.2.

[55] *Apol.* 55.8. For the metaphor of initiation, see Kaster, *Guardians of Language,* 16: "The literary culture was a mystery, of the Muses or the ancients: its acquisition was an initiation, by which 'the things not to be spoken' were revealed."

Let us begin with magic, the point where our two questions come together. In the *Apology* Apuleius opens his defense on the charge of magic with the question "How do you define 'magician'?"[56] He suggests a definition himself with a digression on the "magicians," or *magi*, of the Persians—priests who are so venerated that they are entrusted with the education of future kings. *Their* magic, if that is what he is accused of, is both pleasing to the gods and so highly prized that few are allowed to learn its secrets (*Apol.* 25.9–26.3). But perhaps, he suggests, his adversaries have in mind the common definition, that a magician is someone who through communication with the gods can accomplish whatever he wills by the mysterious power of his incantations. In that case, he professes amazement at his opponents' audacity, for surely anyone who believed that he had such superhuman powers would be afraid to accuse him (*Apol.* 26.6–9).

If both modern readers and Apuleius' real (or supposed) audience in the courtroom are confused by now, that is what he intends. He continues to blow smoke, and the fog grows thicker and thicker as he explains how he will defend himself:

> I won't deny any of the things they claim I have done, whether the charges are true or false, but I will proceed as if they were true, so that this great assembly, which has come to hear the case from near and far, can understand that neither a true charge nor a false allegation can be made against philosophers that they would not be prepared to defend even if they could deny it—such is their confidence in their innocence. First then, I will refute their arguments and prove that they have nothing to do with magic. Then, I will show—even assuming that I was the greatest magician in the world—that there has been neither cause nor opportunity for them to catch me in some act of black magic.[57]

Apuleius' language is deliberately murky and convoluted, but his line of defense is simple enough: he admits the various actions he has been charged with (such things as buying fish, having a slave with a tendency

---

[56] "Quae quidem omnis Aemiliano fuit in isto uno destinata, me magum esse, et ideo mihi libet quaerere ab eruditissimis eius advocatis quid sit magus." *Apol.* 25.8.

[57] "Atque ego omnia obiecta, seu vera seu falsa sunt, non negabo, sed perinde atque si facta sint fatebor, ut omnis ista multitudo, quae plurima undique ad audiendum convenit, aperte intellegat nihil in philosophos non modo vere dici, sed ne falso quidem posse confingi, quod non ex innocentiae fiducia, quamvis liceat negare, tamen potius habeant defendere. Primum igitur argumenta eorum convincam ac refutabo nihil ea ad magian pertinere; dein etsi maxime magus forem, tamen ostendam neque causam ullam neque occasionem fuisse, ut me in aliquo maleficio experirentur." *Apol.* 28.2–4.

to fainting spells, keeping secret objects under a linen cloth, and owning a black ebony statue of Mercury), argues that they are all related either to his activities as a scientific philosopher or to his practice of religious mysteries, and maintains that even if the objects in question did have magical uses, he is not necessarily a magician on that account.

In each case he teases his audience with his expert knowledge of magic—slyly dropping technical terminology, daring his adversaries to give away their own illicit knowledge by challenging him, and even uttering strings of words that sound like magical curses.[58] Then he backs away in a show of innocence. A single example will suffice: the case of the ebony statue that the prosecution described as a hideous skeleton made for the practice of magic.[59] Apuleius shows the court his beautiful little statuette, denies that it is anything but an object of religious devotion, and expatiates on its charms. But in fact the statue is of Mercury (Greek Hermes), the god of magic and escort of the dead to Hades. Although Apuleius does not openly acknowledge Mercury's connection with magic, he clearly confirms it in his attack on Aemilianus—a magical curse if ever there was one:

> In payment for this lie, Aemilianus, may this god [Mercury] who goes between the lords of heaven and hell bestow on you the hatred of both, and may he always send phantoms of the dead to meet you, and heap up before your eyes every ghost, spectre, spirit, fiend, all apparitions that walk by night, all dread dwellers in the tomb, all terrors of the sepulchre—although by age and character you are close enough to them already.[60]

Yet almost before these bloodcurdling words have sunk in, Apuleius takes off the mask of the magician and becomes the very picture of an innocent philosopher, piously claiming: "But we of the family of Plato

---

[58] See Hunink, *Apuleius . . . de Magia*, esp. 97–98, 145, 162–63 and *ad* 31.9, 35.6, 43.2, 44.9, 45.2, 54.2, 64.8. For Apuleius' "curses," see *Apol.* 38.7, 64.1–2, 90.6, and Hunink ad loc.

[59] *Apol.* 61–64.2. See Hunink, *Apuleius . . . de Magia*, ad loc.; Abt, *Die Apologie des Apuleius*, 296–303.

[60] "At tibi, Aemiliane, pro isto mendacio duit deus iste superum et inferum commeator utrorumque deorum malam gratiam semperque obvias species mortuorum, quicquid umbrarum est usquam, quicquid lemurum, quicquid manium, quicquid larvarum, oculis tuis oggerat, omnia noctium occursacula, omnia bustorum formidamina, omnia sepulcrorum terriculamenta, a quibus tamen aevo et merito haud longe abes." *Apol.* 64.1–2. For parallels with ancient curses, see Abt, *Die Apologie des Apuleius*, 303–6. For the formal and archaic language, see Hunink, *Apuleius . . . de Magia*, ad loc. My translation owes several turns of phrase to Butler's translation, *The Apology and Florida of Apuleius of Madaura*, 107–8.

know nothing except what is festive and joyful and majestic and pertains to the upper world and to the heavens."[61]

Magician? Philosopher? Or a bit of both? Apuleius satisfied the court of his innocence, but in the *Apology* he leaves a whiff of magic in the air, suggesting more than a passing acquaintance with the dark arts and adding a *frisson* of danger to his image. Perhaps that is all he intended, but the scent of sulphur was strong enough to convince later generations of his magical powers, especially when they considered the role of magic in the *Golden Ass*, whose hero and first-person narrator readers from late antiquity to the twentieth century almost universally identified in varying degrees with Apuleius himself.

The identification of Apuleius with his hero Lucius was largely a natural consequence of using a first-person narrator: the "I" of a novel, like the "I" of an oration or poem, invites an autobiographical reading. But Apuleius exploits this effect and plays with it, creating in Lucius a character whose features both differ from and resemble those of his own persona. The differences are great enough to prevent us from eliding Lucius with Apuleius; the resemblances are great enough to encourage the identification (and as we shall see presently, one detail positively requires it).

From the beginning of the novel Apuleius depicts a hero fundamentally different from himself. Lucius is a Greek from Corinth and a relation of the famous Plutarch,[62] whereas Apuleius is a Roman from North Africa. Lucius is credulous and foolish, both as a man and as an ass; Apuleius presents himself as a sophisticated man of the world. Lucius bungles his efforts at magic—or has them bungled for him, when Fotis gives him the wrong ointment (*Met.* 3.24). The Apuleius we see in the *Apology* may or may not be an actual magician; he could never be an incompetent one. But Lucius also resembles Apuleius.[63] Both men are peripatetic provincial intellectuals of good family. Both have an interest in magic. Both are eloquent orators in both Greek and Latin. Both have ties to Platonic philosophy: Apuleius is an avowed Platonist, and Lucius is related to Plutarch and Sextus, both Middle Platonic philosophers. Perhaps most important, both are initiated more than once into mystery cults, and Lucius' conversion to Isis is told so powerfully that it has often been taken to reflect Apuleius' own religious experience.[64]

---

[61] "Ceterum Platonica familia nihil novimus nisi festum et laetum et sollemne et superum et caeleste." *Apol.* 64.3.

[62] *Corinth*: *Met.* 1.22.4, 2.12.3. *Plutarch*: *Met.* 1.2.1. For the text of the *Metamorphoses*, I cite the text of Robertson: *Apulée: Les Métamorphoses*.

[63] See Harrison, *Apuleius*, 217–18.

[64] E.g., by Nock, *Conversion*, 138–55; Griffiths, in *Apuleius of Madauros: The Isis Book*, 3–7.

These resemblances in themselves, however, are not enough to identify Lucius with Apuleius. Lucius' experiences need not even be derived or adapted from those of Apuleius.[65] In the social and intellectual world of the second century, there must have been many young men not unlike Lucius—aspiring sophists at the beginning of their careers, traveling the world, dabbling in religion and philosophy (and perhaps magic), and eager for sexual and other adventures. If Apuleius had been such a youth, so were many others. It is important to remember, too, that ultimately the figure of Lucius has its origin in the lost Greek *Metamorphoses* by "Lucius of Patrae," from which the plots of both Apuleius' *Metamorphoses* and the *Onos* of Pseudo-Lucian were derived.[66]

To some extent, however, it is naive to seek Lucius' identity and relation to Apuleius. He is Apuleius' creature if not entirely his creation, a persona like that of the magician in the *Apology*, which the author may assume or set down at will. In the *Metamorphoses*, too, just as in the *Apology* and *Florida*, Apuleius' real aim is self-display.[67] The object is not to identify the "real Apuleius" (or the "real Lucius," for that matter) but to dazzle the reader by assuming multiple and contradictory personae.[68] Not only Lucius' transformation to an ass and eventual recovery of his human form, but also the changes and confusions in the identities of author, narrator, and other speakers, justify the title *Metamorphoses*.[69]

Apuleius draws attention to his impersonations in the *Metamorphoses* in two famous passages, strategically placed at the beginning and end of the novel. In each he presents the question of his own identity vis-à-vis that of his speaker as a conspicuous and unsolvable problem. In the first passage he gives us too few clues to arrive at an answer; in the second the clue leads to an impossible contradiction.

The proem (*Met.* 1.1) explicitly raises the question of the speaker's identity.[70] "Quis ille?" (Who is this?), the speaker asks, and then proceeds

---

[65] *Pace* Harrison, *Apuleius*, 218.

[66] See Mason, "Greek and Latin Versions of the Ass-Story," with earlier bibliography. Lucius of Patrae was probably the name of the first-person narrator of the Greek *Metamorphoses*, wrongly identified with the author by the ninth-century patriarch Photios (our only source for the work). See Mason, 1669–71; Winkler, *Auctor & Actor*, 255.

[67] Harrison reaches much the same conclusion: "The problem for a self-promoting sophistic intellectual in writing fictional narrative is that of how to keep the spotlight on himself when not talking about himself. . . . The . . . complex presentation of narrative voice . . . is precisely the kind of strategy which draws attention to the existence and virtuoso status of the work's author." *Apuleius*, 232–33.

[68] See especially van der Paardt, "The Unmasked 'I.'"

[69] Cf. Winkler, *Auctor & Actor*, 200: "The entire AA is a playful game of multiple identities."

[70] There is a large bibliography on the prologue. For a starting point, see Kahane and Laird, eds., *A Companion to the Prologue of Apuleius' Metamorphoses*.

to describe himself—unhelpfully—as a Greek of Attic, Corinthian, and Spartan stock who has learned Latin in Rome with great difficulty and begs pardon for any faults in the language with which he will tell his "Greekish tale" (*fabulam Graecanicam*). The description fits neither the North African Apuleius nor the Greek Lucius (whose Latin seems perfectly adequate for his career in the Roman law courts at the end of the novel).[71] Other answers have been proposed (the speaker is an actor outside the story, like the *prologus* in Plautine comedy, or perhaps even the book itself, etc.);[72] but in fact Apuleius has given us no way to decide. The unidentifiable speaker is another of Apuleius' personae, made deliberately mysterious and intriguing in order to announce and advertise the writer's protean powers at the opening of his novel. The important detail is the question itself ("quis ille?"): Apuleius is the speaker; what part is he playing now?

Near the end of the novel (*Met.* 11.27) Apuleius ostentatiously forces the reader to confront the problem of his relation to his hero.[73] The puzzle is laid out in a vision, which Lucius says was related to him by a priest of Osiris named Asinius Marcellus. (The name is significant, as he points out unnecessarily.)[74] Asinius says that Osiris himself had urged Lucius' initiation into his rites:

> For the previous night, while he was arranging garlands for the great god, he thought he heard from his mouth (with which he pronounces each one's destiny) that a man from Madauros was being sent to him, a very poor one. He should at once prepare his initiation rites for him; for by his providence the glory of learning was in store for the man and a great reward for himself.[75]

The subject of the prophecy must be our hero, the Greek Lucius, but as the "man from Madauros" he can be only Apuleius, the North African author. The paradox is a red herring wrapped up in indirect statement,

---

[71] *Met.* 11.28.6. The point is made by Harrison (*Apuleius*, 228).

[72] For the *prologus* answer, see Smith, "The Narrative Voice in Apuleius' *Metamorphoses*," and the supporting arguments of Winkler, *Auctor & Actor,* 200–203. For the book answer, see Harrison, "The Speaking Book."

[73] For other, less conspicuous references to Apuleius at *Met* 2.12 and 4.32, see van der Paardt, "The Unmasked 'I,'" 105.

[74] "Reformationis meae <minime> alienum nomen." *Met.* 11.27.7. Since *minime* is a supplement by Robertson, the modern reader is left to decide whether the name Asinius is or is not appropriate to Lucius' reformation.

[75] "Nam sibi visus est quiete proxima, dum magno deo coronas *exaptaret*, de eius ore, quo singulorum fata dictat, audisse mitti sibi Madaurensem, sed admodum pauperem, cui statim sua sacra deberet ministrare; nam et illi studiorum gloriam et ipsi grande compendium sua comparari providentia." *Met.* 11. 27.9. (I print Hanson's text here. F reads "exaptat et," printed by both Helm and Robertson, who follow it with a lacuna.)

and it smells appropriately fishy.⁷⁶ Apuleius holds on to it just long enough to put on the mask of Lucius, or perhaps to let Lucius put on the mask of Apuleius, giving the reader a final reminder of his powers as an impersonator.⁷⁷

LASTING IMPRESSIONS

Apuleius' role-playing in the *Apology* and the *Golden Ass* superimposed the overlapping images of magician and alter ego of Lucius on his basic persona of philosopher and celebrity. It would be interesting to know how his public reacted to this complex and carefully constructed personality. Unfortunately, the sources are silent: Apuleius is not mentioned by name by any of his contemporaries or by anyone else until the beginning of the fourth century, nearly 150 years after his death.⁷⁸

Nevertheless, there are some hints that his works were being read in North Africa in the late second and third centuries. A second-century papyrus seems to illustrate the story of Cupid and Psyche, and it has been argued that Tertullian and Arnobius may have been influenced by the philosophical works.⁷⁹ Moreover, according to the author of the *Historia Augusta*, Apuleius was also known to the African emperors Clodius Albinus (d. 197) and Septimius Severus (d. 211). In the *Life of Albinus* Severus attacks Albinus in a letter to the Roman senate; among his complaints is that Albinus is an enthusiastic reader of Apuleius. Severus says: "It was even more irritating that many of you thought that he deserved to be praised as a man of letters, when he was busying himself with old wives' nonsense and growing senile among literary trifles and the Carthaginian Milesian tales of his friend Apuleius."⁸⁰ But unfortunately

---

⁷⁶ Harrison (*Apuleius*, 231) points out "the extraordinarily ambiguous use of pronouns, possessive adjectives, and indirect speech" in the passage: "Here, if anywhere, is a context where identities might become confused and misinterpreted."

⁷⁷ See van der Paardt ("The Unmasked 'I,' " 106): "What does the author of an 'I'-novel do? He dons . . . a mask, he becomes someone else: Apuleius of Madauros becomes Lucius of Corinth! . . . [The great god Osiris performs] the last, definitive metamorphosis: he changes the narrator into what he used to be, the author!"

⁷⁸ Apuleius is first mentioned in Lactantius, *Div. inst.* 5.3.7. See the next section.

⁷⁹ The papyrus (PSI VIII 919) shows Psyche (with her lamp?) beside a reclining Cupid. It seems to have been a cartoon for a textile or fresco. See Coppolla, "PSI VIII.919," 85–87, plate 2; Bassi, "Amore e Psyche"; Cavallo et al., eds., *Scrivere libri e documenti nel mondo antico*, 2 (color plate), 231–32. For Tertullian and Arnobius, see Moreschini, *Apuleio e il Platonismo*, 219–40. (But Moreschini's parallels between Tertullian and Apuleius have been rejected by Barnes; see his *Tertullian*, 256–58).

⁸⁰ "Maior fuit dolor, quod illum pro litterato laudandum plerique duxistis, cum ille neniis quibusdam anilibus occupatus inter Milesias Punicas Apulei sui et ludicra litteraria consenesceret." *HA. Alb.* 12.12. (Albinus also seems to have written Milesian tales himself;

this gratifyingly circumstantial reference is inconclusive. Perhaps Albinus really was wasting his time with Apuleius' stories and was criticized for it by Severus, but there is no way to be sure that the story antedates the late fourth century, usually taken to be the time of composition of the *Historia Augusta.*

Even without firm *testimonia,* however, we can still infer that Apuleius did make an impression on his immediate posterity and that his efforts to create and manage his image had largely succeeded, for the persona that emerges in the fourth century bears a strong resemblance to the one we saw in the second—although with his features more sharply delineated, as if his second- and third-century audience had silently accepted, consolidated, and embellished the picture that he had presented to them. The late antique Apuleius is still a philosopher, still a celebrity in his native North Africa, and now unquestionably both a famous magician and the alter ego of Lucius. He has also acquired some new features while we weren't looking, for he is now a figure in both Christian and pagan polemic and Constantinian art. In these new theaters of operation he shares the stage with more important actors, appearing with Apollonius of Tyana in the former and Vergil in the latter.

The late-antique persona of Apuleius, however, is by no means consistent or stable, for it varies with the eye (and the purposes) of the beholder, and it changes over time. The dominant facets of his personality are always the magician and the philosopher, but in different proportions and with different emphases from one age to another. In the rest of this chapter we will consider the reception of Apuleius' image in three periods: the fourth century and first decade of the fifth (Lactantius to Jerome), the second and third decades of the fifth century (Augustine), and the early Middle Ages.

Divided Self?

In the period from Lactantius to Jerome, Apuleius is still both magician and philosopher, but with one interesting exception he is no longer both at once. We might almost say that for most of the century he has a split personality: he is a magician in Christian and pagan polemic and a philosopher in Constantinian art. Although he was being read (as subscriptions in our oldest manuscript of the *Apology, Metamorphoses,*

---

see *HA Alb.* 11.8.) The term "Milesian tales," derived from the racy *Milesiaca* of Aristides of Miletus (ca. 100 BC), seems originally to have referred to short, obscene stories but was later used almost as a generic term for fiction. Apuleius describes the style of the *Golden Ass* as "sermone . . . Milesio" (*Met.* 1.1.1).

and *Florida* attest), it is important to note that no one who writes about him in this period either quotes him or shows a close familiarity with his works.[81] The situation is different, however, in the case of our two extant artistic representations. Neither can be taken as a portrait of the "real" Apuleius, but, as we shall see, each seems to be inspired by his writings.

Apuleius appears first as a magician. Our source is a fellow North African, the Christian apologist Lactantius, who mentions him briefly in his *Divine Institutes* somewhere between 305 and 313.[82] Lactantius, a sufferer in Diocletian's Great Persecution of the Christians, is arguing against the pagan Hierocles, who is usually identified as one of the prime movers of the persecution.[83] In his now lost polemical work *To the Christians,* Hierocles had claimed that Apollonius of Tyana performed wonders even greater than the miracles attributed to Christ.[84] Now Lactantius professes to be amazed that he had not named Apuleius as well: "It's a wonder that Hierocles overlooked Apuleius," he exclaims, "for people like to talk about *his* many marvels, too."[85]

Apollonius of Tyana, whom Hierocles had deemed so superior to Christ, was a first-century neo-Pythagorean and holy man famous as a wonderworker.[86] His asceticism, wisdom, miraculous cures, and resurrection

---

[81] For the subscriptions in the archetype of the text of the *Apology, Metamorphoses,* and *Florida,* see chapter 2.

[82] The dates 304–312 are given by Barnes, "Porphyry *Against the Christians*: Date and the Attribution of Fragments," 439. In *Constantine and Eusebius,* 291 n. 96, Barnes fixes the date at 308–9. In a personal communication, Oliver Nicholson more conservatively dates the work between 305 and 313. For a modern translation, see Lactantius, *Divine Institutes,* trans. Bowen and Garnsey.

[83] We know too little about the life and movements of Lactantius (ca. 250–325). For convenient accounts, see Lactantius, *De Mortibus Persecutorum,* ed. Creed, xxv–xxix; Bowen and Garnsey, trans., in Lactantius, *Divine Institutes,* 1–6. He was teaching rhetoric in Nicomedia in Bithynia in 303 when the Great Persecution began (*Div. inst.* 5.2.2) and lost his position. He apparently left Nicomedia and wrote and published the first edition of the *Divinae institutiones* in the western part of the empire, either in Gaul or in his native Africa. (Barnes, in *Constantine and Eusebius,* 291 n. 96, argues for North Africa.) For Hierocles, see Barnes, "Sossianus Hierocles."

[84] Forrat believes that Hierocles wrote his tract while he was serving as *vicarius,* well before the beginning of the persecution in 303, implying a date sometime in the late 290s (Eusebius, *Contre Hiéroclès,* 11–20). Barnes dates the tract to around 303 ("Sossianus Hierocles").

[85] The section reads as follows (the italicized words are translated in the text): "Idem [i.e., Hierocles] cum facta eius [i.e., Christi] mirabilia destrueret nec tamen negaret, voluit ostendere 'Apollonium vel paria vel etiam maiora fecisse.' *Mirum quod Apuleium praetermisit, cuius solent multa et mira memorari*" *Div. inst.* 5.3.7.

[86] See Philostratus, *The Life of Apollonius of Tyana,* trans, Jones. For later accounts, see Speyer, "Zum Bild des Apollonius von Tyana"; Bowie, "Apollonius of Tyana"; Forrat, in Eusebius, *Contre Hiéroclès,* 29–55.

from the dead made him a natural rival to Christ in anti-Christian polemics. Perhaps best of all from the pagan point of view was the story that he had escaped the wrath of the emperor Domitian by disappearing into thin air, thus showing himself a better magician than Christ, whose encounter with Roman authority had ended so differently.[87] It is impossible to be sure when Apollonius made his first appearance in religious polemic. The difficulty arises because our only evidence for the pagan side comes from the refutations of Christian apologists, who were always partisan and sometimes had only indirect or hearsay access to the work of their pagan opponents. Perhaps Hierocles was the first to invoke Apollonius, as Eusebius claimed in his polemic *Against Hierocles* around 311–12.[88] Or perhaps the famous pagan apologist Porphyry had invoked him a few years earlier in his work *Against the Christians*.[89] The important point for us is that at the end of the third century Apollonius had the prestige and qualifications to be presented as a match for Christ and the apostles and that at least one pagan apologist (Hierocles) took advantage of the fact.

But Hierocles did not mention Apuleius, and it is likely that no one else did either until Lactantius invoked his name in the *Divine Institutes*. Apuleius' fame was no match for that of Apollonius, and he had no biographer like Philostratus to preserve his memory. But he was known in North Africa, and Lactantius brings him into the debate, invoking him not as a writer but as a personality and figure of the popular imagination. Perhaps Lactantius had read some of Apuleius' works (although we cannot be sure of it); but in the *Divine Institutes* he is clearly recalling North African tales and oral tradition. Apuleius himself

---

[87] Philostratus, *Vita Apoll.* 8.5. See also Lactantius, *Div. inst.* 5.3.9, and Eusebius, *Contra Hier.* 38, both evidently quoting Hierocles.

[88] *Contra Hier.* 1.2: "Only he [Hierocles], among all those who have ever written against us, has produced a formal contrast and comparison of Apollonius with our savior" (Jones, trans., *Eusebius's Reply to Hierocles*, in Philostratus, *Apollonius of Tyana*, 157). For the date, see Forrat, in Eusebius, *Contre Hiéroclès*, 25; Barnes argues for ca. 303 ("Sossianus Hierocles").

[89] Porphyry's work is dated between 270 and 303. For a date of ca. 271–72, see Croke, "The Era of Porphyry's Anti-Christian Polemic." Barnes favors a date of around or after 300: "Porphyry *Against the Christians*"; "Scholarship or Propaganda?" Fragments 4, 46, 60, and 63 of Porphyry mention Apollonius (fragments 4 and 46 also mention Apuleius); but all these fragments date from the late fourth or fifth century, and only fragment 4 is now considered authentic (see the discussion of Jerome later in this section). Fragments 60 and 63 belong to a group of texts from the fourth- or fifth-century apologist Makarius of Magnesia that most modern scholars consider wrongly attributed to Porphyry; see Barnes, "Porphyry *Against the Christians*," 428–30; Meredith, "Porphyry and Julian Against the Christians," 1126–28. Benoit relegates these fragments, as well as fragment 46 (from Augustine, *Ep.* 102.32; see below), to the general stock of anti-Christian polemics ("Le 'Contra Christianos' de Porphyre").

cannot have been Lactantius' source, since he claims no marvelous or supernatural accomplishments in any of his works.

After Lactantius the linking of Apuleius and Apollonius became a fixture in Christian polemic. Jerome, writing a hundred years later, at the beginning of the fifth century, again mentions the pair as magicians.[90] He is refuting Porphyry, who had evidently argued that Christian claims were based primarily on miracles and that the apostles worked their wonders for the sake of gain.

> Someone might say, "They did all this for money." For this is what Porphyry says: "The poor and uneducated men, since they had nothing, worked some wonders with magic arts. But it is no great thing to perform wonders. The magicians in Egypt also performed wonders against Moses. Apollonius performed wonders, and so did Apuleius: in fact, they performed boundless wonders." I grant you, Porphyry, that they performed wonders with their magic arts in order to get money from silly rich women whom they had seduced. For this is what you say.[91]

The passage is interesting on several counts: as a contribution to the fragments of Porphyry's lost *Against the Christians*, as an example of Jerome's polemical method, and as evidence for the late-antique knowledge of Apuleius.

Jerome's quotation of Porphyry (listed as fragment 4 of *Against the Christians*) begins with the words "The poor and uneducated men" and concludes three sentences later with the clause "in fact, they performed boundless wonders."[92] This is the only unquestionably authentic fragment of Porphyry that mentions Apollonius and Apuleius. The authenticity of the fragment as a whole, however, does not guarantee the authenticity of everything in it. Barnes claims that Jerome knew Porphyry only indirectly.[93] But it is just as likely that he was using or remembering

---

[90] For the date, see Jay, "Jérôme à Bethléem," 377–78.

[91] "Dicat aliquis: Hoc totum lucri causa fecerunt. Hoc enim dicit Porphyrius: Homines rusticani et pauperes, quoniam nihil habebant, magicis artibus operati sunt quaedam signa. Non est autem grande facere signa. Nam fecerunt signa et in Aegypto magi contra Moysen. Fecit et Apollonius, fecit et Apuleius: et infinita signa fecerunt. Concedo tibi, Porphyri, magicis artibus signa fecerunt, ut divitias acciperent a divitibus mulierculis, quas induxerant: hoc enim tu dicis" Jerome, *Tractatus de Psalmo lxxxi*, 225–32.

[92] "Homini rusticani et pauperes . . . infinita signa fecerunt." See Meredith, "Porphyry and Julian Against the Christians," 1130 n. 16. The standard edition of the fragments is still that of Harnack, "Porphyrius 'Gegen die Christen.'" Harnack (pp. 46–47) treats the words "divitias . . . induxerant" as a quotation, as if from Porphyry.

[93] Barnes, "Scholarship or Propaganda?" 54. Barnes also argues (53) that Porphyry's *Contra Christianos* was suppressed by Constantine and asserts: "It is extremely hard to find authors writing after 325 who report the contents of the work at first hand."

an interpolated text, for it would be surprising if some changes had not crept into it during the intervening century of religious polemic. Jerome was also capable of adding touches of his own if it suited his satirical purposes, as the name of Apuleius does here. With the reference to Apuleius' use of magic to achieve his mercenary marriage, Jerome manages not only to make a last-minute riposte to Porphyry's slur on the supposed venality of the apostles (and to trump it) but also to allude to the allegation made by Porphyry's detractors that he, too, had married a rich elderly widow for her money.[94]

It is important to note, however, that Jerome's citation of Apuleius as a magician is different in kind from that of Lactantius. Even if he is invoking only Apuleius' image, the image is at least one clearly related to his works and not merely a piece of apocryphal flotsam. Jerome knows about the *Apology* even if he has not read it—or at least he knows enough to be familiar with its charge that Apuleius won his rich wife by sorcery. If he also knows the fact that Apuleius claimed to be innocent, his satirical nature and polemical purposes are such that he happily overlooks it.

Apuleius appears as a philosopher very soon after he is first mentioned as a magician, in the early decades of the fourth century. The evidence this time is both artistic and literary, and the context is Constantinian. Apuleius has been identified on a painted ceiling in Trier, and he had a bronze statue in the Baths of Zeuxippos at Constantinople, as we have seen. In both cases Vergil is part of the program.

Trier was one of Constantine's capital cities. In the early fourth century it housed some of the imperial family, including the emperor's son Crispus, and perhaps Crispus' tutor Lactantius as well. The last point is unverifiable, since we do not know the date or locale of Lactantius' service.[95] It is tantalizing because of the suggestion that Lactantius might have had a part in determining the program of the ceiling, which probably belonged to a reception room in an imperial residence.[96]

The room was constructed after 315 and demolished in 326, when work began on the foundations of Trier Cathedral.[97] At that time the ceiling collapsed, and the pieces fell down more or less in place, a happy

---

[94] The story appears in a fragment of the *Theosophia* of Aristokritos (fifth century) quoted by Buresch, *Klaros*, 124. See Harnack, "Porphyry 'Gegen die Christen,'" 40–41 (Zeugnis xxvi b). Harnack (p. 4) argues that it is derived from Eusebius' work against Porphyry.

[95] Lactantius' service probably began before 317, when Crispus was appointed Caesar. See Creed, in Lactantius, *De mortibus persecutorum*, xxvii.

[96] Simon, *Die konstantinischen Deckengemälde in Trier*, 19.

[97] See Weber, *Constantinische Deckengemälde*; Simon, *Die konstantinischen Deckengemälde*.

circumstance that has permitted a nearly complete reconstruction (see plate 1).[98] The rectangular painting is divided into fifteen panels—three on the short sides and five on the long. Seven panels showing busts of male and female figures alternate checkerboard fashion with eight panels showing pairs of putti or Erotes with different attributes. The putti appear on each of the four corners, in the centers of the long sides and on either side of the central bust in the middle row. Three of the busts represent elderly men (apparently poets or philosophers); the other four seem to be either portraits or personified virtues. There are no inscriptions to identify the figures in any of the panels.

Several interpretations of the ceiling's program have been proposed, but the most convincing is that of Erika Simon, who has identified the three "philosophers" as Vergil, Apuleius, and Heraclitus, one of the "portraits" as Apollo, and the others as personified virtues associated with Constantine's wife, Fausta.[99] Simon dates the painting not long after 315 and reads its message as predominantly solar and imperial rather than overtly Christian (although she notes that the panels of putti around the central bust are arranged in a cruciform pattern).

The essential part of her argument for the present discussion is her identification of the elderly men on the two short sides as Vergil and Apuleius. Each is identified by the attributes of the putti juxtaposed with his portrait. The putti around the image of Vergil have attributes appropriate to the *Fourth Eclogue*, which prophesies a new golden age of Apollo: the horn of plenty; a standing vessel, perhaps for wine; and a whip and charioteer's cloak evoking Apollo, the charioteer of the sun.[100] The corresponding bust at the other end is marked as a philosopher by his cloak and beard. The paired figures above him are not the same putti as in the other panels, but rather Cupid and Psyche from the *Golden Ass* (see plate 2). The philosopher, therefore, can only be Apuleius (see plate 3). The panel of Cupid and Psyche illustrates a particular moment in the story, as Simon has deduced from the flat box or tray in Psyche's hand.[101] It is the object of her last labor: the box of beauty that she was to fetch from Proserpina in Hades and present—unopened—to Venus. But she violated the taboo. When she opened the box, she was immediately engulfed in a Stygian sleep, in which she would have remained if Cupid had not awakened her with a painless touch of his arrow (*Met.* 6.21.3). The panel shows Psyche and Cupid just after

---

[98] For color illustrations of the reconstructed ceiling, see Weber, *Constantinische Deckengemälde*, and Simon, *Die konstantinischen Deckengemälde*.

[99] Simon, *Die konstantinischen Deckengemälde*, 19–37.

[100] The images are also appropriate to the prophetic passages in the *Aeneid* anticipating the reign of Augustus. See Rodgers, "Constantine's Pagan Vision."

[101] Simon, *Die konstantinischen Deckengemälde*, 20–21.

her awakening and their joyous reunion. She is about to complete her task, after which she will be taken to Olympus and receive the gift of immortality.

Simon has seen that the image of Cupid and Psyche identifies the philosopher in the adjacent panel as Apuleius, but we can also turn the argument around to say that Apuleius' character as a philosopher is linked to Cupid and Psyche. We can infer both that the author of the ceiling's program has derived his conception of Apuleius as a philosopher from the novel and, conversely, that he sees the story of Cupid and Psyche as important and serious. The panel represents not merely the happy ending of a romance but an event of philosophical and religious significance. Its meaning is clear enough: Psyche ("Soul")—though undeserving, as her box reminds us—has been saved by Love and will soon achieve eternal happiness. This message, like Vergil's prophecy of a new golden age, is not necessarily Christian but still consistent with Christian ideas—a nice compromise for a Constantinian work so soon after the emperor's famous conversion in 312.

Psyche's presence on the ceiling in Trier, like her appearance on the second-century papyrus, is precious evidence of early interest in Apuleius' story. The image in Trier, however, is more informative, for its context and placement also allow us to infer the artist's interpretation and to see it as an important anticipation of later allegorical treatments, like those of Martianus Capella and Fulgentius to be examined in the next chapter.

About a decade or so after the painting in Trier, Apuleius appeared in another Constantinian installation. His statue was placed in a large collection of sculpture arrayed in the Baths of Zeuxippos in Constantinople for the dedication of the city in 330 AD.[102] Our source is the late fifth-century Byzantine poet Christodorus, who describes eighty-one statues in the baths.[103] Although Christodorus lists many Greek poets, historians, and philosophers in his ecphrasis, he names only two Roman writers: Apuleius and Vergil.[104] The program of the statues has not been satisfactorily explained, and perhaps Christodorus, writing 150 years after the fact, did not understand it himself. The points that matter for our purposes, however, are Apuleius' depiction as a philosopher and the fact that he and Vergil are the only Roman writers whose statues we

---

[102] For Christodorus' description of the statue, see p. 14. For the baths and their program, see, with earlier bibliography, Bassett, "*Historiae custos*" and *The Urban Image of Late Antique Constantinople*, 51–57, 160–85.

[103] Christodorus' ecphrasis as we have it is probably incomplete: it lacks both preface and conclusion, and it is conceivable that descriptions of some statues have dropped out. See Bassett, "*Historiae custos*," 495.

[104] Apuleius: *Anth. Pal* 2.303–5; Vergil: *Anth. Pal* 2.414–16.

know appeared in the collection. The singling out of Apuleius and Vergil, so soon after the installation of the ceiling in Trier, suggests that the designer of the program was associating them in a similar way, or at the very least that he was recalling their appearance in Trier. Christodorus himself, however, does not treat the two statues as a pair, and there is no evidence that they appeared next to each other.[105]

Apuleius makes his last appearance in the visual arts of antiquity at the end of the fourth century. This imaginary portrait, on a Roman contorniate, or circus medal, is the only surviving ancient image accompanied by an identifying inscription (see plate 4).[106] The contorniate shows Apuleius in profile as a beautiful beardless youth, wide-eyed, and with shoulder-length curls held neatly in place by a fillet. The depiction was surely inspired by passages in the *Florida* and *Apology*. The fillet alludes to the priesthood he mentions in *Florida* 16, while the artfully casual coiffure recalls both the beautiful long hair criticized by his opponents in the *Apology* and the flowing locks of his alter ego Apollo in *Florida* 3.[107] The portrait surely would have been more to Apuleius' taste than those in Trier and Constantinople, for it is one he might have commissioned himself: "Apuleius the Platonic philosopher as Apollo."

But of course Apuleius did not commission the portrait. The contorniate is a product of the complex social, intellectual, and religious world of late fourth-century Rome, and its iconography was selected by a fourth-century designer or patron to reflect contemporary interests. The image is by no means a generic portrait. It is not only unlike the previous representations of Apuleius that we know about (the bearded philosopher shown on the Trier ceiling and probably in his various statues as well), but also without parallel among the hundreds of real and imaginary portraits on the contorniates. No doubt one of the designer's motives for choosing Apuleius' verbal self-portait as his model in preference to the existing material representations and conventional philosopher portraits was that he knew Apuleius' text and wanted to advertise it. In the 390s Apuleius was of some interest in Rome, as we shall see in the next chapter. But he may have had something else in mind as

---

[105] The two descriptions are handled differently, and they are separated by over a hundred lines.

[106] There are two copies of the medal. See Alföldi, *Die Kontorniat-Medaillons* 1.1.32; 1.2: plate 37.12; 2: 101–2, 371, plate 214.12. See also Schefold, *Die Bildnisse*, 428–29.

[107] "Immo etiam docuit argumento suscepti sacerdotii summum mihi honorem Carthaginis adesse" *Fl.* 16.38. "Capillus ipse, quem isti aperto mendacio ad lenocinium decoris promissum dixere." *Apol.* 4.11 (and see Hunink, *Apuleius . . . de Magia* 2:22). "Crines eius praemulsis antiis et promulsis caproneis anteventuli et propenduli." *Fl.* 3.10.

well, for the likeness on the contorniate has a close parallel in an unexpected quarter—in fourth-century representations of Christ.

The iconography of Christ in this period is rich and complex, but the most important points for us are that the young, beardless Christ, like Apuleius, has Apollonian antecedents and that he is an otherworldly "intellectual wunderkind" (the phrase is Zanker's), who has aspects of both the philosopher and the wonder-worker.[108] Among the closest parallels to our Apuleius are a small statue of Christ in the Terme Museum in Rome dated around 380 and two figures of Christ (one in profile) on a column sarcophagus in the Vatican Museum dated around 370.[109] Both monuments show Christ holding a book roll. In both he appears with fine, youthful features, a tunic and pallium, and shoulder-length hair neatly covering his ears—just like Apuleius on the contorniate, except that Apuleius wears the fillet of a pagan priest.

The meaning and purpose of the contorniate will be explored more fully in the next chapter when we consider Apuleius' place in the world of late fourth-century Rome. For now it is sufficient to note that the portrait alludes both to the second-century text of Apuleius and to fourth-century Christian iconography, overlaying the image of "the Platonic philosopher as Apollo" with that of "the charismatic holy man and wonder-worker." The resulting multivalent picture of Apuleius finally reunites the personalities of philosopher and magician that had been separated throughout the fourth century.

"This Platonic Philosopher"

A much more complex and detailed picture of Apuleius appears in Augustine than in the literary or artistic works of his predecessors. Augustine's greater knowledge and greater interest are not surprising, for he

---

[108] See Zanker, *The Mask of Socrates,* 289–300 (for "intellectual wunderkind," see 299). See also Gerke, *Christus in der spätantiken Plastik,* 31–48; Dinkler, *Christus und Asklepios,* 35–37; Mathews, *The Clash of Gods,* 54–91.

[109] For the statuette (Rome, Museo Nazionale Romano 61565), see Zanker, *The Mask of Socrates,* 290–92, 390 n. 42, plate 157; Mathews, *The Clash of Gods,* 128–29; Gerke, *Christus in der spätantiken Plastik,* plates 56–59; Ensoli and La Rocca, *Aurea Roma,* 361–62. For the sarcophagus (Vatican S. Pietro I.677, formerly Lat. 174), see Deichmann, *Repertorium der christlich-antiken Sarkophage* 1.677 (pp. 274–77), plate 106; *The Vatican Collections,* 30–31; Gerke, 37–38, plates 53–54; Mathews, *The Clash of Gods,* fig. 68. The sarcophagus was much restored in the eighteenth century. See Bartoli, "Bartolomeo Cavaceppi," 36–45; see also the discussions and bibliographies in Koch, *Frühchristliche Sarkophage,* 320, 615; Deichmann, *Repertorium*; *The Vatican Collections.* For other parallels, see Deichmann, 1:45 (plate 15), 2:151 (plate 63), 2:152 (plate 64).

had much in common with Apuleius, including background, education, and youthful ambition. He was a fellow North African; he went to school in Apuleius' hometown, Madauros, and later studied and taught rhetoric at Carthage. In the period from about 412 to 427, we find him citing Apuleius as both a magician and a philosopher, taking for granted his identity with Lucius, revealing details of his career, and quoting and discussing his *De mundo* and *De deo Socratis*.[110]

Augustine differs from his literary predecessors in acknowledging both of Apuleius' personalities. He does not explicitly unite or integrate the magician and the philosopher (the two figures generally appear in separate contexts), but he implies a necessary relation between them, viewing Apuleius' magic as a corollary of his philosophy.[111] The link is Apuleius' work *De deo Socratis*, which sets out the Platonic conception of *daimones* as intermediaries between gods and mortals. For Augustine these *daimones* have no status as intermediaries. They are simply demons, evil spirits and purveyors of the magic arts, with which they delude and destroy their devotees. By professing to revere them, Apuleius is inevitably implicated in their supernatural activities. The connection between demons and magic, implied in Augustine's correspondence, becomes more important in the *City of God*, in which two books are devoted to refuting *De deo Socratis*.

Augustine pairs Apuleius with his fellow magician Apollonius three times in his correspondence, but he also refers to him as a magician without mentioning Apollonius in both the letters and the *City of God*.[112] In the letters the context is always the now familiar debate about Christian miracles and pagan magic. Unlike Lactantius and Jerome, however, Augustine is openly skeptical about Apuleius' powers and doubts that he could match the miracles related in scripture. In *Epistola* 102, probably written around 412,[113] Augustine responds to a pagan attack on the credibility of the story of Jonah and the whale. He implies that such a miracle would be too great for Apuleius and Apollonius and casts a slur in passing on the specious magic of demons:

> And yet if what has been written about Jonah were said to have been accomplished by Apuleius of Madauros or Apollonius of Tyana, whose

---

[110] See Hagendahl, *Augustine and the Latin Classics* 1:17–33, 2:680–89. See also O'Donnell, "Augustine's Classical Readings," 149–50. For discussion, see Moreschini, *Apuleio e il Platonismo*, 221–25, 240–54; Horsfall Scotti, "Apuleio tra magia e filosofia"; Hunink, "*Apuleius, qui nobis Afris Afer est Notior.*"

[111] But in *Ep.* 102.32 (see below) he seems to lump together philosophers and magicians.

[112] Apuleius and Apollonius: Augustine, *Ep.* 102.32, *Ep.* 136.1, *Ep.* 138.18. Apuleius alone: *Ep.* 137.13, *Ep.* 138.19, *Civ.* 8.19, *Civ.* 18.18.

[113] O'Donnell, "Augustine's Classical Readings," 149 n. 15.

many wonders they boast of without any trustworthy authority (although demons do some things like the holy angels—not in truth but in appearance, not by wisdom but clearly by trickery)—if any such thing were told about these men, as I have said, whom they praise as magicians or philosophers, not derision but a cry of triumph would sound in their mouths.[114]

Augustine's skepticism continues in his famous correspondence of 412 with Marcellinus and Volusianus that led up to the *City of God*. In *Epistola* 137 to Volusianus, Augustine challenges the supporters of Apuleius and other magicians to consider whether their heroes, like the biblical prophets, had ever resurrected anyone from the dead.[115] In *Epistola* 136 Marcellinus asks Augustine to counter the arguments of pagans claiming that Apollonius, Apuleius, and other magicians had performed wonders greater than Christ's. The question is an old chestnut, Marcellinus admits, but he still hopes that Augustine will respond to it.[116] Although he considers the argument scarcely "worthy of derision," in *Epistola* 138 Augustine replies at length, again linking demons and magic in an aside.[117] In this letter he is particularly concerned with Apuleius, who, as he says, "as an African is better known to us Africans."[118] Quickly sketching Apuleius' biography, including his priesthood, marriage, lawsuit, and statue in Oea, Augustine notes that he in fact achieved little with all his magic powers, in spite of his excel-

---

[114] "Et tamen si hoc, quod de Iona scriptum est, Apuleius Madaurensis vel Apollonius Tyaneus fecisse diceretur, quorum multa mira nullo fideli auctore iactitant, quamvis et daemones nonnulla faciant angelis sanctis similia non veritate sed specie, non sapientia sed plane fallacia, tamen, si de istis, ut dixi, quos magos vel philosophos laudabiliter nominant, tale aliquid narraretur, non iam in buccis creparet risus, sed typhus." Augustine, *Ep*. 102.32. This passage is listed as fragment 46 of Porphyry's *Against the Christians*, but it does not mention Porphyry, and Benoit attributes the references to Apollonius and Apuleius to the general stock of anti-Christian polemic ("Le 'Contra Christianos' de Porphyre," 71).
[115] "Nam de magorum miraculis, utrum etiam mortuos suscitaverint, illi viderint, qui et Apuleium se contra magicarum artium crimina copiosissime defendentem conantur non accusando sed laudando convincere." Augustine, *Ep*. 137.13.
[116] "Quae quidem quaestio usque quaque detrita est et eorum super hac parte satis nota calliditas, qui dispensationem dominicae incarnationis infamant. Sed tamen etiam ego in hac parte, quia plurimis, quicquid rescripseris, profuturum esse confido, precator accesserim, ut ad ea vigilantius respondere digneris." [Augustine], *Ep*. 136.1.
[117] *Worthy of derision*: "Quis autem vel risu dignum putet, quod Apollonium et Apuleium ceterosque magicarum artium peritissimos conferre Christo vel etiam praeferre conantur?" Augustine, *Ep*. 138.18. *Demons and magic*: "Horum daemonum perversitatem atque fallaciam, per quos et magicae artes humanas mentes decipiunt." Ibid.
[118] "Apuleius enim, ut de illo potissimum loquamur, qui nobis Afris Afer est notior." Ibid. 138.19.

lent birth, education, and rhetorical skill: "In the matter of earthly success, that well-known magician was what he was able to be. From this it is clear that he was nothing more, not because he was unwilling but because he was unable."[119] He then delivers his knock-out punch: those who tell stories of Apuleius' magical powers are in fact contradicting their hero, for he emphatically denied being a magician.[120] The point is important to his argument, and he also makes it in another letter from the same correspondence.[121]

In the *City of God* Apuleius appears twice as a magician. Here Augustine is interested not in the debate about miracles and magic but in magic itself and Apuleius as its devotee.

In book 8 (composed around 415–17), one of his major purposes is to refute the demonology of *De deo Socratis*. Apuleius' denial of magic is again part of the argument, but now Augustine uses it differently: to point out what he judges to be both the hypocrisy and the inconsistency of Apuleius' position.[122] Since Augustine considers reverence for *daimones* tantamount to subscribing to magic, he regards Apuleius' denial as hypocritical (or at least fainthearted): by denying magic Apuleius renounced his faith. In *City of God* 8.19 Augustine contrasts his denial with the steadfastness of the Christian martyrs: "If he knew that these [magic arts], at least the ones that he was charged with, were divine and pious and consistent with the works of the divine powers, he ought not only to have confessed but to have professed them."[123] If he were punished for his belief by death, Augustine continues sarcastically, "the demons would pay his soul worthy recompense, since he did not fear to have his human life taken away for proclaiming their divine works."[124] Apuleius, however, was no martyr for his faith in demons; instead, we have the copious and eloquent defense of "this Platonic philosopher,"[125] as Augustine calls him, against the charge of magic. But Apuleius' denials

---

[119] "Quod ergo ad istam terrenam pertinet felicitatem, fuit magus ille, quod potuit. Unde apparet nihil eum amplius fuisse, non quia noluit, sed quia non potuit." Ibid.

[120] "Quamquam et adversus quosdam, qui ei magicarum artium crimen intenderant, eloquentissime se defendit. Unde miror laudatores eius, qui eum nescio qua fecisse miracula illis artibus praedicant, contra eius defensionem testes esse conari. Sed viderint, utrum ipsi verum perhibeant testimonium et ille falsam defensionem." Ibid.

[121] Ibid. 137.13. See n.115 above.

[122] See Horsfall Scotti, "Apuleio tra magia e filosofia," 307–10.

[123] "Quas [magicas artes] utique sibi obiectas si divinas et pias esse noverat et divinarum potestatum operibus congruas, non solum eas confiteri debuit, sed etiam profiteri." Augustine, *Civ.* 8.19.

[124] "Digna animae illius daemones dona rependerent, pro quorum divinis operibus praedicandis humanam vitam sibi adimi non timeret." Ibid.

[125] "Huius . . . philosophi Platonici." Ibid.

are not only self-serving. By his defense (which Augustine claims was based "on denying things that cannot be committed by an innocent man"),[126] Apuleius also revealed the flaw in the argument of *De deo Socratis*: since by condemning magic he also condemns the *daimones* who teach and promote it, how can he explain why they should be honored and esteemed?[127]

In *City of God* 18.18 (composed around 425) Augustine brings the connection between magic and demons into the discussion of metamorphosis. If such transformations ever took place, he argues, they would be mere illusions produced by the trickery of demons, who "change only in appearance things created by the true God so that they seem to be what they are not."[128] Apuleius is brought into the discussion, if not as a magician, at least as someone in touch with the magic arts, when Augustine relates his own acquaintance with present-day tales of metamorphosis. He says that he himself has heard (but does not believe) stories of men being transformed into animals and keeping their human reason, "just as Apuleius either declared or pretended happened to him in the books which he entitled the *Golden Ass*—that after taking a magical substance he became an ass, but with his mind remaining human."[129]

The passage is often quoted, since it is our earliest evidence for the title *Golden Ass*, which Augustine says was awarded by Apuleius himself.[130] But it is also the earliest evidence for the way in which the novel was understood by a specific, identifiable reader. Augustine clearly takes it as autobiography, whether real or fictitious; for although he denies the possibility of metamorphosis and doubts the sincerity of Apuleius' account, he assumes without question that Apuleius is claiming to relate his own experience—that he is, in fact, the Lucius of his novel. The assumption continued to be unquestioned for at least a thousand years, and the identity of Apuleius and Lucius was to play a major role in the interpretation of the *Golden Ass*. As we shall see, the identification was

---

[126] "Ea negando, quae non possunt ab innocente committi." Ibid.

[127] "At omnia miracula magorum, quos recte sentit esse damnandos, doctrinis fiunt et operibus daemonum, quos viderit cur censeat honorandos." Ibid.

[128] "Specie tenus, quae a vero Deo sunt creata commutant, ut videantur esse quod non sunt." Ibid. 18.18.

[129] "Sicut Apuleius in libris, quos asini aurei titulo inscripsit, sibi ipsi accidisse, ut accepto veneno humano animo permanente asinus fieret, aut indicavit aut finxit." Ibid.

[130] The title *Metamorphoses*, preserved in Florence, Biblioteca Laurenziana 68.2 (F), goes back at least to the end of the fourth century; see Pecere, "Esemplari con *subscriptiones*," 122–25. But the novel may have had a double title (*Metamorphoses / Asinus Aureus*); see Münstermann, *Apuleius*, 45–56; Harrison, *Apuleius*, 210 n. 1, with earlier references. For *Asinus Aureus* as an appropriate title, see Winkler, *Auctor & Actor*, 292–321; Bitel, "*Quis ille Asinus aureus*?"

so deeply ingrained that Renaissance scribes regularly awarded Apuleius the praenomen Lucius, and annotators generally called the novel's hero either Apuleius or Lucius Apuleius.[131] (There is no literary evidence for Apuleius' actual praenomen, and no praenomen appears in our oldest manuscripts, which call him Apuleius Madaurensis or Apuleius philosophus Platonicus or some combination of the two.)[132]

In Augustine's view Apuleius the magician is ineffective and incompetent because magic itself is no more than the deceptive trickery of demons; true marvels are brought about by piety and simple faith, not by magic.[133] But he has more respect for Apuleius the Platonic philosopher. Augustine praises the Platonists as supreme among pagan philosophers for their conception of god as the source of creation, truth, and felicity.[134] Apuleius, as a follower of the school—and one from Augustine's homeland, writing in Latin—enjoys a prominent place among them: "Among these [later Platonists], the Greeks Plotinus, Iamblichus, and Porphyry were renowned; but the African Apuleius was prominent as a famous Platonist in both languages—that is, in both Greek and Latin."[135]

But if Apuleius wins Augustine's praise for his Platonism, he also incurs his polemical criticism for the same reason. In Augustine's eyes the Platonists are guilty of a fundamental error: even though they entertain nearly Christian ideas about the supreme deity, they are nevertheless adherents of polytheism.[136] Apuleius' convenient exposition of the taxonomy of gods, *daimones*, and mortals in *De deo Socratis* gave Augustine the material on which to base his detailed point-by-point criticism of the Platonic view in books 8 and 9 of the *City of God*. He quotes Apuleius extensively and subjects his views to ruthless and biting polemic, reserving his greatest scorn for the Platonic conception of

---

[131] See p. 69 below.

[132] If Coarelli is right to identify the L. Apuleius Marcellus of Ostia with our Apuleius (see n. 5 above), we would have to say that Lucius actually was Apuleius' praenomen. But since the Renaissance scribes could have had no knowledge of the house at Ostia, we can be sure that they arrived at the praenomen from their autobiographical reading of the novel. For Apuleius' name in the oldest manuscripts, see n. 19 above.

[133] "Fiebant autem simplici fide atque fiducia pietatis, non incantationibus et carminibus nefariae curiositatis arte compositis, quam vel magian vel detestabiliore nomine goetian vel honorabiliore theurgian vocant." *Civ.* 10.9.

[134] "Isti Deo cognito reppererunt ubi esset et causa constitutae universitatis et lux percipiendae veritatis et fons bibendae felicitatis." *Civ.* 8.10.

[135] "Ex quibus sunt valde nobilitati Graeci Plotinus, Iamblichus, Porphyrius; in utraque autem lingua, id est et Graeca et Latina, Apuleius Afer extitit Platonicus nobilis." *Civ.* 8.12.

[136] "Sed hi omnes et ceteri eius modi et ipse Plato diis plurimis esse sacra facienda putaverunt." Ibid.

daimones as intermediaries between gods and mortals.[137] The Platonists maintain that the gods are too sublime to mingle with mortals.[138] Augustine replies that the demons are too evil and base to deserve either intercourse with gods or reverence from men. Moreover, he argues, the Platonic premise is wrong to begin with:[139] God in the person of Christ *does* mingle with mortals, and he is our only intermediary—divine in that he is equal to the father, and partaking in humanity in that he is like ourselves.[140]

Augustine pours scorn on Apuleius' demonology, but his long and detailed refutation indicates the importance he attributed to him. Apuleius figures prominently in the correspondence of 412 between Augustine in Hippo and Marcellinus and Volusianus in Carthage, and it seems quite possible that his works were being read and debated in Carthage by both Christians and pagans.[141] We can never be sure on this point, however, since the surviving correspondence treats Apuleius only in general terms and as a miracle-worker. But whether or not Marcellinus and Volusianus and their friends in Carthage had a manuscript of Apuleius, it is clear that Augustine in Hippo did, and that he studied it closely in preparation for writing the *City of God*.

His manuscript surely included *De deo Socratis*, which he quotes frequently and at length, and probably also *De mundo* (quoted once at some length in *City of God* 4.2). It is more difficult to be certain of the rest of its contents. Augustine knows the general outlines of the *Apology* (enough to make the obvious point, ignored by Jerome, that Apuleius denied being a magician), and he knows that Lucius was transformed into an ass in the *Metamorphoses*. But these are details that he could have easily picked up either as matters of general knowledge or from reading the two works in his youth; he did not need to possess a manuscript. He never mentions or cites *De Platone*, but it has been plausibly suggested that he used it "silently" in his treatment of Platonism in *City of God* 8.[142] He relates some biographical details not preserved in other

---

[137] See especially *Civ.* 8.20 and Hagendahl, *Augustine and the Latin Classics* 2:684 n. 3.

[138] "Nullus deus miscetur hominibus." Apuleius *DDS* 4.128 (translating Plato, *Symp.* 203A).

[139] "Non enim verum est, quod idem Platonicus ait Platonem dixisse: 'Nullus Deus miscetur homini.'" *Civ.* 9.16.

[140] "Hic est, sicut eum sancta scriptura praedicat, 'mediator Dei et hominum homo Christus Iesus,' de cuius et divinitate, qua patri est semper aequalis, et humanitate, qua nobis factus est similis, non hic locus est ut competenter pro nostra facultate dicamus." *Civ.* 9.17.

[141] See O'Donnell, "Augustine's Classical Readings," 149–50.

[142] Horsfall Scotti, "Apuleio tra magia e filosofia," 318–19 n. 96.

sources (*Epistola* 138), but it is not clear whether he found them in works now lost to us or whether they were known generally in North Africa. He also quotes in detail from the pseudo-Apuleian *Asclepius* (*City of God* 8.23–26).[143] This fourth-century work was transmitted with Apuleius' philosophical texts from an early period, which may or may not have been as early as the time of Augustine.[144] Augustine discusses it immediately after his refutation of Apuleius in *City of God* 8, but he clearly does not attribute it to Apuleius himself. Perhaps the *Asclepius* was included in his manuscript, but it seems just as likely that later readers, seeing it so closely linked with Apuleius in the *City of God*, incorporated it into their texts and brought it into the tradition. It appears immediately after *De deo Socratis* in the earliest witness to both the *Asclepius* and Apuleius' philosophical works, the ninth-century manuscript Brussels, Bibliothèque Royale Albert Ier 10054–10056.[145]

Apuleius was interesting to Augustine as a fellow North African and important to him as a Latin Platonist providing material for discussion and refutation in the *City of God*. But Augustine was even more important to Apuleius—at least to Apuleius the philosopher, for it was largely Augustine's interest that brought the philosophical works to the attention of later readers and secured their rich *fortuna* in northern Europe during the Middle Ages.[146] At this point, however, we must part company for a time with Apuleius the philosopher. After around 500 Apuleius' reception becomes two stories: the *fortuna* of the philosophical works (*De deo Socratis, De mundo, De dogmate Platonis*, and the rest) and the tale of the "literary" works (*Metamorphoses, Apology*, and *Florida*), which travel in quite different circles. It is the path of the latter that we will follow in the next chapter. First, however, we must see what happened to Apuleius the magician.

The Magician Vanishes

From Lactantius, Jerome, and Augustine it is clear that Apuleius' character as a magician was well established in late antiquity, and that

[143] See Hagendahl, *Augustine and the Latin Classics* 1:29–33, 2:687–89.

[144] For the date, see Horsfall Scotti, "Apuleio tra magia e filosofia," 313–15, with earlier bibliography.

[145] See Marshall in Reynolds, ed., *Texts and Transmission*, 16–18; Klibansky and Regen, *Die Handschriften*, 60–62; Munk Olsen, *L'Étude des auteurs classiques latins*, 13. We have no clues about the intermediate history of the *Asclepius;* according to Nock (*Corpus Hermeticum* 2:266), there are no testimonia to it between Augustine and the beginning of the twelfth century.

[146] Moreschini, *Apuleio e il Platonismo*, 254; Klibansky and Regen, *Die Handschriften*, 35–38.

stories of his feats were current in North Africa and perhaps elsewhere. But the details are elusive. Although Jerome refers to the charge from the *Apology* that Apuleius won his wife by sorcery, and Augustine recalls the magic transformation in the *Golden Ass*, none of the three Christian writers relates a single example of the popular stories he alludes to. The "many marvels" and "boundless wonders" that they say people (especially pagans) liked to talk about have entirely disappeared. Although we can scarcely blame the Christian apologists for not preserving them—after all, it was not their business to pass on tales of pagan magic—it would still be interesting to know exactly how Apuleius' carefully constructed persona was treated and transformed in oral tradition.

Apuleius' reputation as a magician survives into the Middle Ages, but the stories attached to his name are both late and anachronistic. The image that emerges from them is almost embarrassingly unimpressive. In the Latin west his powers are memorialized in a single example, a charm against nosebleeds preserved in the medical writings of Pseudo-Theodorus: "[You write] the following [in the sufferer's blood] on a sheet of paper and hold it up to his ear: 'Blood, Apuleius of Madaura commands you to stop your flow.'"[147]

More stories are told about him in Byzantium, where he always appears with either Apollonius of Tyana or Julian the Chaldaean or both at once. In the company of these more competent and famous magicians he is usually ineffective.

Apuleius' powers are essentially worthless in a story told in the *Quaestiones et Responsiones*, ascribed to the Byzantine theologian and saint, Anastasios of Sinai (d. after 700).[148] (The date and authorship of the work are uncertain, and some parts of it may be much later than the time of Anastasios.)[149] *Quaestio* 20 concerns magic: "As a consequence of what power do heretics and wicked men often prophesy and work marvels?"[150] The response provides several explanations, ending with the power of demons and the following story: "So too in the time of the emperor Domitian the magicians Julianus, Apollonius, and Apuleius performed wonders of different kinds, and one such performance

---

[147] "Item in chartas (sc. scribis) ad aurem ipsius Sanguis, imperat tibi Apuleius madaurensis, ut cursus tuus stet." *Additamenta Pseudo-Theodori ad Theodorum Priscianum* 276, 21–22. See also Önnerfors, "Magische Formeln," 207.

[148] For Anastasios, see Beck, *Kirche und theologische Literatur*, 442–47.

[149] Ibid., 444–45.

[150] Ἐκ ποίας δυνάμεως οἱ τὰ ἐναντία φρονοῦντες [καὶ πράττοντες] προφητεύουσι πολλάκις καὶ θαυματουργοῦσιν; Anastasios Sinaites, *Quaestiones et responsiones* (Patrologia Graeca 89: col. 517).

appears in the tales of our elders."[151] It seems that Domitian and the great men of his court had called upon the three magicians to save Rome from a terrible plague that was ravaging the city. Apuleius said that he would save a third of the city within fifteen days, and Apollonius promised to save a third within ten. Julian, however, "the best among them and much closer to the devil through this vanity,"[152] saved his third on the spot, as well as the thirds assigned to Apuleius and Apollonius. The story concludes with a list of various marvels performed by Apollonius with the help of demons. Apuleius is clearly the least important of the three magicians, for he is soon forgotten and all our attention is directed to Julian and Apollonius. The story may be an old one, as the author suggests, but if so, Apuleius is only a latecomer in it. The author does not know that the three magicians were not contemporaries (a fact that would have been obvious, at least in the West, as late as the fifth century). Apparently he does not know any stories about Apuleius' magic (if he did, we could expect to hear them, since he is so forthcoming with details about Julian and Apollonius). He does know of Apuleius' reputation as a magician, but that is perhaps all he knows. Apuleius is only a name, no doubt included to bring the number of contesting wonder-workers up to the canonical three.[153]

The eleventh-century polymath Michael Psellos pairs Apuleius with Julian in two stories. In one he characterizes Apuleius as grounded in mere matter and Julian as "more intelligent and godlike."[154] Accordingly, Apuleius' amulets and spells are unable to restrain the wild animals harassing Trajan's army, while Julian, unaided by either spells or amulets, gets rid of them altogether. In the other, Apuleius is more successful than usual.[155] He is a talented theurgist, able to bind and loose the chthonic gods with charms and spells, and he even forces one not to consort with his fellow theurgist Julian. But even here Apuleius seems less impressive than his colleague. Apuleius' power is a negative one that interferes with a single rival, while Julian creates a magic image that routs the entire Dacian army with thunderbolts.

---

[151] Ὡσαύτως δὲ καὶ ὁ Ἰουλιανὸς, καὶ Ἀπολλώνιος, καὶ Ἀπολέϊος οἱ μάγοι, ἐπὶ Δομετιανοῦ τοῦ βασιλέως, διαφόρους φαντασίας εἰργάσαντο. ὧν μία ἐργασία τοιαύτη φαίνεται ἐν τοῖς τῶν ἀρχαιοτέρων ἀνδρῶν διηγήμασι. Ibid. (cols. 524–25).

[152] ὁ ἀκροθήνιος παρ' αὐτοὺς, καὶ πλεῖον ἐγγίων τῷ διαβόλῳ διὰ τῆς ματαιότητος. Ibid. (col. 525).

[153] Three is of course the usual number in folktales, but we might also remember the three rival philosophers (Apollonius, Euphrates the Stoic, and Dio Chrysostom) before Vespasian in Philostratus, *Vita Apoll.* 5.27–38.

[154] νοερώτερος καί θειότερος. Michael Psellos, *Scripta minora* 2:102.

[155] Michael Psellos, *Philosophica minora* 1.3, ll. 137–47.

• • •

Like his fellow sophists, Apuleius was a performer as well as a writer. He worked hard to make himself interesting to his audience, creating what he hoped would be a distinctive and memorable image—not only with his words but also with his delivery and performance, and probably with his appearance and mannerisms as well. To a large extent his efforts were successful. The impressions he made on his contemporaries and immediate posterity have not survived, but they were evidently strong enough to preserve his memory—or rather the memory of the image he had so carefully created—to the time of Lactantius in the early fourth century and at least to the beginning of the fifth century, nearly 250 years after his death.

Apuleius' writings undoubtedly played a significant part in the preservation of his image as a philosopher. The designer of the Trier ceiling knew at least the story of Cupid and Psyche. The designer of the contorniate knew at least the *Apology* and some of the *Florida*. Augustine carefully studied *De deo Socratis* and had probably read the *Metamorphoses* and *Apology* in his youth. But stories about Apuleius the magician evidently circulated independently of his writings. A local legend seems to have grown up around him, created by his ambiguous manipulation of smoke and mirrors in the *Apology* and encouraged by his stories of magic in the *Metamorphoses* and perhaps even by his own behavior.

It is impossible to tell how long such stories circulated and whether any were ever written down. They no doubt gained some renewed interest during the religious controversies of the fourth century. (We know that Augustine's friends in Carthage were still being regaled with them by their pagan rivals as late as 412.) But with the end of pagan polemic, they were no longer useful; the oral tradition, perhaps not strong to begin with, was lost, and pagan writings were destroyed. Apuleius' image as a magician, however, lived on, preserved like a fly in amber by references in the Christian apologists and disembodied both from his writings and from the ancient tales of his marvels. Now only a name, "Apuleius the magician" became a useful "extra" for Byzantine writers to include in their anachronistic stories of Julian and Apollonius.

CHAPTER 2

Exemplary Behavior: The *Golden Ass* from Late Antiquity to the Prehumanists

> A discussion of wisdom thrusts out of its sanctuary and into the nursery this whole class of tale, which offers only pleasure to the ear.
> —Macrobius, Commentarii in Somnium Scipionis

While Apuleius' vivid and durable image was enjoying its independent existence from the late second to the early fifth century, texts of his works were circulating in North Africa and making their way to other parts of the empire.[1] We know too little about this earliest phase of Apuleius' reception. With the obvious exception of Augustine, we have few clues as to the identity and purposes of his readers, the works they were interested in (and why), or the formats in which they were reading them.

It seems clear, however, that Apuleius' own interests were more catholic than those of most readers and that his works found different audiences (or perhaps in the case of those no longer extant, no audience at all).[2] His surviving oeuvre has come down to us in two separate traditions dubbed for convenience the "philosophical" and the "literary," a division that may well be as early as the transfer from roll to codex in the fourth century.[3] Little is known about the late-antique and medieval reception of either group, but both our information and our inferences are somewhat more secure in the case of the philosophical works.

---

[1] See appendix 1. For a useful discussion of Apuleius' *fortuna* in late antiquity, see Stramaglia, "Apuleio come *auctor*," with a detailed bibliography.

[2] See appendix 1.

[3] The philosophical group includes *De deo Socratis*, *De Platone*, *De mundo*, and the pseudo-Apuleian *Asclepius*; the literary group includes *Apology, Metamorphoses*, and *Florida*. See Marshall in Reynolds, ed., *Texts and Transmission*, 15–18. But the division between the groups is unclear: many scholars believe that the opening sections in the philosophical group, transmitted as a prologue to *De deo Socratis*, actually belong to the *Florida* (at the end of the literary group). See pp. 46–47. Although the literary and philosophical works were transmitted in separate traditions, the compiler of the late seventh- or early eighth-century *Abolita* Glossary seems to have had works from both groups, in an unknown number of manuscripts. See pp. 60–61.

We know that Augustine read at least *De deo Socratis* and *De mundo* and perhaps *De Platone* as well; and we can be sure that these works would also have been studied by other philosophically inclined readers, particularly as the knowledge of Greek declined in the western empire.[4] The "literary" works present more difficulties. This group is descended from an archetype corrected in Rome and Constantinople by a certain Sallustius at the end of the fourth century. It contains two quite different genres: rhetorical works (the *Apology* and *Florida*) and fiction (the *Golden Ass*). The composition of the group is puzzling. Why was the *Golden Ass* put with the rhetorical works, and, perhaps even more to the point, why was it preserved at all?

The answer is not to be found in the high literary standing of novels in antiquity. On the contrary. Fiction in both Greek and Latin enjoyed a poor reputation—at least among the few writers who deign to mention it. Most of our testimonia in both languages are to be dated within a few decades of Sallustius' archetype.[5] Among the Latin sources, Augustine alone expresses no open criticism; his reference to the *Golden Ass* (ca. 425) is relatively neutral.[6] The rest disdain fiction as silly and puerile. The fourth-century author of the *Historia Augusta* has Septimius Severus characterize his rival's fondness for Apuleius' "Carthaginian Milesian tales" as senile foolishness.[7] In 401 Jerome speaks of "curly-haired dandies reciting the fictions of Milesian tales in school," an activity he lumps with other low amusements, like the notorious "Testament of the Pig" and similar inanities.[8] In his commentary on the *Somnium Scipionis* (ca. 430), Macrobius distinguishes between *fabulae* that are edifying (those of philosophy) and those that are merely amusing (Menander's plays and the tales of Petronius and Apuleius):

> Comedies like those that Menander and his imitators brought to the stage caress the ear, and so do plots full of the fictitious calamities of lovers on which even [Petronius] Arbiter spent so much effort or with which Apuleius, to our surprise, sometimes amused himself.

---

[4] For Augustine, see pp. 35–36. For the *fortuna* of the philosophical works in late antiquity, see Klibansky and Regen, *Die Handschriften*, 29–42.

[5] For testimonia to Greek fiction, see Stephens and Winkler, eds., *Ancient Greek Novels*, passim. Among the few positive comments is that of the physician Theodorus Priscianus (ca. 400), who suggests Greek erotic stories as a remedy for impotence—which might be termed an endorsement (*Euporiston* 2.34). See Stephens and Winkler, 476.

[6] Augustine, *Civ.* 18.18. See pp. 33–34.

[7] "Milesias Punicas" (*HA. Alb.* 12.12). See pp. 20–21.

[8] "Quasi non cirratorum turba Milesiarum in scholis figmenta decantent, et Testamentum Suis Bessorum cachinno membra concutiat, atque inter scurrarum epulas nugae istiusmodi frequententur!" Jerome, *Contra Rufinum* 1.17.

A discussion of wisdom thrusts out of its sanctuary and into the nursery this whole class of tale, which offers only pleasure to the ear.⁹

Two details are worth noting in Macrobius' comment: first, his surprise that Apuleius wrote fiction (the clear implication being that it was unworthy of him), and, second, his odd characterization of the works of both Petronius and Apuleius as "full of the fictitious calamities of lovers." The description easily fits all five extant Greek novels,¹⁰ but it is not the obvious way to characterize either the *Golden Ass* (with the possible exception of the story of Cupid and Psyche) or what is left of the *Satyricon* (even bearing in mind the erotic adventures of its disreputable heroes). Macrobius disapproves of Apuleius' and Petronius' novels, to be sure, but it is not clear that he has actually read them.

But even if Macrobius did not read fiction, others did. "Many more scroll through Milesian tales than through the books of Plato," observes Jerome.¹¹ We know little about these readers, except that they were probably drawn from the same highly educated minority that produced the audience for other literary genres.¹² Some of them may have begun to read fiction at an early age. The novels were not written for children, but evidence is beginning to mount that both grammarians and rhetoricians used them for teaching purposes (a fact that may account for the comments on their puerile nature by Jerome and Macrobius).¹³ For the

---

⁹ "Auditum mulcent vel comoediae, quales Menander eiusve imitatores agendas dederunt, vel argumenta fictis casibus amatorum referta, quibus vel multum se Arbiter exercuit vel Apuleium non numquam lusisse miramur. Hoc totum fabularum genus, quod solas aurium delicias profitetur, e sacrario suo in nutricum cunas sapientiae tractatus eliminat." Macrobius, *Somn. Scip.* 1.2.8. For Macrobius' date, see Cameron, "The Date and Identity of Macrobius."

¹⁰ Cf. Stephens and Winkler's description: "Their action . . . centers on an erotic pair of high station, scarcely postpubescent, who fall in love at first sight, may or may not be immediately married, . . . undergo a series of harrowing adventures and testings of their faithfulness—kidnapping, shipwreck, slavery, even marriage to another party—before being reunited, presumably to live happily ever after." *Ancient Greek Novels*, 4.

¹¹ "Multoque pars maior est Milesias fabellas revolventium, quam Platonis libros. In altero enim ludus et oblectatio est, in altero difficultas et sudori mixtus labor." Jerome, *Commentariorum in Esaiam Liber* 12, *prologus*.

¹² Modern scholars tend to reject the old idea that fiction was a genre for children or women or the "popular reader," positing instead a sophisticated and highly literate readership. See, with earlier bibliography, Wesseling, "The Audience of the Ancient Novels"; Stephens, "Who Read Ancient Novels?"; Bowie, "The Readership of Greek Novels."

¹³ There is enough evidence from papyri to document the use of novels in schools in the Greek world; presumably they were also used in the Latin west (Stramaglia, "Fra 'consumo' e 'impegno'"). For two third-century fragments of Achilles Tatius that seem to have been part of the library of a rhetorical school, see idem, 131–36.

most part, however, fiction readers have left little trace in the historical record. The only securely identified readers of the *Golden Ass* in the late fourth or early fifth century are Augustine and Sallustius; neither has given an account of his reasons for reading the novel or what he thought of it. All the evidence (that is, the admittedly slender testimony of the *Historia Augusta*, Jerome, and Macrobius) is on the other side: serious people disdained fiction—or claimed to—however amusing and popular it might be.

Given this attitude, it is hardly surprising that ancient fiction became an endangered species. Fewer than half of the Greek novels survive.[14] The *Milesiaca* of Aristides of Miletus are lost, and their translation by Sisenna exists only in a few fragments. Only a small fraction of Petronius' *Satyricon* survives. Apuleius' *Hermagoras* is lost; its half-dozen fragments suggest that it was probably a novel.[15] The losses occurred at different times and under various circumstances, but no doubt much of the wreckage took place in and around the fourth century. This was the period when ancient literature was being transferred from roll to codex—the critical point at which a work's survival depended on its seeming important or interesting enough to justify the active step of making or commissioning a copy in the new medium. Being admitted into the Noah's ark of the new technology did not ensure a text safe passage through the Middle Ages, but missing the boat in the first place was a virtual guarantee of oblivion.

The *Golden Ass* survived because someone in the fourth century wanted it to: someone, whether Sallustius or another, had it copied from its rolls into a codex, along with the *Apology* and perhaps the *Florida* as well. This chapter will follow the fortunes of the *Golden Ass* and its companions from the formation of Sallustius' manuscript to the eve of the Renaissance. The discussion will treat two distinct but intersecting themes subsumed under the rubric "exemplary behavior": the transmission of Apuleius' text and the interpretation of the *Golden Ass*.

Apuleius in Rome

Apuleius was a figure of some interest in late fourth-century Rome. That much is clear both from Sallustius' manuscript and from the contorniate portrait discussed in chapter 1. Both the contorniate and the

---

[14] We have 5 complete Greek novels, fragments of 7 or 8 others, and scraps of 12 works that might be novels. See Stephens and Winkler, *Ancient Greek Novels*, 6.

[15] See Harrison, *Apuleius*, 21–22.

manuscript are products of the senatorial aristocracy—a class whose ideology and motives in this period have come under renewed scrutiny in the last generation.

The fourth-century aristocracy used to be characterized as predominantly and militantly pagan, and its activities, whether producing contorniates or transcribing classical authors, were seen as ideological acts of resistance to Christian authority.[16] For some time, however, scholars have favored a less dramatic and more complicated picture, pointing out that aristocratic pagans and Christians in the later fourth century were not invariably in bitter opposition, and that through much of the period the tendency was toward mutual accommodation rather than conflict.[17] Pagans and Christians intermarried, and individual members of pagan families converted to Christianity. Christians celebrated pagan holidays and used pagan imagery in their artifacts and sometimes even in their tombs; pagans enjoyed high office and high status and tended to avoid religious activities—like animal sacrifice—that were repellent to Christians. Religion mattered, at some times more than others, and to some individuals more than others; but the senatorial class had other, equally important concerns: Roman patriotism and love of the classical past, but, above all, maintaining and augmenting its traditional status under changing conditions.

The contorniates reflected these interests. Roman aristocrats put on games and circuses as their ancestors had done, and it is likely that they issued the contorniates as souvenirs.[18] We might think of them as promotions—not quite like T-shirt day at the baseball game, but rather as demonstrations of aristocratic largesse commemorating the games and their sponsors. The reverses of the contorniates ("tails," we might say) generally show images connected with games and spectacles—chariots, racehorses, scenes from shows and pageants. The reverse of

---

[16] Alföldi, for example, regarded the contorniates as pagan propaganda, as the title of the first edition of his work on contorniates indicates: *Die Kontorniaten: Ein verkanntes Propagandamittel der stadtrömischen heidnischen Aristokratie in ihrem Kampfe gegen das christliche Kaisertum.* See also Bloch, "The Pagan Revival in the West."

[17] Alföldi's thesis was criticized at the time by Toynbee in an influential review (*JRS* 35 [1945]: 115–21) and twenty years later by Cameron ("Paganism and Literature"). Without directly challenging the thesis of a pagan resistance, Brown argued for a "drift into a respectable Christianity" on the part of the senatorial aristocracy, pointing out the long survival of secular traditions in Rome itself ("Aspects of the Christianization of the Roman Aristocracy," esp. 9–10). O'Donnell argued that Christians and pagans were not rigidly polarized, demonstrating that a range of zeal and opinion existed on both sides ("The Demise of Paganism"). See also Salzman, *On Roman Time,* 193–246 and esp. 193–96. But recently Hedrick has suggested that the subscriptions cannot be ideologically neutral: *History and Silence,* 197–213.

[18] See Toynbee's review of Alföldi.

the Apuleius contorniate shows a warrior and a temple—probably from a dramatic tableau. The obverses ("heads") picture various subjects: emperors past and present, gods and scenes from mythology, Roman legends, and Greek and Roman literary figures. The latter include Homer, Pythagoras, Horace, and Sallust as well as Apuleius and Apollonius of Tyana.

The contorniates began to appear in the mid-350s and continued well into the fifth century; the Apuleius contorniate is dated around 390.[19] The date is significant, for at almost the same time, the text of Apuleius was being studied and corrected in both Rome and Constantinople, as the subscriptions in our oldest manuscript of the *Golden Ass* attest. This manuscript, Florence, Laurenziana 68.2 (called "F"), contains three works of Apuleius: the *Apology*, the *Golden Ass* or *Metamorphoses,* and the *Florida*.[20] It was written near the end of the eleventh century, but it preserves eleven subscriptions by a fourth-century corrector testifying to his study of the text.[21] (The subscriptions are confined to the *Apology* and *Metamorphoses*, an important point that will concern us presently.) Eight of the subscriptions are identical: "Ego Sallustius legi et emendavi Rome felix" (I, Sallustius, successfully read and corrected [the text above] in Rome).[22] Another is very similar: "Ego Sallustius emendavi Rome felix."[23] But two subscriptions in the manuscript are different. The first, which appears at the end of book 1 of the *Apology*, gives Sallustius' full name: Gaius Crispus Sallustius.[24] The other, at the end of book 9 of the *Metamorphoses*, adds the dates and places of his work: "I, Sallustius, successfully read and corrected [the text above] in Rome in the consulship of Olibrius and Probinus when I was studying

---

[19] See Schefold, *Die Bildnisse*, 428. Alföldi suggested that the contorniates could be separated into three periods (*Die Kontorniaten*), and a detailed chronology was worked out by Curtis Clay in Alföldi, *Die Kontorniat-Medaillons* 1.1:216–32.

[20] See Marshall in Reynolds, *Texts and Transmission*, 15–16; Lowe, "The Unique Manuscript of Apuleius' *Metamorphoses* (Laurentian. 68.2) and Its Oldest Transcript." The essential modern discussion is Pecere, "Esemplari con *subscriptiones*." F also contains a text of Tacitus. See pp. 94–95.

[21] See Jahn, "Über die Subscriptionen," 331–32; Zetzel, *Latin Textual Criticism in Antiquity*, 213–14. For discussions of the context, see Marrou, "La vie intellectuelle"; Pecere, "Esemplari con *subscriptiones*"; idem, "La tradizione dei testi latini."

[22] Florence, Bibl. Laur. 68.2, fols. 134v, 138v, 143v, 149r, 154r, 159r, 164v, 178r. The subscription appears at the ends of books 2–8 and 10 of the *Metamorphoses*.

[23] Florence, Bibl. Laur. 68.2, fol. 126r. The subscription appears at the end of book 2 of the *Apology*. It is illustrated in Tatum, *Apuleius and the Golden Ass*, plate 1; Pecere, "Esemplari con *subscriptiones*," plate 3b.

[24] "Ego G(aius) Crispus Sallustius emendavi Rome felix." Laur. 68.2, fol. 118r. See Pecere, "Esemplari con *subscriptiones*," plate 2a. It may be worth noting that both subscriptions to the Apology read *Ego Sallustius emendavi*, etc., whereas all of those to the *Metamorphoses* read *Ego Sallustius legi et emendavi*, etc.

rhetoric under Endelechius in the forum of Mars. I went over it again in Constantinople in the consulship of Caesarius and Atticus."[25]

This last subscription fairly bristles with clues about Sallustius and his world. Sallustius worked on Apuleius first in Rome in 395 and again in Constantinople in 397. His family, the Sallustii, belonged to the recent senatorial aristocracy, and in 395 Sallustius would have been completing the rhetorical studies obligatory for a young man of his class.[26] His choice of school is emblematic of this transitional period. The religion of Sallustius is unknown; his teacher, Endelechius, is known to have been a Christian.[27] At the end of his studies Sallustius went to Constantinople—perhaps on family business or imperial service—taking his manuscript of Apuleius with him. Sallustius has not been securely identified, but some scholars believe that he is the same Sallustius whose wedding in Ostia was mentioned by Symmachus in 398.[28] If they are correct, we must imagine that he returned to Rome after only a short stay in Constantinople.

Both the extent of Sallustius' text and what he did for it are unclear. His manuscript included both the *Apology* and the *Metamorphoses*, as the subscriptions in F attest. But F contains no subscriptions to the *Florida*. The fact is suggestive, but we do not have enough information to be confident about what it suggests. Perhaps the subscriptions were lost in the course of transmission (and we should remember that F also lacks subscriptions to books 1 and 11 of the *Metamorphoses*).[29] Perhaps

---

[25] "Ego Sallustius legi et emendavi Rome felix Olib<r>io et Probino v(iris) c(larissimis) cons(ulibus) in foro Martis controversiam declamans oratori Endelechio. rursus Constantinupoli [sic] recognovi Caesario et Attico cons(ulibus)." Laur. 68.2, fol. 171v. See Pecere, "Esemplari con *subscriptiones*," plate 4a. For the sense of "controversiam declamans," see Marrou, "La vie intellectuelle," 94–95. For the context, see also Pecere, "La 'subscriptio' di Statilio Massimo," 109–12.

[26] Jones, Martindale, and Morris, *Prosopography of the Later Roman Empire (PLRE)* 1:800. For the Sallustii, see *PLRE* 1:796–98; Pecere, "Esemplari con *subscriptiones*," 115–18.

[27] The Sallustii were pagans in the time of Julian, but it is possible that they had converted in the interim. Our Sallustius is probably the son of the homonymous correspondent of Symmachus (*Ep.* 3.30–31, 5.55–57, 6.35) who was urban prefect in 384 or 387 (*PLRE* 1:797.4), a man identified as a pagan by Chastagnol (*Les fastes de la préfecture de Rome au Bas-Empire*, 216–18) and a Christian by Pietri (*Prosopographie chrétienne du Bas-Empire* 2:1982). The rhetorician and poet Severus Sanctus Endelechius (*PLRE* 2:975) taught in Rome at the end of the fourth century and was a friend of Paulinus of Nola. See Marrou, "La vie intellectuelle," 94. He is the author of a bucolic Christian poem, *De mortibus boum* (*Anthologia Latina* 1.2.335–39); see Alimonti, *Struttura, ideologia ed imitazione virgiliana*.

[28] Pecere, "Esemplari con *subscriptiones*," 117. Symmachus, *Ep.* 6.35: "Ipsi haec de nuptiis Ostiensibus ad quas nos viri inlustris Sallustii filius iunior evocavit contulimus in paginam." See Bloch, "The Pagan Revival," 206, 214.

[29] Pecere originally rejected this explanation using the argument that F is the product of a closed reception ("Esemplari con *subscriptiones*," 132). But a few years later he argued

Sallustius added the *Florida* excerpts at a later date for purposes of his own, as Pecere once suggested.[30] Or perhaps Sallustius' manuscript did not include the *Florida* at all, and the excerpts were added by a later scribe to a descendant of Sallustius' manuscript at some point before the transcription of F. The whole question is complicated by the fact that the *Florida* may not be confined to F and the so-called literary tradition. *De deo Socratis*, the first work in the philosophical group, is preceded by several excerpts of uncertain identity: some scholars consider them a preface to *De deo Socratis*; others argue that they belong to the *Florida*, and that their presence at the opening of the philosophical group is the result of an incorrect division between the works at an early stage of the whole tradition.[31] If this last idea is correct, it would have important implications for our understanding of the antecedents and formation of Sallustius' manuscript. At this point, however, the only points that we can be sure of are that the presence of the *Florida* in F is not surprising (a collection of oratorical excerpts is an obvious companion piece for the *Apology*) and that its format in F differs from those of the *Apology* and *Metamorphoses*.

We can be only a little more confident about the exact nature of Sallustius' work on the text of Apuleius. He says that he "corrected" it in Rome and "revised" or "went over" it in Constantinople. The words he uses are *emendavi* and *recognovi*. In this period neither term has the technical sense that it would acquire in later text criticism, and each embraces a rather large number of activities ranging from simple proofreading to correction of the text against another exemplar to glossing it with marginal notes.[32] All that we can be sure of is that Sallustius first "corrected" Apuleius with the help of his teacher Endelechius and later either proofread his text by himself or checked it against another copy

---

in favor of it on codicological grounds: "I colofoni alla fine delle *Metamorfosi* e dei *Florida* erano dunque già scomparsi quando il Laur. 68, 2 fu allestito" ("Qualche riflessione," 109). See p. 62.

[30] Pecere, "Esemplari con *subscriptiones*," 134–35.

[31] For arguments that the excerpts belong to *De deo Socratis*, see Hunink, "The Prologue of Apuleius' *De deo Socratis*"; Sandy, *The Greek World of Apuleius*, 192–96. The idea that the *Florida* and *De deo Socratis* were incorrectly separated early in the tradition was espoused by Goldbacher in *Apulei Madaurensis opuscula quae sunt de philosophia*, xv, and Thomas in "Remarques critiques sur les oeuvres philosophiques d'Apulée," 155–56. It has been argued again recently by Regen ("Il *De deo Socratis*") and Harrison (*Apuleius*, 90–92, and *Apuleius: Rhetorical Works*, 177–80). For earlier bibliography, see especially Hunink, *Apuleius*, and Harrison, *Apuleius*.

[32] For *emendare*, see Zetzel, "The Subscriptions in the Manuscripts of Livy and Fronto"; Pecere, "Antichità tarda e trasmissione dei testi," 66–67. Sallustius seems to be using *recognoscere* (a technical term in legal documents) as a synonym for *emendare*; see Pecere, "La tradizione," 238–39 n. 288.

in Constantinople. In either case, presumably he brought his manuscript back to Italy, where it eventually made its way into the family library of the Sallustii.

Aristocrats like Sallustius corrected texts, just as they issued contorniates—to assure themselves and others that they were guardians of the classical past. The luxury manuscripts they collected advertised not only their wealth and status but also their cultural superiority. The source of their intellectual prestige was the rhetorical school; and, to judge from the surviving subscriptions of the period, it was largely the rhetorical school that drove and promoted their activity as correctors. Ancient subscriptions are preserved in twenty-seven manuscripts of secular works.[33] Six of these subscriptions can be dated to the period 395–405; 3 of the 6 were written by aristocrats, and 5 of the 6 explicitly mention rhetoricians or rhetorical schools.[34] Four of the writers were very young—either still in their student days or in the early phases of their careers.[35] Of the 6 works accompanied by subscriptions, only 1—Livy, the heirloom text of the ostentatiously pagan Symmachi—is as old as the Augustan period; interestingly enough, it is the only work whose subscription makes no allusion to a rhetorician or school. The others are from the silver age and later: Martial, Juvenal, Pseudo-Quintilian, Persius, and Apuleius. The list testifies to a decidedly "modern" taste

---

[33] The classic study of the subscriptions is Jahn, "Über die Subscriptionen." For a modern summary and discussion, see Zetzel, *Latin Textual Criticism*, 206–31, 288. For the subscriptions around 400, see Pecere, "La tradizione."

[34] The six subscriptions are to the following texts: Apuleius (395 and 397), written by an aristocrat, Sallustius, the student of Endelechius; Martial (401), written by an aristocrat, Torquatus Gennadius, a student in the rhetorical school in the Forum of Augustus; Persius (402), written by an aristocrat, Tryphonianus Sabinus, saying that he has corrected his text without his teacher's help; Pseudo-Quintilian (very late fourth century), written by a presumed rhetorician, Domitius Dracontius, probably for use in his school; Juvenal (around 400), written by Nicaeus, a student of Servius; and Livy, books 1–10 (before 401), written by Victorianus for the Symmachi. (I have omitted the two slightly later subscriptions to Livy by Nicomachus Flavianus and Nicomachus Dexter, which are probably to be dated between 408 and 431; see Hedrick, *History and Silence*, 181–82.) The class of Nicaeus is unknown; Pecere speculates that he was an aspiring careerist of modest background ("La tradizione," 45–46). Victorianus identifies himself as a man of senatorial rank (*v[ir] c[larissimus]*), but he was probably a grammarian who had been promoted for his literary talents and services (see idem, 61, with bibliography). For the texts of the subscriptions, see Zetzel, *Latin Textual Criticism*, 211–15, 223, 225. For the identities of the subscribers, see Pecere, "La tradizione," 30–69. For the dating of the subscriptions to Pseudo-Quintilian, Livy, and Juvenal, see idem, 49, 60, 43.

[35] Sallustius and Gennadius identify themselves as students of rhetoric. Nicaeus would have been younger still, as Kaster notes: "In the normal course of events in a Roman education, he is not likely to have been more than fifteen years old" ("Servius and *Idonei Auctores*," 208 n. 65). Tryphonianus Sabinus says that he is thirty years old (Zetzel, *Latin Textual Criticism*, 214).

on the part of rhetoricians and their pupils, who evidently preferred recent classics to the venerable works of earlier periods.[36]

Not surprisingly, they chose texts appropriate to the rhetorical school. Martial and the satirists suited the late fourth-century interest in moral teaching because of their criticism of vice and human foibles. The declamations of Pseudo-Quintilian and the *Apology* (and *Florida*) of Apuleius were obvious choices.[37] The *Golden Ass* might seem to fit our pattern less comfortably: it is very long, it belongs to a genre not highly valued in intellectual circles, and its undoubted satiric and rhetorical elements are probably not concentrated or pervasive enough for Sallustius and Endelechius to have selected it on those grounds alone. Nevertheless, both the young aristocrat and his teacher must have seen something—although perhaps not the same thing—in the *Golden Ass* to justify their efforts. It is likely that Sallustius' interest in the work was personal and Endelechius' professional, but their purposes must have been compatible—an obvious point that rules out the old idea that Sallustius' correction of Apuleius was an act of pagan resistance.[38] Whatever Sallustius' motives might have been, we cannot imagine that his Christian teacher promoted a polemical pagan agenda.[39] Endelechius' purposes must have been connected in some way to the rhetorical school, although he probably would not have intended to treat the work in the same way as the *Apology* (or *Florida*).[40]

We can only speculate about the motives of Sallustius and Endelechius, but it is fair to venture some suggestions, since any insight into their reasoning would also help us to understand the reasons for the survival of the *Golden Ass*. I speculate, then, that Sallustius may have been drawn to the *Golden Ass* by its presentation of Isis—not as an act of resistance, and perhaps not even out of religious enthusiasm, but primarily because the goddess and her colorful rites were very much in vogue at the time; and I suggest that both Sallustius and Endelechius may have been attracted by its potential for allegorical interpretation.

It is Isis, we remember, who saves the undeserving Lucius from his asininity and restores his humanity in the last book of the novel. The fortunes of the Ass reach their nadir at the end of book 10, when he

---

[36] For the interest in later authors in this period, see also Kaster, "Servius and *Idonei Auctores*."

[37] Pseudo-Quintilian seems to have been copied by a rhetorician for use in his school; see Pecere, "La tradizione," 46–51.

[38] Alföldi, *A Festival of Isis in Rome*, 46 n. 105; Bloch, "The Pagan Revival," 214.

[39] As Cameron points out ("Paganism and Literature," 5–6). Cameron also notes that 395, only a few months after the pagan defeat at the battle of the Frigidus, "would have been about as inappropriate a moment for pagan propaganda as could well be imagined" (6).

[40] For the suggestion that Apuleius had become a school author as early as the fourth century, see Stramaglia, "Apuleio come *auctor*."

faces the degradation of being exhibited as a spectacle in the arena, where his masters intend to have him copulate with a condemned murderess. He flees to the seashore and falls into an exhausted sleep. Book 11, the "Isis book," opens with the full moon rising out of the sea and his vision of the goddess.

> First, her hair was thick and long, flowing in soft curls spread over her divine neck and shoulders. A crown intricately shaped with many kinds of flowers encircled her head, and in its center above her forehead a flat round disk like a mirror—or rather a symbol for the moon—gleamed with a shining light.[41]

The beautiful goddess tells him that on the next day there will be a procession and festival to dedicate a new ship in her honor, a first offering for the new sailing season. Lucius is to present himself at the procession and eat from the garland of roses carried by one of the priests. He will be restored to himself, and in return he must pledge himself to Isis forever. For once Lucius does what he is told. He returns to his human shape and is duly initiated in the mysteries of Isis and Osiris. The novel ends with our hero a prosperous and somewhat complacent priest of Isis: "Shaving off all my hair, I gladly performed the duties of that ancient college founded in the time of Sulla, not covering or concealing my baldness, but leaving it exposed wherever I went."[42]

The mysteries of Isis, after being forbidden in the republic and early empire, began to enjoy acceptance and widespread popularity in the first century and persisted side by side with Christianity long after the conversion of Constantine. Lucius regained his humanity at a festival called the Isidis navigium, or "Ship of Isis," which continued to be celebrated well into the sixth century—even though the emperor officially banned pagan worship and closed the temples in 391 and removed pagan holidays from the calendars in 395.[43] We do not know whether Sallustius

---

[41] "Iam primum crines uberrimi prolixique et sensim intorti per divina colla passive dispersi molliter defluebant. Corona multiformis variis floribus sublimem destrinxerat verticem, cuius media quidem super frontem plana rutunditas in modum speculi vel immo argumentum lunae candidum lumen emicabat." *Met.* 11.3.4.

[42] "Rursus denique quaqua raso capillo collegii vetustissimi et sub illis Syllae temporibus conditi munia, non obumbrato vel obtecto calvitio, sed quoquoversus obvio, gaudens obibam." *Met.* 11.30.5.

[43] For the laws (*Cod. Theod.* 16.10.10 and 2.8.22), see Bloch, "The Pagan Revival," 198; Salzman, *On Roman Time*, 236. But O'Donnell notes ("The Demise of Paganism," 59–60): "What is remarkable about the imperial legislation against paganism is its matter-of-fact quality: the order was given, assumed to be executed, and promptly forgotten." For the persistence of the festival, see Degrassi, *Inscriptiones Italiae* vol. 13, *Fasti et elogia*, fasc. 2, *Fasti Anni Numani et Iuliani*, 420; Lydus, *De mensibus* 4.45. See also the little

himself was a devotee of Isis, and it probably does not matter. For many years, Isis, Osiris, and Serapis had been fashionable among the Roman aristocracy, who ostentatiously issued coins in their honor, joined their priesthoods, and celebrated their feasts, particularly the Isidis navigium.[44] At the end of the fourth century, Isis was in the air, and it would have been only natural for young Sallustius to take an interest in the novel in which she figures so prominently. If that was his motive, his Christian teacher Endelechius indulged, or at least allowed, his interest, as his presence in the subscription indicates.

But if Isis appealed to Sallustius, it is likely that allegory interested both men. In the 360s, in the time of Julian the Apostate, another Sallustius, certainly a kinsman and perhaps the grandfather of our Sallustius, wrote a Neoplatonic handbook, *Concerning the Gods and the Universe*, which presents allegorical interpretations of myths like the judgment of Paris and the death of Attis.[45] Allegory, we could say, was a family tradition of the Sallustii. For Endelechius, on the other hand, an interest in allegory would have been not hereditary but professional.[46] Intellectuals of every stripe practiced allegorical interpretation of literary works.[47] We know that grammarians and rhetoricians used novels in schools, and it would not be surprising if they occasionally allegorized them.

The most tantalizing bit of evidence is a fragmentary discussion of Heliodorus' novel *Ethiopica* by a certain Philip the Philosopher, whose work is now dated to fifth-century Constantinople.[48] Philip is otherwise

---

hymn *De Isidis Navigio*, which Cameron (*Claudian*, 204–5) attributes to Claudian; the poem commemorates a celebration of the Isidis navigium, probably held in Rome after 394: "Carmina vel spuriorum vel suspectorum app. 11," in *Claudii Claudiani Carmina*.

[44] Isis and Serapis appear on contorniates, but especially on the *vota publica* coins issued until 394, many of which feature the Isidis navigium; see Alföldi, *A Festival of Isis* and "Die alexandrinischen Götter." For priesthoods held by aristocrats, see Alföldi, *A Festival of Isis*, 43; Bloch, "A New Document." For celebrations of the Isidis navigium, see the previous note. Rutilius Namatianus tells of witnessing another festival, the Heuresis of Osiris, in Faleria in 417 (*De Red.* 1.373 f.); for the date, see Cameron, "Rutilius Namatianus."

[45] For this Sallustius, see *PLRE* 796–98.1, 5; Pecere, "Esemplari con *subscriptiones*," 115–16. For the handbook, see Sallustius, *Concerning the Gods and the Universe*; Lamberton, *Homer the Theologian*, 139–43.

[46] The connection of Endelechius with an interest in allegory would be strengthened if one could be sure that he was to be identified with the Sanctus to whom Paulinus of Nola addresses his complex allegorical reading of the pelican, owl, and sparrow in *Ps*. 102.6–7 (*Ep*. 40). See Schmid, "Tityrus Christianus," 121–22 n. 51; Alimonti, *Struttura, ideologia ed imitazione*, 19–21 n. 4, with further bibliography.

[47] For examples, see Jones, "Allegorical Interpretation in Servius"; Lamberton, *Homer the Theologian*; Hays, *Fulgentius the Mythographer*, 93–141.

[48] For the date and locale, see Acconcia Longo, "Filippo il filosofo a Costantinopoli." See also Stramaglia, "Fra 'consumo' e 'impegno,'" 141–43, with earlier bibliography. The work

unknown.⁴⁹ Perhaps he was a rhetorician, but one cannot be sure: the title *philosophos* may identify him only as a respected intellectual. He presents his allegory to a group of informed listeners (*philologoi*) in the heart of the city, in a district near the schools and library around the Basilike frequented by students and their teachers, palace functionaries, lawyers, and bureaucrats.⁵⁰ Urged by his friends to defend Heliodorus' novel, Philip at first dismisses romances as "the milk . . . of our infant education."⁵¹ But he soon warms to his topic, proposing that the work contains a higher, mystical meaning for those who are philosophical enough to perceive it. He argues that the *Ethiopica* "is educational and teaches ethics by mixing the wine of contemplation into the water of the tale"—a claim he goes on to demonstrate by means of a Neoplatonist Christian allegory.⁵² The novel's heroine, Chariclea, Philip explains, "is a symbol of the soul and of the mind that sets the soul in order."⁵³ The name Chariclea is a synthesis of the words *charis* (grace) and *kleos* (fame), and the synthesis comes about "because the soul is united . . . with the body and becomes a single substance with it."⁵⁴

It is tempting to imagine that Sallustius or Endelechius (or both) contemplated a comparable allegorical reading of the *Golden Ass*, especially of the story of Cupid and Psyche. Perhaps Endelechius might have planned to expound an allegory to his students, or perhaps Sallustius thought of following in the footsteps of his allegorizing kinsman, the Sallustius of *Concerning the Gods and the Universe*. Whatever their intentions, however, no trace of any such works remains. To move from hypothetical to actual allegorical readings of Apuleius, we must look to the next century and back to Apuleius' native North Africa.

---

has been edited by Hercher (1895) and Colonna (1938). For an English translation, see Lamberton, *Homer the Theologian*, 306–11. For a detailed discussion of the allegory, see Tarán, "The Authorship of an Allegorial Interpretation," 216–28; Hunter, "'Philip the Philosopher'"; Sandy, "A Neoplatonic Interpretation."

⁴⁹ Acconcia Longo convincingly argues against the old idea that he is to be identified with Filagato da Cerami, an Italo-Greek active in Reggio Calabria in the eleventh or twelfth century ("Filippo il filosofo," 5–10).

⁵⁰ For the *ambiente*, see Acconcia Longo, "Filippo il filosofo," 16–20.

⁵¹ γάλα τῆς νηπιώδους . . . παιδεύσεως. Colonna 366, translated by Lamberton, *Homer the Theologian*, 307.

⁵² παιδαγωγικὴ γὰρ ἡ βίβλος καὶ ἠθικῆς φιλοσοφίας διδάσκαλος, τῷ τῆς ἱστορίας ὕδατι τὸν οἶνον τῆς θεωρίας κεράσασα. Colonna 367, Lamberton, *Homer the Theologian*, 307.

⁵³ Χαρίκλεια σύμβολόν ἐστι ψυχῆς καὶ τοῦ ταύτην κοσμοῦντος νοός. Colonna 368, Lamberton, *Homer the Theologian*, 309.

⁵⁴ ὅτι συντίθ<εται> κ<αὶ ψυχὴ σ>ώματι, μία μετ' αὐτοῦ γινομένη ὑπόστασις. Colonna 368, Lamberton, *Homer the Theologian*, 309.

Psyche and Fulgentius

Apuleius and the *Golden Ass* were certainly known in North Africa at the beginning of the fifth century, as Augustine's references in the *City of God* attest. The novel was still being read in Apuleius' homeland at the end of the century, when Cupid and Psyche attracted the allegorizing zeal of Martianus Capella and Fulgentius the Mythographer.[55] We know very little about either—except that Martianus was a pagan and Fulgentius a Christian. Martianus' work is probably to be dated in the 470s or 480s.[56] Fulgentius wrote somewhat later—certainly after the 480s and perhaps even in the reign of Thrasamund (496–523).[57] He is not to be identified with Saint Fulgentius, the bishop of Ruspe.[58]

Martianus allots Cupid and Psyche, but especially Psyche, a cameo role in his strange allegorical work *The Marriage of Mercury and Philology*. Psyche was one of the figures considered by Mercury as a possible bride, but she was out of the running, since, as Martianus tells us, "she was held captive by Cupid with unbreakable bonds."[59] Martianus' Psyche is allegorical, but her story is not the one told by Apuleius. She does not even have the same parents. In Apuleius her parents are the unnamed "king" and "queen" of fairy tale. In Martianus her father is Apollo and her mother Endelichia, a name we might translate as "continuous or perennial motion."[60] We will leave Martianus' Psyche for now, but we must not forget her; in the next chapter we will find her playing an important role in Renaissance interpretations of Apuleius.

Fulgentius, however, does follow Apuleius—even to the point of imitating his language and turns of phrase.[61] He treats the story of Cupid and Psyche in the *Mythologies*, a collection of fifty myths and their allegorical interpretations.[62] Since his main interest is allegory, Fulgentius

---

[55] See appendix 1.
[56] See Shanzer, *A Philosophical and Literary Commentary*, 8–17.
[57] See Hays, *Fulgentius the Mythographer*, 1–24.
[58] For the arguments, see ibid., 263–91, with bibliography.
[59] "Captivamque adamantinis nexibus a Cupidine detineri." Mart. Cap. 1.7.
[60] The name of Psyche's mother appears (correctly) as Endelichia in the manuscripts but was wrongly changed in the tenth century to Entelechia (Aristotelian "entelechy"). See Shanzer, *A Philosophical and Literary Commentary*, 68, with earlier bibliography; see also Dronke, *Fabula*, 109–10, with earlier bibliography.
[61] Here is a partial list of echoes in the order of their appearance in *Mit.* 3.6: *Met.* 4.28.1; 4.31.2; 5.24.4; 5.1.6; 5.8.1; 5.21.5; 5.19.2; 5.20.2. For a detailed analysis, see Mattiacci, "Apuleio in Fulgenzio," 239–44.
[62] *Mit.* 3.6. Fulgentius also refers to Psyche at *Mit. prol.* 1.4 and 1.20. For the allegory, see Gaisser, "Allegorizing Apuleius"; Mattiacci, "Apuleio in Fulgenzio," 244–45. Moreschini has surveyed interpretations of Psyche from Fulgentius to the nineteenth century in *Il mito di Amore e Psiche in Apuleio* (for Fulgentius, see 26–30). See also Moreschini, "Towards a History of the Exegesis of Apuleius"; idem, "Una 'Piacevole storia.'" I cite the

generally devotes little attention to the myths themselves: he keeps his narrative to a minimum and almost never attributes a story to a particular author. There are only two exceptions; the one that concerns us is the tale of Cupid and Psyche, which Fulgentius both attributes to Apuleius and tells in copious detail before proceeding to his allegorical explanation.[63] This different treatment sets Cupid and Psyche apart: for Fulgentius Apuleius' story is clearly something special.[64]

The story as Fulgentius tells it falls into three parts or sections—each related in a different style. (It is important to note that the name Psyche never appears in his narrative.)

Part 1 is straight narrative and goes like this. The king and queen of a certain city had three daughters. The two older ones were pretty enough, but the youngest was so beautiful that she was believed to be an earthly Venus. The older daughters married, but no one dared to court the youngest. Instead, she was worshiped like a goddess with prayers and sacrifices. Venus was outraged and commanded Cupid to punish the girl, but instead he fell in love with her the moment he saw her. Apollo commanded that she be placed alone on a mountain peak and escorted as in a funeral procession to her marriage to a winged serpent. Zephyr wafted her down from the cliff into a beautiful golden house, where she was waited on by invisible servants whom she perceived only as voices. Her husband came to her at night, made love to her in the darkness, and departed at dawn unseen. The section ends with a neat little summary in very Apuleian style: "Habuit ergo vocale servitium, ventosum dominium, nocturnum commercium, ignotum coniugium" (Fulg., *Mit.* 3.6.115). [In short, she had voices for servants, an insubstantial domain, nocturnal intercourse, and an unknown husband.]

Part 2 continues the narration but adds moralizing comments. The two sisters climbed the mountain and loudly lamented her death. Her husband forbade her to see them, but, as Fulgentius says, "the unbreakable ardor of kindred affection overshadowed her husband's command."[65]

Latin text from Helm's Teubner edition. Helm's text of *Mit.* 3.6 is reprinted in Binder and Merkelbach, *Amor und Psyche*, 435–37. The English translation of Whitbread, *Fulgentius the Mythographer*, is convenient but unreliable; it should be used with great caution. Fulgentius' allegorical explanation and the end of the story of Cupid and Psyche are translated in *The Story of Cupid and Psyche as Related by Apuleius*, ed. Purser, 129–30.

[63] The other exception is the first story in the collection, "On the Origin of Idols" (*Mit.* 1.1), which Fulgentius attributes to the otherwise unknown "Diophantus Lacedemonum auctor."

[64] *Pace* Relihan, who argues that "the myth of Cupid and Psyche . . . is treated very contemptuously." *Ancient Menippean Satire*, 266 n. 18.

[65] "Tamen consanguineae caritatis invincibilis ardor maritale obumbravit imperium." Fulg. *Mit.* 3.6.115.

Zephyr wafted the sisters down, and she agreed to their poisonous advice to find out what her husband looked like. Fulgentius says: "She seized curiosity, a stepmother of her safety, and she seized easily credulity, which is always the mother of deception, neglecting the voice of caution."[66] Her sisters told her that she was married to a serpent. Believing them, she planned to kill him and "hid a dagger under the pillow and covered a lighted lamp with a bushel."[67] When her husband was asleep, she armed herself with the steel and uncovered her lamp. She recognized Cupid— it is important to remember here that *Cupido*, "Cupid," also means "erotic desire"—and while "she was on fire with the licentious passion of love,"[68] she burned her husband with a drop of oil from her lamp. Cupid fled, chastising her curiosity, and left her homeless and a refugee. In the end, after she had been greatly persecuted by Venus, he accepted her in marriage at the urging of Jupiter.[69] The section ends with a rush, omitting much of the story, and differing from Apuleius' account, in which it is Cupid who desires the marriage and Jupiter who agrees to allow it.

Part 3 summarizes the girl's trials in an elegant *praeteritio*: "I could run through the whole story in this chapter—how she went down to the underworld and fetched a little jar from the waters of the Styx and stole fleece from the flocks of the Sun and sorted the seeds and nearly died when she took a bit of Proserpina's beauty for herself, but . . ."[70] Having just related these matters, Fulgentius declines to relate them, explaining that they have already been told at length by both Apuleius and an otherwise unknown author called Aristophontes the Athenian.

Although Fulgentius closely follows Apuleius, his account nevertheless omits several interesting details—some more important than others. We hear nothing, for example, of the husband's forbidding the girl to see his face, but this is a point Fulgentius will make presently in his allegorical explanation.[71] In Apuleius the sisters make repeated visits,

---

[66] "Curiositatem, suae salutis novercam, arripuit et facillimam credulitatem, quae semper deceptionum mater est, postposito cautelae suffragio arripit." Ibid.

[67] "Novaculam sub pulvinal abscondit lucernamque modio contegit." Ibid. In Apuleius Psyche is to hide the lamp under the cover of a jar ("aliquo claudentis aululae tegmine," *Met.* 5.20.2); see p. 58.

[68] "Dum inmodesto amoris torretur affectu." Fulg. *Mit.* 3.6.115.

[69] "Tandem multis iactatam Veneris persecutionibus postea Iove petente in coniugio accepit." Ibid. 116.

[70] "Poteram quidem totius fabulae ordinem hoc libello percurrere, qualiter et ad infernum descenderit et ex Stygiis aquis urnulam delibaverit et Solis armenta vellere spoliaverit et seminum germina confusa discreverit et de Proserpinae pulchritudine particulam moritura praesumpserit; sed . . . " Ibid.

[71] He may also be hinting at the prohibition when he calls him "coniux luci fuga." Ibid. 115. Cf. Psyche's contemptuous reference to her husband at Apuleius, *Met.* 5.19.2: "maritum incerti status et prorsus lucifugam."

and their malice increases with each sight of Psyche in her luxurious surroundings. Fulgentius gives us only the last, decisive encounter. This omission, like his omission of the girl's subsequent revenge on her sisters, keeps his abbreviated narrative sharp and uncluttered. Apuleius tells the story in two books; he can afford to be expansive. Fulgentius, sketching it in two pages, cannot.

Other omissions, however, not only suit Fulgentius' reduced format but give his narrative a different emphasis and direction from that of his model. In Apuleius the husband, who is prescient as well as divine, sees that malignant Fortune presents a terrible danger to his young wife and urges her to be on guard against her envious sisters.[72] Cruel Fortune is omnipresent in the *Golden Ass*; her evocation here links Psyche's misfortunes with those of Lucius and other characters, and suggests the vulnerability of frail and foolish humanity to malignant supernatural forces. To put it bluntly, Psyche's simplicity (some would say her stupidity), like Lucius' curiosity, lays her open to the machinations of Fortune. In Fulgentius there is no Fortune to blame—only disobedience (the girl's affection for her blood kin, we remember, overshadowed her husband's command), curiosity ("the stepmother of her safety"), and credulity ("the mother of deception"). There is also no sign of the affectionate and worried husband we see in Apuleius; Fulgentius tells us only that "the husband who avoided the light of day, threatening her, forbade the sight of her sisters."[73]

Fulgentius has also omitted every detail connected with Psyche's redemption and final happiness: her pregnancy, Cupid's assistance in completing the tasks set by Venus, her divinity and joyous marriage. The pregnancy of Apuleius's Psyche is essential to the plot and its resolution. Her fear for herself and her unborn child makes her forget her promise to Cupid when her sisters tell her that her unknown husband is not only a serpent but a carnivore—adding the deliciously gruesome detail that he is just waiting for her to grow still greater with child so that there will be more of her to eat.[74] Her pregnancy increases the anger of Venus, who does *not* look forward to becoming a grandmother and decides to avoid it by the simple expedient of declaring Psyche's marriage invalid. "This child of yours will be born illegitimate," Venus gloats, "*if* I let you bring it to birth at all."[75] But Psyche's pregnancy also adds the final touch to the happy ending: she gives birth to a child, Voluptas (Pleasure),

---

[72] *Met.* 5.5.2–3 and 5.11.3–6.

[73] "Ille coniux luci fuga sororios ei comminando vetaret aspectus." Fulg. *Mit.* 3.6.115.

[74] "Nec diu blandis alimoniarum obsequiis te saginaturum omnes adfirmant, sed cum primum praegnationem tuam plenus maturaverit uterus, opimiore fructu praeditam devoraturum." *Met.* 5.18.1.

[75] "Spurius iste nascetur, si tamen partum omnino perferre te patiemur." Ibid. 6.9.6.

an emblem of her joyous and everlasting union with Cupid.[76] Even in his absence Apuleius' Cupid constantly protects and helps Psyche, orchestrating the assistance she receives in her various tasks.[77] In her final trial, when she fails to heed the prohibition against opening Proserpina's casket of beauty and falls into a deathlike sleep, he flies to her rescue and awakens her with a painless prick of his arrow.[78] He then flies to Olympus and pleads his case with Jupiter. Psyche is made immortal, and hence a suitable bride for the marriage between partners of equal status as required by Roman law. In true fairy-tale fashion, Cupid and Psyche get married and live happily ever after.

In Fulgentius' narrative, by contrast, there is no pregnancy and no baby Voluptas, no help and protection by the absent husband, and no plea to Jupiter. All we have is a shotgun wedding: "At last, at Jupiter's urging, he took her in marriage."[79] Fulgentius (or a later scribe) suggests the girl's immortality in the title of the chapter, "The Story of the Goddess Psyche and Cupid," but no hint of it appears elsewhere either in his narrative or in the subsequent allegory.[80]

The result of Fulgentius' omissions is a darker and more pessimistic story than that in Apuleius—one that is focused far more on the girl's error than on her subsequent sufferings and final redemption. It is this story, subtly but surely different from Apuleius' *Cupid and Psyche*, that he explains in his allegory. We might allegorize Apuleius' tale as the story of the union of the Soul with Love. Fulgentius' allegory is about the sins of the flesh and the evils of sexual desire. Here it is:

The city of the girl's birth represents the world, and her parents, the king and queen, are God and Matter. The three daughters are Caro (Flesh), Ultronietas (a very rare word that Fulgentius defines as Free Will), and Anima or Psice (Soul).[81] Soul is younger because the body is already made when the soul is placed in it. She is more beautiful because Soul is both superior to Free Will and nobler than Flesh. She is envied by Venus, that is, Lust, who sends Cupiditas, or Desire, to

---

[76] "Sic rite Psyche convenit in manum Cupidinis et nascitur illis maturo partu filia, quam Voluptatem nominamus." Ibid. 6.24.4.

[77] See *Apuleius: Cupid and Psyche*, ed. Kenney, on *Met.* 6.10.5, with further references. Venus explicitly acknowledges that Cupid is helping Psyche (see *Met.* 6.11.2 and 6.13.3, with Kenney's notes ad loc.).

[78] For this and the following details, see ibid. 6.21–24.

[79] "Postea Iove petente in coniugio accepit." Fulg., *Mit.* 3.6.116.

[80] "Fabula deae Psicae et Cupidinis." Ibid. 3.6. Given that in the chapter itself Fulgentius calls the girl Psice only once (at 3.6.117, when he explains her name at the beginning of the allegory) and that he nowhere refers to her immortality, the title is quite possibly a late addition. As Hays notes, "Such items are particularly vulnerable to scribal interference" (*Fulgentius the Mythographer*, 173).

[81] *Mit.* 3.6.117.

destroy her.[82] Desire, which can be of either good or evil, esteems Soul and joins with her as if in a marriage and persuades her not to see his face—that is, says Fulgentius, not to learn the delights of desire.[83] Fulgentius expands this explanation with one of the most fascinating and revealing comments in the allegory: "Whence also Adam, although he sees, does not see that he is naked until he eats from the tree of concupiscence."[84] Fulgentius does not explain the connection, but leaves it to us to infer that seeing the face of Desire is equivalent to eating the apple: each is a fall from innocence into carnal awareness and lust; each is a sin.

The allegory continues. Desire urges Soul not to be persuaded by her sisters, Flesh and Free Will, to satisfy her curiosity about his appearance. But terrified by their urging, she takes the lamp from beneath the bushel—"that is," says Fulgentius, "she reveals the flame of longing hidden in her heart, sees that it is sweet, and falls in love with it."[85] Fulgentius' heroine sees what has been there all along—her own sexual longing, its light unfortunately no longer hidden under a bushel. Apuleius' heroine hid her lamp under a jar lid, but Fulgentius' "bushel" (*modio*) recalls the New Testament and its repeated injunction *not* to keep one's light hidden under a bushel. Thus, in the Sermon on the Mount, Jesus says: "Neither do men light a candle, and put it under a bushel, but on a candlestick: and it giveth light unto all that are in the house. Let your light so shine before men, that they may see your good works, and glorify your father which is in heaven" (Matthew 5:15–16).[86] Fulgentius wants his readers to remember this good light, which *should* be revealed, and to contrast it with the sinful flame of carnal desire, which should remain hidden from us.[87] The flame does double duty in his allegory: it is

---

[82] "Huic invidet Venus quasi libido; ad quam perdendam cupiditatem mittit." Ibid.

[83] "Sed quia cupiditas est boni, est mali, cupiditas animam diligit et ei velut in coniunctione miscetur; quam persuadet ne suam faciem videat, id est cupiditatis delectamenta discat." *Met.* 3.6.117–18.

[84] "Unde et Adam quamvis videat nudum se non videt, donec de concupiscentiae arbore comedat." Fulg., *Mit.* 3.6.118.

[85] "Id est desiderii flammam in pectore absconsam depalat visamque taliter dulcem amat ac diligit." Ibid.

[86] "Neque accendunt lucernam et ponunt eam sub modio, sed super candelabrum ut luceat omnibus qui in domo sunt: sic luceat lux vestra coram hominibus, ut videant vestra bona opera et glorificent Patrem vestrum qui in caelis est." See also Mark 4:21 and Luke 11:33.

[87] Fulgentius also associates Psyche's lamp with lust and its dangers twice in his prologue. He promises that his work will not follow such lights: "Neque enim illas Eroidarum arbitreris lucernas meis praesules libris, quibus aut Sulpicillae procacitas aut Psices curiositas declarata est." *Mit. prol.* 1.4. And he declares (falsely, as it turns out) that he will not deal with the "light-carrying girls" (*lignides puellas*) Hero and Psyche: "Dum haec lumen queritur extinctum, illa deflet incensum, ut Psice videndo perderet et Ero non videndo perisset." Ibid. 1.20. (Hero is treated at *Mit.* 3.4.)

Soul's desire, but it also sets fire to Soul's desire. We might say that the flame burns and damages itself. Here is the way Fulgentius puts it: "[Soul] is said to kindle the flame with the spurting of the lamp because every Desire burns as much as it is loved and fixes the stain of sin on its own flesh."[88] He continues: "Therefore, as if made naked by Desire, she is deprived of her mighty fortune and tossed by dangers and driven from her royal palace."[89] Here the allegory ends—with Fulgentius implicitly keeping the example of Adam before us. Soul, like Adam, has succumbed to temptation and gained forbidden knowledge; and like Adam, she is driven from her Eden.

Medieval Sightings

Fulgentius undoubtedly had a manuscript of at least part of the *Metamorphoses*, for he closely imitates phrases from both the story of Cupid and Psyche and the prologue.[90] He seems to have known some of Apuleius' lost works as well.[91] His fellow North African, Martianus Capella, probably had texts of the *Metamorphoses* and *De deo Socratis*.[92] But Fulgentius and Martianus were not the only ones reading Apuleius in the decades around 500. In Gaul, Sidonius Apollinaris mentions Apuleius

---

[88] "Quam ideo lucernae ebullitione dicitur incendisse, quia omnis cupiditas quantum diligitur tantum ardescit et peccatricem suae carni configit maculam." Fulg., *Mit.* 3.6.118.

[89] "Ergo quasi cupiditate nudata et potenti fortuna privatur et periculis iactatur et regia domo expellitur." Ibid.

[90] For Cupid and Psyche, see n. 61 in this chapter. In his own prologue, Fulgentius echoes the first sentence of the *Metamorphoses*: "Tuarum aurium sedes lepido quolibet susurro permulceam" (*Mit. prol.* 1.3: cf. "auresque tuas benivolas lepido susurro permulceam," *Met.* 1.1.1); see Carver, "*Quis ille?*" 169. It is harder to be sure about echoes from other parts of the novel. Mattiacci believes that Fulgentius draws on passages in both *Met.* 2 and *Met.* 3 ("Apuleio in Fulgenzio," 236–37, 252–53), but Bradford Gregory Hays tells me that so far he has found "no unequivocal evidence" that Fulgentius knew either parts of the *Metamorphoses* other than the prologue and Cupid and Psyche or any of the other extant works (personal communication, May 19, 2002).

[91] In *Expositio sermonum antiquorum* he cites five passages from Apuleius. Two are from lost or spurious works: *Hermagoras* (cited in *Expos.* 3) and *De re publica* (*Expos.* 44). The other three are from Cupid and Psyche: *Met.* 5.9.8 (*Expos.* 17); *Met* 4.35.2 (*Expos.* 36); and *Met.* 5.8.1, 5.15.1, or 6.19.4 (*Expos.* 40). For a detailed discussion, see Mattiacci, "Apuleio in Fulgenzio," 245–52. All of Fulgentius' quotations from the *Metamorphoses* differ markedly from the text transmitted by F (Laur. 68.2), a fact that led Mazzarino to argue that his text was from a separate tradition (*La Milesia e Apuleio* 22–42). Most scholars, however, would agree with Robertson that he simply cited carelessly (see Robertson's *apparatus* at 4.35.2 and "The Manuscripts of the *Metamorphoses* of Apuleius," 31–32).

[92] See Willis' *apparatus* to Martianus, passim; Klibansky and Regen, *Die Handschriften*, 33–34. For elements from *De deo Socratis* in Martianus' demonology, see Lenaz, ed., *Martiani Capellae De nuptiis*, 81–100.

with approval (although with no indication of firsthand knowledge), and his friend Claudianus Mamertus (who never mentions the name Apuleius) closely imitates passages from the *Apology* in his own *De statu animae*.⁹³ Neither writer alludes to the *Metamorphoses*. In Constantinople some decades later, Priscian knew and cited five different works of Apuleius of which only *De deo Socratis* is extant.⁹⁴ The interesting and important point, however, is that of all our sources in this period, only Martianus and Fulgentius can be shown to have known the *Metamorphoses*. The other works in the literary group seem to have been almost entirely unknown outside North Africa: we have no citations for the *Florida*, and only Claudianus Mamertus can be shown to have studied the *Apology*.

After Priscian and Fulgentius, Apuleius becomes almost invisible for several hundred years, until the copying of F in the eleventh century. But the operative word is *almost*. For there is excellent evidence that someone in Spain, probably in a monastic library, had access to his works as late as the end of the seventh or beginning of the eighth century. The medieval Spanish *Abolita* Glossary, now only partly preserved, includes rare words not only from the *Metamorphoses, Florida,* and *Apology* but also from *De mundo, De deo Socratis,* and *De dogmate Platonis*.⁹⁵ This is an extremely important piece of evidence. All of the other ancient readers of Apuleius we have been considering—from Sallustius to Fulgentius—were interested in only a portion of his large production. Sallustius corrected the *Apology*, the *Metamorphoses*, and probably the *Florida*. Augustine mentions several works, but quotes only *De deo Socratis* and *De mundo*.⁹⁶ Claudianus Mamertus imitated the *Apology* and perhaps used his translation of the *Phaedo*. Martianus knew some of the philosophical works and the *Metamorphoses*. Priscian cites

---

⁹³ See appendix 1. Sidonius (d. before 490) mentions Apuleius in *Ep.* 2.9.5, 2.10.5, 4.3.1, and 9.13.3. The only works he mentions by name are the translation of Plato's *Phaedo* (*Ep.* 2.9.5) and *Quaestiones conviviales* (*Ep.* 9.13.3). For Claudianus Mamertus (d. ca. 474), see the important discussion of Alimonti, who argues that he not only uses individual Apuleian words and phrases but has created a deliberate and artistic imitation of the *Apology* ("Apuleio e l'arcaismo"). It is also possible that Claudianus used Apuleius' *Phaedo* in the passage from the *Phaedo* in *De statu animae* 2.7. See Alimonti, "Apuleio e l'arcaismo," 224–26; Klibansky and Regen, *Die Handschriften*, 39 n. 120.

⁹⁴ See appendix 1. For discussions with detailed bibliography, see Stramaglia, "Apuleio come *auctor*," 144–46, 157–59; idem, "Prisciano e l'*Epitome historiarum* di Apuleio."

⁹⁵ The glossary is called *Abolita* from its first entry. See the important discussion of Klibansky and Regen, *Die Handschriften*, 39–42. Apuleius glosses have been identified by both Weir ("Apuleius Glosses") and Klibansky and Regen (*Die Handschriften*, 41 n. 134). The *Abolita* Glossary is printed in *Glossaria Latina* 3, ed. Lindsay and Thomson, 97–183. See also Lindsay, "The 'Abolita' Glossary."

⁹⁶ See pp. 35–36.

various works, all outside the literary group. Fulgentius was interested above all in Cupid and Psyche. But our Spanish glossator seems to have had a text of the entire surviving corpus (and possibly of some lost works as well).[97] It is not clear that he actually read all these works himself, but someone (or several someones) before him did: our compiler, like all glossators, gathered his entries from the glosses in annotated manuscripts.[98] Perhaps the Apuleius text he used was contained in a single manuscript, perhaps in two or three. In either case, the compiler had at his disposal works from both the literary and the philosophical traditions—from now on, separate streams not to be reunited in a single manuscript until the fourteenth century.

It is impossible either to estimate how many manuscripts of Apuleius' several works were in circulation in late antiquity and the early Middle Ages (six? ten? a dozen?) or to decide whether the same manuscript was used by any two of our readers. For the literary group, however, it came down in the end to one—the manuscript corrected by Sallustius in 395 and 397 that preserved the *Apology, Metamorphoses,* and *Florida* to posterity. No one knows what happened to Sallustius' manuscript between the fourth and eleventh centuries. Perhaps it passed from the Sallustii into the hands of some other great family and from there into a monastic library. The best guess is that it spent the centuries in the area between Rome and Naples, a locale rich in both aristocratic villas and monastic centers.[99] But at last either this manuscript or a copy of it arrived at the great monastic library at Monte Cassino in southern Italy, probably during the cultural resurgence of the monastery in the eighth century.[100] And there it remained.

The oldest surviving copy of it (Florence, Laurenziana 68.2, called F) was probably made between 1060 and 1075, during the golden age of the monastery, in the time of its famous bibliophile abbot Desiderius.[101] In this "mirabile xi secolo di Montecassino," as Cavallo calls it, the

---

[97] Weir, "Apuleius Glosses," 42; Klibansky and Regen, *Die Handschriften,* 41.

[98] "Vocabula igitur ferme nulla in glossariis tractantur nisi ea quibus interpretatio in margine codicis alicuius, puta Vergilii, fuerat adscripta." Lindsay in *Glossaria Latina* 4, 77–78.

[99] For this area as a general source of classical texts, see Guglielmo Cavallo, "La trasmissione dei testi," 412–13.

[100] It probably did not arrive during the first period of the monastery (529–77), when its intellectual activities seem to have been concerned exclusively with sacred literature. For the history of the library before the eleventh century, see Bloch, "Monte Cassino's Teachers and Library," and Cavallo, "La trasmissione dei testi," with earlier bibliography.

[101] Cavallo ("La trasmissione dei testi," 387) dates the manuscript to the abbacy of Richerius (1038–55), but Newton convincingly argues that it belongs to the first half of Desiderius' rule, i.e., ca. 1060–75 (*The Scriptorium and Library at Monte Cassino,* 96–107, 108, and see 266 fig. 1).

monks embarked on a campaign of recopying their ancient manuscripts, especially those that were mutilated or damaged.[102] They no doubt had various motives, but Newton points out that they were especially interested in acquiring or restoring books and authors associated with Augustine.[103] The philosophical works of Apuleius were beyond their reach outside Italy, but the monks had their own ancient manuscript of the literary group, and they recopied that. Augustine's interest had already been important for the preservation of the philosophical works in northern Europe; Newton's argument suggests that we can also credit him, at least indirectly, with the restoration and preservation of the *Golden Ass* in Monte Cassino. We cannot know the precise condition of the ancient manuscript, but Pecere has demonstrated that it lacked one or more folios between the *Metamorphoses* and the *Florida*. The scribe of F indicated the lacuna both by crowding the end of the *Metamorphoses* to make it end at the bottom of one folio (fol. 183v) and by beginning the *Florida* at a place several lines down on the next (184r). He included neither a colophon or subscription for the *Metamorphoses* nor a title for the *Florida*, since neither appeared in his model.[104] The lacuna soon became undetectable, for later scribes ignored or concealed it either by supplying a title for the *Florida* or by running the *Metamorphoses* and *Florida* together as a continuous work.[105]

Pecere's demonstration of the mutilated state of F's exemplar has an important and inescapable corollary: either the beginning of the *Florida* or the end of the *Metamorphoses* or both are lost. Since the *Metamorphoses* seems complete as it stands, with Lucius' description of himself in his final incarnation as a priest of Isis, it is probably safe to conclude that the damage was confined to the final subscription of the *Metamorphoses* and the opening of the *Florida*—although one must also confess that in a work of so many twists and turns as the *Metamorphoses* we might never suspect the loss of one more episode or even of a final surprising denouement.[106]

---

[102] Cavallo, "La trasmissione dei testi," 397–98. He suggests that there was an effort in the eleventh century to renew and preserve the ancient manuscripts collected in the eighth and ninth centuries: "Si sana in tal modo il contrasto tra la fioritura di studi attestata nella Montecassino dell'viii–ix secolo e le scarse testimonianze librarie a noi pervenute di quei secoli."

[103] Newton, *The Scriptorium and Library at Monte Cassino*, 319–21.

[104] Pecere, "Qualche riflessioni," 107–9 and plates 1–2. The title *Floridorum Liber* on fol. 184r is a later addition, as Pecere observes. See also Pecere, "Una pista di attualità," 507–25, esp. 512. The absence in F of a subscription at the end of the *Florida* is susceptible of several explanations, including damage to the archetype; but see pp. 46–47.

[105] Pecere, "Qualche riflessioni," 109–12.

[106] For an argument that the *Metamorphoses* as we have it is incomplete, see van Mal-Maeder, "*Lector, intende*," esp. 112–17.

F remained in Monte Cassino until the middle of the fourteenth century, when it was taken to Florence. But it was not the only Apuleius manuscript at Monte Cassino. Its exemplar was copied at least once more in the eleventh century—perhaps twice, as Pecere argues.¹⁰⁷ A copy of F itself was transcribed around 1200; this manuscript (Laurenziana 29.2, called φ) is now also in Florence.

We will return to F and its fellows presently. The important point for our present discussion is that from around the middle of the eleventh century on, the literary and rhetorical works of Apuleius were available in a way that they had not been for several hundred years. The first readers seem to have been at Monte Cassino itself, for unmistakable echoes of the *Florida* appear in the works of Guaiferius, one of its eleventh-century monks.¹⁰⁸ It is probably also to Monte Cassino—although a generation or so later—that we owe the so-called *spurcum additamentum*, or "dirty addition," to book 10 of the *Golden Ass*.

In book 10 the Ass at last finds himself happy and well treated. His current master has discovered that he has human qualities and tastes: he has him taught to recline politely at table and to eat and drink like a gentleman. News of the Ass's accomplishments spreads—indeed, rumor has it that he can even wrestle and dance. Eventually his keeper finds that people will pay to see the Ass's tricks. One of his besotted admirers is a wealthy matron, a Pasiphae, Lucius tells us—albeit one in love with an ass.¹⁰⁹ The keeper sells the matron the Ass's services for

---

¹⁰⁷ The other copies would be C (Assisi, Biblioteca Comunale 706, "the Assisi fragments" of the *Apology*) and (X), a hypothetical copy not showing F's lacuna at *Met.* 8.7–9. See Pecere, "Qualche riflessioni," esp. 100–104. If Pecere is shown to be correct, the Class I manuscripts would be descended from (X), and F could no longer be considered the archetype. The question is still open; see Graverini's survey "Note di aggiornamento," 183–85. For earlier discussions, see Lowe, "The Unique Manuscript of Apuleius' *Metamorphoses*"; Robertson, "The Manuscripts of the *Metamorphoses*" and "The Assisi Fragments"; Marshall, in L. D. Reynolds, ed., *Texts and Transmission*, 15–16.

¹⁰⁸ Guaiferius (d. before 1080) echoes *Florida* 18.3 in *Vita Sancti Secundini* (PL 147.1295D) and *Florida* 23.1–2 in *S. Lucii Papae et Martyris Vita* (PL 147:1301–2). See Manitius, *Geschichte der lateinischen Literatur des Mittelalters*, esp. 486 and 489. For discussion, see Pecere, "Qualche riflessioni," 119 n. 34; Newton, *The Scriptorium and Library*, 288. For other echoes of the *Florida* in Guaiferius, see Piovesan, "Per il testo e le fonti di Guaiferio," esp. 76–80. It is sometimes thought that the monks also knew the philosophical works, since Guaiferius' contemporary Alfanus (d. 1085), in his life of Saint Christina, has the saint claim a particular interest in *De deo Socratis*: "In illo namque libello Apuleii, qui de Deo Socratis [sacratis, *ed.*] titulatur, in quo propter incredibilem copiam suavitatemque dicendi saepe et multum studere solebamus." (*Vita et Passio Sanctae Christinae*: PL 147:1272B). But the passage shows no particular knowledge of Apuleius and in fact quotes some lines not found in *De deo Socratis* or anywhere else; Alfanus no doubt knew of the work from reading Augustine. See Manitius, *Geschichte*, 635.

¹⁰⁹ "Nec ullam vaesanae libidini medelam capiens ad instar asinariae Pasiphaae complexus meos ardenter expectabat." *Met.* 10.19.3.

the night, and he does so well with her that the keeper and master decide that he should repeat his performance in the arena, this time with a condemned murderess. This is the prospect, we remember, that precipitated the Ass's flight and ultimate redemption by Isis.

The *spurcum additamentum* is inserted in the account of the Ass's night with the amorous matron. It appears at the moment when the woman has disrobed and anointed both herself and the Ass with fragrant oils in preparation for their lovemaking, which Apuleius will go on to describe in explicit detail.[110] Here it is:

> And, by Hercules, she cleansed the swollen scrotum of my testicles with washings of fragrant wine and Chian rosewater. And then with her fingers—thumb, index, middle, ring, and pinky—she pushed back my foreskin and purified the shaft of my snowy-white penis of no little filth. And while the beautiful woman was quickly coming from my testicles to the head of my penis, I, whimpering and raising my teeth to the sky, was extending my penis because of the frequent rubbing, and again and again touching my belly with it as it bobbed up and down. And she herself, seeing what my penis had discharged amid her flowery lotions, asserted that the little delay during which she had ordered the bed to be laid seemed as long as a year.[111]

Modern scholars are in general agreement that the passage is not Apuleian.[112] It contains too many neologisms, and too much culled from later authors and grammarians, to be the work of any ancient author.

---

[110] Lucius' encounter with the matron appears at *Met.* 10.19.3–10.22. The *spurcum additamentum* was probably meant to be inserted between *Met.* 10.21.1 and 10.21.2.

[111] "Et ercle orcium pigam perteretem Hyaci fragrantis et Chie rosacee lotionibus expiavit. ac dein digitis, hypate licanos mese paramese et nete, hastam mei inguinis nivei spurci<ti>ei pluscule excoria<n>s emundavit. et cum ad inguinis cephalum formosa mulier concitim veniebat ab orcibus, ganniens ego et dentes ad Iovem elevans Priapo<n> frequenti frictura porrixabam ipsoque pando et repando ventrem sepiuscule tactabam. ipsa quoque, inspiciens quod genius inter antheras excreverat, modicum illud morule, qua lustrum sterni mandaverat, anni sibi revolutionem autumabat." The text is that of Mariotti, "Lo *spurcum additamentum*, 231–32." My translation is based on Mariotti's commentary.

[112] Winkler is an exception (*Auctor & Actor*, 193). He asserts that the passage has been banished by prudish scholars "for inadequate critical reasons" and lists it in his index under the rubric "Castration: of text." For the decisive arguments favoring medieval authorship, see Fraenkel, "A Sham Sisenna," and especially the detailed discussion of Mariotti ("Lo *spurcum additamentum*") with earlier bibliography. See also Zimmerman, in *Apuleius Madaurensis Metamorphoses, Book X*, 433–39; Martos, *Las Metamorfosis o El Asno de Oro* 1:cli–cliv. Recently Lytle has argued for the authenticity of the passage with reference to ancient methods of animal breeding: "Apuleius' *Metamorphoses* and the *Spurcum Additamentum* (10.21)." His argument is handily refuted by Hunink: "The 'spurcum additamentum.'"

It is a late medieval production, probably to be dated somewhere in the twelfth or thirteenth century.[113] The passage does not appear in our eleventh-century manuscript F; rather, we find it first in the margin of φ, in the hand of a fourteenth-century humanist named Zanobi da Strada, an interesting figure whose important role in Apuleian studies will concern us presently.[114] Zanobi's friend Giovanni Boccaccio transcribed it into the margin of his manuscript, too, as we shall see in the next chapter.

The unknown author of the passage (scholars affectionately call him "Spurcus")[115] undoubtedly had a taste for the obscene, but he was also a learned man, widely read in medieval scholarly and medical texts. Most important, however, Spurcus knew and appreciated his Apuleius. He uses Apuleian-sounding words that are not found in Apuleius—words like *perteretem* ("swollen"), *concitim* ("quickly" or "passionately"), and *sepiuscule* ("again and again").[116] He makes the delighted Ass whimper with pleasure at the matron's caresses and toss his head to the sky with his teeth bared—actions that seem human and asinine at the same time. His use of *ganniens* ("whimpering") is a particularly nice touch: we are to imagine, I think, not a hee-haw but something like a delighted snuffle or whinny.[117] Another fine detail is his having the matron bathe the Ass with rosewater—a teasing reference to the long-sought rose remedy that will change him back to a man.

Spurcus also had a fine sense of humor. As Fraenkel pointed out, his source for the names of the matron's fingers ("hypate licanos mese paramese et nete": thumb, index, middle, ring, and pinky) is Boethius' treatise *De institutione musica* 1.20.[118] In Boethius, of course, the names refer not to fingers but to the strings of the lyre. Spurcus omits two of Boethius' names (the lyre has seven strings, the matron only five fingers), but otherwise he presents the names in order from the lowest and most resonant (*hypate*) to the highest and shortest (*nete*). The matron may not be playing a tune on the Ass, but at the very least she is practicing her fingering. We will never know just how Spurcus thought of calling fingers by the names of strings. Perhaps he was inspired by

---

[113] Mariotti, "Lo *spurcum additamentum*," 248.

[114] For the identification of Zanobi's hand in φ, see Giuseppe Billanovich, *I primi umanisti*, 29–33.

[115] Fraenkel seems to have coined the name: "Spurcus (as I shall call him for short)" ("A Sham Sisenna," 151).

[116] See Mariotti, "Lo *spurcum additamentum*," 234, 239, 242.

[117] As Mariotti notes, *ganniens* in Spurcus anticipates the matron's *gannitus* in Apuleius' narrative at 10.22.2 ("Lo *spurcum additamentum*," 240).

[118] Fraenkel, "A Sham Sisenna," 153–54. For the text, see Boethius, *De institutione arithmetica, De institutione musica*. For a translation, see *Fundamentals of Music,* by Bower.

Boethius' comment that *licanos* (*lichanos*) means "index finger" in Greek or by the suggestive diagram he would have seen in his Boethius manuscript.[119] Perhaps he saw the manuscript itself at Monte Cassino.[120]

Spurcus' lines are Apuleian in spirit, though not in reality. They are a creative imitation in tune with Apuleius' manner and with the tone of the episode of the amorous matron. They are also quite different in kind from the echoes of specific passages in the *Florida* that Guaiferius culled from his reading to use in his saints' lives, not because they are obscene but because they draw on their author's understanding and interpretation of his sources (Apuleius and Boethius) to create a new work, however small and unworthy it may be. It seems pleasantly ironic that the first creative use of Apuleius in seven hundred years—that is, since the time of Fulgentius—should be such a cheerfully asinine obscenity.

Coming to Light

After Spurcus, all is quiet—but only for a time. By the end of the thirteenth century someone had removed or copied a manuscript from Monte Cassino and brought it to northern Italy. One manuscript of the *Apology, Metamorphoses*, and *Florida* survives from this period, but undoubtedly there were more.[121] Soon the cat was out of the bag: in the few years from about 1320 to 1332, Apuleius appears in the works of several important encyclopedists and commentators, all clearly familiar with one or more of the works from Monte Cassino.

Our earliest reference appears in the *Chronicon* of Benzo of Alessandria, a North Italian notary who worked in Milan, Como, and Verona

---

[119] As Fraenkel suggests in "A Sham Sisenna," 153. These diagrams generally show a vertical line on the left to which are attached horizontal lines indicating the strings, each neatly labeled on the right. The appearance is not unlike that of fingers attached to a hand.

[120] In a personal communication, Francis Newton has told me that *De institutione musica* is not among the Monte Cassino manuscripts from the period 1050 to 1300 that he has seen, but he has drawn my attention to a handbook of the liberal arts, now in Venice, containing excerpts from the work (Venice, Biblioteca Marciana MS Lat. Z. L. 497). This eleventh-century manuscript was copied from a Beneventan exemplar, and the handbook itself was probably put together by Lorenzo d'Amalfi, who was at Monte Cassino in the 1020s. See Newton, "Tibullus in Two Grammatical *Florilegia* of the Middle Ages." The Venice manuscript itself does not contain *Mus.* 1.20; for its contents, see Bower, "Boethius' *De institutione musica*, 246.

[121] The manuscript is Milan, Biblioteca Ambrosiana N 180 sup, the best witness to the Class I tradition. It is now dated in the late thirteenth century; see Petoletti, in Baglio, Ferrari, and Petoletti, "Montecassino e gli umanisti," 227. See also appendix 2.

Exemplary Behavior • 67

from about 1311 to 1330. He probably composed the *Chronicon* around 1320.[122] Benzo has this to say in his chapter on Apuleius:

> Vincent [of Beauvais] says that he has discovered two books of this Apuleius: one *De vita et moribus Platonis* and another, which has the title *De deo Socratis*. But I have read another book of the same Apuleius that has this title: *Apulei Platonici Floridorum [liber]*. I have also learned of another book of the same man that has the title *Asini aurei [liber]* or, according to others, *Lucii Apulei Platonici Madaurensis methamorfoseos liber*. He tells many amusing tales of various kinds, but in a rhetorical and exotic style, explaining that he had been changed into the form of an ass by magic arts, and that he had seen the things that he reports and that they happened to him while he was in the form of an ass. For this reason Macrobius in the *Somnium Scipionis* speaks of "plots full of the fictitious calamities of lovers on which even [Petronius] Arbiter spent so much effort or in which Apuleius to our surprise sometimes excelled." I would not even repeat these things, for fear that they might arouse the scorn of readers or listeners, except that I have learned that even the outstanding doctor Augustine also has written about it. For Augustine mentions the same thing in book 18 of the *City of God*, where he discusses the trickery of demons.[123]

The chapter goes on to quote Augustine's argument in *City of God* 18.18 that metamorphosis is a deception perpetrated by demons that changes

---

[122] For Benzo (d. around 1330), see Sabbadini, *Le scoperte dei codici latini e greci* 2:128–50; Ragni, "Benzo d'Alessandria"; Petoletti, "Montecassino e gli umanisti," 224–26, 236–38; idem, *Il "Chronicon" di Benzo d'Alessandria*. For the date, see Petoletti, *Il "Chronicon,"* 13: "Risulta abbastanza chiaro che il nucleo dei libri superstiti venne elaborato negli anni intorno al 1320." Benzo's *Chronicon* is partly preserved in Milan, Biblioteca Ambrosiana B24 inf. Book 24 has been edited by Petoletti, *Il "Chronicon."*

[123] "Huius autem Apulei duos se repperisse libros dicit Vincentius, unum scilicet *De vita et moribus Platonis*, alium qui intitulatur *De deo Socratis*. Ego vero alium eiusdem Apulei librum legi, qui intitulatur sic: Apulei Platonici *Floridorum*; alium quoque librum eiusdem comperi qui intitulatur *Asini Aurei* vel, secundum alios, intitulatur sic: Lucii Apulei Platonici Madaurensis *Methamorfoseos* liber. Qui multas et varias ac iocosas quidem fabulas stilo tamen rethorico peregrinoque recitat, insinuans se in asini formam magicis artibus fuisse conversum seque vidisse que refert atque ei contigisse, dum in asini forma esset. Unde Macrobius in *Sompnio Scipionis* dicit: 'Argumenta fictis casibus amatorum referta, quibus se vel multum Arbiter exercuit, vel Apuleium nonnumquam luxisse miramur.' Que quidem etiam non recitarem, ne derisui legentibus aut audientibus essent, nisi et eximium doctorem Augustinum etiam de illo scripsisse comperissem; etenim de eodem mentionem facit Augustinus libro *De civitate Dei* XVIII°, ubi de ludificatione demonum agit." Benzo, *Chronicon* 24.79.1–23. Milan, Biblioteca Ambrosiana B24 inf., fol. 280r-v, quoted from Petoletti, *Il "Chronicon,"* 336. Benzo's text of Macrobius (*Somn. Scip.* 1.2.8) differs slightly from that in modern editions, which read "lusisse." See n. 9 in this chapter.

only the appearance (but not the reality) of beings created by God.¹²⁴ It concludes:

> Augustine tells this and other marvels, which I have followed up (even at the cost of digressing to some extent), so that those reading what they might be likely to believe concerning the transformation of this Apuleius and similar cases, might know what such a great doctor thought in these matters.¹²⁵

Benzo's detailed remarks—the first discussion of Apuleius since antiquity—are full of clues, not only about what he saw and read but also about what he thought of it. He says nothing about having seen the *Apology*, but he does know (or know about) the *Florida* and the *Metamorphoses*, for he tells us that he has read (*legi*) the one and learned about (*comperi*) the other.¹²⁶ The distinction between "reading" and "learning about" seems intended to point to a real difference in his knowledge of the two works. Benzo's account of the plot and style of the *Metamorphoses*, though accurate enough, is very general: it is about what one would expect from someone who had merely "learned about" the novel. But he clearly did "read" the *Florida*, for he uses substantial quotations and citations from the *Florida* (but not from the *Metamorphoses*) in his *Chronicon*.¹²⁷

Benzo derived his comments on the *Metamorphoses* from Macrobius and Augustine: from the one he learned to consider its content trivial ("plots full of the fictitious calamities of lovers"), and from the other he gained a precedent for mentioning such trivia ("even the outstanding doctor Augustine has also written about it"). Augustine, however, also had another, more profound influence on both Benzo and other early fourteenth-century humanists, for he not only taught them that the transformation in the *Golden Ass* was an illusion but supported (and supplied) their assumption that the novel was to be read as autobiography. That Apuleius is relating his own experience, whether real or imaginary, is assumed in Benzo's plot summary ("[he explains] that he had been changed into the form of an ass by magic arts, and that he had seen the things that he reports and that they happened to him while

---

¹²⁴ For Augustine's discussion, see pp. 33–34.

¹²⁵ "Hoc et alia mira recitat Augustinus, que ideo, licet quodammodo digrediendo, prosecutus sum, ut legentes que de transformatione huius Apulei et similium credere habeant, sciant quod in hiis senserit tantus doctor." Benzo, *Chronicon* 24.79.77–80, quoted from Petoletti, *Il "Chronicon,"* 338.

¹²⁶ The distinction is noted by both Petoletti ("Montecassino e gli umanisti," 226 n. 32) and Carver ("The Rediscovery of the Latin Novels," 260).

¹²⁷ The passages have been identified and listed by Petoletti, "Montecassino e gli umanisti," 236–37. See also idem, *Il "Chronicon,"* index.

he was in the form of an ass"), just as it had been in Augustine's ("Apuleius either declared or pretended [it] happened to him in the books which he entitled the *Golden Ass*—that after taking a magical substance he became an ass, but with his mind remaining human.")[128]

Benzo certainly either saw a manuscript of the *Metamorphoses* or learned of its title from someone who had, for he calls the author of the *Metamorphoses* Lucius Apuleius, a name that first began to appear in manuscripts in the early fourteenth century. The earliest appearance I know of is in a manuscript dated around 1316, just a few years before Benzo composed the *Chronicon*. This manuscript, Vatican Library, Ottob. lat. 2091, introduces the novel thus: *Lucii Apuleii Platonici Maudorensis Methamorphoseon liber primus incipit*.[129] It is risky to identify Ottob. lat. 2091 as Benzo's source (if it were, we would expect him to mention Apuleius' *Apology*, since the manuscript includes some fragments of it).[130] Benzo (or his informant) could have seen a manuscript now lost to us. In any case, we can be sure that the name Lucius was supplied by a fourteenth-century scribe who wanted to find a praenomen to fill out the traditional "Apuleius Madaurensis" in the incipit of his manuscript. Although Apuleius' praenomen appears neither in ancient literary sources nor in the Monte Cassino manuscripts, Lucius was the obvious choice. Since no less an authority than Augustine himself had identified Apuleius with the first-person narrator of his novel, what could be more natural than for someone to award him the hero's praenomen as well? It was probably inevitable that the praenomen would soon take on a life of its own in both manuscripts and discussions of the novel: when readers saw the name Lucius Apuleius, they naturally assumed the identity of novelist and hero and worked out their interpretations accordingly.[131]

At almost the same time that Benzo was writing his *Chronicon*, Apuleius made an appearance in another work, *Liber de vita et moribus philosophorum*, formerly ascribed to the English scholar Walter Burley (1275–1345?).[132] The attribution has been refuted, but the important

---

[128] "[Sicut] Apuleius in libris, quos asini aurei titulo inscripsit, sibi ipsi accidisse, ut accepto veneno humano animo permanente asinus fieret, aut indicavit aut finxit." *Civ.* 18.18.

[129] Fol. 30r. For a description, see Pellegrin, *Les manuscrits classiques latins de la Bibliothèque Vaticane* 1:785–6. For the date, see Butler and Owen, *Apuleii Apologia*, xxxix–xl. See also appendix 2.

[130] Vatican Library, Ottob. lat. 2091, fols. 10r–13r. But in Pellegrin's transcription of the incipit (*Les manuscrits classiques latins* 1:785), the work is not attributed to Apuleius: "Liber de magia incipit apud Claudium Maximum Maurinum" (fol. 10r).

[131] And they continued to do so for several hundred years: Apuleius was still sometimes called Lucius well into the twentieth century.

[132] For Burley, see Thomas Andrew Archer in *DNB* 3 (1921): 374–76. A good critical edition of *De vita* is much to be desired. I cite the 1886 edition of Hermann Knust.

point for our purposes is not so much the identity of the author as the date and background of his work.¹³³ The date is certainly before 1326 and perhaps as-early as the period 1317–20; the work was composed in northern Italy by someone (I shall call him Pseudo-Burley) in close contact with the cultural milieus of Bologna and Padua.¹³⁴ Pseudo-Burley knows works from the philosophical tradition like *De deo Socratis* and *De Platone*, but he is also familiar with the *Apology* and *Metamorphoses* (although apparently not with the *Florida*). He quotes short passages from the *Apology* in his chapters on Socrates and Demosthenes and a longer extract in the chapter on Apuleius.¹³⁵ The chapter begins: "Apuleius of Madaura, African, Platonic philosopher, most learned in Greek and Latin, was famous in Athens. He succeeded Plato and wrote many books."¹³⁶ Pseudo-Burley goes on to list Apuleius' works, pausing briefly over the *Metamorphoses*:¹³⁷

> And another that he divided into twelve books and called the *Golden Ass*, where he wrote that it happened to him that when he had taken a magical substance given to him by some woman, he thought he had been changed into an ass, but with his mind remaining human. Afterward he was cured of this illusion.¹³⁸

Modern scholars have been much intrigued by Pseudo-Burley's comment that the *Golden Ass* has twelve books, but the number is probably

---

¹³³ See the convincing discussion of Grignaschi, "Lo pseudo Walter Burley." For recent bibliography on Burley, see Krieger, "Studies on Walter Burley."

¹³⁴ Grignaschi has determined the *terminus ante quem* from a manuscript (Wolfenbüttel 200) containing a text dated 1326 that draws heavily on *De vita*, but he would put the composition of *De vita* itself as much as a decade earlier ("Lo pseudo Walter Burley," 158–69). For the *ambiente*, see idem, 147–48. Over forty years ago Stigall argued from the date and provenance of Pseudo-Burley's manuscripts that the work was composed in northern Italy; being unaware of the evidence of Wolfenbüttel 200, however, he dated *De vita* to a period late in Burley's career ("The Manuscript Tradition"). The combination of date and place of composition rules out the attribution to Walter Burley, who would have come into contact with Italian circles only during his embassies to Avignon in 1327 and 1330.

¹³⁵ He quotes twice from Apuleius' discussion of the mirror: *Apol* 15.4–6 in *De vita* 30 "Socrates" (Knust 120) and *Apol.* 15.8–9 in *De vita* 37 "Demosthenes" (Knust 160). In *De vita* 58 "Apuleius" (Knust 258), he quotes from the discussion on poverty (*Apol.* 18.1–4, 6–8).

¹³⁶ "Apuleius, madaurensis, afer, philosophus platonicus, Athenis claruit in greca et latina lingua doctissimus. Hic Platoni successit et libros plures scripsit." *De vita* 58 (Knust 254).

¹³⁷ The list includes *De vita et moribus Platonis*, *De deo Socratis*, *Cosmographia* (*De mundo*), *Asinus aureus*, and *Librum oratorium contra Emilianum* (*Apology*).

¹³⁸ "Item alium quem in .XII. libros distinxit quem "Asinum aureum" intitulavit, ubi scripsit sibi accidisse quod, accepto veneno a quadam muliere sibi dato, humano animo permanente, visum illi fuit quod in asinum fuisset mutatus, a qua illusione postmodum est curatus." *De vita* 58 (Kunst 254).

only a careless error.¹³⁹ Pseudo-Burley's account need not have been based on any more than hearsay, for it betrays no evidence that he actually saw a manuscript or read the novel.

Pseudo-Burley knows (or tells) more of the story than Benzo did, but almost all of his account (and much of his wording) comes from Augustine.¹⁴⁰ He adds to Augustine's account only the detail that the substance was provided by a woman, a point that he probably learned indirectly. He uses Augustine's title for the novel (*Golden Ass*), and the phrases "it happened to him," "when he had taken a magical substance," and "with his mind remaining human" are all from the *City of God*. But Pseudo-Burley also took something else from the *City of God*. Both the turn of phrase "he thought he had been changed into an ass" and his reference to Apuleius' experience as an "illusion" (*illusione*) are derived from Augustine's argument that metamorphosis is a deception of demons. Whatever his independent knowledge of the novel, Pseudo-Burley, like Benzo, used Augustine to interpret it.

Pseudo-Burley's work greatly influenced other early humanists, including the author of an important Veronese anthology of pithy sayings entitled *Flores moralium auctoritatum,* compiled in 1329.¹⁴¹ But the author of the *Flores* did not depend on Pseudo-Burley for Apuleius, for he quotes both from the *Florida* (apparently unknown to "Burley") and from the *Metamorphoses* (not quoted by either Benzo or Pseudo-Burley). The implication of the last point is important: the author of the *Flores* is the first person since antiquity (apart from scribes) who can be shown to have read much or all of the novel. He cites *Florida* 2 twice: first for the observation that "one witness with eyes is worth more than ten with ears," and then for its converse.¹⁴² The rest of his quotations come from various parts of the *Metamorphoses*, which he calls either *Asinus* or *Asinus aureus*.¹⁴³ Like Benzo, he gives Apuleius the praenomen Lucius.

---

¹³⁹ Van Mal-Maeder plays with the idea that he might have seen a manuscript copied before the lacuna demonstrated by Pecere at the end of F (*"Lector, intende,"* 114 n. 85). Carver thinks of a mistake, hearsay, or possibly a manuscript in which the *Florida* was included at the end of the *Metamorphoses* ("The Rediscovery of the Latin Novels," 261).

¹⁴⁰ As both van Mal-Maeder and Carver observe (see previous note).

¹⁴¹ Verona, Biblioteca Capitolare CLXVIII (155). For the *Flores*, see Sabbadini, *Le scoperte*, 90–97; and esp. Petoletti, "Montecassino e gli umanisti," 232–34, with earlier bibliography. For Pseudo-Burley's influence, see Grignaschi, "Lo pseudo Walter Burley," 167–69. Idem, "Corrigenda et Addenda sulla questione dello Ps. Burleo," 326–28. *De vita* became enormously popular; Prelog lists over 270 manuscripts ("De Pictagora phylosopho").

¹⁴² "Pluris est oculatus testis unus quam auriti decem" (*Florida* 2.3); "Pluris est auritus testis unus quam oculati decem" (*Florida* 2.4; but this citation continues through 2.5). See Petoletti, "Montecassino e gli umanisti," 233.

¹⁴³ He quotes from *Met.* 3, 5, 8, and 10. See Petoletti, "Montecassino e gli umanisti," 233–34.

The author of the *Flores* is anonymous, but in 1997 Giuseppe Billanovich argued that he was to be identified as the early Veronese humanist Guglielmo Pastrengo (d. 1362), a friend of Petrarch and the author of an alphabetical encyclopedia entitled *De viris illustribus*, which was probably composed around 1350.[144] The identification is possible even though the *Flores* and *De viris illustribus* have few points in common in their treatment of Apuleius (we would not expect much overlap between a florilegium and an encyclopedia in any event). We will return to Guglielmo presently. For now it is enough to note that if Billanovich is correct, Guglielmo da Pastrengo must be called not only the author of the *Flores* but also the first person in the Renaissance we can identify by name as a reader of the *Golden Ass*.

Apuleius makes his next appearance in 1332, in a commentary on the *City of God* by Thomas Waleys, a Welsh Dominican.[145] Waleys, a peripatetic and learned man, lectured at Oxford and Bologna and served as a cardinal's chaplain in Avignon (ca. 1331–33). He probably became acquainted with the works from Monte Cassino either in Bologna or in Avignon.[146] In his note on *City of God* 4.2 Waleys claims to have seen five books of Apuleius. His list includes three from the philosophical tradition: *De dogmate Platonis, De deo Socratis*, and *De cosmographia (De mundo)*. He gives pride of place, however, to the *Apology* and *Metamorphoses*:

> [Apuleius also wrote a book] *De magia* in which he defends himself against his accusers who said he used magic. Augustine mentions this book below in book 8, chapter 19. [He also wrote] a book *De asino aureo*, which is also called *Methamorphoseos*, in which he relates marvelous transformations accomplished by magic and how he himself was changed into an ass. Augustine mentions this book below in book 18, chapter 18.[147]

---

[144] Giuseppe Billanovich, "Petrarca e i libri della cattedrale di Verona," 127–35. For Guglielmo, see Guglielmo da Pastrengo, *De viris illustribus et De originibus*, ed. Bottari, ix–xciv, with earlier bibliography.

[145] For Waleys (d. ca. 1350), see Smalley, *English Friars*, 75–108. See also Mary Bateson, "Wallensis," *DNB* 20 (1921): 578–79.

[146] Both Smalley (*English Friars*, 91) and Carver ("The Rediscovery of the Latin Novels," 261) opt for Avignon.

[147] "Item de magia in quo defendit se contra accusatores suos, qui eum uti arte magica dicebant, de quo libro facit Augustinus mentionem infra libro viii capitulo xix. Item librum de asino aureo, qui et methamorphoseos appellatur, in quo narrat mirabiles transmutationes factas arte magica et de seipso quomodo in asinum conversus erat. De quo libro facit Augustinus mentionem infra libro xviii capitulo xviii." Thomas Waleys on *Civ.* 4.2, in Augustine, *De civitate dei* (Basel, 1479).

On *City of God* 8.19 Waleys mentions the two works again, this time in connection with Augustine's discussion of magic. After providing an accurate but general description of the *Apology* and quoting its opening line, he expatiates on its success: "But Apuleius denied the charges against him and refuted everything both vividly and eloquently, so that all those present in the court were amazed, and no misgiving remained in anyone's heart concerning his innocence."[148] Waleys himself, however, does entertain some doubts about Apuleius' innocence, and he thinks Augustine did, too. Augustine found Apuleius' defense hypocritical, since he considered the reverence for demons advocated in *De deo Socratis* to be nothing short of devotion to magic.[149] Waleys' misgivings arise from Apuleius' account of Lucius' dealings with magic in the *Metamorphoses*: "Apuleius also says in regard to himself in the book he made *De asino aureo*, that he was very willing to learn that art; but it turned out badly for him as a consequence, as he relates, because while he was attempting to learn that art, he was changed, as he thought, into an ass."[150]

Waleys, like his predecessors, is influenced by Augustine in his interpretation of the *Golden Ass*: he regards the transformation into an ass as an illusion ("he was changed, as he thought, into an ass"), and he assumes that the novel is a record of Apuleius' own experience. But his approach is different. Waleys attempts not only to characterize Apuleius' individual works but also to see thematic links between them; in his view the *Metamorphoses* refutes Apuleius' denial of the charge of magic in the *Apology*, while *De mundo*, as well as the *Metamorphoses*, deals with transformation. Not surprisingly, Augustine's arguments in the *City of God* provide the inspiration for Waleys' thematic parallels. As we have seen, Augustine's doubts about Apuleius' sincerity in the *Apology* at *City of God* 8.19 lead Waleys to point to his adventure with magic in the *Golden Ass*. When Augustine comments at *City of God* 4.2 that Apuleius in *De mundo* "observes that all terrestrial things are liable to change, overturning, and destruction,"[151] Waleys links its theme

---

[148] "Sed Apuleius sibi obiecta negavit, et omnia tam evidenter quam eloquenter repulit, ut omnes astantes in iudicio mirarentur, et etiam in nullius corde de eius innocentia scrupulus remaneret." Waleys on *Civ.* 8.19, in Augustine, *De civitate dei*.

[149] For Augustine's comments in *Civ.* 8.19, see pp. 32–33.

[150] "Apuleius etiam in libro quem fecit de asino aureo dicit de seipso quod artem illam libentissime didicerit, sed male sibi cessit ex hoc ut narrat, quia dum artem illam volebat discere in asinum ut sibi videbatur conversus est." Waleys on *Civ.* 8.19, in Augustine, *De civitate dei*.

[151] "Terrena omnia dicens mutationes, conuersiones et interitus habere." Augustine, *Civ.* 4.2.

with that of the *Metamorphoses*. In the *Golden Ass*, he says, Apuleius "relates marvelous transformations [*transmutationes*]." In *De mundo* "Apuleius wants to show that all terrestrial things are subject to transformations [*transmutationes*] so that they do not remain in the same arrangement, even though the earth itself at all events remains in its essence, but in now this, now that arrangement."[152]

After a flurry of interest in late antiquity and the early Middle Ages by readers from Sallustius to Martianus Capella to Fulgentius and the compiler of the *Abolita* Glossary, the "literary" Apuleius of the *Apology*, *Metamorphoses*, and *Florida* slumbered quietly through the centuries at Monte Cassino, blinking his eyes and stretching in the eleventh and twelfth centuries as he was turned over by a scribe or two, briefly quoted by the monk Guaiferius, and scandalously imitated by the egregious Spurcus. But in the early trecento he was well and truly brought to light. Within only a dozen years he was examined and discussed in close succession by four important early humanists: Benzo, PseudoBurley, the author of the *Flores* (Guglielmo da Pastrengo?), and Thomas Waleys. All four were active in northern Italy (Verona, Milan, Bologna) or Avignon, or both.

We have no way of knowing either what manuscripts they saw or how many manuscripts might have been available, although there must have been more than one. The fact that none of our humanists mentions all three works might point to their circulation either individually or in pairs, as has been recently suggested.[153] But we can also localize the sightings. Benzo and the author of the *Flores*, both active in Verona, know the *Metamorphoses* and the *Florida*. Both call the novel's author Lucius Apuleius. Waleys, active in Bologna and Avignon, knows the *Metamorphoses* and the *Apology*, as does Pseudo-Burley, who seems to have been in touch with intellectual activity in Bologna and Padua.[154]

---

[152] "Et vult Apuleius ostendere quod omnia terrena habeant transmutationes ita quod non maneant in eadem dispositione quamvis saltem ipsa terra maneat in substantia, sed in dispositione alia et alia." Waleys on *Civ.* 4.2, in Augustine, *De civitate dei*.

[153] Carver, "The Rediscovery of the Latin Novels" 261.

[154] But Waleys, unlike Pseudo-Burley, probably actually saw the *Metamorphoses*. He says he did; and, like Benzo, he refers to the works from Monte Cassino by titles like those found in early manuscripts. His use of the singular "methamorphoseos" (on *Civ.* 4.2) recalls the title in Benzo and in some fourteenth-century manuscripts, including Vatican Library, Vat. lat. 2193. He calls the *Apology De magia*, part of its title in many manuscripts, including F and φ (see Munk Olsen, *L'Étude des auteurs classiques latins* 1:11). He also uses the word *transmutationes* in his description of the plot of the *Metamorphoses* (the word *transmutatio* appears as a title in the late thirteenth-century manuscript Milan, Biblioteca Ambrosiana N 180 sup, fol. Ir: "Apuleius de Magia et Transmutatione sive de Asino aureo et Florida"). Pseudo-Burley, interestingly enough, seems not to know a title for the *Apology*; he refers to it as "librum oratorium contra Emilianum." *De vita* 58 (Knust 256).

Pseudo-Burley and Waleys constitute a pair in another important way as well, for in addition to talking about the *Metamorphoses* and quoting the *Apology*, both also clearly know works from the philosophical tradition. Pseudo-Burley quotes *De deo Socratis* and *De Platone*.[155] Waleys claims to have seen them. Both mention *De mundo*, and both call it *Cosmographia*, a title that appears in early manuscripts but not in Augustine.[156] Waleys, moreover, has read enough of the work to know that Augustine is quoting it inexactly at *City of God* 4.2.[157] In short, Pseudo-Burley and Waleys are the first readers in over six hundred years—that is, since the compiler of the *Abolita* Glossary—to know both the "literary" and the "philosophical" Apuleius.

None of our four humanists, however, had more than a superficial knowledge of the works of Apuleius he discussed. They were busy culling the works of many ancient authors, some as recently discovered as Apuleius, for their encyclopedias, anthologies, and commentaries; and they were happy to find out what they could and move on. They mined Apuleius for information or *sententiae*, and they tried to see where his work, especially the *Golden Ass*, might fit into their own religious and moral universe. Augustine greatly simplified their task: they read the novel entirely through his chapter in the *City of God*, where they found its title and plot, as well as the assumption that the work is autobiographical and the theological comfort that the hero's transformation is only a demonic illusion.

---

[155] Pseudo-Burley quotes passages cited earlier by Vincent of Beauvais and John of Wales, but sometimes he supplies their omissions. See Grignaschi, "Lo pseudo Walter Burley," 127.

[156] For the title in Pseudo-Burley, see n. 137 in this chapter. The title appears in Leiden, Bibliotheek der Rijksuniversiteit Voss. Lat. Q 10 (eleventh century), and Munich, Bayerische Staatsbibliothek Clm 621 (twelfth century); see Klibansky and Regen, *Die Handschriften*, 83, 90.

[157] "Illa ergo que Augustinus hic adducit sunt in cosmagraphia [*sic*] sua, et recitat Augustinus magis sententiam quam verba." Waleys on *Civ.* 4.2, in Augustine, *De civitate dei*.

CHAPTER 3

A Mixed Reception: Interpreting and Illuminating the *Golden Ass* in the Fourteenth Century

> Who in our time could penetrate the hearts of the ancients and shake to wakefulness minds taken so long ago from mortality into another life? Who could summon forth their thoughts?
> —*Boccaccio*, Genealogie deorum gentilium

Apuleius made his entrance into the Renaissance modestly enough, quietly slipping out of Monte Cassino at the end of the thirteenth century and making his way north and into the notice of scholars in northern Italy and Avignon. His appearance does not seem to have created much of a stir, especially in comparison with the excitement that greeted the rediscovery of other long-lost ancient authors. One thinks at once of Catullus, for example, whose reappearance at about the same time was heralded in Benvenuto Campesani's famous riddling poem "On the Resurrection of the Veronese Poet Catullus."[1] But the situations were different. Perhaps most obviously, the North African Apuleius, unlike Catullus, was not "coming home." But it is also important to remember how slight a reputation Apuleius brought with him in contrast with the renown from antiquity that surrounded Catullus and other newly discovered authors. Through no fault of his own, self-promoter that he was, Apuleius had been scarcely mentioned by later writers in antiquity. It is fair to say that virtually everything known about him at the beginning of the fourteenth century depended on the not entirely favorable testimony of Augustine, who had been principally interested in refuting the demonology of *De deo Socratis* and had little to say about the works transmitted at Monte Cassino.

Within a very few years, however, Apuleius' fortunes changed dramatically. In 1332 Thomas Waleys proudly noted his acquaintance with the *Golden Ass* but could summarize and interpret its contents only with the assistance of Augustine's brief notice in *City of God* 18.18.

---

[1] "De resurectione Catulli poetae Veronensis." For the text, see Catullus Carmina, ed. Mynors, 105. For a discussion and earlier bibliography, see Gaisser, *Catullus and His Renaissance Readers*, 18, 283–84 n. 76.

But before the decade was out, Apuleius had come to the attention of the two greatest literary men of the age: Francesco Petrarch and Giovanni Boccaccio, both of whom owned and annotated manuscripts and used Apuleius creatively in their own writing. By around 1360 at least eight new manuscripts of the *Golden Ass* were available in northern Italy and Avignon, including those of Petrarch and Boccaccio.[2] By the end of the century, there were at least eleven more.[3] Throughout the century scholars read, transcribed, allegorized, imitated, and argued about Apuleius, coming at him in different ways and without reaching a consensus on the meaning—or the merits—of his work.

This chapter is concerned with the varied—one might almost say picaresque—adventures of the *Golden Ass* from about 1340 to around 1375. Boccaccio's use of the novel will be the centerpiece of our story, but Petrarch also plays an important role, as do the Bolognese scribe Bartolomeo de' Bartoli and the manuscript illuminator with whom he collaborated. There are also four bit parts in this tale of "mixed reception": the somewhat enigmatic Zanobi da Strada, an anonymous allegorist, and two little-known, but disagreeable clerics. We will begin with Petrarch.

Petrarch and His Manuscript

Francesco Petrarch (1304–74) is probably best known today as one of the great Italian poets, but he was also a major humanist and book collector, amassing what one modern scholar has termed "the greatest library in Christendom."[4] Petrarch studied, corrected, and annotated almost all of his manuscripts; and his annotations were so highly regarded by other scholars that they often copied them word for word.[5] Among his many books were important manuscripts of Homer, Plato, Cicero, Vergil, and Livy, as well as a manuscript of Catullus, now lost.[6]

---

[2] See appendix 3.2.

[3] See appendix 3.3.

[4] "In fine la sua crebbe a biblioteca massima della cristianità." Giuseppe Billanovich, "L'altro stil nuovo," 35. For Petrarch's library, see de la Mare, *The Handwriting of Italian Humanists* 1.1:5–6, with further bibliography.

[5] De la Mare, *Handwriting* 1.1:5. The annotations in Petrarch's Apuleius manuscript (Vat. lat. 2193) are duplicated in Vatican Library, Ottob. lat. 2091; see Tristano, "Le postille del Petrarca," 371. For a list of volumes annotated by Petrarch, see Petrucci, *La scrittura di Francesco Petrarca*, 115–29.

[6] From the large bibliography I note a small selection, all with further references. For Homer, see Pertusi, *Leonzio Pilato fra Petrarca e Boccaccio*, 43–72. For Plato, see Diller, "Petrarch's Greek Codex of Plato." For Cicero, see Reeve, "The Rediscovery of Classical Texts in the Renaissance." For Vergil, see Buonocore, *Vedere i classici*, 257–58;

He also owned—and annotated—a beautiful illuminated manuscript of Apuleius, now in the Vatican Library. This manuscript, Vat. lat. 2193, is a landmark in the reception of Apuleius, for in addition to the *Apology*, *Metamorphoses*, and *Florida* transmitted at Monte Cassino, it contains the philosophical works *De deo Socratis*, *De Platone*, and *De mundo*, as well as the pseudo-Apuleian *Asclepius*.[7] Pseudo-Burley and Waleys knew works from both traditions, as we have seen; but they undoubtedly found them in separate manuscripts. Petrarch's manuscript is the earliest we have to unite the literary and philosophical works in a single volume: from now on, Apuleius would be available in a unified tradition.

The manuscript was written in northern Italy, perhaps in Verona, at some time between 1330 and 1340.[8] Petrarch acquired it in the early 1340s, together with three other manuscripts from the same scriptorium.[9] Just how he acquired it is an open question; perhaps he commissioned the manuscript himself, or perhaps it was a gift obtained through the good offices of Guglielmo da Pastrengo, as Giuseppe Billanovich asserted.[10] In any event, Petrarch read Apuleius—*all* of Apuleius—with considerable interest, as his numerous annotations demonstrate.[11] He was doing so by 1340–43, a date guaranteed by both paleographic and literary evidence: the script of the majority of his notes belongs to this period, as do echoes from Apuleius (some from passages marked in his

---

Giuseppe Billanovich, "L'altro stil nuovo," 1. For Livy, see idem, "Petrarch and the Textual Tradition of Livy." For Catullus, see Gaisser, *Catullus and His Renaissance Readers*, 19–20; Guido Billanovich, "Petrarca e il Catullo di Verona."

[7] Vat. lat. 2193 also contains Cicero, Frontinus, Vegetius, and Palladius. See Nolhac, *Pétrarque et l'humanisme* 2:98–102; Vattasso, *I codici petrarcheschi della Biblioteca Vaticana,* 161–62 and plates 1–2. For a detailed description, see Pellegrin, *Les manuscrits classiques latins* 3.1:514–17, with earlier bibliography. For the illuminations, see Nolhac, "Manuscrits à miniatures de la bibliothèque de Pétrarque"; and especially Buonocore, *Vedere i classici,* 268–74, with earlier bibliography. The manuscript had passed into the papal library by the early fifteenth century; see Giuseppe Billanovich, *Petrarca letterato,* 396.

[8] For the place and date, see Giuseppe Billanovich, "Quattro libri del Petrarca," 239.

[9] The other three manuscripts are Troyes, Bibliothèque Municipale 552 (Cicero); Paris, Bibliothèque Nationale lat. 8500 (a large miscellany of late-antique authors); Paris, Bibliothèque Nationale lat. 5054 (Josephus). See Giuseppe Billanovich, "Quattro libri del Petrarca"; Zanichelli, "'Non scripsit set miniavit.'"

[10] Noting that the guide letters for the miniatures were all written in the same period and in Petrarch's hand, Tristano suggested that Petrarch put the manuscript together himself ("Le postille del Petrarca," 367). For the claim that all four manuscripts were presented to Petrarch in 1342 by Mastino II della Scala with Guglielmo as an intermediary, see Giuseppe Billanovich, "L'altro stil nuovo," 31.

[11] The Apuleius annotations are edited and discussed by Tristano, "Le postille del Petrarca," 365–439.

manuscript) both in his *Rerum memorandarum libri* and in portions of the *Africa*.¹²

But although Petrarch annotated and used Apuleius, he did not claim him as a favorite author. That honor was reserved for writers like Vergil and Cicero and Horace. In a famous letter to Boccaccio, he says that he has read Apuleius and Plautus and others "once, in a hurry, lingering only as in someone else's domain."¹³ He continues:

> So it happened that I saw many things in passing, excerpted a few, stored away fewer still—and those as of general application—in the open and in the vestibule of memory, so to speak. Thus, whenever I happen to hear or produce them, I know at once that they are not mine, and I am not deceived as to their owner. That is, I possess them from another, and as another's property—which they truly are.¹⁴

Petrarch's comment is not disingenuous.¹⁵ He wants to convey a major distinction between the ways in which he uses an author like Apuleius and one like Vergil. He will take ideas and commonplaces from the one, but he will make the other a part of himself. The writings of Vergil and the rest, he says, "have been attached not merely to my memory, but to my marrow, and they have been made one with my nature."¹⁶ The essential

---

¹² The notes were written in two periods: ca. 1340–43 and ca. 1347–50. See Petrucci, *La scrittura*, 117–18 and plates 9 and 10; Tristano, "Le postille del Petrarca," 369. For Apuleian echoes, see ibid., 267–68.

¹³ "Legi semel apud Ennium, apud Plautum, apud Felicem Capellam, apud Apuleium, et legi raptim, propere, nullam nisi ut alienis in finibus moram trahens." Petrarca, *Familiarium rerum libri* 22.2.11. The text is cited from *Le familiari* 4:105. (But clearly Petrarch read Apuleius more than once, as his annotating the text on separate occasions demonstrates.)

¹⁴ "Sic pretereunti, multa contigit ut viderem, pauca decerperem, pauciora reponerem, eaque ut comunia in aperto et in ipso, ut ita dixerim, memorie vestibulo; ita ut quotiens vel audire illa vel proferre contigerit, non mea esse confestim sciam, nec me fallat cuius sint; que ab alio scilicet, et quod vere sunt, ut aliena possideo." Petrarca, *Familiarium rerum libri* 22.2.11 (*Le familiari* 4:105–6).

¹⁵ *Pace* Carver, "The Rediscovery of the Latin Novels," 262.

¹⁶ The passage is worth quoting in full (the words translated in the text are in italics). "Legi apud Virgilium apud Flaccum apud Severinum apud Tullium; nec semel legi sed milies, nec cucurri, sed incubui, et totis ingenii nisibus immoratus sum; mane comedi quod sero digererem, hausi puer quod senior ruminarem. Hec se michi tam familiariter ingessere et *non modo memorie sed medullis affixa sunt unumque cum ingenio facta sunt meo*, ut etsi per omnem vitam amplius non legantur, ipsa quidem hereant, actis in intima animi parte radicibus, sed interdum obliviscar auctorem, quippe qui longo usu et possessione continua quasi illa prescripserim diuque pro meis habuerim, et turba talium obsessus, nec cuius sint certe nec aliena meminerim." Petrarca, *Familiarium rerum libri* 22.2.12–13 (*Le familiari* 4:106).

80 • Chapter 3

difference is between observation and collection on the one hand and transformative imitation on the other.[17]

Petrarch did not make Apuleius "one with his nature." The many hundreds of annotations in his manuscript bear out the description of his method in his letter to Boccaccio. They are brief—usually two or three words at most—sometimes correcting the text or marking or repeating a hard word or catchy phrase, sometimes noting a parallel passage from another author. Some of the passages he has marked can be matched with tags or quotations from Apuleius in his work.[18] But this does not mean that his study of Apuleius was superficial. Petrarch, even working quickly and "lingering in another's domain," has thought about what he has read and taken care to use Apuleius allusively and creatively, as in this letter describing his first impressions of Paris:

> I entered the city of Paris, the capital of the kingdom, which boasts Julius Caesar as its founder, with the same emotions as those of Apuleius when he went around the Thessalian city Hypata long ago. I spent much time in a state of excited amazement and looking around at everything, eager to see and find out whether what I had heard about the city was true or fictitious, and whenever I ran out of daylight for my task, I added the night, too.[19]

Petrarch is recalling the beginning of book 2 of the *Golden Ass*, where Lucius awakens on his first morning in Hypata, dazzled by its reputation for magic and sure that everything he sees has mysterious and marvelous properties (*Met.* 2.1.1–5). The passage in his letter, which borrows very little of Apuleius' language, is a true allusion that evokes the context and spirit of its model; we know immediately that the young Petrarch saw his new city as mysterious and magical, too.[20]

---

[17] See Pigman, "Versions of Imitation in the Renaissance." *Fam.* 22.2.12 is discussed on 12–14. See also McLaughlin, *Literary Imitation in the Italian Renaissance*, 27–29.

[18] E.g., *Ep. fam.* 2.9.22 (cf. *Apol.* 90.5 and Tristano, "Le postille del Petrarca," no. 851, pp. 429–30); *Ep. fam.* 3.9.4 (cf. *Fl.* 20.3–4 and Tristano, no. 559, p. 412); *Ep.* fam. 9.13.27 (cf. *Met.* 9.13.4 and Tristano, no. 984, p. 437); *Ep. fam.* 20.1.21 (cf. *Met.* 9.18.2 and Tristano, no. 988, pp. 437–38). Petrarch used Apuleius' *De Platone* throughout *Rerum memorandarum* 1.25; see Giuseppe Billanovich, ed., ad loc. (pp. 26–31).

[19] "Pariseorum civitatem, regni caput, que auctorem Iulium Cesarem pretendit, introii non aliter animo affectus quam olim Thesalie civitatem Ypatham dum lustrat, Apuleius. Ita enim solicito stupore suspensus et cuncta circumspiciens, videndi cupidus explorandique vera ne an ficta essent que de illa civitate audieram, non parvum in ea tempus absumpsi, et quotiens operi lux defuit, noctem superaddidi." Petrarca, *Familiarium rerum libri* 1.4.4 (*Le familiari* 1:25).

[20] The dramatic date of the letter is 1333, when Petrarch would have been twenty-nine. But the passage may have been added when he was revising this section of his correspondence in 1350–51. For both the date and the allusion to Apuleius, see Rizzo,

An allusion like this is very different from the ways in which Petrarch's immediate predecessors, from Benzo to Waleys, read and used Apuleius. It is also very different from the way in which Petrarch's friend and contemporary Guglielmo da Pastrengo used Apuleius in his encyclopedia *De viris illustribus*—writing at about the same time or even some years after our passage in Petrarch.[21] Guglielmo begins his entry on Apuleius with a summary of the *Metamorphoses* that has a familiar ring:

> Apuleius, a philosopher of Madaura, a Platonist, distinguished in Latin and Greek literature, was smeared with a magic ointment and changed into the likeness of an ass, yet retained his human intellect. But when a year had passed, he was returned to his original form. He composed a book about this illusion and the things he suffered while it lasted and called it the *Golden Ass*.[22]

Guglielmo may have read the *Metamorphoses*. He certainly did if he is the author of the *Flores moralium auctoritatum*, and he probably did if he in fact supplied Petrarch with his manuscript.[23] He has little more to say about it, however, than Benzo, Pseudo-Burley, and Waleys did a generation earlier; he adds only the magic ointment and the duration of the metamorphosis, details that undoubtedly came from an acquaintance—whether at first- or secondhand—with the novel. Guglielmo's entry is most interesting, however, not for what it says about Guglielmo but for what it says about Petrarch, who had already moved well away from Augustine's jejune summary in the *City of God* to an independent study and use of the novel in his own writing.

Even Petrarch, however, was not entirely free of Augustine—or, it might be better to say, he was not free of the autobiographical reading promulgated by him. Like all his contemporaries, he takes Apuleius himself for the hero of the novel. He does so not only in the letter quoted above ("I entered the city of Paris . . . with the same emotions as those

---

"Note alle *Familiari* del Petrarca," 607–11, with earlier bibliography. This passage in Apuleius is not marked in Petrarch's manuscript.

[21] Guglielmo's work is dated ca. 1350. For the chronology of *Ep. fam.* 1.4.4, see the previous note.

[22] "Apuleius, philosophus Madaurensis, Platonicus, Latina Grecaque litteratura insignis, unctus veneno in asini effigiem conversus est, humano tamen animo permanente; sed anno decurso, forme pristine redditus est; de qua illusione et hiis que interim passus est librum composuit, quem Asinum aureum intitulavit." Guglielmo da Pastrengo, *De viris illustribus*, 9.

[23] He apparently read at least *Met.* 1.2.2, which he imitates in two letters to Petrarch; see Frasso, "Tre lettere," 104–14. He also seems to have some direct knowledge of two works in the philosophical tradition: *De deo Socratis* and *De mundo*. See, Guglielmo da Pastrengo, *De viris illustribus*, 10 n. 13; 90 *ap. crit*. For Guglielmo and the *Flores* see pp. 71–72.

of Apuleius when he went around the Thessalian city Hypata long ago") but also elsewhere in his correspondence.[24] Petrarch's autobiographical reading was reflected (and confirmed) by what he saw in his manuscript. Four of the Apuleian works in the manuscript have illuminated initials; each depicts Apuleius in an appropriate character. At the beginning of *De deo Socratis* he is shown as a bearded philosopher (see plate 5).[25] In the *Florida* he appears as a busy writer, a pen in one hand and a scraper or eraser in the other (see plate 6).[26] At the beginning of the *Apology*, we see him in the pose of an orator and dressed as a magician or scholar in a wonderful fur-trimmed robe (see plate 7).[27] In the initial for the *Metamorphoses*, he is shown as Lucius, the work's asinine hero (see plate 8).[28] The illumination shows Apuleius/Lucius above the bar of the initial *A*, his alter ego the Ass below, his brown hide lightly flecked with gold in allusion to the popular title of the novel. The arrangement perhaps indicates his dual nature as man and beast—human above the waist and animal below. The autobiographical interpretation of the artist is echoed by that of the scribe, for in the title of the novel he awards Apuleius the praenomen of his hero: "Here begins book one of the Metamorphosis of Lucius Apuleius the Platonist of Madaura" (*Lucii Apulegii Platonici Maudarensis Methamorphoseos liber primus incipit*).[29]

Illuminating Apuleius

The illuminations in Petrarch's manuscript show the several personae of Apuleius that the artist or scribe perceived in his works. Those in another manuscript, just a few years later, both illustrate and interpret the *Golden Ass*. This manuscript, also now in the Vatican Library, is Vat. lat. 2194, transcribed in 1345 by the Bolognese scribe Bartolomeo de' Bartoli and dedicated to Bruzio Visconti, illegitimate son of Luchino Visconti, duke of Milan.[30] Bartolomeo, brother of the artist Andrea

---

[24] Cf. *Ep. fam.* 1.10.3 ("hospitem Apuleii Milonem"); *Ep. fam.* 9.10.4 ("ut apud Milonem Ypathe olim Apuleius").

[25] Vat. lat. 2193, fol. 1r. The same image is probably to be understood as presiding over the other philosophical works that follow, since none has an initial.

[26] Ibid., fol. 19v; illustrated in Nolhac, "Manuscrits à miniatures," plate 8a.

[27] Vat. lat. 2193, fol. 27r.

[28] Ibid., fol. 43r; illustrated in Buonocore, *Vedere i classici*, 269 fig. 192.

[29] The praenomen Lucius appears only in the title of the *Metamorphoses*. In the titles of the other works in Vat. lat. 2193, Apuleius is called Apuleius Mauderensis (*De deo Socratis*), Apuleius Platonicus (*Florida*), and Apuleius Platonicus Madaurensis (*Apology*).

[30] For a detailed description, see Pellegrin, *Les manuscrits classiques latins* 3.1.517–18, with earlier bibliography. For the illuminations, see Buonocore, *Vedere i classici*, 267–68 with earlier bibliography.

de' Bartoli, collaborated on manuscripts with some of the most celebrated illuminators in Bologna.[31] Bruzio, described by contemporaries as a very wicked prince, was also a powerful and highly cultivated one.[32] Both men took a special interest in literature of a moral, religious, or edifying character. Bartolomeo's other works include manuscripts of the *Office of the Virgin Mary*, the Roman Missal, the *Divine Comedy*, and a work of his own composition, *La Canzone delle Virtù e delle Scienze* (The Poem of the Virtues and the Arts), also dedicated to Bruzio.[33] Bruzio's library contained (in addition to the *Canzone* and the *Golden Ass* copied by Bartolomeo) Augustine's *City of God* and *Compendium of Moral Philosophy*, compiled at Bruzio's request by Luca de' Mannelli, a Dominican monk.[34]

Offices, Augustine, Dante, missals, virtues—these choices of scribe and patron seem strange company for the *Golden Ass*. But in the presentation and iconography of their manuscript, Bartolomeo and his illuminator have made Apuleius' novel a worthy shelf mate for these edifying texts.[35] The tone is established on the elaborately decorated first folio, which contains both a very brief dedication to Bruzio and the opening chapters of the novel.[36] Two themes dominate the illumination: the Visconti arms and emblems, shown in the upper and lower margins, and the seven virtues, which appear in two miniatures, one centered in the lower margin, the other in the initial *A*, which begins the novel.[37] In the lower miniature the Visconti stemma is surrounded by four female figures representing the cardinal virtues (Prudence, Temperance,

---

[31] See Orlandelli, "Bartolomeo de' Bartoli." For an important discussion of the ways in which scribes worked with illuminators, see Alexander, *Medieval Illuminators*, 52–71.

[32] For a discussion of contemporary accounts, see Dorez, *La Canzone delle Virtù e delle Scienze*, 18–19.

[33] *Officium*: Kremsmünster, Stiftsbibliothek, Res. 4. Missal: Munich, Bayerische Staatsbibliothek, Clm. 10072. *Divine Comedy*: Vatican Library, Chigi L.V.167. *Canzone*: Chantilly, Musée Conde 599. Bartolomeo also collaborated in the correction of a manuscript of Gratian's *Decretum* (Paris, Bibliothèque Nationale, Nouv. acq. lat. 2508); see Dorez, *La Canzone*, 12.

[34] Augustine: Paris, Bibliothèque Nationale lat. 2066. *Compendium*: Paris, Bibliothèque Nationale lat. 6467. See also Pellegrin, *La bibliothèque des Visconti et des Sforza* (1955), 403-4; eadem, *La bibliothèque (supplement)*, 27, plate 91. A portion of Mannelli's dedication of the *Compendium* is reproduced by Dorez: *La Canzone*, 19.

[35] The illuminator was probably "il Maestro del 1346" (Conti, *La miniatura bolognese*, 94–96, plates 288–93), rather than Bartolomeo's brother, Andrea de' Bartoli (Pellegrin, *La bibliothèque [supplement]*, 27).

[36] The dedication reads "Magnifico et excelso militi ac domino domino Bruto Vicecomiti per suum familiarem Bartolomeum de Bartolis de Bon<onia>." Vat. lat. 2194, fol. 1r.

[37] The folio is illustrated in Pellegrin, *La bibliothèque (supplement)*, plate 91; eadem, *Les manuscrits classiques latins* 3.1, plate 2; and Conti, *La miniatura bolognese*, plate 286. For a detailed description, see Pellegrin, *Les manuscrits classiques latins* 3.1.517.

Justice, and Fortitude), each with her appropriate attributes. Within the initial *A* (see plate 9), Bruzio is shown on the right, facing a kneeling Bartolomeo, who presents an open book to his patron. Between them stands a winged female figure representing the theological virtue Charity. On the left, outside the *A,* are the winged figures of the other theological virtues, Faith and Hope.

The decoration of the page firmly establishes an association between Bruzio and the virtues, seemingly one of his favorite themes, to judge from the subject and iconography of two other works dedicated to him at roughly the same time: Luca de' Mannelli's *Compendium of Moral Philosophy* (ca. 1344) and Bartolomeo's *Canzone delle Virtù e delle Scienze* (dated ca. 1339–49).[38] Luca's *Compendium* is subtitled *Tract on the Four Cardinal Virtues.* Bruzio appears twice on its first folio: first receiving the book from Luca and then—depicted as the virtue Justice—seated on a throne and trampling Pride (Superbia) underfoot.[39] Bartolomeo's *Canzone* treats the seven virtues and the seven liberal arts. Its first folio shows Bruzio on horseback accompanied by seven figures: two male riders (labeled Vigor and Sensus); four female figures (labeled Circumspectio, Intelligentia, Discretio mater virtutum, and Docilitas mater scientiarum); and the kneeling Bartolomeo (labeled *compositor operis*), again presenting his book.[40] Docilitas, "mother of the arts," has her hand placed protectively on Bartolomeo's shoulder to indicate that he is under her patronage.

But Vat. lat. 2194 does something different from the manuscripts of these moral treatises. In the manuscripts of the *Compendium* and the *Canzone,* the decoration on the first folio both matches the contents of the works and associates Bruzio Visconti with the virtues. In Vat. lat. 2194, by contrast, the decoration still associates Bruzio with the virtues, but it does more, implying—or creating—a match between itself and the contents of the manuscript. To put it another way, the opening decoration in Vat. lat. 2194 treats the *Golden Ass* as if it, too, were a moral treatise, suggesting that the novel is to be interpreted in a religious—or at least in a moral—light. The seriousness of Bartolomeo's reading is announced by placing the first chapters of the *Golden Ass* on the same page with Bruzio and the virtues. It is further emphasized

---

[38] For the date of the *Canzone,* see Orlandelli, "Bartolomeo de' Bartoli," 560; since Bartolomeo mentions Luchino Visconti as the (living) duke of Milan, the work must have been dedicated before his death in 1349.

[39] Illustrated by Dorez, *La Canzone,* plate 3; Pellegrin, *La bibliothèque (supplement),* plate 92.

[40] The folio is illustrated by Dorez, *La Canzone*; Pellegrin, *La bibliothèque (supplement),* plate 90.

by the words highlighted in the decorative pattern to the right of the initial (plate 9): *(a)t ego tibi sermone.* These are the first words of the novel, but they gain a heightened significance in their visual context, which makes them seem to be addressed not only by Apuleius to the reader but also by Bartolomeo to his patron. We can almost see him saying as he holds out his book to Bruzio: "But I [say] to you in [my] discourse."

Bartolomeo's "discourse" is his book, the *Golden Ass*, which he has both transcribed and interpreted for his patron. The interpretation is expressed not in words but in the initials placed by Bartolomeo and his illuminator at the beginning of each book. The illuminated initial for book 1, as we have seen, shows Bruzio and Bartolomeo with the theological virtues. The other initials illustrate the first chapter or so of each book.[41] In most cases the image follows the story very closely; sometimes it reflects almost Apuleius' exact words. In what follows I will look most closely at the initials to books 2, 5, 6, 9, and 11. These images either share similar themes or show (or imply) supernatural intervention in the story.

The initial *U* of book 2 shows Lucius on his first morning in Hypata (see plate 10).[42] He is shown outside, but sitting up in bed. A tower stands behind him, and he looks up at the sky, where a winged figure clad in pink emerges from the clouds. The eyes of the figure are fixed on Lucius, and its arm is drawn back, perhaps in warning or dismay. Lucius' body is tense, his look surprised and perhaps apprehensive. The scene takes place in what may be a garden, although it lacks grass and flowers. A running fountain sits on the ground next to two palm trees. A bird sits in one of the trees, and next to it is another bird, seemingly suspended in midair. The image differs from Apuleius' account in one obvious respect: it shows Lucius still in bed (and in a bed placed outside at that), whereas Apuleius describes him as "having emerged from both sleep and bed at the same time."[43] This is an interesting point that will concern us presently. In other respects, however, the image is a close

---

[41] The initials are described by Pellegrin, *Les manuscrits classiques* 3.1.517 and (in greater detail) by Stok in Buonocore, *Vedere i classici*, 267–68. The initials of books 2, 7, and 9 are shown in Buonocore's figs. 189–91. The only image not illustrating the beginning of a book is that for book 7 (fol. 36r); see below and n. 58 in this chapter.

[42] Vat. lat. 2194, fol. 5v. As in book 1, the opening words are highlighted in the pattern adjacent to the initial: *(u)t primum nocte*; but here the third word is divided between the pattern and the regular text: *noc-te*. It is tempting to suspect a visual pun, since the whole phrase reads "ut primum nocte discussa" (as soon as the night had been broken up). But it should be noted that the last word in the pattern is also divided in books 4 (fol. 17r: *me-dium*), 9 (fol. 48v: *ma-nus*), and 11 (fol. 65v: *vigi-liam*).

[43] "Et somno simul emersus et lectulo." *Met.* 2. 1.1.

86 • Chapter 3

illustration of the first chapter of book 2, eerily reflecting not real events[44] but Lucius' thoughts as he moves through the streets of Hypata.

> Nor was there anything in that city that I looked at and believed to be what it was, but I thought that every single thing had been changed into another form by a deadly utterance, so that I believed the pebbles I tripped over had been hardened from a man to stone and the birds I heard had grown their feathers on a human form, and the trees surrounding the city wall had their leaves in the same way and the waters of the fountains had their flowing streams from human bodies. I imagined that the statues and images were about to walk, that the walls of houses were on the verge of speech, that the cattle and farm animals of that sort were going to utter a portent, and that from the very sky itself and the radiant sphere would suddenly come an oracle.[45]

The image is selective (it omits the pebbles, statues, and cattle), but everything in it—birds, trees, streaming fountain, the walls of the tower—has its counterpart in Lucius' account. These are the things Lucius sees on that first morning, and he imagines that each has been transformed from human flesh into its present form. In Apuleius the trees and fountains and the rest are apparently genuine, their transformation only a function of Lucius' imagination. We could read the contents of the image in the same way as well—ordinary trees, birds, fountain, and the rest—except for the winged figure coming down from the clouds. This must be the "oracle" that Lucius believes about to come to him "from the very sky itself and the radiant sphere." Perhaps in the illumination, as in Apuleius, this heaven-sent oracle exists only in Lucius' imagination and only as a likely future apparition; or perhaps—and this is the more interesting idea—the oracle in the image is intended as an actual presence. If the oracle is not merely a fantasy but a genuine apparition, its presence vouches for the truth of Lucius' other imaginings, demonstrating that the fountain, trees, birds, and walls of the illumination are in fact human beings transformed by "a deadly utterance" and that their ordinary appearance conceals a frightening reality.

The initial for book 5 is a P, for *Psyche*, and contains Psyche herself (see plate 11).[46] She had been carried down from her cliff by Zephyr at

---

[44] *Pace* Stok in Buonocore, *Vedere i classici*, 267, who relates the garden to Byrrhena's atrium at *Met.* 2.4 and the birds to Pamphile's transformation at 3.21.

[45] "Nec fuit in illa civitate quod aspiciens id esse crederem quod esset, sed omnia prorsus ferali murmure in aliam effigiem translata, ut et lapides quos offenderem de homine duratos et aves quas audirem indidem plumatas et arbores quae pomerium ambirent similiter foliatas et fontanos latices de corporibus humanis fluxos crederem; iam statuas et imagines incessuras, parietes locuturos, boves et id genus pecua dicturas praesagium, de ipso vero caelo et iubaris orbe subito venturum oraculum." *Met.* 2.1.3–5.

[46] Vat. lat. 2194, fol. 24r. The opening words are highlighted in the pattern adjacent to the initial: "(P)syche teneris et herbosis."

the end of book 4 and placed in a flowering meadow. Book 5 begins: "Psyche softly reclined in a delicate and flowering place on a couch of dewy grass, her great distress and anxiety at rest, and gently fell asleep."[47] The illumination shows Psyche fast asleep in a garden—an enclosed garden, in fact; for the loop in the letter *P* surrounds it like a wall, symbolizing and protecting her virginity (at least for now). Perhaps in a moment she will awake and look around her as Apuleius' Psyche does: "She sees a grove planted with tall trees of great size; she sees a spring shining with clear water; in the very middle of the grove near the running spring there is a royal house built not with human hands but with divine skill."[48] For now, however, our painted Psyche is unaware of her surroundings.[49] They are almost like the scene in Apuleius (two palm trees, a running fountain, and a tower correspond to Apuleius' grove, spring, and "royal house"); but the image contains two unexplained additions: a lion and a deer reclining next to the sleeping Psyche.

It is important to note, however, that the elements in this initial also closely match those in the initial to book 2: a reclining figure, a tower, two palm trees, a running fountain, and two animals. Lucius is awake, Psyche asleep; and he is visited by the figure from the clouds. Otherwise, the two scenes exactly correspond. The correspondence draws attention to the essential parallels between Lucius and Psyche that lie at the heart of the novel. Any modern critic could easily spell them out: two naive figures, each placed in a new and strange environment, each curious to explore the unknown, each warned of the dangers of curiosity and heedless of the warnings, each exiled (Lucius from his humanity, Psyche from her divine marriage), and each finally redeemed by divine favor. Whether Bartolomeo and his illuminator would have gone this far is unclear, but they are certainly assimilating the figures of Lucius and Psyche at the beginning of their adventures and downfall. And they have gone out of their way to do it, for they have brought Lucius and his bed outside in order to make his position correspond to Psyche's. They have also given Psyche two animals to match Lucius' birds, but the lion and deer may have another point as well: their peaceful and unrealistic coexistence emphasizes the fact that Psyche's

---

[47] "Psyche teneris et herbosis locis in ipso toro roscidi graminis suave recubans, tanta mentis perturbatione sedata, dulce conquievit." *Met.* 5.1.1.

[48] "Videt lucum proceris et vastis arboribus consitum, videt fontem vitreo latice perlucidum; medio luci meditullio prope fontis adlapsum domus regia est aedificata non humanis manibus sed divinis artibus." *Met.* 5.1.2.

[49] *Pace* Pellegrin, *Les manuscrits classiques*, 517 ("Psyche . . . contemple la maison de l'Amour"), followed by Stok in Buonocore, *Vedere i classici*, 267 ("Psiche . . . guarda la casa di Amore"). Psyche's eyes are closed, and her head is turned away from everything in the garden, including the tower.

garden (like Lucius' in the image for book 2) is an unnatural and magical place.

But the parallels between the two scenes also highlight the major difference between them that we have already noted: Lucius is awake, receiving (if not heeding) a divine warning, whereas Psyche is asleep, oblivious to Cupid's wonderful garden and as yet unwarned of any danger. Psyche's sleep, like her walled garden, is part of the symbolism of her virginity. But it also makes a contrast with Lucius' wakefulness and emphasizes a difference in their natures. Lucius is looking for trouble before his catastrophe, while Psyche is unable (or unwilling) to believe in it, foolishly trusting her wicked sisters. Lucius goes into disaster with his eyes open, Psyche with hers determinedly shut.[50]

The initial for book 6 gives us our last glimpse of Psyche, now deep in her troubles. The initial *I* shows the goddess Ceres pushing Psyche away from her temple (see plate 12).[51] At the beginning of the book, Psyche, desperately looking for Cupid, comes with great difficulty to the temple of Ceres, where she piously tends and arranges the offerings. Ceres arrives, recognizes Psyche, hears her prayer for sanctuary, and rejects it on the grounds that she is unwilling to offend Venus. She concludes: "Depart immediately from this house and consider yourself lucky that I have not taken you into custody."[52] It is this cold rejection that we see in the initial. The letter *I* is formed by two narrow columns surmounted by a trefoil arch representing Ceres' temple. The goddess stands between the columns, adorned with a golden halo and wings, and garbed in a golden dress the color of her grain. Although she is identified by the sickles and bundle of grain hanging from the arch above her, she seems as much angel as goddess. (Except that she wears a halo rather than a crown, she might even be one of the winged theological virtues from the first folio of the manuscript.) She faces us, holding a column with her left hand and pushing Psyche away with her right. Psyche grasps the same column with both hands, her gaze fixed on the averted face of the goddess. She seems to be bracing her whole body as if against a great force even though Ceres is barely touching her.

This is not the only scene that Bartolomeo could have chosen to illustrate book 6. (Psyche's sight of the temple on the mountaintop at 6.1, for example, and her struggle to reach it, would also have made an interesting and memorable picture.) But the image of the rejecting goddess

[50] For an important discussion of Psyche's sleep in Apuleius, see Dowden, "Cupid & Psyche," 11–22.

[51] Vat. lat. 2194, fol. 30r. The first words of the book are highlighted in the pattern adjacent to the initial: "(I)nterea Psyche variis iactabatur discursibus dies."

[52] "Decede itaque istis aedibus protinus et quod a me retenta custoditaque non fueris optimi consule." *Met.* 6.3.2.

powerfully expresses the theme of the book—Psyche's fall and the trials she must undergo before she can propitiate the angry Venus and regain her divine marriage. This is a serious theme with moral and religious implications, and Bartolomeo and his illuminator have emphasized its importance by giving Ceres an appearance that is both "angelic" and reminiscent of the theological virtues.

The initial S of book 9 shows the Ass at a dangerous moment (see plate 13).[53] His present owners, thinking that he may be suffering from hydrophobia (literally "fear of water"), have shut him up overnight for observation, and now they are about to put him to the test with a pail of water. If he shuns it, they will conclude that he is rabid and leave him to die. The image is divided into two zones by the horizontal center stroke of the S. In the lower zone we see the Ass in the open doorway of his room, a pail of water in front of him, and a nervous keeper peering at him through a hole in the door. The Ass has his head thrown back, and he is looking into the upper zone, staring at a pink-clad, haloed figure emerging from the clouds. The eyes of the figure are fixed on the Ass, and his arms are stretched down to him as if in protection. The Ass seems to sense an uncanny presence: he bares his teeth and throws back his ears; his hair seems to be standing on end. His keeper, meanwhile, is unaware of the upper zone and its apparition, conscious only of the Ass, the door, and the pail of water.

The image in the lower zone corresponds closely to the situation in Apuleius. The protective figure of the upper zone also appears in the text, but only as an aside in Lucius' ex post facto comment on the events. Here is the relevant passage (the keepers are just about to have their first look at the Ass since his incarceration the night before):

> So they end their argument by deciding to see for themselves, and peeking through a crack, they see me standing quietly, sound and in control of my faculties. And they risk opening the door a little further, to see if I am now tame. But one of them, a savior clearly sent to me from heaven, demonstrates the following plan to the rest for testing my sanity: that they should offer me a pail filled with fresh water to drink, and if I should take the water willingly and without alarm as usual, they would know that I was healthy and free of all disease.[54]

---

[53] Vat. lat. 2194, fol. 48v. The first words of the book are highlighted in the pattern adjacent to the initial: "(S)ic ille nequissimus carnifex contra me ma-(nus)."

[54] "Sic opinionis variae terminum ad explorationem conferunt ac de rima quadam prospiciunt sanum me atque sobrium otiose consistere. Iamque ultro foribus patefactis plenius, an iam sim mansuetus, periclitantur. Sed unus ex his, de caelo scilicet missus mihi sospitator, argumentum explorandae sanitatis meae tale commonstrat ceteris, ut aquae recentis completam pelvem offerrent potui meo, ac si intrepidus et more solito sumens aquis adlibescerem, sanum me atque omni morbo scirent expeditum." *Met.* 9.3.2–3.

Bartolomeo and his illuminator have singled out the words "a savior clearly sent to me from heaven" in order to interpret the scene. Lucius' comment refers only half seriously (if that) to the keeper who suggested the water test, but the artist and scribe manufacture from it a different and more august heavenly protector, who appears to the Ass alone and guides his actions. If we look again at the image, we can see that the savior's fingers are slightly pointed down, as if he were gesturing toward the pail below, urging the Ass to drink.

This pictorial intervention by the savior gives the hydrophobia incident more emphasis than it has in Apuleius—too much, we might think, for its small role in the plot of the novel. But the image is important for the interpretation that Bartolomeo and his illuminator are developing, for it both recalls the supernatural warning to Lucius in book 2 and foreshadows the ultimate redemption of the Ass in book 11. In Apuleius the events at the beginnings of book 2 and book 9 have little in common, and most modern critics would probably find the opening scene of book 2 far more significant. But Bartolomeo and his illuminator have given them similar themes and put them on the same level. In book 2 Lucius looks up at a warning figure in pink flying down from the clouds, an "oracle" (as the text has it) vouching for the dangerous and magical nature of Hypata. In book 9, Lucius, long since transformed into an ass through his neglect of good advice, again looks up at a supernatural visitor in pink appearing out of the clouds. This time, however, the figure is not an oracle but a savior, and his presence seems to promise more to the Ass than escape from his immediate difficulties.

That promise is fulfilled, of course, in book 11. The image in the initial C shows Lucius bathing in the sea in the moonlight (see plate 14).[55] The C is closed by a curved bar to make a circle enclosing the scene. Above is a starry sky dominated by a down-facing crescent moon. Below is the streaming sea, its waters filled with fish and reflecting the image of the moon. The points of the reflected crescent are facing up (if we brought the two crescents together, they would form another circle). A naked man stands almost to his waist in the streaming water; he leans forward into it so that his chest and arm and face are below the surface. He seems to be splashing water on his face, but perhaps he is also feeling the shape of his features with his fingers. His head is framed—we could almost say encircled—by the crescents above and below. He makes a strange figure as we see him both in and out of the water, and it is not always easy to be sure of what we are seeing. He seems to have a beard and long hair. (But the water may be deceiving us—what

---

[55] Vat. lat. 2194, fol. 65v. The opening words are highlighted in the pattern next to the initial: "(C)irca primam ferme noctis vigi-(liam)."

one thought at first might be a tail turns out to be a stream of water running past his chest, up over his lower back, and down behind his legs.)

The image illustrates the moment at the beginning of book 11 when Lucius awakens from his exhausted sleep, sees the radiant full moon rising out of the sea, and believes that his "hope of salvation" *(spem salutis)* is at hand:

> And immediately shaking off my drowsiness, I rose up quickly and joyfully, and, eager to purify myself, I gave myself to the sea's cleansing. Submersing my head seven times in the waves (because the divine Pythagoras proclaimed that number above all most suited to religious observance), I prayed with tearful face to the all-powerful goddess. "O Queen of heaven . . ."[56]

But Bartolomeo and his illuminator have taken some liberties. The moon is not full, as in Apuleius, and the bathing figure is a man, not an ass. Perhaps changing the moon was a technical decision: a crescent moon is more obviously moonlike than a full one, which might have looked too much like a sun. But the change has also allowed Lucius' head to be placed between the real crescent moon and its reflection, as if underscoring his halfway state: both in and out of the cleansing water, and perhaps not yet entirely human. Whether partly or wholly restored, however, he is not the ass we see in Apuleius. His form in the image either anticipates his later transformation (which is guaranteed at this point in any event) or suggests that his recognition of the divinity and his purification in the sea have already given back his humanity.

The complex pictorial interpretation of the *Golden Ass* in Vat. lat. 2194 by Bartolomeo and his illuminator is a remarkable achievement. The illuminations represent individual books and episodes, accurately reflecting Apuleius' text and exploring its implications. But they are also related to each other and tell a story of their own in a kind of parallel or hypertext that presents a reading of the novel as a whole. The illuminations to books 2 and 5 show Lucius and Psyche as analogous figures at the beginning of their adventures. The illuminations to books 3 and 4 (not discussed above) show Lucius in difficulties, first in his own person, being arrested for murder, and then as an ass, in the custody of

---

[56] The words in italics are translated above. "Fato scilicet iam meis tot tantisque cladibus satiato et spem salutis, licet tardam, subministrante augustum specimen deae praesentis statui deprecari; *confestimque discussa pigra quiete <laetus et> alacer exurgo meque protinus purificandi studio marino lavacro trado septiesque summerso fluctibus capite, quod eum numerum praecipue religionibus aptissimum divinus ille Pythagoras prodidit, deam praepotentem lacrimoso vultu sic adprecabar: Regina caeli* . . ." Met. 11.1.3–2.1.

the bandits.⁵⁷ We see the corresponding troubles of Psyche in the initial to book 6, where she is driven away by Ceres from her temple and deprived of divine assistance. The image for book 7 (not discussed above) in fact illustrates the end of book 6 and sends us back to Lucius at a moment of terrible danger. We see the Ass standing before the bandits' cave carrying two heavy packs and a bound female prisoner (Charite); the bandits are deciding on the cruelest way to kill them.⁵⁸ The initial to book 8 (not discussed above) continues the sad story of Charite, showing the hunt during which her husband is treacherously murdered by his rival.⁵⁹ The image for book 9 is related to those of books 2 and 11, emphasizing Lucius' protection by divine forces and anticipating his redemption. The initial for book 10 (not discussed above) picks up the theme of treachery depicted in the image for book 8, but here the treachery backfires.⁶⁰ The initial shows two scenes from one of the secondary tales in the novel. In the first scene, a woman vainly tries to seduce her stepson; in the second, her own son drinks the poison she intended for the virtuous stepson. The stepmother is a figure like that of the condemned murderess at the end of book 10; the stepson rejects her embraces just as the Ass will flee his scheduled copulation with the murderess in the arena. Like the image in book 9, then, the initial for book 10 also prepares for Lucius' redemption. Book 9 shows him under divine guidance; book 10 presents a scene that prefigures his escape from degradation and his subsequent flight to the goddess. The initial for book 11, as we have seen, shows Lucius regaining his humanity.

Bartolomeo reads the novel in moral and religious terms. Events occur on the mortal plane, shaped by human actions and choices. But there is also a divine plane, of which only Lucius and Psyche (and the reader of the manuscript) are aware. We see its forces in action only at critical moments for Lucius and Psyche, but presumably it is to be understood as watching over everything that happens in the novel. In the episodes where they appear, the supernatural forces do not cause events; rather, they comment on them or illustrate their consequences. Apparitions from the sky warn and guide Lucius; the goddess rejects Psyche.

⁵⁷ Vat. lat. 2194, fols. 12r and 17r. Cf. *Met.* 3.2.1 and 4.1 and 3. The image for book 4 is misinterpreted by both Pellegrin (*Les manuscrits classiques*, 517) and Stok (in Buonocore, *Vedere i classici*, 267). The initial on fol. 17r shows two scenes: the Ass first arriving with the bandits (*Met.* 4.1.1), and then fleeing after he has trampled a peasant in his garden (*Met.* 4.3.6–7). *Pace* Pellegrin and Stok, his pursuers are not shown.

⁵⁸ Vat. lat. 2194, fol. 36r. Cf. *Met.* 6.31–32. *Pace* Pellegrin (517), followed by Stok (267–68), the person on the Ass is not a brigand riding it but a prisoner bound to it.

⁵⁹ Vat. lat. 2194, fol. 42r. Cf. *Met.* 8.4.

⁶⁰ Ibid., fol. 57v. Cf. *Met.* 10.4–5.

Although the interpretation presented in the illuminations is not overtly Christian (it contains no biblical scenes or characters), it is clearly in harmony with Christian ideas, including those symbolized by the seven virtues depicted on the opening page of the manuscript.

BOCCACCIO AT MONTE CASSINO: A FAMOUS STORY

Giovanni Boccaccio (1313–75) began to study Apuleius in the 1330s, five or ten years before Petrarch and Bartolomeo started work on their manuscripts, and he continued to use and interpret the *Golden Ass* for many years. Boccaccio, like his friend Petrarch, is best known today for his great contribution to Italian literature. He is most famous, of course, for his racy *Decameron*, but he also composed many other Italian works in both prose and poetry, as well as scholarly works of an encyclopedic type in Latin.[61] Boccaccio was also like Petrarch in being a serious humanist and book collector as well as a writer; for him, too, there was a fruitful and creative symbiosis between scholarly and literary pursuits. The two men differed, however, in their approach to Apuleius. Petrarch, as we have seen, did not include Apuleius in the inner circle of the writers whose works had become, as he says, "one with his nature."[62] But Boccaccio might well have described Apuleius in exactly these terms. He became acquainted with Apuleius' works as a very young man, assiduously annotated his text, imitated the *Golden Ass* in several genres over a period of years, transcribed a manuscript, and wrote (and rewrote) an allegorical treatment of the story of Psyche, which he was still revising near the end of his life.

Contrary to long-cherished scholarly opinion, however, Boccaccio did not "discover" Apuleius or the *Golden Ass*, and he did not remove F, the oldest manuscript of Apuleius' literary works, from Monte Cassino. As we saw in chapter 2, a manuscript (or manuscripts) of Apuleius had appeared in northern Italy in the late thirteenth or very early fourteenth century, probably before Boccaccio was born.[63] Boccaccio himself was imitating Apuleius by 1339.[64] It was only many years later, in the late 1350s, that F was brought to Florence, along with several other important manuscripts from Monte Cassino. The bearer of these manuscripts

---

[61] For Boccaccio's life and works, see Branca, *Giovanni Boccaccio*.

[62] See n. 16 in this chapter.

[63] The early humanists were reading and quoting from the texts transmitted at Monte Cassino as early as 1320. We have at least two manuscripts from before 1320: Milan, Ambrosiana N180 sup, and Vatican Library, Ottob. lat. 2091; see appendix 3.1–2.

[64] See the discussion below.

was not Boccaccio but his friend and fellow humanist Zanobi da Strada, as Giuseppe Billanovich demonstrated over fifty years ago.⁶⁵

We might summarize Billanovich's argument using the criteria of motive, means, and opportunity familiar from old-fashioned detective stories. Boccaccio had motive, for he is known to have been an ardent book hunter; but he lacked both means and opportunity, since he was a relatively poor man without great power or influence. He could get into Monte Cassino, as we will see presently, but he lacked the ability to carry away whole manuscripts. Zanobi, on the other hand, not only was a serious humanist and book collector but had all the means and opportunity in the world. From 1355 to 1357 he was vice bishop of Monte Cassino with full control of the monastery and everyone in it. He could take what he liked and evidently did.⁶⁶ Moreover, we have the paleographic equivalent of fingerprints to clinch the case: there is no sign of Boccaccio's hand in F, but Zanobi's has been identified among its numerous annotations.⁶⁷ The busy Zanobi probably took the other two surviving Monte Cassino manuscripts of Apuleius at the same time: both φ and C are in Tuscany (φ in Florence, C in Assisi), and both have annotations in his hand.⁶⁸

The idea that Boccaccio took F from Monte Cassino seems to have originated as an almost accidental corollary to another mistaken idea: that he took Tacitus from Monte Cassino.⁶⁹ In 1892 Pierre de Nolhac hinted at Boccaccio's discovery and removal of Tacitus, but the suggestion was given its most authoritative expression by Enrico Rostagno a decade

---

⁶⁵ Giuseppe Billanovich, *I primi umanisti*, 29–33. For a fuller account, see idem, "Zanobi da Strada tra i tesori di Montecassino." Billanovich, however, was by no means the first to question the story of Boccaccio's removal of manuscripts from Monte Cassino. Five years earlier Coulter had pointed out the chronological and logistical problems in an important article: "Boccaccio and the Cassinese Manuscripts." She argued that "the person actually responsible . . . may have been a man of far greater importance than he in the history of fourteenth-century Italy" (218). Her candidate was Niccolò Acciaiuoli, grand seneschal of Naples.

⁶⁶ Giuseppe Billanovich, "Zanobi da Strada tra i tesori di Montecassino."

⁶⁷ For the lack of notes in Boccaccio's hand, see Casamassima, "Dentro lo scrittoio del Boccaccio," 255. (Rafti's assertion that the title of the *Florida* in F [Laur. 68.2, fol. 184r] is in the hand of Boccaccio may be discounted: "Riflessioni sull'*usus distinguendi*," 293–94.) For Zanobi's annotations, see Giuseppe Billanovich, *I primi umanisti*, 33.

⁶⁸ See Giuseppe Billanovich, *I primi umanisti*, 31–33, 40, and plate 3. But Billanovich was mistaken in his claim that only Zanobi annotated φ, which also contains notes by Boccaccio and others. See the discussion below.

⁶⁹ Again, Zanobi da Strada seems to have been the culprit; see Giuseppe Billanovich, *I primi umanisti*, 40; idem, "Zanobi da Strada tra i tesori di Montecassino." For a full discussion of Zanobi's annotations of Tacitus in Laur. 68.2, see Baglio, "Tacito e Zanobi da Strada," in Baglio, Ferrari, and Petoletti, "Montecassino e gli umanisti," 205–24.

later.[70] Both men supported the theory with a story of Boccaccio's visit to the library at Monte Cassino ascribed to Boccaccio himself. Subsequent scholars readily accepted the idea and uncritically extended it to other Monte Cassino manuscripts in Florence, including F.[71] They were convinced not only by the known and verifiable connections that Nolhac and Rostagno adduced between Boccaccio and Tacitus but also (and perhaps even more) by the story of Boccaccio at the great library.

The case for Tacitus does indeed have its starting point in several facts. Boccaccio used Tacitus as a source in his later work (after around 1361).[72] He is known to have left a Tacitus manuscript to the convent of Santo Spirito in Florence.[73] A Monte Cassino manuscript of the *Historiae* and *Annales* 11–16 (the so-called Second Mediceus of Tacitus) is contained in the same volume (Laur. 68.2) with F.[74] (Tacitus is bound at the beginning, Apuleius at the end; the two were put together at an unknown date.) The inference from these facts seemed obvious enough: Boccaccio must have acquired a text of Tacitus from Monte Cassino around 1360 or so, kept it in his possession, and finally willed it to Santo Spirito, from which it finally made its way to the Biblioteca Laurenziana. But the argument has been shown to be fallacious at its essential point: the description of the manuscript Boccaccio left to Santo Spirito does not fit the Tacitus in Laur. 68.2.[75]

The story of Boccaccio's visit to Monte Cassino does not prove or even suggest that he removed F or Tacitus or any other manuscript, but it is valuable for other reasons. First and most important, it presents a complex perspective on the reception of the written word. But it also says something about the condition of the monastery and its library in the fourteenth century, conveys the eagerness and excitement of the early book hunters, and demonstrates the related interests and close ties between individual humanists. The relation in this case is that between

---

[70] Nolhac, "Boccacce et Tacite," 129, 145–46; Rostagno, ed., *Tacitus: Codex Laurentianus Mediceus 68I[-II]*, iii–vi. But the idea goes back at least to Voigt in 1880: *Die Wiederbelebung des classischen Alterthums* 1:252. (Voigt was convinced that Boccaccio discovered Tacitus at Monte Cassino, but cautious about whether he had taken the manuscript to Florence.)

[71] See Coulter's account: "Boccaccio and the Cassinese Manuscripts," 217.

[72] See Zaccaria, "Boccaccio e Tacito," with earlier bibliography.

[73] Mazza, "L'inventario," 41–42.

[74] For Tacitus, see Tarrant in Reynolds, ed., *Texts and Transmission*, 406–9 (but Tarrant seems almost inclined to accept the Nolhac-Rostagno theory). See also the facsimile in Rostagno, ed., *Tacitus: Codex Laurentianus Mediceus 68I[-II]*. For a description of Laur. 68.2 with earlier bibliography, see Casamassima in *Mostra di manoscritti, documenti e edizioni* 1:129–31.

[75] See Coulter, "Boccaccio and the Cassinese Manuscripts," 222; Mazza, "L'inventario," 41–42. The manuscript Boccaccio left to Santo Spirito is apparently lost.

Boccaccio and his friend and admirer Benvenuto da Imola, from whom we have the story.

Benvenuto da Imola (ca. 1330–ca. 1387) was almost a generation younger than Boccaccio.[76] Like Boccaccio, he was interested in Apuleius; he owned and annotated a manuscript of Apuleius' philosophical and literary works now in the Vatican Library (Vat. lat. 3384).[77] But he is most famous for his commentary on Dante, and it was through Dante that he probably made his acquaintance with Boccaccio, who lectured on the *Divine Comedy* in Florence in 1373–74. The story of Boccaccio's visit to Monte Cassino appears in Benvenuto's own commentary on Dante, composed a few years later.

Monte Cassino in the fourteenth century was no longer the bustling intellectual and religious center it had been some two hundred years earlier when F and the other Apuleius manuscripts were produced in the scriptorium presided over by the abbot Desiderius and his successors.[78] Dante, writing around 1320, has the abbey's founder, Saint Benedict himself, mourn its present condition and the moral degradation of its monks. In the *Paradiso* Benedict recalls the ladder crowded with angels that the patriarch Jacob once saw reaching up into highest heaven. He laments:

> But no one now would lift his feet from earth
>   to climb that ladder, and my Rule is left
>   to waste the paper it was written on.
> What once were abbey walls are robbers' dens;
>   What once were cowls are sacks of rotten meal.[79]

Commenting on these verses, Benvenuto remarks that Monte Cassino now "is truly quite deserted and desolate."[80] He goes on to explain that Dante's Benedict considers his rule a waste of paper "because it takes up space on parchment in vain and unproductively when it is not kept."[81]

---

[76] For Benvenuto's life and works, see Paoletti, "Benvenuto da Imola." For his use of Boccaccio, see Uberti, "Benvenuto da Imola dantista."

[77] See appendixes 2 and 3.3. For a description, see Klibansky and Regen, *Die Handschriften*, 118–19. The attribution of the notes in Vat. lat. 3384 to Benvenuto has been questioned (without discussion) by Rossi, "Benvenuto da Imola lettore di Lucano," 166 n. 4.

[78] For the condition of the monastery in the thirteenth and early fourteenth centuries, see Leccisotti, *Montecassino*, 71–77.

[79] "Ma, per salirla, mo nessun diparte / da terra i piedi, e la regola mia / rimasa è per danno de le carte. / Le mura che solieno esser badia / fatto sono spelonche, e le cocolle / sacca son piene di farina ria." Dante, *Paradiso* 22.73–78. The translation is by Allen Mandelbaum.

[80] "De rei veritate est valde desertus et desolatus." Benvenuto da Imola, *Comentum* 5.301.

[81] "Quia frustra occupat chartas sine fructu cum non servetur." Ibid. The "rule" (*regola*) is the famous rule of Saint Benedict that established the Benedictine order.

Using the idea of wasted paper as his opening, he begins what was to become the famous story of Boccaccio at Monte Cassino: "And for a clearer understanding of this line, I want to report here a thing my venerable teacher Boccaccio of Certaldo told me in jest."[82]

It seems that Boccaccio had gone to the monastery in hopes of seeing its famous library. When he humbly asked one of the monks to open it for him, he was told roughly that it was already open and was directed to a steep staircase—another Jacob's ladder, we might say. "He climbed up happily," Benevenuto continues,

> and found the place of such great treasure without door or key, and as he entered he saw weeds growing through the windows and all the books and tables thick with dust. Marveling, he began to open and turn over one book after another, and he found there many different volumes of ancient and exotic works. From some of them several gatherings had been removed; from others the edges of the pages had been cut away; and thus they were mutilated in many ways. At last, he went away grieving and in tears, regretting that the toil and effort of so many famous intellects had come into the hands of such corrupt and wasteful men. Running into the cloister, he found a monk and asked him why those precious books had been so foully mutilated. He replied that some monks, hoping to make a few *soldi*, would scrape off a gathering and make cheap psalters to sell to boys, and that they made gospels and breviaries out of the margins to sell to women.[83]

Benvenuto ends with a sentence that we are probably to understand as Boccaccio's own conclusion to the story: "Now, O scholar, go break your skull to make books!"[84] The ironic words pick up and help to explain Benvenuto's otherwise mysterious comment at the beginning that Boccaccio told his story "in jest" (*iocose*). The anecdote is by no means amusing, but it has a bitter irony that would not have been lost

---

[82] "Et volo hic ad clariorem intelligentiam huius literae referre illud quod narrabat mihi jocose venerabilis praeceptor meus Boccaccius de Certaldo." Ibid.

[83] "Ille laetus ascendens invenit locum tanti thesauri sine ostio vel clavi, ingressusque vidit herbam natam per fenestras, et libros omnes cum bancis coopertis pulvere alto; et mirabundus coepit aperire et volvere nunc istum librum, nunc illum, invenitque ibi multa et varia volumina antiquorum et peregrinorum librorum; ex quorum aliquibus detracti erant aliqui quaterni, ex aliis recisi margines chartarum, et sic multipliciter deformati: tandem miseratus labores et studia tot inclytissimorum ingeniorum devenisse ad manus perditissimorum hominum, dolens et illacrymans recessit; et occurrens in claustro petivit a monacho obvio quare libri illi pretiosissimi essent ita turpiter detruncati. Qui respondit quod aliqui monachi, volentes lucrari duos vel quinque solidos, radebant unum quaternum et faciebant psalteriolos, quos vendebant pueris; et ita de marginibus faciebant evangelia et brevia, quae vendebant mulieribus." Ibid. 5.302.

[84] "Nunc, vir studiose, frange tibi caput pro faciendo libros." Ibid.

on the old Boccaccio as he told it to his friend.[85] Boccaccio, like the ancient authors in the library, had spent his life studying and writing books that he hoped would last, and in Monte Cassino he could see what such effort amounted to in the end.

Benvenuto's story of Boccaccio in the library neatly complements the lament of Dante's Benedict, for both passages demonstrate the fragility and vulnerability of the written word. As in the case of Benedict's *Rule*, words can be preserved ("on paper," as we would say), but not kept or observed. Like the words of Boccaccio's ancient authors, they can be seen as "not worth the paper they are written on," and so annihilated for the sake of what was supposed to preserve them. But in either case they are effectively lost—"through a waste of paper," in Dante's words (*per danno de le carte*). The story has nothing to do with the removal of manuscripts from Monte Cassino and everything to do with the artistic purposes of Benvenuto da Imola in this section of his *Comentum super Dantem*.

That is not to say, however, that the story is a fiction or that Boccaccio never visited Monte Cassino. Given his interests and opportunities, it would be surprising if he had not done so. He was in Naples from 1327 to 1341—that is, for most of his boyhood and youth—and he returned to Naples on several occasions in later life.[86] Monte Cassino is only about seventy miles from Naples, a possible excursion in the fourteenth century, if not an easy one. Nevertheless, to some extent Benvenuto's anecdote is a red herring, for Boccaccio's most important connection with Monte Cassino is not with the library itself but with its manuscripts—and specifically, in the case of Apuleius, with φ (Laur. 29.2). As a young man in Naples Boccaccio came into at least temporary possession of this manuscript, which he annotated so copiously that scholars have been able to correlate his notes with Apuleian borrowings and imitations in several of his works, including three Latin letters he wrote in Naples in 1339.[87] His annotations are spread throughout the

---

[85] The date of Boccaccio's visit to Monte Cassino is unknown; see Coulter for a good account of the possibilities: "Boccaccio and the Cassinese Manuscripts." Modern scholars are inclined to follow Leccisotti, who dates it to 1362: "Ancora a proposito del viaggio del Boccaccio a Montecassino." But Boccaccio would have told the story to Benvenuto in 1373–74, just a year or so before his death.

[86] See Branca, *Giovanni Boccaccio*, 12–15.

[87] For Boccaccio's hand in φ, see Casamassima, *Mostra* 1:132–3. For the relation between Boccaccio's annotations and his borrowings from Apuleius, see idem, "Dentro lo scrittoio del Boccaccio," 256–58. See also the important studies of Vio ("Chiose e riscritture") and Fiorilla ("La lettura apuleiana"). For the letters (*Ep.* 1–3), see Boccaccio, *Opere latine minori*, ed. Massèra, 109–17. For *Ep.* 2 with a commentary and Italian translation, see Boccaccio, *Opere in versi*, ed. Ricci, 1065–73. Boccaccio's use of Apuleius in *Ep.* 2 was demonstrated a hundred years ago by Vandelli in his review of Zingarelli's

manuscript, but they are most numerous in the story of Psyche and in books 7–9 of the *Metamorphoses*, an interesting point that will concern us presently.[88]

The date and circumstances of Boccaccio's use of φ are unknown, although he was obviously reading Apuleius' literary works by 1339, as the imitations in his letters attest.[89] The detailed study of φ demonstrated by the annotations was not a matter of a day or so, and it surely was not carried out in the filthy and inhospitable library at Monte Cassino. We must imagine a period of reflection and comparative leisure in Naples itself, where the young Boccaccio moved in rather exalted political and literary circles.[90] Perhaps either one of his influential friends got the manuscript out of the monastery for him, or—and this is more likely—someone in Naples already had it in his possession and gave Boccaccio the use of it.[91] In my scenario, when Boccaccio left Naples for Florence in 1341, he took a copy of his annotations (and perhaps other notes on Apuleius as well) and left the manuscript behind—he seems not to have had access to it in Florence. The fate of φ in the years after 1339–41 is unclear, but apparently Zanobi da Strada brought it to Florence with his other manuscripts in the late 1350s, since his annotations, as well as Boccaccio's, appear in its margins.[92] (And it is to Zanobi, we must remember, that the world owes the text of the medieval *spurcum additamentum* to book 10 of the *Metamorphoses*.)[93]

Although Boccaccio seems to have been forced to abandon φ, he did not abandon his study of Apuleius. For the rest of his life he returned to Apuleius, and especially to the *Golden Ass*, many times and in various ways. In what follows we will look most closely at three of his Apuleian projects: his use of the *Metamorphoses* in the *Decameron*, his transcription of a manuscript of the *Apology*, *Metamorphoses*, and *Florida*, and his allegory of Psyche in the *Genealogies of the Pagan Gods*.

"L'Epistola di Dante a Moroello Malaspina"; and see Coulter, "Boccaccio and the Cassinese Manuscripts," 223 n. 21.

[88] Casamassima, "Dentro lo scrittoio del Boccaccio," 257. Boccaccio's annotations to the story of Psyche (Laur. 29.2, fols. 39r–47v) have been edited by Vio, "Chiose e riscritture," 149–55. His notes on the two adultery stories imitated in the *Decameron* (fols. 57r–v and 58v–60r) have been edited by Fiorilla, "La lettura apuleiana," 650–53.

[89] He also had access to a text of *De deo Socratis* by around 1339. See p. 108.

[90] For Boccaccio's life in Naples, see Branca, *Giovanni Boccaccio*, 16–39.

[91] Perhaps it was Zanobi da Strada or Niccolò Acciaiuoli who gave Boccaccio the use of φ, if Giuseppe Billanovich was correct in his assertion that the two acquired an Apuleius manuscript from Monte Cassino in 1332 (although he was thinking of a now lost copy of F). See Billanovich, "L'altro stil nuovo," 22–23.

[92] For the difficulties in distinguishing between the hands of Boccaccio and Zanobi (and others) in Laur. 29.2, see Fiorilla, "La lettura apuleiana," esp. 636–37, 654–59.

[93] See p. 65.

Two Adultery Stories in the *Decameron*

In the years just before and after his departure from Naples, Boccaccio began to extend his imitation of Apuleius from Latin to Italian. The Latin letters of 1339 present what is essentially a pastiche of Apuleian phrases and vocabulary. But in the *Comedia delle ninfe fiorentine* (1341–42) and the *Teseida* (1339–41), he adopts and adapts ideas and longer passages, naturalizing them in his own Italian literary context. In the *Comedia delle ninfe* he plays especially with the passage on Fotis' hair from *Met.* 2.8–9.[94] In the *Teseida* he presents a brief allegorization of the story of Psyche, which I will treat below in the discussion of the *Genealogies of the Pagan Gods*. It was the *Decameron* (1349–51), however, that provided Boccaccio with the greatest scope for creative exploitation and emulation of his model, allowing him to imitate Apuleius' style and to use and transform pieces of the Latin novel throughout his own Italian prose narrative.[95] His use of Apuleius is most obvious and ambitious in the two adultery stories that he has taken from book 9 of the *Golden Ass*.[96]

Both of Apuleius' tales probably originated in the adultery mime, a favorite genre on the ancient stage. The mime has a simple plot, with almost infinite variations.[97] A wife and her lover are interrupted by the unexpected return of her husband. She hides the lover, he is discovered, and then almost anything can happen—as long as it is amusing at someone's expense. The fun derives from the situation itself—the husband unaware (or not, as the case may be), the wife nervous, the lover concealed—but especially from comic suspense: how will the lover be revealed this time, and what jest will ensue?

In the second story of book 7 of the *Decameron*, Boccaccio borrows Apuleius' famous "tale of the tub."[98] In the *Golden Ass* Lucius calls it

---

[94] See Vio, "Chiose e riscritture," 144–47; McLaughlin, *Literary Imitation*, 62–63. The passage is marked in Laur. 29.2, fol. 29r: "Nota de laude capillorum"; but Fiorilla believes that the note is not by Boccaccio but in a different fourteenth-century hand ("La lettura apuleiana," 649 n. 31).

[95] See Branca's notes in Boccaccio, *Decameron*, passim. See also Rossi, ed., *Il Decameron*, 32–36.

[96] For a point-by-point comparison, see Sanguineti White, *Boccaccio e Apuleio*. See also Klesczewski, "Erzählen als Kriegskunst." For *Met.* 9, see Bechtle, "The Adultery Tales."

[97] Reynolds, "The Adultery Mime," esp. 81–84. See also McKeown, "Augustan Elegy and Mime"; Kehoe, "The Adultery Mime Reconsidered." Among the most important classical sources are Horace, *Sat.* 1.2.127–34, 2.7.53–61; Ovid, *Tr.* 2.497–506; Juvenal 6.41–44. On mime in general, see Fantham, "Mime: The Missing Link."

[98] Apuleius *Met.* 9.5–7. Boccaccio, *Decameron* 7.2. The two stories are discussed by Bajoni in "La novella del *dolium*." See also Sanguineti White, *Apuleio e Boccaccio*, 155–98; Klesczewski, "Erzählen als Kriegskunst," 387–93.

a "witty tale of the cuckolding of some impoverished man"; Boccaccio places it among the stories of "tricks women have played on their husbands either for love or for their own preservation, whether their husbands were unaware of it or not."⁹⁹ Here is how Apuleius tells it. A wife is entertaining her lover, when her husband comes home unexpectedly. She quickly hides the lover in a large jar in the corner. The husband comes in and tells her he has sold their jar for five silver pieces.¹⁰⁰ The buyer is ready to take it away. Disaster! But the wife is quickwitted. She claims that *she* has sold it for seven; even now her buyer is in the jar inspecting it. The clever lover pops out of the jar, claims that it's filthy, and the foolish husband gets into it himself to clean it out—whereupon the wife bends over the jar to direct him, and the lover continues his business from behind. Afterwards the unknowing husband carries the jar home for his wife's lover.

Boccaccio closely follows Apuleius: his plot is virtually the same, and his tone, like that of Apuleius, is light. But he is no slavish imitator. As Filippo Beroaldo was to observe in his commentary 150 years later, "he has most neatly included and quoted this Apuleian story—not as a translator, but as an author."¹⁰¹ Boccaccio transposes Apuleius' story from a nameless and squalid hamlet to fourteenth-century Naples and gives Neapolitan names (Giannello Scrignario and Peronella) to the lover and the wife (both unnamed in Apuleius).¹⁰² But his essential change is to the character of the wife. In Apuleius she is "notorious for the worst kind of sexual misconduct"; Boccaccio's Peronella, by contrast, is a pretty and charming young thing enjoying what seems to be her first lover.¹⁰³ Apart from her modest circumstances, she is not unlike several of Boccaccio's straying wives—tempted by a handsome young

---

⁹⁹ *Met.* 9.4.4: "Lepidam de adulterio cuiusdam pauperis fabulam." *Decameron* 7, *praef.*: "Si ragiona delle beffe, le quali, o per amore o per salvamento di loro, le donne hanno già fatte a' lor mariti, senza essersene avveduti o sì." The text is cited from Boccaccio, *Decameron*, ed. Branca.

¹⁰⁰ Most modern editors of Apuleius print "sex denariis," but both φ and some manuscripts of Class I, including the one transcribed by Boccaccio himself (Laur. 54.32), read "cinque denariis." Boccaccio gives the sum as "cinque gigliati" (*Dec.* 7.2.20), no doubt from his recollection of φ. See Fiorilla, "La lettura apuleiana," 651 n. 36.

¹⁰¹ It is worth quoting Beroaldo in full (the words in italics are translated in the text): "Iohannes Boccacius eloquio vernaculo disertissimus condidit centum fabulas argumento et stilo lepidissimo festivissimoque, inter quas *Apuleianam hanc inseruit transposuitque commodissime, non ut interpres, sed ut conditor*; quam foeminae nostrates non surdis auribus auditant neque invitae legunt." Beroaldo, *Commentarii*, fol. 193v.

¹⁰² Cf. *Met.* 9.4.4–9.5.1 (presumably the story takes place in the same miserable village where it is told) and *Dec.* 7.2.7. Peronella was a frequent female name in Naples, and fourteenth-century documents record a real Giovanni Scrignario; see Branca ad loc.

¹⁰³ Cf. *Met.* 9.5.1 ("postrema lascivia famigerabilis") and *Dec.* 7.2.7 ("una bella e vaga giovinetta").

man who has made advances to her, but neither criticized as immoral nor really ill disposed to her husband.[104] The experienced wife in Apuleius, being "practiced and artful at peccadillos of this sort," knows just what to do when her husband returns, whereas poor Peronella is all atwitter.[105] But it is precisely her inexperience that makes her trick so impressive. She thinks of it on the spot—"quasi in un momento di tempo," as Boccaccio says (*Dec.* 7.2.6)—and not only saves the day but turns a profit for the household at the same time, pleasing her husband, satisfying her lover, and getting the best of both.[106]

The great vat or jar is the central prop in both stories. It hides the lover, presents the necessity and opportunity for the wife's trick, and provides the chance for some much needed cash—all in preparation for the final shocking vignette. Apuleius and Boccaccio present the same picture: the husband inside the jar, the lover outside, and the wife conveniently disposed between, dealing with both at the same time. Apuleius describes the scene with a dirty joke appropriate to the whorish wife and the squalid setting: while the naked husband was hard at work cleaning out the jar, "the pretty little lover leaned over the workman's wife as she bent forward over the jar and hacked at her [*dedolabat*] without a care in the world."[107] The wife, meanwhile, was servicing both men at once, as the double entendre in the next sentence suggests: "But she put her head down into the jar and with a prostitute's skill was playfully handling [*tractabat*] her husband."[108] Boccaccio dispenses with Apuleius' double entendre, since his less experienced (and more wholesome) Peronella satisfies only one man at a time. Explicit but not obscene, he describes the picture with a bold image from the world of nature: Giannello "satisfied his youthful lust in the way that the stallions, unbridled and hot with passion, mount the mares on the broad

---

[104] E.g., inter alias, the wives of *Dec.* 3.5, 3.7, 3.8.

[105] *Met.* 9.5.4: "Mulier callida et ad huius modi flagitia perastutula." Compare Peronella's anxious dithering: "Oimé! Giannel mio, io son morta, ché ecco il marito mio, che tristo il faccia Iddio, che ci tornò, e non so che questo si voglia dire, ché egli non ci tornò mai più a questa otta: forse che ti vide egli quando tu c'entrasti! Ma per l'amore di Dio, come che il fatto sia, entra in cotesto doglio che tu vedi costì, e io gli andrò a aprire, e veggiamo quello che questo vuol dire di tornare stamane così tosto a casa." *Dec.* 7.2.12–13.

[106] See Sanguineti White, "Boccaccio e Apuleio," 197–98.

[107] "At vero adulter bellissimus ille pusio inclinatam dolio pronam uxorem fabri superincurvatus secure dedolabat." *Met.* 9.7.5. For the phrase *secure dedolabat* as "a nasty ambiguity," see Hijmans et al., in *Metamorphoses Book IX*, 80. But the obscenity of *dedolabat* was noted already by Beroaldo in 1500: "*Dedolabat*: subagitabat expolibat complanabat in obsceno significatu. fabrorum verbum est, qui dolando incurvati complanant materiarum asperitatem." *Commentarii*, 195r.

[108] "Ast illa capite in dolium demisso maritum suum astu meretricio tractabat ludicre." (Met. 9.7.6). See Hijmans et al., in *Metamorphoses Book IX*, 80–81.

plains of Parthia."[109] The substitution is a memorable riposte to Apuleius' joke, as is his conclusion to the scene. Apuleius ends it with a quick ablative absolute still using imagery from the workshop with sexual overtones: "when both jobs were finished" (*utroque opere perfecto*).[110] Boccaccio, like an elegant clockmaker, stops the action all at once and returns the three figures to their places: "His lust reached its fulfillment at almost the same point that the jar was scraped out, and he withdrew and Peronella took her head from the jar and the husband came out of it."[111] The jar has one last role to play—in Apuleius as the emblem and instrument of the poor husband's humiliation and in Boccaccio as the source of Peronella's profit at the expense of her lover. Apuleius achieves his effect by making the husband carry the jar on his back to the house of the adulterer (*Met.* 9.7.6), Boccaccio by fixing our attention on Giannello and his payment of the seven silver coins to the husband.[112]

In *Decameron* 5.10 Boccaccio borrows a second adultery tale from the *Golden Ass*, again using the same plot elements we find in Apuleius.[113] An amorous wife makes friends with an old woman who provides her with lovers. Just as the wife and her latest lover are sitting down to supper, her husband comes home unexpectedly and she quickly hides the lover—under a grain trough (in Apuleius) or a chicken coop (in Boccaccio). The husband explains his early return by telling another adultery story: he had been about to sup with his neighbor, when loud sneezing alerted them to a lover hidden in a cleaning closet by the neighbor's wife. His own wife hypocritically attacks her neighbor's unchastity, but soon afterwards an ass steps on her lover's fingers where they stick out from his hiding place. He shrieks, and all is discovered. Surprisingly, the husband reacts with perfect good humor. But here the similarities between Apuleius and Boccaccio end. Their stories differ markedly in tone and characterization, and their endings are entirely different. As we shall

---

[109] "E in quella guisa che negli ampi campi gli sfrenati cavalli e d'amor caldi le cavalle di Partia assaliscono, a effetto recò il giovinil desiderio." *Dec.* 7.2.34.

[110] *Met.* 9.7.6. Cf. Beroaldo: "Perfecit opus suum maritus cum dolii sordes erasit, et item adulter, dum inclinatam fabri uxorem dedolavit." *Commentarii,* fol. 195r. But of course *utro opere* also refers to the activity of the double-dealing wife. For the sexual sense of *opus,* see Hijmans et al., in *Metamorphoses Book IX,* 81.

[111] "Il quale [sc. desiderio] quasi in un medesimo punto ebbe perfezione e fu raso il doglio, e egli scostatosi e la Peronella tratto il capo del doglio e il marito uscitone fuori." *Dec.* 7.2.34.

[112] See Sanguineti White, *Boccaccio e Apuleio,* 197, who notes that Boccaccio neglects to say how the jar was delivered. The last words of the story are "He had it brought to his house" ("A casa sel fece portare," *Dec.* 2.7.36).

[113] *Met.* 9.14–31, *Dec.* 5.10. See Walters, "'No More Than a Boy'"; Sanguineti White, *Apuleio e Boccaccio,* 69–154; Klesczewski, "Erzählen als Kriegskunst," 393–400.

see presently, Boccaccio has written a comedy, Apuleius a tragedy—or at least a melodrama.

In Apuleius the story appears as the Ass is on a downward slide: his circumstances are growing worse with each successive owner, and the moral landscape is darker and more hopeless. Several adultery stories are told in book 9, but only this one has the Ass at its center. He is both the would-be hero and the fatal meddler of the tale, and it is through his eyes that we witness and assess its events. But he does not reveal himself as an intelligent or sensitive moral observer; from beginning to end his reactions and instincts remain as they have been—asinine.

His owner is a miller whose wife is a paragon of vice: "saeva scaeva viriosa ebriosa pervicax pertinax" (cruel, perverse, man-crazy, drunken, headstrong, intransigent).[114] She may even be a Jew or a Christian, since she pretends to believe in a single god.[115] To top it off, she has taken a dislike to the Ass and cruelly mistreats him—increasing both his natural curiosity and his desire to expose her activities. He observes with interest as the wife's drinking companion, a vicious old woman, brings her a new lover, a smooth-cheeked boy still young enough to attract male lovers. As he sees her adulterous adventure unfold, he becomes ever more outraged and determined to expose her. Finally Providence, as he thinks, gives him his chance. As he is being led past the grain trough, he spies the lover's exposed fingers and maliciously grinds them to a pulp with his hoof. Shrieks ensue. The miller coolly grabs the boy, comments on his youth and good looks, and promises not to harm him. He says: "I will treat you as property held jointly with my wife. . . . I will settle the affair by splitting our common property, so that without any dissension or strife the three of us can come to an agreement in a single bed."[116] And he adds, with ominous good humor: "I always lived so harmoniously with my wife that . . . the same things pleased us both."[117] He carries the terrified boy off to bed and duly takes his share

---

[114] *Met.* 9.14.4. Rossi (*Il Decameron*, 33) notes that Boccaccio has marked this passage in ϕ and imitated its effect in his description of Fra Cipolla's worthless servant in *Dec.* 6.10.17: "Egli è tardo, sugliardo e bugiardo; negligente, disubidente e maldicente; trascutato, smemorato e scostumato." See also Sanguineti White, *Boccaccio e Apuleio*, 41–42.

[115] Met. 9.14.5. For discussion and further bibliography, see Hijmans et al., in *Metamorphoses Book IX*, 140.

[116] "Plane cum uxore mea partiario tractabo . . . communi dividundo formula dimicabo, ut sine ulla controversia vel dissensione tribus nobis in uno conveniat lectulo." *Met.* 9.27.4–5. For the obscene double entendre of *dividundo*, see Hijmans et al., in *Metamorphoses Book IX*, 240. Beroaldo had already explained the obscenity: "Potest videri subesse huic verbo [sc. dividundo] obscenus intellectus. . . . Dividere verbum est obscenae significationis, et ad pedicones refertur, et puerorum concubitores, quorum in libidine propostera et infanda nates quasi dividuntur." *Commentarii*, fol. 209r.

[117] "Nam et ipse semper cum mea coniuge tam concorditer vixi ut . . . eadem nobis ambobus placerent." *Met.* 9.27.5.

of the community property. The next day he completes his punishment by beating the boy, who "fled in tears with his white buttocks laid open during the night and again in the daytime."[118] The miller concludes his joke about splitting joint assets by putting his wife out of the house and sending her a bill of divorce.

As devotees of the adultery mime, we might expect the story to end here: the miller has put the boy in his place, given his wife her comeuppance, and enjoyed a jest at the expense of both. But Apuleius surprises us by adding a melodramatic reversal that turns the miller's triumph into catastrophe and reveals the Ass as the inadvertent and indirect agent of his master's destruction. The evil wife hires a witch to do away with her husband, and shortly afterward his corpse is found hanging from a beam in a locked room. His goods are sold off, and the Ass goes to another owner, whom he will also bring to disaster.

Boccaccio has created a different story by transplanting it from its context in Apuleius to the setting of the *Decameron*. The literary transplanting entails some obvious but important changes. In Boccaccio the story is no longer an episode in a novel but a self-contained entity; and the ass, so central in Apuleius, is relegated to a bit part: he belongs to a visiting workman, and he treads on the lover's fingers purely by accident. The husband's destruction is necessary in the novel, where it not only follows the work's regular pattern of apparent success overtaken by sudden disaster but also demonstrates the consequences of the Ass's self-righteous behavior and propels him into a new adventure. But Boccaccio's short story has no need of these elements. He divests the tale of its final episode and places it among the stories of "what has turned out well for a lover after cruel or unhappy misfortunes."[119]

A strange placement, we might think; for Apuleius' story, even without its unhappy ending, does not fit the pleasant rubric of "what has turned out well for a lover." But Boccaccio's tale does match the description—and in a wonderfully ironic way. The irony is suited to its narrator, Dioneo, the most complex and subtle of the *Decameron*'s young storytellers, who claims the privilege of departing from the prescribed theme at will but often, as here, adheres to it in an oblique or paradoxical fashion.[120]

---

[118] "Nates candidas illas noctu diuque dirruptus, maerens profugit." *Met.* 9.28.4. See Hijmans et al., in *Metamorphoses Book IX*, 247: "The sensus obscenus is to be found with *noctu* primarily; *dirruptus* without sensus obscenus refers to *diu*. The verb thus combines sex and spanking."

[119] "Si ragiona di ciò che a alcuno amante, dopo alcuni fieri o sventurati accidenti, felicemente avvenisse." *Decameron* 5, *praef.*

[120] See the important study of Duranti, "Le novelle di Dioneo," esp. 15–18. Days 1 and 9 have no prescribed theme. On days 3, 6, and 8 Dioneo says he will follow the theme; on days 4, 7, and 10 he announces that he will depart from it. He does not announce his intentions on days 2 and 5.

In order to see how Dioneo (and Boccaccio) have adhered to the theme, we must consider the effects of moving the story—and especially its essential element, the miller's jest—into the moral and social world of the *Decameron*.

When the miller in Apuleius sodomizes his wife's would-be lover, he is within his rights as a wronged husband, since in antiquity rape, like flogging, mutilation, and even castration, was a recognized way to punish an adulterer.[121] But by his action the miller also degrades the boy and asserts his own superior masculinity and status.[122] The issue is not the "sexual orientation" of the miller, as we might put it, but rather the humiliation of the lover. The miller makes a jest of his act with the conceit that the boy is a joint property to be split with his wife in the dissolution of their marital partnership.

But the husband's behavior, so unremarkable in Apuleius, becomes problematic in the world of the *Decameron,* which is imbued with different sexual attitudes and has been shaped by thirteen centuries of Christianity.[123] In this world a man who performs a sexual act on another male is by definition a pervert with abnormal desires and appetites. To put it another way, Apuleius' punishing husband is Boccaccio's homosexual.[124] His homosexuality is the essential fact of the story. It necessitates a redrawing of the characters of both husband and wife, puts the plot in motion, and—most important—sets up the obligatory jest at the end.

In Boccaccio the husband, Pietro, is of necessity wicked, since in Boccaccio's world homosexuality is a sin. His wife is no monster as in Apuleius but a lusty young woman, "who would have found two husbands more to her liking than one," as Boccaccio tells us.[125] Since her husband cares only for boys, she satisfies her desires with a series of lovers, kindly procured for her by an old lady of her acquaintance.[126] After he discovers the latest one under the chicken coop, the wife angrily

---

[121] See Richlin, *The Garden of Priapus*, 215, 256 n. 5.

[122] For a discussion of these matters in connection with Apuleius' story, see Schmidt, "Ein Trio im Bett," 71–72; Walters, "'No More Than a Boy.'"

[123] For the shift in attitudes, see Walters, "'No More Than a Boy.'" Dante puts homosexuals in hell (*Inferno* 15), and Boccaccio, in his commentary on the canto, describes homosexuals as those "che contro a natura bestialmente adoperarono" (*Esposizioni sopra La Comedia di Dante,* 669).

[124] As Sanguineti White observes: "Il 'momentaneo sfogo di vendetta' [sc. of the miller] diventa un'abitudine, un modo di vivere di Pietro." *Apuleio e Boccaccio*, 153.

[125] "La quale due mariti più tosto che uno avrebbe voluti." *Dec.* 5.10.7.

[126] As Radcliff-Umstead notes, Boccaccio has turned Apuleius' drunken procuress into "a fascinating religious hypocrite counting beads and arranging assignations." "Boccaccio's Adaptation of Some Latin Sources for the *Decameron*," 173.

takes the offensive. "Understand well, Pietro," she says. "I am a woman like other women, and I want what the others want, and if I don't get it from you, I am not to blame for going after it."[127] But Pietro, well pleased by the looks of the young man, shrugs off her attack. "Just make sure that we all get our supper," he promises, "and I'll see to it that you have no grounds for complaint."[128] The narrator concludes: "What Pietro arranged to the satisfaction of all three after supper has slipped my mind. I only know that the next morning when he was finally escorted back to the town square, the young man was not at all sure which part he had played more that night—the wife or the husband."[129] Pietro's jest, like the miller's, is fully revealed the next day, and we see how the story does indeed fit the rubric of "what has turned out well for a lover after cruel or unhappy misfortunes." In fact, all has turned out well for *three* lovers—the homosexual husband, his lusty wife, and the accommodating young man. Although Pietro's jest is quite different from the miller's—of necessity, as we have seen—it still takes its cue from Apuleius and, as I would argue, from a particular passage in Apuleius, the miller's words in *Met.* 7.27.4–5 and his famous promise "without any dissension or strife the three of us can come to an agreement in a single bed."[130] The passage apparently made a strong impression on the young Boccaccio, for he annotated it heavily in ϕ.[131]

---

[127] "E intendi sanamente, Pietro, che io son femina come l'altre, e ho voglia di quel che l'altre, sì che, perché io me ne procacci, non avendone da te, non è da dirmene male." *Dec.* 5.10.58.

[128] "Or va dunque ... fa che noi ceniamo, e appresso io disporrò di questa cosa in guisa che tu non t'avrai che ramaricare." Ibid. 61.

[129] "Dopo la cena quello che Pietro si divisasse a sodisfacimento di tutti e tre m'è uscito di mente; so io ben cotanto, che la mattina vegnente infino in su la Piazza fu il giovane, non assai certo qual più stato si fosse la notte o moglie o marito, accompagnato." Ibid. 63.

[130] "Sine ulla controversia vel dissensione tribus nobis in uno conveniat lectulo." *Met.* 9. 27.5. *Pace* Pastore Stocchi, who argued that Boccaccio derived the homosexual husband and his arrangement to satisfy his wife from a Latin poem on a similar topic, "Conquestio uxoris Cavichioli," which he dates to the twelfth or thirteenth century ("Un antecedente latino-medievale di Pietro di Vinciolo"). For the text, see Franceschini, "Due testi latini inediti del basso medioevo." But the poem is probably to be dated in the fifteenth century; see Gualandri and Orlandi, "Commedia elegiaca o commedia umanistica?" with earlier bibliography.

[131] Laur. 29.2, fol. 60r–v. Fiorilla ("La lettura apuleiana," 653) mentions only the gloss on *partiario* on fol. 60r, but there is also a note on Apuleius' legalisms *herciscundae familiae ... formula* (fol. 60r). Vio ("Chiose e riscritture," 155 n. 23) lists an interesting comment on the miller's stated intention at *Met.* 9.27.4 (fol. 60r): "Q.d. nolo me totaliter ab uxore mea separare vel divortium cum ea facere propter adulterium per eam commissum, sed puellum adulescentem tamquam comunem inter nos dividere eo utendo." There is also a faint vertical line next to the words "ut sine ulla controversia vel dissensione tribus nobis in uno conveniat lectulo" (fol. 60v).

108 • Chapter 3

BOCCACCIO THE SCRIBE

At about the same time that he was finishing the *Decameron* or a little later, Boccaccio transcribed his own manuscript of Apuleius' *Apology, Metamorphoses*, and *Florida* (Laur. 54.32).[132] The date of the manuscript is uncertain, but it is probably safe to place it somewhere around the mid-1350s.[133] Some years earlier, probably around 1339, when he was still in Naples, the young Boccaccio had transcribed the text of *De deo Socratis*, which is now bound with the other works in Laur. 54.32. Thus, Boccaccio is the first person we know of by name—after Apuleius himself—to have transcribed works from both the literary and the philosophical groups; and his is one of only four fourteenth-century manuscripts to contain works from both groups.[134]

Boccaccio's manuscript is not an important witness to the text of either group, for he was a careless and inattentive scribe.[135] In the case of the *Golden Ass*, the interest of the manuscript lies elsewhere: in the questions it raises about his motives, his exemplar, and what drew his attention as he transcribed and annotated the novel. Boccaccio's motive for transcribing Apuleius is obvious: he wanted his own manuscript. But this answer suggests a further major question: if he did not already have a manuscript, what was the immediate source for his detailed allusions and imitations of Apuleius in the *Decameron*? It was not φ, for he had left that manuscript behind in Naples in 1341. Perhaps, as I have suggested, he relied on notes based on his annotations in φ. Perhaps he had access to someone else's manuscript in Florence. Perhaps he used notes together with his borrowed manuscript. The question is still open. The exemplar of Boccaccio's manuscript has not been identified. Again, it was not φ (or its parent F). Rather, his transcription belongs to the family of manuscripts called Class I, a group descended from an exemplar that did not have the large lacuna in *Met.* 8 that mars F and φ and their descendants.[136] The fact is further evidence, if evidence were needed,

[132] See appendixes 2 and 3.2. The manuscript is described by Casamassima in *Mostra* 1.152–54 and plate 36; de la Mare, *Handwriting* 1.1.26–27 and plate 6g; Klibansky and Regen, *Die Handschriften*, 69–70.

[133] Klibansky and Regen would date it shortly after 1350 (*Die Handschriften*, 69–70).

[134] The others contain the full philosophical group as well as the literary works. The four are, in order of age, Vat. lat. 2193 (Petrarch's manuscript); Laur. 54.32 (Boccaccio's ms.); Vat. lat. 3384 (owned by Benevenuto da Imola); and Naples IV.G.55. See appendix 3.

[135] His carelessness even in transcribing his own works is notorious. See Klibansky and Regen, *Die Handschriften*, 176–77, with earlier bibliography.

[136] According to Robertson, Boccaccio's manuscript, one of the "least respectable" of the Class I group, is descended from British Library Add. ms. 24893. ("The Manuscripts of the *Metamorphoses* of Apuleius," 86.)

for the late arrival of φ in Florence: if Boccaccio's old friend φ had been available, surely he would have used it as his exemplar.

Boccaccio was well acquainted with Apuleius by the time he sat down to transcribe his manuscript. He added few annotations, and those mostly on *Metamorphoses*, book 1—a fact that some scholars have taken as a sign of lack of interest in this once favorite author.[137] Perhaps. But we should remember that Boccaccio had already annotated Apuleius once, and rather thoroughly. He already knew the hard words he had glossed in φ, for he had used many of them in his own Latin works. He knew the plots of his favorite stories in book 9 by heart; he had the story of Psyche well in mind, as we shall see presently. Perhaps he still had copies of his earlier annotations and did not want to reproduce them.[138] Whatever his level of interest, however, he was coming back to a work and an author he knew very well; he could afford to annotate sparingly.

Both his notes and the manuscript itself have something to say about how he read the *Golden Ass*. Like several other fourteenth-century scribes, Boccaccio awards Apuleius the praenomen Lucius in the incipit of the novel: "Here successfully begins the first book of the *Metamorphoses* or the *Golden Ass* of Lucius Apuleius, the Platonic philosopher of Medauros" (Incipit liber primus methamorphoseon seu asini aurei lucii apulei medaurensis philosophi platonici feliciter).[139] Not surprisingly, he also considers Apuleius to be the hero. "Apuleius arrives at Hypata," he tells us on *Met.* 1.21.2, and a few lines later, "Apuleius arrives at the house of Milo" *(Met.* 1.22.1), "Apuleius buys fish" *(Met.* 1.24.4), and "Apuleius comes upon his old friend Phytias" *(Met.* 1.24.5).[140] Boccaccio's notes show an eye for narrative structures, and—at least in one case— for human psychology. In book 1 Lucius falls in with a pair of travelers, one of whom is about to tell a fantastic story, while the other refuses to listen. Lucius asserts his own belief in magical and fantastic events and quickly tells a story of his own. Boccaccio's comment is worthy of

---

[137] See Casamassima, "Dentro lo scrittoio," 256: "Il tempo ha compiuta la sua opera: nel Boccaccio molto è mutato, anche verso Apuleio; . . . la confezione del Laur. 54.32 . . . è dunque come l'adempimento di un dovere." Boccaccio's annotations in Laur. 54.32 have been edited by Fiorilla, "La lettura apuleiana," 659–67.

[138] But a few notes in Laur. 54.32 do have counterparts in φ; see Fiorilla, "La lettura apuleiana," 649.

[139] Laur. 54.32, fol. 18r. The name Lucius Apuleius also appears in the incipit of *De magia* (fol. 1r), and in those of the *Florida* (fols. 62v, 64r, 65v, 67v), as well as in the subscriptions of Sallustius (fol. 11v, 18r, 21r, etc.). More interesting, however, is the fact that it also appears in the title of *De deo Socratis*, transcribed in ca. 1339–40 (fol. 70r).

[140] "Pervenit Apuleius Ypatam" (Laur. 54.32, fol. 20v); "Pervenit ad domum Milonis Apuleius" (fol. 20v); "Emit Apuleius pisces" (fol. 21r); "Invenit Apuleius Phytiam sotium suum quondam" (fol. 21r).

the author of the *Decameron*: "Apuleius begins his own story in order to make the one companion willing to say what he had begun and the other willing to listen."[141] Once or twice he gives a running plot summary as he had done in the margins of φ (the notes on "Apuleius'" arrival in Hypata mentioned above are a case in point); but now for the most part he is content to note the beginnings and endings of stories and changes of narrators. After Lucius' story to the travelers in book 1, he notes: "Apuleius ends. Aristomenes begins a story about the innkeeper Socrates."[142] As the tale concludes, he duly notes: "The end of Aristomenes' story."[143]

Boccaccio's most famous annotation is the *spurcum additamentum* to book 10.[144] Although the passage seems a natural addition in the margin of his manuscript given both his own interests and his friendship with Zanobi da Strada, its paternity is appropriately unclear. Boccaccio apparently added the passage around 1367, that is, about a decade after Zanobi brought φ to Florence.[145] Neither of the friends, however, seems to have taken his version from the other.[146] Zanobi probably took his copy from an original in Monte Cassino, perhaps from the margin of a manuscript now lost. If Boccaccio copied from the same text (now in Florence courtesy of Zanobi), the differences between his version and Zanobi's could be attributed to the difficulty of the script of their original.[147]

Boccaccio's Psyche

Boccaccio had always been interested in Psyche. When he was still in Naples, he made a running summary of her story in the margins of φ.[148] Not long afterward he included her in a short allegory in the commentary on his *Teseida*.[149] The text describes Cupid making his arrows, and his

---

[141] "Apuleius suam incipit fabulam ut comites alterum ad dicendum quod ceperat alterum ad audiendum faciles reddat." Bibl. laur. 54.32, fol. 18r. Boccaccio's note caught the eye of a later reader, for it also appears in Laur. 54.24, fol. 1v. (Laur. 54.24 is dated 1422.) See p. 140.

[142] "Finit Apuleius. Incipit Aristomenes fabulam de Socrate caupone." Laur. 54.32, fol. 18v.

[143] "Finis fabule Aristomenis." Laur. 54.32, fol. 20v.

[144] Laur. 54.32, fol. 56r.

[145] The date is Coulter's ("Boccaccio and the Cassinese Manuscripts," 225). She is followed by Casamassima, *Mostra*, 153.

[146] See Mariotti, "Lo *spurcum additamentum*," esp. 230–31, 247–48.

[147] The obvious candidate would be Assisi, Biblioteca Comunale 706, which now contains only fragments of the *Apology*. See Mariotti, "Lo *spurcum additamentum*, 247 n. 4.

[148] See Vio, "Chiose e riscritture," 148–155.

[149] Branca dates *Teseida* to 1339–41 and suggests that much of the work and its commentary should probably be dated after Boccaccio's return to Florence (*Giovanni Boccaccio*, 49).

daughter Voluttà (Pleasure) tempering them in a nearby fountain.[150] Boccaccio's note explains:

> Amore [Cupid] took a young woman called Psyche to wife, and had of her a daughter, namely, Pleasure. By Psyche the author means hope [*speranza*]. Whenever she comes and stays with love in the mind of the lover, they conceive this daughter, Pleasure, which here means a singular delight that the soul [*anima*] feels within itself, hoping to attain the thing it loves; and delight of this sort is what tempers the arrows of love—that is, what makes them strong enough to be able to empassion the heart.[151]

Psyche makes another brief appearance in the *Comedia delle ninfe fiorentine* (ca. 1341–42).[152] There, one of the amorous nymphs describes her own response to seeing the beautiful Cupid: "Oh, how often I thought of Psyche and considered her both fortunate and unfortunate—fortunate in such a husband and unfortunate to have lost him, then most fortunate to have got him back again from Jupiter."[153] In both *Teseida* and *Comedia delle ninfe fiorentine*, Psyche plays only a tiny part in the footnotes or asides of a much larger erotic drama, and in supporting roles at that: as the mother of Pleasure in the one and as the lucky wife of the desirable Cupid in the other. Within a few years, however, Boccaccio was to give her a very different and much more important role, this time as the subject of a profound and serious religious allegory in his *Genealogie deorum gentilium* (Genealogies of the Pagan Gods).[154] Her story appears in *Gen.* 5.22: "On Psyche the fifteenth daughter of Apollo."[155]

---

[150] "Tra gli albuscelli, ad una fonte allato, / vide Cupido fabricar saette, / avendo alli suoi piè l'arco posato, / le quai sua figlia Voluttà selette / nell' onde temperava." Boccaccio, *Teseida* 7.54, 1–5.

[151] "Amore prese per moglie una giovane, la quale fu chiamata Psice, e ebbe di le' una figliuola, cioè questa Voluttà; per la quale Psice intende qui l'autore la speranza, la quale quante volte viene e dimora con amore nella mente dello innamorato, cotante volte generano questa figliuola, cioè questa Voluttà; la quale s'intende qui per uno diletto singulare che l'anima sente dentro a sé, sperando d'ottenere la cosa amata; e questa cotale dilettazione è quella che tempera le saette d'Amore, cioè che le fa forti a potere bene passionare il cuore." *Teseida*, ad 7.54 (Boccaccio, *Tutte le opere* 2:464–65).

[152] For the date, see Branca, *Giovanni Boccaccio*, 59.

[153] "Oh quante volte ricordandomi di Psice, la reputai felice e infelice; felice di tale marito e infelice d'averlo perduto, felicissima poi d'averlo riavuto da Giove." *Comedia delle ninfe fiorentine* 32.43 (Boccaccio *Tutte le opere* 2:778).

[154] For *Genealogie* (plural) as the correct title, see Zaccaria, "Ancora per il testo," 243–44.

[155] "De Psyce XV^a Apollinis filia." The following discussion revises and expands that in Gaisser, "Allegorizing Apuleius," 29–33.

The *Genealogie* is a massive Latin encyclopedia of classical mythology in fifteen books—thirteen books of myths arranged according to the family trees of the gods and two books in defense of poetry and fiction.[156] Boccaccio started to work on it before 1350 (even as he was still writing the *Decameron*) and continued to work on and revise it for the rest of his life.[157] The final revisions were not complete at the time of his death. The *Genealogie* exists in two principal versions, which scholars have dubbed the "autograph" and the "vulgate." Neither is fully authoritative, but in the case of Psyche it has been established that the vulgate supersedes and corrects the autograph.[158] The autograph, however, had already revised and corrected the allegory of Fulgentius that we considered in the last chapter. As a consequence, we find in the three versions (Fulgentius, Boccaccio in the autograph, and Boccaccio in the vulgate) three different and distinct readings of Apuleius' story.

In what follows I shall consider first Boccaccio's revisions to Fulgentius in the autograph and then his revisions to the autograph in the vulgate.[159] The principal points of difference are Psyche's parentage, the identity of Psyche and her sisters, the identity of Psyche's husband, and the ending of the allegory.

Although elsewhere in the *Genealogie* Boccaccio frequently cites, quotes, and criticizes Fulgentius, in *Gen.* 5.22 he avoids all mention of his name and almost all echoes of his language and style.[160] He undoubtedly knew Fulgentius' allegory of Psyche and set out to refute or

---

[156] For the general nature of the work, see Coulter, "The Genealogy of the Gods"; Osgood, *Boccaccio on Poetry*, xi–xlviii.

[157] See Branca, *Giovanni Boccaccio*, 83–84, 106–7; Romano, *Genealogie deorum gentilium libri* 2:847–57.

[158] See Martellotti, "Le due redazioni delle *Genealogie* del Boccaccio"; Pier Giorgio Ricci, "Contributi per un'edizione critica." For the textual complexities of the work as a whole, see especially the important articles of Zaccaria: "Per il testo"; "Ancora per il testo"; Griggio, review of Zaccaria's edition. The edition of Romano (*Genealogie deorum gentilium libri*) is based on the autograph; that of Zaccaria (*Genealogie deorum gentilium*) takes into account the vulgate.

[159] For the autograph, I refer to Romano's edition, taking into account Zaccaria's corrections ("Ancora per il testo," 262); for the vulgate, I refer to Zaccaria's. Romano's text of the autograph is printed and discussed by Hijmans ("Boccaccio's *Amor and Psyche*"). The text of the vulgate from the 1497 Venice edition is printed, translated, and discussed by Haight, *More Essays on Greek Romances*, 125–30, 196–201.

[160] Boccaccio often invokes Fulgentius (see Romano's index s.n. Fulgentius) and occasionally criticizes his interpretations as far-fetched (e.g., at *Gen.* 2.52, 4.24, 4.30, 10.10, and 11.7). He does echo Fulgentius on one point: like Fulgentius, but unlike Apuleius, he has Psyche hide her lamp under a "bushel" (*modio*). Boccaccio says: "Novaculam paravit et lucernam abscondit sub modio" (*Gen.* 5.22.7); cf. Fulgentius: "Novaculam sub pulvinal abscondit lucernamque modio contegit" (*Mit.* 3.6.115). In Apuleius the lamp is to be hidden "aliquo claudentis aululae tegmine" (*Met.* 5.20.2).

correct it—albeit tacitly—in his own.[161] He ostentatiously departs from Fulgentius (and Apuleius) at the outset. In Apuleius, Psyche's parents were the unnamed king and queen of fairy tale, in Fulgentius God and Matter. But Boccaccio follows Martianus Capella and identifies them as Apollo and Endelichia.[162] Apollo, according to Boccaccio, is the sun— "the god which is the true light of the world, since it is for no other power except god to create a rational soul."[163] Endelichia is *perfecta etas*, "maturity," who brings to fulfillment the rational soul that we have from "the father of light" even in the womb.[164] By changing Psyche's parents to Apollo and Endelichia from Fulgentius' God and Matter, Boccaccio achieved two results. First, the change allowed him to fit Psyche into the genealogical scheme of his work, as the "fifteenth daughter of Apollo." Second, and more important, it brought her birth into line with an important point in medieval theology.[165] This doctrine, which maintained that God created each soul ex nihilo, made it impossible for Psyche to be the daughter of Matter. Boccaccio also makes changes to the identities of Psyche and her sisters. In the autograph they are no longer Fulgentius' Soul, Flesh, and Free Will (Anima, Caro, Ultronietas), entities somehow separate from each other and different in kind, but rather three souls: Psyche is the rational soul, her sisters the vegetative and sensitive souls.[166] They are different in age because they have been placed into the body at different times; first the vegetative, then the sensitive, and finally the rational soul.[167]

---

[161] Hijmans suggests that Boccaccio "opposes" Fulgentius ("Boccaccio's *Amor and Psyche*," 33, 40 n. 8).

[162] "Psyces, ut dicit Martialis [sic] Capella in libro, quem De nuptiis Mercurii et phylologie scripsit, filia fuit Apollinis et Endelichie [ed. Endilichie]." *Gen.* 5.22 (Romano 255). Cf. Mart. Cap. 1.7; Fulg., *Mit.* 3.6.

[163] "Qui mundi vera lux est deus, cum nullius alterius potentie sit rationalem creare animam, nisi dei." *Gen.* 5.22 (Romano 259).

[164] "Endelichia autem, ut dicit Calcidius super Tymeo Platonis, perfecta etas interpretatur; cuius ideo rationalis anima dicitur filia, quia et si in utero matris illam a patre luminum suscipiamus, non tamen eius apparent opera, nisi in etate perfecta." *Gen.* 5.22 (Romano 259). Boccaccio has inherited an old confusion of Martianus' Endelichia ("continuous motion") with Aristotelian Entelechia ("entelechy"). See chapter 2, n. 60. For the sense of *perfecta etas*, see Padoan's note on Boccaccio's *Esposizioni sopra La Comedia di Dante*: (ad *Canto 13*) "Qui l'"età perfetta' sta ad indicare la raggiunta maturità fisica e spirituale"; Boccaccio, *Tutte le opere* 6:954–55 n. 7.

[165] As Hijmans suggests; see "Boccaccio's *Amor and Psyche*," 40 n. 8.

[166] "Sunt huic due sorores maiores natu, quarum una est anima vegetativa, altera vero sensitiva, sed Psyces pulchritudine illas excedit, et hoc ideo quia vegetativa anima communicamus cum plantis, sensitiva autem cum brutis, rationali quidem cum angelis et Deo, quo nil pulchrius." *Gen.* 5.22 (Romano 259–60).

[167] "Psyces vero ideo dicitur iunior, quia longe ante eam vegetativa conceditur fetui, et inde tractu temporis sensitiva, postremo a deo rationalis infunditur." Ibid. (Romano 260).

114 • Chapter 3

Boccaccio's most important change to Fulgentius is in the identity of Psyche's husband. In Apuleius, of course, he was Cupid. Fulgentius calls him Cupiditas (Desire), but in Boccaccio Psyche enjoys a divine marriage with God himself. The change radically alters the meaning of the husband's prohibition—and consequently of the allegory. Fulgentius tells us that for Psyche to see her husband's face is "to learn the delights of desire," that is, to awaken to carnal awareness and lust.[168] The prohibition given to Boccaccio's Psyche, by contrast, concerns not carnal but divine knowledge:

> He forbids his wife to desire to see him, unless she wants to destroy him, that is, she must not wish to see into the reasons concerning his eternity, or the first causes of things, or his omnipotence—things that are known to him alone. For whenever we mortals examine such matters, we destroy him, or rather we destroy ourselves, by straying from the right path.[169]

The sisters in Boccaccio together represent *sensualitas*, the capacity for sensation; and they envy Psyche because, as Boccaccio tells us, "It is nothing new for *sensualitas* to be at odds with reason."[170] First they try to persuade her "to see her husband, that is, to wish to see what she loves by means of natural reason, and not to know it through faith."[171] When their persuasions fail, they terrify her with the serpent story, which Boccaccio allegorizes as the argument "that spiritual contemplation into the cause of unknown things not only takes away sensory delights but heaps up the greatest toils and untimely miseries and brings in the end no agreeable compensation."[172] Psyche "puts her faith in arguments like these";[173] and we are probably to understand that she has now redirected the faith through which she formerly knew her husband, placing it instead in the unworthy blandishments of *sensualitas*. When she does so, "she sees a beautiful likeness of a man, that is, the external works of God, but she cannot see his true form or divinity, since no one has ever

---

[168] Quam persuadet ne suam faciem videat, id est cupiditatis delectamenta discat." Fulg. *Mit.* 3.6.117–18.

[169] "Hic coniugi prohibet, ne eum videre cupiat, ni perdere velit, hoc est nolit de eternitate sua, de principiis rerum, de omnipotentia videre per causas, que soli sibi nota sunt; nam quotiens talia mortales perquirimus, illum, imo nosmet ipsos deviando perdimus." *Gen.* 5.22 (Romano 260).

[170] "Minime novum est sensualitatem cum ratione [*ed.* rationem] discordem." Ibid. The opposition is very old (the only citation for *sensualitas* in Lewis and Short is Tertullian, *De anima* 17.38: "Plato irrationalem pronuntiat sensualitatem").

[171] "Ut virum videat, id est velit naturali ratione videre quod amat, et non per fidem cognoscere." Ibid.

[172] Anime contemplationes incognitarum rerum per causam, non solum delectationes sensitivas auferre, sed labores maximos et angores minime oportunos ingerere, et nil demum placide retributionis afferre." Ibid.

[173] "Talibus demonstrationibus fidem adhibet." Ibid.

seen God."[174] The catastrophe is immediate: "When she wounds and harms with the spark [from her lamp], that is, with the haughty desire through which she has become disobedient and trusting in *sensualitas*, she destroys the good of contemplation and is thus separated from her divine marriage."[175] Boccaccio provides no object for his verbs "wounds" and "harms." But we can easily supply one if we recall his earlier comment: "Whenever we mortals examine such matters, we destroy him, or rather we destroy ourselves." Psyche's arrogant desire to know through her senses what she is allowed to know only through faith and contemplation wounds and harms her divine husband, and also herself.

In the end, however, all is well. Psyche is loving and penitent and destroys her sisters, thereby overpowering the vegetative and feeling souls "so that they have no power against reason."[176] Here is how the allegory ends:

> When she is purged through toil and suffering of her haughty presumption and disobedience, she regains the good of divine love and contemplation and is joined to it forever, until, having put away transitory things, she is carried to everlasting glory and there gives birth to Pleasure, or eternal joy and delight, the child of love.[177]

The contrast with the end of Fulgentius' allegory could not be greater. Fulgentius ends with the catastrophe of the lamp and Psyche's subsequent exile: "Therefore, as if made naked by Desire, she is deprived of her mighty fortune and tossed by dangers and driven from her royal palace."[178] Fulgentius suppressed Psyche's happy ending. Boccaccio has restored it—and that makes all the difference. Boccaccio, like Apuleius, has told a story of redemption (although in a way Apuleius would never have imagined), and his allegory powerfully corrects Fulgentius, who presented only the Fall.

Boccaccio's treatment of Psyche in the autograph produces a more optimistic, but also a more religious and more overtly Christian, reading than that of Fulgentius. His revisions in the vulgate to his earlier treatment in the autograph work to the same end, refining and clarifying the

---

[174] "Videt effigiem viri pulcherrimam, id est extrinseca Dei opera, formam, id est divinitatem, videre non potest, quia Deum nemo vidit unquam." Ibid. As Zaccaria notes ad loc., Boccaccio is quoting John 1.18: "Deum nemo vidit unquam."

[175] "Et cum favillula ledit et vulnerat, id est superbo desiderio, per quod inobediens facta, et sensualitati credula, bonum contemplationis amittit, et sic a divino separatur coniugio." *Gen.* 5.22 (Romano 260).

[176] "Easque adeo opprimit, ut adversus rationem nulle sint illis vires." Ibid.

[177] "Et erumnis et miseriis purgata presumptuosa superbia atque inobedientia, bonum divine dilectionis atque contemplationis iterum reassumit, eique se iungit [*ed.* iniungit] perpetuo, dum perituris dimissis rebus in eternam defertur gloriam, et ibi ex amore parturit Voluptatem, id est delectationem et letitiam sempiternam." Ibid. (Romano 260–61).

[178] Fulg. *Mit.* 3.6.118. See p. 59.

Christian vision of his interpretation. His most important changes are in the identity of Psyche and her sisters and in the narrative.

In the autograph Boccaccio had changed the identities Fulgentius had given to Psyche and her sisters, making them three souls. In the vulgate he changes their identities again. The three sisters, he now explains, are not three souls but three *faculties* of the soul: "Her sisters are older, not because they were born first, but because they employ their potentiality first. One of these is called vegetative, the other sensitive. They are not souls, as some would have it, but faculties of this soul."[179] Boccaccio has changed his conception to conform with fourteenth-century religious orthodoxy, which insisted on the essential singleness of the soul; and he gives a very similar account in his Dante lectures, which he was writing when he was still revising and editing the *Genealogie* (that is, between around 1372 and the time of his death).[180]

These facts demonstrate the importance of the vulgate for determining Boccaccio's final intentions, as scholars have noted.[181] But they may also say something about his motives for the revision. We can imagine that he used the familiar conception of three souls in the autograph without too much serious thought. That it was heretical occurred to him later, and he revised accordingly. He could have discovered his unorthodoxy in several ways, but I suspect that it occurred to him as he was preparing his Dante lectures. Dante explicitly points out that the conception of multiple souls is mistaken, referring in the *Purgatorio* to "that error that believes that one soul is kindled in us on top of another."[182] Although Boccaccio did not live to write lectures on the *Purgatorio*, he surely reread it attentively in the early 1370s, along with the rest of the *Comedia*. He makes use of the orthodox doctrine in his allegorical discussion of *Inferno*, canto 13, to explain why the souls of the suicides are changed into plants: they have lost or given up their rational and sensitive faculties and retain only the vegetative.[183]

---

[179] "Sunt huius due sorores maiores natu, non quia primo nate sint, sed quia primo potentia utuntur sua, quarum una vegetativa dicitur, altera vero sensitiva; que non anime sunt, ut quidam voluerunt, sed huius anime potentie." *Gen.* 5.22.13 (Zaccaria).

[180] See Martellotti, "Le due redazioni," 145–46; Pier Giorgio Ricci, "Contributi per un'edizione," 210–11. The idea of multiple souls was condemned as heretical by the Council of Vienne in 1311–12 in favor of the doctrine of the soul as *simplex in substantia* favored by Aquinas and others. For Boccaccio's account of the single but tripartite soul in *Esposizioni sopra la Comedia di Dante*, see below.

[181] In addition to Martellotti and Ricci (see previous note), see Zaccaria, "Per il testo," esp. 202 n. 33.

[182] "Quello error che crede / ch'un'anima sovr' altra in noi s'accenda." Dante, *Purgatorio* 4.5–6.

[183] "È adunque da sapere, acciò che si conosca qual ragion movesse l'autore a fingere l'anime di questi dannati convertirsi in piante, l'anime nostre avere tre potenzie principali,

In the vulgate Boccaccio also revises his narrative. He drastically condenses the story but also changes and suppresses some important details.[184] In the autograph, as in Apuleius, Psyche is pregnant when she spies on the sleeping Cupid, her tasks are related at length, and she is given an official wedding. Here is how the narrative in the autograph ends:

> But Cupid, tired of the misfortunes and labors of the girl he loved, beseeched Jupiter to allow her to become his wife. Jupiter, granting his prayers, assembled the gods and in their presence ordered that Psyche should be Cupid's wife forever. At Jupiter's command Mercury conveyed her to heaven, and when she had been made immortal, the nuptials were celebrated on the spot. And she bore Cupid a daughter, Pleasure herself.[185]

The narrative in the vulgate, by contrast, omits any mention of Psyche's pregnancy, condenses her tasks, and omits both her wedding and her gift of immortality. Boccaccio relates Psyche's labors and happy ending in a single long sentence.

> Then after she had been harshly reprimanded by Venus and scourged with whips by her servants, when she was enmeshed by her order in toils no mortal could extricate herself from, with the aid of her husband she accomplished what had been enjoined upon her; and at last through his prayers to Jupiter it was brought to pass that she came into favor with Venus, and when she had been received into heaven, enjoyed an eternal union with Cupid, to whom she bore Pleasure.[186]

---

delle quali è la prima la potenzia vegetativa. . . . La seconda potenzia è la sensitiva. . . . La terza e ultima potenzia è la rationale. . . . Puote adunque aparere quegli cotali, che se medesimi uccidono, aver perduto quello per che chiamati debbiamo essere animali razionali; oltre a questo . . . non pare che colui . . . si possa o si debba giustamente dire sensibile animale: e per ciò che pure animale è, resta ad essere animale di quella spezie la quale non ha né ragione né sentimento, cioè vegetativo." Boccaccio, *Esposizioni*, 630–32.

[184] Boccaccio's condensed narrative leaves out some details important for the sense, particularly the fact that Psyche's sisters claim that her lover is a snake. See Martelloti, "Le due redazioni," 143–44.

[185] "Cupido autem impatiens infelicitatum et laborum puelle a se dilecte, Iovem oravit, ut pateretur illam sibi coniugem fore. Qui precibus annuens, congregatis diis, eorum in presentia iussit ut Psyces coniunx esset perpetua Cupidinis. Quam Mercurius Iovis iussu devexit in celum et ibidem, immortalis effecta, nuptie celebrate sunt. Ipsam autem Cupidini peperit voluptatem filiam." *Gen.* 5.22 (Romano 259).

[186] "Inde a Venere obiurgata acriter et a pedissequis eius lacessita verberibus, in labores mortali inexplicabiles iussu implicata, opera viri adiuta perfecit iniuncta; cuius postremo ad Iovem precibus actum est ut in Veneris deveniret gratiam et in celis assumpta, Cupidinis perpetuo frueretur coniugio, cui peperit Voluptatem." *Gen.* 5.22.10 (Zaccaria).

This second ending is abstract and metaphysical, where the first had been concrete and matter-of-fact. Psyche's tasks, beyond the powers of any mortal, can be accomplished only with divine aid. She is received into heaven but not conveyed or taken there, and there is no wedding or assembly of gods as witnesses. Since the preceding narrative has omitted her pregnancy, we can imagine that Pleasure, the child of her divine union, was not only born in heaven but also conceived there. But the most important change in the vulgate narrative (and the one most significant for its deeper Christian vision) is its treatment of Psyche's immortality. In the vulgate Psyche is not "made immortal" as in the autograph (and in Apuleius). She needs no such gift, since in general Christian doctrine, the soul is immortal by definition and (if not damned) is ultimately "received into heaven."

Boccaccio's interpretation of Psyche in the vulgate version of the *Genealogie* is a complex intertextual production, informed by (and revising) the treatments of Apuleius and Fulgentius and his own earlier treatment in the autograph. Both of his versions, like the treatment of Fulgentius before him, are also shaped by his other reading, as well as by his time and place and all the cultural influences around him. Many of these factors (probably most of them) cannot be recovered for either author, but some at least are obvious. The essential fact is that both Fulgentius and Boccaccio are seeing Psyche's story from a Christian perspective, but not same Christian perspective; for one is writing at the very end of late antiquity and the other (over eight hundred years later) on the eve (or rather at the dawn) of the Renaissance. Fulgentius, still viewing classical mythology from a defensive position, sees its fables as "lying fictions"; Boccaccio, by contrast, is concerned to vindicate them. Fulgentius uses biblical texts as the armature of his interpretation, making Psyche's fall parallel to that of Adam in the Book of Genesis, and her fatal uncovering of her lamp a perversion of the New Testament admonition not to hide one's light under a bushel.[187] Boccaccio has no single major subtext but draws on a complex tradition of Christian ideas, including those of his favorite poet, Dante.

Boccaccio's interpretation of Psyche and her story had an interesting afterlife in fifteenth-century Florence. There, artists under the patronage of the Medici painted his version of the story on marriage chests (*cassoni*).[188] The use of Boccaccio on the cassoni was demonstrated over a

---

[187] See pp. 58–59.

[188] See Cavicchioli, *The Tale of Cupid and Psyche*, 64–79, 83–84; eadem, *Le metamorfosi di Psiche*, 45–55; Vertova, "Cupid and Psyche in Renaissance Painting before Raphael"; eadem, "La favola di Psiche riscoperta a Firenze"; Nützmann, "Verschlüsselt in Details"; Schubring, "Zwei Cassonetafeln"; Gaisser, "Allegorizing Apuleius," 33–34; Weiland-Pollerberg, *Amor und Psyche in der Renaissance*, 27–41. The definitive study of

hundred years ago by Richard Foerster, who noted that they follow Boccaccio in presenting Psyche's parents as Apollo and Endelichia.[189] There is more than that to be said, however, for the cassoni follow Boccaccio not only at the beginning of the story but at the end as well—although with an interesting correction, as we shall see.[190]

There are several sets of these paintings, all similar but not identical in iconography.[191] Most interesting for our purposes is the earliest—a pair of cassone frontals now in Berlin generally attributed to the Master of the Argonauts and dated around 1470.[192] The cassoni apparently commemorate a Medici marriage (one displays the Medici stemma), probably that of Lorenzo de' Medici and Clarice Orsini in 1469.[193] The painter tells Psyche's story in two parts: the first panel takes us from Psyche's conception to Cupid's flight; the second panel shows her wanderings and the happy ending.[194]

The first frontal contains three principal scenes: the marriage chamber of Psyche's parents on the left, the marriage chamber of Cupid and Psyche on the right, and the mountain in the center, from which Psyche will be carried to her bridegroom (see plate 15). The chamber on the left shows a woman in bed—and a golden spherical object just above her. These are the parents of Psyche in Boccaccio's allegory: her mother, Endelichia, and her father, Apollo, the sun. In the chamber on the right

---

cassoni is Schubring, *Cassoni*. See also Hughes, *Renaissance Cassoni*; Baskins, *Cassone Painting, Humanism, and Gender*.

[189] Foerster, "Amor und Psyche vor Raffael," 221. Foerster discusses only the panel by Jacopo Sellaio now in the Fitzwilliam Museum in Cambridge, England.

[190] *Pace* Vertova, "Cupid and Psyche," 112: "The painted narrative draws on the Christian mythographers and on Boccaccio's *De genealogiis* (*editio vulgata*) only at the beginning of the story."

[191] For a list, see Callman, "Subjects from Boccaccio in Italian Painting," 57–60.

[192] See especially Nützmann, "Verschlüsselt in Details," with earlier bibliography.

[193] Bode noticed the Medici stemma and believed that the wedding was that of Piero de' Medici and Lucrezia Tornubuoni: "Zwei Cassone-Tafeln," 150–51. Vertova agrees ("Cupid and Psyche" and "La favola di Psiche"). Cavicchioli (*Le metamorfosi di Psiche*, 46–47) suggests that the marriage was of someone in the Medici circle. Nützmann identifies the couple as Lorenzo and Clarice: "Verschlüsselt in Details." In my earlier discussion ("Allegorizing Apuleius," 33–34) I followed Vertova's dating and identification of the couple, but at that time I had not seen Nützmann's important paper. For a recent evaluation of the evidence that favors Nützmann's dating, see Weiland-Pollerberg, *Amor und Psyche in der Renaissance*, 27–30.

The panels are discussed and illustrated by Schubring, *Cassoni*, 422–23, plates 193–95; Vertova, "Cupid and Psyche," plates 30a–b, 33a. For fine color illustrations, see Cavicchioli, *The Tale of Cupid and Psyche*, plates 35–36; Hughes, *Renaissance Cassoni*, 134–35.

[194] Scenes from Psyche's journey to Hades have been identified in a panel fragment now in Cracow (formerly in the Lanckoronski collection in Vienna) by Vertova, "Cupid and Psyche," 110–12 and plate 31a. For a color illustration, see Cavicchioli, *The Tale of Cupid and Psyche*, plate 37. Also see Callmann, "Subjects from Boccaccio," 58.

Psyche stands over the sleeping Cupid; he flies out the window as she holds on to his ankle. The second frontal focuses on Psyche's encounters with the gods (see plate 16). On the left she is scolded by Cupid from his cypress tree, rejected by Ceres and Juno, and scourged by a minion of Venus. On the right, the action is shown in two registers corresponding to heaven and earth. In the upper right a kneeling Cupid pleads with Jupiter for Psyche's hand. The marriage takes place below, but still in heaven, as the clouds underfoot are meant to indicate.[195] (I will return to this point presently.) Jupiter performs the ceremony, which looks for all the world like a nice Christian wedding—except for the wings and nudity of the bridegroom.

The story of Psyche is obviously an appropriate subject for wedding chests and panels in marriage chambers, and certainly much more cheerful than many from the standpoint of the bride. (The Sabine women, Lucretia, and Dido, for example, appear on cassoni with depressing regularity.)[196] But the painter of the Medici cassoni and his patron had something more in mind than just a love story with a happy ending. They followed Boccaccio in depicting Psyche's parents as Endelichia and Apollo, the sun—"the god which is the true light of the world," as Boccaccio says. But they also followed him by omission, for the scene of Psyche's happy ending does not show her either being escorted to heaven or drinking the cup of immortality, as in Apuleius. The artist, like Boccaccio, takes Psyche's immortality for granted.

But the artist also revises Boccaccio. Boccaccio omits the official wedding of Cupid and Psyche; the artist includes it, and for an obvious reason: he is painting the story on a wedding chest. Boccaccio treats the marriage of Psyche as the union of the soul with God. The cassone presents this allegory as a model or symbol for human marriage—specifically, in this case, for the marriage of Lorenzo de' Medici and Clarice Orsini. To put it another way, the marriage of Lorenzo and Clarice is to be seen as an earthly or mortal reflection of the everlasting oneness of the soul with God. The conflation of the divine and human unions is reflected in the placement of Psyche's wedding on the cassone: the members of the wedding party are standing on the ground, but with clouds under their feet, so that the wedding seems to take place in heaven and earth at the same time.

Apuleius' encounter with Boccaccio is the high point of his fortunes in the fourteenth (and perhaps any) century. He had come at last into the

---

[195] Vertova ("Cupid and Psyche," 112) suggests that the wedding is placed on earth because the painter lacked room for it in the upper register.

[196] For a sophisticated discussion of Dido and Lucretia (and other female subjects on cassoni), see Baskins, *Cassone Painting*.

hands of a man whose interests were as catholic as his own, whose imagination was as fantastic and free ranging, and who cared as much not only for literary style but also (if in different proportions) for religion and philosophy. The three works of Boccaccio that we have looked at in this chapter constitute three ways of reading Apuleius: first, two stories in Italian brought into a new setting, the *Decameron*, and into a new moral and social world; second, a manuscript, a physical manifestation of reading transmitting the author as literally as possible, but in a form shaped and interpreted by the scribe; and third, an allegorical interpretation in a Latin encyclopedia that revises earlier allegories, revises itself, and is revised again in Florentine art.

Boccaccio used, imitated, and interpreted Apuleius so easily and confidently that we might almost imagine him in possession of all the apparatus of classical scholarship, including a modern text and commentary. All he had, however, was intermittent access to some corrupt manuscripts, a profound interest and affinity with his author, and his own powerful intellect and imagination. His contemporaries were less gifted, as we might expect. The two short sections that follow will demonstrate, if nothing else, that the sublime does not always triumph over the ridiculous.

A CONFUSION OF CLERICS

In the last years of Boccaccio's life, sometime between 1371 and 1375, two Italian clerics exchanged an acrimonious correspondence about Apuleius that is preserved in several sixteenth-century editions of Petrarch.[197] The correspondents are Stefano Colonna and Simone da Brossano. They were more or less equally matched. Brossano was a well-known canon lawyer, a member of the papal court in Avignon, and an archbishop soon to become a cardinal.[198] Colonna, provost of the chapter of Saint-Omer, held a lesser ecclesiastical rank but a greater social one, for he was one of the powerful nobility, a member of the grand and haughty Roman family of the Colonna.[199] Neither man spent much time on his pastoral duties. At the time of the correspondence, Brossano,

[197] The best and fullest account is that of Coville, "Une correspondence." Coville reports that the correspondence appears in the editions of Petrarch of 1501, 1503, 1554, and 1581. I have consulted the editions of Venice, 1501, and Basel, 1581.

[198] See Coville, "Une correspondance," 203–4; Walter and Becker, "Brossano." Brossano became archbishop of Milan in 1371 and was named cardinal at the end of 1375, a fact that Coville (206) used to date the correspondence (Colonna addresses him as archbishop).

[199] See Coville, "Une correspondance," 204–6; Cochin, "Recherches sur Stefano Colonna." Colonna was named cardinal in 1378 but died before he could receive the title (Coville, "Une correspondance," 211 n. 6).

archbishop of Milan, was in Avignon, attached to the pope, and Colonna was probably in some Colonna domain in central Italy.

The story as it is preserved to us begins in medias res. In the first letter Colonna reminds Brossano of his promise (in person? in an earlier letter?) to lend him a book of Apuleius. In the second, Brossano replies; his long and patronizing refusal impugns both Colonna's sanity and his piety for wishing to read such a book. In the third, the enraged Colonna comes back with an even longer attack, justifying his own taste in reading and responding point by point to Brossano's arguments with vicious and sometimes witty rhetoric. Previous scholars have treated the disagreement as a conflict between the new humanist spirit and old-fashioned narrow scholasticism, with Colonna on one side and Brossano on the other.[200] That is undoubtedly true, as far as it goes. More interesting, however, especially at this point in the fourteenth century, is the fact that neither opponent seems to have any idea what he is talking about.

Colonna begins his first letter thus: "I know, excellent father, that I have begged you eagerly enough to lend me the book of Apuleius that it is pleasing to call *De monarchia moderni temporis*, because you claimed (and you cannot deny it) to have it in Babylon [i.e., Avignon]."[201] In his reply Brossano chastises Colonna's interest in fiction ("How can you seek the fabulous and false, which the Holy Spirit shuns?"[202]), and then turns to the work itself: "It pleases you to call the book *De monarchia temporis praesentis*, but it would be more pleasing if you called it simply *De monarchia*. . . . Indeed, among some people it is called *De asino*, and that is the nature of the book."[203]

Colonna, after taking some time to frame his response, comes back with the defense that he is not interested in fables and fiction but in philosophical truths:

> Under bitter leaves are hidden sweet fruits. Should they not be gathered through dislike of the leaves? Or is there any sane person who does not know that they are ripe with desirable sweetness? What intelligent man would not eat them greedily? I would say that it is

[200] Ibid., 210–15, followed by Carver, "The Rediscovery," 262–63. Colonna's humanist credentials are vouched for by his long friendship with Petrarch (Coville), but he was not the author of a book, *De viris illustribus*, as Carver asserts (the work is by Giovanni Colonna).

[201] "Satis a me cupide pater optime scio te oratum, ut librum Apuleii quem intitulare iuvat, de Monarchia moderni temporis accommodares, quod abnuere minime valens, habere te illum in Babylone asseruisti." Colonna, in Petrarca, *Opera* 1581, 1117.

[202] "Quomodo ergo fabulosum et fictum ambis, quem Spiritus sanctus effugit?" Brossano, in Petrarca, *Opera* 1581, 1118.

[203] "Iuvat te librum intitulare de Monarchia temporis praesentis, sed plus iuvaret si dixisses de Monarchia simpliciter. . . . Nam apud quosdam est de Asino, et sic est libri textura." Ibid.

the same in the case of the book of Apuleius. Perhaps it contains curious and fabulous and frivolous matter under which, just as under the covering of verdant and luxuriant leaves, is hidden a most pleasing fruit, and a deep and profound meaning. . . . I do not care for fiction or embrace artificiality, but I sensibly pursue the true thoughts of philosophers, and descending through various tunnels right to the center of the earth, under the framework of the world I eagerly seek out veins of gold. And this is in part what I planned to do, when I could obtain from you the book of Apuleius *De aureo asino* (as you say some people call it), not intending to search out fables, but to acquire the philosophy of that ancient poet, just like pearls under a dung heap.[204]

The most curious detail in this exchange is the way in which the two antagonists refer to Apuleius' work, calling it first *De monarchia moderni temporis* (Colonna), then *De monarchia temporis praesentis* and *De asino* (Brossano), and finally *De aureo asino* (Colonna). The obvious (but incorrect) explanation is that *De monarchia* is an alternate, mistaken, or ironic title for the *Golden Ass*.[205] But this cannot be the case, since the work *De monarchia* actually exists, although it is not by Apuleius.[206] The only known copy of it is preserved in a manuscript in the Vatican Library, in which it is attributed (wrongly) to Lucius Apuleius and bears the title *De principatu quem Romani monarchiam appellant*.[207] The manuscript is from the middle of the fourteenth century, but the work itself was perhaps written somewhat earlier, around 1300.

How then are we to explain the dispute of Colonna and Brossano? I think that the only answer is that neither knew very much about Apuleius. On that assumption, we might reconstruct the story as follows.

---

[204] "Subtus amara folia dulcia latent poma, an non legenda odio foliorum? Aut madenda dulcoris cupidine, sanus quis ignoret? Prudens quis avide non comederet? Haud aliter de Apuleii libro dicere velim. Curiosam forte et fabulosam continet et lascivam, sub qua, veluti sub virentium et luxuriantium foliorum umbraculis, gratissimus fructus absconditur, profunda et altissima iacet sententia. . . . Nam fictum haud ambigo, nec fucum amplector, sed philosophantium veras cum ratione insector sententias, et variis cuniculis usque pene ad centrum terrae descendens, cupidus sub mundi machina, auri venas exquiro. Quod cum in parte fecisse rebar, cum a te de aureo asino Apuleii librum, quem sic apud quosdam intitulatum asseris, obtinere potuissem, non equidem perscrutaturus fabulas, sed illius antiqui Poetae adepturus philosophiam, haud aliter, quam sub sterquilinio margaritas." Colonna, in Petrarca, *Opera* 1581, 1119–20.

[205] Thus Coville ("Une correspondance," 212): "*De monarchia moderni temporis* qui ne peut être que l'*Ane d'or*." Carver (following Coville?) says that Colonna had asked for the *Golden Ass* ("Rediscovery," 262–63).

[206] See the edition and discussion of Kohl and Siraisi, "The *De Monarchia* Attributed to Apuleius."

[207] Vat. lat. 1520. For a description, see ibid.; Pellegrin, *Les manuscrits classiques latins* 2.2.172–73.

124 • Chapter 3

At some point before our correspondence begins, Brossano (unaware of its recent origin) told Colonna that he had a manuscript of Apuleius' *De monarchia*, perhaps thinking that he could get one if necessary. When Colonna asked for it, he put him off for as long as possible. When he could not get it, he went on the defensive, claiming that the work in question was in fact the *Golden Ass* ("indeed, among some people it is called *De asino,* and that is the nature of the book"), and trotting out the standard objections to fiction. What he says about it shows no knowledge of its contents. Colonna, who knew nothing about either *De monarchia* or the *Golden Ass,* postponed his response long enough to do some research. In his reply, he uses the title *De aureo asino* (compare Brossano's *De asino*); and having learned of its racy reputation, he suggests that this apparent dung heap, if turned over assiduously enough, might contain pearls of philosophical wisdom.

We can see the exchange between Colonna and Brossano both as a conflict between humanism and scholasticism and as an example of uninformed intellectual and personal one-upsmanship. Above all, however, it is a useful demonstration of how little even highly educated people in the fourteenth century knew not only about Apuleius but about ancient authors in general. So far in this chapter we have been looking at the peaks represented by Petrarch, Boccaccio, and (more surprisingly) Bartolomeo de' Bartoli. With Colonna and Brossano we come down to earth for a more realistic view, to be reminded both that the ancient authors were difficult to attain or even to learn about (the crux of the matter in their dispute), and that not everyone considered it even worth the effort. Or as Brossano says: "You seek an abundance of books; you don't have it, and neither do I, and there is not a large number. And if there is not, perhaps it is not a disadvantage."[208]

An Interesting Allegory

Stefano Colonna was ready to descend even to the center of the earth or to turn over the dung heap of fable to seek out what he was sure would turn out to be the gold and pearls of Apuleius' philosophy. He was not alone in his enthusiasm, for the Biblioteca Nazionale in Florence preserves an allegory of Lucius of just the kind he suggests.[209]

---

[208] "Quaeris copiam librorum, tibi non adest, et mihi abest, et numerus non est. Et si non adest, forte non obest." Brossano, in Petrarca, *Opera* 1501. (The last sentence has been omitted in the 1581 edition.)

[209] Florence, Biblioteca Nazionale ms. II. VI. 2, fols. 2r–16r. The allegory was first noticed by Garin, "Noterelle sulla filosofia del rinascimento," 320. It was edited by Garfagnini, who also describes the manuscript: "Un accessus ad Apuleio e un nuovo codice

The allegory—in a fourteenth-century hand—is written in the margins of a fourteenth-century manuscript of the Third Vatican Mythographer. Since its author knows *De deo Socratis* as well as the *Apology* and the *Metamorphoses*, the work was almost certainly composed no earlier than the middle of the fourteenth century, when the philosophical and literary traditions of Apuleius were first reunited.

The author, like almost everyone in the fourteenth century, refers to Lucius Apuleius and takes the *Metamorphoses* as autobiographical. He begins his discussion with what he considers the all-important fact of Apuleius' Platonism. In *De deo Socratis*, he notes, Apuleius "asserted the heedlessness of the human race, especially of the ignorant."[210] His premise is that in the *Apology* and the *Metamorphoses* Apuleius demonstrates this human failing from his own experience: "And so with the example of his own asinine misery which he encountered, wishing people to be on their guard against other assaults of this kind, he placed the book *De magia* before the volumes of the *Metamorphosis* that were added to it directly below".[211] Accordingly, he presents allegories of both works, arguing that the story of Lucius' transformation is part of his (that is, Apuleius') defense.[212]

It is easy for a modern reader to point out the nonsensical and bizarre in the author's complicated interpretation. He identifies the characters of the *Apology* as allegorical abstractions with qualities suggested by their names: Emilianus is a "demon, emulous and envious"; Pudentilla is "matrimonial knowledge" (sex within marriage?); Lucius (Apuleius) himself, "the shining man," is "blessed understanding."[213] The author tells us that the erotic verses brought up by Apuleius' accusers contain disguised profound truths, just like the Song of Songs.[214] We are to learn from Lucius' experiences that there are "three stupid dumb animals" and a fourth "altogether detestable and perverse": the ass, woman, "the man skilled in letters who acts contrary to the evidence of his expertise," and

---

del Terzo Mitografo vaticano." The work is briefly treated by Gaisser, "Allegorizing Apuleius," 35–36. I cite the work from Garfagnini's edition, which I have checked against the manuscript.

[210] "humani negligentiam generis asserit, imperitorum maxime." "Accessus," ed. Garfagnini, ll. 5–6. Cf. Apul. *DDS* 3.

[211] "Exemplo itaque proprie quam incurrit miserie asinine, cupiens ceteros incursus eiusmodi homines precavere, librum *De magia* preposuit *Metamorphoseos* voluminibus immediate subiunctis." "Accessus," ed. Garfagnini, ll. 16–18.

[212] "Lucius sui transformationem immiscuit, refellere accusantem conatus." Ibid., l. 70.

[213] "Emilianus, demon scilicet, quasi emulianus et invidus." Ibid ll. 118–19. "[Emilianus] . . . Pudentille hoc est matrimonialis scientie, pudicitiam criminatur" (ll. 122–23). "Lucido . . . viro" (l. 178). "Lucius, id est beatus intellectus" (l. 160).

[214] Ibid., ll. 125–35.

"the hireling, who is the vile servant of tyrants."[215] And so on. But we should note that much in the author's method would not have seemed strange to his contemporaries. No less an authority than Coluccio Salutati would have found both his reference to the Song of Songs and his allegorical interpretation of proper names perfectly appropriate. Salutati says in his defense of poetry, *De laboribus Herculis*:

> When the mystical interpreter reveals the hidden meanings of the poets, and modifies each detail by referring it to God, nature, or customs, he may certainly suppose that he has hit upon an acceptable interpretation, even though what he has found can be said to have been unintended by the author. But if he can fit the significance of the proper names to the meaning he has found, I would boldly assert that he has unquestionably elicited the author's true meaning, or if this is not the case, and the names do not fit what the author has intended, I would assert that he has found a much more fitting sense than that which the author meant.[216]

Nonetheless, however admissible the details of its approach, the allegory as a whole does not hang together. Unlike Boccaccio's equally Christian and moral interpretation, it does not present a coherent reading or give us a second story that reflects on and deepens the meaning of the first—as Boccaccio's story of the soul's union with God stands beside and retells Apuleius' story of Psyche and her marriage with Cupid. The incoherence of the interpretation arises from the author's attempt to allegorize the *Apology* (which of course is not a story) and to treat it as essentially a single work with the *Metamorphoses*.

The story of Lucius by itself is much more amenable to allegorical treatment. In fact, it is so easily understood as an allegory that the author is able to entertain several different readings of it at the same time. He tells us first that Lucius is transformed into an ass because he tried to learn about magic and that he at last regained his freedom by the

---

[215] Ibid., ll. 19–25: "Tria esse animalia stulta bruta, quartum omnino detestabile ac perversum. . . . Primum est animal asinus . . . secundum femina . . . tertium litterarum peritus, agens contraria peritie documentis; quartum vero perversum animal stipendiarius dicitur, qui tyrannorum vilis est famulus."

[216] "Cumque poetarum abdita misticus interpres aperiet, et ad deum, naturam, vel mores singula referens adaptaverit, sine dubitatione reputet se, quamvis incogitatum ab autore dici queat id quod invenerit, in sententiam tolerabilem incidisse. Quod si ad illa que senserit adaptare poterit propriorum nominum rationem, audacter affirmem ipsum sine controversia veram autoris eliciusse sententiam, aut si forsitan illa non fuerit, et ad id quod autor intendisset nomina non accedant, longe commodiorem sensum quam autor cogitaverit invenisse." Salutati, *De laboribus Herculis* 2.14. The translation is that of Kallendorf: *Virgil and the Myth of Venice*, 99.

grace of heaven.[217] A few lines later he says that Lucius' asinine imprisonment symbolizes the misery of human existence—from the vileness of conception to the frightening and lamentable finality of death.[218] On the next page he asserts that it signifies the enslavement of the inner man to anxious passions of the mind, or "bestial anxieties," and that the man regains his human shape when he has recovered his lost grace.[219] His favorite idea, however, seems to be that Lucius' transformation is caused by lust—symbolized by the kiss of his mistress, Photis: "The kiss of Photis is the idle delight of this world, which [gives] human souls into the hands of demons and twists them into the appearance of beasts."[220] In all of these interpretations, however, Lucius' sufferings as an ass are a necessary penance—it is hardly going too far to call them a kind of earthly purgatory. The author says: "Condemned for his mistakes, he cannot eat the fresh roses until he endures much trouble and distress."[221] Lucius' sufferings are not merely a punishment but a spur to the repentance that will save him.

> In many cases God by his wonderful dispensation allows stupefying troubles to be put in motion for the space of correction; and when most people are overwhelmed by the depth of their faults, he generally provides the sudden grace of relieving repentance. From the remedy of his flight he deserves the counsel of prayer; and when he has chosen it he succeeds in having the rose remedy, that is, the sedation of lascivious passion and his restoration to a man, so that he may no longer live like an animal, but preserve himself in religion and chastity.[222]

The allegory, strange as it is, is a work of great historical interest, not least as tantalizing evidence of early discussions and interpretations of Apuleius that are otherwise unknown to us. It sometimes gives the

---

[217] "Accessus," ed. Garfagnini, ll. 25–30.

[218] Ibid., ll. 42–51.

[219] Ibid., ll. 82–85. "Peiores preterea patitur quas ignorat erumnas [*ms.*; erumnis, *ed.*] donec reparat post anxietates gratiam bestiales amissam" (ll. 82–84.)

[220] "Osculum istud Photis est otiosa deliciositas huius mundi, que in manus demonum et in facies brutorum animas pervertit humanas" (ll. 243–45). Her kiss is also the kiss of Judas (ll. 241–43).

[221] (The italicized words are translated in the text.) "Est igitur in predam latronum ductus, honeribus sarcinatus et multis anxietatibus et erumnis oppressus, *nec potest rosas recentes comedere donec plures patiatur damnatus errorum.*" ll. 246–48.

[222] "Mirabili Deus dispensatione in multis stupendas erumnas permittit ad correctionis spatium agitari, et ubi profunditate plurimi premuntur culparum, ibi gratiam compunctionis relevative subitam plerumque ministrat. Ex fuge remedio consilium orationis meretur, quo selecto impetravit habere rosarum medelas, scilicet sedationem ardoris lascivi et reformationem in hominem [*ms.*; nature humane, *ed.*,], ne amplius bestialiter vivat sed religiose casteque se servet" (ll. 263–69).

impression of being part of a continuing scholarly discussion,[223] and its presence in the margins of another manuscript, though thrifty, suggests that it may have been copied from an earlier source. The text itself has been carefully, if sparingly, annotated and corrected, in some cases by a second hand. The author had a manuscript of the *Apology* and the *Metamorphoses*, and if he did not have a text of *De deo Socratis*, he at least had the beginning of the work well enough in mind to use it to introduce his discussion. He gives only a few hints about his manuscript: it contained the *Apology* and *Metamorphoses* (which he calls *Metamorphosis*) in the usual order, but whether it also contained the *Florida* is impossible to tell; it is just conceivable that, like Boccaccio's manuscript, it included *De deo Socratis*.

The work is perhaps most interesting, however, for presenting the first interpretation of the story of Lucius—or, rather, the first *written* interpretation, since the illuminations executed for Bartolomeo de' Bartoli in Vat. lat. 2194 certainly constitute an interpretation. But if the work of our anonymous author is the first allegory of Lucius, it would by no means be the last. In this respect his allegory anticipates the direction that Apuleian interpretation was to take in the fifteenth century, when scholarly readers would leave Psyche and her divine union to artists and poets and turn their attention to the human failings and redemption of Lucius.

---

[223] The most striking example is the author's discussion of the first word in the *Apology*, ll. 51–56. It should be *certus*, he says, although some ("quorumdam expositione decepti," ll. 51–52) read *cecus*, perhaps as an indication of Apuleius' troubles.

CHAPTER 4

Making an Impression: From Florence to Rome and from Manuscript to Print

> And so we shall demonstrate that we are really from the family of Plato, for it knows nothing except what is festive, joyous, heavenly, divine.
> —*Marsilio Ficino*, Commentarium in Convivium Platonis, De Amore

Two events in the early fourteenth century determined the fortunes of Apuleius for over 150 years: Boccaccio's decisive encounter with the *Metamorphoses* in the late 1330s and the reappearance of the philosophical works in Italy a generation earlier. Boccaccio discovered not the manuscript of the *Golden Ass* but its literary riches, and he brought his find back to Florence a decade or so before Zanobi da Strada arrived with the manuscripts from Monte Cassino. The newly discovered philosophical works, overshadowed in the fourteenth century by their literary siblings, came to the fore in the fifteenth, fueling the reception of all of Apuleius' works and finally propelling them into print in 1469 in one of the earliest editions of a classical author printed in Italy.

The reappearance of the philosophical works at last reunited the two strands of Apuleius' oeuvre. They had been separated for nearly a thousand years: while the literary works lay unnoticed in Monte Cassino, the philosophical works enjoyed a rich *fortuna* in northern Europe but were essentially unknown in Italy.[1] But by the early decades of the fourteenth century texts from both traditions had become available to readers like Pseudo-Burley and Thomas Waleys in northern Italy. The literary works came to these early scholars—at an unknown number of removes—from Monte Cassino; but they almost certainly saw the philosophical works not in Italian manuscripts but in texts brought from France (or even England or Germany), perhaps by way of Avignon.[2]

---

[1] Of the twenty-six extant philosophical manuscripts written before 1200, not one is known to be of Italian origin; only three were written in Italy before 1300. See Klibansky and Regen, *Die Handschriften*, 49–50.

[2] At least one manuscript of the philosophical works is known to have been brought to Italy from Avignon: Milan, Biblioteca Ambrosiana N 266 sup. See Klibansky and Regen, *Die Handschriften*, 88–89.

As the fourteenth century progressed, Italian scribes began to copy works from both traditions, although with a distinct preference for the literary works and especially the *Metamorphoses*.[3] Between around 1340 and 1343, the scribe of Petrarch's manuscript (Vat. lat. 2193) took the obvious step of uniting the two traditions in a single volume, but there was no great rush to follow him. Although three more manuscripts containing both literary and philosophical texts were completed by the end of the century, none was designed and executed as a single volume; in each case the literary and philosophical works were written separately, either by different scribes or in different periods.[4] In the fifteenth century manuscripts of Apuleius became more numerous, but now the philosophical works moved into the ascendant. The figures tell the tale: from the fifteenth century we have 18 manuscripts of the *Metamorphoses* but 52 philosophical manuscripts, 35 of which were written in Italy.[5] Texts from the two traditions still appealed to different readers: only 7 fifteenth-century manuscripts contain both the *Metamorphoses* and philosophical works.[6]

In the first half of the fifteenth century the chief beneficiary of both Boccaccio's legacy and the new interest in the philosophical works was Florence, now in its full glory as the foremost center of humanist activity in Italy. Florentine or Tuscan scholars owned or transcribed at least 11 of the 40 existing manuscripts of the *Metamorphoses*; 15 manuscripts of philosophical works still remain in Florentine libraries.[7]

---

[3] There are nineteen fourteenth-century Italian manuscripts of the *Metamorphoses*; see appendix 3.2–3. Thirteen manuscripts of philosophical works were copied in the same period, of which only seven are Italian. (I have arrived at figures for the philosophical works using the manuscript descriptions in Klibansky and Regen, *Die Handschriften*. Here and elsewhere I follow Klibansky and Regen in including manuscripts of the *Asclepius*.)

[4] See appendix 3.2–3. The three are Laur. plut. 54.32; Vat. lat. 3384; and Naples, Biblioteca Nazionale IV.G.55.

[5] For the literary manuscripts, see appendix 2; 2 of the 18 could also belong to the very late fourteenth century (Oxford, Laud. lat. 55 and Wolfenbüttel Gud. lat. 30). For the philosophical manuscripts, see Klibansky and Regen, *Die Handschriften*, 50. Klibansky and Regen list 111 philosophical manuscripts as a total for all periods, but the number also includes some annotated editions.

[6] The seven are Florence, Biblioteca Laurenziana, Laur. plut. 54.12; Laur. plut. 54.13; Laur. plut. 84.24; Naples, Biblioteca Oratoriana CF. 3.7; Olomouc, Státní Vědecká Knihovna M II 58 (formerly I.IV.8); St. Gallen, Kantonsbibliothek Ms. 483; Vatican Library, Urb. lat. 199. In addition, Vatican Library, Vat. lat. 3082 includes the *Apology* and the philosophical works; see Klibansky and Regen, *Die Handschriften*, 117.

[7] For the literary manuscripts, see appendix 4.1. For the philosophical manuscripts, see Klibansky and Regen, *Die Handschriften*, 67–78. But some Florentine philosophical manuscripts have migrated to other libraries. One copied by Marsilio Ficino, for example, is now in Milan (Biblioteca Ambrosiana S 14 sup); see Klibansky and Regen, 89.

In Florence, as elsewhere, Apuleius had readers for both his literary and philosophical works, but even in Florence the philosophical readers predominated. The reason was Platonism, newly emerging in the Renaissance as a rival to the long-entrenched Aristotelianism of the Middle Ages. The Latin works of Apuleius, "the Platonic philosopher of Madauros" were considered potentially valuable as summaries of Platonic thought, especially when Plato's own works were still hard to find and still largely untranslated. But both in Florence and elsewhere in Italy, interest in the philosophical works continued even when scholars were able to read Plato himself either in Greek or (more often) in Latin translations.

In this chapter we will follow Apuleius from Florence to Rome and from manuscript to print. Our account will pay attention to both books and readers, to manuscripts and their annotations and interrelations as well as to the humanists who studied them, and to the first edition and the forces and scholars who produced it.

THE FLORENTINE CONNECTION

The humanists, like their modern counterparts, undoubtedly talked to each other about the authors they were reading. We cannot overhear their conversations, but some sense of them is preserved not only in the texts but in the annotations of their manuscripts, which were often copied or reflected in the annotations of other humanists, some near contemporaries and others removed by generations. The phenomenon is general and well attested for many authors and periods, but it is particularly conspicuous in the numerous Florentine manuscripts of the *Metamorphoses*, most of which still remain close to their birthplace.[8] By looking at annotations appearing in two or more of the Florentine manuscripts, we can see what the humanists found interesting in Apuleius and what ideas about his novel were circulating in this closely interconnected intellectual community.[9]

By the middle of the fourteenth century (1350–60) there were at least three manuscripts of the *Metamorphoses* in Florence: Boccaccio's transcription (Laur. 54.32) and F and φ from Monte Cassino. Before the end of the century there were at least three more: Laur. 54.14, Santa Croce 24

---

[8] The annotations of Petrarch were often copied (see chapter 3, n. 5). There are at least eighteen copies of Francesco Pucci's notes on Catullus (see Gaisser, "Catullus," 243–49). For the manuscripts in Florence, see appendix 4.1.

[9] The following discussion is an expansion of my earlier comments in "Apuleius in Florence."

sin 11, and British Library, Harley 4838. Most of these manuscripts are annotated to some degree, but the notes of the fourteenth-century annotators have few points in common (although Santa Croce 24 sin 11 and Harley 4838 share one important idea, as we shall see presently). The serious copying of annotations began in the first decades of the fifteenth century, when both manuscripts and the humanists who studied them became more numerous. This new generation of readers copied each other's notes as well as those of their predecessors.

The principal interrelations can be observed in six manuscripts, four from the group available at the end of the fourteenth century (Laur. 29.2 [φ], Laur. 54.32, Harley 4838, Santa Croce 24 sin 11) and two copied in the fifteenth (Laur. 54.12 and Laur. 54.24). Although it is not possible to be sure of the attribution of every note, we know or can guess the names of several of the principal annotators (or the scribes, in the cases of 54.32 and 54.12): Zanobi da Strada and Boccaccio (φ), Boccaccio (54.32), Coluccio Salutati and Zomino da Pistoia, called Sozomeno (Harley 4838), and Antonio di Mario (54.12). The annotators of Santa Croce 24 sin 11 and Laur. 54.24 remain unidentified.

What follows is not an exhaustive analysis of the complex interrelations of the Florentine manuscripts and all their annotations but something much more modest: a summary account of the manuscripts' readers and some of the points that interested them. We will consider the work of several fifteenth-century annotators, looking at the ways in which each incorporated the ideas of his predecessors into his own understanding of Apuleius. Our protagonists are the scribe Antonio di Mario, the humanist teacher Sozomeno, and the anonymous annotators of Laur. 54.24. Antonio di Mario is the only known Florentine in the group, but Sozomeno had strong connections with Florentine humanists and manuscripts, as did Mattia Lupi, the owner of Laur. 54.24.

Antonio di Mario (fl. 1417–56) was an extraordinarily prolific Florentine scribe who copied texts for a distinguished roster of patrons over a long career.[10] Among his fifty-odd manuscripts is Laur. 54.12, which he completed and signed on 20 June 1425.[11] The manuscript belonged to Piero de' Medici, but Antonio probably wrote it for Piero's father, Cosimo.[12] Laur. 54.12 is beautifully presented in clear humanistic script on fine creamy parchment, with vine-stem initials of blue, white,

---

[10] See Ullman, *The Origin and Development of Humanistic Script*, 98–109; de la Mare, "New Research on Humanistic Scribes," 417, 425, 482–84, 595.

[11] "Antonius Marius Florentinus transcripsit Florentię xii Kalendis Iulii MCCCCXXV." Florence, Biblioteca Laurenziana 54.12, fol. 198r.

[12] Ames-Lewis, *The Library and Manuscripts of Piero di Cosimo de' Medici*, 279; de la Mare, "Cosimo and His Books," 130–31, 152. For a description, see Klibansky and Regen, *Die Handschriften*, 68–69.

and gold—an elegant but not ostentatious addition to a rich man's library. It contains both the literary and the philosophical works, the latter no doubt at Cosimo's request, since he had a serious interest in philosophy.[13] Antonio, "Cosimo's favorite scribe,"[14] had ready access to the riches of the Florentine libraries, and he used four of the six manuscripts of the literary works available in the city at the end of the fourteenth century. He no doubt had equal access to manuscripts of the philosophical works.[15]

For the *Metamorphoses* he employed three different manuscripts, as he tells us in his subscription:

> The end of the last book of the *Metamorphoses* of Apuleius the Platonist of Madauros, which I transcribed with two highly corrupt exemplars, although I did not know or recognize it. Then it was taken up and emended by me, the scribe himself, with an excellent and most ancient exemplar. 1425. May you prosper and flourish.[16]

Antonio does not name his three manuscripts, but Robertson identifies Laur. 29.2 (φ) as his "excellent and most ancient exemplar" and suggests that his corrupt sources were Laur. 54.14 and Santa Croce 24 sin 11.[17]

---

[13] Cosimo's library is itemized by de la Mare in "Cosimo and His Books." Among his philosophical books were the dedication copy of Plato's *Letters* and the *Apology*, *Crito*, and *Phaedo* translated by Leonardo Bruni and copied by Antonio di Mario (the dialogues are dated July 1427; see de la Mare, 145–46); Aristotle's *Ethics*, translated by Leonardo Bruni (146); Seneca's *Letters* and philosophical works, both manuscripts copied by Antonio di Mario in 1426 (147), Aristotle's *Nicomachean Ethics* (147); Pseudo-Aristotle's *Economics*, copied by Antonio in 1419–20 (147–48); Aristotle's *Posterior Analytics* (148); Plato's *Gorgias* and *Phaedo* (152). Near the end of his life Cosimo encouraged the young Marsilio Ficino to translate all of Plato; see Hankins, *Plato in the Italian Renaissance* 1:267–68, 300–304, with earlier bibliography.

[14] The phrase is Hankins' (*Plato in the Italian Renaissance* 1:368).

[15] There are five manuscripts of the philosophical works still in Florence that were written before 1400. In the Biblioteca Laurenziana: Laur. 54.32 (Boccaccio's transcription of *De deo Socratis*); Laur. 76.36 (12th c.); San Marco 284 (11th c.); San Marco 341 (12th c.). In the Biblioteca Nazionale Centrale: Conventi Soppressi i.IX.39 (12th c.). Three of the five were once owned by Coluccio Salutati (the exceptions are Laur. 54.32 and San Marco 341). See Klibansky and Regen, *Die Handschriften*, 67–78.

[16] "Apulei Platonici Madaurensis Methamorphoseon liber ultimus explicit quem transcripsi cum duobus incorruptissimis exemplaribus me inscio neque cognito. Correptus deinde et emendatus per me ipsum scriptorem cum optimo atque vetustissimo exemplari MCCCCXXV. Valeas feliciter." Laur. 54.12, fol. 146r. I agree with Robertson that by *incorruptissimis* Antonio means "most corrupt" ("The Manuscripts" 38 n. 1). Although I find no parallel for this meaning, the sense of the passage demands it. It is conceivable that Antonio meant to write *corruptissimis* or that he was thinking of *incorrectissimis* and carelessly wrote *incorruptissimis* instead. (For examples of comparative and superlative degrees of *correctus/incorrectus*, see Rizzo, *Il lessico filologico*, 215 and 224.)

[17] Robertson, "The Manuscripts," 38.

Robertson did not do a full collation, but he believed that Santa Croce 24 sin 11 was Antonio's source for book 1.[18] This is an important point, and we will return to it presently. For the *Apology* Antonio used Laur. 68.2 (F); for the *Florida* Laur. 29.2 (φ).[19] Given the order of the literary works in 54.12 (*Metamorphoses, Apology, Florida*) and the fact that the sources Robertson proposes for its text of the *Metamorphoses* contain neither the *Apology* nor the *Florida*, we can reconstruct the sequence of events as follows.[20] When he needed to find an exemplar for the *Apology* after he had transcribed the *Metamorphoses* using Laur. 54.14 and Santa Croce 24 sin 11, Antonio turned to the venerable Laur. 68.2 (F). For the *Florida*, however, he required yet another exemplar (the *Florida* portion of F is nearly illegible), and this time he settled on Laur. 29.2 (φ).[21] As he paged through φ, he realized that its text for the *Metamorphoses* was far superior to those of his two original exemplars and took the opportunity to go back and correct the text he had already copied.

Antonio studied not only the text in φ but also its annotations, importing at least two of its more distinctive notes on the *Metamorphoses* into his margins. The first is a comment at *Met.* 3.24 by Boccaccio or another fourteenth-century reader on Lucius' transformation: "Apuleius hic induit asinum credens induere bubonem" (Here Apuleius, believing he is taking on the shape of an owl, takes on that of an ass).[22] The second is Zanobi da Strada's text of the *spurcum additamentum*.[23] The additamentum had been copied by both Zanobi and Boccaccio into their manuscripts, perhaps (but not necessarily) from a common exemplar. Their two versions differ enough at several points both to make it clear that neither is dependent on the other and to allow later copies to be traced back to their source.[24] The additamentum enjoyed a very limited *fortuna* in fifteenth-century manuscripts, all either Florentine or of Florentine descent. Zanobi's version appears in Laur. 54.12, Boccaccio's

---

[18] Ibid.

[19] Butler, in Apuleius, *Apologia*, xxxv–xxxvi.

[20] Santa Croce 24 sin. 11 does contain a few folios of the *Florida* but breaks off at *Fl.* 9.29, with the comment (fol. 117r): "Amen. non complevi quia corruptum exemplar nec intelligebam."

[21] For the explanation of Antonio's change from F to φ for the *Florida*, I am following Butler, in Apuleius, *Apologia*, xxxvi.

[22] Laur. 29.2, fol. 35r; Laur. 54.12, fol. 72v.

[23] Laur. 29.2, fol. 66r; Laur. 54.12, fol. 132v. For the pedigree of Antonio's text of the *additamentum*, see Robertson, "The Manuscripts," 31.

[24] For the text of the *additamentum*, see chapter 2, n. 111 and the discussion of Mariotti ("Lo *spurcum additamentum*," 231–32). The principal differences are as follows. Zanobi in φ reads *ercle, fragrantis, expiavit, paramese, conatim*. Boccaccio in Laur. 54.32 reads *hercle, fragantis, expurgavit, parmese, concitim*.

in Laur. 54.24, which we shall consider presently, and in Vatican Library, Urb. lat. 199, where it was copied from Laur. 54.24.²⁵ Only the scribe of Urb. lat. 199 incorporated it into the text; other annotators and scribes kept it safely segregated in the lower margin.

Neither of Antonio's other exemplars for the *Metamorphoses* is heavily annotated: there are only a handful of notes in Santa Croce 24 sin 11, and almost none in Laur. 54.14. But Santa Croce 24 sin 11, which Antonio used for book 1, did provide him with a detail that was to have an interesting and acrimonius reception: the mistaken idea that the prologue of the *Metamorphoses* was written in verse.²⁶ The theory, however, did not originate with the annotator of Santa Croce 24 sin 11. The verse prologue is found first in some annotations by the famous Florentine humanist Coluccio Salutati (1331–1406), who seems to be its author.²⁷ Salutati was most interested in Apuleius' philosophical works.²⁸ But he also had a copy of the *Metamorphoses* (British Library, Harley 4838).²⁹ He annotated its first few pages, probably in the 1370s, and supplied his own prefatory material, which consists of a transcription of the prologue in verse, a brief profile of Apuleius, and an explanation of the meter.³⁰ (See appendix 4.2 for a transcription of Salutati's discussion.)

Salutati's profile of Apuleius is reminiscent of the descriptions given by the early humanists Benzo, Pseudo-Burley, and Waleys several decades

---

²⁵ Robertson, "The Manuscripts," 31.

²⁶ For the history of the verse prologue in the printed editions, see Carver, "*Quis ille?*"; May, "The Prologue to Apuleius' *Metamorphoses*," 300–8.

²⁷ For Salutati, see especially Ullman, *The Humanism of Coluccio Salutati*; de la Mare, *Handwriting*, 30–43; Witt, *Hercules at the Crossroads*.

²⁸ See n. 15 above and the discussion in the section titled "Apuleius and the Latin Platonic Library," below.

²⁹ See de la Mare, *Handwriting*, 1.1:42. As far as I know, Salutati's sole use of the *Metamorphoses* in his own works is a reference to the description of Fotis' hair at *Met.* 2.8.9 in *De laboribus Herculis* 3.11, in which he allegorizes Medusa's hair as rhetorical ornament. Medusa is more beautiful than her sisters, he says: "Decore presertim in crinibus, quoniam ornamentis (que per crines significantur, qui sunt, ut demonstrat Apulegius, precipuum mulierum decus. Nam si tollantur, nulla fuerit adeo pulcra quin turpissima videatur)." But Salutati may also have been thinking of Boccaccio's imitation of the same passage in *Comedia delle ninfe fiorentine*: compare Boccaccio's phrase "della donna speziale bellezza" (*Comedia*, p. 932) with Salutati's "precipuum mulierum decus." There are two notes on *Met.* 2.8.5 in Harley 4838, fol. 141r: "De capillis" (in the hand of Sozomeno; see below) and "hic laudat capillorum ornatum" (in Coluccio's?).

³⁰ Harley 4838, fols. 134v–135r. De la Mare (*Handwriting*, 1.1:42) noted that Salutati had written the prologue in verse, suggesting that his annotations perhaps belong to the "middle period" of his script, i.e., the 1370s. Later both Dr. Regina May and I began to study Salutati's annotations independently. See May, "The Prologue"; Gaisser, "Apuleius in Florence." May does not consider the *fortuna* of the verse prologue in the Florentine manuscripts.

earlier, drawing as it does on the familiar passages from Macrobius and Augustine.[31] Two points in his account should be noted. First, Salutati reveals a surprising ignorance of the *Apology*, which he claims to have read. Here is what he says: "[Apuleius] was also an outstanding orator, and we have read his orations on magic, composed in defense of his wife, who had been accused of service of the magic art."[32] Clearly, whatever he says, Salutati has not read the *Apology*, and it is worth noting that there is no record that he ever owned a manuscript of it. The second point is more interesting. As May has observed, Salutati characterizes Apuleius as a writer of comedy.[33] (His opening words are "Hic autem autor comicus fuit.")[34] May is surely correct in her argument that this characterization has led him to present Apuleius' prologue in verse, and in the most characteristic verse of Roman comedy at that: iambic trimeter. His metrical explanation starts: "The author begins with a preface of twenty-five verses. The meter is iambic trimeter, consisting of six feet. But the poet freely substitutes feet."[35] The discussion that follows (see appendix 4.2) fits the prologue into Salutati's scheme with procrustean zeal, substituting, trimming, and stretching both quantities and the rules of scansion in order to interpret Apuleius' prose as verse. It is important to note, however, that all of these metrical acrobatics are performed in the explanation; Salutati has not revised the text to make it fit his metrical scheme but tailored his explanation to fit the text.[36]

Both Salutati's transcription of the verse prologue and his profile of Apuleius appear on fol. 134v of the manuscript. The facing page (fol. 135r) contains his metrical explanation in the upper margin, just above the beginning of the *Metamorphoses*.[37] Someone—probably Sozomeno, who later owned the manuscript—has annotated the prose text of the prologue with Salutati's verses in mind (see below). The scribe of the manuscript had indicated no paragraphs or internal divisions in

---

[31] Macrobius, *Somn. Scip.* 1.2.8; Augustine, *Civ.* 8.12, 8.14.

[32] "Fuit etiam orator eximius, cuius orationes de magia legimus, in defensionem uxoris compositas, quae de magicę artis ministerio fuerat accusata." Harley 4838, fol. 134v.

[33] May, "The Prologue," esp. 293–300.

[34] Harley 4838, fol. 134v. Salutati has derived this idea from Macrobius, *Somn. Scip.* 1.2.8.

[35] "Viginti quinque versus praemittit autor. Genus carminis trimetrum iambicum, constans ex sex pedibus. Excipit autem poeta licentiose pedes." Harley 4838, fol. 135r.

[36] In this he differs from several sixteenth- and seventeenth-century editors; see Carver, "*Quis ille?*" But Salutati either emended the text he found in Harley 4838 as he wrote his verse prologue or used a source whose text differed slightly from that of Harley 4838. For a comparison, see appendix 4.3.

[37] Harley 4828, fols. 134v and 135r are illustrated in Gaisser, "Apuleius in Florence," plates 1 and 2. Fol. 135r is shown in May, "The Prologue," plate 2.

his text, but the annotator has marked a separation between the prologue and the narrative by enlarging the T of *Thessaliam*, the first word of the narrative (*Met.* 1.2.1). He has also indicated divisions in the prose text that exactly correspond to the lines of the verse prologue and made several textual corrections that match readings in the verse text.[38]

Salutati's manuscript was probably the source for the annotator who added a verse prologue to Santa Croce 24 sin 11. The scribe of this manuscript, if we can rely on Bandini's eighteenth-century catalog of the Biblioteca Laurenziana, may be Tedaldo della Casa (ca. 1330–ca. 1410), a Franciscan monk of the convent of Santa Croce in Florence who was an acquaintance of Salutati's.[39] The identity of the annotator is unknown, but he was not the scribe. His script is not the same as that in the rest of the manuscript, and his verse prologue is clearly a later addition, for the folio on which it appears has been pasted in separately. As in Salutati's manuscript, the verse prologue appears on a verso facing the opening page of the *Metamorphoses*.[40] The annotator's verses are like Salutati's (the line breaks are identical), but his text is slightly different, not only from Salutati's but also from the text on the facing page of the manuscript.[41] Unlike Salutati, he provides neither title nor comment to accompany his rendition of the prologue. In fact, his verses look so isolated and anonymous that Bandini did not even recognize them as the beginning of the *Metamorphoses*, commenting in his catalog: "On the first page is read a prologue to some comedy, written in a later hand."[42]

Antonio di Mario, however, did recognize the verse prologue in Santa Croce 24 sin 11. He was so convinced by it that he not only transcribed it into the manuscript he was copying for Cosimo de' Medici but also

---

[38] May attributes the marks indicating verse divisions to Salutati ("The Prologue," 297), but Sozomeno also uses gallows marks (see below), and he has taken notice of Salutati's preface in other notes. (The names "Augustinus" and "Macrobius" in the margin of fol. 134v are in his hand, as are the words "prohemium" and "tractatus" in the margin of fol. 135r.) For the prose and verse texts in Harley 4838, see appendix 4.3.

[39] Della Casa is best known for copying several of Petrarch's works in the late 1370s, probably at the suggestion of Salutati. See Casnati, "Tedaldo della Casa," and Feo, *Codici latini del Petrarca*, 361–64, both with earlier bibliography. For della Casa as the scribe of Santa Croce 24 sin 11, see Bandini, *Catalogus codicum latinorum* 4:177. As far as I know, the identification has not been discussed by modern paleographers. It is plausible on historical grounds, since Tedaldo did transcribe a number of manuscripts, owned a small library that he turned over to his convent in 1406, and moved in Florentine humanist circles.

[40] The verse prologue appears on fol. Vv, the prose text on fol. 1r.

[41] See appendix 4.3. Line breaks have not been marked in the prose text on fol. 1r.

[42] "In prima pagina recentiori manu scriptus legitur Prologus quidam in aliquam Comoediam." Bandini, *Catalogus* 4:177.

omitted the prose version entirely.⁴³ In Antonio's manuscript the verses have an impressive and authentic look. They are neatly laid out in two columns headed with a handsome vine-stem initial of blue, white, and gold and separated by a space of several lines from the narrative (*Met.* 1.2), which begins with another initial of the same kind. Like the verses in Santa Croce 24 sin 11, Antonio's have neither title nor comment. When he was copying the verse prologue from Santa Croce 24 sin 11, Antonio no doubt compared its text, at least cursorily, with that of the prose version on the facing page.⁴⁴ After studying the text of φ, however, he made several major corrections to his verses, as the erasures and additions in his manuscript attest.⁴⁵

At about the same time that Antonio was transcribing Laur. 54.12 in Florence, other humanists were annotating manuscripts of their own nearby. The manuscripts in question are Laur. 54.24, owned by Mattia Lupi, and Harley 4838, Salutati's manuscript, which was later acquired and annotated by Sozomeno of Pistoia.

Mattia Lupi (1380–1468), a cleric and schoolmaster, was born in San Gimignano and spent his entire life in Tuscany.⁴⁶ He taught in San Gimignano and Pistoia, but mostly in Prato, just ten miles from Florence. Lupi was not a distinguished humanist, but he had literary ambitions (manifested in his unfinished epic on the history of San Gimignano), and he owned a large library, which he presented to his native town.⁴⁷ Among his books were two manuscripts of Apuleius: Laur. 51.9, which contains *De deo Socratis* and Macrobius' *Saturnalia*, and Laur. 54.24,

---

⁴³ Laur. 54.12, fol. 54r. The prose preface is also omitted from St. Gallen, Kantonsbibliothek 483.

⁴⁴ His use of the verses in Santa Croce 24 sin 11 is confirmed by his reading "spartica" in line 11. The other versions all read "spartiaca"; see appendix 4.3. (Modern editions print "Spartiatica".) But he includes "vetus" in line 13 (omitted in the verse version of Santa Croce 24 sin 11 but included in the prose).

⁴⁵ See appendix 4.3. Antonio has added "accipe" (l. 9) in darker ink, writing the last two letters above the line, since there was not enough space for the whole word; "isthomos" (l. 10) is written over an erasure, as are "Tenaros" (l. 11) and "inqua" (φ reads "inquam," indicating the *m* with a horizontal line that would have been easy for Antonio to miss). He has lengthened "grecam" (l. 24) to "grecanicam," placing the letters *nicam* above the line for lack of space. Antonio could have imported "accipe" and "grecanicam" from Santa Croce 24 sin 11 ("accipe" appears—but deleted—in its prose version, "grecanicam" in the verse), but in that case one would have expected him to have done so at the beginning when he was laying out the columns of his text.

⁴⁶ For Lupi, see Davies, "The Senator and the Schoolmaster," and Fioravanti, "Librerie," both with earlier bibliography.

⁴⁷ His unpublished epic, *Annales Geminianenses*, though unfinished, still amounts to about 12,500 hexameters (about the length of the *Odyssey*). It has not been admired; see Davies, "The Senator and the Schoolmaster," 8–9. For the library, see Fioravanti, "Librerie"; Davies, 9–11.

which includes the *Metamorphoses* and *Florida* and a summary of the *Apology*.[48]

The scribe of Laur. 54.24, unlike Antonio di Mario, does not give his name or say anything about his exemplar (or exemplars). But he does give us a very precise date, stating that he completed the *Florida* "on 26 January 1422, in the sixteenth hour."[49] Perhaps he copied the manuscript for Lupi, who is known to have commissioned at least two other manuscripts, including Laur. 51.9 and Laur. 36.23 (Ovid's *Fasti* and Catullus).[50] I suspect, however, that Lupi acquired it from a previous owner, since its copious annotations do not seem to be in his hand.[51] The notes in Laur. 54.24 are closely related to two different sets of marginalia: those of Boccaccio in Laur. 54.32 and those of Sozomeno in Harley 4838. They are written in at least three hands: those of the scribe and of the first and second annotators. For the most part, the notes like those in Boccaccio's manuscript can be ascribed to the scribe and the first annotator, and the notes like those in Sozomeno's to the second annotator; but it is not always possible to distinguish among the hands or even to be sure that only three are involved.[52] Lupi's relation to the annotations is unclear.

Both the scribe of Laur. 54.24 and the first annotator consulted Boccaccio's manuscript, which had remained in Florence after his death.[53] The scribe did not use Laur. 54.32 as his exemplar, but he did enter some of Boccaccio's readings—not very systematically.[54] In book 10 he added Boccaccio's text of the *spurcum additamentum* in the

---

[48] These manuscripts, along with the bulk of Lupi's library, were brought to Florence by Duke Cosimo I in 1568—hence their present location in the Laurenziana. For Laur. 51.9, see Klibansky and Regen, *Die Handschriften*, 67–68; de la Mare, "Humanistic Script," 98–100. Laur. 54.24 (unlike Laur. 51.9) does not have Lupi's arms, but a note on fol. 1 identifies it as "dalla Comunità di S. Gemignano." It is almost certainly part of Lupi's library; see Fioravanti, "Librerie," 69.

[49] "Completus die xxvi{a} Ianuari mccccxxii hora xvi{a}" (Laur. 54.24, fol. 85r).

[50] Lupi's texts of both Macrobius and Catullus were corrected or copied from manuscripts owned by Salutati. See de la Mare, "Humanistic Script," 98–100; Davies, "The Senator and the Schoolmaster," 11.

[51] I find no similarity between the hands in Laur. 54.24 and the photographs of Lupi's cursive and formal scripts in Davies, "The Senator and the Schoolmaster," figs. 1 and 2.

[52] The scribe of Laur. 54.24 uses a small, open, and very regular script. The script of the first annotator, by contrast, is very compact, but still neat and quite regular. That of the second annotator is somewhat looser and less well aligned. Examples of all three can be found on Laur. 54.24, fol. 1v.

[53] Boccaccio left his books to the convent of Santo Spirito in Florence. Laur. 54.32 appears in the inventory of the library made in 1451. See Mazza, "L'inventario," 47.

[54] Given the quality of Boccaccio's text, we might prefer to call the scribe discriminating rather than unsystematic. In *Met.* 1.1 he has added the following from Laur. 54.32 as variants: "papirum"; "egiptiam"; "accipe" (omitted in his text); "ysmos" (modern editions read "Isthmos"). See Gaisser, "Apuleius in Florence," plate 3.

lower margin.⁵⁵ His most striking imitation of Boccaccio, however, is at the end of the manuscript (fol. 85v), where he presents a summary of the *Apology* modeled on the rubrics preceding *De deo Socratis* in Laur. 54.32. Boccaccio's rubrics—fourteen summary statements, each numbered and preceded with a red paragraph mark—appear on a verso facing the opening page of *De deo Socratis*.⁵⁶ The rubrics in Laur. 54.24, written in red and each preceded with a blue paragraph mark, itemize the contents of the *Apology*. The list (which is not numbered) begins, "The reply of Apuleius to the charges against him of good looks and eloquence," and ends twenty-one rubrics later with "comparison of a virgin and a widow."⁵⁷ The manuscript ends here, and we cannot know whether the scribe planned to begin the *Apology* on the recto of a new gathering so that his rubrics, like Boccaccio's, would face the first page of his text and serve as a table of contents, or whether he simply substituted the rubrics for the work itself.⁵⁸

The first annotator of Lupi's manuscript was equally attentive to Laur. 54.32, carefully reproducing almost every note (and all of the longer notes) on Boccaccio's first four folios.⁵⁹ He includes Boccaccio's comments framing Lucius' story to his fellow travelers in *Met.* 1.4: "Apuleius begins his own story in order to make the one companion willing to tell what he had begun, and the other willing to listen"; "Apuleius concludes. Aristomenes begins a story about Socrates the innkeeper."⁶⁰ A few folios later he enters Boccaccio's summary of Lucius' first hours in Hypata: "Apuleius arrives in Hypata" (*Met.* 1.21.2); "Apuleius arrives at the house of Milo" (*Met.* 1.22.1); "Apuleius buys fish" (*Met.* 1.24.4); "Apuleius comes upon his old friend Phytias" (*Met.* 1.24.5).⁶¹

---

⁵⁵ Laur. 54.24, fol. 63v. Cf. Laur. 54.32, fol. 56r.

⁵⁶ Laur. 54.32, fol. 69v. The rubrics are edited and discussed by Klibansky and Regen in *Die Handschriften*, 176–95, and shown in plate 5 there.

⁵⁷ "Responsio Apuleii ad obiecta contra se de forma corporis et eloquentia"; "Comparatio virginis et vidue" (Laur. 54.24, fol. 85v).

⁵⁸ Fol. 85v ends a gathering of ten leaves. The manuscript contains nine gatherings: 12, 2 (8), 4 (10), 8, 10. But the first leaf of the first gathering has been removed. See below.

⁵⁹ Fiorilla lists thirty seven notes by Boccaccio in Laur. 54.32, fols. 18r–21v ("La lettura apuleiana," 664–66). All but six are reproduced in Laur. 54.24. (The omitted notes are numbers 44, 51, 53, 65, and 71 in Fiorilla's edition.)

⁶⁰ On *Met.* 1.4.1: "Apuleius suam incipit fabulam ut comites alterum ad dicendum quod ceperat, alterum ad audiendum faciles reddat" (Laur. 54.24, fol. 1v). On *Met.* 1.5.1: "Finit Apuleius. Incipit Aristomenes fabulam de Socrate caupone" (Laur. 54.24, fol. 1v). The annotator has also included Boccaccio's note on the end of Aristomenes' story at *Met.* 1.20.1 ("finis fabule Aristomenis," fol. 4v). For these notes in Laur. 54.32, see pp. 109–10 and Fiorilla, "La lettura apuleiana," 664–65.

⁶¹ "Pervenit Apuleius ypatam"; "pervenit ad domum Milonis Apuleius" (Laur. 54.24, fol. 5r). "Emit Apuleius pisces"; "Invenit Apuleius Phytiam sotium suum quondam" (fol. 5v). See pp. 109–10 and Fiorilla, "La lettura apuleiana," 666.

The relation between the annotations in Lupi's manuscript and those in Boccaccio's is obvious: the scribe and first annotator of Laur. 54.24 copied from Laur. 54.32. Matters are much less clear in the case of Lupi's manuscript and Sozomeno's, since the owners are virtual contemporaries. I am inclined to think that Sozomeno and the second annotator of Laur. 54.24 influenced each other, for some of their shared notes seem to have originated in Lupi's manuscript, others in Sozomeno's. But it is also important to note that each manuscript has many notes not found in the other (or in other manuscripts, as far as I know). Whether they studied each other's notes or one copied the other, both annotators also read and interpreted Apuleius independently and in accordance with their own interests.

Zomino of Pistoia (1387–1458)—who preferred to be called by the Greek name Sozomeno—was just a few years younger than Mattia Lupi. He was more accomplished than Lupi, but resembled him in some important respects. Like Lupi, he was a cleric and teacher; and, like Lupi, he is known both for writing a mediocre literary work and for presenting a distinguished library to his native town.[62] It is quite likely that the two men were acquainted with each other: they had similar interests and knew some of the same important Florentine humanists; both were in Pistoia in the mid-1440s.[63] Unlike Lupi, however, Sozomeno is known to have spent much of his life in and around Florence: he lived there from about 1418 to 1431 and visited often when he was living in Pistoia, only about twenty miles away. It was probably in Florence, perhaps around 1430, that he acquired Salutati's manuscript of the *Metamorphoses*.[64]

Sozomeno was an enthusiastic annotator, and the margins of his books are full of notes of every kind, from variant readings and simple glosses to mythological explanations and references to other works. He even kept track of many of his notes by a system of cross-references to annotations in other manuscripts.[65] But he did not annotate all of his

---

[62] For Sozomeno, see de la Mare, *Handwriting*, 1.1: 91–105, and Cesarini Martinelli, "Sozomeno" both with earlier bibliography. His literary work is a history, *Chronicon universale aa. 1411–1455*. For his library, see Sabbadini, "La biblioteca di Zomino da Pistoia"; Savini, "La libreria di Sozomeno da Pistoia."

[63] For Lupi's Florentine acquaintances, see Davies, "The Senator and the Schoolmaster"; for Sozomeno's, see de la Mare, *Handwriting*. Lupi was a vicar for the bishop of Pistoia in the early 1440s (Davies, 8). Sozomeno held a similar position in the late 1430s and perhaps again in 1446 (de la Mare, 94; Cesarini Martinelli, "Sozomeno," 10 n. 3).

[64] Salutati's library was dispersed after his death (1406); see Ullman, *The Humanism*, 278–80. Sozomeno owned at least five of Salutati's manuscripts, and he is known to have bought two other second-hand manuscripts in Florence in 1429 and 1431; see de la Mare, *Handwriting*, 1.1: 97 n. 3.

[65] See de la Mare, *Handwriting*, 1.1: 93–94 and plate 21.f.

manuscripts to the same degree. He wrote full commentaries on Ovid's *Metamorphoses* and Seneca's *Tragedies* and detailed notes on Terence and Lucan—all standard texts in the fifteenth-century curriculum that he probably used in his teaching.[66] Texts not taught in schools, like Quintilian and Livy, received a different treatment.[67] These were texts that he read for himself, and he annotated them more sparingly, focusing on points of interest or interpretation as they occurred to him. Apuleius' *Metamorphoses* in Harley 4838 clearly belongs to this last category, as his annotations attest.

Among Sozomeno's notes not shared with Laur. 54.24, two examples must suffice. Both concern Boccaccio, who seems to have been one of Sozomeno's favorite "modern" authors.[68] In a terse note on the first adultery tale of book 9, Sozomeno refers to the *Decameron*: at the point where the wife bends over the vat in order to handle her husband and service her lover, he says, "This is where Boccaccio got it."[69] In his note at the beginning of the story of Cupid and Psyche in book 4, he supplies a cross-reference: "For the interpretation of this story, look in the end of the tragedies, [fol.] 61."[70] Sozomeno's cross-reference is to a manuscript still in Pistoia, one of the few to survive the dispersion of his library. The manuscript, Fort. A.46, contains his commentaries on Ovid's *Metamorphoses* and Seneca's tragedies.[71] At the end of the tragedies, just as Sozomeno tells us in Harley 4838, we find the promised interpretation of Cupid and Psyche: Boccaccio's allegory from *Genealogie deorum gentilium* 5.22.[72] Sozomeno evidently wrote this note in Harley 4838 (and perhaps his others as well) after transcribing Fort. A.46, that is, at some time in the 1430s or later.[73]

At least two notes that Sozomeno shares with Laur. 54.24 seem to have originated with Lupi's first annotator—or, rather, with Boccaccio's

---

[66] See Cesarini Martinelli, "Sozomeno," 38.

[67] Ibid.

[68] For Sozomeno's use of Boccaccio's *Genealogie deorum gentilium*, see Cesarini Martinelli, "Sozomeno," 64–67.

[69] "Bocacius hinc accepit" (Harley 4838, fol. 176r), *ad* "At illa capite in dolium" (*Met.* 9.7.6). Cf. *Decameron* 7.2 and pp. 100–103 above.

[70] "De interpretatione huius fabule quaere in fine tragediarum. 61" (Harley 4838, fol. 155r), *ad* "Erant in quadam civitate" (*Met.* 4.28).

[71] Biblioteca Comunale Forteguerriana A.46. For a description, see Murano et al., *I manoscritti medievali*, 92. For the commentaries, see Coulson, "Lives of Ovid," 162–64; Cesarini Martinelli, "Sozomeno," 39–45, 64–80. I must express my thanks to Frank Coulson for his assistance with this manuscript.

[72] Biblioteca Comunale Forteguerriana A.46, fols. 61v–62r (= 167v–168r in the present foliation of the manuscript).

[73] Fort. A.46 is dated between 1430 and 1440 by Cesarini Martinelli ("Sozomeno," 37). Coulson suggests a date around 1431 ("Lives of Ovid," 162).

notes in Laur. 54.32 by way of Lupi's annotator. In Laur. 54.32 Boccaccio numbers the crimes of the witch Meroe: "Primum Meroen malefitium . . . secundum . . . tertium . . . quartum . . . quintum . . . sextum.[74] In Laur. 54.24 either the scribe or the first annotator (it is impossible to be sure) has exactly copied Boccaccio's list.[75] The numbers appear again in Sozomeno's manuscript, but now without comment of any kind. The annotator has simply placed a series of Arabic numbers from 1 to 5 (instead of 1–6) in his margin, and he has slightly misplaced them at that, beginning his count at *Met.* 1.8.6 instead of 1.9.1 with Boccaccio and the annotator of Laur. 54.24.[76] The second example is still further removed from Boccaccio and Laur. 54.24. As we have seen, at the beginning of Lucius' story to his fellow travelers (*Met.* 1.4), Boccaccio and Lupi's annotator both remark: "Apuleius begins his own story in order to make the one companion willing to tell what he had begun, and the other willing to listen." Sozomeno abbreviates and rephrases, but the paternity of his comment is obvious: "Digression. The author reports these marvels in order to induce him to talk."[77]

We can also see an exchange of notes between Sozomeno and the second annotator of Laur. 54.24. Sozomeno is the borrower in the case of a note on book 1. In *Met.* 1.4 Lucius tells of seeing a boy climb up out of the throat of a sword swallower and twine himself around the sword like the serpent around the "staff of the god of medicine."[78] The annotator of Laur. 54.24 comments: "He is talking here about Aesculapius, the son of the sun and Coronis, who was a very great doctor and brought Hippolytus back to life and is worshiped in the likeness of a serpent, as is shown in Valerius [Val. Max. 1.8.2] when he came to Rome to free it from an epidemic."[79] Sozomeno has two notes on Aesculapius, one so close above the other that we could take them for a single comment, except that the beginning of each is marked with the paragraph sign (or "gallows") that he often uses to indicate a note.[80] The one below is only a cross-reference: "We have spoken about

---

[74] Laur. 54.32, fol. 19r; see Fiorilla, "La lettura apuleiana," 665 nn. 56–60 and 64.

[75] The annotator's numbers appear at the same places as Boccaccio's (*Met.* 1.9.1, 1.9.3, 1.9.4, 1.9.5, 1.10.1, 1.10.5). Laur. 54.24, fol. 2v.

[76] Harley 4838, fol. 136r.

[77] "Digressio. Hec mira refert auctor ut inducat illum ad dicendum." Harley 4838, fol. 135r.

[78] "Dei medici baculo" (*Met.* 1.4.5).

[79] "De Esculapio filio solis et Coronidis loquitur qui maximus medicus fuit et resuscitavit Ypolitum et colitur in spetie serpentis ut patet in Valerio quando venit Romam ut liberaret eam ab epidemia." Laur. 54.24, fol. 1v.

[80] For examples, see de la Mare, *Handwriting*, 1.1: plates 19.e and g (bottom), 20.d.

Aesculapius in book 2 of Ovid's *Metamorphoses*. 18."[81] Above it is the note from Laur. 54.24. Sozomeno evidently wrote the cross-reference first, marking it with his usual sign. At that point his chief sources for Aesculapius were Ovid's *Metamorphoses* and Boccaccio's chapter in *Genealogie*. He added the other note later, after he learned from the comment in Laur. 54.24 that the god was also mentioned by Valerius Maximus.[82] In a note on book 4, however, the annotator of Laur. 54.24 is the beneficiary. At *Met.* 4.28.1 Sozomeno comments: "Incipit fabula psycen pulcerrima valde" (The most exceedingly beautiful story of Psyche begins).[83] Lupi's manuscript has a note in red at the same place— "Incipit fabula psycen"—to which the annotator later added Sozomeno's phrase "pulcerrima valde," writing it in black and in slightly smaller letters.[84]

But the most important contribution of Sozomeno's manuscript to the annotator of Laur. 54.24 was really Salutati's: the idea that the prologue of the *Metamorphoses* was written in verse. Lupi's manuscript, unlike Harley 4838, Santa Croce 24 sin 11, and Laur. 54.12, does not contain a verse version of the prologue. But the annotator, like Sozomeno (or conceivably Salutati) in Harley 4838, has both marked off line divisions in the prose text corresponding to Salutati's verses and enlarged the T of *Thessaliam*, the first word of the narrative.[85] It is tempting to speculate, moreover, that the annotator might also have followed Harley 4838 in providing a verse transcription facing the first folio of the text. We will never know, however, since the page that would have contained it has been removed, perhaps because its recto contained Lupi's arms or a note of ownership.

The fifteenth-century Florentine and Tuscan scribes and annotators of the *Metamorphoses* borrowed and shared manuscripts with an ease that would have been impossible for all but the most important or best-connected scholars of previous generations. In the fourteenth century a Boccaccio or a Salutati could find or borrow a manuscript or two; a Stefano Colonna might never see one at all.[86] In the 1420s, however,

---

[81] "De Esculapio diximus libro II Ovidii *Metamorphoseon*. 18." Harley 4838, fol. 135r. The reference again is to Fort. A. 46, this time to his commentary on Ovid, where he quotes a long passage from Boccaccio's *Genealogie* (*Gen.* 5.19, fol. 18r–v).

[82] Boccaccio does not mention Valerius.

[83] Harley 4838, fol. 155r.

[84] Laur. 54.24, fol. 23v.

[85] Laur. 54.24, fol. 1r. See Gaisser, "Apuleius in Florence," plate 3.

[86] For Boccaccio and Colonna, see chapter 3. Assuming that Salutati did not emend the text of Harley 4838 while he was writing out his verse preface, he probably had access to two manuscripts: Harley 4838 and whatever text he used for his verse prologue.

Antonio di Mario was able to consult four different manuscripts, and the scribe of Laur. 54.24 had access to Boccaccio's manuscript as well as to his own exemplar. A few years later the second annotator of Laur. 54.24 and Sozomeno benefited from seeing each other's manuscripts and all their annotations. In spite of all their access to texts, however, Apuleius' Florentine readers took only a limited interest in the novel. Their notes, without exception, are concentrated in the first folios of their manuscripts, growing ever sparser as the work proceeds.[87] The annotators focus on rare words, plot details, and mythological references; the only nod to anything one might term *interpretation* is Sozomeno's reference to Boccaccio's allegorical reading of the story of Psyche. Their major and most frequently repeated contributions are either irrelevant (the *spurcum additamentum*) or wrong (the verse prologue).

The reasons for the annotators' lack of interest are not far to seek. The *Metamorphoses* was out of their experience. It was both unfamiliar in genre and abstruse (even bizarre) in language. Most of it was not even serious. Since it was not part of the curriculum, the annotators felt no need to study it deeply; they read the novel with enough attention to make them seek out and study the texts and notes of other humanists, but they were not preparing either to imitate it or to explain it to anyone else. The *spurcum additamentum* remained essentially a Florentine phenomenon, but the verse prologue made its way into at least one non-Florentine manuscript (St. Gallen 483).[88] It went on to a complex *fortuna* in editions from the fifteenth to the nineteenth century.

---

[87] The same is true of Boccaccio and Salutati in the fourteenth century. Boccaccio, of course, had already annotated Laur. 29.2 before transcribing and annotating Laur. 54.32; and he interpreted Apuleius extensively in his writings. Salutati refers only once to the *Metamorphoses* in his writings (see n. 29 in this chapter), and he annotated only the first few folios of Harley 4838.

[88] For St. Gallen, Kantonsbibliothek 483, see appendixes 2 and 4.3. I have not been able to determine the exact pedigree of the verse preface in this manuscript, but it is surely inspired by one of the Florentine manuscripts. St. Gallen 483 contains three sections, each in a different hand: Apuleius, *Metamorphoses* and *De deo Socratis* (fols. 7r–293r); Theophrastus, *De nuptiis* (295–97); and Petrarch, miscellaneous poetry (fols. 1r and 308r). The date 1424 appears on fol. 308r, but it may not apply to the manuscript as a whole. In a personal communication, Professor Virginia Brown dates the manuscript to the first half of the fifteenth century, placing it in northern Italy—perhaps Bologna or Milan. The text of the preface does not exactly match that in any of the Florentine manuscripts, although it has points in common with each (see appendix 4.3). May considers the manuscript an apograph of Harley 4838 ("The Prologue," 300–301), but the text of the prologue at least has more similarities with that in Santa Croce 24 sin 11 and Laur. 54.12 (see appendix 4.3). As in Laur. 54.12, it replaces the prose preface.

Apuleius and the Latin Platonic Library

Although the Florentine humanists did not delve deeply into Apuleius' novel, they took a serious interest in his philosophical works. They owned even more manuscripts of the philosophical than of the literary works, and they studied them with greater care, since they considered Apuleius an important source for Platonic philosophy.[89] Their reception of the philosophical works is closely tied to their reception both of Plato and of other Latin Platonist texts.

Apuleius had been described by no less an authority than Augustine as "a famous Platonist in both Greek and Latin."[90] The recommendation was enough to persuade the Greekless scholars of the Middle Ages to include his philosophical works in their library of Latin works on Platonic philosophy.[91] The works in this rather sizable collection most closely related to the fortunes of Apuleius included—in addition to the always indispensable Augustine—Macrobius' commentary on the *Somnium Scipionis*, Calcidius' fourth-century commentary and translation of the first part of the *Timaeus*, the twelfth-century translation of the *Phaedo* by Aristippus, a twelfth-century Platonist tract called *Liber Alcidi*, and the pseudo-Apuleian *Asclepius*, which had been transmitted with Apuleius' philosophical works from at least the ninth century. These texts were often read with Apuleius, for they appeared in the same libraries and sometimes even in the same manuscripts with his works.

The fourteenth-century humanists, who had as much reverence for Augustine and Plato (and as little Greek) as their medieval predecessors, continued to read Apuleius and the other Latin sources. By the end of the century, however, they also hoped to reach Plato more directly—through study of the dialogues themselves, both in Greek and in contemporary Latin translations. The effort began in Florence, propelled and promoted especially by its humanist chancellor, Coluccio Salutati, who brought the Greek émigré Manuel Chrysoloras to the university of Florence in 1397 and thereby established the study of Greek in Italy.[92] Salutati himself managed to learn little Greek and seems to have owned no Greek manuscripts.[93] He did, however, own and annotate three

---

[89] See pp. 130–31, n. 7 in this chapter, and appendix 4.1. Today the Vatican Library has more philosophical manuscripts than Florence does (18), but many have migrated there from other cities. See Klibansky and Regen, *Die Handschriften*, 108–20.

[90] "In utraque autem lingua, id est et Graeca et Latina, Apuleius Afer extitit Platonicus nobilis." Augustine, *Civ.* 8.12.

[91] This paragraph drastically simplifies the complex subject of medieval Latin Platonism and its sources. For a fuller discussion, see Klibansky, *The Continuity of the Platonic Tradition*, 21–37, 51–53. See also Gersh, *Middle Platonism and Neoplatonism* 1:1–26; Hankins, "Plato in the Middle Ages."

[92] Ullman, *The Humanism*, 118–22.

manuscripts of Apuleius' philosophical works.⁹⁴ In the 1390s he used Apuleius in two works of his own, quoting and discussing one passage from *De Platone* in his treatise *De fato et fortuna* and paraphrasing another in *De laboribus Herculis*.⁹⁵ Salutati also owned several of Apuleius' companions in the Latin Platonic library, including Macrobius' commentary on *Somnium Scipionis, Asclepius, Liber Alcidi,* Calcidius' *Timaeus,* and the *Phaedo* of Aristippus.⁹⁶

After 1400 Greek studies proceeded apace in Florence, providing both more humanists competent in Greek and more Latin translations of Plato's dialogues. The younger generation of humanists still read Apuleius' philosophical works, but now increasingly as an adjunct to Plato rather than as a source for his thought. Giannozzo Manetti (1396–1459) used Greek sources, including Plato himself, for his *Vita Socratis* (ca. 1440), but he also cited Apuleius' *De Platone* and quoted extensively from *De deo Socratis,* especially for his discussion of Socrates' famous daimon.⁹⁷ Manetti's manuscript of the philosophical works (if he had one) has not been identified, but he did own a handsome manuscript of the *Metamorphoses*—although perhaps only to complete his library, since it contains not so much as a single annotation.⁹⁸

Although Renaissance translations of Plato began to appear very early in the fifteenth century, the first translation of all the dialogues was completed only in 1469. The translator was Marsilio Ficino (1433–99), the most important translator of Plato in the Renaissance and a major Neoplatonic philosopher in his own right.⁹⁹ Before mastering Greek,

⁹³ Ullman found none (ibid., 120).

⁹⁴ Florence, Biblioteca Laurenziana 76.36 and San Marco 284; Florence, Biblioteca Nazionale Centrale, conventi soppressi i. IX.39. See Ullman, *The Humanism,* 150, 155, 174, 215–16. See also n. 15 in this chapter.

⁹⁵ He quotes from *De Platone* 1.12 at *De Fato et fortuna* 2.2 and loosely paraphrases *De Platone* 1.5 and 1.6 at *De laboribus Herculis* 3.16. For Salutati's use of the *Metamorphoses* in *De laboribus Herculis,* see n. 29 in this chapter.

⁹⁶ Macrobius' commentary: Florence, Biblioteca Laurenziana 77.6. See Ullman, *The Humanism,* 235–36. *Asclepius*: Laurenziana 76.36; Florence, Biblioteca Nazionale Centrale, conventi soppressi i.IX.39. *Liber Alcidi*: Biblioteca Laurenziana, Strozzi 72. See Ullman, 52–53; Hankins, *Plato in the Italian Renaissance* 1:34 n. 8. (Strozzi 72 was later owned by Marsilio Ficino; see Gentile et al., *Marsilio Ficino,* 5–7.) *Timaeus* and *Phaedo*: Vat. lat. 2063. See Ullman, 186–87, 245–46.

⁹⁷ In *Vita Socratis* 1.15 (ed. De Petris) Manetti cites *De Platone* 1.187; in 2.35–42 he closely follows *De deo Socratis,* 17–20; see De Petris' discussion, pp. 82–83. See also Moreschini, *Apuleio e il Platonismo,* 264–65. For a translation of the *Vita Socratis,* see Manetti, *Biographical Writings,* ed. Baldassari and Bagemihl, 177–233.

⁹⁸ Vatican Library, Pal. lat. 1574. See appendix 3. The manuscript has only a note of Manetti's ownership on fol. Iv written by Tommaso Tani; see Pellegrin, *Manuscrits classiques latins* 2.2:233.

⁹⁹ For Ficino and Plato, see especially Hankins, *Plato in the Italian Renaissance* 1:267–359, and Vasoli, "Marsilio Ficino," both with earlier bibliography. Although Ficino

however, Ficino began his studies with Apuleius and the other Latin Platonists.[100] In his twenties he began to acquire his own library of Latin Platonism. In 1454 he transcribed and annotated a manuscript containing Calcidius' commentary on the *Timaeus*, Leonardo Bruni's Latin translation of the *Gorgias*, and *De deo Socratis* (Milan, Biblioteca Ambrosiana S 14 sup).[101] In 1456 he copied another Apuleius manuscript, this time with the help of two other scribes. This manuscript, which he also annotated, includes *De Platone, De mundo*, and portions of *Asclepius* and the *Liber Alcidi* (Florence, Biblioteca Riccardiana 709).[102] In 1456 he also composed a work entitled *Institutiones Platonicae disciplinae*, aided, as he wrote many years later, "partly by chance discovery and partly by reading some of the Latin Platonists."[103] The work is no longer extant, but no doubt the Latin Platonists he mentions included Apuleius and the other Latin sources whose works he had copied and annotated in his manuscripts. But Ficino was not an uncritical reader of Apuleius. In an annotation in Riccardiana 709, he (or the scribe with whom he was closely associated) remarks testily after the Orphic hymn in *De Mundo* (*Mu.* xxxvii.372): "The end of Apuleius on the god, which he has stolen word for word from Aristotle, from his book *On the Universe*."[104]

Ficino seems not to have owned a manuscript of Apuleius' literary works, but he had some acquaintance with them, for he quotes both the *Apology* and the *Metamorphoses* in his commentary on Plato's *Symposium* (*Commentarium in Convivium, de Amore*, ca. 1469).[105] In each case he has chosen the passage for its Platonic associations. After noting in *De Amore* 1 that the combination of physical and spiritual beauty

---

completed his translation in 1469, it was not printed until 1484; see the discussion in Hankins, 300–11.

[100] According to Kristeller, Ficino began to study Greek in 1456 ("Marsilio Ficino," 42). For Ficino's manuscripts, see Gentile et al., *Marsilio Ficino*.

[101] For a description, see Klibansky and Regen, *Die Handschriften*, 89. See also Gentile et al., *Marsilio Ficino*, 7–8. Ficino's dated subscription appears on fol. 172r.

[102] For descriptions, see Klibansky and Regen, *Die Handschriften*, 77–78; and in more detail, Gentile, "In margine all'epistola *De divino furore*," 73–77. See also Gentile et al., *Marsilio Ficino*, 15–17.

[103] "Partim fortuita quadam inventione, partim Platonicorum quorundam Latinorum lectione adiutus." Ficino, *Opera omnia* 1.2:929. The passage appears in the letter accompanying a revision of the work that he sent to Filippo Valori in 1491.

[104] "Finis Apuleii de deo quem de verbo ad verbum ab Aristotele furatus est ex libro eius de mundo." Riccardiana 709, fol. 42v, quoted in Gentile, "In margine," 62. The comment appears in a portion of the manuscript copied by one of Ficino's scribes, as Gentile points out. See also Gentile et al., *Marsilio Ficino*, 15–17.

[105] It is just conceivable that Ficino saw the two works in the first edition (1469).

inspires a more powerful love than either one by itself, he concludes, echoing the *Apology*: "And so we shall demonstrate that we are really from the family of Plato, for it knows nothing except what is festive, joyous, heavenly, divine."[106] In *De Amore* 7 he comments on the power of a younger person to fascinate an older one with his gaze, capping his discussion with a passage from the *Metamorphoses*:

> This, my excellent friends, is the subject of the lament of the Platonist Apuleius. "You yourself," he says, "are the whole cause and source of my present suffering and also my healing and sole salvation. For those eyes of yours, having penetrated by way of my eyes into my inmost heart, are kindling a raging fire in my marrow. Therefore, pity the one who is dying for your sake."[107]

Ficino's attribution of this "lament" is not quite correct. Apuleius is the author, to be sure; but the speaker is the stepmother in one of the embedded tales of the novel, and she is trying, Phaedra fashion, to seduce her young stepson. The important point, however, is Ficino's epithet "the Platonist Apuleius"; for the idea of love's being transmitted into the heart from the eyes is in fact from Plato's *Phaedrus*, as Ficino recognized.[108] Ficino is not just quoting a few apposite lines as if from a commonplace book. Rather, he has used his knowledge of Plato to interpret a passage in the *Metamorphoses*, which he then uses to illustrate his own Platonic argument on the genesis of love.[109]

In the three generations of Florentine humanists from Salutati to Ficino, we can observe an increasing knowledge of Plato and a continuing, but ultimately not uncritical, interest in Apuleius' philosophical works. In Ficino we can also observe a sense of the philosophical element in the *Metamorphoses*. But the humanists were not the only Florentines

---

[106] "Atque ita ex platonica familia revera nos esse testabimur. Ea quippe nihil novit, nisi festum, letum, celeste, supernum." Ficino, *Commentarium in Convivium Platonis, De Amore* 1.4 (p. 21, ed. Laurens). Cf. Apuleius, *Apol.* 64.3: "Ceterum Platonica familia nihil novimus nisi festum et laetum et sollemne et superum et caeleste." The echo was noted by Moreschini, *Apuleio e il Platonismo*, 265–66.

[107] "Hoc illud est, o amici optimi, de quo Platonicus Apuleius conqueritur: Causa, inquit, omnis et origo presentis doloris, et etiam medela ipsa et salus unica mihi tute ipse es. Isti enim tui oculi, per meos oculos ad intima delapsi precordia, acerimum meis medullis commovent incendium. Ergo misere tua causa pereuntis." Ficino, *Commentarium in Convivium* 7.4 (pp. 221–23, ed. Laurens). Cf. Apuleius, *Met.* 10.3.5–6.

[108] The conceit was frequently used in the Greek novels and probably derives from *Phaedrus* 251b. See Zimmerman, *Metamorphoses* 10, 91.

[109] Ficino refers in more general terms to Apuleius' philosophical works in *Platonic Theology* 13.2.33, 16.5.4, and 17.4.4. See index of sources in vol. 6 of the Allen-Hankins edition.

interested in Apuleius' philosophical works. Florence's ruling family, the Medici, also commissioned and owned manuscripts of Apuleius. Over a period of several generations, from 1425 to around 1490, the Medici commissioned three manuscripts of the complete works. Cosimo probably commissioned Laur. 54.12 in 1425, as we saw in the previous section. His son Piero acquired the manuscript around 1450, but within a few years commissioned an Apuleius manuscript of his own: Laur. 54.13.[110] Piero's manuscript, like Cosimo's, is a handsome production. Its text, although "very corrupt," is elegantly written on expensive white parchment.[111] A fine portrait of Apuleius appears in the initial for *De deo Socratis*, the first work in the manuscript (see plate 17).[112] Apuleius is shown in profile, holding his book in one hand. His gray beard and clothing are in the fashion of fifteenth-century Constantinople, and he wears a Byzantine cap.[113] Strange garb, one might think, for Apuleius, so far removed in space and time from the contemporary Byzantine world. But it is less strange than it seems, for the Greeks were thought not to have changed their costume from the time of antiquity, and Renaissance artists often depicted authors and philosophers in Byzantine dress.[114] The costume identified the artist's subject—of any nationality or of any period in the past—as ancient, venerable, and wise.

---

[110] Laur. 54.12 has Piero's ex libris and appears in the 1456 inventory of his manuscripts; see Ames-Lewis, *The Library and Manuscripts of Piero di Cosimo de' Medici,* 279. De la Mare has identified the scribe of 54.13 as Ser Benedetto, who worked for the Medici in the late 1450s and early 1460s ("New Research," 433, 490).

[111] "The whole MS is very corrupt." Butler and Owen, eds., *Apologia,* xxxvi.

[112] The illuminated page is probably the work of the miniaturist Francesco d'Antonio del Chierico, perhaps with the assistance of other artists. I owe this attribution to a personal communication from Dottoressa Angela Dillon Bussi of the Biblioteca Laurenziana. For Francesco d'Antonio and his work for the Medici, see Garzelli, "Le immagini, gli autori, i destinatari," 99–112. For an author portrait in a similar style attributed to Francesco d'Antonio (Florence, Biblioteca Medicea Laurenziana 68.16), see Brown, "Portraits of Julius Caesar," 343–44 and fig. 4c.

[113] I must thank Dr. Elfriede Knauer for her helpful comments on this illumination and for directing me to much of the essential bibliography on Byzantine costume.

[114] For the continuity in Greek costume, see Vespasiano da Bisticci's comments on the garb of the Greek ambassadors at the Council of Union in Florence in 1439: "E' Greci, in anni mille cinquecento o più, non hanno mai mutato abito, quello medesimo abito avevano eglino in quello tempo, ch'eglino avevano avuto nel tempo detto" ("Vita di Eugenio IV," in *Le vite* 1:19). For the use of the costume by Renaissance artists, see Knauer, "Ex oriente vestamenta," 692–97, esp. 694–95 n. 370; Lazzi, "Novità e persistenze"; eadem, "L'immagine dell' autore 'classico,'" 102. Apuleius is also shown in Byzantine dress in Vatican Library, Urb. lat. 199, fol. 2r (see appendix 3). This manuscript from Urbino was written nearly a generation later than Laur. 54.13 (it is dated between 1474 and 1482). It also contains both the philosophical and the literary texts. For other author portraits in Byzantine costume, see Buonocore, ed., *Vedere i classici,* fig. 37 (Eusebius); Alexander, ed., *The Painted Page,* 48 (Livy).

Yet even if the Byzantine costume is an "iconographical topos,"[115] it is nonetheless appropriate for the Apuleius shown in this Florentine manuscript. To be sure, the garb identifies him as "an ancient author," but it also assimilates him to the contemporary Byzantine scholars who brought Greek and Plato to Florence in the fifteenth century, reminding the reader that Apuleius, like them, is an intermediary between ancient Platonism and the "modern" world.

Many years after the completion of Laur. 54.13, perhaps around 1490, Lorenzo de' Medici ("the Magnificent") commissioned a still more elaborate manuscript: Laur. 84.24. This manuscript, described in Bandini's eighteenth-century catalog as "of remarkable beauty," is splendidly decorated in gold and lapis by the famous illuminator Attavante.[116] Like the other Medici manuscripts, Laur. 84.24 contains both the *Metamorphoses* and the philosophical works, but it also includes two of Apuleius' usual companions in the Latin Platonic library, Calcidius and the *Liber Alcidi*, as well as two Platonizing commentaries on Boethius by Thomas Aquinas.[117] Apuleius' works are surrounded by their Platonic companions, for the order in the manuscript is Calcidius, Apuleius (*De deo Socratis, Asclepius, De Platone, De mundo, Metamorphoses*), *Liber Alcidi*, Aquinas on Boethius. The emphasis, however, is on Calcidius, as Attavante's title page indicates (see plate 18). On this page, a verso facing the first page of Calcidius, the artist has arrayed the titles of the works in an elegant design: a central tondo encircled by seven smaller ones. Calcidius has pride of place in the central tondo and in the smaller one directly above it, while Apuleius and the other authors appear in the remaining satellites. The design neatly conveys two essential points about the nature of the manuscript: the centrality of Calcidius and the fact that the collection was conceived as a unity each of whose parts contributes to the design of the whole. The design of the whole, of course, is Platonic, and probably owes much, as scholars have argued, to the influence of Ficino, even though by the time of the manuscript his own studies had extended far beyond the concerns of the Latin Platonists.[118]

---

[115] The phrase is Lazzi's: "L'abbigliamento 'alla grecanica' diviene quindi un topos iconigrafico" ("L'immagine dell' autore 'classico,'" 102).

[116] "Mirae pulchritudinis," Bandini, *Catalogus* 3:255. For descriptions of the manuscript, see Klibansky and Regen, *Die Handschriften*, 72–73, and Gentile et al., *Marsilio Ficino*, 7–8. For Attavante, see Garzelli, "Le immagini, gli autori, i destinatari," 219–45.

[117] According to Robertson, the text of the *Metamorphoses* in Laur. 84.24 was copied from Santa Croce 24 sin 11 ("The Manuscripts," 38). For the Platonic character of the Aquinas texts, cf. Garin (*Studi sul Platonismo medievale*, 99 n. 2): "Non a caso sono scelti gli stessi commenti di San Tommaso. Nelle *quaestiones super librum Boetii de Trinitate* si trovano riferimenti a Macrobio e alle dottrine dei Platonici, molto simili a testi del *Liber Alcidi*."

[118] See Gentile et al., *Marsilio Ficino*, 7–8.

The Latin Platonic library was surprisingly durable throughout the fifteenth century, existing as a complement both to the new Greek studies and to the work of Renaissance Neoplatonists. But the core collection was by no means monolithic, and works could be included or omitted depending on a scholar's purposes and interests. Apuleius has a very large place in the Platonist collection in Laur. 84.24, and a much smaller one in the roughly contemporary list of writers and works that Ficino compiled in a letter of around 1489.[119] This list, which one could call not a library but a survey of Platonism, covers a large array of philosophical writers from late antiquity to Ficino's own time, including only what Ficino deems the most important Platonic works of each. In such an overview, *De deo Socratis* is the only work of Apuleius that merits a mention.

The last authors on Ficino's list of important Platonists are two important fifteenth-century humanist churchmen: Cardinals Basil Bessarion and Nicholas of Cusa.[120] Both had connections with Florentine Platonism, and Bessarion had been in correspondence with Ficino in the 1460s.[121] Both had also been associated (in different ways) with the first edition of Apuleius in 1469. We shall turn presently to the *princeps* and its origin as a kind of Platonist manifesto, but first we must linger a bit longer in Medici Florence in order to consider an interesting event of the previous generation: the discovery that the *Onos* (*The Ass*) of Pseudo-Lucian has the same plot as the *Metamorphoses*.

Poggio's Discovery

What should have been the greatest advance in reading the *Metamorphoses* in the first half of the fifteenth century was made by a humanist who had little interest in the novel and perhaps never actually read it: Poggio Bracciolini. Poggio (1380–1459) is justly renowned as a scribe and manuscript hunter, as an important figure in the papal curia in the early quattrocento, as a writer (of dialogues, invectives, and jests as well

---

[119] The letter, entitled "Responsio petenti Platonicam instructionem et librorum numerum," is edited by Klibansky, *Continuity*, 42–47. The list of Latin Platonists (pp. 46–47) includes Dionysius the Areopagite, "much of Augustine" (*Augustini multa*), Boethius' *Consolatio*, Apuleius' *De deo Socratis* (which Ficino calls *De daemonibus*), Calcidius on the *Timaeus*, and Macrobius on the *Somnium Scipionis*. It continues with medieval thinkers, including Avicenna and Duns Scotus, and concludes with Ficino's contemporaries, Bessarion and Nicholas of Cusa. For discussion, see Klibansky, p. 36.

[120] "Extat insuper Defensio Platonis a Bessarione cardinali Niceno facta; quaedam speculationes Nicolai Cusii cardinalis." Ficino in Klibansky, *Continuity*, 47.

[121] For an exchange of letters in 1469 between Bessarion and Ficino, see Ficino, *Lettere* 1 (ed. Gentile), letters 11 and 12 (also in Ficino, *Opera omnia* 1:616–17).

as of a *History of Florence*), and finally as a chancellor of Florence.¹²² He is not known, however, as a student of Apuleius. He mentions Apuleius' name only a few times in his works.¹²³ A reminiscence of the *Florida* has been detected in a speech he made at the Council of Constance in 1417, but the echo is faint and isolated.¹²⁴ A single cryptic (and perhaps erroneous) reference to Apuleius appears in the inventory of his library made after his death.¹²⁵

But if Poggio took little interest in Apuleius, he was very interested in Apuleius' Greek contemporary Lucian, whose writings were in tune with his own satirical nature. He cited, quoted, and paraphrased Lucian in several of his works.¹²⁶ He also translated him. At some time before 1444 he translated Lucian's dialogue *Zeus Catechized,* calling it *The Cynic, or On Fate.*¹²⁷ Around 1450 he translated another work that he believed to be by Lucian, *Onos (The Ass),* and dedicated it to Cosimo de' Medici.¹²⁸ Here is what he says in his preface to Cosimo:

> Poggio with best wishes to the distinguished Cosimo de' Medici. Long ago when I had read that book of Apuleius entitled *De asino*

---

¹²² The definitive biography is by Walser, *Poggius Florentinus*. See also de la Mare, *Handwriting*, 1.1: 62–84; Ullman, *Origin and Development,* 21–58; Bigi and Petrucci, "Poggio Bracciolini." Poggio's letters to Niccolò Niccoli are translated by Gordan, *Two Renaissance Book Hunters*.

¹²³ I know of only two places where Poggio mentions Apuleius: *Ep* 5.23 and his translation of Lucian (see below). But since most of Poggio's works are not indexed, there may be additional references.

¹²⁴ "Deponite opes, fastum, superbiam, avariciam, libidines et ceteras animi pestes" ([*Oratio ad patres reverendissimos,*] in Fubini, "Il 'Teatro del Mondo,'" 121); cf. *Florida* 22.3–4: "Adversum iracundiam et invidiam atque avaritiam atque libidinem ceteraque animi humani monstra et flagitia philosophus iste Hercules fuit: eas omnes pestes mentibus exegit." I owe this reference to David Marsh.

¹²⁵ Item 14 in the inventory reads "tusculane lapuleius in;° [*sic*] volumine in pergameno copertum corio viridi" (Walser, *Poggius,* 419). If it is not in error, the reference must be to Cicero's *Tusculans* and some work of "L[ucius]" Apuleius. The *Tusculans* appear in no extant manuscript of Apuleius' literary works, but they are sometimes found with the philosophical works (e.g., in Cambridge Fitzwilliam Museum, McLean 169; Escorial, Real Biblioteca O.III.16; British Library, Egerton 2516; Saint-Omer, Bibliothèque Municipale 652). See Klibansky and Regen, *Die Handschriften,* ad loc. None of these manuscripts matches the description in Poggio's inventory.

¹²⁶ See Marsh, *Lucian and the Latins,* 37–40, with earlier references. See also Fubini, "Il 'Teatro del Mondo,'" 20–25; Mattioli, *Luciano e l'umanesimo,* 127–35.

¹²⁷ *Cinicus sive De fato.* The work has been edited by Marsh ("Poggio and Alberti"), who also discusses its date (189–90). It is preserved in a single manuscript (Vat. lat. 3082), which also contains Apuleius' *Apology* and several of his philosophical works; for a description, see Klibansky and Regen, *Die Handschriften,* 117. A translation of Lucian's *Vera historia* by Lilius Tifernas in Vat. lat. 1552 has been wrongly attributed to Poggio; see Marsh, *Lucian and the Latins,* 40, with further bibliography.

¹²⁸ See Marsh, *Lucian and the Latins,* 37–38; idem, "Alberti and Apuleius," 406–7; Mattioli, *Luciano e l'umanesimo,* 127–30. For the date, see Walser, *Poggius Florentinus,*

aureo, I supposed that either what he had written had happened to him in person or that it had come into existence as his invention and fabrication; and the words of St. Augustine confirmed me in this opinion. In the eighteenth book of the *City of God* when he was talking about the transformations of men into various forms, he said: "Thus, Apuleius either declared or pretended it happened to him in the books which he entitled The Golden Ass—that after taking a magical substance he became an ass, but with his mind remaining human." And so I remained of this opinion, that the whole thing, whether true or fictitious, should be attributed to Apuleius. But recently in a certain volume of the works of Lucian—a man of keen intellect and many-sided talent—I discovered among the rest a little book entitled "The Ass of Lucian." Eager to know what the book contained, I read that what Apuleius declares happened to him also befell the other, so that there is no doubt that this story was invented by Lucian or some other Greek. For the sake of practice I took upon myself the task of turning it into Latin—not so that in translating this work I might do what is forbidden by the old proverb and plead a case already decided, but to show that this old comedy reworked by Apuleius must not at all be taken for the truth, but rather considered to have been introduced by Lucian with the desire of mocking the magic arts, in accordance with his habit of making fun not only of men but even of the gods. Moreover, since I knew that those who suffer painful episodes of gout are generally pleased by jests in an easing of their pain, and since nature has made you humorous and responsive to jests, I have sent you this little story full of asinine enjoyment and playfulness, in which I did not venture to change the sense or take away anything, lest I seem to wish to appear more skillful than Apuleius, who transformed it into his own work. Therefore, you will read this little work for relaxation when you are at leisure at home and free from cares of state. Farewell.[129]

---

231 n. 2. The translation is most conveniently available in the 1964 facsimile of the 1538 edition, *Opera omnia* 1:138–55.

[129] "Poggius plurimam salutem dicit Cosmo de Medicis viro insigni. Cum eum quondam qui de asino aureo inscribitur Appulei librum legissem, extimabam, aut sibi ipsi quod scripserat accidisse, aut extitisse inventum, et comentum suum, qua in opinione me confirmarunt beati Augustini verba, qui in decimo octavo de civitate Dei libro, cum de transmutationibus hominum in varias formas loqueretur inquit: 'Sicut Apuleius in libris quos asini aurei titulo inscripsit sibi ipsi accidisse, ut accepto veneno humano permanente animo asinus fieret, aut indicavit, aut finxit' [*Civ.* 18.18]. Itaque in ea sententia permanebam, hanc totam vel veram vel fictam rem Apuleio esse tribuendam. At vero nuper cum in quodam volumine operum Luciani [Luciam, *ms.*] (qui varii acerrimique ingenii vir fuit) reperissem inter cetera libellum, cuius titulus erat Luciani asinus, noscendi quid is liber contineret cupidus, legi quod Apuleius sibi evenisse affirmat, et illi contigisse, ut haud

Poggio says that he has read the *Golden Ass*, and perhaps he has; but even the best humanists' claims about their reading matter are not always reliable, as we saw in the case of Coluccio Salutati and the *Apology*. At any event, Poggio says nothing in his preface to demonstrate much familiarity with the novel, presenting only what is by now the very old chestnut from Augustine, which conveniently reveals enough of Apuleius' plot to make its similarity to the Greek story obvious.[130] He certainly could have read the *Golden Ass* in either Rome or Florence, for there were plenty of manuscripts in both cities by the 1450s.[131] If so, it is a little surprising that he did not consult it as he translated the *Onos*. Since Poggio's Greek was not strong, and he is known to have relied on Latin works as aids to translation, we might have expected him to cannibalize Apuleius' distinctive Latin to convey the very similar events of the *Onos*.[132] But he does not: none of Apuleius' vivid phrasing or vocabulary has crept into his flat and simple translation, even in places where using it would have been almost irresistible to anyone (especially to an indifferent student of Greek) with a good knowledge of the *Golden Ass* and a handy manuscript. Poggio's renditions of Lucius' arrival in Thessaly, his meeting with his mother's old friend, his amorous encounters with the maid, his witnessing of the witch's transformation, and his own metamorphosis into an ass—all are devoid of the Apuleian touch.[133]

---

dubium sit ab Luciano aut alio ex Graecis eam fabulam adinventam. Ego sane exercitii gratia laborem michi desunsi ut eum facerem latinum, non ut id quod veteri verbo prohibetur, acta agerem in hoc opusculo traducendo, sed ut ostenderem hanc veterem et ab Apuleio [Apuleo, *ms.*] velut inovatam comediam nequaquam esse pro vero accipiendam, sed extimandam potius ab Luciano introductam studio artes eludendi magicas, prout suus mos est, non tantum homines, sed etiam deos irridendi. Cum autem scirem eos quos aliquando podagra dolore afficit, solere in doloris remissione delectari iocis, te autem facetum fecerit natura et ad iocos prontum, misi ad te hanc fabellam asinine iocunditatis et lascivie plenam, in qua re non sum ausus sententias inmutare, aut aliquid demere, ne videar velle videri prudentior Apuleo, qui eadem in suum opus convertit. Leges igitur hoc opusculum laxandi animi gratia cum eris otiosus domi, et vacuus ab reipublicae curis. Vale." Florence, Biblioteca Riccardiana, ms. 137, fol. 1r–v. The most easily available edition of Poggio's works prints the letter with some alterations, the most important of which is the substitution of the name Lucius for Lucianus throughout: Bracciolini, *Opera omnia* (Basel, 1538), 1:138.

[130] Poggio's reference to Apuleius in *Ep.* 5.23 mentions only the basic plot of the novel. Writing to Giovanni Tortelli in 1454, he says: "Unum tamen dicam, nimiam sanctissimo domino nostro in nonnullos indulgentiam multos preter Apuleium in asinos non aureos sed stuppeos reddidisse." Bracciolini, *Lettere* 3:215.

[131] See appendix 3.

[132] For Poggio's knowledge of Greek, see Walser, *Poggius Florentinus*, 229–31. For his use of Latin translations, see Marsh, *Lucian and the Latins*, 39. For his handling of the Greek of the *Onos*, see Mattioli, *Luciano e l'umanesimo*, 129–30.

[133] Two examples will suffice, both from the witch's transformation. First, the maid's announcement. Poggio: "Paucis diebus post nunciat mihi Palestra patronam invenisse

But Poggio did not have to know (or care) much about the *Golden Ass* to recognize its similarities with the *Onos* and to understand the implications of his discovery: that the story was not original with Apuleius and consequently that it had to be fictional, or, as he says, that "it must not at all be taken for the truth." The modern reader is inclined to go further, to point out that this work that is neither original nor "true" cannot be autobiographical, that the "I" of the novel is not Apuleius; in short, that Apuleius is not Lucius. But Poggio did not spell it out in these terms, perhaps because he considered it obvious, or perhaps because he was primarily interested in the question of originality.

Poggio's discovery should have made the humanists completely rethink their autobiographical interpretation, but it did nothing of the sort. His successors dutifully cited his preface—and went on reading the story of Lucius as before, as the real or fictitious adventures of Apuleius himself. Part of the difficulty was their deeply rooted and natural assumption that a first-person narrator must be talking about himself, an assumption, as we have seen in the case of Apuleius, that goes back at least to Augustine. This assumption had led fourteenth-century humanists to award Apuleius the praenomen of his hero, calling him Lucius Apuleius. The name set the stage for confusion; for when Poggio pointed out the existence of the Greek story, the humanists were so bemused both by the fact that its hero is also a Lucius (Loukios) and by the identification of its author as Lucian (or, in Latin, Lucianus) that they gave little thought to the implications of his discovery for the interpretation of the *Golden Ass*. There were too many Luciuses (both authors and heroes) to keep them all straight. The names were especially confusing to printers of Poggio's work. Most printed editions of his preface call the author of the *Onos* "Lucius" rather than "Lucianus," and the printer of the German translation of Poggio's Latin takes both the hero and the author of the *Onos* to be Lucius Apuleius.[134]

But confusion was not limited to printers. Editors of Apuleius also presented muddled accounts of the *Onos* and its author. In his preface

---

conversuram, ut ad suum amatorem adiret" (*Opera omnia*, 142). Apuleius: "Quadam die percita Photis ac satis trepida me accurrit indicatque dominam suam . . . nocte proxima in avem sese plumaturam atque ad suum cupitum sic devolaturam" (*Met.* 3.21.1). Second, the maid takes Lucius to spy on her mistress. Poggio: "Me apprehensum manu ad ostium domus ducit in qua illi dormiebant, meque iubet per rimulam ostii introspicientem quae fierent animadvertere. Video patronam deposita veste nudam prodire" (142). Apuleius: "Me perducit ipsa perque rimam ostiorum quampiam iubet arbitrari, quae sic gesta sunt. Iam primum omnibus laciniis se devestit Pamphile" (*Met.* 3.21.3–4).

[134] The first edition of Poggio's translation (Augsburg, ca. 1477) correctly reads "Lucianus," but the editions of Poggio's works printed in 1513 and 1538 both read "Lucius." For the German translation of Poggio's translation (Augsburg, ca. 1478), see chapter 7.

to the first edition (1469), Giovanni Andrea Bussi sees the *Onos* as an autobiographical fiction, taking the first-person narrator for Lucian himself. He tells us: "Among other works, this Lucian wrote the *Golden Ass* in jest, and pretended that he had been changed into it."[135] Bussi does not seem to notice that the name of the hero of the *Onos* (Lucius) is not the same as that of its purported author (Lucianus). But a generation later the great Apuleian commentator Filippo Beroaldo did notice, and in the preface of his commentary (1500) he solved the problem in the by now familiar way, by awarding the author the praenomen (and also the toponym) of his hero. He calls him "Lucius Lucianus Patrensis" and treats him as a serious devotee of magic:[136] "Not a few have put their trust in the teaching of magic as if it were the most powerful of all things. Among these (to pass over the rest), Lucius Lucianus of Patrae, an expert in divination and an elegant and biting sophist, has written that he sought Thessaly, on fire with a longing to learn about magic."[137]

Apuleius in Print

Poggio's discovery, interesting and potentially important as it was, had little immediate impact. The most important event in Apuleius' reception in the second half of the fifteenth century was the result not of literary considerations or of interest in the *Golden Ass* but of philosophical controversy. The humanist enthusiasm for Plato had been unpopular in some quarters from the time of Coluccio Salutati in the first years of the century: while the humanists yearned to recover and understand Platonic philosophy, conservative clerics saw Plato as epitomizing all the evils they considered inherent in the study of pagan authors.[138] The dispute intensified as the century wore on, until by the late 1450s it had developed into a full-fledged and angry controversy. The study of Platonism became a lightning rod for disagreements over theology, morality, and politics. It pitted the new humanism against the old scholasticism

---

[135] "Hic Lucianus asinum, inter cetera, aureum lusit seque in eum finxit esse commutatum." Bussi, *Prefatio* to Apuleius, in Miglio, ed., *Prefazioni*, 13. Hereafter all references to Bussi's prefaces are to this edition.

[136] Beroaldo, *Commentarii*, fol. A1v. (The hero of the *Onos* is from Patrae; *Onos* 55 [in Pseudo-Lucian, *Lucius, or The Ass*].)

[137] "Ceterum non parum multi credulitatem suam addixerunt magicae doctrinae, perinde ac rerum cunctarum potentissimae. Inter quos, ut ceteros preteream, Lucius Lucianus patrensis divinationis gnarus nec minus elegans sophista quam mordax scripsit se petiisse Thessaliam desiderio noscendae magiae flagrans." Beroaldo, *Commentarii*, fol. A1v.

[138] See Hankins, *Plato in the Italian Renaissance* 1:29–40.

and the Greek church against the Roman, but above all it pitted Plato against Aristotle as the true servant of Christian theology.[139] Apuleius benefited mightily from the debate, which thrust him into the limelight as one of the first classical authors to appear in print, and only the second to be printed in Italy.[140] On 28 February 1469 the editio princeps of his works was published in Rome by Sweynheym and Pannartz, the earliest printers operating on Italian soil.[141]

By this time the controversy over Plato had been simmering for many years. The particular debate that catapulted Apuleius into print began in 1458 when George of Trebizond, a Greek émigré and prominent anti-Platonist, circulated an attack on Plato entitled *A Comparison of the Philosophers Aristotle and Plato*.[142] The most important Platonist to respond to it was another Greek émigré, Cardinal Basil Bessarion (1408?–1472).[143] Bessarion was a convert from the Greek church who rose to such prominence in Italy that he was nearly elected pope on two separate occasions. He was also a major intellectual figure in Rome. He amassed the largest library of Greek manuscripts in Italy, and he

---

[139] For detailed accounts, see ibid. 1:163–263 and Monfasani, *George of Trebizond*, 201–29. Hankins warns against seeing the controversy in simplistic terms: "It is quite impossible to divide the partisans of Aristotle and Plato neatly into ideological or ecclesiological camps, as has sometimes been done in the older literature; in reality, the significance of the contest changed from one year to the next, and from one protagonist to another" (*Plato* 1:216). He goes on to note, however, that the controversy had "a single predominating theme"—the question "whether Platonic philosophy could indeed take the place of Aristotelianism as the philosophical handmaid of Christian theology" (*Plato* 1:216–17). Hankins dates the origin of the Plato-Aristotle controversy to the Council of Union in Florence in 1439 and the criticisms of Aristotle by Gemistus Pletho (*Plato* 1:205). The dispute continued in the Greek East and among the Greek émigré community in Italy and finally erupted into Latin in the work of George of Trebizond (see below).

[140] Cicero's *De officiis* was printed in Cologne in 1465–66 (GKW 2272), and Terence in Strassburg perhaps as early as 1469 (Cop. 5736); see Hirsch, *Printing, Selling and Reading*, 138. In Italy only Cicero seems to have been printed before Apuleius: Sweynheym and Pannartz printed *De oratore* in 1465 and 1468 (GKW 6742 and 6744), *Epistolae ad familiares* in 1467 (GW 6799), *Brutus* and *Orator* in January 1469 (GKW 6754), and *De officiis*, *Paradoxa*, and *De amicitia* in January 1469 (GKW 6924). See Feld, "Sweynheym and Pannartz," 286.

[141] GW 2301. For Sweynheym and Pannartz, see Scholderer, "Printers and Readers in Italy," 202–4; idem, "The Petition of Sweynheym and Pannartz to Sixtus IV." For the edition of Apuleius, see Miglio, in Bussi, *Prefazioni*, xxxvii–liii; Feld, "Sweynheym and Pannartz," esp. 299–301.

[142] *Comparatio philosophorum Aristotelis et Platonis*. See Monfasani, *George of Trebizond*, 156–66; Hankins, *Plato in the Italian Renaissance* 1:236–45.

[143] See Labowsky, "Bessarione"; Zorzi, "Cenni sulla vita e sulla figura di Bessarione." For a discussion of Bessarion's date of birth, see Monfasani, "Platina, Capranica, and Perotti," 112–24.

headed a circle frequented by many distinguished clerics and humanists.[144] Bessarion began to work on his rebuttal almost immediately after George's attack. In 1459 he completed a draft in Greek, but he continued to labor over his work for a decade. By early 1469 he had completed the Latin version of his refutation, *In calumniatorem Platonis* (Against the False Accuser of Plato), more commonly called *Defensio Platonis*. It was published by Sweynheym and Pannartz in August 1469.[145] Announcing and advertising the publication of Bessarion's work was one of the chief purposes of the editio princeps of Apuleius, which was, as Hankins puts it, "part of a concerted press campaign to promote the reputation and authority of Plato, the first such campaign in the history of printing."[146] Bessarion's copy of the editio princeps (richly illuminated and on vellum like a luxury manuscript) is preserved in the Biblioteca Marciana in Venice.[147]

No one knows who encouraged the German printers Sweynheym and Pannartz to make their way to Rome in 1465 and to set up their press in nearby Subiaco. But Bessarion is an obvious candidate.[148] He was a shrewd practical politician as well as a philosophically inclined cleric, and he had been quick to see and exploit the powers of the new technology. Another candidate, almost equally plausible, is Bessarion's fellow cardinal and longtime ally in the promotion of Platonism, Nicolas of Cusa (Nicolaus Cusanus, 1401–64), who was based in Rome from 1458 until 1464.[149] Cusanus, a German, was well acquainted with printing

---

[144] For Bessarion's library, see Labowsky, *Bessarion's Library*. Bessarion also owned two Apuleius manuscripts: Venice Marciana lat. 467 (coll. 1557), which contains the philosophical works and the *Asclepius* with his annotations, and Marc. lat. 469 (coll. 1856), which contains Calcidius, Apuleius' *Apology*, Cicero's *De natura deorum*, and Macrobius' *Saturnalia*. For Marc. lat. 467, see Klibansky and Regen, *Die Handschriften*, 122; Bianca, *Da Bisanzio a Roma*, 70–71. For Marc. lat. 469, see Fiaccadori et al., eds., *Bessarione e l'umanesimo*, 498–99; and Bianca, 103–4 (who notes that Bessarion acquired it around the time of the publication of Apuleius). For Bessarion's sodality and its activities, see Bianca, "Roma e l'accademia bessarionea."

[145] For the date, see Monfasani, *George of Trebizond*, 219.

[146] Hankins, *Plato in the Italian Renaissance* 1:214.

[147] Venice, Bibl. Marciana, membran. 15bis. See Labowsky, *Bessarion's Library*, 481. The illuminated first page of the *Metamorphoses* with Bessarion's arms is illustrated by Zorzi, "Stampatori tedeschi a Venezia," 121; see also Fiaccadori et al., eds., *Bessarione e l'umanesimo*, 495–96. Another copy of the first edition with Bessarion's arms (this time on the first page of the preface), formerly in the collection of Beriah Botfield, was sold by H. P. Kraus to a private collector in the 1990s. It is described and illustrated in color in Kraus' catalog, *The Greek Book*, frontispiece, pp. 1–2.

[148] See Zorzi, "Stampatori tedeschi a Venezia," 115; idem, "Cenni," 15.

[149] See Balsamo, "I primordi della tipografia," 233–36. See also Feld, "Sweynheym and Pannartz," 303; Zorzi, "Cenni," 6: "È probabile che i due [stampatori] siano giunti in Italia chiamati da alti personaggi della Chiesa romana: si pensa a Niccolò da Cusa o al Bessarione." For Cusanus and Bessarion, see Lotti, "Cultura filosofica di Bessarione," 80–82.

from an early period, and he is known to have expressed the hope that the technology would be brought to Rome.[150] Since Sweynheym and Pannartz arrived only after the death of Cusanus, the more lasting influence was undoubtedly Bessarion's; but Cusanus would surely have favored the Platonist program adopted by the two printers in selecting works for publication, and no doubt he would have been as pleased as Bessarion to have them print Bessarion's *Defensio Platonis*.[151]

The printers' principal editor, Giovanni Andrea Bussi (1417–75), was the client of both Cusanus and Bessarion and something of a Platonist in his own right.[152] He was a member of Bessarion's circle. He had also been Cusanus' secretary in Rome from 1458 to 1464 and had joined the cardinal in reading and emending philosophical texts, including Cusanus' important ninth-century manuscript of Apuleius' philosophical works, now Brussels, Bibliothèque Royale Albert Ier 10054–56.[153]

Bussi dedicated most of his editions to Pope Paul II, and Apuleius is no exception. But Bussi's real audience is much wider than a single addressee. With the advent of printing, a dedication or preface was no longer essentially a private matter but rather a form of large-scale communication: a potential audience was now to be measured no longer in tens or twenties but in hundreds.[154] Bussi uses his preface to address the humanist community at large—not only to introduce Apuleius but also to advertise Bessarion's *Defensio Platonis* and to praise both Bessarion and Cusanus. Contrary to custom, his opening words mention neither his addressee (the pope) nor the author of the work he has edited (Apuleius).

---

[150] Cusanus' enthusiasm for printing is reported by Giovanni Andrea Bussi in his preface to the *Epistolae* of Saint Jerome printed by Sweynheym and Pannartz in 1468: "Eiusmodi est enim impressorum nostrorum et characteres effingentium artificium ut vix inter hominum inventa, non modo nova sed ne vetera quidem, quicquam excellentioris inventi possit referri. Digne honoranda saeculisque omnibus magnifacienda profecto Germania est, utilitatum inventrix maximarum. Hoc est quod semper gloriosa illa et caelo digna anima Nicolai Cusensis, cardinalis Sancti Petri ad Vincula, peroptabat, ut haec sancta ars, quae oriri tunc videbatur in Germania, Romam deduceretur." Bussi, *Prefazioni*, 4.

[151] For the agenda behind the editions, see Feld, "Sweynheym and Pannartz"; Miglio, in Bussi, *Prefazioni*, xxv, xlv–xlvi; Zorzi, "Cenni," 15.

[152] For Bussi, see Miglio, in Bussi, *Prefazioni*, xvii–xxix; Miglio, "Giovanni Andrea Bussi."

[153] Arfé has recently identified Bussi's hand along with that of Cusanus throughout the manuscript; see "The Annotations of Nicolaus Cusanus." For descriptions of the manuscript, see ibid., 29–30; Klibansky and Regen, *Die Handschriften*, 60–62. Cusanus also owned (although he did not annotate) another early manuscript of Apuleius' philosophical works now in Brussels: Bibliothèque Royale Albert Ier 3920-3923 (eleventh century). See ibid., 59–60; Arfé, 31 n. 10. For Bussi's collaborations with Cusanus and his work on Platonist manuscripts, see Miglio, in Bussi, *Prefazioni*, xxiv and xxxiii nn. 32–33; Arfé, 50 n. 77; Bianca, "La biblioteca romana di Niccolò Cusano."

[154] For the printed dedication as "an open letter," see Miglio, in Bussi, *Prefazioni*, xvii.

Instead, he immediately calls our attention to the august figure of Bessarion: "Bessarion, cardinal bishop of Sabina of the holy Roman church and patriarch of Constantinople, known everywhere in the world by the venerable appellation 'the Nicaean.'"[155] It is by Bessarion and his work, Bussi continues, that he has been inspired to produce an edition of Apuleius:

> As I read through the writings of the most illustrious Bessarion in recent months—both the rest and especially those in defense of Plato—I thought it would be an excellent idea if I were to make available to Latin readers a few Platonists particularly outstanding in authority and learning who are unknown to many of the Latins because of the scarcity of books and also unknown to many because of the archaism, or rather the unbelievable elegance of their language. Digging them out as if from bookworms rather than from bookcases, I would labor to correct them with my usual effort, not to say skill, and with as much care as I could.[156]

The edition Bussi describes is in the tradition of the familiar Latin Platonic library. Like several of the manuscripts made by or for the Florentine Platonists, it contains Apuleius' literary works along with the philosophical texts (including the pseudo-Apuleian *Asclepius*). Like them, it also includes a Platonic work not by Apuleius. But while the Florentine manuscripts combine Apuleius with Calcidius or the *Liber Alcidi*, Bussi has selected a different work, complimenting both Bessarion and Cusanus by including a recent translation of a Platonic handbook by a second-century Platonist named Alcinous.[157] The work's translator, Pietro Balbi (1399–1479), was a client of Bessarion's in the 1450s and 1460s; he probably used a Greek manuscript in Bessarion's library for his translation.[158] But the work is even more closely connected with Cusanus, for he was its dedicatee, as Bussi proudly points out, adding a long and

---

[155] "Bessarion sanctae Romanae Ecclesiae episcopus cardinalis Sabinensis et Constantinopolitanus patriarcha, Nicaeni veneranda nuncupatione terrarum ubique celeberrimus." Bussi, *Prefazioni*, 11.

[156] "Equidem scripta a clarissimo Bessarione, tum cetera, tum pro Platone maxime, superioribus mensibus perlegens, putavi optimo consilio factum iri, si Platonicos nonnullos, eosque gravitate et doctrina in primis excellentes, Latinorum multis propter librorum raritatem, multis item propter linguae vetustatem, immo vero incredibilem elegantiam, ignotos, veluti ex tineis, potius quam scriniis erutos, ea qua consuevi opera, ne dicam sollertia, nostris hominibus traderem perlegendos, quantulacunque valerem, in tollendis mendis laborans diligentia." Bussi, *Prefazion*, 12.

[157] *Disciplinarum Platonis epitome*. For this work, see Alcinous, *The Handbook of Platonism*. As the editor Dillon notes (p. xli), Alcinous' epitome is the first Greek work to appear in print (albeit in Latin translation).

[158] See Pratesi, "Pietro Balbi." For Balbi's translation, see Saffrey, "Pietro Balbi," esp. 426–28. Bessarion owned at least three manuscripts of Alcinous, two of which are still

affectionate eulogy of Cusanus that neatly balances his opening tribute to Bessarion.[159]

Bussi's preface, heavily larded with both praise of Plato and his devotees and castigation of modern anti-Platonists, concludes with a polemical grand finale: when Plato is defended by such pillars of Christianity and learning as Bessarion and Cusanus, Bussi argues, surely no one should be foolish or wicked enough to attack him.[160] Plato's detractors, like men trying to darken the sun by throwing dust into the air, have been blinded by their own folly, but Bussi piously hopes to help them see the light:

> Nevertheless, because we do not desire triumph over the wretched (since we have been illuminated both by the combined rays of Christianity and Plato and by human feeling) and because we pity those blind men, let us give the hand of kindness to the errant and stupid and to those who perceive and understand nothing at all. Let us conduct them to all the springs of penitence and good conscience, so that bathing in the water of correction and anointing their inflamed eyes, by the relief of their pain they may learn better ways at last and bemoan their error.[161]

Both Bussi's preface with its inflammatory conclusion and Bessarion's *Defensio Platonis* stirred up further controversy. Before the end of the year, George of Trebizond had sent Bessarion a letter replying to the *Defensio*, his son Andreas had written an angry response to both Bussi and Bessarion (which he addressed to Pope Paul II and predictably called *Platonis Accusatio*), and Bussi had replied to Andreas in the preface of his edition of Strabo.[162] The dispute ended only with the deaths of both Bessarion and George of Trebizond in 1472.[163]

---

to be found in the Biblioteca Marciana in Venice: Mg. 513 (770) and Mg. 525 (775). See Labowsky, *Bessarion's Library*, index (529).

[159] Bussi, *Prefazioni*, 17. Given their shared association with both Bessarion and Cusanus, Bussi and Balbi were undoubtedly acquainted. They both appear as interlocutors in Cusanus' dialogue *Directio speculantis seu de non aliud* (1462); see Miglio, in Bussi, *Prefazioni*, xxxiii n. 32.

[160] Bussi, *Prefazioni,* 18–19.

[161] "Nos tamen non de miseris triumphum optantes, christianisque et Platonis simul radiis et humanitate illustrati, caecos istos miserati, demus errantibus et stupidis et nihil cernentibus nihil intelligentibus omnino veniae manum; ad fontesque omnes poenitentiae conscientiaeque deducamus, ut loti retractationis aqua lippientesque oculos inuncti, doloris medicamento aliquando discant meliora ingemiscantque errasse." Ibid., 19.

[162] George's letter has been edited by Monfasani: *Collectanea Trapezuntiana*, 161–88. The preface and some excerpts of Andreas' *Accusatio* were published by Zaccaria, *Iter litterarium per Italiam*, 126–34. See also Monfasani, *George of Trebizond*, 216–18. For Bussi's response, see his *Praefatio* to Strabo, (*Prefazioni*, 34–40).

[163] Hankins, *Plato in the Italian Renaissance* 1:216.

The first edition of Apuleius came into existence as a salvo in the Platonist controversy, but it was also of monumental importance for the reception of Apuleius himself, for it both provided an intelligible introduction to his works and made them available to more readers than at any time in their history. The guidance that Bussi provides to his readers is of great interest. Before the editio princeps, Apuleius' works had been the subject of annotations, allegories, literary imitations, and artistic interpretations, but Bussi presents the first direct expository treatment since Augustine's comments in the *City of God*, over a thousand years earlier. Aware that many readers will be seeing Apuleius for the first time, Bussi uses his preface to provide landmarks, orienting and encouraging them, as he says, like travelers on a previously untried road.[164] Bussi's road map is deliberately modest, for he makes no pretense of giving a full interpretation of his author; but it is fairly complete nonetheless, listing Apuleius' works in the order of their appearance in the edition and giving a brief account of the nature and principal qualities of each. He begins with the literary works: first the *Metamorphoses*, followed by the *Florida* and *Apology*. Then the philosophical works: *De deo Socratis*, *De Platone*, *De Mundo*, and *Asclepius*, followed by Alcinous. This ordering, although seemingly surprising in view of Bussi's Platonist agenda, actually promotes it, for it allows him to close the preface with his memorable tribute to Cusanus and equally memorable polemics against the anti-Platonists.

Bussi emphasizes the Platonism of the philosophical works, directing his comments on each to the support of his (and Bessarion's) position. *De deo Socratis*, he notes, was "very often usefully cited by our Saint Augustine in his excellent books on the City of God for evidence of the most important divine matters."[165] The work shows quite clearly "who and how great a teacher our Plato was in the first philosophy of religion."[166] With his parallel phrasing ("our Saint Augustine" and "our Plato"), Bussi aligns the two as pillars of Christian thought; his phrase "first philosophy of religion" presents Plato as a (pre-Christian) theologian. He treats *De Platone* as a platform to attack Plato's contemporary critics: "As if portending that someday there would be false accusers of

---

[164] "De quo [Apuleio], pater beatissime, quaedam fortassis lecturis non ingrata, huic inserere ad te epistolae statui, non tam ut faciliore opera Apuleius intelligeretur (id enim longioris lucubrationis indiget) quam ut in novam materiam, veluti inaccessam prius viam, recens ingressos, indiciis quibusdam et quasi certioribus signis, quo magis et confiderent et procederent, admonerem, ne rei ignoratione plus iusto trepidarent." Bussi, *Prefazioni*, 13.

[165] "A divo nostro Augustino saepius in praeclaris voluminibus De civitate Dei ad rerum primarum et caelestium opportune citatus testimonia." Ibid., 15.

[166] "Quis et quantus magister in ipsa divinarum rerum prima philosophia noster fuerit Plato." Ibid.

Plato, it can be thought to have been written and prepared almost with an eye to the defense of the divine man."[167] The words "false accusers of Plato" (*calumniatores. . . . Platonis*) and "defense" (*defensio*) neatly allude to the contemporary debate and to the title of Bessarion's work, *In calumniatorem Platonis,* and its alternative designation, *Defensio Platonis.* In the long discussion that follows, Bussi execrates Plato's *calumniatores* and exalts Plato himself. He ends his list of philosophical works with the three translations: *De mundo, Asclepius,* and Alcinous. He uses *De mundo* as an opportunity to mention Aristotle:

> In the sixth position [in the edition] is the book *De Mundo,* written to King Alexander by Aristotle, the wisest and greatest of natural philosophers, and presented by our Apuleius to the Latins in order that a single man of the family of the Platonists could be counted as both a Platonist and an Aristotelian, devoted to each as the greatest and most preeminent in his own class of philosophers, and an unfailing proclaimer of the praise of both. And rightly. For in this way he tacitly expressed the verdict that both held the same opinion with a correct assessment and that they did not at all disagree, as certain people think.[168]

Bussi's point—that a Platonist could value Aristotle and that the two ancient philosophers, although different in kind, were often in essential agreement—was of considerable importance not only to Bessarion but also to Bussi's beloved patron Cusanus.[169] He passes quickly over *Asclepius* and Alcinous: *Asclepius* as a translation of "an ancient and divine philosopher" that will be a basis for others trying to translate out-of-the-way material, and the translation of Alcinous as the first translation of a work explaining the principles of Plato's philosophy.[170]

But it is the literary works that come first in Bussi's edition, and he makes no attempt to argue for their Platonism. He accurately and

---

[167] "Quasi calumniatores futuros Platonis aliquando praesagiens veluti dedita opera ad defensionem divini hominis putari potest esse perscriptus atque praeparatus." Ibid.

[168] "Sextum locum obtinet De mundo liber ab Aristotile sapientissimo et physicorum maximo ad Alexandrum regem scriptus, ab Apuleio nostro Latinis exhibitus, ut unus vir ex Platonicorum familia uterque posset et Platonicus et Aristotelicus esse censeri, maximo utrique et in suo genere philosophorum primario affectissimus atque laudis utriusque praedicator indefectus. Et merito. Utrunque enim idem recta expensione sentire minimeque, quod quidam arbitrantur, dissentire, eo modo tacitus iudicabat." Ibid., 16.

[169] For Bessarion, see Hankins, *Plato in the Italian Renaissance* 1:222–9. Cusanus' interest in both philosophers is noted later in Bussi's preface: "Philosophiae Aristotelicae acerrimus disputator fuit; theologiae vero christianae summus interpres et magister et caelestis arcani antistes sapientissimus. At Platonis nostri et Pythagoraeorum dogmatum ita cupidus atque studiosus ut nemo magis illi scientiae putaretur intendisse." Bussi, *Prefazioni,* 18.

[170] See Bussi, *Prefazioni,* 19.

enthusiastically characterizes the *Florida* (short "panegyrics" on varied subjects and full of interest on that account) and rather vaguely describes the *Apology* (a most learned defense against the false charge of magic).[171] But he gives pride of place to the *Metamorphoses* and awards it the most detailed discussion, deeming it of greater significance and importance than the rest.[172]

He begins by pointing out that Apuleius has derived his plot from Lucian:

> The Syrian Lucian, an especially clever sophist (or philosopher, as all the Greeks assert), yet a satirist against philosophers, agreeably writing many things in sport rather than in calumny, spared not one of the philosophers. Among other works, this Lucian wrote the *Golden Ass* in jest, and pretended that he had been changed into it. The plot of this work is handed down in various ways, but to explain it is outside the time and scope of our discussion. Setting out to emulate this *Ass*, our Lucius—a man with an exuberant nature anyway and a most passionate disposition (since he was an African), and the most subtle philosopher of that time—says that . . . while he was attempting to be turned into a bird, he was made into the form of an ass.[173]

Although Bussi does not mention the name of Poggio, he is clearly aware of his discovery (indeed, given Poggio's celebrity and Roman connections, it would be surprising if he were not). It is less clear, however, that he has actually read Poggio's work or knows much about either Lucian or the work Poggio had attributed to him. He thinks that the title of "Lucian's" story is the *Golden Ass,* and his comments about its contents are suspiciously vague: "The plot of this work is handed down in various ways, but to explain it is outside the time and scope of our discussion." Bussi does not explicitly say that Apuleius' work must be a fiction, since its story has been taken from another author; but he seems to understand the fact, for he tells us not that Apuleius experienced the events related in the novel but that he says he did. He punctuates his plot summary with indirect statements and references to

---

[171] Ibid., 15.
[172] "Ab ea [*Metamorphosi*] ego, uti a maioris operae libello, initium feci." Ibid.
[173] "Lucianus ille Syrus, argutulus in primis atque elegans, vel sophista, vel philosophus, ut omnes Graeci suffragantur, satyrus tamen quidam in philosophos, lusu verius quam calumnia, multa scribens cum gratia, nemini philosophorum pepercit omnino. Hic Lucianus asinum, inter cetera, aureum lusit seque in eum finxit esse commutatum; cuius rei varie traditur argumentum, quod non est huius dictionis et temporis explicare. Hunc asinum noster Lucius aemulaturus, ingenii alioqui exuberantis et, ut Afer, acerrimi, philosophus omnium illius aevi subtilissimus . . . dicit . . . dum in avem affectaret verti, sese in asinum esse figuratum." Ibid., 13.

Apuleius' narration: "Our Lucius . . . says that he was made into the form of an ass"; "He says that he kept the mind he had as a man"; "He introduces amazing stories relevant to the situation"; "At last, after suffering many miserable labors, as he himself says, . . . he was restored to his former human self and initiated in the great religions."[174]

A modern reader might be inclined to explore the implications of the fact that Apuleius (or "our Lucius," as Bussi calls him) has made himself the hero of someone else's adventures, but this is not what interests Bussi. Rather, he is eager to explain what he thinks the reader should take away from the work, for he believes that it offers valuable instruction about both life and literary style.

From Lucius' adventures the alert reader can learn not exactly a moral lesson but rather—as Agatha Christie's Miss Marple used to say—"not to underestimate the depravity of human nature." Here is how Bussi puts it:

> In his ass's body he says he kept the mind he had as a man and so—hiding under the Ass—easily learned many things that would otherwise have been difficult to discover. But before he is covered by the ass he introduces amazing stories relevant to the situation. Then, concealed by the Ass, he falls into various miserable calamities, which he relates in a lively style. In this whole story the attentive reader will clearly see human nature depicted and revealed, and he will learn the unexpected cunning of deceit, by which even cautious men are often taken in, since, as Plautus cleverly observes, "man is no man but a wolf to a man as long as it is not recognized what kind of man he is."[175]

Bussi does not spell out from which direction the "cunning of deceit" might come, but presumably the treachery he has in mind is double-edged. Any unknown man is a threat—a potential "wolf," as Plautus put it;

---

[174] "Noster Lucius . . . dicit . . . sese in asinum esse figuratum." Ibid. "Mentem hominis sui ait se retinuisse." Ibid. "Fabellas mirificas ad rem pertinentes inducit." Ibid. "Tandem exanclatis multis aerumnosisque laboribus, ut ipse ait, . . . homini est priori suo restitutus et religionibus magnis initiatus." Ibid., 14.

[175] "In corpore tamen asinino mentem hominis sui ait se retinuisse atque ita sub asino latitantem multa commoditate, difficilia alioqui cognitu, didicisse. Verum priusquam asino vestiatur fabellas mirificas ad rem pertinentes inducit. Asino exinde contectus, in aerumnosas ac multifarias incidit calamitates, quas festiva dictione commeminit. Quo in toto sermone, si quis recte intendat, mores humanos effictos liquido perspiciet explicari et impraemeditatas fallaciarum argutias discet, quibus etiam cauti saepissime capiantur, cum non homo homini, sed lupus sit potius homo, ut scite Plautus inquit, dum qualis sit homo, non noscitur." Ibid., 13. Cf. Plautus, *Asinaria*, 495: "Lupus est homo homini, non homo, quom qualis sit non novit," translated in the Loeb edition as "Man is no man, but a wolf, to a stranger."

but he is also in danger of being preyed on by "wolves," as Lucius is when his humanity is unrecognized. Bussi is still thinking of human treachery in his account of Lucius' physical and spiritual conversion.

> At last, after suffering many miserable labors, as he himself says—that is, after surviving and surmounting them with the greatest anxiety and physical distress, and passing through the manifold tricks and trials of treacherous men of this life—when he had taken and eaten roses from the hand of the Egyptian priest with the assistance of the helpful moon, he was restored to his former humanity and initiated in the great religions.[176]

The interpreters of the *Golden Ass* before Bussi were allegorists, and so were most of his successors; but there are no allegories here. Bussi makes no moral judgment on Lucius. He sees him as both a witness to human wickedness and a victim of it, but not as wicked himself or in need of correction. For Bussi, Lucius' transformation is an accident rather than a punishment, and his restoration is not a matter of redemption but of simple survival—and of living through the worst that human beings can plot either against each other or against unfortunate asses.

This reading is not morally edifying, but it has an element of dark realism that is tempting to read against Bussi's own experiences. In the struggle between the Sforza and the Savoia for control of Vigevano, Bussi's native city, Bussi's father had favored the losing Savoia, bringing the wrath of Duke Francesco Sforza down on himself and his sons.[177] As a result, Sforza malevolently persecuted Bussi for many years, using his considerable influence with a series of popes to keep him from ecclesiastical preferment and to deprive him of the modest income to which the small sinecures he did have would have entitled him. In order to eat, Bussi was reduced to copying supplications and other small documents on the street corners.[178] His fortunes improved dramatically after he became Cusanus' secretary in 1458, but it was only with Sforza's death in 1466 that the persecution ended. From the relative security of his position with Sweynheym and Pannartz three years later, Bussi might well have thought of Lucius as a kindred spirit, for he too had suffered

---

[176] "Tandem exanclatis multis aerumnosisque laboribus, ut ipse ait, id est cum summa animi anxietate et corporis molestia superatis ac victis, transcursisque multiplicibus vitae huius fallacium hominum machinamentis atque excitiis, lunae auxiliatricis ope, rosis de manu Aegyptii sacerdotis acceptis ac devoratis, homini est priori suo restitutus et religionibus magnis initiatus." Ibid., 14.

[177] See Miglio, in Bussi, *Prefazioni*, xx–xxix.

[178] See ibid., xxi.

from the cruel machinations of his fellow men and survived, his fortunes and life at last transformed.[179]

But for Bussi the *Golden Ass* is not merely a practical demonstration of human nature. It is also a manual of style. Apuleius' baroque and exuberant Latinity was to become embroiled in controversy at the end of the fifteenth century and throughout the sixteenth (and beyond) as humanists debated the criteria of correct Latin style and argued about what authors to imitate, and to what degree.[180] But even before the dispute reached its height, Apuleius' style inspired extreme reactions. Over a dozen years before Bussi's edition, Lorenzo Valla (1407–57), the famous *arbiter elegantiae* who exposed the Donation of Constantine as a counterfeit by stylistic analysis, had denounced Apuleius' Latin as thoroughly asinine: "What shall I say about Apuleius, especially in the work called the *Golden Ass*? If anyone were to imitate its language, he would seem not so much to speak golden words as to bray."[181] Bussi does not say that he is reacting to Valla's verdict, but he was undoubtedly aware of it, since both men were active in Rome at the same time and moved in some of the same circles (even though Valla's was always the more exalted orbit). His appreciation of Apuleius' style is worth quoting in full.

> Here is that *Golden Ass,* composed with such verbal charm and wit and agreeableness of language that whoever makes a habit of reading it attentively can become both more polished and fuller in Latin style. For because its subjects are so diverse, Lucius pours out in it all the more recondite treasures of language and discloses them to the full extent of his verbal ability in words so suitable and appropriate that he seems not to write, but to paint his story clearly. Few things, I suppose, can happen to a person in the midst of life that could not be brought out adequately from this storeroom if he wanted to express

---

[179] Bussi was undoubtedly compensated for his editorial work, which must have occupied his every waking moment from the end of 1468 to March 1472, even though he claims to have edited Aulus Gellius, at least, for nothing. The claim in the colophon of Gellius is printed by Lee, who is inclined to extend it to all of Bussi's editorial activity; see Lee, *Sixtus IV and Men of Letters*, 108 n. 103. Bussi lived long enough to be appointed papal secretary and librarian of the Vatican Library by Pope Sixtus IV in 1474, but not long enough to enjoy his new distinctions, for he died in 1475. See Miglio, in Bussi, *Prefazioni*, xxviii–xxix.

[180] See especially D'Amico, "The Progress of Renaissance Latin Prose."

[181] "Quid dicam de Apuleio, in eo praesertim opere, cuius nomen est de asino aureo? Cuius sermonem si quis imitetur, non tam auree loqui, quam nonnihil rudere videatur." Valla, *In errores Antonii Raudensis adnotationes*, in *Opera* 1:414. The bibliography on Valla is immense. For useful summaries, see Pfeiffer, *History of Classical Scholarship*, 35–41; Grafton and Jardine, *From Humanism to the Humanities*, 66–82. For bibliography, see Osmond and Ulery, "Sallusius," in *Catalogus Translationum et Commentariorum* 8.241–43.

or write them in Latin. Everywhere he is witty, controlled, graceful, apt, varied, eloquent, elegant, ready, so that his language seems to be born on the spot, not adopted from outside. Perhaps someone might say that the diction of our Apuleius is not familiar or in common use. That is the very thing that I wonder at, that I praise, that I extol: that in language not hackneyed, not emasculated, not clumsy, not slovenly or redundant, not low—in short, not commonplace—he relates everyday things taken from the midst of life. He writes not for cookshops or lodging houses or for idle street corners or for the gathering places of rabble, but for sophisticated men who care about elegance and polished learning.[182]

Bussi is struck as much by Apuleius' ability to write about ordinary reality as by his useful lessons in survival. From Lucius' adventures an attentive reader can learn how to cope in a hostile world; in their language an aspiring writer can find a way to express everything that happens "in the midst of life." But Bussi's zeal for stylistic realism has its limits. We might say that it is one step removed from reality: the language he admires is not that of "cookshops or lodging houses" but rather of a highly educated man writing for a sophisticated audience about cookshops or lodging houses, which is a very different matter. Bussi valued this sort of recherché language for everyday life so much that he hoped one day to put together a glossary for the benefit of novice writers, collecting and defining rare words not only from Apuleius but also from Pliny the Elder and other difficult authors.[183]

---

[182] "Hic est asinus ille aureus, tanto dicendi lepore ac sale et linguae gratia compositus ut quisquis illum studiosius lectitarit, in dictione Latina fieri tersior queat atque cumulatior. Nam quod res sunt diversissimae, omnes secretiores linguae thesauros in eo Lutius effundit, ac quantum in dicendo valuerit, reserat, verbis adeo propriis et accommodatis, ut non scribere, sed pingere plane historiam videatur. Perpauca sane, uti ego arbitror, in media vita homini possunt accidere, quae latine proferre aut scribere cupienti, hinc depromi sufficienter non valeant. Ubique enim est lepidus, castigatus, venustus, aptus, varius, copiosus, concinnus, praesto, ut nasci ibidem non extra adscisci videatur oratio. Dixerit fortassis aliquis, minus tritam esse atque usurpatam Apuleii nostri dictionem. Idipsum est, quod ego demiror, quod laudo, quod extollo, quia non detrita quadam, non succida, non rustica, non squalenti et laciniosa oratione, non proculcata, non vulgatissima denique, res cotidianas ex media vita sumptas edisserit; quippe qui non popinis aut meritoriis tabernis, aut nugalibus triviis, aut misticorum compitis scribit, sed elegantiae ac cultioris doctrinae urbanis hominibus atque studiosis." Bussi, *Prefazioni*, 14.

[183] "Ubi a recognitionum munere pauxillum quivero respirare, animus est mihi, rudibus inexpertisque et litterarum tyrocinia ingredi incipientibus, aliquid scribere. . . . Si tamen Deus dederit mihi . . . ut aliquando C. Plinium difficillimum illum omnium qui scripserunt propter mendas autorem . . . vel mediocriter absolvam, propositum est in noticiam ferre, tam Plinii ipsius nonnulla quam Apuleii et eiusmodi reliquorum quorundam verba desueta ex fragmentis veterum scriptorum quae licebit colligendo, recentioribus etiam nostris adiunctis amicorumque undique imploratis auxiliis, ut hodie certe manca latinitas in verborum desitorum prope explicatione plus aliquantulum habeat adiumenti." Ibid., 14–15.

It would be interesting to see Bussi's glossary, but his editorial duties were apparently so onerous that he never found time to compile it. In less than four years he oversaw the printing of thirty-three books, of which he edited at least twenty-six.[184] Shut up in this "prison of paper," as he describes it, he was always working at top speed and often on several authors at once.[185] Predictably, his work has been harshly criticized, and modern scholars have had much to say about his deficiencies as an editor, their mildest charges being carelessness and lack of discernment.[186] It is a mistake, however, to think of Bussi as an editor in our sense of the word. He found manuscripts of the texts he wanted to print and corrected them as well as he could with the aid of other available manuscripts, with his own instincts, and sometimes with the help of friends.[187] Getting manuscripts was always a problem, for even when they existed, owners were reluctant to lend them to be copied by the new technology.[188]

In the case of Apuleius, Bussi had to find not one manuscript but several, as he notes in his preface:

> I have brought together into a single corpus the Platonist Lucius Apuleius, in whom exceptional command and agreeableness of language are joined to the highest erudition. I have done so fairly carefully, as well as was allowed in the paucity of exemplars, seeking him out piece by piece in various places, and I have handed him over to our printers for copying.[189]

The number of Bussi's exemplars is unknown, and none has been securely identified, but some points are clear. At a minimum, he used two manuscripts (in addition to his exemplar for Alcinous), for he speaks of bringing Apuleius' works together "into a single corpus" and "piece by piece"

---

[184] See Feld, "Sweynheym and Pannartz," 289, 284.

[185] Bussi's phrase "quasi in custodia carceris chartarii seclusum" is quoted by Miglio in Bussi, *Prefazioni*, xxvii.

[186] See, for example, the comments of Kenney, *The Classical Text*, 12–17. Kenney introduces his discussion in these words: "Bussi was one of the entourage of scholars of (it should be said) the second rank collected by Pope Nicholas V; his own scholarly and critical gifts were certainly not of a very high order" (12). Bussi's contemporaries were also critical, especially of his edition of Pliny (1470); see Monfasani, "The First Call for Press Censorship."

[187] Bussi's preparation of Pliny is a case in point. See Casciano, "Il MS. Angelicano 1097"; Marucchi, "Note sul manoscritto [Vat. lat. 5991]"; Martin Davies, "Making Sense of Pliny," 242–47.

[188] See Miglio, in Bussi, *Prefazioni*, xxix, xli; Kenney, *The Classical Text*, 16.

[189] "Lucium Apuleium Platonicum, in quo uno summae eruditioni praecipua linguae copia et gratia coniuncta est, mediocri vigilantia, ut in exemplariorum penuria licuit, redegi in unum corpus, variis in locis membratim perquisitum, eumque impressoribus nostris tradidi exarandum." Bussi, *Prefazioni*, 12–13.

as he would not have done if his source had been a manuscript of all the works. But we can go further than that, for in his text of the philosophical works scholars have traced affinities with at least three separate manuscripts or manuscript families: Brussels, Bibliothèque Royale Albert Ier 10054–56; Vatican Library, Reg. lat. 1572; and the manuscript group designated NPLU.[190] The Brussels manuscript should be an obvious candidate for Bussi's exemplar, since it was owned by Cusanus and annotated by both Cusanus and Bussi. By the time Bussi was editing Apuleius, however, it was no longer available, for Cusanus had died in 1464, and the manuscript was returned to Germany with the rest of his books. Nonetheless, Bussi's text is linked to it at several points—no doubt, as Arfé suggests, because Bussi recalled some of its readings as he was preparing his edition.[191] The Vatican manuscript seems to be most closely related to Bussi's text of the other philosophical works, but not to that of *De deo Socratis*, which Moreschini claims is closest to the text of NPLU.[192] For the *Metamorphoses* Bussi used a now lost manuscript from the group Robertson designated as Class I—a fortunate choice, since the Class I manuscripts are free from the major lacuna in book 8 that mars all the rest.[193] Presumably he took the *Apology* and *Florida* from the same source.[194] In all, Bussi must have drawn from at least four or five manuscripts as he prepared his edition. More than this it is hard to say.

Bussi's period, like our own (and like that of Sallustius and the archetype of Apuleius), was at the border between two methods of book production.[195] Such periods are dangerous for the survival of works inscribed in the older technology. Bussi's exemplars may well be unknown to us now because someone—perhaps even Bussi himself—did not think it important to preserve them. Perhaps Bussi was careless with his exemplars—editors and printers often were.[196] If so, his negligence is understandable (however unforgivable to modern scholars). Bussi had

---

[190] See Moreschini, *Dall'Asclepius al Crater Hermetis*, 281–82. *N* is Leiden, Bibliotheek der Rijksuniversiteit Vossianus Lat. Q. 10; *P* is Paris, Bibliothèque Nationale Lat. 6634; *L* is Florence, Biblioteca Laurenziana 76.36 (owned and annotated by Salutati); and *U* is Vatican Library, Urb. lat. 1141. For descriptions, see Klibansky and Regen, *Die Handschriften*, 83–84, 99–100, 71–72, 112–13.

[191] Arfé, "The Annotations of Nicolaus Cusanus," 53–54.

[192] Moreschini, *Dall'Asclepius al Crater Hermetis*, 281. But Vat. Reg. lat. 1572 itself was probably not one of Bussi's exemplars, since it was apparently at the Sorbonne in the fifteenth century. See Pellegrin, "Possesseurs français et italiens," 285; eadem, *Manuscrits classiques latins* 2.1:295–96.

[193] Robertson, "The Manuscripts," 30, 36.

[194] As far as I know, this point has not been taken up by modern editors.

[195] For Sallustius, see chapter 2.

[196] See Kenney, *The Classical Text*, 17–18, 81–84.

suffered at firsthand from the expense and scarcity of manuscripts. He had laboriously copied more than his share of them, for both his own use and that of others; and he had been driven by poverty to being a public scribe on the street corner. But with the advent of printing, texts were suddenly available and cheap, and manuscripts correspondingly less precious. Bussi is eloquent about the advantages of the new technology. Books now cost little more than the price of the paper, he tells the pope in a preface.[197] In Rome, "books can generally be bought for less than the cost of binding anywhere else."[198] Students can now spend the time reading and learning that they used to be forced to waste in the drudgery of copying their books.[199] Both his contemporaries and later scholars would justly complain that printing promulgated and perpetuated textual errors, but for Bussi price and availability were everything.

In the case of Apuleius, at least, his enthusiasm was justified. Today we have 40 manuscripts of the *Golden Ass* and 111 of various philosophical works, including the *Asclepius*. In Bussi's day no doubt there was a somewhat larger number of manuscripts from both traditions, but even in Rome, as Bussi attests, texts were not always easy to find. With a single stroke, Bussi's edition changed everything. His text of the *Golden Ass*, fortunately based on the best branch of the tradition, became the base text for the next four hundred years.[200] He claims a press run of 275 copies—a figure that instantly made all of Apuleius' works available in a way that would have been unimaginable even a decade earlier.[201] The edition was reprinted three times by the end of the century.[202] Apuleius had been let loose on the world.

[197] "Verum hoc quoque magnum est, pater beatissime et Deo amabilissime pontifex, quod tuo tempore non minus valet paene papyrus vacua et nuda pergamenave quam hodie optatissimi libri emantur." Bussi, *Praefatio* to Jerome (*Prefazioni*, 5).

[198] "Ego posteris . . . trado praestantissimos characterum imprimendorum autores . . . Romae artem exercere coepisse tanto artificio et industria hominum . . . ut minoris libri emi fere possint quam alias soleret redimi ligatura." Ibid.

[199] "Nunc patrum in liberos promptas voluntates invitemus ad hos libros levi patrimonii onere coemendos, filios autem ad studendum alacrius atque ferventius incitemus et quicquid temporis describendo insumpsissent, quae prius emere propter vim pretiorum non valebant, nunc illud omne in perdiscendo terant." Ibid., 9.

[200] Robertson, ed., *Les Métamorphoses*, xlix.

[201] Bussi listed the number of copies of each of his editions in a petition to Sixtus IV (printed in *Prefazioni*, 82–84). See Feld, "Sweynheym and Pannartz," 284–85; Scholderer, "The Petition of Sweynheym and Pannartz to Sixtus IV." Bussi's numbers have been questioned; see Hirsch, "The Size of Editions of Books"; idem, *Printing, Selling and Reading*, 65–66.

[202] The reprints are Vicenza 1488 (GKW 2302), Venice 1493 (GKW 2303), and Milan 1497 (GKW 2304).

CHAPTER 5

Telling Tales: The *Golden Ass* in Ferrara and Mantua

> Psyche had patience in her misfortunes.
> —*Matteo Maria Boiardo*, Tarocchi

Bussi's edition was a major turning point in the reception of Apuleius. Before 1469, Apuleius' fortunes in the fifteenth century were modest and driven for the most part by interest in his philosophical works. The first edition itself was the product of a philosophical controversy. After Bussi's edition, the floodgates were open. With the wide availability of the text, readers with other interests came to the fore—philologists, translators, novelists, and poets—all with a greater interest in the literary than in the philosophical works, and all eager to appropriate Apuleius' style and narrative for their own purposes.[1] There must have been a few such readers throughout the fifteenth century, although they have left few traces.[2] Printing both multiplied their numbers and preserved their works.

Even before Bussi there were signs that interest in Apuleius was turning in a new direction. In the period between 1462 and 1467, Francesco Colonna, author of the bizarre masterpiece *Hypnerotomachia Polifili*, mined both the literary and philosophical works, using Apuleius' ornate and recherché Latin as the basis for his own strange Latinate vernacular.[3] Colonna used a manuscript (or manuscripts) for this early part of his work (book 2 of the *Hypnerotomachia* in its present form). When he composed book 1 many years later, he used the 1488 reprint of Bussi's edition as his source for Apuleius.[4]

---

[1] For a useful summary of the many treatments of Psyche in this period and into the sixteenth century, see Moreschini, *Il mito di Amore e Psiche*, esp. 11–26.

[2] There is tantalizing evidence, for example, that Feltrino Boiardo (d. 1456) translated the *Golden Ass*; see below.

[3] The identity of Francesco Colonna is controversial. His modern editors identify him as a Venetian monk (Pozzi and Ciapponi, eds., *Hypnerotomachia Polifili* 2:3 n. 1), but others insist that he should be identified with Francesco Colonna of Palestrina, a member of the powerful Colonna family and an associate of Pomponio Leto and the Roman Academy (see Calvesi, *La "Pugna d'Amore in Sogno,"* 140–45, with earlier bibliography).

[4] See the important article of Fumagalli, "Francesco Colonna." Echoes of Apuleius in both books are listed in Pozzi and Ciapponi, eds., *Hypnerotomachia Polifili* 2:323–24.

Apuleius' language was also the concern of Niccolò Perotti (1429–80), who included over two dozen passages from his works in *Cornu copiae sive commentarii Linguae latinae* (published posthumously in 1489).⁵ Although *Cornu copiae* was undoubtedly the product of many years of reading and research, Perotti probably found most or all of his Apuleius passages in the 1469 edition of Bussi.⁶ If so, he used the edition out of necessity and convenience rather than because he respected Bussi. The two men undoubtedly knew each other in Rome, for both were members of Bessarion's circle: Perotti was Bessarion's secretary from 1447 to 1464, and Bussi was Cusanus' secretary from 1458 to 1464. But the secretaries were not such good friends as their masters had been. Perotti mounted a savage attack on Bussi's 1470 edition of Pliny's *Natural History*, and Bussi soon answered him in the usual humanist fashion: without mentioning his name.⁷ Both were probably motivated as much by professional rivalry as by scholarly zeal, for Perotti was preparing his own edition of Pliny, and both men were interested in producing studies of rare words.⁸ Bussi thought of writing a glossary for the use of novice writers—an intention he apparently never fulfilled. Perotti's plans were more ambitious: in the *Cornu copiae* he intended to elucidate every word of Martial's epigrams with synonyms, parallels, and derivatives from authors of every period.⁹ He did not live to finish his great work, but the small portion we have (which covers only Martial's *Liber spectaculorum* and part of the first book of epigrams) became a valuable compendium of Latin usage for generations of lexicographers.¹⁰

Colonna and Perotti exemplify the two main types of Apuleius' readers in this period: the literary/artistic on the one hand and the scholarly/pedagogical on the other. Readers of the one type studied Apuleius in order to create new works in the literary or visual arts, those of the other to gain a better understanding of Apuleius himself, whether from

---

⁵ For Perotti's life, see Mercati, *Per la cronologia della vita e degli scritti di Niccolò Perotti*. Twenty-six passages are listed by Prete (23 from the *Metamorphoses* and one each from *De mundo*, *De deo Socratis*, and *De Platone*): "Frammenti di Apuleio." But Perotti attributed at least 161 passages to Apuleius that have not been identified. For a detailed analysis, see Brancaleone, *Citazioni "apuleiane"*; see also Prete, "Frammenti di Apuleio." On the general question of Perotti's unidentified citations, see Oliver, " 'New Fragments' of Latin Authors."

⁶ Brancaleone implies as much (*Citazioni "apuleiane,"* 4). Furno suggests that the actual time of composition might have extended from 1468 to 1479 (*Le Cornu copiae*, 47).

⁷ Monfasani, "The First Call for Press Censorship," esp. 3–11. See also Nauert, "Gaius Plinius Secundus," 325–29.

⁸ Perotti's Pliny was printed by Sweynheim and Pannartz in 1473. For Bussi's projected glossary, see p. 169.

⁹ See especially Furno, *Le Cornu copiae*, and Brancaleone, *Citazioni "apuleiane,"* both with earlier bibliography.

¹⁰ Furno, *Le Cornu copiae*, 14.

a historical, stylistic, or textual perspective. Through the efforts of both, in the years from 1469 until 1500 Apuleius received more attention in more quarters than at any previous time in his history. In this and the following chapter we will look at these two distinct strains of Apuleius' reception, focusing our attention on the work of the men most associated with them. This chapter concerns the retellings of tales from the *Golden Ass* by the poet Matteo Maria Boiardo and his successors for the courts of Ferrara and Mantua. In the next we will consider the commentary of the great teacher and scholar Filippo Beroaldo of Bologna.

BOIARDO: TRANSLATING AND TRANSFORMING APULEIUS

Matteo Maria Boiardo, count of Scandiano (1440 or 1441 to 1494), was a noble by birth and a courtier by profession, but his greatest talents were literary. He is best known today for his long epic romance, *Orlando Innamorato*.[11] In the 1470s Boiardo was in Ferrara, whose duke, Ercole I d'Este, presided over a glittering and sophisticated court and encouraged both the literary and the visual arts.[12] Ercole, not an intellectual or a scholar himself, knew little Latin, but he enjoyed translations of exciting or entertaining tales from the classics. Boiardo translated several works for him in this period, including Herodotus' *Histories* and the *Lives* of Cornelius Nepos, but *Apulegio volgare*, his translation of the *Golden Ass*, was the most important.[13] This work enjoyed a special position in Ferrara, becoming a favorite with Ercole and his family and soon inspiring literary and artistic treatments of the story of Cupid and Psyche.

Boiardo completed *Apulegio volgare* by early 1479. There is some evidence that his grandfather Feltrino Boiardo (d. 1456) had translated the *Golden Ass* a generation earlier, but this translation may well have been lost by Boiardo's time.[14] In any event, it could have exerted little

---

[11] See Forti, "Matteo Maria Boiardo." Biographical surveys are also given by Ross, trans., in Boiardo, *Orlando Innamorato*, 10–19; Ulivi, in Boiardo, *Opere di Matteo Maria Boiardo*, xxxv–xli.

[12] For Ercole and his court, see Gundersheimer, *Ferrara*, 173–228; Ross, in Boiardo, *Orlando Innamorato*, 10–19.

[13] The essential study of *Apulegio volgare* is by Fumagalli, *Matteo Maria Boiardo*. See also idem, "Amore e Psiche in centri padani." There is no modern edition of the work as a whole, but Fumagalli (*Matteo Maria Boiardo*, 217–345) has edited Boiardo's translation of the story of Psyche (*Met.* 4.28–6.24).

[14] In Angelo Decembrio's dialogue *De politia litteraria* 1.6, the interlocutor Feltrino Boiardo says: "Quid autem de Apuleio et asino nostro aureo? De quo, ut abundantius cum meis ridere possem, eum ego ipse in vernaculum sermonem transtuli." The passage is quoted by Fumagalli (*Matteo Maria Boiardo*, 15) from Vat. lat. 1794, fol. 17r. Fumagalli (15 n. 24) dates the dialogue between 1461 and 1464.

or no influence on *Apulegio volgare*, which is based, as Fumagalli demonstrated, on the 1469 edition of Bussi, a work not available until thirteen years after Feltrino's death. The precise copy of Bussi's edition that Boiardo used has not been identified, but Fumagalli suggests that it had been corrected against a manuscript (not by Boiardo himself), and that its corrections were similar to those in the copy now in the Huntington Library.[15]

Boiardo was not a faithful translator, for he glossed over difficult passages and took little interest in trying to reproduce Apuleius' style. For Boiardo, as for Ercole, it seems, the story was everything—and not all the story at that. He omitted book 11 and with it Lucius' redemption and conversion to Isis, substituting the farcical conclusion of the *Onos (Ass)* of Pseudo-Lucian.[16] There, Loukios, restored to human shape by his own efforts, returns to the amorous matron only to be summarily rejected because he is no longer the beautiful ass she loved but only "an ugly monkey without a tail."[17] The use of "Lucian's" conclusion changes the tone of the novel, firmly keeping *Apulegio volgare* away, not only from any taint of "paganism" but also from the serious questions raised by Lucius' transformation and conversion in Apuleius. But "Lucian" is not Boiardo's only addition to Apuleius. As Fumagalli has noted, Boiardo often uses both phrasing and content from Boccaccio's imitations in the *Decameron* (7.2 and 5.10) in his translations of Apuleius' "tale of the tub" and "miller's tale" in *Met.* 9 (5–7 and 14–28).[18] Fumagalli calls the process "contaminatio." I would put it differently: that by using Boccaccio as an intertext, Boiardo has incorporated the imitation into the original, giving his tales a double resonance. The incorporation of Boccaccio, like the substitution of "Lucian," not only made *Apulegio volgare* something more (and more interesting) than a mere translation, but also suited the interests of Ercole and his court. Boiardo could be sure that they would recognize and savor his echoes of Boccaccio and smile at his sardonic and racy ending.

Boiardo's artistry did not stop here. If he used Boccaccio's imitations of Apuleius as an intertext in *Apulegio volgare*, he also used both Apuleius

---

[15] Fumagalli, *Matteo Maria Boiardo*, 1–28, 31–91.

[16] For Pseudo-Lucian, he seems to have relied on the Italian translation of Niccolò Leoniceno, who was also at Ercole's court in the 1470s. See Acocella, *L'Asino d'oro nel Rinascimento*, 17–75.

[17] "Una brutta simia senza coda," Boiardo, *Apulegio volgare*, quoted from Acocella, *L'Asino d'oro*, 66. The phrase "senza coda" is an obscene addition to "Lucian" in both Leoniceno and Boiardo. (Pseudo-Lucian says only "monkey" [*pithekon*].)

[18] Fumagalli, *Matteo Maria Boiardo*, 137–44. For Boccaccio's versions of the adultery stories, see pp. 100–107.

PLATE 1. Trier ceiling overview. Bischöfliches Museum, Trier.

PLATE 2. Cupid and Psyche on Trier ceiling. Bischöfliches Museum, Trier.

PLATE 3. Apuleius on Trier ceiling. Bischöfliches Museum, Trier.

PLATE 4. Apuleius Contorniate. Cabinet des Médailles, Paris 17163. Bibliothèque Nationale de France.

PLATE 6. Apuleius as a writer. Vat. lat. 2193, fol. 19v.

PLATE 5. Apuleius as philosopher. Vat. lat. 2193, fol. 1.

Plate 8. Apuleius as the ass. Vat. lat. 2193, fol. 43r.

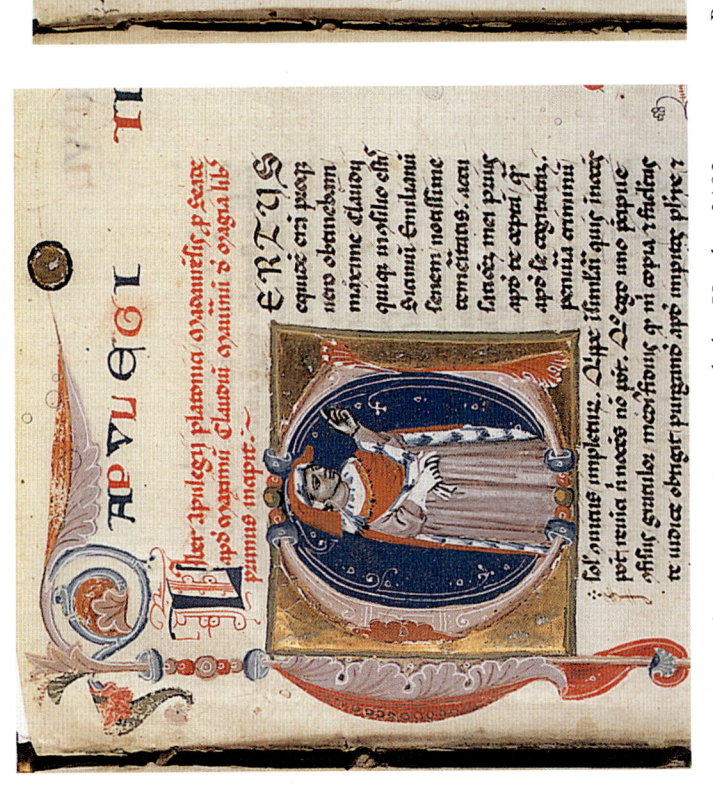

Plate 7. Apuleius as a magician or scholar. Vat. lat. 2193, fol. 27r.

PLATE 9. The Theological Virtues in the initial *A* of the *Golden Ass*. Vat. lat. 2194, fol. 1r.

PLATE 10. Lucius in bed. Vat. lat. 2194, fol. 5v.

PLATE 11. Psyche in Cupid's garden. Vat. lat. 2194, fol. 24r.

PLATE 12. Psyche in Ceres' temple. Vat. lat. 2194, fol. 30r.

PLATE 13. The ass and the bucket of water. Vat. lat. 2194, fol. 48v.

PLATE 14. Lucius bathing by moonlight. Vat. lat. 2194, fol. 65v.

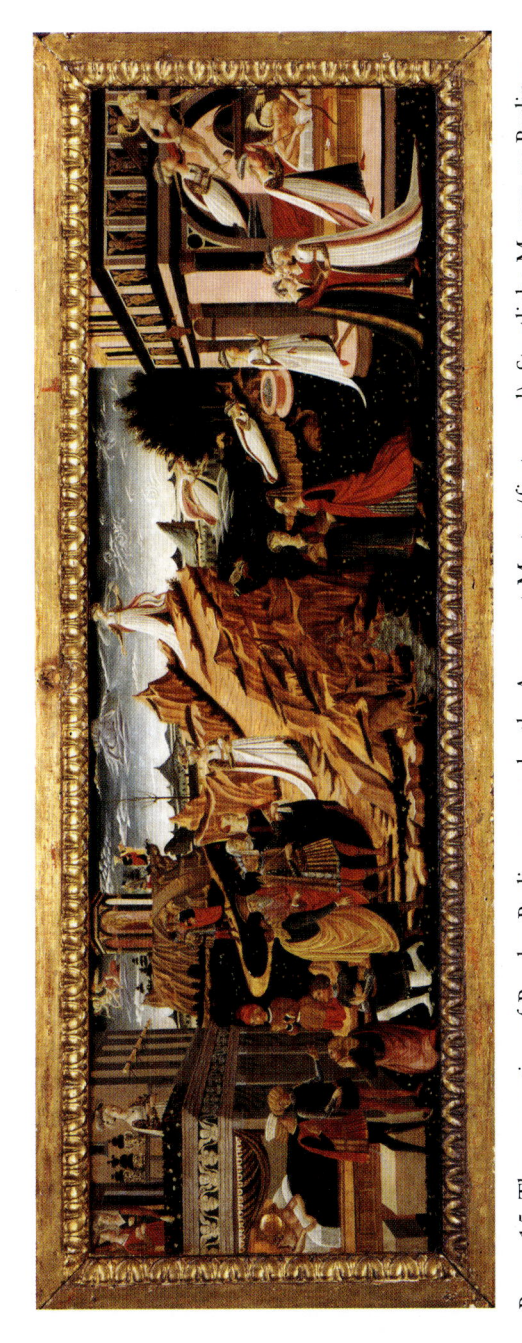

Plate 15. The conception of Psyche. Berlin cassone by the Argonaut Master (first panel). Staatliche Museen zu Berlin—Gemäldegalerie (cat. 1823).

PLATE 16. The wedding of Cupid and Psyche. Berlin cassone by the Argonaut Master (second panel). Staatliche Museen zu Berlin— Gemäldegalerie (cat. 1824).

PLATE 17. Apuleius in a Byzantine cap. Firenze, Biblioteca Laurenziana ms. Laur. Plut. 54.13, fol. 1r.

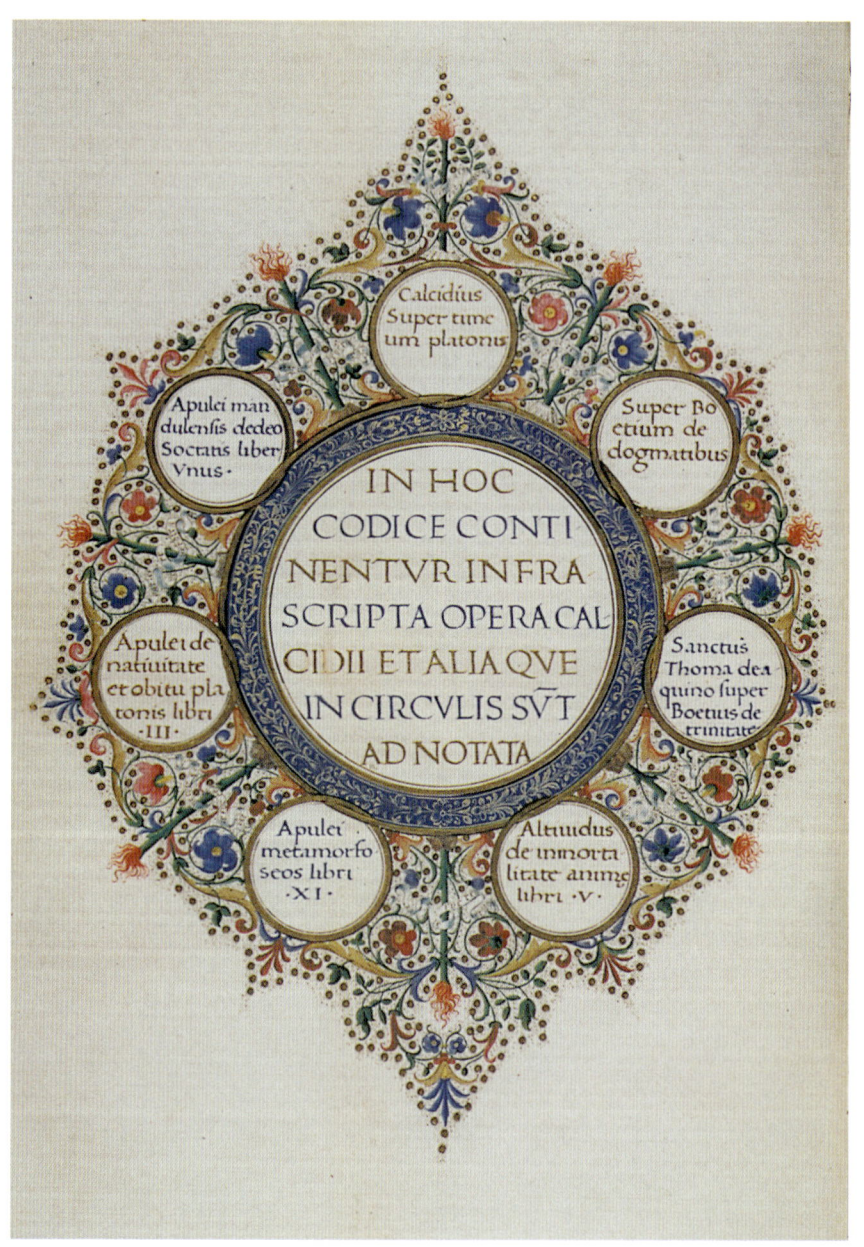

Plate 18. Apuleius's works in a Platonic context. Firenze, Biblioteca Laurenziana ms. Laur. Plut. 84.24, fol. 1v.

¶ Wie lucius Apuleius in gestalt eins esels verkert ward

O mir aber zůviele die vrsach meins beleibens vñ was ich gerñ erlernē wolt zc̄ Sprach ich O aller liebste palestra · ich bit dich zeig mir dem frowē do sy sich gebruchi jr zauberey vnd sich in ein and̄ form vñ gestalt werd verkerē· Deñ ich lange zeit her gewunst vñ begert habe solicher wund̄licher ding zesechē vñ allerliebst vō dir· ob du dz icht kūdest den ich gelaub dz du diser kūst mit gar vnwissent sielt· dorum ich dis vō niemant lieб dan von dir die yetz wordē bist mein selleren vñ habē wolte · denn du mich vō lieb we gē d' myn vf kein frowen mein au ge ie gekert han

PLATE 19. Transformation of Lucius in Niklas von Wyle's *Der goldene Esel* (Straßburg, ca. 1478). Herzog August Bibliothek Wolfenbüttel: 130 Quodl. 2º (3).

PLATE 20. Psyche and her sisters in Andreas Ernnst's edition of *Cupid and Psyche*. [Erfurt, ca. 1515]. Herzog August Bibliothek Wolfenbüttel: G 507.4º Helmst. (10)—frontispiece.

and *Apulegio volgare* as an intertext in *Orlando Innamorato*.[19] The most striking example is yet another adultery tale from *Met.* 9—this time, interestingly enough, one *not* used in the *Decameron*. Apuleius uses it as an embedded story in the "miller's tale" (*Met.* 9.16–21), Boiardo as a novella in *Orlando Innamorato* (2.26.20–52).[20] The plot is the same in both. A lover gains access to a married woman by bribing the slave set to guard her. While he is enjoying her favors, the husband comes home unexpectedly. The lover escapes, but in his haste he leaves behind an article of clothing (slippers in Apuleius, a cloak in Boiardo). The husband discovers the clothing, sees that he has been betrayed, and angrily binds the treacherous slave and drags him off (to the forum in Apuleius, to the gallows in Boiardo). The lover sees them, realizes what has happened, and at once devises a clever ruse. He furiously throws himself at the slave and begins to berate him for stealing his clothing on the previous day. The husband, of course, is taken in.

But the plot is all that Boiardo has taken from Apuleius. The two tales differ in tone, characterization, and emphasis, but above all in their narrator and position in the larger work.

In Apuleius the story is told to the miller's wife by her elderly procuress in order to tout the merits of a possible new lover. This paragon is desirable in every respect, the old woman claims, but especially because he is such a champion at foiling the precautions of jealous husbands. She tells her story to support this assertion, claiming that for this exploit alone "he single-handedly deserves to enjoy the favors of every married woman."[21] In her version, the lover pays both the slave and the wife for their services, the wife is last heard of in the lovemaking interrupted by the arrival of her husband, and the husband never confronts her. The story ends with the husband convinced of his slave's loyalty and persuading him to return the slippers to their owner. Each detail is designed to appeal to the already adulterous miller's wife. The wife in the story gets paid, remains inconspicuous except for her sexual encounter, and is unquestioned by her cuckolded husband. Best of all, she enjoys a bold and quick-thinking lover. Naturally the miller's wife is won over. Persuaded that her present lover is timid and weak by comparison

---

[19] See Fumagalli, *Matteo Maria Boiardo*, 150–56; for verbal echoes in *Orlando Innamorato* from Boiardo's translation of the story of Psyche, see 217–345. The first two books of *Orlando Innamorato* were published in 1482–83; the third was unfinished at Boiardo's death. See Bruscagli, "Matteo Maria Boiardo," 675–76, with earlier bibliography.

[20] The same story was also used by Mantovano in his comedy *Il Formicone*, which was "perhaps performed for the first time in November 1503 at the court of Francesco Gonzaga in Mantua" (Scobie, "The Influence of Apuleius' *Metamorphoses*," 213–14). The point is interesting, given the enthusiasm for Apuleius in Este/Gonzaga circles; see below.

[21] "Dignus hercules solus omnium matronarum deliciis perfrui." *Met.* 9.16.3.

with the bawd's candidate, she commissions her to arrange an assignation (*Met.* 9.22.1–2). But the old woman turns out to be guilty of false advertising, for the young boy she presents is nothing like the lover in her tale. When the miller comes home unexpectedly, the lover hides ignominiously under a grain trough. He quakes with fear on being discovered and is finally sent off in disgrace after being both sexually and physically humiliated.

Apuleius' story of the quick-witted lover is one of venality and deceit; the "miller's tale" in which it is embedded—equally sordid—ends in the mistreatment of the lover and the murder of the miller by witchcraft.[22] Boiardo takes the embedded story out of its squalid context and brings it into the romantic world of *Orlando Innamorato* (*OI*), placing it in a new frame story, where it becomes a tale of true love triumphant, culminating in marriage and conversion to Christianity. The frame story is that of the lovers Fiordelisa and Brandimarte, whose adventures are entwined with several other stories in books 1 and 2 of the poem. The story of the quick-witted lover is related to them by Doristella, a damsel they have rescued from an enchanted castle (*OI* 2.26.21–52).[23] As the three ride off together, Doristella tells her story to explain her presence in the castle and to entertain her companions by demonstrating that "no shield protects a jealous man, /—that's good, since he deserves the worst."[24]

With his choice of narrator, Boiardo has turned Apuleius' story inside out. We are not given the tale by a third-person (and demonstrably unreliable) narrator but brought inside it by one of the actors. In Apuleius the wife was the least important of the four characters. Boiardo makes her central and lets us see everything from her perspective. Doristella's true love, Teodoro, asks for her hand on the very day that her father has betrothed her to another. Her husband proves to be jealous (like the husband in Apuleius), but he is also impotent.[25] His impotence provides an additional motive for Doristella's unfaithfulness, but it also invalidates the marriage, since intercourse is crucial to the enactment of marriage.[26] Even before her marriage, however, Doristella has vowed to love where she wished, and when Teodoro appears in her

---

[22] For Apuleius' treatment of the fates of the lover and the husband, see pp. 104–5.

[23] Doristella's story is discussed by Jo Ann Cavallo, *Boiardo's Orlando Innamorato*, 130–36. See also Reichenbach, *L'Orlando Innamorato di M. M. Boiardo*, 75–82.

[24] "Come a un geloso mai scrimir non vale, / E ben gli sta, che degno è d'ogni male." *OI* 2.26.21. The text is that of Tissoni Benvenuti, in Boiardo, *L'Inamoramento de Orlando*. The translation is that of Ross, in Boiardo, *Orlando Innamorato*.

[25] Like the husband in Boccaccio, *Dec.* 2.10, which Cavallo sees as Boiardo's model for Doristella's story (*Boiardo's Orlando Innamorato*, 130–36). But the impotence of the jealous husband is the only point of resemblance between the two tales.

[26] See Cavallo, *Boiardo's Orlando Innamorato*, 133, with bibliography.

husband's absence, she is all too willing to act on her resolution. The slave is duly bribed, the lovers enjoy their sport, and the husband comes home unexpectedly—but not quite as in Apuleius, for Doristella engineers Teodoro's escape and feigns sleep when her husband enters the bedroom. For the sake of verisimilitude, she even snores. The sleeping and snoring are absent from Apuleius, who says nothing about the wife's actions after the husband's return, but both details appear in Boiardo's *Apulegio volgare*.[27]

Doristella's story continues after Teodoro manages to explain the telltale cloak: she continues her assignations under the nose of her increasingly suspicious husband until he is finally convinced of her infidelity and locks her up in the enchanted castle. The embedded tale ends at this point, for the three travelers are set upon by robbers. With the interruption, we find ourselves back in the frame story, which goes on to relate the happy ending of Doristella's adventures (*OI* 27.8–35). The travelers reach the kingdom of Doristella's father and find it under siege by Teodoro, but the lovers are soon reunited and peace is proclaimed. Fiordelisa is discovered to be the long-lost sister of Doristella. Doristella marries Teodoro and Fiordelisa Brandimarte, and the two sisters, who "both were Catholic and Christian," convert everyone in their Islamic Armenian homeland to Christianity.[28]

The most distinctive aspects of Doristella's tale counter and rebut the worldview presented in Apuleius. Two points of contrast are particularly important: truth and marriage. In both Apuleius and Boiardo, the truth or falsity of the embedded story is revealed by its sequel in the frame. At the end of the "miller's tale" the bawd is exposed as a liar by the inadequacy of her protégé. We see that the old woman fabricated her story as a come-on: there was no adventure with the wife, the slave, and the slippers; and the quick-witted lover never existed. Doristella, by contrast, is shown to have told the truth. The conclusion of her adventures related in the frame story explicitly confirms what she has said of her parentage, her forced marriage, her love of Teodoro, and his having followed her to her husband's country.[29] Her story of the quick-witted

---

[27] See Fumagalli, who compares the two passages (*Matteo Maria Boiardo*, 150–55): "Scorpione ne va cridando a la camera e trova la moglie nel lecto: *molto sonachiosa se mostrava*" (*Apulegio volgare*, at Met. 9.20.4) and "il mio marito in camera saliva, / et io queta mi stava come sposa, / *mostrandomi adormita e sonochiosa*" (*OI* 2.26.40). On the authority of the Pisa manuscript of *Apulegio volgare* (Pisa, Biblioteca Universitaria, ms. 979), Fumagalli would read "sornacchiosa" (snoring) instead of "sonochiosa"(sleepy) in both passages.

[28] Reichenbach points out that the poet has neglected to tell us how the women themselves were converted (*L'Orlando Innamorato*, 82).

[29] Even the kidnapping of her sister that she mentions in passing at the outset (*OI* 2.26.22) is confirmed by the recognition of Fiordelisa.

lover is implicitly confirmed by the presence of the lover himself in the person of Teodoro. In the stories of both authors the question of truth bears also on the theme of marriage. Apuleius in both the embedded story and its frame presents marriage as an opportunity for deception, open to corruption by money and adultery—or rather by adultery solicited by money, a point made explicit in the bawd's tale and implied for the miller's.[30] In Boiardo, Doristella's story asserts the importance of marriage.[31] Her arranged marriage is invalidated in her own mind both by the fact that it is forced upon her and by her husband's inability to consummate it.[32] She chooses her own mate, who is well suited to her by mutual affection, similarity of character, and even similarity of name.[33] This is her true marriage, which is formally celebrated at the end and gains the further validation of her reunion with her family and the conversion of her country to Christianity.

It would be difficult to imagine anything more unlike the adultery tale in the *Golden Ass*. In *Orlando Innamorato* Boiardo has radically transformed Apuleius' story—pouring old and bitter wine into a new bottle whose shape and chemistry have turned it into a romantic elixir. But Boiardo's story has not lost touch with its source. We might better say that it is in competition with it, and that Boiardo has engaged in a dialectical or emulative imitation of Apuleius, advertising and exploiting both the distance and the dissonance between their affective landscapes.[34]

Playing Cards

Boiardo translated Apuleius for Ercole d'Este and wrote *Orlando Innamorato*—if not *for* the court, then certainly with its approval and enjoyment.[35] He also drew on Apuleius in a much smaller project for the court, a verse description of a pack of tarot cards entitled

---

[30] Money also figures in Apuleius' first adultery story, the "tale of the tub." See p. 100.

[31] On this point, see Cavallo, *Boiardo's Orlando Innamorato*, 131–34.

[32] For Doristella this arranged marriage is also unnatural, and she laments that she has less choice in her mate than the animals do (*OI* 26.27–28).

[33] Cavallo points out that both names have the root *dor* ("gift"): Doristella, Teodoro (*Boiardo's Orlando Innamorato*, 132). We could go further and note that Teodoro's name ("gift of God") suggests divine sanction for the match.

[34] For dialectical or emulative imitation, see especially Greene, *The Light in Troy*, 43–48. See also the discussion of imitation in Gaisser, *Catullus and His Renaissance Readers*, 196–99, with earlier bibliography.

[35] For courtly elements in the poem, see Ross, trans., *Orlando Innamorato*, 14–19, with earlier bibliography.

Tarocchi o Capitoli (Tarot Cards or Chapters).[36] This little work consists of five chapters, one for each suit (Fear, Jealousy, Hope, Love, and Triumph), and two sonnets. A tercet is devoted to each card. Boiardo's allusion to Apuleius is brief: a single tercet in the chapter on the suit of Triumphs. In this suit each card apart from the joker (Il Matto) illustrates a quality (for example, Faith, Error, Trickery, or Fortitude) with a personage from the Bible, history, or myth. Patience, the eighth card in the suit, is represented by Psyche:

> Psyche had patience in her misfortunes
> And for that reason was aided in her distress,
> And in the end was made a Goddess who is an example to us.[37]

The cards themselves have vanished, but fortunately we have an account of them by a near contemporary, Pier Antonio Viti (ca. 1470–1500), who described them for an unidentified lady at the court of Urbino who wanted to have a similar deck made for herself.[38] Viti discusses each card in detail, describing its appearance and giving his own interpretation of Boiardo's verses. Here is what he has to say about Psyche:

> Patience, in the eighth place, follows Anger [the seventh card]. She is represented by Psyche, who, suffering her misfortunes most patiently, won the right of being placed in the number of the saints.[39] She is our soul, most illustrious lady, which raising itself with the greatest labors from the filth of the world, takes wings granted by the grace of Jove, rising with divine assistance all the way to Heaven, where partaking of a blessed life by right of her labors, she becomes a saint. This will not happen to you after death, my patroness, since deservedly you have already been placed among the saints through the labors you have sustained; and your intercessions with our Lord will be of assistance to *my* poor Psyche, which now finds itself in the midst of labors, so that I might follow the path of your mind (which is divine and blessed in every part), my most illustrious lady, and distance myself from earthly desires, and be seen clearly by all to raise myself to Heaven on full-fledged wings of passionate longing.

The picture of Psyche is of a beautiful young woman clad in a violet mantle with a white dress underneath, and she holds part of her mantle

---

[36] The work is edited and discussed by Foà. See also Renier, "I Tarocchi." It should probably be dated to the 1470s; see Foà, 9–10.

[37] "*Pazienza* Psiche ebbe ne i casi soi, / E però fu soccorsa ne li affanni / E facta Dea nel fin, ch'è exempio ad noi" Boiardo, *Tarocchi* 5.25–7 (ed. Foà, 57).

[38] For Viti, see Renier, "I Tarocchi," 245–47.

[39] I translate "Dea" in Boiardo as "Goddess," but "Dee" or "Dea" in Viti as "saints" or "saint." See the discussion below.

with both hands, and she has at her feet on one side a broken bow with a reversed inscription below it, and on the other side two wings stripped of their feathers and a dapple-gray horse with a violet bridle, which, being patiently valiant, would endure every labor. And above the head of the aforesaid Psyche are three verses that tell about her.[40]

The Psyche of Boiardo's verses is one-dimensional—of necessity, given the tiny space allowed her by the tercet. Hers is a success story ("an example to us," as Boiardo puts it), and a short one at that: she is patient in misfortune and thereby wins assistance and is ultimately made immortal ("a Goddess"). But we must remember that Boiardo's tercet is only part of the "text" presented on the card: the verse and picture were to be read together. The picture described by Viti shows her as young and beautiful. The color of her cloak presents her as a lover, for purple is the color of the suit of Love.[41] The attributes at her feet (the broken bow and unfeathered wings) take us further into her story, alluding to a particular moment in Apuleius' account: the scene in which Venus lists the punishments she would like to inflict on Cupid for loving Psyche (*Met.* 5.30.5–6). Among the penalties she mentions are the unstringing of his bow and the clipping or shearing of his wings.[42] The image on the card shows these penalties fulfilled and tells us how to read the scene: with Cupid powerless, the painted Psyche is alone and without resource—that is, precisely in the situation in which she is to

---

[40] "*Pazienza*, al *Sdegno*, nel octavo loco segue, per Psiche significata, la quale li adversi casi soi pazientissimamente soffrendo, meritò de essere nel numero de le Dee collocata. Questa è, Illustrissima Madonna, l'anima nostra, che cum grandissime fatiche da le brutture del mondo levandose, piglia l'ale, da Iove per grazia concesseli, pogiando col divino adiuto insino al Cielo, dove, per merito de le sue fatighe, la felice vita prendendo, diventa Dea. Il che a voi, Patrona mia, non adverrà doppo morte; essendo già nel numero de le Dee, per le sustenute fatiche, meritevelmente collocata; le intercessione de la quale apresso el nostro S.^re Dio, a la mia povera Psiche, che nel mezo de le fatiche ora se ritrova, potranno in modo giovare, che io l'orme e del divino animo vostro e del graziato in ogni sua parte de la mia Illustrissima Madonna seguendo, da le terrene voglie partendomi, visibilmente da ciascuno, cum l'ale de caldo disio impennate, levarmi al Cielo serò veduto. La pictura de Psiche è in forma di Nynfa, di morello manto vestita, con il bianco camiso di sotto, e tiene cum ambedue le mane parte del suo manto; et ha a suoi piedi, da l'un de canti, uno arco ropto, con uno scrito riverso a lui di sotto; e da l'altro canto due ali spenachiate et uno cavallo leardo, col freno morello, che pazientemente essendo generoso, patisse ogni fatica. E sopra el capo di dicta Psiche sono tre versi che di lei ragionano." Viti, *Illustrazione*, in Boiardo, *Tarocchi*, ed. Foà, 51–52.

[41] "El campo de le qual carte è colore morello nel gioco de *Amore*, che significa Amore, cioè colore violaceo." Ibid., 31.

[42] Venus suggests destruction of two sorts: to Cupid's equipment (undoing his quiver, blunting his arrows, unstringing his bow, and putting out his torch) and to his person (shaving his hair and clipping his wings). The artist has selected an easily depicted item from each list, substituting a broken bow for an unstrung one for clarity.

show the quality of Patience she represents. The horse beside her also embodies long-suffering endurance, for Psyche, like all the characters in the suit of Triumphs, is accompanied by an animal signifying her quality.[43] If we read back from the picture to the tercet, however, we see that despite appearances, Psyche is not alone after all: even at the moment shown on the card she is "aided in her distress" (as she was in Apuleius), and she will achieve her reward of immortality.

Viti lets us read the verbal and visual texts of the card together, but he also adds an elaborate interpretation of his own. Boiardo tells us that for her patience Psyche was assisted in her distress and made immortal and that she is an example to us. Viti takes these details from Boiardo, ascribes to Psyche the wings of Cupid pictured on the card, and confects not only a complex Christian allegory with himself at the center but also an ornate compliment to his patroness.

He begins by explicitly identifying Psyche as "our soul" and goes on to depict her experience in specifically Christian terms, first granting her a spiritual ascent from "the filth of this world" to Heaven on God-given wings and then surreptitiously redefining the nature of her immortality. Both Viti and Boiardo call the transformed Psyche "Dea," but Viti's "Dea" is not the same as Boiardo's . In Boiardo the word can be given its usual translation, "goddess," since neither the tercet nor the picture on the card moves his Psyche out of the realm of mythology. In Viti, however, "Dea" must mean "saint." He applies the term to both Psyche and his patroness, who must be a saint, since she can intercede with the Christian God ("our Lord") on behalf of Viti's soul ("my poor Psyche"). Her intercession is necessary, for Viti's soul—just like Psyche herself before her canonization—"finds itself in the midst of labors." The parallel between Viti's labors and Psyche's (both called *fatiche*) recalls Boiardo's concluding point, that Psyche is "an example to us"; but just as in the case of the word "Dea," Viti has another card up his sleeve. Psyche is indeed an example for Viti in his labors and also at the end of the allegory, for he aspires to raise himself to Heaven in an ascent that mirrors hers, wings and all.[44] But she is not the example for the endurance of toil by which he is to win his ascent. He assigns this role to his human patroness, who for *her* labors (*fatiche*) is already in the number of the saints—not after death, like Psyche, but in her own lifetime. As we ponder this allegory, we may think that Viti has placed us

---

[43] "Et a piede di tucti li Trionfi sono animali di quella medesima natura che è il trionfo." Ibid., 47. Toil (*Fatiga*), for example, is accompanied by ants (48), Reason (*Ragione*) by bees (49), and Anger (*Sdegno*) by a bear (50–51).

[44] His wings are fully fledged (*impennate*) and thus ready for flight, unlike the unused and unfeathered (*spenachiate*) wings on the card.

in an overelaborate hall of mirrors, and so he has. Psyche is a partial example for both Viti and his patroness—for Viti in his labors and ascent and for the patroness in her endurance and sainthood. The sainted patroness is Viti's own example of endurance, whom he can follow through her intercession with God. And Viti himself? His ascent, "seen clearly by all," is implicitly an example to everyone.

Viti's allegory has carried us far away from both Apuleius and Boiardo into the world of his own exalted (or overheated) imagination. But his allegory and Boiardo's are alike in one essential point that sharply distinguishes them from the earlier allegories of Fulgentius and Boccaccio, as well as from the story in Apuleius: Psyche is not marked as guilty or sinful or deserving of her labors in any way. In Boiardo and Viti her story is one of endurance rewarded by immortality, not of curiosity punished and finally redeemed by suffering—naturally enough, we might say, since in Boiardo's cards she is an illustration of Patience, and her story begins with her misfortunes.

Boiardo's version reminds us, however, that the story of Psyche is capable of different tellings and that those tellings yield different meanings: everything depends on the details omitted or included and on where the teller chooses to begin or end the tale. Apuleius' leisurely narration gives us a sort of fairy tale that we can allegorize (or not, if we choose) as the union of the Soul with Love. Fulgentius assimilates Psyche to Adam and makes her illustrate the Fall: he dwells on Psyche's transgressions (her disobedience and the curiosity that awakens her sexual desire), omits every detail connected with her redemption and final happiness, and ends his allegory with her expulsion from the Eden of Cupid's palace.[45] Boccaccio, by contrast, is less interested in Psyche's fault than in her redemption and the ultimate union of the soul with God. The narration in his final version concludes with Psyche in Heaven, her innate immortality implicitly acknowledged by his omission of the cup of divine ambrosia that gives her eternal life and sanctifies her marriage in Apuleius (*Met.* 6.23.5).[46]

Psyche at Court

Boiardo's tercet on Psyche in the *Tarocchi* (and the card accompanying it) lived on in Viti's allegory and description, written, we must remember, for a courtly audience, the aristocratic lady in Urbino. But Boiardo's *Apulegio volgare* was to have a far more important reception and a

---

[45] See chapter 2.
[46] See chapter 3.

much greater influence on both the literary and the artistic reception of Apuleius himself, especially at the court of Ferrara.

Boiardo completed his translation around 1479, but Ercole d'Este drastically limited its circulation. He jealously guarded all his books, but he seemed to take special delight in Apuleius' novel, which he claimed to consult every day.[47] His precautions were successful. *Apulegio volgare* was published only in 1518, long after the deaths of both Ercole and Boiardo, and only two manuscripts are extant.[48] In the 1490s, while Ercole and his family still had what we might term "exclusive rights" to it, *Apulegio volgare* inspired at least three important treatments of Psyche associated with the Este: a long poem entitled *Fabula Psiches et Cupidinis* by Niccolò da Correggio, a fresco cycle in one of Ercole's palaces, and a comedy by Galeotto del Carretto entitled *Noze de Psiche e Cupidine*. Correggio's poem is based on Apuleius, but still more on *Apulegio volgare*; the fresco cycle (now lost) and Carretto's comedy used both Correggio and Boiardo.

Niccolò da Correggio (1450–1508), like his cousin Boiardo, was both a courtier and an accomplished poet.[49] Around 1491 he dedicated his poem on Psyche to Ercole's daughter, Isabella Gonzaga, wife of Francesco Gonzaga, marquess of Mantua. According to the dedication, he did so at her express request.[50] The work—written in Italian despite its Latin title—was an appropriate gift for the new bride (the marriage took place in 1490), and its subject would already have been familiar to her. Isabella had almost surely read Boiardo's translation at her father's court, and she probably had access to it in her husband's, for in 1481, in a rare gesture of generosity, Ercole had presented a copy of it to her future father-in-law, Federico I Gonzaga.[51] Isabella maintained an interest in *Apulegio volgare* and wrote to Ferrara to

---

[47] Ercole made the claim in a letter of 1481 to Federico Gonzaga as an excuse for sending him a copy rather than the original of Boiardo's translation. The letter is quoted by Fumagalli, *Matteo Maria Boiardo*, 10.

[48] They are Naples, Biblioteca Nazionale XIII C 95, and Pisa, Biblioteca Universitaria, ms. 979. But there must have been at least four more, including the dedication copy. See Fumagalli, *Matteo Maria Boiardo*, 161–63; idem, "Amore e Psiche," 79 n. 10. For the publication history, see especially *Fumagalli*, 163–84.

[49] For Correggio's life and works, see Tissoni Benvenuti, in Correggio, *Opere*, 493–505. See also Farenga, "Niccolò da Correggio."

[50] "Pure, astrecto dal comandamento di Vui, mia Signora e Patrona, quelle che sono a le mie mane pervenute vi mando." Correggio, dedication of *Fabula Psiches et Cupidinis*, p. 49. The work seems to have been completed by June 1491; see Tissoni Benvenuti, in Correggio, *Opere*, 499.

[51] Federico was delighted with the work, as his thank-you note to Ercole attests. The correspondence on Boiardo's translation is printed and discusssed by Fumagalli, *Matteo Maria Boiardo*, 10–12.

request another copy some years later (1512), after the Gonzaga copy was lost.[52]

Correggio no doubt had read Apuleius' Latin, but *Apulegio volgare* was his immediate source for *Fabula Psiches et Cupidinis*, as its many parallels and verbal echoes with Boiardo attest.[53] Like Apuleius, Correggio uses the story of Psyche as a tale within a tale.[54] In Apuleius, of course, the story is related by a drunken old woman in the robbers' cave. She tells it to distract and console the girl Charite, kidnapped by the robbers on her wedding day; but it is also heard by the Ass (Lucius), who later relates it to us. Apuleius never says what the old woman's audience thought of her story: Charite shows no reaction, and the Ass, shallow as ever, only calls it "such a pretty tale" (*tam bellam fabulam*) and regrets that he doesn't have tablets and a stylus to write it down (*Met.* 6.25.1). Psyche is never mentioned again in the novel, and Apuleius leaves it to us to infer the relation between her story and that of Lucius. In Correggio, the frame story is related in the first person by the poet-lover, who tells how Cupid afflicted him with an unrequited passion for the nymph Florida, how he pursued her in vain, finally falling into an exhausted sleep in a beautiful garden, and how he saw Cupid himself in his dream. The embedded story is related by the dream Cupid: it is his own history, the tale of Psyche. In the concluding panel of the frame story, the poet wakes and meets the god Pan, a fellow victim of unhappy love. Pan confirms the truth of the poet's vision and invites him to remain in the garden, but the poet refuses, disillusioned by the instability of both love and life itself. Unlike Apuleius, Correggio tightly weaves his two stories together. Cupid and Pan appear in both. In the frame Cupid is the pitiless god of love who causes the poet's sufferings; in the embedded tale he is his own helpless victim. Pan plays the role of wise and kindly helper in both frame and insert—counseling the poet in the one and Psyche in the other.[55] Correggio tightens the connection in other ways as well, both vouching for the truth of the embedded

---

[52] See ibid., 12–15.

[53] Parallels are noted by Fumagalli in his edition of Boiardo's translation (ibid. 217–345, and see also 145–50). See also Fumagalli, "Amore e Psiche," 79–80; Trecca, *La magia rinnovata*, 79–80; Cavicchioli, *Le metamorfosi di Psiche*, 62. Correggio also echoes Boiardo's description of Psyche's reaction to Cupid's announcement of her pregnancy. Boiardo: "Molto di questo Psiche si ralegrava" (*Apulegio volgare* in Fumagalli, *Matteo Maria Boiardo*, 259; cf. *Met.* 5.12.1 and Fumagalli, "Amore e Psiche," 77). Correggio: "Lei di questo mio dir si ralegrava" (*Fabula*, stanza 93, line 7).

[54] For a detailed analysis of Correggio's poem, see Trecca, *La magia rinnovata*, 71–144. See also Stillers, "Erträumte Kunstwelt."

[55] As Trecca notes, Correggio has followed Boiardo in enhancing Pan's role in the Psyche story: *La magia rinnovata*, 104–5. See also Cavicchioli, *Le metamorfosi di Psiche*, 61–62. The meeting of Psyche and Pan in Apuleius appears at *Met.* 5.25.3.

story in the frame and showing the effect the tale has on its hearer. Pan confirms Cupid's story, as we have seen; and the poet, hearing that the god of love himself cannot escape its vicissitudes, renounces love altogether and makes his escape. He concludes by advising his readers to do the same: "Flee fast and far because love's arrow kills and not just stings you."[56]

As Correggio tells it, the story of Psyche is not an allegory of patience or of the just punishment of curiosity and lust, nor yet of the soul's union with either God or Love. Rather, even with its happy ending, it is a cautionary tale of the vulnerability of gods and men alike to the vicissitudes of fortune.[57] More to the point, however, it is not the story of Psyche at all, but the story of Cupid, which is a very different matter. The point of view, the emotions, the misfortunes, all belong to the narrator, who is no third-person storyteller unconnected with the events, like Apuleius' old woman, but one of the principals, giving his own first-person account. The story looks different when we see it through Cupid's eyes. Cupid himself is no longer Psyche's "mysterious husband," as in Apuleius—a figure whose identity, emotions, and even actions are only fleetingly hinted at in the old woman's narration.[58] Instead, as both the protagonist and the teller of the story, he is an open book, his every emotion on display. Psyche, by contrast, is no longer the heroine of the tale. Cupid duly relates her adventures, but keeps himself at center stage, replacing Psyche's feelings and perspective with his own. Cupid's focus on himself, evident everywhere, dominates his account of the fatal night. Apuleius describes Psyche's anguished hesitation before the event: "She hurries, delays, is daring, is fearful, despairs, rages; and (it all comes down to this) in the same body, she hates the beast, and loves the husband."[59] Correggio's Cupid substitutes his own distress for Psyche's:

> O dear Psyche, alas too trusting, alas too ready to harm us both! Your invisible lover does not deserve to have you cut off his head. You will not see any horrible sight, but in fact beauty manifest! Poor girl, how much more you will regret it when you weep for me in vain! Thus I sadly said to myself at the time, seeing my Psyche harden her heart against me with that piercing blade—against me, who made the gods wait on her! I knew everything although I was absent, and what

---

[56] "Fuggiti presto, di buon passo e longie, / ché'l stral d'amor ucide e non pur pongie." Correggio, *Fabula*, stanza 179, lines 7–8. The text is cited from Niccolò da Correggio *Opere*, ed. Tissoni Benvenuti.

[57] For the importance of fortune in Correggio and a comparison with Apuleius' treatment, see Trecca, *La magia rinnovata*, 118–24.

[58] See Kenney's important article: "Psyche and her Mysterious Husband."

[59] "Festinat differt, audet trepidat, diffidit irascitur; et quod est ultimum, in eodem corpore odit bestiam, diligit maritum." *Met.* 5.21.4.

must happen next. But, conquered by the love I bore her, I still returned to her as usual.[60]

When Psyche raises her lamp over the sleeping Cupid, Apuleius has us see his beauty through her eyes (*Met.* 5.22); Correggio's Cupid uses Psyche as a mirror for his own self-description (*Fabula*, stanzas 107–9).

The most important effect of transforming Psyche's story into the story of Cupid, however, is to deprive it of all possibility of religious or moral seriousness. Correggio's Cupid—pitiless in the frame and victim of fortune in the embedded tale—does not lend himself to allegorical improvement. His Psyche, relegated to secondary status, is little more than a peg on which to hang the emotions of her hapless lover. The poem in which they appear is not edifying or susceptible to religious allegory—and it is not intended to be.[61] Rather, it is a piquant and engaging entertainment for courtly readers already familiar with other versions of the story. We can imagine that its novelties would have pleased their fancy.

Correggio's *Fabula Psiches et Cupidinis*, like Boiardo's *Apulegio volgare*, seems to have been closely guarded by the Este, for it was printed only in 1507.[62] The poem was a gift to Isabella Gonzaga, but it was also well known at her father's court in Ferrara, where it may have provided the impetus for a cycle of frescoes at one of Ercole's pleasure palaces, Belriguardo.[63] Belriguardo and its frescoes disappeared long ago, but a contemporary description survives that draws on the poem. The description appears in a work entitled *De triumphis religionis*, dedicated to Ercole in 1497 by a struggling humanist named Giovanni Sabadino degli Arienti.[64] Arienti's work—which, like Correggio's, is in Italian, despite its Latin title—concerns the princely virtues. Book 5, on

---

[60] "—O cara Psiche, ohimè troppo credibile, / al commun danno, ohimè pur troppo presta! / Non merita l'amante tuo invisibile / che tu gli levi dal corpo la testa; / tu non vedrai alcuno aspecto orribile, / ma proprio la bellezza manifesta. / Misera, quanto ancor ti pentirai, / alor che indarno tu mi piangierai!—/ Cusì dicevo alor tra me dolente, / vedendo la mia Psiche incrudelire / contra di me con quel cortel pungente, / di me, ch'io la facevo ai dei servire! / Sapevo tutto, ben ch'io fussi absente, / e como l'ordin doveva seguire, / ma, vinto dall' amor ch'io gli portava, / como era usato, a lei pur ritornava." Correggio, *Fabula*, stanzas 103–4.

[61] For a different view, see Stillers, who argues that Correggio's Cupid has qualities in common with Christ and that Psyche's story is that of sinful man—losing paradise through guilt and folly and finally gaining blessedness through suffering ("Erträumte Kunstwelt," 137–38).

[62] But once in print, it evidently enjoyed great success; by 1521 it had been reprinted five times. See Tissoni Benvenuti, in Correggio, *Opere*, 508, 512–13.

[63] Gundersheimer, *Art and Life at the Court of Ercole I d'Este*, 64 n. 55. See also Cavicchioli, *Le metamorfosi di Psiche*, 63.

[64] Arienti's work survives in a manuscript in the Vatican Library (Ross. 176). Its importance was first recognized by Gundersheimer, who published it in 1972 in *Art and Life*.

magnificentia, includes a room-by-room description of Belriguardo, including the Sala di Psiche and its frescoes.[65] The painter, not named by Arienti, has been identified as Ercole de' Roberti.[66]

Arienti describes the frescoes as a narrative sequence in many scenes, beginning with the "celestial nymph Psyche" and Venus' instructions to Cupid to punish her, and ending with Psyche's having given birth to her daughter, Voluptas.[67] His account, however, is a literary ecphrasis rather than a precise description, and it does not allow us to visualize the appearance of the frescoes.[68] He does not say how many scenes there were or how they were arranged.[69] He gives little information about the contents or design of individual scenes, emphasizing instead elements of narration, feeling, or motivation that could not have been shown by the painter. One example must suffice. In his description of Psyche's wedding night, Arienti shows us Psyche tucked up in the marriage bed and Cupid positioned beside her, his weapons put down at the foot of the bed, "telling her reassuringly not to be afraid of the oracle that has told her that he was a monster."[70] We can almost imagine the scene with its two protagonists and their props (the bed and the weapons); but Arienti says nothing of its colors or of the postures of Cupid and Psyche, the

---

See also Gundersheimer, *Ferrara*, 249–62 (part of Arienti's description of the Sala di Psiche is translated on 259–60). For Arienti, see James, *Giovanni Sabadino degli Arienti*; Ghinassi, "Giovanni Sabadino degli Arienti." For a general discussion of *De triumphis religionis*, see Shepherd, "Giovanni Sabadino degli Arienti."

[65] The fundamental discussions are those of Gundersheimer (*Art and Life*, 21–22; "The Patronage of Ercole I d'Este," 8–17; *Ferrara*, 249–52). See also Cavicchioli, "*Amore e Psiche*"; de Jong, "Il pittore a le volte," 204–13.

[66] See Gundersheimer, "The Patronage of Ercole I d'Este," esp. 8–12. But the identification had already been suggested by Cast: "Review of *Art and Life*," 283.

[67] "Psych celeste nympha" (Arienti, fol. 49v in Gundersheimer, *Art and Life*, 62); Voluptas: fol. 53r, in Gundersheimer, 64.

[68] Compare de Jong: "Sabadino did not aim at an accurate account of Ercole de' Roberti's paintings: what he did was to write an *ekphrasis*" ("Il pittore a le volte," 207).

[69] Arienti's frequent use of the word *vedesi* (one sees) in his description led Gundersheimer to suggest that the word was a "divider" between scenes and that "Sabadino was describing fourteen distinct scenes or panels, though there may have been more" (*Art and Life*, 22). Cavicchioli also thinks of fourteen scenes, but with varying numbers of episodes in each ("*Amore e Psiche*," 143 n. 30). If Gundersheimer is right, some of the scenes demarcated by *vedesi* would be very crowded; the first, for example, would include Psyche's exposure on the cliff, her rescue by Zephyr, Cupid's falling in love with her in spite of his mother's command, a banquet in which Psyche is waited on by nymphs and honored by the songs of the Muses, and her wedding night with Cupid (Arienti, fol. 49v–50r in Gundersheimer, *Art and Life*, 62). It is also unclear, moreover, that Arienti used only *vedesi* as a divider: scenes also seem to be introduced with *si vede* or *se vede* (eight times) and *et vedesi* (once, for the description of the great wedding feast at the end).

[70] "Confortandola non havere timore delo oraculo che decto li havea lui essere mostro" (Arienti, fol. 50r, in Gundersheimer, *Art and Life*, 62).

very elements that would evoke the picture for us as a physical entity. And he concludes the description with Cupid's words of reassurance, which could not have been shown in the fresco at all; this detail, which is not in Apuleius, comes straight from Correggio.[71]

Arienti's account of the Sala di Psiche is both tantalizing and frustrating. On the one hand, it gives us a glimpse of the earliest monumental treatment of the Psyche story in Renaissance art (the precursor, if not the model, for such masterpieces as the frescoes of Raphael and his pupils in the Farnesina in Rome and Giulio Romano's frescoes in the Palazzo Te in Mantua).[72] On the other hand, the glimpse is too limited and imprecise to convey any real sense of the room and its decorations. In the previous section we considered the description of another lost work of art: Viti's account of the tarot cards with Boiardo's verses. Viti's description of Psyche provides all the information we need to make a similar card for ourselves: Psyche's posture, the colors of her dress and mantle, which she holds by both hands, the broken attributes of Cupid at her feet on either side, even Boiardo's tercet written above her head and the dapple-gray horse with its violet bridle next to Cupid's unfeathered wings. Arienti's ecphrasis, by contrast, gives no such details; a reader hoping to reconstruct the Sala di Psiche would not even know where to begin.

But Viti and Arienti were writing for different audiences: Viti for a lady who had never seen the cards and wanted a deck of her own, and Arienti for Ercole d'Este, who knew very well what the Sala di Psiche looked like and had had a hand in its design, as Arienti notes at the end of his description. The passage is worth quoting in full:

> These events and deeds of moral love, full of individual meanings, are represented so successfully that they could have been by the hands of Parrhasius, who defeated Zeuxis with his painting of the curtain over the grapes, as well as by the hands of the excellent Ferrarese painter who painted such a moral thing following your ducal instruction, my dear most talented prince. On this subject Niccolò da Correggio, a distinguished and eloquent gentleman and a capable man of arms, has also portrayed something very felicitous in graceful and sweet verse in his mother tongue, following what the outstanding author Apuleius writes.[73]

---

[71] Compare Correggio, *La fabula*, stanzas 75–77, and esp. 77, lines 5–8: "Ma non aver di l'oracul paura, / ch'io non son fiera uscita di Nemea, / ma giovinetto ancor sul primo fiore, / che per te acceso ha nel suo foco Amore." For a list of Arienti's borrowings from Correggio see de Jong, "Il pittore a le volte," 210–13.

[72] See nn. 97 and 98, below.

[73] "Questi accidenti et acti de morale amore, pieni de singulari sentimenti, sono effigiati con tanta felicitate che Parasio il quale in pictura del velo sopra l'uva vinse Zeusis,

Again Arienti's remarks are surprisingly uninformative. He tells us that the subject of the paintings is moral, that they were the work of an excellent Ferrarese painter, that they were painted according to Ercole's "ducal instruction," and that the story had been treated previously by Niccolò da Correggio and Apuleius. But he does not discuss the moral message, identify the painter, describe Ercole's role, or specify the relation between the paintings and the literary treatments.

All of these details so obscure to us were well known to Arienti's immediate audience: the court of Ferrara and especially Ercole himself.[74] We cannot visualize the Sala di Psiche and its program as they did, but by supplementing Arienti's comments with other contemporary information, we can at least date the paintings and perhaps get some inkling of Ercole's intentions.[75] Ercole and Roberti were working intensively together on the cartoons for the paintings in February 1493, as we learn in a letter from Ercole's secretary to the duchess, Eleonora of Aragon.[76] Since many contemporary accounts, including Arienti's, make it clear that Ercole was a deeply religious man with a great interest in the immortality of the soul, it seems probable that he was directing Roberti to treat the story of Psyche as a religious allegory. The impression is confirmed by a letter of 1498 to Ercole from a kinsman, Niccolò Maria d'Este, suggesting that paintings based on the allegorical *Tabula Cebetis* might provide an appropriate counterpart for the Psyche cycle. After complimenting Ercole's princely enthusiasm for painting, Niccolò Maria continues: "And, having already had the story of Psyche painted, which under a veil means the soul, and the disturbances which accompany it, it remained to find some other invention, which, portraying it with subtlety and secret mystery, might represent human life".[77] At the start of his description Arienti, too, suggests an

---

bastarebbe fusseno de loro mane non che de mane de optimo pictore ferrariense che tanta morale cosa pinse secondo la tua ducal instructione, ingegniosissimo principe mio charo. Di che anchora tanta beata cosa in legiadro e dolce verso materno Nicolao da Coregio, signore claro e facundo e d'arme valido huo[mo] ha depincto, secondo Apoleio auctore prestante scrive." Arienti, fol. 53r–v, in Gundersheimer, *Art and Life*, 64–65.

[74] But Arienti also intended his work for readers beyond Ferrara, as James points out (*Giovanni Sabadino degli Arienti*, 63), for he intended to place a presentation copy in the library of the monastery of San Domenico in Bologna.

[75] See Gundersheimer, who quotes and translates the relevant sources ("The Patronage," 8–18).

[76] Ibid., 8–9. The letter is quoted at greater length by Manca, *The Art of Ercole de' Roberti*, 213–14.

[77] "Et havendo gia facto depingere la Psyche, che sotto velamento significa l'anima, e la perturbatione che drieto li vanno, Restava trovare qualche altra invention, che depingendola con suttile, e secreto misterio rapresentasse l'humana vita." Niccolò Maria d'Este, quoted in Gundersheimer, "The Patronage," 15 n. 28. The translation is Gundersheimer's, slightly modified.

allegorical reading. "On the walls," he says, "we see represented with singular morality, under a poetic veil, the story of the celestial nymph Psyche in most felicitous painting."[78] But that is all he says, and we are left to see for ourselves just what moral meaning Ercole might have intended to convey "under the poetic veil" of Roberti's painting. Since Arienti's description emphasizes Psyche's tasks, her despair, and the help she receives on the way, we can imagine that her story was to be seen as an allegory of the helpless and undeserving soul laboring through trials to immortality.[79] The final image in his description is both suggestive and mysterious: "And then one sees that Psyche has given birth at full term to a charming daughter called Pleasure, fruit of the wretched world."[80] The last phrase, which makes such a despairing comment on the human condition, is consistent with the allegorical reading I have suggested. If it is not merely an addition by Arienti, we can probably attribute the thought to Ercole himself, because it does not appear in any earlier account.[81]

Arienti's description frequently echoes Niccolò da Correggio's *Fabula Psiches et Cupidinis*, and he mentions Correggio's treatment, as we have seen. But Correggio's poem could not have inspired the serious allegorical program of the frescoes suggested by both Niccolò Maria d'Este and Arienti himself, since it deliberately sidesteps all moral or religious allegory. The poem probably influenced the frescoes in a different way, simply by bringing the Psyche story to Ercole's attention. Correggio had dedicated *Fabula Psiches et Cupidinis* to Isabella Gonzaga in 1491; the

---

[78] "In le pariete si vede con moralità singulare, sotto poetico velamento hystoriata con felicissima pictura, Psych celeste nympha." Arienti, fol. 49v, in Gundersheimer, *Art and Life*, 62.

[79] Arienti relates Psyche's trials in detail, as Cavicchioli notes (*Le metamorfosi di Psiche*, 59–60); but I do not understand her assertion that he systematically eliminates the celestial scenes from his description (*Le metamorfosi*, 59; "Amore e Psiche," 133). By itself, his detailed account of Psyche's wedding banquet among the gods would be sufficient to show the importance of heavenly forces in the story. Arienti, fol. 52v–53r, in Gundersheimer, *Art and Life*, 64.

[80] "E poi si vede Psych del suo maturo parto havere parturita una vaga figlia nominata Voluptate, fructo del misero mondo." Arienti, fol. 53r, in Gundersheimer, *Art and Life*, 64.

[81] Apuleius' story ends: "Sic rite Psyche convenit in manum Cupidinis et nascitur illis maturo partu filia, quam Voluptatem nominamus" (*Met.* 6.24.4. Fulgentius does not mention the child at all. In Boccaccio's Christian vision the child is characterized optimistically: "Cupidinis perpetuo frueretur coniugio, cui peperit Voluptatem"; and in the allegorical explanation: "Ex amore parturit Voluptatem, id est delectationem et letitiam sempiternam" (*Gen.* 5.22.10 and 17 [Zaccaria]). Arienti's immediate predecessors, Boiardo and Correggio, give Psyche a *son*, Dilecto. Boiardo: "Lor nacque quello figliolo che Dilecto è chiamato" (*Apolegio volgare* 6.24, Fumagalli, 345). Correggio: "Psiche divenne mia, como io t'ho decto, / e gravida, di nui nacque il Dilecto" (*Fabula* 169.7–8).

tale would still have been of current interest when Ercole and Roberti started to work on the Belriguardo frescoes two years later.

But the Belriguardo frescoes did not exhaust the Este-Gonzaga enthusiasm for Cupid and Psyche. A few years later Galeotto Del Carretto (ca. 1455–1530) treated the theme again, this time in a comedy: *Noze de Psiche e Cupidine* (The Marriage of Psyche and Cupid).[82] Del Carretto, like Boiardo and Correggio, was both an aristocratic courtier and a poet.[83] He came to Mantua in 1494 on a diplomatic mission, resided at the court in 1496–97, and maintained a correspondence with Isabella Gonzaga, which is still preserved.[84] *Noze de Psiche e Cupidine* is not named in the correspondence, but it is perhaps to be identified with the "new comedy" Del Carretto mentioned to Isabella in a letter of November 1499 and sent to Mantua at her insistence in January 1500.[85] Whatever its exact date and destination, however, the comedy belongs to the *ambiente* of Ferrara and Mantua, since it is heavily influenced by both Correggio's *Fabula* and Boiardo's *Apolegio volgare*, and especially the latter.[86]

Del Carretto's comedy presents the familiar story, although with some new wrinkles that we will consider presently. The essential difference between *Noze de Psiche e Cupidine* and its predecessors, however, is that between drama and narrative. In narrative the author may relate the story through his own persona or that of one of the characters, but events come to us ostensibly from a single source (or at least one source at a time), whether an omniscient third-person narrator as in Apuleius or a self-interested first-person narrator as in Correggio.[87] Drama, by contrast, presents many voices and points of view: in theory, at least, a play may have as many perspectives as it has speakers. The plot may be anticipated or summarized in a prologue or *argumentum* (as it is in

---

[82] Edited by Mussini Sacchi in Tissoni Benvenuti and Mussini Sacchi, eds., *Teatro del Quattrocento*, 611–725.

[83] See Ricciardi, "Galeotto Del Carretto."

[84] The correspondence has been published by Turba, "Galeotto del Carretto."

[85] See the discussion of Tissoni Benvenuti, *Teatro del Quattrocento*, 559–67. The general opinion is that Del Carretto wrote the comedy to celebrate the marriage contract of Guglielmo IX Paleologo and Anna d'Alençon in 1502, but as Tissoni Benvenuti points out (564), Del Carretto was in exile from Guglielmo's court from until 1501 until 1503. There are no manuscripts of the play; the earliest edition seems to have been printed in 1520 (Tissoni Benvenuti, 567).

[86] Parallels are noted by Fumagalli in his edition of Boiardo's translation (*Matteo Maria Boiardo*, 217–345, and see also 145–50).

[87] This is an oversimplification, of course, especially for Apuleius. Since Apuleius's narrator is Lucius narrating the story told by the old woman, the tale is filtered through two storytellers (not counting Apuleius himself).

Noze de Psiche e Cupidine), but its details emerge through the actions and words of its characters.

Del Carretto gives all of Apuleius' characters speaking roles in *Noze*: Psyche, Cupid, Venus, Jupiter, Mercury, Psyche's parents and sisters, and all the rest, including the helpful ants, reeds, eagle, and tower. He even brings in the sisters' husbands in the last two acts. But with all these perspectives, the focus is always on Psyche herself. Her parents' grief, her sisters' envy, Venus' jealousy, Cupid's love and anger, even the dismay and confusion of the sisters' husbands, are all responses to Psyche and her adventures. Even Cupid must take a back seat. He is absent during most of the play, and his scenes with Psyche before the catastrophe with the lamp are all offstage: we hear, but are not supposed to see, their bedtime conversations.

Del Carretto's most interesting innovation is in the role he gives to Psyche's family at the end of the play (act 5, lines 119–356). In Apuleius, Psyche's parents appear briefly at the beginning and are barely mentioned later. Her sisters are destroyed immediately after the loss of Cupid, and the husbands they despise never appear at all. Del Carretto, by contrast, brings all these characters together at the house of Psyche's parents, Cosmo and Endilizia,[88] for a grand reunion with Psyche before she is transported to Olympus for her wedding with Cupid. To do so, he makes Mercury resurrect Psyche's sisters, brings their husbands to Cosmo's house, and has Psyche appear out of nowhere, all in the space of about fifty lines. The resulting scene is surprising but effective. The reanimation of the sisters allows them to be reunited with their husbands and contributes, as the editor notes, to the happy ending of the comedy and the theme of legitimate marriage, which is emphasized both in its title and in the epithalamia at the end sung by Apollo and the Graces (act 5, lines 381–465).[89] Its more important function, however, is to allow Psyche to be reconciled with her sisters and forgive them: their resurrection is for Psyche's spiritual benefit. As Mercury tells her: "If pity dwells in your heart, lift from your breast the anger you have conceived, which seems to overwhelm your thoughts with hatred. With a pleasing result and kindly heart allow yourself to pardon the mistake they committed before, since they show signs of penitence".[90]

---

[88] The name Endilizia is derived from Martianus Capella by way of Boccaccio (see chapter 3, n. 162), but Del Carretto seems to have named Cosmo himself (the father, unnamed in Apuleius, is identified as *deus* in Fulgentius' allegory, and as Apollo in Martianus and Boccaccio).

[89] See Mussini Sacchi on *Noze*, act 5, line 84, in *Teatro del Quattrocento*.

[90] "[Però,] se nel tuo cuor pietate alberga, / leva dal petto el conceputo sdegno, / qual par ch'in odio el tuo penser somerga; / fa' che cum grato effetto e cuor benegno / tu gli perdoni el già comesso errore / poi che ti fan de penitenzia segno." *Noze*, act 5, lines 296–301.

In her answering speech (act 5, lines 308–25), Psyche pardons her sisters, accepts Jupiter's summons to immortality, rejoices in the cessation of Venus' anger and in her own coming wedding to Cupid, and bids her parents farewell. The editor justly observes: "She departs triumphant, now superior to earthly things."[91]

At the end of the fifteenth century the *Golden Ass* enjoyed a remarkable reception at the courts of Ercole d'Este in Ferrara and his daughter Isabella d'Este Gonzaga in Mantua. Within a little over twenty years, from around 1479 to 1500, the novel was translated, imitated, illustrated, versified, and dramatized. Boiardo inaugurated the process with *Apulegio volgare*, which made the novel available to a generation of Italian poets and artists. Boiardo himself imitated one of the adultery stories in *Orlando Innamorato*, but his allegorical tercet on Psyche was more in the spirit of his successors, Viti, Correggio, and Del Carretto, who seemed almost obsessed with her story—each presenting a new perspective or interpretation in a different genre and each drawing on his predecessors as he did so. Two Este works of art are known to have represented Psyche or her story: the small tarot card and the great frescoes in Belriguardo. Both soon disappeared, but they were survived by written descriptions that add to our understanding of the literary tradition.

The interest in Apuleius and Psyche that Boiardo had awakened did not end in 1500 or limit itself to Este circles. The story of Psyche was paraphrased in Italian by Giorgio Beccaria around 1503.[92] Mario Equicola presented it as a brief Neoplatonic allegory in *Libro de natura de amore* (composed between 1505 and 1525).[93] Del Carretto used it again (along with the story of Lucius and the Judgment of Paris from *Met.* 10) in the long allegorical drama *Tempio d'Amore*, which he began sometime after 1503 and finally published in 1524.[94] (Each of the episodes is presented as an ecphrasis: Lucius in a mosaic pavement, the Judgment of Paris as a painting, and the story of Psyche as a relief in a loggia in the garden of Amore.)[95] We hear of a comedy of Psyche presented at Carnival in Constantinople by Venetian merchants in 1524.[96] Raphael and his pupils used the story for their frescoes in Agosto Chigi's Villa

---

[91] "Se ne va trionfante, ormai superiore alle cose terrene." Mussini Sacchi, ad loc.

[92] The work is preserved in manuscript with no reference to its author: Milan, Biblioteca Trivulziana 26 (12). The beginning and ending have been edited by De Maria, *La favola di Amore e Psiche*, 263–77. Mussini Sacchi has identified the author as Giorgio Beccaria ("Un amico pavese di Matteo Bandello: Giorgio Beccaria").

[93] See Ricci, *La redazione manoscritta*, 252; Cherchi, "Mario Equicola."

[94] Galeotto Del Carretto, *Tempio d'amore*, ed. Magnani and Caramaschi.

[95] Lucius (called Lucio Apuleio): *Tempio d'amore*, ll. 3021–67; Judgment of Paris: 2112–88; Psyche: 4373–56.

[96] See Acocella, *L'Asino d'oro*, 105; De Maria, *La favola di Amore e Psiche*, 125–26.

Farnesina in Rome in 1518.[97] Within a decade, Giulio Romano, who worked on the Farnesina with Raphael, had made it the subject of his own fresco cycle in the Palazzo Te in Mantua for Isabella Gonzaga's son, Duke Federico Gonzaga.[98]

But enough. The trail of artistic representations and vernacular literary works after 1500 is rich and tempting, but it has been well traveled before us and we can follow it no farther.[99] Instead, it is time to turn our attention to interpretation in a different genre, the Latin scholarly commentary. In the next chapter we will move from the courts of Ferrara and Mantua to a lecture hall of the University of Bologna and the Apuleius commentary of Filippo Beroaldo.

[97] Some details in the Farnesina frescoes are derived from Niccolò da Correggio, as De Maria (*La favola di Amore e Psiche*, 236) and Shearman noted ("Die Loggia der Psyche," 71–4). See also, with earlier bibliography, Acocella, *L'Asino d'oro*, 112–17; Cavicchioli, *Le metamorfosi di Psiche*, 65–83; eadem, *The Tale of Cupid and Psyche*, 87–116 (with color illustrations).

[98] See, with earlier bibliography, Acocella, *L'Asino d'oro*, 125–36; Cavicchioli, *Le metamorfosi di Psiche*, 83–100; eadem, *The Tale of Cupid and Psyche*, 116–44 (with color illustrations). The frescoes in Palazzo Te also show the influence of Niccolò da Correggio, but especially of the *Hypnerotomachia*. For the *Hypnerotomachia*, see Gombrich, "Hypnerotomachiana," 125; Verheyen, "Die Malereien in der Sala di Psiche," 55–58; idem, *The Palazzo Te in Mantua*, 25–56.

[99] For surveys in addition to the books of Acocella and Cavicchioli (see previous note), see De Maria, *La favola di Amore e Psiche*, and Moreschini, *Il mito di Amore e Psiche*, 7–48.

CHAPTER 6

Apuleius Redux: Filippo Beroaldo Comments on the *Golden Ass*

> I am publishing this new likeness of my mind, thoroughly polished with versatile sculpting and careful elegance.
> —*Filippo Beroaldo,* Commentarii in Asinum Aureum

Filippo Beroaldo (1453–1505) was a near contemporary of Correggio and del Carretto.[1] Like them, he was busy with Apuleius in the 1490s, for at about the same time that they were rewriting the story of Psyche for Isabella Gonzaga in Mantua, he was working on his commentary on the *Golden Ass* in nearby Bologna. He published his work—a large folio volume of nearly six hundred pages—on 1 August 1500.[2]

By 1500 Beroaldo had become one of the most prolific scholars of his time. He had already published commentaries on Propertius, Suetonius, and Cicero's *Tusculan Disputations*, editions of Pliny's letters and Cicero's orations, Latin translations of stories from Boccaccio in both prose and verse, several volumes of orations and poems, and *Annotationes centum*, a volume of emendations and interpretations of various authors.[3] He was also one of the busiest and most famous teachers in Europe. He taught his students at the University of Bologna all day long: in large lectures of two or three hundred in the morning and in smaller groups or individual tutorials in the afternoons.[4] Many of these

---

[1] For Beroaldo's life, see especially Krautter, *Philologische Methode*. See also Rose, *Filippo Beroaldo der Ältere*, 4–150; Gilmore, "Filippo Beroaldo, Senior"; Maréchaux, "Béroalde l'ancien (Philippe)."

[2] GKW 2305. The fundamental study is Krautter's *Philologische Methode*. See also Casella, "Il metodo dei commentatori umanistici"; Gaisser, "Teaching Classics in the Renaissance," 1–12; eadem, "Reading Apuleius with Filippo Beroaldo"; eadem, "Filippo Beroaldo on Apuleius"; Küenzlen, *Verwandlungen*, 59–129.

[3] This list is by no means complete. For a bibliography of Beroaldo's works, see Krautter, *Philologische Methode*, 188–92. See also Rose, *Filippo Beroaldo der Ältere*, 70–77. For Beroaldo's translations of Boccaccio, see Viti, "Filippo Beroaldo."

[4] Beroaldo describes his teaching in a letter of 1499 to Péter Váradi, dedicatee of his commentary on Apuleius: "Lectionibus publicis distringor, quarum quottidiani auditores sunt circiter tercenteni; occupatum quoque occupant privatae lectiones, quarum sitientes sunt complusculi principes scholasticorum." Modena, Biblioteca Estense, Ms. Campori App. 324 (γ, S, 5, 25), fol. 24v ff., quoted from Garin, "Note sull'insegnamento," 383.

students were foreign, for Beroaldo's reputation extended far beyond Italy. They came from Spain and France, but above all from Germany and eastern Europe; indeed, a contemporary chronicler tells us both that he had two hundred students "from the other side of the Alps" and that they all left Bologna after his death.[5] Beroaldo's students were undoubtedly attracted not only by his prodigious learning but also by his kindly, genial manner, for the picture of him that emerges from contemporary biographies is of a happy, hospitable man, deeply religious, but also good company and a bit of a bon vivant.[6] Beroaldo presents a similar but not identical image in his own works, which he specifically characterizes as self-portraits. This is an important point, and I shall return to it presently.

It is not clear when Beroaldo first became interested in Apuleius, but he was already looking closely at all three of the literary works as early as 1488, when he published *Annotationes centum*, for five of its chapters are devoted to Apuleian textual and interpretative problems.[7] He introduces this section of the *Annotationes* as follows:

> Apuleius of Madauros is full of errors because much of his vocabulary is unusual, which not only makes the fine and learned writer rough going, but also renders him more error-ridden all the time; in fact, to point out for now a few of the many corruptions that come to mind, is there not an error in the first book of the *Golden Ass* that correctors have deliberately ignored?[8]

Beroaldo's words fall just short of an announcement that he intends a larger work on Apuleius. Krautter inferred from his remark on the

---

[5] "Era in questa terra doxento scholari oltramontani per lui, che dopo la soa morte tutti se partino." Fileno dalla Tuata, in Bologna, Biblioteca Universitaria, ms. 1438, fol. 277v, quoted from Frati, "I due Beroaldi," 212.

[6] Two of Beroaldo's students published short biographies almost immediately after his death: Bartolomeo Bianchini (*Philippi Beroaldi vita*) and Jean de Pins (*Clarissimi viri Philippi Beroaldi Bononiensis vita*). Both tell of his kindness to students (and of his soliciting former students for gifts). Bianchini (ed. 1522, BB 4v) speaks of his good nature, his love of dice (he usually lost), his "profusissima libido in foeminas," and his devout belief in God and observance of rites and holy days.

[7] *Annotationes* 72–76. Annot. 72: *Met.* 1.23; Annot. 73: *Met.* 3.3; Annot. 74: *Flor.* 5; Annot. 75: *Apol.* 31; Annot. 76: *Apol.* 18 and *Met.* 1.7. (References are to Ciapponi's edition; in earlier editions the sections are not numbered.) Beroaldo also frequently refers to all three works in passing (see Ciapponi's index under Apuleius).

[8] "Apuleius Madaurensis plurimis scatet mendis propterea quod plurimi eius lectionis sunt infrequentes, quae res scriptorem loculentum atque eruditum non solum reddit scrupulosum, sed etiam in dies magis mendosum facit et enim, ut in presentiarum pauca ex plurimis depravata atingam quae succurrunt, nonne in primo De asino aureo mendum est quod correctores dissimulanter preterierunt?" Beroaldo, *Annotationes* 72.1.

corrupt state of the text that he might already have been thinking of a commentary.⁹ (Renaissance editors and commentators love to point out that the texts of their authors are impossibly corrupt, the better to shine by repairing them.) But the second part of the passage gives a still bigger hint: when Beroaldo says that he will point out a few corrupt places "for now," he strongly suggests that he intends to treat many more in the future.

Whenever Beroaldo started it, however, the commentary on Apuleius was already well advanced by 1496, when he published his commentary on Cicero's *Tusculan Disputations*. He is eager to go back to his "commentarii Apuleiani," he says in the dedication of the *Tusculans*, and he wants to get the work "hammered into shape on his grammatical anvil."¹⁰ This remark, prominently placed at the end of his dedication, is clearly meant to announce, if not advertise, his next major work, but at this point Beroaldo does not say exactly what that work will include. Perhaps he was commenting only on the *Golden Ass*, but his earlier discussions in the *Annotationes* also treated the *Florida* and *Apology*, and four years later the title page of the commentary on the *Golden Ass* would promise the imminent publication of notes "on the rest of the works."¹¹ (These notes never appeared.) On 22 May 1499 Beroaldo signed a contract with his printer specifically for the *Golden Ass*, and by the middle of December he was correcting his text for publication, as we learn from a letter to Péter Váradi, the Hungarian archbishop and former student to whom the commentary was dedicated.¹² The commentary was finally published, however, only in the following August. We will consider both the reasons for the delay and the interesting provisions of Beroaldo's printing contract in the last section of this chapter.

⁹ Krautter, *Philologische Methode*, 37.

¹⁰ "In manibus sunt commentarii Apuleiani, quos intervallo brevi intermissos ad officinam revocare contendo, ut litteratoria incude formati usui esse possint mercis nostrae negotiatoribus et condimentorum nostrorum alimenta sectantibus." *Commentarii questionum Tusculanarum* (Bologna, 1496), A1v. The *Tusculans* commentary was dedicated to Philippus Cyulanus, on whom see Rose, *Filippo Beroaldo der Ältere*, 135–36.

¹¹ The title page reads: "Commentarii a Philippo Beroaldo conditi in Asinum Aureum Lucii Apuleii. Mox in reliqua opuscula eiusdem annotationes imprimentur" Beroaldo, *Commentarii in Asinum Aureum*, a 1 r.

¹² For the contract, see Sorbelli, *Storia della stampa in Bologna*, 61. On correcting the commentary: "Ad haec [his teaching responsibilities] quottidiana revisitatio recognitioque Apuleianorum Commentariorum horas suas sibi vendicat, namque antequam impressor formis excudat singulas paginas syllabatim pensito, ut opus fiat quam emendatissimum sincerissimumque, iamque viginti amplius quaterniones absoluti consumatique sunt sub incude impressoria. Haec omnia acervatim congesta et citra cessationem quot diebus resurgentia, efficunt ut vix sit interdum respirandi locus." (This passage is from the same letter to Váradi quoted in n. 4 in this chapter.) For Váradi, see Garin, "Note sull' insegnamento," 376–77 n. 1; Rose, *Filippo Beroaldo der Ältere*, 133–35.

Since Beroaldo cared little for manuscripts (he seldom bothered to consult them and had very few of his own), he probably made his first acquaintance with Apuleius in a printed edition.[13] The 1469 princeps is the most likely candidate, since he was already correcting Apuleius' text in 1488, the date of the first reprint of Bussi's edition.[14] The text that Beroaldo printed with his commentary in 1500 must also be based on that of an earlier edition. But the exact paternity of his text is unclear; according to Krautter, it cannot be matched conclusively with either the princeps or any of its reprintings.[15] Krautter speculated that Beroaldo might have used a now unknown reprint, noting that in the eighteenth century Hain listed an edition of 1472 that has not been traced by modern bibliographers.[16] But we do not need to posit an untraceable edition in order to suggest a plausible background for Beroaldo's text. The more likely explanation is that Beroaldo consulted new reprints of Bussi's edition as they appeared and selected readings from other sources as well so that his own text became an eclectic *contaminatio* of his sources. Probably he gave a printed text with his corrections to the printers (a typical practice). They might or might not have returned it; in any case, at his death Beroaldo still owned a copy of one of the earlier printings.[17]

Beroaldo lectured and commented on many authors, but he had a special affinity for Apuleius that drew him to the *Golden Ass* and inspired him to labor over it for many years. He shared Apuleius' love of baroque and recherché language, his close attention to the details of everyday life, his powerful strain of self-promotion, and his interest in religious experience. This chapter will examine Beroaldo's commentary both as an interpretation and as an imitation of Apuleius' work, focusing on Beroaldo's teaching, his interpretation of the story of Lucius, his literary imitation of Apuleius, and his character as a celebrity commentator.

---

[13] Krautter pointed out that although Beroaldo claimed about 380 corrections in the Apuleius commentary, he invoked manuscript readings only seventeen times (*Philologische Methode*, 129). According to the inventory made just after Beroaldo's death, only 13 of his 190 books were manuscripts. See Pezzarossa, "*Canon est litterarum*," 332–48.

[14] Bussi's 1469 edition was reprinted (with some changes) in 1488, 1493, and 1497. See chapter 4, n. 202.

[15] See Krautter, *Philologische Methode*, 126–28. Krautter did not examine the 1497 edition, which according to *Gesamtkatalog der Wiegendrucke* is an exact reprint of the 1493 edition (127 n. 5).

[16] Hain 1315† (printed in Venice by Nicolas Jensen). See Krautter, *Philologische Methode*, 128.

[17] Pezzarossa, "*Canon est litterarum*," 339. The entry ("90. Apuleius") does not identify the book as an edition, but manuscripts are designated as such in the inventory, and Pezzarossa treats the Apuleius as a printed book.

Lecturing on Apuleius

Beroaldo intended his commentary on the *Golden Ass* for several audiences: for his dedicatee Péter Váradi, for contemporary scholars in Italy and throughout Europe, for posterity, and for his students at the University of Bologna. Each audience was important to him intellectually, personally, or financially; but his students were his first concern. Beroaldo wrote his *Apuleius*, as he wrote all his commentaries, for his lectures at the university: he designed it both to please and to instruct the young men who flocked to his lecture hall from all over Europe. The commentary is not a transcript of his lectures, but he lectured from it. If we pay close attention, we can almost imagine ourselves in his lecture room and hear his voice.

Like all Renaissance teachers (and medieval teachers before them), Beroaldo directed his lectures to the text, going through it line by line and word by word, explaining as he went. Many of his comments are textual, for Bussi's text was riddled with errors—understandably enough, given his sources and working conditions. Beroaldo wanted to present his students and readers with the best possible text (and we must remember that he was already correcting Apuleius in his *Annotationes* of 1488), but his approach to editing was not the systematic method approved by his contemporary the great philologist Poliziano or by Poliziano's descendants from Scaliger through the twentieth century.[18] Beroaldo arrived at his corrections by conjecture and paid little attention to manuscript readings and their pedigrees. Krautter has argued that most if not all of his few (and vague) references to manuscript readings are at second hand, and that he probably never looked at either of the two manuscripts that we know might have been easily available to him.[19] But Beroaldo had a method of his own, which he describes more than once as "examining the blood and marrow" of words.[20] He steeped himself in the language, style, and historical context of the ancient author and tried as far as possible to place himself *inside* the world of the text. His own broad and deep knowledge of ancient religion, law, medicine, and daily life did the rest. In the case of Apuleius he was astonishingly successful: almost

---

[18] See Ciapponi, in Beroaldo, *Annotationes centum*, 15–28; Grafton, "The Scholarship of Politian."

[19] Krautter, *Philologische Methode*, 128–34. Beroaldo's student (and rival) Giovanni Battista Pio mentions one manuscript in the library of San Domenico in Bologna and another owned by an unnamed humanist in Ferrara (Battista Guarino?) as the sources for two of his own readings, for which Beroaldo also claims credit. Krautter (132–33) identified Dresden, Sächsische Landesbibliothek Dc 178 as the San Domenico manuscript.

[20] See Ciapponi, in Beroaldo, *Annotationes centum*, 8 nn. 3–4; Krautter, *Philologische Methode*, 144–48.

two-thirds of the readings that he arrived at by conjecture also appear in manuscripts, and a substantial number of his corrections without manuscript authority have been accepted by modern editors.[21]

Beroaldo also commented on Apuleius' style, which he admired and imitated. As he says in the preface:

> There are interspersed in our Lucius not a few words that I enjoy rather than employ, but very many that I employ as much as I enjoy. And he is certainly often a most elegant coiner of words—and with such grace and charm that nothing more graceful or charming could be created. Finally, this Ass of ours is seen to be golden in fact as well as in name, composed and put together with such wit and refinement of style and such elegance of uncommon expressions that it could be said of it with perfect justice that if the Muses wished to speak Latin, they would speak in the language of Apuleius. And to give my opinion: frequent reading of Apuleius can contribute greatly to the cultivation of style and is especially suitable to that part of eloquence which is called conversational. . . . Wherefore, reader, I beseech, I advise, I urge you to let this writer become well known to you and be your manual and handbook.[22]

Beroaldo's statement is programmatic—we might almost call it a manifesto; for he not only expresses his enthusiasm for Apuleius' language but also demonstrates his own use of it, seasoning his passage with unusual words and Apuleian diction. He signals his intention by using a most appropriate Apuleian coinage in the first sentence: "interseminata" (interspersed).[23] He structures his discussion around artfully modified pronouncements on style taken without acknowledgment from Varro and Quintilian.[24] Like Bussi before him, Beroaldo treats Apuleius as a model

---

[21] Krautter, *Philologische Methode*, 133–44.

[22] "Sunt praeterea in Lucio nostro verba non parum multa interseminata, quibus magis delecter quam utar, plurima vero quibus perinde utar ac delecter. Et sane novator plerumque verborum est elegantissimus tantoque cum decore et venere, ut nihil decentius, nihil venustius fieri possit. Denique hic noster Asinus sicut verbo dicitur ita re ipsa aureus conspicitur, tanto dicendi lepore, tanto cultu, tanta verborum minime trivialium elegantia concinnatus compositusque, ut de eo id dici meritissimo possit: Musas Apuleiano sermone loqu<u>turas fuisse si latine loqui vellent, et ut dicam quod sentio plurimum conferre Apuleii frequens lectio ad excolendam linguam potest, et ad eam eloquentiae partem quam sermonatricem appellant maxime est accomodata. . . . Quamobrem te lector, oro, moneo, hortor, ut familiaris tibi fiat hic scriptor, sitque tuum quasi manuale et enchiridion." Beroaldo, *Commentarii*, fol. 1v.

[23] *Interseminata* appears elsewhere only at *Apol.* 40. Other unusual words include *novator* (cf. *novatori verborum* as an epithet of Sallust in Aulus Gellius 1.15.18); *sermonatricem* (cf. *sermocinatrix* at *Met.* 9.17.3; *sermocinatricem*, Quint. *Inst.* 3.4.10); and the unusual and nonclassical *manuale* and *enchiridion* (both used, but not often, by Christian writers).

[24] His first sentence rephrases Varro, *Ling. lat.* 5.9: "Cum poeticis multis verbis magis delecter quam utar, antiquis magis utar quam delecter." He borrows his comment on

of style. Bussi admired Apuleius for writing about everyday reality in an elegant way. Beroaldo believes that his language is especially suited to discourse that is "conversational," by which he seems to mean informal discussion.[25] The essential point, however, is that Beroaldo treats Latin as a language to be mastered and used in the contemporary world—a matter of vital importance, since his students needed to be expert Latinists to succeed in their clerical, university, or professional careers. But not everyone agreed with Beroaldo and Bussi on Apuleius' merits. In Bussi's day Lorenzo Valla had asserted that to write like Apuleius was to bray like an ass.[26] In Beroaldo's, the debate intensified, and the stakes grew correspondingly high. Modern readers can admire Apuleian style as we admire other ancient works of art, intellectually and from a distance; but for Beroaldo and his students, style was no abstract matter. Latin was the written (and often spoken) language of educated Europe, and the purity and correctness of ancient authors was a subject for serious controversy. Beroaldo's championing of Apuleius provoked counterattacks by the partisans of Cicero, who would ultimately carry the day.[27]

Beroaldo wanted to present his students with a correct text and to initiate them into the nuances of Apuleius' style, but he had a more general purpose as well: to provide them not merely with a course on the *Golden Ass* but with an education in every aspect of Roman antiquity, including language, history, law, custom, religion, mythology, custom, and dress.[28] His course (and commentary) was an encyclopedia of the past—diffuse, discursive, constantly straying from the work at hand into other texts and genres.

A look at the first page of his *Apuleius* will illustrate the point (see figure 1). It contains little more than the first four lines of the novel, dwarfed and surrounded by commentary.[29]

> At ego tibi sermone isto milesio vari-
> as fabulas conseram: auresque tuas be-

---

the Muses' choice of model from Quintilian's similar comment on Plautus (*Inst.* 10.1.99). His reference to "that part of eloquence which is called conversational" alludes to Quintilian's identification of a third style, suited for private discussions (*Inst.* 3.4.10): "Plato in Sophiste iudiciali et contionali tertiam adiecit *prosomiletiken*, quam sane permittamus nobis dicere sermocinatricem." I am indebted to Krautter for these identifications: *Philologische Methode*, 93–96.

[25] See Krautter, *Philologische Methode*, 95–96.
[26] See p. 168.
[27] See D'Amico, "The Progress of Renaissance Latin Prose." See also Krautter, *Philologische Methode*, 72–125; Küenzlen, *Verwandlungen*, 86–96.
[28] See Krautter, *Philologische Methode*, 41–42.
[29] The following discussion expands the comments in Gaisser, "Reading Apuleius," 25–26; eadem, "Filippo Beroaldo on Apuleius," 89. See also Sandy, "Two Renaissance Readers of Apuleius," 241–42.

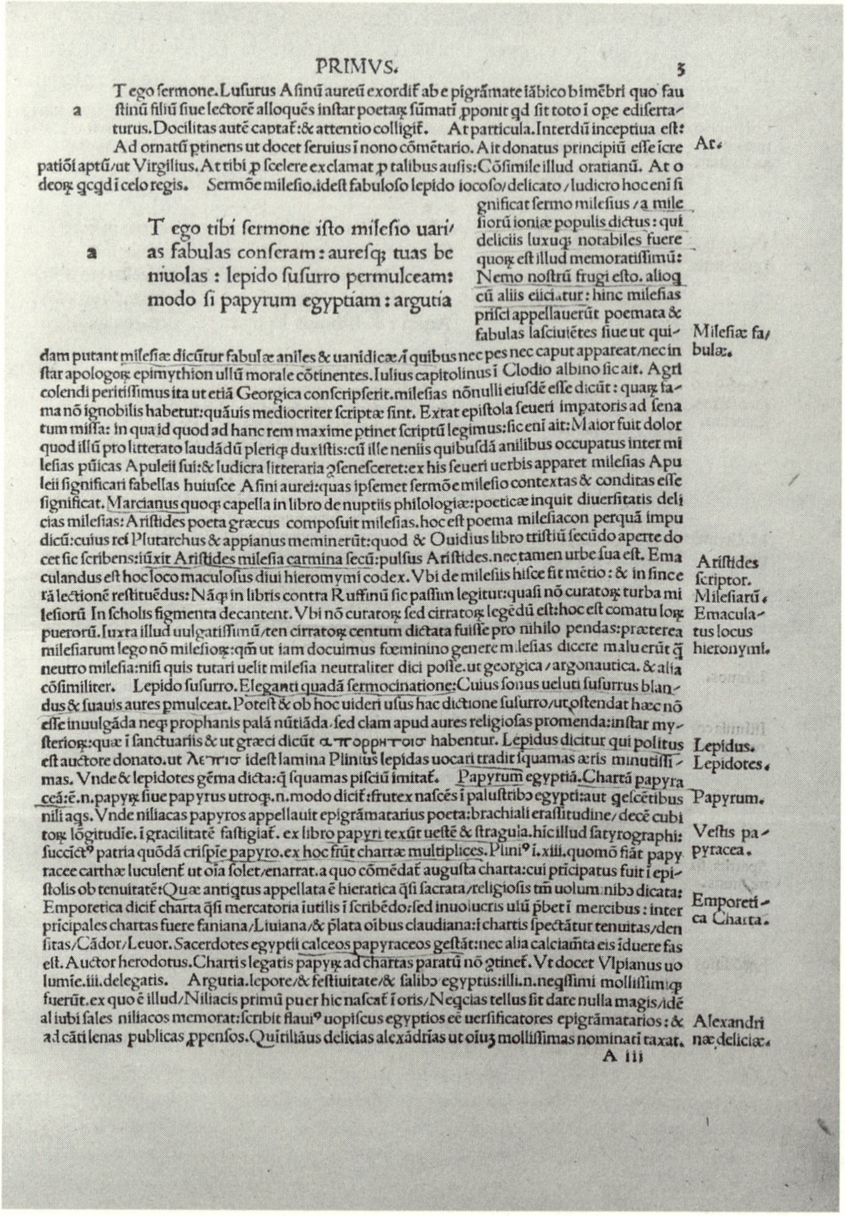
PRIMVS. 5

T ego sermone. Lusurus Asinū aureū exordit ab e pigrāmate iābico bimēbri quo fau
a stinū filiū siue lectorē alloquēs instar poetaꝝ sūmati ꝑponit qd sit toto i ope edisertaturus. Docilitas autē captat:& attentio colligit. At particula. Interdū inceptiua est:
Ad ornatū ptinens ut docet seruius i nono cōmētario. Ait donatus principiū esse icre At.
patiōi aptū/ut Virgilius. At tibi ꝓ scelere exclamat ꝓ talibus ausis: Cōsimile illud oratianū. At o
deoꝝ qcqd i celo regis. Sermōe milesio. idest fabuloso lepido iocoso/delicato/ludicro hoc eni si
gnificat sermo milesius/a mile
siorū ioniæ populis dictus: qui
deliciis luxuq; notabiles fuere
quoꝝ est illud memoratissimū:
Nemo nostrū frugi esto. alioq
cū aliis eiicitur: hinc milesias
prisci appellauerūt poemata &
fabulas lasciuiētes siue ut qui- Milesiæ fa/

T ego tibi sermone isto milesio uari/
a as fabulas conseram: aurésq; tuas be
niuolas: lepido susurro permulceam:
modo si papyrum egyptiam: argutia

dam putant milesiæ dicūtur fabulæ aniles & uanidicæ/i quibus nec pes nec caput appareat/nec in bulæ.
star apologoꝝ epimythion ullū morale cōtinentes. Iulius capitolinus i Clodio albino sic ait. Agri
colendi peritissimus ita ut etiā Georgica conscripserit. milesias nōnulli eiusdē esse dicūt: quaꝝ fama nō ignobilis habetur: quāuis mediocriter scriptæ sint. Extat epistola seueri impatoris ad sena
tum missa: in qua id quod ad hanc rem maxime ptinet scriptū legimus: sic eni ait: Maior fuit dolor
quod illū pro litterato laudādū plerique duxistis: cū ille neniis quibusdā anilibus occupatus inter mi
lesias pūicas Apuleii sui: & ludicra litteraria ꝯsenesceret: ex his seueri uerbis apparet milesias Apu
leii significari fabellas huiusce Asini aurei: quas ipsemet sermōe milesio contextas & conditas esse
significat. Marcianus quoq; capella in libro de nuptiis philologiæ: poeticæ inquit diuersitatis deli
cias milesias: Aristides poeta græcus composuit milesias. hoc est poema milesiacon perquā impu
dicū: cuius rei Plutarchus & appianus meminerūt: quod & Ouidius libro tristiū secūdo aperte do
cet sic scribens: iūxit Aristides milesia carmina secū: pulsus Aristides. nec tamen urbe sua est. Ema Aristides
culandus est hoc loco maculosus diui hieronymi codex. Vbi de milesiis hisce fit mētio: & in fince scriptor.
rā lectionē restituēdus: Nāq; in libris contra Ruffinū sic passim legitur: quasi nō curatoꝝ turba mi Milesiarū.
lesiorū In scholis figmenta decantent. Vbi nō curatoꝝ sed cirratoꝝ legēdū est: hoc est comatu loꝝ Emacula-
puerorū. Iuxta illud uulgatissimū/ten cirratoꝝ centum dictata fuisse pro nihilo pendas: præterea tus locus
milesiarum lego nō milesioꝝ: qm ut iam docuimus fœminino genere milesias dicere maluerūt q̄ hieronymi.
neutro milesia: nisi quis tutari uelit milesia neutraliter dici posse. ut georgica/argonautica. & alia
cōsimiliter. Lepido susurro. Eleganti quadā sermocinatione: Cuius sonus ueluti susurrus blandus & suauis aures pmulceat. Potest & ob hoc uideri usus hac dictione susurro/ut ꝯstendat hæc nō
esse inuulgāda neq; prophanis palā nūtiāda/sed clam apud aures religiosas promenda: instar my-
sterioꝝ: quæ i sanctuariis & ut græci dicūt απορρητοις habentur. Lepidus dicitur qui politus Lepidus.
est auctore donato. ut λεπις idest lamina Plinius lepidas uocari tradit squamas æris minutissi- Lepidotes.
mas. Vnde & lepidotes gēma dicta: q̄ squamas pisciū imitat. Papyrum egyptiā. Chartā papyra
ceā: ē. n. papyꝝ siue papyrus utroq;. n. modo dicit: frutex nascēs i palustrib; egypti: aut gescētibus Papyrum.
nili aqs. Vnde niliacas papyros appellauit epigrāmatarius poeta: brachiali crassitudine/decē cubi
toꝝ lōgitudie. i gracilitatē fastigiat. ex libro papyri texūt uestē & stragula. hic illud satyrographi: Vestis pa-
succinct⁹ patria quōdā crispie papyro. ex hoc fiūt chartæ multiplices. Plini⁹ i. xiii. quomō fiāt papy pyracea.
racee carthæ luculent ut oīa solet/enarrat. a quo cōmēdat augusta charta: cui pricipatus fuit i epistolis ob tenuitatē: Quæ antiqtus appellata ē hieratica q̄si sacrata/religiosis tm̄ uolumnib; dicata:
Emporetica dicit charta q̄si mercatoria iutilis i scribēdo: sed inuolucris ulū pbet i mercibus: inter Emporeti-
pricipales chartas fuere faniana/Liuiana/& plata oibus claudiana: i chartis spectātur tenuitas/den ca Charta.
sitas/Cādor/Leuor. Sacerdotes egyptii calceos papyraceos gestāt: nec alia calciamta eis iduere fas
est. Auctor herodotus. Chartis legatis papyꝝ ad chartas paratū nō ꝯtinet. Vt docet Vlpianus uo
lumie. iii. delegatis. Argutia. lepore/& festiuitate/& salib; egyptus: illi. n. nequissimi mollissimiq;
fuerūt. ex quo ē illud/Niliacis primū puer hic nascat i oris/Neqcias tellus sit dare nulla magis/idē
al iubi sales niliacos memorat: scribit flaui⁹ uopiscus egyptios eē uersificatores epigrāmatarios: & Alexandri
ad cāti lenas publicas ꝑpensos. Quītiliāus delicias alexādrias ut oiu; mollissimas nominari taxat. næ deliciæ.
A iii

Figure 1. First page of Beroaldo's *Commentarii in Asinum aureum Lucii Apuleii* (Bologna, 1500). Rare Book and Manuscript Library, Van Pelt-Dietrich Library, University of Pennsylvania.

nivolas: lepido susurro permulceam:
modo si papyrum egyptiam: argutia.³⁰

Well now, I would like to thread together different tales for you in the Milesian style you like and caress your ears into approval with a beguiling whisper—provided that [you don't mind looking at] an Egyptian papyrus [inscribed] with the sharpness [of a reed from the Nile].³¹

Beroaldo comments on nearly every word in the passage. He starts with an assertion that Apuleius has written his prologue in verse: "As he is about to begin the *Golden Ass*, he opens with an epigram in mixed iambics in which he addresses either his son Faustinus or the reader and, just like the poets, sets out in summary what he will treat in detail in the whole work."³² Beroaldo is not the first humanist to think of a verse prologue.³³ As we saw in chapter 4, the idea originated with Coluccio Salutati about 125 years before Beroaldo's commentary and gained a certain currency among Florentine humanists in the early fifteenth century. The interesting point, however, is that Beroaldo both has a different conception of the meter from his predecessors and terminates the prologue in a different place. Salutati explained the meter as iambic trimeter, a common meter of Roman comedy, but Beroaldo calls the passage an "epigram in mixed iambics," suggesting something like an iambic epode. (He makes no attempt to explain the scansion.) Salutati and his successors continue the verse prologue to its natural end at *Met.* 1.1.6: "lector intende letaberis" (pay attention, reader: you will enjoy it), but Beroaldo ends it much earlier, in *Met.* 1.1.3, with "quis ille? paucis accipe" (who's that? hear in a few words).³⁴ Given these differences, as well as his limited interest in manuscripts, it is unlikely that Beroaldo derived his idea directly from one of the Florentine manuscripts. I suspect that he got it at second-or thirdhand (as he derived some of the readings he attributes to manuscripts).

He continues with a note on the force of the opening word, *at*, which is unusual and abrupt enough at the beginning of a work that some

---

³⁰ *Met.* 1.1.1 in Beroaldo, *Commentarii in Asinum aureum*, fol. 3r.

³¹ For the sake of intelligibility, I have incorporated Apuleius' next words into the translation, showing them in brackets: "Nilotici calami inscriptam non spreveris inspicere" (*Met.* 1.1).

³² "*At ego sermone.* Lusurus Asinum aureum exorditur ab epigrammate iambico bimembri quo Faustinum filium sive lectorem alloquens instar poetarum summatim proponit quid sit toto in opere edisertaturus." Beroaldo, *Commentarii*, fol. 3r.

³³ See pp. 135–38 and appendix 4.2.

³⁴ "*Hymetos Attica.* Post anteloquium epygrammatis ingreditur narrationem prosa oratione." Beroaldo, *Commentarii*, fol. 3v.

early readers (and later editors) were moved to change it.³⁵ Beroaldo merely reports the views of Servius and Donatus with some illustrative passages: according to Servius, he says, "sometimes the particle is inceptive, suiting embellishment"; according to Donatus, "it is an apt beginning for a reproach."³⁶ Next he launches into a long discussion of the phrase "sermone . . . milesio" (Milesian style). Such a style, he says, is "fictitious, witty, funny, frivolous, and playful," and it gets its name from the luxury-loving citizens of the Ionian city Miletus.³⁷ Accordingly, "Milesian" is a designation for racy stories, or for silly old wives' tales full of nonsense and without the sort of moral one finds in fables.³⁸ He quotes the (largely negative) comments of several ancient authors about Milesian tales and concludes with a textual correction of the comment from Jerome.³⁹ In his next note he treats the phrase "lepido susurro" (beguiling whisper), glossing it as "an elegant conversation, whose sound caresses the ears like a coaxing and pleasant whisper."⁴⁰ He explains that *lepidus* means "polished" and speculates that Apuleius may have used *susurro* to show that his words were "not to be disclosed or openly made known to the uninitiated, but revealed in secret in the presence of reverent ears."⁴¹ This last remark is the most literary observation on the page: like many modern readers, it seems, Beroaldo is already looking ahead to the end of the novel and Lucius' initiations into the mysteries of Isis and Osiris. He continues with a long note on *papyrum egyptiam*,

---

³⁵ F reads *at*, but *et* appears in Laur. 54.12 and in Salutati's verse version of the prologue (British Library, Harley 4838, fol. 134v). For *at* and the editors, see Harrison and Winterbottom, "The Prologue to Apuleius' *Metamorphoses*," 10–11; Scobie, in Apuleius, *Metamorphoses I*, 66.

³⁶ "*At*. particula interdum inceptiva est, ad ornatum pertinens ut docet Servius in nono commentario. Ait Donatus principium esse increpationi aptum." Beroaldo, *Commentarii*, fol. 3r. Cf. Servius on *Aeneid* 9.144, Donatus on Terence, *Andria* 666.

³⁷ "*Sermo milesio*. idest fabuloso lepido iocoso delicato ludicro. hoc enim significat sermo milesius, a Milesiorum Ioniae populis dictus, qui deliciis luxuque notabiles fuere." Beroaldo, *Commentarii*, fol. 3r.

³⁸ "Hinc milesias prisci appellaverunt poemata et fabulas lascivientes sive ut quidam putant milesiae dicuntur fabulae aniles et vanidicae, in quibus nec pes nec caput appareat, nec instar apologorum epimythion ullum morale continentes." Ibid.

³⁹ Beroaldo quotes two of the passages discussed earlier (the criticism attributed to Septimius Severus in *Historia Augusta*, *Alb*. 12.12 and Jerome's comment on "curly-haired dandies" at *In Rufinum* 1.17); see pp. 20 and 41. Beroaldo's text of Jerome read "quasi non curatorum turba milesiorum in scholis figmenta decantent." As Sandy points out ("Two Renaissance Readers," 242), he corrects *curatorum* to *cirratorum* and *milesiorum* to *milesiarum*.

⁴⁰ "*Lepido susurro*. Eleganti quadam sermocinatione, cuius sonus veluti susurrus blandus et suavis aures permulceat." Beroaldo, *Commentarii*, fol. 3r.

⁴¹ "Potest et ob hoc videri usus hac dictione susurro, ut ostendat haec non esse invulganda neque prophanis palam nuntianda sed clam apud aures religiosas promenda." Ibid.

discussing the grammatical gender of the word *papyrus*, the size and origin of the papyrus plant, its uses for clothing and books, and the several sizes of papyrus sheets. The last note on the page is on *argutia* (sharpness), which Beroaldo defines as "humor, liveliness, and Egyptian wit."[42]

In half a dozen notes on only four lines of text Beroaldo has touched on Latin usage, text criticism, literary history, the technical details of ancient book production, and something that we could call literary criticism. His comments are designed not only to help readers with Apuleius but also to impart a knowledge of every detail of Roman civilization suggested by the words of the text. Many of Beroaldo's remarks are irrelevant to Apuleius, but they are essential to the main pedagogical purpose of the commentary: to bring Apuleius' world, as well as his words, into the fifteenth-century lecture hall.

In order to do so, he gives detailed and sometimes diffuse explanations of aspects of antiquity, as we have just seen. But he also frequently explains Apuleius' world by comparing it with his own, linking details in the *Golden Ass* to familiar experience or to the life and customs of fifteenth-century Bologna. At the end of book 4 Zephyr fills Psyche's skirts with his breath and gently wafts her from her cliff down to Cupid's garden (*Met.* 4.35.4). Beroaldo notes: "He has described what we see done by the force of the wind: that is, that a garment—especially a woman's—is spread out when the air fills it and raised up almost into a circle."[43] In book 9 the fuller's wife hides her lover under the wicker cage on which clothes were bleached with sulfur fumes.[44] Beroaldo comments: "Our women make use of this today too, so that they put their clothes all around under a wicker cage and safely bleach and whiten them with the fumes of the sulfur below."[45] In book 8 the charlatan priests of the Syrian goddess use a false prophecy to cheat a farmer out of his fattest ram (*Met.* 8.29.2), and Beroaldo inveighs against their contemporary counterparts:

> Good gods! How often we see this going on in our own territory, that certain mendicants, posing on the pretext of religion as servants and priests of Saint Paul and Saint Anthony, wander the towns and

---

[42] "*Argutia*. lepore et festivitate et salibus egyptiis." Ibid.

[43] "Expressit id quod venti vi fieri videmus: ut scilicet vestis et potissimum muliebris reflato sinu expandatur et in orbem quasi sustollatur." Ibid., fol. 100r.

[44] "Eundem illum subiectum contegit viminea cavea, quae fustium flexu tereti in rectum aggerata cumulum lacinias circumdatas suffusa candido fumo sulpuris inalbabat." *Met.* 9.24.2.

[45] "Foeminae nostrates hoc hodie quoque usurpant, ut scilicet sub cavea viminea circumdent velamenta, eaque fumo sulphuris suppositi impune candificent inalbentque." Beroaldo, *Commentarii*, fol. 207r.

countryside and farms; and making up a prophecy with some hocus pocus, announcing good fortune, promising that the saints they boast of will be well disposed, from one foolish and credulous rustic they demand and receive a ram, from a second hens, eggs, cheese, from one a suckling pig, from another superstitious and awe-struck soul a measure of grain.[46]

But although Beroaldo links Apuleius' world with his own, it is not because he is trying to make a dead past live again or because he himself is living in a long-lost world. Rather, he sees the past as still alive in the present, and he is eager to convey this insight to his students. For Beroaldo there is no unbreachable gulf between antiquity and his own time: the past is recoverable, and the scholar steeped in history and philology can recognize and demonstrate its likeness to the present. Beroaldo treats history as a continuum—of natural phenomena (like the power of the wind to puff up a woman's skirts), of human nature, of customs, and even of religious practice.

LUCIUS THE PRIEST

Although Beroaldo's vision of historical continuity is evident throughout the commentary, it is particularly conspicuous in his treatment of religion in book 11, in which Lucius is saved by the goddess Isis and initiated in her mysteries.[47] He uses it to find meaning in Lucius' adventures and to demonstrate their relevance to the religious life of himself, his students, and his dedicatee.

Over and over again in this book Beroaldo links details of Christian and Isiac ritual, not merely comparing them but deriving the one from the other. Apuleius describes the images of the Egyptian gods carried

---

[46] "Dii boni, quam saepe hoc videri contingit in territorio nostro, ut quaedam hominum mendicabula sub religionis praetextu tamquam ministratores sint antistitesque divi Pauli et Antonii, circumeant castella pagos villas et quibusdam affaniis vaticinationem mentientes prospera denunciantes divos quos palam iactant propicios futuros spondentes ab rustico hoc bruto et credulo poscant et accipiant arietem, ab illo gallinas, ova, caseum, ab alio porcellum, ab alio superstiticioso et attonito tritici sestarium." Ibid., fol. 188r. Beroaldo makes striking use of Apuleian vocabulary in this passage. *Affaniae (afannae)* is attested only in Apuleius (cf. *afannas* at *Met.* 9.8.4, and 10.10.2). *Mendicabulum* (used in Plautus) appears three times in Apuleius in the singular or plural (*Met.* 9.4.3; *Apol.* 22.9; *Fl.* 9.9), but not again before the fourth century (*TLL* 8.705).

[47] For Beroaldo's historical approach to religion, see Krautter, *Philologische Methode*, 152–71. But Beroaldo's ideas may also have a philosophical basis. Recently Künzlen has argued that Beroaldo's treatment of book 11 contains elements of Florentine Neoplatonism (*Verwandlungen*, 112–21).

in the procession of Isis as "gods deigning to walk on human feet."[48] Beroaldo comments:

> Spoken humorously and appropriately, for we say that the gods [i.e., "saints"] walk on human feet when men carry masks and titles of the gods ["saints"] in a sacrificial procession. . . . As I keep thinking about these customs of pagan cult I come to the view that almost everything pertaining to the celebration of our rites has been taken over and transferred from them. Undoubtedly from the religion of the pagans are linen vestments, the shaved heads of priests, the turning around at the altar, the sacrificial procession, strains of music. The obeisance, prayers, and many other things of that sort that our priests solemnly employ in our mysteries have undoubtedly been taken over from the ceremony of the ancients. So also among us, men walk in sacred procession under the likenesses of saints and prophets, who could be called gods ["saints"] walking on human feet.[49]

Similar observations appear many times throughout the Isis book.[50] They reflect Beroaldo's keen historical interest and research—Krautter even goes so far as to consider him one of the founders of the comparative study of religions.[51] But Beroaldo's comparisons go beyond the external phenomena of vestments and ceremonial: he sees an essential likeness in religious experience.

He emphasizes the resemblance between Apuleius' portrayal of Isis and the Christian conception of divinity. Isis presents herself to Lucius as "the single embodiment of all gods and goddesses."[52] Beroaldo comments:

---

[48] "Dei dignati pedibus humanis incedere." *Met.* 11.11.1.

[49] "Ioculariter dictum et decenter. Dicimus enim deos incedere pedibus humanis quando homines in pompa sacrificali sustinent personas et nomina deorum. . . . Mecum ego subinde recollens haec instituta sacrorum ethnicorum venio in eam sententiam, ut credam pleraque omnia ad cerimoniarum nostrarum celebrationem pertinentia illinc esse translata transpositaque. Nimirum ex gentilium religione sunt lineae vestes, derasa sacerdotum capita, vertigines in altari, pompa sacrificalis, musica modulamina. Adorationes preces aliaque id genus compluria, quae nostri sacerdotes in nostris mysteriis solemniter usurpant, haud dubie sumpta de cerimonia priscorum. Sic et apud nos homines incedunt in pompa sacrorum sub effigie sanctorum et prophetarum, qui dici possent dei humanis pedibus incedentes." Beroaldo, *Commentarii*, fol. 264v.

[50] Beroaldo mentions linen vestments again on *Met.* 11.10.1 (fol. 263r) and 11.23.7 (fol. 274r); tonsured priests on *Met.* 11.10.1 (fol. 263r); candles in processions at 11.10.2 (fol. 263v); required prayers at the first, third, sixth, and ninth hours on 11.20.5 (fol. 271v); the valedictory formula closing the rites on 11.17.3 (fol. 270r); and hierarchy of priests on 11.30.4 (fol. 280r). Also see Krautter, *Philologische Methode*, 164–71.

[51] Krautter, *Philologische Methode*, 168.

[52] "Deorum dearumque facies uniformis." *Met.* 11.5.1; Walsh's translation; see his *Golden Ass*.

"From this it is clearly shown that all gods and goddesses are traced back to one, who under various names of gods and goddesses is worshiped as the creator of things both in poetic fictions and in the systems of philosophers."[53] On the goddess' simultaneous appearance to Lucius and the priest of Isis (*Met.* 11.6.3), he notes: "God is fully present everywhere, nor does he withdraw from one person when he comes to another. This poetic idea squares with Christian dogma."[54] He considers Lucius' prayer to Isis (*Met.* 11.25.1–6) worthy of the Virgin Mary and superior to all the Christian hymns written in her honor:

> One can see in our Lucius divine prayers composed with such devotion, such dignity, such point that nothing could be spoken more reverently, so that Apuleius' petitions could be applied most appropriately to the goddess [*divam*] of the Christians, so that whatever is said in this place about the moon or Isis could be said reverently and properly about the blessed Virgin. Countless hymns, petitions, and prayers have been composed to the holy Virgin by learned men, but there is nothing (and may they forgive me for saying so) to be compared with this petition of Apuleius. It is filled with learning and every elegance: if she were entreated by it, our goddess [*dea nostra*] would be no less won over and propitiated than by all the prayers of the saints. Look at the language, consider the emotions, ponder the divine mysteries: you will see that nothing more perfect could be devised, and that the prayer is worthy of being incorporated in our rites and of being specifically employed every day to pray to the saving protectress [*sospitatrix*] of the Christian religion.[55]

---

[53] "Hinc evidenter ostenditur deos omnis et deas ad unum referri, qui fabricator rerum variis nominibus deorum et dearum tam figmentis poeticis quam philosophicis rationibus colatur." Beroaldo, *Commentarii*, fol. 256v. And cf. *ad* 11.5.1 (*Commota Luci*): "Responsio Lunae ad Apuleium mysticotera qua evidenter ostenditur unum esse numen nominibus pluribus cultum nominatumque" (fol. 256r).

[54] "Deus ubique locorum praesens est ubique totus, nec dum ad unum accedit ab altero recedens. Dogmati christiano quadrat illud poeticum." Beroaldo, *Commentarii*, fol. 259r.

[55] "Est videre in Lucio nostro orationes divinas tam sancte tam graviter tam sententialiter compositas absolvi, ut nihil religiosius dici quicquam possit, ut Apuleianae precationes possint commodissime aptari ad divam Christianorum, ut quicquid hoc in loco dicitur de Luna sive Iside, idem religiose et conducenter de beata virgine dici possit. Innumeri sunt hymni precationes orationes compositae a doctissimis ad divam virginem, sed nihil est, quod bona cum venia illorum dictum sit, cum hac Apuleiana precatione comparandum: haec doctrinae et elegantiae omnis est refertissima, hac rogata dea nostra non minus placaretur fieretque propitia, quam omnibus sanctorum orationibus. Specta dictiones, pensita sensus, perpende mysteria: videbis nihil quicquam absolutius posse excogitari, dignamque esse precem, quae sacris nostris inseratur et ad exorandam Christianae sectae sospitatricem quottidie peculiariter adhibeatur." Ibid., fol. 275v.

In this remarkable passage Beroaldo anticipates the many historians of religion who have identified similarities between Isis and Mary.[56] He calls Mary not only "goddess" (*diva* and *dea*), but also "saving protectress" (*sospitatrix*), a term coined specifically for Isis by Apuleius: Mary is "the saving protectress of our religion" as Isis was of Lucius's.[57] In the next note he emphasizes the maternal concern of both Isis and Mary for their worshipers.[58]

Beroaldo's real concern, however, is not to claim that Mary is derived from Isis (as he argues that Christian linen vestments and the like are derived from their ancient counterparts). Rather, he wants to show a continuity of religious experience between antiquity and the present—or, to put it more bluntly, that the religious emotions of Lucius are like those of a modern Christian. He argues that Lucius' words and sentiments could and perhaps should be used in Christian worship;[59] but that is not all: Lucius' initiation and eventual priesthood can be equated with the acceptance of a Christian vocation. Lucius is eager to be initiated into the rites of Isis but finds himself putting it off, daunted by the goddess' requirements of abstinence and chastity (*Met.* 11.19.3). Beroaldo compares the hesitation of Augustine to commit himself fully to God and quotes Augustine's rueful words in the *Confessions*: "'Soon.' 'Soon indeed.' 'Wait a little.' But 'soon' and 'soon indeed' never came and 'wait a little' went on for a long time."[60] Lucius closes his prayer to Isis by saying that he has nothing to offer her; he can only keep and imagine her in his heart (*Met.* 11.25.6). Beroaldo comments: "This is the true worship of God and the appropriate offering."[61]

---

[56] See Witt, *Isis in the Greco-Roman World*, 272–74, with earlier bibliography.

[57] Apuleius uses the word at *Met.* 11.9.1 (*sospitatricis deae*); 11.15.4 (*deae sospitatricis*); 11.25.1 (*sospitatrix*). For the word as a coinage, see Griffiths, *The Isis Book*, 181. Beroaldo uses it at least twice of Mary: in the passage quoted above, and in his next comment (see nn. 55 and 58 in this chapter).

[58] "*Matris affectionem* (*Met.* 11.25.1): quid maius in laudem deae nostrae dicitur quam quod materno affectu et indulgentia nos foveat . . . cui eximia propter merita cognomen indidimus maternae venerationis qua Christianorum mater ac sospitatrix passim appellatur." Beroaldo, *Commentarii*, fol. 275v.

[59] Beroaldo's idea found some acceptance. In 1499 Sebastian Brant published a prayer to Mary based on several sections of book 11; see Küenzlen, "Cento und Kontrafaktur." Brant's prayer ("Ad gloriosam virginem mariam: ex verbis Apuleii Precatio") appeared a year before Beroaldo's commentary, but Küenzlen (p. 836) argues that Brant had the idea from Beroaldo by way of a mutual student, perhaps Jakob Locher, who had been in northern Italy from 1493 to 1495. For Locher, see Rose, *Filippo Beroaldo*, 132–33.

[60] "Divus Augustinus libro viii Confessionum hoc idem de se ipso scribens ait. . . . 'modo ecce modo, sine paululum, sed modo et modo non habebat modum, et sine paululum in longum ibat.' (*Conf.* 8.5.12)." Beroaldo, *Commentarii*, fol. 270v.

[61] "Qui verus est dei cultus legitumumque sacrificium." Ibid., fol. 276r.

Lucius describes his initiation as his "birthday of the sacred mysteries."⁶² Beroaldo comments:

> That day on which anyone is consecrated and has been initiated into the sacred mysteries is called the birthday of the sacred mysteries; and we ought to celebrate it no less conscientiously than the day of our birth, since from the one, life alone is brought forth, but from the other, religious and holy life.⁶³

Accordingly, Beroaldo considers it appropriate that Lucius should call the priest who initiated him his parent (*Met.* 11.25.7) or, as Beroaldo puts it, "the agent of his second birth."⁶⁴ Lucius begins the account of his initiation by saying: "I approached the boundary of death."⁶⁵ Beroaldo notes:

> From this we gather that a man who is truly consecrated and has been made a pure and holy priest through a kind of death, puts off this irreligious life and is carried away by the prompting of the divine will through the supernal and infernal regions so that he sees and recognizes the things that the apostle Paul saw and recognized. These things are ineffable, nor is it permitted for a man to divulge things that are not understood even when they have been heard, since they are above the grasp and understanding of mortals.⁶⁶

Beroaldo has no more trouble equating the mystical visions experienced by Lucius in his initiation with those that Paul relates to the Corinthians than he had in comparing Lucius' hesitation with that of Augustine.⁶⁷ For him, Lucius' experiences are comparable with those of the greatest Christians of antiquity, and Lucius' initiation is tantamount to the consecration of a (Christian) priest.

Beroaldo interprets other details of Lucius' several initiations in the same way. He points out that the sacred meal after the initiation (*Met.* 11.24.5)

---

⁶² "Natalem sacrorum." *Met.* 11.24.4.

⁶³ "Natalis sacrorum dicitur ille dies quo quispiam consecratur fitque sacris initiatus, quem non minus religiose celebrare debemus quam diem nativitatis, quoniam ex illo vita tantum, ex hoc vero vita religiosa et sancta producitur." Beroaldo, *Commentarii*, fol. 275r.

⁶⁴ "Merito sacerdotem a quo consecratus fuerat parentem vocat, *quasi auctorem secundae nativitatis*, ut iterum quasi renatus fuisse videatur, quoniam sacris iniciatus est." Ibid., fol. 276r.

⁶⁵ "Accessi confinium mortis." *Met.* 11.23.7.

⁶⁶ "Ex hoc colligimus hominem qui vere consecratur fitque sacerdos integer et sanctus per quandam quasi mortem exuere vitam hanc irreligiosam, rapique numinis instinctu per superna et inferna, ut ea videat et agnoscat quae vidit et agnovit apostolus Paulus: quae ineffabilia sunt, nec licet homini eloqui, quae etiam audita non intelligantur, cum sint supra captum intellectumque mortalium." Beroaldo, *Commentarii*, fol. 274v.

⁶⁷ For Paul, cf. Acts 9.1–9; Corinthians 2.12.1–6.

has its counterpart in the feasts of modern priests: "When our priests are consecrated, when they attain some priestly office, they are accustomed to receive their fellow initiates, that is, fellow priests, with a meal not so much religious as gluttonous, to inaugurate their entering on the priesthood".[68] When Lucius must sell his clothing to finance a second initiation, a divine apparition reassures him that the poverty he faces will not give him cause for regret (*Met.* 11.28.4). Beroaldo agrees:

> We must not regret the poverty we incur for the sake of religion, for which many have thrown away gold and silver, trampling under foot earthly goods in order to be rich in spirit. Many priests now, I say, although they have no goods, yet in accordance with the view of the apostles possess all things of which God is the most generous dispensor. . . . On the other hand, you will find many people who imitate the example of Ananias and Saphira, who, lying to God, sold their field and placed part of the price before the feet of the apostles, keeping part for themselves [*Acts* 5.1–11], . . . worshiping not so much the Savior, that is, our Preserver, as the gods Argentinus and Aesculanus [the god of silver coin and the god of copper coin].[69]

Lucius' garb as an initiate has features in common with those of a Christian priest.[70] At one point it is referred to as "that auspicious garment" (*felici illo amictu*, *Met.* 11.29.5). Beroaldo comments: "Naturally the garment should be called auspicious in which we are made sacred from profane, pure from impure, full of light from full of darkness, and are transferred from this filth of earthly things to a life most whole and likewise most blessed."[71] He continues the note with a compliment to

---

[68] "Quando nostri sacerdotes consecrantur, quando sacerdotium aliquod adipiscuntur, consuevere ientaculo non tam religioso quam guloso accipere symmistas, i. e., consacerdotes, ut auspicentur introitum sacerdotalem." Beroaldo, *Commentarii*, fol. 275r. Beroaldo perhaps took *symmistas* from *Apol.* 55.8, where the 1493 printing of Bussi's edition (fol. lxviii v) reads *liberi patris symmystae* (modern editions print *mystae*).

[69] "Impenitenda est pauperies quam facimus causa religionis, propter quam multi aurum argentumque abiecerunt, bona terrena conculcantes ut animo beatissimi forent. Multi nunc sacerdotes de bonis, loquor, cum nihil habeant omnia tamen possident iuxta apostolicam sententiam, quorum deus dispensator est largissimus. . . . Contra complusculos invenias, qui exemplum Ananiae et Saphyrae imitentur, qui deo mentientes agro divendito partem praecii ante pedes Apostolorum posuerunt, partem sibi reservantes, . . . non tam Sotera hoc est Servatorem nostrum, quam Argentinum deum Esculanumque percolentes." Beroaldo, *Commentarii*, fol. 278r. For Argentinus and Aesculanus, see Augustine *Civ.* 4.21.

[70] Thus on *duodecim . . . stolis* (*Met.* 11.24.1): "Attende hic stolas accipi pro vestibus sacerdotalibus sicut hodie stolas induunt nostri sacerdotes." Beroaldo, *Commentarii*, fol. 274v.

[71] "Nimirum foelix amictus est ille nominandus, quo ex prophanis efficimur sacrati, ex impuris puri, ex tenebricosis luminosi, et ab hac rerum terrenarum colluvione transferimur ad vitam sincerissimam et perinde beatissimam." Ibid., fol. 279r.

Péter Váradi, his dedicatee: "Glorified with this life, most distinguished Bishop, you can be rightly called blessed and fortunate since in you a knowledge of letters is joined with priestly dignity."[72] The comment seems oddly placed, but it is quite relevant to Beroaldo's argument, as we shall see presently.

The novel ends with Lucius, now a full-fledged priest of Isis and Osiris, joyously performing the duties of his office (*Met.* 11.30.5). Beroaldo ends his commentary on a corresponding note:

> Happy and full of joy, he will perform these duties, whosoever is a priest pure in his life and free of crime, whose mind, not bent on earth but raised aloft into heaven, will consider nothing except the divine, nothing except the celestial, who, enjoying the contemplation of God and the divine nature, will lead a joyful and altogether blessed life. And if only we might be able to share in it to some degree![73]

In this closing vision of the "altogether blessed life" of an ideal priest, Beroaldo reinforces the connection he has made many times before, not only between pagan and Christian religious experience in general, but between the experience of the individual Lucius and the immediate experience of himself and his readers, a group that includes posterity and his fellow scholars, but especially his students and his dedicatee, Péter Váradi.

In Beroaldo's view Lucius' story has something to say to everyone. As he says in his valediction to Váradi at the end of the volume: "The text of the Ass of Apuleius is undoubtedly a mirror of human affairs, and in this wrapping one sees the depiction of our character and the portrayal of daily life, whose goal and greatest happiness is religion and the worship of divine majesty, united and joined with learning."[74] If we look into "the mirror of human affairs" as Beroaldo has interpreted it for us, we can see several contemporary religious types: greedy and dishonest religious charlatans, hypocrites like Ananias and Saphira, imperfect mortals who aspire to (or should aspire to) "the blessed life,"

---

[72] "Qua tu Antistes Amplissime illustratus merito dici beatus potes et foelix, cum in te sacerdotali dignitati sit litterarum doctrina coniuncta." Ibid.

[73] "Quae [munia sacerdotalia] laetus obibit et plenus gaudio quisquis fuerit sacerdos integer vitae scelerisque purus, cuius mens non in terris curva sed in caelum sublimata nihil nisi divinum, nisi caeleste cogitabit, qui contemplatu dei ac divinitatis perfruens vitam deget gaudialem ac prorsus beatam, cuius utinam nos aliqua ex parte participes esse possimus." Ibid., fol. 280v.

[74] "Lectio Asini Apuleiani nimirum speculum est rerum humanarum, istoque involucro effecti nostri mores expressaque imago vitae quotidianae conspicitur, cuius finis et summa beatitas est religio cultusque divinae maiestatis una cum eruditione copulata connexaque." Ibid.

and the perfect priest, who has already attained it. The last two types are the most important, for they correspond most closely to the story of Lucius on the one hand and to the situations of Beroaldo's students, Beroaldo himself, and Péter Váradi on the other.

Let us begin with Váradi, the most obvious case. Throughout his discussion of book 11, Beroaldo has been at great pains to characterize Lucius' initiations as the embracing of a religious vocation and ultimately of a priesthood comprehensible in Christian terms. When he describes Lucius at his moment of final glory as the ideal priest, in full attainment of religious joy, Váradi is surely meant to see his own reflection in the image. Beroaldo reinforces the connection in the valediction, for when he describes the fullest purpose of life as "religion and the worship of divine majesty, united and joined with learning," he is alluding in the clearest possible way to Váradi, whom he has saluted repeatedly not only as the epitome of ecclesiastical virtue but as the very embodiment of religion combined with learning. He hailed him in these terms only a folio earlier, in the passage we mentioned above as seeming oddly placed in its context.[75] The comment, as we see now, has an important purpose: to emphasize the link between Váradi and the blessed man of Beroaldo's last note and valediction.

Beroaldo's praise of Váradi reaches its fullest expression at the end of the commentary, but the groundwork for it was laid in the dedication. There Beroaldo opens his tribute by describing Váradi as "one whom we rightly consider blessed, whose abundant piety is united with excellent learning."[76] He continues: "These two qualities, so intimately connected, are undoubtedly productive of supreme happiness. Religion, the expeller of vices, unites us to God and joins us with a most glorious bond. Learning, the seeker of virtue, or rather virtue itself, equips, improves, beautifies our minds."[77] Beroaldo goes on to praise Váradi as the personification of piety and learning for several folios, hailing him near the end of the dedication as "Archbishop Peter, most learned among the foremost bishops, most religious among the learned, most illustrious in both groups."[78] The Váradi leitmotif, as we might call it, is an elegant and elaborate compliment to Beroaldo's dedicatee, identifying him as an

---

[75] Ibid., fol. 279r; and see n. 72 above.

[76] "Tibique nuncupatim dedicamus Archiepiscope Colocensis, quem merito beatum censemus, cuius amplissimae religioni luculenta doctrina coniuncta est." Beroaldo, *Commentarii*, fol. a2r.

[77] "Quae duae sotiabili nodo connexae proculdubio sunt beatitudinis effectrices. Quippe religio vitiorum expultrix Deo nos conciliat et vinculo pulcherrimo connectit. Doctrina vero virtutis indagatrix immo ipsa virtus animos nostros exornat excolit venustat." Ibid.

[78] "Archiepiscope Petre, inter antistites primarios doctissime, inter doctos religiosissime, inter utrosque clarissime." Ibid., fol. a4v. And again at the close: "Vale decus antistitum et columen eruditorum." Ibid.

ideal priest in full possession of spiritual happiness and neatly linking him with the perfected Lucius described in the commentary.[79] But the theme of piety united with learning also has a less exalted subtext. The learned Váradi, as Beroaldo notes in the dedication, is also a patron and host of learned men; surely Beroaldo himself, as a learned man and a dispenser of learning par excellence, deserves his patronage.[80]

Váradi is at one end of the religious and moral spectrum reflected in the "mirror of human affairs" described by Beroaldo. At the other end are religious hypocrites and charlatans, and Beroaldo's particular objects of disdain, ignorant priests.[81] In between we find—in two distinct but closely related categories—Beroaldo's students and Beroaldo himself, imperfect mortals requiring not the praise bestowed on Váradi or the scorn heaped on the charlatans but instruction and exhortation.

Even without Beroaldo's help his students could easily have seen themselves in the unredeemed Lucius, a privileged youth like themselves, far from home, eager for new experiences, and apt to fall into bad company. But Beroaldo's allegorical interpretation makes the connection even clearer. He presents his interpretation in two places: in the preface, in a section entitled "The Intent and Plan of the Author" (*Scriptoris intentio atque consilium*) and in his commentary on the rose cure in book 11 (*Met.* 11.13.2). The two discussions are complementary but not identical: in the preface he treats the story as a whole; in book 11 he focuses on Lucius' restoration.

In the preface Beroaldo presents several different allegories, each of which treats Lucius' experience as a parable of the human condition.[82]

---

[79] Küenzlen relates Beroaldo's emphasis on *religio* and *philosophia* to his use of Ficino (*Verwandlungen*, 96–122, esp. 101 and 117).

[80] On Váradi's patronage, cf.: "Qui cum sis litteratissimus convictoribus litteratis delectaris, habesque in prandio et coena eruditos fabulatores. . . . Tu Platonici praecepti retinentissimus bonos omnis hoc est litteratos diligis ac foves. Et cum eruditis sit amicicia tua vel maxime concupiscenda, tu eruditorum benivolentiam studiose expetis muneribusque concilias. . . . Tu me perinde ac in studiis humanitatis neque postremum, neque imi subsellii professorem muneribus es prosequutus." Beroaldo, *Commentarii*, fol. a4r. Beroaldo makes a thinly veiled request for a valuable present from Váradi on fol. 264r–v.

[81] E.g., in the dedication: "Conditores ecclesiasticae litteraturae celeberrimi prodiderunt caecum animal deo offerri quotienscumque illiteratus sacris initiatur, fitque adscripticius militiae religiosae. Dii boni, quot ceca animalia quotidie Deo dedicantur, quot antistites primarii, quot protomystae, quot episcopi cecutientes sunt et prorsus talpae, hoc est indocti incultique." Ibid., fol. a2v.

[82] See also Krautter, *Philologische Methode*, 64–68; Anselmi, "Mito classico," esp. 36–37; Küenzlen, *Verwandlungen*, 96–102. Cf. Moss (*Renaissance Truth and the Latin Language Turn*, 236), who observes: "Beroaldo's prologue presents . . . an array of interpretative possibilities. He can view the text as a document in literary history, as a moral allegory, as Neoplatonic philosophy dressed . . . in the mantle of fable, or as an example of Latin *eloquentia*."

He begins with his most fully developed idea, and the one that ultimately emerges as dominant.

> We turn into asses when we have sunk into bestial pleasures and are brutish in our asinine stupidity and no spark of reason and virtue shines forth in us, for in this way, as Origen teaches in his books *On First Principles*, a man becomes a horse and a mule, in this way a human body is changed into bodies of sheep or cattle. The reformation from an ass to a man signifies that reason is coming back to its senses, having trampled pleasures underfoot and thrown off bodily delights, and that the inner man, who is the real man, has come back from that dung-filled prison to a shining habitation with the guidance of virtue and religion, so that we can say that young men, possessed by the enticement of pleasure, turn into asses; but when they grow old not long afterward and their mind's eye is active and their virtues mature, they cast off the aspect of a brute animal and resume their humanity. Indeed, Plato writes in the *Symposium* [219A] that the mind's eye begins to see keenly when the eye of the body deteriorates.[83]

In the next breath he moves on to another idea: that in life many men are wolves or pigs or other beasts, since the world is Circe's way station. Her transforming drugs are forgetfulness, error, and ignorance, but the rose cure is knowledge, which restores human shape, that is, rational intelligence.[84] Another explanation, he says, might be that the

---

[83] "[Verum sub hoc transmutationis involucro, naturam mortalium et mores humanos quasi transeunter designare voluisse, ut admoneremur] ex hominibus Asinos fieri, quando voluptatibus belluinis immersi Asinali stoliditate brutescimus, nec ulla rationis virtutisque scintilla in nobis elucescit, sic enim homo ut docet Origenes in libris *periarchon*, fit equus et mullus, sic transmutatur humanum corpus in corpora pecuina. Rursus ex Asino in hominem reformatio significat calcatis voluptatibus, exutisque corporalibus deliciis rationem resipiscere, et hominem interiorem, qui verus est homo ex ergastulo illo cenoso, ad lucidum habitaculum, virtute et religione ducibus remigrasse, ita ut dicere possimus iuvenes illicio voluptatum possesos in Asinos transmutari, mox senescentes, oculo mentis vigente, maturescentibusque virtutibus exuta bruti effigie humanam resumere. Scribit enim Plato in Symposio quod tunc mentis oculus acute incipit cernere cum primum corporis oculus deflorescit." Beroaldo, *Commentarii*, fol. 2v.

[84] "Quod [transformation into beasts] minime mirari nos oportet cum terrenus locus Circes ipsius sit diversorium, cum animae aut unguentis delibutae, aut pharmacis epotis inebriatae transfigurentur in brutas animantes. Pharmaca autem sunt oblivio error inscitia, quibus anima consopita brutescit, donec gustatis rosis, hoc est scientia, quae mentis illustratio est, cuiusque odor suavissimus, avide hausta in humanam formam hoc est rationalem intelligentiam revertatur exuto asinali corio, idest deposito inscitiae et rerum terrenarum crassiore velamento." Ibid. Küenzlen (*Verwandlungen*, 99–100) points out that Circe's drugs (*oblivio, error, inscitia*) correspond to those listed by Proclus (λήθη, πλάνη, ἄγνοια) in his commentary on Plato's *Alcibiades* 1. Beroaldo's comments are very similar to the passage in Proclus: "For truly oblivion, error and ignorance are like some

metamorphosis is caused by the manifold toils and changes of human life by which man is transformed almost every day.[85] Finally, he asserts that the principal reason for the transformation is that Apuleius as a good Platonist and Pythagorean is secretly using the story to set out the doctrine of metempsychosis and transmigration of souls.[86] Beroaldo claims to prefer this philosophical idea, but he does not pursue it; later he quietly reverts to his first explanation, which, unlike metempsychosis, fits both Lucius' story and the all-important rose cure.[87]

Beroaldo was not the first to interpret the story of Lucius. It was allegorized in the fourteenth century, as we saw in chapter 3, and Bussi presented a brief interpretation of it in the preface of his edition.[88] Like Beroaldo, the fourteenth-century allegorist presented several different allegories without reconciling them, but common to all his readings was the idea that Lucius' sufferings as an ass were a necessary penance before he could be restored to humanity. Bussi, by contrast, saw the novel as a depiction of human nature; for him, the asinine Lucius was a victim of others and his restoration a matter of simple survival. Beroaldo follows Bussi in seeing the novel as a reflection of life, but in other respects he is closer to the earlier allegorist: both consider the Ass responsible for his fate, relate his transformation to the vicissitudes of human life, imagine an "inner man" trapped in an alien body, and think of Lucius' asinine shape as a prison. Beroaldo probably did not know the earlier work, which exists only in a single manuscript. Perhaps he had heard or read similar interpretations now lost to us, but there is also no reason

---

use of drugs that drags souls down to the abode of dissimilarity. Why then be surprised if in their way of life there are many who are wolves, many who are swine and many who have put on the likeness of some other kind of irrational animal, since the earthy regions are the residence of Circe and many souls are ensnared by her draught on account of their immoderate desire?" Proclus, *Alcibiades* 1.257, trans. O'Neill Cf. Proclus, *Sur le premier Alcibiade de Platon*, ed and trans. Segonds.

[85] "Potest et metamorphoseos causa referri ad multiiugos humanae vitae labores multiformesque varietates, quibus homo pene quotidie transmutatur." Beroaldo, *Commentarii*, fol. 2v.

[86] "Illa vero eruditioribus principalis huiusce transmutationis causa valdeque probabilis videri potest, ut videlicet sub hoc mystico praetextu Apuleius noster pythagoricae platonicaeque philosophiae consultissimus dogmata utriusque doctoris ostenderet et sub hac ludicra narratione palingenesiam atque metempsychosim idest regenerationem transmutationemque dissimulanter assereret." Ibid.

[87] But he does bring up metempsychosis in his opening lecture on Apuleius: "Quoniam haec Metamorphosis id est Asini Aurei transfiguratio referri conducenter potest ad pythagoricam metempsychosin atque palingenesiam, id est transanimationem regenerationemque, non pigebit de Pythagora, mox de pythagorico Apollonio Tyaneo prolixius fabulari." Beroaldo, "Oratio habita in narratione Lucii Apuleii," in *Orationes et poemata*, fol. n1v.

[88] See pp. 124–28 and 166–68.

to believe that he could not have arrived at his ideas independently. In any case, the differences between Beroaldo's interpretation and that of his predecessor are more important than their similarities. Unlike the earlier allegorist, he remains almost entirely on the moral, human level (the only exception being his isolated reference to metempsychosis). For Beroaldo, Lucius' transformation is not a necessary purgatory from which he can be rescued only by divine grace but a consequence of foolish human conduct that can be remedied by human effort, that is, by the acquisition of knowledge.[89] He also differs from the allegorist, as well as from Bussi, in another essential respect: unlike either, he associates the fall into asininity with youth, which is especially prone to be "possessed by the enticements of pleasure."[90] The several hundred young men in his lecture hall undoubtedly got the point. Those who identified the reference to the mind's eye and Plato's *Symposium* would have enjoyed it all the more, for Beroaldo is quoting from Socrates' rebuke of the pleasure-loving young Alcibiades, who had just unsuccessfully propositioned him.

Beroaldo presents a detailed reading of Lucius' restoration and the rose cure in two long notes in book 11, each keyed to an essential moment in the story. The first is on the phrase "I devoured the garland" (*coronam devoravi*, *Met.* 11.13.2). Beroaldo begins by noting that Apuleius' rose scene differs from that in Lucian; in Lucian the hero merely catches sight of some roses and eats them, but in Apuleius he takes them from the hand of a priest. The figure of the priest is essential to Beroaldo's interpretation.

> But our Lucius . . . says that he devoured the rose garland from the hand of the priest, and that when he had eaten it he was immediately returned to his original human form, so that on the allegorical level you might understand that the rose garland is wisdom. As long as mortals do not aspire to taste it, they are sluggish, like brute animals covered with the hide of an ass. When they have plucked the roses from the outstretched hand of the priest, that is, of the wise man, who is the high priest of learning who invites the hungry to the sweet taste of wisdom, at once they put off their brutal covering and become rich in human reason and truly men, and they themselves are

---

[89] Cf. Anselmi, "Mito classico e allegoresi," 37: "La lettura della metamorfosi di Lucio è intrisa di sapienza laica: come riacquisizione di una 'humanitas' non mistica, ma sapienziale ed etica, di civiltà."

[90] Cf. also Beroaldo's comment at 11.15.1 (*virentis aetatulae*): "Adolescentiae lubricum tam instabile tamque obnoxium est ut qui in eo non cadunt, saltem titubent." Beroaldo, *Commentarii*, fol. 267r.

initiated in the priestly rites. Purged of the stain of their earthly body and divested of their vices, henceforward unpolluted by any taint of crime, they serve God, united with him on the recommendation of virtue. Nothing is more blessed than this life. If only we might achieve it just as our Apuleius most felicitously did at last, after struggling through manifold toils and putting off earthly impurity.[91]

This reading is on a more lofty level than that in the preface. There the rose cure was merely knowledge (*scientia*). Although its source was unspecified, presumably a sufficiently learned man—Beroaldo himself, for example—could administer it. Those it restored would regain their humanity, which Beroaldo equated with rational intelligence. In this passage, however, the cure is wisdom (*sapientia*), which must be presented by the outstretched hand of the priest (*sacerdos*) or wise man (*sapiens*). This "high priest of learning" (*antistes doctrinarum*) not only restores the brutish and asinine to humanity and reason but brings them up to his own level, so that they may become priests themselves and servants of God—just like Apuleius, as Beroaldo says, but we might also add "just like Péter Váradi."

Beroaldo ends his note with a wish for himself and his students: "If only we might achieve this blessed life." Such a life and vocation, attained by Lucius and the archbishop Váradi, is indeed a wonderful aspiration; but Beroaldo shifts to a more modest hope in his second note, which he frames as an exhortation to his readers, but still more, we may be sure, to his immediate audience, the students in his lecture hall. This note treats the opening words of Lucius' reformation: "The animal form fell away" (*delabitur ferina facies*, Met. 11.13.3):

Do you want to put off your animal form? Make the brutish filth that deforms the inner man fall from your mind. Take care, see to it that nothing bestial is seen in you. Strive, as you are called a rational creature, so to follow reason as the guide of your life, treading your appetites under foot, that you might become radiant with the glow of virtue. Thus the hair of the ass will melt away, thus the thick hide

---

[91] "Noster vero Lucius . . . ait se ex manu sacerdotis coronam roseam devorasse, eaque devorata in pristinum hominem fuisse e vestigio reformatum, ut mystice intelligas coronam rosaceam esse sapientiam. Ad quam gustandam quam diu mortales non aspirant, tam diu bruti et asinino corio contecti torpescunt; mox ubi rosas carpserunt ex manu porrigentis sacerdotis, hoc est sapientis, qui antistes est doctrinarum qui esurientes ultro invitat ad gustulum sapientiae dulcissimum, illico exuunt brutale tegumentum fiuntque humana ratione pollentes et vere homines; ipsi quoque sacerdotalibus sacris iniciantur, terreni corporis labe purgati et vitiis exutis nulla deinceps scelerum contagione polluti Deo serviunt, cui conciliante virtute coniunguntur. Qua vita nihil beatius esse potest, ad quam utinam nos quoque pervenire possimus sicut Apuleius noster post exudatos labores multiiugos post exutas terrenas sordes aliquando felicissime pervenit." Ibid., fol. 266r.

will thin out into more delicate skin, thus the fat of your belly will contract. Finally, with every brutish feature annulled, you will be remade into a man whom all might justly admire and look up to with respect. In the same way, men are transformed into wolves and become werewolves when they take on wolfish appetite. In the same way, they soon turn back from wolves into their original form and resume their original garb when, after putting off their shameless ways and laying aside their wolfish nature, they return, with the mind's eye grown more keen, to human ways and to human reason, embracing upright behavior and putting on again the virtue they had laid aside.[92]

Here the goal is not religious perfection but a simple return to humanity and reason, achieved, as it seems, not with the aid of an externally acquired cure but by personal effort. Those so restored attain not the blessed life of Lucius the priest but rather the respect of their fellow men. The goal can be reached by discipline and also by just growing up, for that is the point of Beroaldo's reference to "the mind's eye" (*oculo mentis*), which takes us back to the association of the keen mind's eye with maturity in his first allegorical statement in the preface.

Beroaldo's students are young and thereby prone to asininity, but they may yet attain humanity and even religious excellence. Péter Váradi, already in possession of the blessed life, is the ideal priest. Beroaldo positions himself somewhere in between. On the scale of religious accomplishment, he is like neither the asinine nor the perfected Lucius; although fully rational and beyond youthful stupidity, he is not yet in possession of purity and blessedness. Sometimes he places himself with the aspiring students (and readers) with a hortatory "we": "If only we might achieve this blessed life!" But he also separates himself from them with his second-person instructions: "Do you want to put off your animal form? Make the brutish filth that deforms the inner man fall from your mind." His position is well calibrated to win over dedicatee and students alike: deferential to the superiority of the one and yet not too remote from the human frailty of the other.

---

[92] "Cupis exuere faciem ferinam? Facito ut ex animo tuo brutales sordes, quae interiorem hominem deformant, delabantur. Curato provideto ut in te nihil belluinum conspiciatur, da operam, ut sicuti diceris animal rationale, ita rationem vitae ducem sequaris, appetitionibus conculcatis, ut virtutis fulgore fias luminosus. Ita pilus asininus defluet, ita corium crassum in cutem subtiliorem tenuabitur, ita obesitas ventris cohibebitur. Denique omni abolita brutali effigie reformaberis in hominem, quem cuncti merito mirentur et cum veneratione suspiciant. Sic homines transfigurantur in lupos fiuntque versipelles, quando induunt lupinam voracitatem; sic mox ex lupis in pristinam faciem revertuntur, pristinamque vestem resumunt, quando exutis improbis moribus et lupina deposita natura ad humanos mores et humanam rationem oculo mentis vegetiore regrediuntur probitatem amplexantes et virtutem quam deposuerant resumentes." Ibid.

Beroaldo amusingly demonstrates his own middle religious and social position in a long digression on vegetarianism near the end of the commentary. In preparation for his final initiation, Lucius refrains for many days from eating meat, or, as he says, "I submit to the yoke of meatless chastity."[93] Beroaldo observes that such a yoke is very hard for meat eaters, "and especially for me, who would rather be counted among the carnivores [*creophagos*] than the vegetarians [*carpophagos*]."[94] The contrast between Beroaldo's learned Grecisms and his down-to-earth personal admission sets the tone for the passage that follows, in which everything is designed to appeal to both the erudition and the humor of his audience. Pythagoras cried out against the eating of meat, Beroaldo admits, supplying a sample of the philosopher's vegetarian preaching; but he himself prefers "the well-known statement of the church" that "to the pure all things are pure."[95] Naturally, the pronouncement of "the church" trumps that of the pagan philosopher, but Beroaldo leaves it to his audience to identify his quotations (the one from the speech of Pythagoras in Ovid and the other from Paul's Epistle to Titus) and to enjoy his piquant juxtaposition of the philosopher's imaginary rant with Paul's dismissal of Jewish dietary laws.[96] He continues:

> If anyone should prevent me from eating meat and relegate me to inanimate food, I would waste away in a minute and become inanimate myself. Perhaps at this point someone might run up, saying, "Look here, you, our teacher and commentator—is this your teaching? Is this how you instruct us? You are a gourmand and a greedy and insatiable glutton. You tell us that we should frequent cookshops and dives. You do not know that wholesome study cannot be conducted without self-restraint; you don't know that a sparing and slender diet is necessary for students of the disciplines of which you are considered such a great and celebrated professor. How can you have time for the body and the mind at the same time? How can you frequent the cookshop and books at the same time?"[97]

---

[93] "Inanimae . . . protinus castimoniae iugum subeo." *Met.* 11.30.1.

[94] "Talis autem vitae et castimoniae iugum plerisque omnibus durissimum est assuetis carnibus vesci *et mihi imprimis, qui malim inter creophagos quam carpophagos annumerari.*" Beroaldo, *Commentarii*, fol. 279v.

[95] "Ego illud ecclesiasticum probo: omnia munda mundis." Ibid.

[96] Ovid, *Met.* 15.75–76, 81–82; Epistle to Titus 1.15.

[97] "Si quis mihi interdiceret esu ca<r>nium et ad inanimos cibos relegaret, citissime tabescerem; fieremque et ipse inanimis. Hic occurrat forsitan quispiam dicens heus tu magister et commentator noster heccine tua est disciplina? Sic nos instruis? Ganeo es et lurco et edax et vorax. Tu nobis popinam et ganeam colendam praecipis. Nescis studium salutare fieri non posse citra frugalitatem, nescis parco victu et tenuiculo opus esse studiosis disciplinarum, quarum tu haberis professor, tam magnus tam famigeratus. Quomodo potes

Beroaldo responds to the charges of his hypothetical student with professorial gravitas: he is no glutton, he claims, but moderate in his tastes, preferring simple but dainty food that benefits both mind and body. Anyway, he adds, vegetables and fruits and beans are unwholesome (*cacochyma*); as both Galen and everyday experience demonstrate, they bloat the body and dull the mind.[98] Beroaldo closes his digression with an address to Váradi:

> Now let us return from our detour back to the path, so that—if gods and men approve—the final touches might be placed on these commentaries, in order that our Lucius, changed from obscurity to Lucidity, might fly forth into the world and come quickly, O greatest bishop, into your hands, which will receive him courteously, eagerly, and affectionately.[99]

Beroaldo's digression appeals to both the absent Váradi and the crowd of students in his lecture hall, and it lightens the serious religious tone of his long commentary on Lucius' transformation and subsequent devotion to Isis and Osiris. But it has another function as well. Beroaldo uses it to put the spotlight on himself and to remind us who he is: the all-important professor and commentator standing outside or, we might say, presiding over the text before us. His students and Váradi have their counterparts in Lucius, the one in the foolish youth, the other in the perfect priest. Beroaldo's counterpart, as we shall see in the next section, is Apuleius himself.

Straying from the Path

As we consider Beroaldo's treatment of book 11, it is easy to see why he was one of the most popular teachers in Europe. He provides an interpretation of Apuleius and an education in antiquity, but also something more: a running conversation on the present that emerges as a sort of metatext from his notes and especially from his digressions. In the commentary on book 11, the theme of the conversation is contemporary

---

corpori simul et animo vacare? Quomodo popinam simul et libros colis?" Beroaldo, *Commentarii*, fol. 279v.

[98] "Et profecto longe conducibilius salutariusque est modico cibo et eo quidem precioso viriculas refocillare recreareque, quam oleribus et pomis atque leguminibus implere ventrem ad saturitatem, quae omnia sunt cacochyma, ut Galenus docet et argumenta quotidiana evidenter ostendunt, quibus corpus distentum languet et animus hebetescit." Ibid.

[99] "Iam a diverticulo in viam regrediamur ut ext<r>ema manus, diis hominibusque faventibus, hisce commentariis imponatur, ut tandem Lucius noster ex tenebroso Lucidus factus provolet in publicum, et in manus tuas Antistes Maxime festinanter conveniat, quae illum comiter desyderanter amanter excipient." Ibid.

moral and religious experience, which both gives meaning to the story of Lucius and is given meaning by it. But Beroaldo does not confine his contemporary discourse to religion or to book 11. His commentary contains several such metatexts or conversations. In this section we will look closely at two: one on the nature of art and the other on the meaning of the story of Psyche.[100] In each, Beroaldo presents himself as both an interpreter and a modern-day counterpart of Apuleius.

The principal building block of Beroaldo's metatexts is the digression—an excursion from the line-by-line exposition of the text into the world of fifteenth-century Bologna and the life and views of Beroaldo himself. The commentary is studded with such excursuses.[101] Beroaldo included them, as Krautter noted long ago, not only to bring the past to life for his students but also to imitate Apuleius' technique and to make philological commentary into a literary genre in its own right.[102] The digressions we will be looking at confirm Krautter's observation, for in every case Beroaldo both presents himself as a worthy emulator of Apuleius and creates his own small but self-conscious work of literary art.

Digressions are a part of the design of Beroaldo's work, as he says in the preface: "Sometimes in accordance with my particular custom I have neatly woven in little flowers plucked from the meadow of learning, and I have frequently added extra details [*parerga*] as painters do, so that the flagging reader might be refreshed."[103] Beroaldo describes Apuleius' embedded tales in similar terms. In one passage he observes that these tales refresh the flagging reader and provide variety with artfully disposed "little flowers."[104] In another, he claims for Apuleius the

---

[100] I have published earlier versions of the discussion in this section in "Reading Apuleius" and "Filippo Beroaldo on Apuleius."

[101] For a useful but incomplete list of Beroaldo's digressions, see Casella, "Il metodo dei commentatori umanistici," 685–701. Casella points out that Beroaldo imitates the themes and styles of the authors he discusses; see 660–69, esp. 661, 667.

[102] Krautter, *Philologische Methode*, 40–52. And compare his comment (p. 50): "Denn offensichtlich betrachtet er den philologischen Kommentar nicht nur als gelehrtes Hilfsmittel, sondern geradezu als literarische Gattung mit durchaus künstlerischen Ansprüchen."

[103] "Interdum ex instituto prope peculiari, flosculos ex doctrinarum prato decerptos decenter intexui, et more pictorum parerga frequenter adieci, quibus lassescens lector reficeretur." Beroaldo, *Commentarii*, fol. 2v.

[104] On the story of the adulterous slave and his terrible punishment related at *Met.* 8.22: "Hac narrationis varietate quibusdam quasi flosculis exornat venustat Lucius noster suum hoc opus, ne lectores morosa continuatae narrationis aequalitate lassescant." Ibid., fol. 180r. Also see Krautter, *Philologische Methode*, 50. Apuleius' digressions refresh the commentator as well, as Beroaldo points out in his elaborate introduction to the first adultery tale in book 9 (*Met.* 9.5–7): "Nos quoque mythopoion, hoc est opificem fabellae, Lucium nostrum latialiter personantem et graphice lepidissimeque explicantem inaudiamus legamus pensitemus auribus oculis animis lubentibus, cum talibus egressionum amoenitatibus non solum lectores verum etiam commentatores reficiantur" (fol. 193v).

painter's license to embellish his work with extra details (*parerga*); both the word and the comparison echo Beroaldo's description of his own additions.[105] Many of Beroaldo's digressions are used in a general imitation of Apuleius, breaking up the steady stream of his line-by-line exposition as Apuleius breaks up the forward march of his narration, and often highlighted with Apuleian diction and vocabulary.[106] But he develops others more fully for use in his literary metatexts, as in the cases we are about to examine.

Beroaldo's discussion of the nature of art grows out of a single complex digression inspired by the description of a statue of Diana and Actaeon in book 2 (*Met.* 2.4.3–10), a major turning point in the novel. Lucius has been invited to the house of his mother's old friend Byrrhena, where he sees a sculpture of Diana and Actaeon, which he describes in a detailed ecphrasis. He admires the sculpture but fails to understand its obvious warning of the dangers of curiosity. The statue depicts Diana standing in a grotto with her dogs on either side. The image of the voyeur Actaeon appears twice—once in stone and again reflected in the pool beneath the goddess's feet—"already animal-like, on the point of becoming a stag."[107] Modern readers shiver with ominous anticipation a line or so later when the kindly Byrrhena tells Lucius, "Everything you see belongs to you."[108] But this is not what concerns Beroaldo, who uses the description as an excuse for a discourse on his own contemporary and literary interests. He is fascinated by Apuleius' insistence on the naturalistic quality of the statue, and a single phrase in the description—"ars aemula naturae" (art rivaling nature)—prompts him to launch into a digression on a contemporary example of artistic realism—a recently completed religious painting by the Bolognese artist Francesco Francia. He comments: "While I was writing this commentary, my fellow townsman Francia clearly demonstrated that art rivals nature."[109] Beroaldo has a

---

[105] On the tale of the condemned murderess (*Met.* 10.23–28): "Inseritur tempestiviter haec fabula . . . quae narratione lepida et speciosa demulceat aures animosque lectorum, et sicut pictoribus datum est excurrere in parerga, idem quoque ius plausibiliter conceditur luculentis auctoribus, ut in parecbases in egressiones favorabiliter exspacientur. Qua in re prope eximius est Lucius noster, qui fabellis intextis et id genus parergis reficit lectorem nauseamque discutiens omne tedium levat." Beroaldo, *Commentarii*, fol. 239r. Compare the phrase *more pictorum parerga* on fol. 2v, quoted in n. 103.

[106] The digression on religious charlatans at *Met.* 8.29.2 is a case in point. See n. 46 in this chapter.

[107] "Iam in cervum ferinus." *Met.* 2.4.10; Walsh's translation.

[108] "'Tua sunt' ait Byrrhena 'cuncta quae vides.'" *Met.* 2.5.1.

[109] "Me ista condente artem emulam naturae esse evidenter ostendit municeps meus Francia." Beroaldo, *Commentarii*, fol. 34v. The digression is translated and discussed by Baxandall and Gombrich, "Beroaldus on Francia." (But they wrongly render "me ista condente" as "in my opinion" [113].)

definite painting in mind—an *Adoration of Christ* that Francia painted for a church in Bologna around 1499. The religious message conveyed by Francia's tender picture of the infant Christ is antithetical to that of Apuleius' imaginary statue of the vengeful goddess. But, again, this is not what concerns Beroaldo. His interest is in an exciting contemporary event in Bologna, the dedication of Francia's painting and its occasion, the return of Antongaleazzo Bentivoglio, a member of Bologna's reigning family, from a pilgrimage to Jerusalem.[110] Beroaldo's digression pays an obvious compliment both to his friend Francia and to the ruling Bentivogli, but it was also designed to make a vivid impression in the lecture hall. Antongaleazzo's return, the painting, and the ceremonies attending its dedication would all have been fresh in the minds of his students, and Beroaldo could have expected his allusion to the event to catch and hold their interest.

But he had a literary purpose as well. Beroaldo's discussion of Francia's painting is the centerpiece in an excursus on the topic "ars aemula naturae" in which he not only compliments Francia but also suggests that he himself is an artist—with words. The digression is symmetrically structured, framing the account of Francia and his work with general comments on art and nature and illustrative quotations. Beroaldo begins with a striking gloss on the phrase *ars aemula naturae*: "Imitatrix studiosa effectrix" (imitator, devotee, creator). He continues: "Indeed, art imitates nature and strives to portray and recall her in every possible respect."[111] Three quotations follow: from *Ad Herennium*, the elder Pliny, and Plato. The quotations are different in kind, and each is directed to a different point: the quotation from *Ad Herennium* to the guiding power of nature, that from Pliny to the importance of following nature, not other artists, and that from Plato to the creative power of art. The quotations from *Ad Herennium* and Plato are taken out of context and rephrased, as Baxandall and Gombrich have noted.[112]

Now let us look more closely. First, Beroaldo's quotation from *Ad Herennium*: "In book three of the *Rhetorica ad Herennium* the author

[110] The painting is to be dated between Antongaleazzo's return (23 October 1498) and the publication of Beroaldo's commentary. See Baxandall and Gombrich, "Beroaldus on Francia," 114 n. 7. It was placed over the altar of S. Maria della Misericordia, but is now in the Pinacoteca in Bologna. For an illustration, see Baxandall and Gombrich, plate 18a. The painting shows Antongaleazzo Bentivoglio kneeling next to the Virgin. Some art historians believe that the shepherd standing at the far right is another member of the Bentivoglio family.

[111] "Ars enim naturam imitatur eamque usquequaque effingere ac representare contendit." Beroaldo, *Commentarii*, fol. 34v.

[112] Baxandall and Gombrich, "Beroaldus on Francia," 114–15.

says, 'Art imitates nature and will discover what nature requires if she follows her example.' "[113] The quotation is not exact. The sentence in *Ad Herennium* reads: "Therefore, let art imitate nature, let her discover what nature requires, and let her follow her example."[114] For the exhortation in *Ad Herennium,* Beroaldo has substituted a general principle: for him it is not that art *should* imitate nature but that she *does,* and that she will succeed by doing so. He has obviously "misquoted," but he has not done so carelessly.[115] Rather, he has tailored the "quotation" to suit his own context, and to bolster his opening assertion: "Indeed, art imitates nature and strives to portray and recall her in every possible respect." It is tempting, however, to suspect that Beroaldo has not completely ignored the context in *Ad Herennium.* He has taken his quotation from a passage on the role of nature and art in memory: by nature, the ancient author tells us, unusual events are more memorable than ordinary ones.[116] The idea provides an appropriate background for Beroaldo's digression on Francia's painting, concerned as it is to evoke a striking and out-of-the-way occasion that was, as we might say, naturally memorable.

Beroaldo's quotation from Pliny is more straightforward. Quoting very closely, but not quite exactly, from *Naturalis historia* 34.61, he recalls the story of the painter Eupompus, who was asked which of his predecessors he followed. Pointing to a great crowd of people, he replied: "Nature herself is what one should imitate—not an artist."[117]

Beroaldo's quotation from Plato is a partial and selective citation, not of Plato himself but of Ficino's Latin translation: "In the tenth book of his *Laws* Plato teaches that all things are made by nature

---

[113] "Libro tertio rethoricorum ad herennium. Imitatur inquit ars naturam et quod ea desiderat inveniet si quod ostendit sequatur." Beroaldo, *Commentarii,* fol. 34v.

[114] "Imitetur ars igitur naturam, et, quod ea desiderat id inveniat, quod ostendit sequatur." *Rhet. Her.* 3.22.

[115] *Pace* Baxandall and Gombrich ("Beroaldus on Francia," 114): "The interest of the piece [Beroaldo's digression] lies . . . in the clarity with which it brings into view some aspects of the relationship between humanist criticism and its sources in ancient literature: the dependence on memory in quotation, the degree of misacceptation, and the curious standards of relevance." Humanist reading practices are more complicated than this comment suggests. For a useful summary, see Hankins, *Plato in the Italian Renaissance* 1:18–26.

[116] In the sentence just before our passage, for example: "Docet ergo se natura vulgari et usitata re non exsuscitari, novitate et insigni quodam negotio commoveri." *Rhet. Her.* 3.22.

[117] "Celebratum est Eupompi pictoris responsum qui interrogatus quem sequeretur antecedentium, dixisse fertur, demonstrata hominum multitudine *naturam ipsam imitandam esse, non artificem.*" Beroaldo, *Commentarii,* fol. 34v.

and art, and that art herself has created images of reality."[118] Compare Ficino:

> Some say that all things that are made, will be made, or have been made, are made by nature, by chance, or by art. . . . From these, art, a mortal entity made afterward by mortals, created secondary things not fully partaking of reality, but images of it related to herself—the sort of things that painting, music, and other similar arts create.[119]

We can easily convict Beroaldo of quoting out of context, for he wrongly attributes to Plato views that Plato cites as those of the materialists with whom he disagrees.[120] He is also guilty of misrepresenting his source: in Plato there are three creative forces (nature, chance, and art), not only nature and art, as Beroaldo asserts. Again, Beroaldo's changes are deliberate. He has tailored his "quotation" for his own rhetorical purposes: to emphasize the link between nature and art, to demonstrate art's creative power, and to characterize its productions as "images of reality."[121]

It is at this point—after his preamble and three quotations—that Beroaldo introduces Francia and his painting as a modern and vivid demonstration of the proposition "ars aemula naturae." In the Francia section, too, he artfully employs quotations, this time to compliment Francia and Antongaleazzo. Echoing Statius' characterization of his wealthy patron and friend Atedius Melior, he describes Antongaleazzo as "most cultivated in every aspect of life."[122] Quoting Pliny's comment on Phidias, he begins his concluding sentence on Francia: "Let these things be said in passing about an artist who can never be praised enough".[123]

Beroaldo ends his digression with a final quotation, this time from his favorite model, Apuleius himself (the source is *De mundo* 20): "Indeed,

---

[118] "Plato volumine decimo de legibus tradit omnia natura et arte fieri, artemque ipsam simulacra veritatis genuisse." Ibid.

[119] "Res omnes nonnulli aiunt, quae fiunt, quae futurae, quaeque factae sunt, vel natura, vel fortuna, vel arte fieri. . . . Ex quibus artem postea mortalem a mortalibus factam, posteriores quasdam res genuisse, non penitus veritatis participes, sed simulacra quaedam sibi ipsi cognata, qualia pictura, musica, caeteraeque artes his similes generant." *Omnia divini Platonis opera tralatione Marsilii Ficini emendatione, et ad graecum codicem collatione Simonis Grynaei* (Lugduni, 1548), 590–51. Cf. Plato, *Laws* 888–89.

[120] Baxandall and Gombrich, "Beroaldus on Francia," 114.

[121] For Beroaldo's deliberate misquotation of Plato, see also Garin, "Note in margine," 439–41.

[122] "In omni vitae colore tersissimus" (Beroaldo, *Commentarii*, fol. 34v). Cf. "vir optime nec minus in iudicio litterarum quam in omni vitae colore tersissime" (Stat. *Silv.* 2, *praef.*).

[123] "Haec obiter dicta sint de artifice nunquam satis laudato" (Beroaldo, *Commentarii*, fol. 34v). The translation is that of Baxandall and Gombrich, in "Beroaldus on Francia," 114. Cf. "Haec sint obiter dicta de artifice numquam satis laudato" (Plin., *Nat. Hist.* 36.19).

the arts themselves in imitation of nature make like things from unlike. But painting, in a particular way—from clashing colors of paint mixed in the right proportions—makes images like the things it imitates."[124] This conclusion achieves both a complimentary and a literary purpose. Its complimentary purpose is obvious: the reference to painting indirectly praises Francia and his imitative and creative powers. The literary purpose is more subtle, and it is achieved through both the source and the content of the quotation. By quoting Apuleius, and specifically in the context of a digression (or, we might better say, of a digression on a digression, since Beroaldo has been commenting on Apuleius' ecphrastic excursus on Byrrhena's statue group), Beroaldo alludes to his imitation of Apuleius' technique. Indeed, his whole digression embodies and exemplifies what he has said of both his own and Apuleius' digressions. I give only one example, the programmatic announcement from his preface quoted above: "Sometimes in accordance with my particular custom I have neatly woven in little flowers plucked from the meadow of learning, and I have frequently added extra details [*parerga*] as painters do, so that the flagging reader might be refreshed."

In the digresssion on the theme "ars aemula naturae," Beroaldo has indeed "woven in little flowers plucked from the meadow of learning" and "added extra details as painters do," but his technique has also been like the one Apuleius attributed to painting in the passage from *De mundo*. Subtly identifying himself as Francia's literary counterpart, he has painted a picture with words, using a palette of different, if not clashing, sources: *Ad Herennium*, Pliny, Ficino's Plato, Statius, and Apuleius.

Beroaldo creates an even more elaborate metatext on the story of Cupid and Psyche. This episode, Apuleius' most important embedded tale, appears at the heart of the novel (*Met.* 4.28–6.24). In three long digressions, strategically placed, Beroaldo makes his commentary on it the centerpiece of his *Apuleius*. He opens his own "Cupid and Psyche" with an elaborate discussion of Fulgentius and allegory at *Met.* 4.28.1, punctuates it near the middle with a description of the villa of his friend Mino de' Rossi at the beginning of *Met.* 5, and closes it with an autobiographical account of his own marriage at *Met.* 6.24.4. The digressions are different in kind. The first is an essay on hermeneutics, the second an ecphrasis, and the third an autobiographical idyll that functions as a sphragis or seal. All are metaliterary and self-referential—interpreting

---

[124] "Artes autem ipsae naturam imitantes ex imparibus paria faciunt. Pictura vero peculiariter ex discordibus pigmentorum coloribus confusione modica temperatis imagines his quae imitatur similes facit." Beroaldo, *Commentarii*, fol. 34v. (Beroaldo has slightly abridged Apuleius, omitting his words *atris atque albis, luteis et puniceis* after *coloribus*.)

the story of Psyche, but also commenting on Beroaldo commenting on Apuleius.

In the first digression (on hermeneutics) Beroaldo presents a programmatic statement in three parts: a discussion of the word *fabula*, a quotation of Fulgentius, and a declaration of his own method.[125]

Beroaldo's long discussion of *fabula* is ostensibly motivated both by the words of the old woman telling the story (she characterizes her narrative as "old wives' tales"—*anilibus fabulis*, *Met*. 4.27.8) and by her fairy-tale opening: "There were a king and queen in a certain city."[126] But Beroaldo also has something else in mind, for *fabula* was a hermeneutically loaded word, as both he and his audience were well aware. Discussion of the *fabula* had a rich and convoluted history, and its legitimacy and correct interpretation had been argued by not only late-antique authorities like Macrobius, Martianus Capella, and Fulgentius but also their medieval and Renaissance counterparts.[127] Beroaldo completely sidesteps this debate, both by treating *fabula* as a lexical item to be defined instead of a genre to be discussed, and by systematically omitting any definition that would necessitate interpreting it philosophically or metaphysically. Macrobius and his successors had categorized, valued, and argued about the various types of fables.[128] Beroaldo, however, although ostensibly giving a systematic account of the meaning and use of *fabula* and its synonyms, in fact does nothing of the sort. Although he gives many definitions, he recognizes only three categories of fable: the practical story with its concluding moral, the obvious untruth, and the plausible plot of a play.[129] This treatment of *fabula* deliberately undercuts the next section of his digression, the allegorical account of "Cupid and Psyche" by Fulgentius the Mythographer, for the type of tale assumed by Fulgentius' reading—a "decent and dignified conception of holy truths, with respectable events and characters . . . presented beneath a modest veil of allegory," as Macrobius terms it[130]— is conspicuously absent from Beroaldo's lexicon. Beroaldo goes on to quote Fulgentius' entire allegory without comment (the city of the girl's

---

[125] Ibid., fol. 95r–v.

[126] "Erant in quadam civitate rex et regina" (*Met*. 4.28.1).

[127] See Dronke, *Fabula*, 14–78; Demats, *Fabula*, 5–60; Lev Kenaan, "*Fabula anilis*."

[128] Macrobius' taxonomy, for example, divided *fabulae* into the merely amusing and those encouraging the listener to virtue, and the latter class into Aesopic fables and a higher type labeled *narratio fabulosa*, which could be further subdivided using the criteria of seemliness and suitability for allegory (*Somn. Scip.* 1.2.7–11). See the schema in Dronke, *Fabula*, 26 n. 1.

[129] Beroaldo, *Commentarii*, fol. 95r.

[130] "Sacrarum rerum notio sub pio figmentorum velamine honestis et tecta rebus et vestita nominibus" (Macr., *Somn. Scip.* 1.2.11). The translation is that of Stahl, in *Commentary on the Dream of Scipio*, 85.

birth is the world; her parents are God and Matter; the girl is soul, her sisters Flesh and Free Will, and so on).[131]

In the last part of the digression Beroaldo contrasts the allegorical method with his own approach. Using the familiar example of Jerusalem, he explains the medieval fourfold system of allegory employed by interpreters of scripture: on the historical level Jerusalem is the city of Judaea, on the allegorical or tropological level the church, on the moral level the soul, and on the spiritual level "the heavenly city to which the prayers of all aspire and desire to be made its inhabitants."[132] For him, however, the historical level is sufficient: "But I will not pursue allegories in the explanation of this story [*huiusce fabulae*] so much as the historical sense, and I will explain the meaning of words and obscure matters, lest I appear a bad philosopher instead of a commentator."[133]

Beroaldo has accomplished both pedagogical and programmatic purposes in this long preamble to "Cupid and Psyche." On the pedagogical level, he has both reviewed the fourfold system of *allegoresis* (a staple of medieval and Renaissance education) and reminded his students of Fulgentius' allegory (first printed in 1498 by a former student and present rival, Giambattista Pio).[134] He endorses neither Fulgentius nor the allegorical system but—good teacher that he is—explains them fully before putting them aside. On the programmatic level, he has taken a stand that would have been familiar to his students and readers; for although he was a deeply religious man, he cared little for metaphysics, always preferring to explain the things of this world rather than to speculate about those of the next.[135] He has also intentionally insulted Pio, a proponent of Fulgentius and someone easily recognizable as a philosophaster.[136] Most important, however, he has presented a complex statement of his own hermeneutical method. In his (admittedly slanted)

---

[131] Fulg. *Mit.* 3.6. Beroaldo, *Commentarii*, fol. 95r–v. For Fulgentius' allegory, see pp. 57–59.

[131] "Hierusalem historice significat civitatem Iudaeae metropolim, allegorice ecclesiam, moraliter animam, spiritaliter celestem civitatem, ad quam cunctorum vota suspirant, et illius coloni effici concupiscunt." Beroaldo, *Commentarii*, fol. 95v.

[133] "Sed nos non tam allegorias in explicatione huiusce fabulae sectabimur, quam historicum sensum, et rerum reconditarum verborumque interpretationem explicabimus, ne philosophaster magis videar quam commentator." Ibid.

[134] Fulgentius, *Mitologiae*. For Pio, see Rose, *Filippo Beroaldo*, 108–14.

[135] Or as he would put it: "Divinis sepositis humana scrutari." The phrase comes from one of Beroaldo's many similar pronouncements: "Socrates ille philosophorum fons ... dixisse fertur: quae supra nos, nihil ad nos. Ex hoc socratico documento commonemur, omissis rebus sublimioribus, circa humiliora versari et a coelestibus ad terrena descendere et divinis sepositis humana scrutari." Beroaldo, *Oratio proverbialis* (Bologna, 1500), quoted from Garin, "Note in margine," 443. And see Garin's important discussion at 442–45).

[136] See Dionisotti, "Giovan Battista Pio e Mario Equicola," 89–91. See also Raimondi, "Il primo commento umanistico," 101–40.

discussion of *fabula*, he has treated the word like a lexicographer rather than a theorist, defining it from its use in ancient authors. His emphasis on the practical and moral fable at the expense of more metaphysical types not only invalidates Fulgentius' allegory in advance but implicitly identifies "Cupid and Psyche" as a moral rather than a philosophical tale. His final statement is the capstone: not as a "bad philosopher" but as a "commentator," he will undertake to explain "the historical sense" and "the meaning of words and obscure matters." His approach, in other words, is that of a philologist. Of course, this is his approach throughout his *Apuleius* (and in all his commentaries). But he states it at this particular point both to contrast his method with the kind of speculation represented by Fulgentius (and Pio) and to herald a reading of "Cupid and Psyche" based primarily on an understanding of its language and mythological and historical background.

True to his word, Beroaldo does explain the tale on "the historical level" of language, plot, and what he regards as universal human psychology. Reading the story in terms of human emotions and behavior, he points out the indulgence of mothers toward their sons, the universal hostility between mothers-in-law and daughters-in-law, and—in a very odd reading of Venus' response to Psyche's pregnancy—the desire for grandchildren and its softening effect on mothers-in-law.[137] Along the way, he indulges in more than a few misogynist stereotypes.[138] He situates the story in its Roman historical context with detailed explanations of essential points of Roman marriage law: paternal consent, marriage between persons of unequal status, legitimacy of offspring, and marriage by *manus*.[139] A philologist to the core, he is ever alert not only to unusual and difficult words but also to the nuances of common words in their contexts. He notes almost every occurrence of the word *anima* and points out its relation to Psyche. Thus, on Psyche's addressing Cupid as "sweet soul of your Psyche" (*tuae Psyches dulcis anima,*

---

[137] *Indulgence* (*Met.* 6.5.4): "Probabile videtur et satis credibile Cupidinem filium reperiri posse in materno domo, cum matres in filios sint longe quam patres indulgentiores" (Beroaldo, *Commentarii*, fol. 120r). *In-law hostility* (*Met.* 6.9.2): "Inter socrus et nurus quoddam quasi genuinum et naturale dissidium est" (fol. 122v). *Grandchildren* (*Met.* 6.9.4): "Uterus foeminae turgidus et praegnatio conciliat favorem et quodam quasi lenocinio blandimenta conquirit; idque potissimum apud socrum quae futura est avia. Tales enim imprimis foeminae nepotulorum desiderio capiuntur" (fol. 122v).

[138] I give only two examples. On *Met.* 5.10.6: "Mulierum est proprium invidere irasci furere ultionem parare; iuxta illud vindicta nemo magis gaudet quam foemina" (Beroaldo, *Commentarii*, fol. 105v). On *Met.* 6.23.3: "sed plerumque nova nupta ab alio praeflorata ad maritum venit. Tanta est morum corruptela ut virgines fiant mulieres in aedibus parentum exuantque pudiciciam, qua amissa omnis virtus in foemina ruit" (fol. 132r).

[139] Beroaldo, *Commentarii*, fols. 123r, 132r–v, 134r.

Met. 5.6.9), he comments: "The allusion is to the name of Psyche, which means soul, as if her husband was the soul of her soul."[140] He points out the wordplay in "Psyche fell in love with Love" (*Psyche . . . in amoris incidit amorem*, *Met.* 5.23.3): "The one signifies the god Cupid, the other love."[141] When Cupid flees Psyche after the catastrophe and addresses her from the top of a cypress tree, Beroaldo (more acutely than the modern commentators, who fail to notice its significance) sees why he alights in that particular tree. His note reads: "The cypress, clearly a tree associated with death and sacred to Dis, and for that reason placed before houses as a funeral sign."[142]

Beroaldo's second and third digressions in "Cupid and Psyche" are also learned, highly personal, and characterized by close attention to words and wordplay. In each he uses significant words from Apuleius as the jumping-off point into his self-referential metatext. Common to both are *psyche* (soul) and *voluptas* (pleasure—the child of Cupid and Psyche).

The second digression appears at the beginning of *Met.* 5. Psyche, awakening from her exhausted sleep, finds herself in the garden of a beautiful country house. An ecphrasis of the house follows, which Beroaldo imitates in an ecphrasis of the villa of his friend Mino de' Rossi. His description is explicitly intended to match Apuleius', as his introduction indicates.

> This is an artistic description of the splendid dwelling in which Psyche [*psyche*] is received by divine agency [*divinitus*]. But since timely digressions rest and restore readers to a greater degree, it seems timely and opportune in this place in particular to give a summary account of the villa at Pontecchio of my dear friend Mino de' Rossi, the depiction of which is not far from this description of Cupid's retreat [*cupidinei diversorii*].[143]

[140] "Allusio est ad Psyches nomen, quo Anima significatur, quasi anima animae maritus sit." Ibid., fol. 103v. Cf. Kenney's note ad loc.: "*Anima* and ψυχή were common lovers' endearments, but . . . [she is ignorant] of what *Psychae . . . anima* implies—that only a complete and perfect union with Love can save her."

[141] "Alterum deum cupidinem, alterum dilectionem significat." Beroaldo, *Commentarii*, fol. 111r. He continues: "ex eadem elegantia est *cupidine cupidinis flagrans*, id est cupiditate dei amoris exestuans."

[142] "Cypressum. Arborem scilicet feralem et diti sanctam, et ideo funebri signo ad domos positam." Ibid.

[143] "Descriptio est graphica luculenti domicilii quo psyche divinitus accipitur. Caeterum cum egressiones tempestivae maiorem in modum reficiant recreentque lectores, tempestivum videtur et oportunum hoc potissimum loco Roscii mei Mini Ponticulanum summatim explicare, cuius topothesia haud sane multum distat ab hac cupidinei diversorii descriptione." Ibid., fol. 100v.

Beroaldo promises a restorative digression and a description, both emulating Apuleius. But he is also emulating Apuleius' wordplay. He uses both *psyche* and *cupidinei* in a double sense: we can understand the subject of the verb "is received" in the first sentence above as either "Psyche" or "the soul" and translate the end of the last sentence as "Cupid's retreat," "the retreat of love, or even "the charming retreat" (if we take *cupidinei* as a simple adjective). Beroaldo's wordplay continues with *diversorium* (retreat).[144] A diversorium is a temporary abode or stopping place—a place to which one turns aside (*diverto*) from one's journey or usual business. Beroaldo has taken the word from Apuleius' description (*Met*. 5.1.3) and uses it, as we will see, as a major theme for his digression.

Beroaldo's description of Mino's villa has two primary intertexts: Apuleius and Pliny the Younger (*Ep*. 2.17 and 5.6). He conspicuously evokes both authors early in his account. In the *Golden Ass* Cupid's house obviously belongs to someone important: "You would know the moment you entered that you were seeing the splendid and delightful retreat of some god," says Apuleius.[145] Beroaldo echoes his words: "At once, from the very moment you enter, you will surely declare that it is the splendid retreat of some prince of the highest nobility."[146] Pliny's Laurentine villa (*Ep*. 2.17) is close to the city; so is Mino's retreat. One can travel the seventeen miles to Pliny's villa after a full day's work and arrive in time to spend the night, or ride the seven miles to Mino's after doing business in the morning and arrive for dinner.[147] In each case, there is more than one way to get there.[148] These allusions to Pliny and Apuleius pay an elegant compliment to Mino. By referring to Pliny, Beroaldo implies that his friend's villa is on a par with that of the ancient Roman grandee.[149] By echoing Apuleius' reference to the villa's owner, he hints that Mino is worthy of comparison with Cupid himself.

---

[144] I have borrowed "retreat" from Walsh's translation.

[145] "Iam scires ab introitu primo dei cuiuspiam luculentum et amoenum videre te diversorium" (*Met*. 5.1.3).

[146] "Statim ab ipso introitu haud dubie asseverabis principis id cuiuspiam et summatis viri luculentum esse diversorium." Beroaldo, *Commentarii*, fol. 100v.

[147] Pliny, *Ep* 2.17.2: "Decem et septem milibus passuum ab urbe secessit, ut peractis, quae agenda fuerint, salvo iam et composito die possis ibi manere." Beroaldo, *Commentarii*, fol. 100v: "Secessit ab urbe plus minus septem millibus passuum. . . . Potesque peractis quae agenda in urbe fuerint matutinis negociis illuc transcurrere ad horam prandii."

[148] Pliny, *Ep* 2.17.3: "Aditur non una via." Beroaldo, *Commentarii*, fol. 100v: "Aditur via non una."

[149] It may even be better. Pliny's Laurentinum "lacks a running stream" ("deficitur aqua saliente," *Ep*. 2.17.24). Mino's villa has them in profusion: "Ex omnibus villae membris supernae infernaeque iuxta scaturiunt aquae salientes erumpuntque." Beroaldo, *Commentarii*, fol. 100v.

Beroaldo could count on his students and readers to appreciate the allusions. They had the text of Apuleius before them, and many would have seen the edition of Pliny's letters that Beroaldo had published in 1498 and again in 1500, just a few months before his lectures and commentary on Apuleius.[150] (The young dedicatee of his Pliny, Johannes von Wartenberg, was probably in Beroaldo's audience for the Apuleius lectures.)[151] Some readers might even have heard Beroaldo lecture on Pliny's letters on his villas, for a list of his explanations of "vocabula obscuriora" from *Ep.* 2.17 and 5.6 survives—perhaps from a student's notes.[152]

Beroaldo's principal subject, however, is not the architecture of Mino's villa but the enjoyment it affords its owner and his guests. It offers boating, fishing, fowling, walking, and even morning mass—each activity measured and watched over by the great clock near the roof that marks the hours with its bell.[153] But Beroaldo does not use *voluptas* for any of these enjoyments. He reserves that word for the account of his own annual visit to Mino at the end of the digression. The concluding passage is full of elaborate wordplay that looks back to the beginning, bringing Apuleius, Mino, himself, and the reader together in a grand finale.

> Every year, almost as a solemn rite, after the university holidays have been proclaimed, he summons me into that most delightful refuge (I know of nothing more delightful). And there we practice good cheer and indulge in purest pleasure [*voluptati*], refreshing mind and body in turn—but not without the most agreeable companionship and sustenance of books, without which there is no true pleasure [*voluptas*].
>
> It was agreeable to make a detour [*divertere*] deliberately into this retreat [*diversorium*], so that you who attentively read all my books (and through you other readers) might know who the de' Rossi in my volumes is, whose castle at Pontecchio can appear—not

---

[150] For these editions, see Krautter, *Philologische Methode*, 190; Rose, *Filippo Beroaldo*, 73 n. 481. The second edition of Pliny's letters was printed in April 1500; Beroaldo's *Apuleius* appeared in August.

[151] Beroaldo lists him among his current noble foreign students in the dedication to Váradi (*Commentarii*, fol. a4v): "Inter quos ad praesens est gemma scholasticorum et illibatus eloquentiae candidatorum flos Johannes Vartimbergensis Boemus." Wartenberg (ca. 1480–1508) was in Bologna from 1497 or 1498 to 1500; see Rose, *Filippo Beroaldo*, 122–23.

[152] "Vocabula obscuriora in duabus epistolis Plinii existentia declarata ut infra per Philippum Beroaldum de anno 1484"; published by Frati, "I due Beroaldi," 227–78. Several of these words (all architectural terms) appear in his description: e.g., *cavum aedium, andronites, gynecea, maceria*; Beroaldo, *Commentarii*, fols. 100v–101r.

[153] Beroaldo, *Commentarii*, fol. 101r.

inappropriately—as a dwelling of pleasure [*voluptatis*] and a lodging of Psyche [*psyches*].

Our Ass has given a detailed account of this artistically and excellently in this place—not with asinine but with philosophic curiosity. But now let us carry on with the commentary we have begun, since it is not out of place to give friends their due in passing, to embellish commentaries with varied elements, and to seek delightful byways [*diverticula*] (so to speak) for our readers.[154]

This passage, like the digression as a whole, is both an affectionate tribute to Mino and a self-conscious assertion of Beroaldo's own literary achievement. The digression began with Cupid's retreat (*cupidinei diversorii*), the imaginary dwelling in which Psyche/Soul was received, and where her child, Pleasure (*Voluptas*), was conceived. Mino's (real) villa—also called a diversorium[155]—is the metaphorical embodiment of Cupid's, for it is both "the lodging of Psyche/Soul," and "the dwelling of pleasure" for Mino and his friends. But Beroaldo has also created his own diversorium: the digression itself. The idea is latent in the familiar language of rest and refreshment introducing the digression; it is brought to life by the wordplay on *diversorium* and its cognates *divertere* and *diverticula* at the end. In the last sentence Beroaldo calls his digressions *diverticula*, which I have translated as "byways" (his usual word for "digressions" is *egressiones*).[156] He uses it, of course, to echo and suggest *diversorium*. But he comes even closer to *diversorium* in the preceding paragraph: "It was agreeable to make a detour [*divertere*] deliberately into this retreat [*diversorium*]." The wordplay nicely blurs the distinction between Mino's retreat and Beroaldo's digression—the one a physical refuge from the everyday world, the other (which describes the first) a literary respite from the task at hand, but both providing rest

---

[154] "Idem me quotannis prope solemniter in illum amoenissimum secessum, quo nihil amoenius novi, evocat post indictas ferias litterarias. Ubi et genialia colimus et voluptati meracissimae indulgemus tum corpus tum animum vicissatim refoventes, non tamen sine suavissimo librorum comitatu et pastu, sine quibus nulla est solida voluptas. Libuit in hoc diversorium de industr<i>a divertere, ut tu qui libellos meos omnis studiose lectitas, ut per te caeteri lectores norint qui sit Roscius in meis voluminibus, cuius praetorium Ponticulanum non absurde domicilium voluptatis atque hospitium psyches videri potest. quod graphice et luculenter hoc in loco Asinus noster non asinali, sed philosophica curiositate perscribit. Sed nos institutas iam commentationes exequamur, cum non ab re sit in transcursu amicis satisfacere, varietatibus commentarios distinguere, et legentibus velut amoena diverticula quaerere." Ibid., fol. 101r–v.

[155] Its temperate climate makes it an excellent "summer retreat" (*diversorium . . . aestivum*). Ibid., fol. 101r.

[156] But he uses *diverticulo* for his digression on vegetarianism at *Met* 11.30.1; see n. 99). In this passage Beroaldo has borrowed his phrasing from Livy 9.17.1: "Et legentibus uelut deuerticula amoena et requiem animo meo quaererem."

and enjoyment to others. Both the description and Beroaldo's claims for it result from Beroaldo's affinity with Apuleius and desire to imitate him. The digression is the emulative counterpart of Apuleius' ecphrasis, matching the creative power of the novelist with the literary skill of his commentator.

Beroaldo's third digression appears in book 6, at the end of "Cupid and Psyche."[157] Again he plays on *soul* and *pleasure*, but now he adds a major new theme, marriage, taking his cue from Apuleius as before.[158] "Cupid and Psyche" ends: "So Psyche was duly married to Cupid, and in the fullness of time a daughter was born to them, whom we call Pleasure [*Voluptatem*]."[159] Beroaldo notes:

> Both wisely and cleverly they say that Pleasure [*Voluptatem*] was born of the marriage of Cupid [*cupidinis*] and Psyche [*psyches*], since pleasure [*voluptas*]—by which the most notable philosophers measure the highest good—comes into being from the desire [*cupiditate*] and love of the soul [*animae*].[160]

He continues:

> While I was writing these things and commenting on this marriage of Psyche and Cupid, it so happened . . . that I took a wife—it was fated by the stars, I believe. . . . May the gods make this marriage fertile and happy and fortunate for us, so that from it pleasure [*voluptas*] may be born. . . . May the offspring born of us be pleasure-bringing [*voluptifica*], like that born of Psyche and Cupid.[161]

A few lines later he proudly announces that his young wife is pregnant. The digression concludes: "I hope and predict that in this memorable jubilee year a son will be born, to be the pleasure [*voluptati*] and ornament of his parents."[162]

---

[157] Beroaldo, *Commentarii*, fols. 134r–v, 135r.
[158] See Gaisser, "Allegorizing Apuleius," 38–39.
[159] "Sic rite Psyche convenit in manum Cupidinis et nascitur illis maturo partu filia, quam Voluptatem nominamus." *Met.* 6.24.4.
[160] "Conducenter et scite voluptatem ex connubio cupidinis et psyches natam esse finxerunt, cum ex cupiditate animae et dilectione voluptas progignatur, qua summum bonum clarissimi philosophorum metiuntur." Beroaldo, *Commentarii*, fol. 134r.
[161] "Condentibus haec nobis et has psyches ac cupidinis nuptias commentantibus siderali opinor decreto factum est, ut ego . . . uxorem ducerem . . . . Dii faxint, ut hoc connubium sit nobis foelix faustum ac fortunatum, utque ex eo voluptas gignatur. . . . gignaturque ex nobis soboles voluptifica, qualis ex psyche et cupidine progenerata est." Ibid., fols. 134r–v, 135.
[162] "Spero et ominor filium anno hoc Iubilei memorando nasciturum, qui parentibus sit voluptati futurus et ornamento." Ibid., fol. 135r.

In this digression Beroaldo's marriage both reenacts the union of Cupid and Psyche and explains it—not in metaphysical terms but in the language of human experiences and feelings. His explanation is at once universal and intensely personal. It begins with what Beroaldo presents as a philosophic truth ("pleasure" is the "child" of "desire" and soul") and continues with wishes appropriate to any marriage ("May the gods make this marriage fertile and happy and fortunate for us"). But the digression is also full of personal detail—biographical information about his wife and her family and musings on his own earlier reluctance to marry.[163] It is personal in another way as well, for if Beroaldo's marriage reenacts Cupid and Psyche's, it also reflects those of several ancient authors, including Apuleius himself. His wife is not an impediment to his literary studies, Beroaldo says, but a comfort and a stimulus, making him believe the old story that "long ago, Marcia held a candle and candlestick for Hortensius as he read and studied, as Terentia did for Tullius, Calphurnia for Pliny, and Pudentilla for Apuleius."[164] The authors are exemplary for Beroaldo (and we should remember that he had edited all of them except for Hortensius), and Beroaldo is exemplary for his students and readers: "Through my marriage, to the studious I have afforded an opportunity for learning and to the lazy a justification."[165]

The Celebrity Commentator

With his metaliterary asides and digressions, Beroaldo moves at will between Apuleius' world and his own. His purposes are largely pedagogical, for his method breathes modern life into the ancient novel, making the past real and vivid for his students. But the metaliterary by nature is also self-referential and attention getting: when Beroaldo exhorts his students, inserts contemporary references, or assembles "flowers from the meadow of learning," he turns the spotlight on himself. He is the man at the podium, presiding over the text as well as the lecture hall, and displaying the literary works he has created from it. In this chapter we have looked at three such metaworks: the extended discourse

---

[163] Ibid., fols. 134v–135r.

[164] "Olim Martia Hortensio, Terentia Tullio, Calphurnia Plino, Pudentilla Apuleio, legentibus meditantibusque candelas et candelabra tenuerint." Ibid., fol 135r. Beroaldo is quoting Sidonius Apollinaris, *Ep.* 2.10.5, but he omits Sidonius' last pair, Rusticiana and Symmachus.

[165] "Studentibus discendi per nuptias occasionem tribui, desidibus excusationem." Beroaldo, *Commentarii*, fol 135r.

on priesthood and moral transformation in the commentary on book 11, the short treatment of art in book 2, and the three-part discussion of the story of Psyche spread over books 4 to 6. In each, Beroaldo imitates Apuleius' language and technique, presenting himself as not only an interpreter but a literary artist.

Beroaldo's readings and metatexts bear the stamp of the personality described by his biographers and revealed in his other works. They show a man intensely interested in the world around him, religious but down-to-earth, and supremely confident of his ability. He compliments patrons and fellow artists and uses the occasion to showcase his own talents, as we have seen in his evocations of Váradi, Francia, and Mino di Rossi. He avoids allegory as a way of interpreting the story of Psyche, but eagerly allegorizes the transformations of Lucius—not because of his ideas about allegory or even religion but because he avoids metaphysical explanations and likes moral ones. His intellectual outlook differs greatly from those of Apuleius' previous Latin interpreters. Fulgentius, Boccaccio, the anonymous fourteenth-century allegorist, and even Bussi, all seem to be writing in a historical vacuum, quite unconcerned with the realities of Apuleius' time and saying very little about their own. Beroaldo, however, is historical in both senses, a fact that allows him—to take only one example—both to understand the details of ancient Isiac religion and to relate them to contemporary Christian practice.

The elaborate content of Beroaldo's lectures and commentaries was enough to attract students and readers, but he did not rely on content alone. He ensured his popularity by showmanship, personality, and self-promotion—the very qualities, in fact, that we observed in Apuleius himself in chapter 1. The similarity should not surprise us, for the circumstances of Beroaldo, the fifteenth-century humanist, and Apuleius, the second-century sophist, for all their obvious differences, nevertheless had much in common. The world of the humanists, like that of the sophists, placed a premium on personal charisma combined with knowledge of the classical past, on oratory for entertainment, and on the ability to attract large numbers of followers. In short, it placed a premium on celebrity. Beroaldo and Apuleius also shared a passion natural to their circumstances: humanist and sophist alike sought and pursued money and fame. Beroaldo, at least, was very good at acquiring both.

He gave rich former students the chance to bid on the dedications to his works, and the negotiations seem to have been accomplished with perfect good humor on both sides. Péter Váradi supposedly placed his bid for the Apuleius commentary with the remark: "If you send me that

Ass of yours that you have kindly promised me, I will send it right back, laden with gold."[166]

He also made money on the sale of his books. In the case of Apuleius we are fortunate enough to have the contract Beroaldo signed with his printer in the spring of 1499. Its provisions included a print run of twelve hundred copies, equal division of the profits between Beroaldo and the printer, and the stipulation that Beroaldo was to lecture on this book and only this at the University of Bologna, and that he was to promote it as much as possible.[167] The twelve hundred copies stipulated in the contract is a very large number—two or three times as large as a typical press run for a commentary on a classical author in this period.[168] As we might say today, the Apuleius commentary was expected to be a blockbuster. Beroaldo planned to lecture from it in the fall of 1499, but publication was postponed by a paper shortage, and he had to lecture on Cicero instead.[169] He explained the matter to his students in the first lecture of the school year, using it as a demonstration of the Greek proverb ἀνάκη δ'οὐδὲ θεοὶ μάχονται: Not even the gods struggle against Necessity.[170] His purpose, however, was not only to explain but also to advertise. In the same lecture he promoted a book of his own orations, touted the usefulness of his Cicero lectures ("the only Cicero you'll ever

---

[166] The story is told by Beroaldo's contemporary biographer, Jean de Pins, who presents it as hearsay: "In Apulejani asini commentariis nuper, quos dum se Thomae colocensi archiepiscopo, viro bonarum artium studioso, dicare velle scriveret, tale accepisse responsum dicitur: 'Asinum istum, quem tam benevole nobis es pollicitus, si ad nos propere miseris, denuo ipse ad te onustum auro remittam.'" (*Clarissimi viri Philippi Beroaldi bononiensis vita* 1:133–34). As Krautter points out (*Philologische Methode*, 24 n. 58), de Pins is confusing another Hungarian friend of Beroaldo's, Tamás Bakócz ("Thomae"), with Váradi. For other requests by Beroaldo for gifts, see Garin, "Note sull'insegnamento," esp. 371, 378.

[167] The contract between Beroaldo and his printer, Benedetto d'Ettore, was signed on 22 May 1499. For its terms, see Sorbelli, *Storia della stampa in Bologna*, 61. See also Bühler, *The University and the Press*, 39.

[168] We do not know enough about the size of editions in the fifteenth century. Bühler characterizes the press run of 1,200 as "an unusually large one for those days" (*The University and the Press*, 39). Haebler mentions a Plato edition of 1,025 copies in the mid-1490s (*The Study of Incunabula*, 175); the other very large editions he cites are of religious and legal texts. Hirsch (*Printing, Selling and Reading*, 66–67) cites figures from 200 to 400 copies for specific classical texts. The 1502 Aldine of Catullus, Tibullus, and Propertius was printed in an extraordinarily large edition of 3,000 copies, but it was an octavo, not a folio edition, and contained the works of all three poets. (See Lowry, *The World of Aldus Manutius*, 174 n. 96; Gaisser, *Catullus and His Renaissance Readers*, 64–65, 309 nn. 153–54.) But many more copies of Beroaldo's Apuleius may have been printed than the 1,200 stipulated in the contract. In his dedication Beroaldo gives the number as around 2,000: "Et sane impressor optimus operam dedit, ut volumina commentariorum circiter duo millia formis excussa divulgarentur." Beroaldo *Commentarii*, fol. a4v.

[169] See Krautter, *Philologische Methode*, 38–39.

[170] Beroaldo, *Oratio proverbiorum*, fols. c4v–c7r.

need," he claims), and promised to lecture on Apuleius "in the memorable and auspicious Jubilee year."[171] His Apuleius finally appeared in August 1500, in time for the next academic year, and sold well from the start.[172]

Beroaldo worked as hard for his fame as he did for his fortune. He basked in his renown and took pains to impress his image both on his current public and on posterity—just like Apuleius, we might say, even though their images are very different. That of Apuleius, as we saw in chapter 1, is ostentatiously complex and ambiguous. Beroaldo's is studiously simple and sincere. The monuments they crave are different, too. Apuleius, devotee of physiognomy that he was, wanted to be memorialized in statues conveying his beauty, eloquence, and philosophical wisdom. Beroaldo, steeped in Christian doctrine, refused to believe in the link that Apuleius insisted on between the inner and outer self, or that a statue could convey his real character to posterity. Instead—philologist to the core—he pinned his hopes on the power of the written word. In the opening paragraph of his dedication he argues that monuments of the intellect are more durable than those of the body—books, the true and breathing likenesses of men, last longer than statues.[173] He has

---

[171] *Orations* (Beroaldo, *Oratio proverbiorum* fol. c6v): "De quorum [Virgilii et Tullii] laudibus melius est ad praesens tacere quam pauca dicere, cum ad laudandum pro merito Virgilium et Tullium, Virgilio et Tullio laudatoribus opus fit. Praeterea in libro orationum mearum extant utriusque scriptoris luculenta praeconia." *Cicero lectures* (fol. c7r): "Erit autem haec procrastinatio scholasticis oppido quam conducibilis. Namque interea aliquot Ciceronis orationes explicabuntur a nobis, ea diligentia, eaque omnifaria eruditione, ut ianua laxissime reserata reliquis deinceps orationibus omnibus videri possit, ut qui vel paucissimas audierit, caeteras sine interprete citraque doctorem adire ipse et per se intelligere queat haud sane difficulter." *Apuleius lectures* (fol. c7r): "Anno autem a salute domini milesimo quingentesimo quem iubileum nominitant, perinde ac auspicatissimo et memorando anno Apuleium fauste ac feliciter initiabimus."

[172] Krautter, in *Philologische Methode*, 39, infers as much from a comment in Beroaldo's opening lecture on Apuleius: "Afficior gaudio non mediocri, cum video commentarios diutinis vigiliis absolutos per ora virorum et manus volitantes circumferri, cum labores nostros neque cassos neque penitendos fuisse conspicio." Beroaldo, "Oratio habita in narratione Lucii Apuleii," fol. m8v. In the same oration (fol. n1r) Beroaldo boasts of the sale of all his works: "Quae omnia nisi mihi bibliopolae blandiuntur, expetuntur a studiosis, probantur a doctis, teruntur manibus scholasticorum tam provincialium quam Italicorum."

[173] "Siquidem statuae et imagines intereunt aut vi convulsae aut vetustatis situ decoloratae, volumina vero quae sunt vera spirantiaque hominum simulacra nulla vi convelluntur, nullo senio obliterantur. Fiuntque vetustate ipsa sanctiora durabilioraque." Beroaldo, *Commentari*, fol. a2r. The theme is a favorite one of Beroaldo's. It appears in his account of the paper shortage that delayed the publication of his Apuleius: "Itaque haec civitas, quae alioque chartam finitimis populis affatim solet subministrare, inopiam chartae sensit, cuius usu constat immortalitas hominum" *Oratio proverbiorum*, fol. 6r. He uses it again in his poem "Quod veriores sunt imagines ex libris quam ex nomismatis" (*Orationes et poemata* / fols. q2v–q3r): "Est scriptis vivax facies: est forma perennis 'Magnorum Regum

already hammered out several self-portraits of this kind, he claims.[174] Now his Apuleius—"this new image of my mind, thoroughly polished with versatile sculpting and careful elegance"—will be another.[175]

Beroaldo's commentary on the *Golden Ass* did turn out to be his monument. It is a major landmark in the history of classical scholarship, and it does portray the mind of its author. The two facts are closely related, for at this point in his reception Apuleius required someone exactly like Beroaldo and a little like himself—that is, a charismatic promoter who was also a passionate philologist and an interested student of everyday life both past and present. The success of the commentary was instant and long lasting. Beroaldo's international reputation and connections, together with the power of printing, immediately secured it an international audience. The commentary was reprinted ten times in the sixteenth century.[176] Soon Apuleius—or, we should say, Beroaldo's Apuleius—made his way over the Alps to all of Europe.

---

nobiliumque ducum / Scriptis Caesarei proceres sanctique Catones / Scriptus Pompeius noscitur atque Numa / Haec verae effigies: haec sunt simulacra virorum / Hi spirant vultus; haec monimenta vigent. Id tibi scripta dabunt: quod nulla nomismata possunt / Sic oculos poteris pascere: sic animum" (ll. 7–14).

[174] "Ego iam pridem aliquot id genus effigies sub litteratoria incude procusas mihi ipsemet publice posui, quibus non minus opinor ingenii mei similitudo expressa conspicitur quam Olympionicarum simulacris perfecta corporum liniamenta spectabantur quae iconica auctores appellant." Beroaldo, *Commentarii*, fol. a2r.

[175] "Hoc vero novicium animi nostri simulacrum vario effigiatu cultuque laborioso perpolitum." Ibid.

[176] See the bibliography in Krautter, *Philologische Methode*, 193–94. The commentary continued to be printed into the nineteenth century (the last edition mentioned by Krautter was printed in 1823).

CHAPTER 7

Speaking in Tongues: Translations of the *Golden Ass*

> I have not so exactly passed through the Author, as to pointe every sentence accordinge as it is in Latine, or so absolutely translated every woorde, as it lieth in the prose.
> —*William Adlington*, The Golden Asse

After its rediscovery in the early fourteenth century, the *Golden Ass* soon traveled throughout the Italian peninsula. Perhaps it crossed the Alps as well, but it is difficult to see signs of such movement in the manuscript evidence. The fourteen extant manuscripts now in libraries outside Italy are almost all of Italian origin.[1] Although some of these manuscripts might well have been owned by readers outside Italy in the fourteenth and fifteenth centuries, the point would be hard to demonstrate. I know of no manuscript now outside Italy whose Renaissance movements can be traced from its origin to its present home. The first concrete evidence for Apuleius' novel outside Italy is found in the age of print. In 1471 the German humanist Hartmann Schedel was either offered or purchased a copy of the first edition along with several other books printed by Sweynheym and Pannartz; the list he made of the books and their prices has been preserved.[2] It is likely but not certain that Schedel actually bought Bussi's edition.[3] What is important, however, is that it was available to him. It would also have been available to many

---

[1] See appendix 2. The only exception seems to be Olomouc, Státní Vědecká Knihovna M II 58, identified by Kristeller as in a "Northern hand" (*Iter italicum* 3.161b). The scribe of Urbana ms. 7 was a non-Italian, Holt de Heke d'Osnabrük, but the text was copied in Rome for a Roman patron, Salvator de Achille, a papal abbreviator.

[2] Hirsch, *Printing, Selling and Reading*, 139 n. 34; see also 69–71. For a facsimile of Schedel's list, see Burger, *Buchhändleranzeigen*, no. 6. The document is also discussed and illustrated by Miglio in Bussi, *Prefazioni*, lv–lviii and plate xxvii.

[3] The catalog of Schedel's library includes several texts of Apuleius. One has this description: "Apuleius de asino aureo: libri floridarum: apologie sive defensionis magie: de deo Socratis ad Trismegistum: Epitoma Alcinoi disciplinarum Platonis." See Stauber, *Die Schedelsche Bibliothek*, 111. The contents sound like those of Bussi's edition, which included Alcinous (see chapter 4, n. 157); but Schedel's copy could also have been a later imprint of Bussi. Schedel also owned Beroaldo's commentary (Stauber, 138) and a twelfth-century manuscript of the philosophical works: Munich, Bayerische Staatsbibliothek Clm 621. See Stauber, 108; Klibansky and Regen, *Die Handschriften*, 90. Apuleius is named and

244 • Chapter 7

others in Europe, for from the beginning printed books were far more mobile than manuscripts had ever been. From the 1470s on, Italian imprints, like their German cousins, were widely advertised and sold throughout Germany and the Low Countries.[4]

Copies of the *Golden Ass* in Bussi's 1469 edition and its reprints undoubtedly made their way out of Italy in the last decades of the fifteenth century, but the novel seems to have attracted little attention from non-Italian readers. Their interest increased dramatically after 1500, largely as a consequence of the publication of Beroaldo's commentary.[5] Beroaldo's interpretations were important, but so was his celebrity and prestige, which other European editors and translators relied on to give their own works legitimacy and cachet. They invoked Beroaldo for their discussions of the meaning of the *Golden Ass*—and they did so even when they altered or misunderstood his views, reading Apuleius through Beroaldo, and both writers through the lenses of their own time and place.

The *Golden Ass* probably crossed the Alps in a printed book. It owed its diffusion in Europe, however, not only to the printing press but also to translation, which moved the novel out of the humanist lecture hall and into the hands of vernacular readers of various backgrounds, intellectual interests, and degrees of literacy. This chapter follows the adventures of the *Golden Ass* outside Italy in the sixteenth century. My principal focus will be on translators. I will consider their use of Beroaldo, their interpretation of the story of Lucius and his transformations, and the ways in which their work was designed to appeal to vernacular readers. Early in the century Apuleius enjoyed separate fortunes in Germany, Paris, and Spain, but as time went on, the borders of both art and language became less distinct: by the end we will find translators translating each other.

TEACHING THE ASS TO SPEAK GERMAN

Although the *Golden Ass* attracted little interest in Germany in the fifteenth century, things were quite different with its near relation, the *Onos* (or *Ass*) of Pseudo-Lucian, which Poggio had discovered around

---

pictured as a Platonic philosopher in Schedel's *Liber chronicarum* (*Nuremberg Chronicle*), fol. LXXIIIIv. The work is accessible in a modern facsimile: Schedel, *Chronicle of the World*, ed. Füssel.

[4] See Hirsch, *Printing, Selling and Reading*, 61–65.

[5] Erasmus is an interesting case in point. He knew something of Apuleius before 1500, probably from one of Bussi's editions, and he occasionally cites or refers to him in his early works. But he draws on Apuleius and especially on the *Golden Ass* in a more complex way in *The Praise of Folly*, *Lingua*, and the third *Chilias* of his *Adagia*, all written after the publication of Beroaldo's commentary. See Elsom, "Apuleius in Erasmus' *Lingua*." For Erasmus' views of Apuleius' fictions, see Carver, "'True Histories,'" 332–35.

1450 and translated into Latin.⁶ In the 1470s the commercial possibilities of Poggio's translation were recognized by an enterprising printer in Augsburg named Ludwig Hohenwang.⁷ He published it around 1477 in an attractive edition illustrated with a series of lively woodcuts, including a charming rendition of the Ass in bed with the amorous matron (see figure 2).⁸ In the next year he published a German translation of Poggio's Latin by Niklas von Wyle (ca. 1415–79)—obviously hoping to attract a wider audience.⁹ The German edition included the same woodcuts—except for that of the Ass and the matron, an interesting point that we will return to presently.

Niklas von Wyle was best known for translating not classical works but the writings of Italian humanists, and he had probably been brought to "Lucian" by his interest in Poggio. He translated the *Ass* in 1469, claiming in his preface that he had often been asked to do so, "in order that people ignorant of Latin might also understand this amazing tale and use it for amusement."¹⁰ He interprets the story accordingly. Poggio had seen it as a satirical treatment of magic, but Wyle presents it as an amusing allegory of human folly. To wit: by making his hero turn into an ass, Lucian shows that he has become a dupe and a fool; and anyone is well off if he manages to spend no more than a year in this condition.¹¹

Wyle probably had little influence on the way in which his work was presented in Hohenwang's edition, since it appeared when he was in poor health and near the end of his life.¹² Wyle had omitted the episode

---

⁶ See pp. 152–57.

⁷ For Hohenwang, see Schmidtchen, "Ludwig Hohenwang."

⁸ Goff L-321; ISTC i100321000. The edition is very rare: ISTC gives only the Pierpont Morgan Library in New York and the Augsburg Staats- und Stadbibliothek as locations.

⁹ Goff Suppl. L-321a; ISTC i100321500. I quote from the facsimile of this edition published by Weil in 1922. The text is most accessible in Niclas von Wyle, *Translationen*, ed. Keller, 248–82. For a detailed description of the Hohenwang edition, see Rosenthal, "Die Erstausgabe von Apulejus' 'Goldenem Esel.'" Wyle's translation had appeared a few months earlier in an edition of his collected translations printed in Esslingen by Konrad Fyner soon after 5 April 1478; see Ohly, "Ein unbeachteter illustrierter Druck Eggesteins," 56–60. For Wyle's biography, see Worstbrock, "Niklas von Wyle."

¹⁰ "Da mitt die menschen der latin vngelert dise wunderbar geschicht auch mochten versten vnnd sich darczů kůrczweil gebrauchen." Wyle, *Der goldene Esel*, (facsimile) [2r]. I must express my grateful thanks to Professors Anna Grotans and Lawrence Buck for their assistance with the German in this section.

¹¹ "Aber die poeten pflegent offt etliche ding verdackt vnder gestalt ainer fabel zebeschreiben so sy noch dann darinne die warheyt vermainen, also mag auch hie sein, das lucianus gemainet habe disen menschen von dem er schreibet in seiner bůlschaft zů ainem esel worden sei, das ist zů ainem toren und narren. Als an me enden geschehen mag, wol dem der nitt v̌ber ain iar dar inne beharret." Wyle, *Der goldene Esel*, (facsimile) [4v].

¹² He would also have been busy overseeing the edition of his collected translations printed by Fyner in Esslingen. See n. 9 in this chapter and Ohly, "Ein unbeachteter illustrierter Druck Eggesteins," 56.

Figure 2. The Ass and the amorous matron in Pseudo-Lucian's *Asinus Aureus* (Augsburg, 1477). The Pierpont Morgan Library, New York. PML 145.

of the amorous matron as "unchaste" ("unke sch"), and Hohenwang duly (and, one suspects, reluctantly) omitted the woodcut showing her in bed with the Ass. But two other details seem to reflect Hohenwang's own ideas: a jocular poem adorning the title page and captions accompanying the woodcuts at high points of the story. Both were obviously designed to amuse readers and sell books.

The poem is a bit of false advertising:

> If a woman has no ass,
> no matter how much
> she wants one to take care of her,
> she'll find age-old instructions here
> about how to keep a house ass,
> kicking him thoroughly on both sides.[13]

The captions, like the woodcuts, make the book attractive and help to explain the plot, but they also reflect a cheerful unconcern for factual detail. Poggio's discovery had made it impossible either to take the *Golden Ass* as autobiographical or to see Apuleius as Lucius. He had pointed out as much in the preface to his translation—which Hohenwang himself had printed only a few months earlier. Wyle seems to have extended Poggio's lesson to "Lucian" and *his* Lucius, for he carefully distinguishes the author from his hero, "this man about whom he writes."[14] But all such distinctions were lost on Hohenwang. One of his most attractive woodcuts shows the asinine hero at the moment of transformation—a dandy to the points of his shoes—dubiously exploring his new muzzle with his fingertips (see plate 19). The astounding caption reads: "How Lucius Apuleius was changed into the form of an ass."[15] The colophon of the work compounds the confusion: "Here ends the *Golden Ass* written by Lucius Apuleius in the Greek tongue, afterward translated into Latin by Poggio the Florentine and most recently put into German by Niklas von Wyle."[16]

"Lucian's" *Ass* in Wyle's translation was as popular as anyone could have wished, for it was reprinted twice before 1500 and several times

---

[13] "Wölche fraw kein esel hatt / Unnd ir begird dar czŭ stat / Das sy ye einen will haben / Der fŭr sy sorg solle tragen / Wie von alter ist kommen her / Die findet hier inn sŏliche ler / Wie man hauss ŏsel halten sol / Ze beyden seiten sporen wol." Wyle, *Der goldene Esel*, (facsimile) [1r].

[14] "Disen menschen von dem er schreibet." See n. 11. Küenzlen makes the same observation (*Verwandlungen*, 191).

[15] "Wie Lucius apuleius in gestalt eines esels verkert ward." Wyle, *Der goldene Esel*, (facsimile) [8v].

[16] "Hye endet der guldin esel durch lucium apuleium in kriechischer zungen beschriben darnach durch poggium florentinum in latin transferiert vund zŭ letst von niclas von wyle geteŭtschet." Ibid., [28r].

in the sixteenth century.¹⁷ Its success paved the way for a similar translation of Apuleius and perhaps inspired Johann Sieder (ca. 1460–before 1535), a little-known ecclesiastical secretary in Würtzburg, to undertake the task.¹⁸

Sieder was the secretary of one important humanist bishop (Lorenz von Bibra, d. 1519) and dedicated his work to another: Johann von Dalberg (1455–1503).¹⁹ The presentation copy of his manuscript is preserved in the Staatsbibliothek in Berlin.²⁰ It is not clear why Sieder chose Dalberg rather than Bibra as his dedicatee, but he probably thought Dalberg was more likely to favor his project and hoped that he would arrange for its publication and perhaps provide future patronage. But Dalberg did not publish the translation, and it was finally printed only in 1538, after the deaths of both men. The printed edition differs in several important respects from Sieder's own version, as we shall see presently.

Sieder is Apuleius' first northern translator and the only one to have interpreted the *Golden Ass* without benefit of Beroaldo's commentary. He dedicated his work in Würzburg on 29 September 1500, and he must have been laboring to "make the Ass speak German" long before that.²¹ By the time that Beroaldo's commentary was published in Bologna on 1 August 1500, Sieder's work would have been nearly completed. He could not have seen Beroaldo's work in time to make any real use of it, and his translation shows no sign that he did.²² The translation cannot be traced to a particular Latin text.²³ Plank suggests that Sieder used a now lost manuscript; but since we have so little evidence for manuscripts outside Italy, it seems more likely that he relied on one of Bussi's editions.²⁴ It was probably also from Bussi that Sieder gained his firm conviction that Apuleius was above all a Platonic philosopher, for Apuleius' Platonism was the raison d'être for Bussi's edition and the point most

---

[17] See Worstbrock, *Deutsche Antikerezeption*, 1:99–101. For the first reprint (Strassburg, ca. 1478–79), see Ohly, "Ein unbeachteter illustrierter Druck Eggesteins"; Harlfinger, ed., *Graecogermania*, 198–99, 211–13.

[18] For Sieder's biography, see Worstbrock, "Johann Sieder." For his translation, see especially Plank, *Johann Sieders Übersetzung*. See also Küenzlen, *Verwandlungen*, 130–203; Häfner, "*Ein schönes Confitemini.*"

[19] For Dalberg, see Morneweg, *Johann von Dalberg*; Plank, *Johann Sieders Übersetzung*, 44–45, with bibliography.

[20] Berlin, Staatsbibliothek Ms. germ. fol. 1239. Häfner ("*Ein schönes Confitemini,*" 133–36) provides a transcription of Sieder's dedication.

[21] "Des wurdet der esel nu tewtsch reden." Berlin, Staatsbibliothek Ms. germ. fol. 1239, fol. 2r, quoted from Häfner, "*Ein schönes Confitemini,*" 133.

[22] *Pace* Häfner, "*Ein schönes Confitemini,*" 98.

[23] See Plank, *Johann Sieders Übersetzung*, 64–66.

[24] Plank's list of translated words that clearly suggest readings not in the editions (*Johann Sieders Übersetzung*, 66 n. 96) is too short to demonstrate more than simple error on Sieder's part.

emphasized in his preface.[25] Sieder found a more immediate inspiration, however, in Niklas von Wyle's "Lucian": he mentions Wyle's translation in his dedication, follows Wyle's word-for-word style of translation, and even borrows from Wyle's discussion about the reality of metamorphoses.[26] He leaves large spaces for illustrations in his manuscript, probably in hopes of an eventual edition with woodcuts like those in Wyle's "Lucian." We can also see Wyle's influence in the fact that Sieder prefaces his translation of the *Golden Ass* with a version of Lucian's satirical *True Histories*, which he asserts will get Apuleius' work off to a "good start."[27]

The modern reader might see some cognitive dissonance between Sieder's views of Apuleius as both a Platonic philosopher and a suitable companion for the satirical Lucian, but Sieder does not go into things so deeply. The main points of interpretation that emerge from his discussion are that the *Golden Ass* is a fable "more like poetry than philosophy," that it is serious and funny at the same time, and that Apuleius uses fable to convey his meaning because young people by nature avoid the serious and lofty ideas of philosophy.[28] Sieder never spells out, however, what he thinks Apuleius' meaning is.

[25] See pp. 157–62. Sieder opens his discussion with Plato: "Gnediger herr, Plato der hochgelert, der uorderst und gerümbtest aller philosophen, und darumb der philosophen got genant, hat (als ewrn gnaden bas dann mir wissend) uil hochgeachter discipul und nachuolger seiner kunste gehabt, unter denselbig<en> gewest Lucius Apuleius, des büchlin so er beschriben, so uoller kunste sind, das sie in der werckstat Platonis geschmidet, uon denen die Platonis buchere gelesen haben, wol erkannt worden." Berlin, Staatsbibliothek Ms. germ. fol. 1239, fol. 2r, quoted from Häfner, "*Ein schönes Confitemini*," 133.

[26] See Plank, *Johann Sieders Übersetzung*, 52–57, 85, 117; Küenzlen, *Verwandlungen*, 160, 190–94.

[27] Unnd damit gnediger herr, der guldin Esel seinen rechten anfangk gewonne, hab ich darfur gesetzt die ersten zwey buchlin Luciani uon der waren sage." Berlin, Staatsbibliothek Ms. germ. fol. 1239, fol. 4r, quoted from Häfner, "*Ein schönes Confitemini*," 135. See Plank, *Johann Sieders Übersetzung*, 118. Sieder's Lucian translation appears on fols. 7r–46r of the manuscript. Küenzlen suggests that Sieder perhaps used the *Golden Ass* to fill out and complete the first-person narrative of the *True Histories* (*Verwandlungen*, 177–80).

[28] "Aber unter den Buchern Apuleÿ ist eins, mere der Poetrey, dann philosophey einlich, der guldin esel genant. . . . Also das sich die hohe uernunfft und meisterschafft dem leser entgegen tragen, ie bißweilen mit so ernnsthafftem gedicht, das dem leser die hare mochten zu berg steigen, und die stirn uol runtzeln werden. Dann so mit lecherlichem geschwetz, das es nit on uerclerung des angesichts, und milterung ernstlicher geberde, unnd etwas mit lachen mag gelesen werdenn [fol. 2r]. . . . Das wiewol die Jugent allerbequembst ist zur lernung, doch ab ernstleich der philosophey, und heiligen dapfferkeit so hochbetrachter synne, angeborner weichmutigkeithalben schewet, mere dahin geneigt ist, dahin sie jr plödigkeit laitet. Deßhalb Apuleius gleich uil andre getan, fabel ertrachtet, unnd erfunden in kurtzweilichs gedicht, hohe synne zuuerleiben, unnd wie in ein kostlich gestickt gewandt, edle gestein und perle zuuersetzen, damit die Jungen gleichsam betrogen, dem lusst der fabel nachuolgend, in das Jhen, das man wil sie konnen und wissen sollen, gelaitet werdenn." Berlin, Staatsbibliothek Ms. germ. fol. 1239, fol. 2r–v, quoted from Häfner, "*Ein schönes Confitemini*," 133–34.

Nothing is known about the immediate fate of Sieder's translation, which evidently existed not only in the manuscript presented to Johann Dalberg but in at least one or two others.[29] It is clear, however, that Sieder's ideas about Apuleius had some influence. The evidence is an oblique criticism, which—typical of its kind—never mentions its target by name. The critic is an otherwise unknown schoolmaster in Erfurt named Andreas Ernnst, who published a Latin edition of the story of Psyche around 1515.[30] In the preface addressed to his pupils, "the studious young people of Erfurt," Ernnst corrects certain mistaken ideas about Apuleius' novel, which are easily recognized as those we have just seen expressed by Sieder. Sieder had described the *Golden Ass* as "a fable" (he calls it both *Fabel* and *Gedicht*) and as "more like poetry than philosophy."[31] Ernnst's title states an opposing position: *Lucii Apuleii fabulosa enarratio de nuptiis Psyche non minus theologica quam poetica* (The No Less Theological Than Poetical Fictional Narrative of Lucius Apuleius concerning the Marriage of Psyche). In his preface Ernnst attacks the designation "fable," as well as the idea implicit in Sieder that Apuleius' work is entertaining: "Therefore, those men are far from the truth who think that Apuleius turned to these fictional matters for nothing or only to be entertaining. . . . But the worst and most unbearable of all are those who call Apuleius' great effort 'a fable.' "[32] It is not a fable, Ernnst maintains, but something very different: a *fabulosa narratio* (fictional narrative or narrative like a fable), in which Apuleius "has hidden divine mysteries" from ordinary men but revealed them "to people of understanding . . . through the agency of wisdom."[33] He attributes this insight to "the interpretation of most learned Beroaldo."[34]

Ernnst's invocation of Beroaldo is significant. Beroaldo's commentary was his acknowledged masterpiece, the most famous work of the most

---

[29] Plank deduces the existence of at least a second manuscript from the fact that the 1538 edition omits a long passage from book 11 that had been inserted—apparently by the original scribe—as a supplement to Dalberg's manuscript. *Johann Sieders Übersetzung*, 57–64.

[30] *Lucii Apuleii fabulosa enarratio de nuptiis Psyche non minus theologica quam poetica* [Erfurt, ca. 1515]. This work seems to exist in a single copy: Wolfenbüttel, Herzog August Bibliothek G507. 4° Helmst. (10).

[31] "Mere der Poetrey, dann philosophey einlich." See n. 28 above.

[32] Quo fit ut a vero longe absint qui frustra vel ut oblectet ad hec fabulosa Apuleium se convertisse putant. . . . At vero omnium pessimi minusque ferendi qui fabulam Apuleii hunc sudorem vocant." *Lucii Apuleii fabulosa enarratio*, fol. a2r.

[33] "Divina misteria figurarum cuniculis ingeniose adeo operuit ut et vulgaribus hominum sensibus subtraxerit et summatibus (:Prudentes dico:) sapientia interprete veri arcani consciis patefecerit." *Lucii Apuleii fabulosa enarratio*, fol. a2r.

[34] "Quod Beroal. doctissimi interpretatio ostendit." *Lucii Apuleii fabulosa enarratio*, fol. a2r.

famous teacher in Europe. Printed—and reprinted—in thousands of copies, it must have made its way to Germany soon after its first appearance, especially since Beroaldo's great number of present and former students "from the other side of the Alps" would have provided it with a large and enthusiastic audience. But although Beroaldo's work must have been circulating in Germany for many years, Ernnst's comment is the earliest reference to it that I have been able to discover.

But Ernnst did not read his great predecessor with much care. The "divine mysteries" he invokes have nothing to do with Beroaldo, who had categorically refused to look for metaphysical readings in the story of Psyche. Ernnst's source for the distinction between "fable" and "fictional narrative" is Macrobius, and the "mystery" he refers to is that of Fulgentius' allegory, which Beroaldo had quoted but not embraced. The labels on the frontispiece of his work clearly direct us to Fulgentius. (see plate 20).[35] Psyche and Cupid are shown in their castle, separated by the sea from Psyche's sisters on their cliff. The sisters are neatly labeled with the names awarded to them by Fulgentius: "Libertas" and "Caro" (Free Will and Flesh). Ernnst's carelessness is easily explained. He no doubt saw Fulgentius' allegory in Beroaldo's commentary, which would have been the easiest place to find it, but did not take the time to notice what Beroaldo actually said about it. What he really wanted was to capitalize on Beroaldo's name and lend luster to his own not very illustrious work.

Beroaldo was invoked more knowledgeably some years later, in the revised version of Sieder's translation published in Augsburg in 1538.[36] The translation was revised and paid for by a certain Johann Lucas, who was apparently Sieder's brother, and it was published by a well-established Augsburg printer, Alexander Weissenhorn. The work is illustrated with seventy-eight handsome woodcuts.[37] Beroaldo's influence on this edition is obvious. His commentary is mentioned in the printing privilege that serves as a copyright; he is cited—once almost verbatim—as an authority on the meaning of the work; versions of his short book summaries appear (in German) before each book; and a few of his comments appear (usually in German) in the margins of the first book and the beginning of the second.[38] But the editor, though more conscientious

---

[35] See Klibansky and Regen, *Die Handschriften*, 53–54.

[36] See Worstbrock, *Deutsche Antikerezeption* 1:23; Plank, *Johann Sieders Übersetzung*; Küenzlen, *Verwandlungen eines Esels*, 130–203; Häfner, *"Ein schönes Confitemini."*

[37] Dodgson, *Catalogue of Early German Woodcuts* 2:14 and 199. The woodcuts were made by two different artists at different periods. The first thirty-seven are by an unidentified artist (the monogrammist NH) active in Augsburg ca. 1516–22. Dodgson dates them to ca. 1520. The others are attributed to Hans Schäufelein and dated ca. 1537.

[38] Plank, *Johann Sieders Übersetzung*, 66.

than Andreas Ernnst, still did not make a thorough study of either Beroaldo's text or his commentary.[39] He paid close attention to Beroaldo's interpretation of Lucius' transformation but changed it in some important respects.

The work opens with an elaborate title page (see figure 3). The title reads:

> A quite delightful and amusing fable of Lucius Apuleius of a golden ass, wherein is taught how human nature, [which is] so entirely foolish, weak, and corrupt that it sometimes lives brutishly, imprudently, and carnally, without reason, just like the horse and mule as David says, may also recover again with God's help and become a man instead of an ass—pious, upright, and rational.[40]

The Latin epigraph below the title is from the thirty-second Psalm: "Be ye not as the horse, or as the mule, which have no understanding: whose mouths must be held in with bit and bridle, lest they come near unto thee."[41]

This interpretation does not appear in Sieder's manuscript. It is an addition by the editor, who—not surprisingly—invokes Beroaldo as his source.[42] Beroaldo, we remember, says that "we turn into asses when we have sunk into bestial pleasures" and that the return to our humanity "signifies that reason is coming back to its senses, having . . . thrown off bodily delights, and that the inner man, who is the real man, has come back from that dung-filled prison to a shining habitation with the

---

[39] Ibid.

[40] "Ain Schön Lieblich auch kurtzweylig gedichte Lucii Apuleii von ainem gulden Esel, darinn geleret, wie menschliche Natur so gar blöd, schwach, und verderbet, das sy beweilen gar vihisch, unverstendig und fleischlich, on verstand dahin lebet, gleich wie die Pferdt und Maul, wie David sagt, auch herwiderumb sich möge auss Gottes beystand erholen und auss ainem Esel ein Mensch werden, Gott gefellig, auffrecht und verstendig." *Ain schön lieblich auch kurtzweylig gedichte Lucii Apuleii von ainem gulden Esel*, fol. a1r.

[41] Psalm 32.9, but identified as "Psalmo XXXI," its number in the Vulgate: "Nolite fieri sicut equus et mulus, in quibus non est intellectus, in chamo et freno maxillas eorum constringe, qui non adproximant ad te [est]."

[42] In his fuller statement of the interpretation, he paraphrases Beroaldo (but also misrepresents his ideas): "Es haben auch solche weise leüte diss damit verstanden, wie Fulgentius und lenge nach auch Beroaldus schreibendt, das der merer tail der menschenn esel, das ist vihische, wie gesagt, wollustig und unverstendig gleich verwilden, das nicht ain fünklin mer der vernunft sin und witz verhanden on menschliche gestalt, lautere thiere hie auff erden beweylen werden, sich weder auff gottes ehere, noch fraintlicher gesellschafft der menschen begeben herwiderumb, so auss esel menschen werden." *Ain schön lieblich auch kurtzweylig gedichte*, fol. a4r. Cf. Beroaldo, *Commentarii*, fol. 2v, quoted on p. 217.

guidance of virtue and religion."⁴³ But the editor has made some important alterations to Beroaldo to produce a much more religious and overtly Christian reading.⁴⁴ For him the fall into brutishness is not caused by animal pleasures and the follies of youth. Rather, it is a consequence of our very nature: humanity in its essence is foolish and corrupt and thus prone to become "like the horse and the mule." And the return to human form is not achieved as in Beroaldo through the rejection of pleasures and the reawakening of reason or even "with the guidance of virtue and religion," but simply with the help of God. Beroaldo was working on the moral, ethical, human level, but Sieder's editor is on another plane entirely, for he is thinking of original sin and the grace and pity of God. The difference is summed up neatly in the meaning each attributes to the restorative roses. In Beroaldo the rose cure is described as both knowledge and wisdom.⁴⁵ In the German author the roses are the gospel and word of God, "whose fragrance, going out into the whole world, refreshes, delights, and preserves in eternal glory all those who taste it, believe it, and put their trust in it."⁴⁶

There is more to be said, however, about the German author's reading. It is not only religious and Christian but specifically Lutheran. Augsburg had gone over to the Lutheran cause in 1537, and Weissenhorn's Apuleius, with its emphasis on original sin and God's grace, is firmly on the Lutheran bandwagon.⁴⁷ We might say that even the Ass himself has a Lutheran cousin. The fine woodcut showing Lucius midway through his transformation on the title page bears comparison with another, far more notorious figure, the so-called Papstesel (or Pope Ass), which Lawrence Buck calls "one of the most famous pieces of propaganda for the early Lutheran reformation"(see figure 4).⁴⁸ The Papstesel, a

---

⁴³ "[Ut admoneremur] ex hominibus Asinos fieri, quando voluptatibus belluinis immersi [Asinali stoliditate brutescimus]. . . . Rursus ex Asino in hominem reformatio significat . . . exutis[que] corporalibus deliciis rationem resipiscere, et hominem interiorem, qui verus est homo ex ergastulo illo cenoso, ad lucidum habitaculum, virtute et religione ducibus remigrasse." Beroaldo, *Commentarii*, fol. 2v.

⁴⁴ See also Küenzlen, *Verwandlungen*, 195.

⁴⁵ *Knowledge*: "Anima consopita brutescit, donec gustatis rosis hoc est scientia." Beroaldo, *Commentarii*, fol. 2v. *Wisdom*: "Noster vero Lucius . . . ait se ex manu sacerdotis coronam roseam devorasse . . . ut mystice intelligas coronam rosaceam esse sapientiam," fol. 266r.

⁴⁶ "Solcher verenderung dextere dei excelsi sollen wir danckbar sein, unnd alweg ein schönes Confitemini für dise rosen seines Evangelii und wortes singen, welcher gerücht aussgeen in alle welt, erquicket, ergetzt, und erhelt bei ewiger glori alle die daran schmecken, glauben, unnd vertrauen." *Ain schön lieblich auch kurtzweylig gedichte*, fol. a4r.

⁴⁷ See Plank, *Johann Sieders Übersetzung*, 72, 125. Küenzlen disagrees, arguing that although the work has Lutheran touches, it is not Protestant in its orientation (*Verwandlungen*, 194–203).

⁴⁸ Buck, "The Roman Monster of 1496."

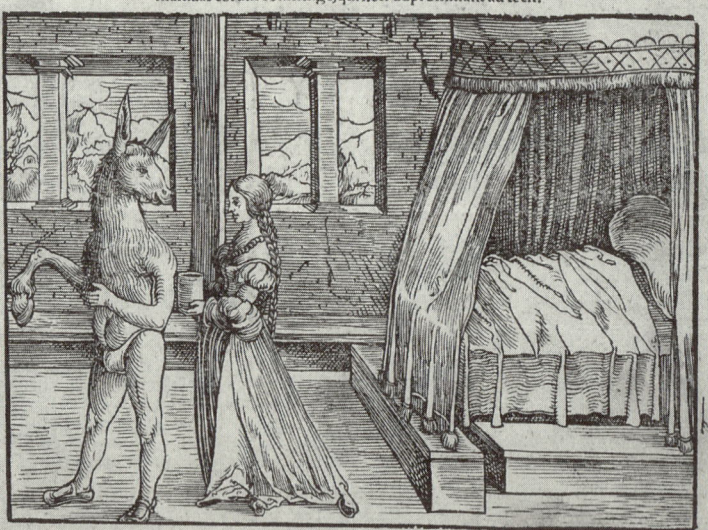

Figure 3. Title page of Johann Sieder's *Ain schön lieblich auch kurtzweylig gedichte Lucii Apuleii von ainem gulden Esel* (Augsburg, 1538). Herzog August Bibliothek. Lh4° 7.

Figure 4. Melanchthon's Bapstesel. Cornell University Library.

monstrous *Mischwesen* representing papal corruption, was a well-known Lutheran image, employed by Melanchthon in a 1523 pamplet of the same name and widely reproduced afterwards.[49] The woodcutter for this part of Weissenhorn's edition probably did his work in the early 1520s.[50] But he could have seen the Papstesel even before it appeared in Melanchthon's pamphlet: the image was printed in Bohemia around 1498, and its presence in Germany is documented as early as February 1522.[51] If we compare the Papstesel with the half-asinine Lucius in the Weissenhorn edition, we can easily discern a close family resemblance. Lucius' head is turned, and he's missing a tail, but otherwise the two have a similar pose. Our Lucius, of course, lacks the breasts of the Papstesel, but the artist has used the outline of the *Esel*'s *mons veneris* to create a sort of jockstrap for his masculine figure.

We can interpret the resemblance between the Papstesel and Weissenhorn's illustration of Lucius in two ways. The weak reading would be that Weissenhorn's artist, looking for a way to depict Lucius at the point of transformation, remembered the Lutheran icon and simply took it as the basis for his own figure. The strong interpretation—which I favor—would be that regardless of the artist's intention in the 1520s, Weissenhorn's readers in 1538 were supposed to notice the resemblance and associate the two figures, and that the figure was supposed to tickle their Lutheran sympathies and their funny bone at the same time.

But the Lutheranism of Weissenhorn's edition, though obvious, is only skin deep. Along with other touches added to Sieder's original work, it is intended to make the work appealing to readers and so to sell books. Let us look again at the title page (see figure 3). Its first words are "Ain schön lieblich auch kurtzweylig gedichte" (A quite delightful and amusing fable). These are followed by the pious description of its meaning: that bestial mankind can be restored to humanity with God's help. The description goes on: "fun to read, prepared with fine pictures, completely translated into German by Herr Johann Sieder," and so on.[52] Below this description we see our half-asinine Lucius, the pretty

---

[49] Melanchthon and Luther, *Deutung der zwo greulichen Figuren*. The image originated in Italy in 1496 as a prodigy associated with the flood of the Tiber in December 1495, but it had developed an antipapal character as early as 1498. Buck, "The Roman Monster of 1496," 1–9. See also Lange, *Der Papstesel*.

[50] See n. 37.

[51] The earliest extant engraving with antipapal imagery is attributed to Wenzel von Olmütz and dated to 1498. Buck, "The Roman Monster of 1496." Luther mentions the image in a sermon dated to February 1522, and perhaps received it from Bohemia in February 1521 (ibid., 20–23), but other prints of it could have arrived earlier.

[52] "Lustig zůlesen, mit schönen figuren zůgericht, grundtlich verdeutscht, durch herren Johan Sieder." *Ain schön lieblich auch kurtzweylig gedichte*, fol. a1r.

maidservant, and a rumpled bed suggesting their amatory adventures. A little religion, pretty pictures, fun, and a touch of sex. What more could anyone want?

Weissenhorn and his editor did not rely on the title page alone to appeal to readers. They presented an illustrated plot summary by using woodcuts with explanatory captions to emphasize the high points of the story. They also made their book accessible by simplifying both Apuleius' language and Sieder's throughout, especially in the elaborate prologue, which posed a potential stumbling block at the very beginning of the novel. Sieder had translated the prologue rather closely, but Weissenhorn's editor smoothes out all its difficulties, banishing the "Milesian language," "Egyptian papyrus," and "Nilotic reed" of Apuleius.[53] In his rewriting, the novel is introduced as an amusing tale of wonders illustrating the turns of the wheel of fortune.[54]

Weissenhorn, like Hohenwang before him, clearly wanted his book to sell, but given the religious situation in Augsburg in 1538, he may have been particularly eager for a profitable book. He seems to have been a Catholic, and he specialized in printing Catholic polemics, including the works of Johann Eck, whom he followed to the Catholic city of Ingolstadt in the summer of 1539.[55] After Augsburg became Lutheran, Weissenhorn's Catholic market undoubtedly shrank, and we find him printing several classical works besides Apuleius in quarto format in 1538, surely in the hope of appealing to a new audience.[56] But his efforts seem to have been unsuccessful, if we can judge not only from his move to Ingolstadt but also from another fact: the *Druckprivileg* of the *Golden Ass* lists several of Sieder's works turned over to Weissenhorn by Johann Lucas, but of these he printed only Apuleius.[57]

If we may judge from its printing history, Sieder's Apuleius was much less popular than Wyle's "Lucian" had been. It was reprinted only once in the next century, in a small edition published in Frankfurt in 1605 that further simplified its language and erased the complexities of Apuleius' story.[58]

---

[53] Häfner juxtaposes Apuleius, *Met.* 1.1.1–2, with the translations of Sieder and the 1538 edition ("*Ein schönes Confitemini*," 109). For a detailed account of stylistic changes throughout the novel, see Plank, *Johann Sieders Übersetzung*, 85–109.

[54] Plank, *Johann Sieders Übersetzung*, 127–31; Küenzlen, *Verwandlungen*, 187–88.

[55] Plank, *Johann Sieders Übersetzung*, 71.

[56] Ibid.

[57] *Ain schön lieblich auch kurtzweylig gedichte*, a2r. (The list is also quoted by Worstbrock, "Johann Sieders," 1196; Häfner, "*Ein schönes Confitemini*," 103.)

[58] See Plank, *Johann Sieders Übersetzung*, 79–135. Küenzlen (*Verwandlung*, 190) mentions a 1665 reprint of the Frankfurt edition. It is not mentioned by Plank or listed in the online catalogs WorldCat or *VD17* (= Das Verzeichnis der im deutschen Sprachraum erschienenen Drucke des 17. Jahrhunderts).

258 • Chapter 7

The Ass in Paris

Although the *Golden Ass* had been available in northern Europe for decades—first in Bussi's edition or one of its reprints, and then in Beroaldo's edition and commentary—it was first printed outside Italy around 1510. The Latin text was printed in Paris by an unidentified printer, and it was edited, or perhaps I should say promoted, by a Belgian humanist from Ghent named Robert de Keysere (Robertus Caesaris Gandavus).[59] This edition was soon followed by another, which was printed in Paris in 1512 for the German booksellers Hornken and Hittorp and edited by an Alsatian scholar named Johann Kierher.[60] Both Paris editions made extensive use of Beroaldo; both were aimed at students; and both were intended to sell.

De Keysere's edition contains the Latin text, together with a biography of Apuleius, summaries of individual books, and an interpretation of the work—all borrowed with only a few changes from Beroaldo.[61] But de Keysere has added some promotional touches. A poem by Guillermus Piel at the beginning praises the *Golden Ass* and ends with a commercial exhortation: "Its modest price recommends this book. Buy this work, reader, if you favor your studies."[62] A note at the end touts the book again, adding the address of the bookseller in the usual sixteenth-century fashion.[63] And in a final, jocular letter, de Keysere goes all out to interest and charm the students for whom the work is intended. He begins with

---

[59] *Lucii Apuleii de Asino Aureo Libri XI* (cited below as *Apuleius: Paris, 1510*). See *Index Aureliensis**106.599. This work seems to have been issued for two booksellers: Jean Petit and Robert de Keysere. The copy in the Beinecke Library (Gna66 c510) has Petit's printer's mark and includes his name and address in the colophon. The copy in the British Library (1080.m.2) has a different printer's mark (unidentified), and the colophon offers the book for sale at a different address; see Renouard, *Les marques typographiques*, 1137, p. 366. The only indication of date in either copy is given in de Keysere's letter to the reader, dated 13 November 1510. For de Keysere (d. 1532), see *Contemporaries of Erasmus* 2:258–59; Renouard, *Répertoire des imprimeurs parisiens*, 64; van der Haeghen, *L'humaniste-imprimeur Robert de Keysere*. For Jean Petit, see Renouard, *Répertoire*, 339–41. I quote from the copy in the British Library.

[60] *Accipe candidissime lector philippi Beroaldi* (cited below as Apuleius: Paris, 1512). See *Index Aureliensis* *106.603; for description, see Mortimer, *Harvard College Library . . . French 16th Century Books* 1:39–40. For Kierher (d. 1519), see *Contemporaries of Erasmus* 2:261; Jöcher, *Allgemeines Gelehrten-Lexicon* 3:321-22.

[61] Beroaldo is credited with the interpretation: "Authoris intentio ex Beroaldo deprompta." *Apuleius: Paris, 1510*, fol. A1r. De Keysere uses Beroaldo's other material without attribution.

[62] "Hunc tenuis census librum sibi vendicat: usquam / Si favor est studiis hoc eme lector opus." *Apuleius: Paris*, 1510, fol. A1r.

[63] "Lucii Apuleii Platonici philosophi praestantissimi Libri XI de Asino aureo (in quibus totius Romanae linguae eloquentiam decoremque elegantissime complexus est) finiunt. Quare studiose lector tuis noli deesse commodis: Librosque hos summa diligentia quotidie

a boast: "Here you have, honest reader, the *Golden Ass* of Lucius Apuleius, now printed in Gaul for the first time and formerly known to very few booksellers of the University of Paris."[64] He goes on to speculate on the reasons for the novel's late appearance: perhaps the Ass was avoiding the company and unpleasant burdens of the asses of Paris, or perhaps learned men have just kept the best works for themselves.[65] He pretends that the Ass at first refused to come:

> And braying again and again, he seemed to say, "Surely you aren't leading me to that place where so many asses run around in the schools every day!" ... Then I answered him, goading him again, harder: "Go on, keep moving, and visit the University of Paris. And by the authority of this goad I promise you: you will never carry Parisian mud; you will never touch the pavement unless you fall out of the hands of some lazy [readers]; you will never carry any burden except yourself—if you linger too long in the houses of the booksellers.[66]

The Ass, of course, was persuaded, and de Keysere rejoices.

> And so I am pleased to be as useful as I can to the studious with this labor and to look after the interests of the University of Paris. ... It is pleasing to summon the students who had run away to the country and rusticated there and grown more asinine (may they pardon me for saying so), and to call them to the braying of this Ass and set them on fire for their studies and fill up the school again to make it more crowded.[67]

De Keysere's edition has a certain charm, but Kierher's would probably have been more useful. It includes Beroaldo's commentary as well as

---

revolve quibus in doctum virum, diis suffragantibus evadere potes: Vale. Impressi sunt et venundantur e regione Collegii Italorum in intersignio divae Agnetis." Ibid., fol. R5v.

[64] "Habes hic candide lector L. Apuleii Asinum aureum, nunc primum in Gallia impressum et Academie Parrhisine librariis paucis admodum ante cognitum." Ibid., fol. R6r.

[65] "Sive quod hic asinus lutum lutetianum tam inordinatum tam pestigenum in hanc usque diem semper abhorruerit et lutigerorum asinorum onera ... sive quod docti viri optimos quosque authores sibi reservant atque custodiunt a turba vulgari." Ibid.

[66] "Et identidem ruditans visus est dicere. Num me illuc ducis: ubi tot asini quotidie in scholis cursitant. ... Tum ego illi, repungens acrius, respondi: prorepe et perge et vise academiam Parrhisinam. Ex hoc stimulo tibi polliceor his verbis. Tu nunquam lutum lutetianum perferes, numquam pavimentum tanges nisi quorum desidum manibus excideris, nunquam sarcinam aliquam geres nisi forte teipsum si in domibus librariorum diutius moratus fueris." Ibid.

[67] "Iuvat igitur me quoque pro viribus hoc labore studiosis prodesse et achademie Parrhisine consulens, ... discipulos qui rus confugerant ibique rusticati et (ut cum pace eorum dicatur) asiniores facti sunt, ad huius asini ruditum vocare et ad studia inflammare rursumque academiam pleniorem refarcire." Ibid.

his text (which Kierher claims to have improved) and the interpretation, dedication, and other material from Beroaldo's edition. The commentary was an important addition, but Kierher made the edition even more helpful to students by compiling a detailed vocabulary list at the end. He includes a dedication to two of his students, urging them to read Apuleius as a relaxation from their more serious studies—presumably in philosophy and theology. He also instructs them to skip over the racy parts, or as he puts it:

> In this delightful recess from your studies, I would caution you on this one point, dearest students . . . that like the clever bee, as you pass through the soft meadows of Apuleius' language, you should taste of whatever is excellent and nourishing, bypassing a number of immoral and lewd things with deafened ears as if they were the songs of the Sirens. . . . Indeed, as Aristotle says, obscene language must be completely banished, for from license of base speech—as the same man says most virtuously along with Saint Paul—also follows base action.[68]

I have been calling this Kierher's edition, but in fact his role seems to have been subordinate to those of the booksellers and printer, for he has no mention in the title page or colophon. The title page features the printer's mark of Ludwig Hornken.[69] Above, serving as a title, is an announcement of the book:

> Receive, most honest reader, the commentary of the most learned Philippo Beroaldo on the *Golden Ass* of L. Apuleius, reprinted from the original by the skill and singular diligence in printing books of the honorable Master Jean Philippe.[70] If you approve it, expect to get in a short time in the most perfectly corrected form the books of the *Florida* of the same author in this attractive type, along with several other works of Apuleius.[71]

---

[68] Quo in studiorum vestrorum iucundissimo secessu, hoc unum vos admonitos velim charissimi discipuli, . . . ut in morem argumentose apis, per mollicula Apuleiani sermonis prata transeuntes, optima quaeque succulentioraque delibetis: deteriora nonnulla lascivioraque obturata aure veluti Syrenum cantus pretereuntes. . . . Siquidem omnino, ut Aristoteles ait, verborum obscoenitas exterminanda est. Ex turpiter enim loquendi, ut idem cum Divo Paulo sanctissime dixit, licentia: sequitur et turpiter facere." *Apuleius: Paris, 1512*, fol. ccvii r.

[69] The title page is shown in Mortimer, *Harvard College Library . . . French 16th Century Books* 1:39. For Hornken, see Renouard, *Répertoire*, 208.

[70] For Philippe, see Renouard, *Répertoire*, 344–45.

[71] "Accipe candidissime lector Philippi Beroaldi viri doctissimi in asinum aureum L. Apulei ex archetypo redimpressa (arte singularique in imprimendis libris industria: honesti viri Magistri Ioannis Philippi) commentaria, quod si probaveris, spera te brevi, hac venustissima litera, eiusdem Floridorum libros, cum plerisque aliis Apulei monumentis quam emendatissime consecuturum." *Apuleius: Paris, 1512*, fol. A1r.

Below Hornken's mark appear the addresses of the bookseller: "They are sold on the Rue Saint Jacques under the sign of the three crowns and at Cologne behind the larger church under the sign of the white rabbit."[72] The colophon informs us that the work was "Printed in Paris in very attractive type at the expense of the most upright associates Ludwig Hornken and Gottfried Hittorp and by the diligence of the most honorable Master Jean Philippe in 1512."[73]

Together the title page and colophon allow us to reconstruct the history of the edition. Hornken and Hittop bore the expense, hiring the printer Jean Philippe to print it and Kierher to do the editorial work. They expected Beroaldo to be their chief selling point, for the first words on the title page feature him prominently in two lines of very large black print: "Accipe candidissime lector Philippi Beroaldi viri doctissimi." The work was designed primarily for students (hence Kierher and his dedication and vocabulary lists) and was to be sold at Hornken's shops in Paris and Cologne. It is hard to know how well the edition sold, but evidently the booksellers did not do well enough with the *Golden Ass* to go ahead with the *Florida* as they had hoped: three editions of the *Florida* appeared in the next few years, but none was associated with Hornken, Hittop, Jean Philippe, or Johann Kierher.[74]

The first two French editions of the *Golden Ass* introduced the novel to new readers in northern Europe, but were probably less than a success for the booksellers who sponsored them. They seem also not to have done much to further the careers of either de Keysere or Kierher. De Keysere had had a successful Latin school in Ghent, but left it around 1508 in order to establish himself in Paris as a printer and bookseller. He became head of the Collège de Tournai and seems to have issued a few books in addition to Apuleius. But by 1513 he was back in Ghent, where he printed books for other booksellers for a few years, before taking up the study of Roman law and Greek and trying without success for an appointment at the newly established Collegium Trilingue in Louvain. Kierher came to Paris from Speyer in 1509, took an MA at the University in 1510, and edited Suetonius and Boccaccio's *Genealogie* as well as Apuleius. He returned to Germany in 1512 and finally became a vicar in the cathedral of Speyer.

---

[72] "Venundantur in vico sancti Iacobi sub intersignio trium coronarum et Colonie retro maiorem ecclesiam sub intersignio cuniculi albi." Ibid.

[73] "Impressum Lutecie charactere admodum venusto expensis Ludovici Hornken et Gottifredi Hittorpii sociorum virorum integerrimorum, industria vero cum primis honesti viri Magistri Ioannis Philippi Anno a partu virgineo millesimo quingentesimo duodecimo." Ibid., fol. ccvii r. For Hittorp, see Renouard, *Répertoire*, 205–6.

[74] Paris, 1514; Strasbourg, 1516; Paris, 1518; see *Index Aureliensis* s.n. Apuleius: *106.604, *106.605, *106.607.

But if the Latin editions of de Keysere and Kierher attracted only limited interest, greater success and a wider audience awaited the *Golden Ass* in translation. The novel was translated into French three times in the sixteenth century, and it received yet another important translation at the beginning of the seventeenth.[75] Three of the four translations were popular enough to be reprinted several times.

The first translator was Guillaume Michel, commonly known as Michel de Tours.[76] Michel, a prolific author and translator specializing in religious allegory, first appeared on the literary scene in Paris in 1516, when he published both an original religious work and a translation of Vergil's *Eclogues*.[77] Many other translations followed, including Apuleius' *Golden Ass* (1518), Vergil's *Georgics* (1519), Suetonius (1520), and Sallust (1532).[78] In each author Michel was able to find hitherto unsuspected moral and religious meanings, which, to judge by the popularity of his translations, struck a responsive chord with contemporary readers.

Michel completed his translation and interpretation of Apuleius in 1517.[79] His work was published by the Paris bookseller Galliot Du Pré in July 1518.[80] The title page begins with this description (see figure 5):

> Lucius Apuleius On the Golden Ass, otherwise called On the Crown of Ceres: containing many pretty stories, delightful fables, and subtle inventions concerning various matters, especially philosophy. Translated from Latin into the French language and newly explained in an allegorical sense, as will be seen at the end of the book.[81]

---

[75] See Le Maitre, *Essai sur le mythe de Psyché*, 38–50.

[76] See Weinberg, "Guillaume Michel,"; Armstrong, "Notes on the Works."

[77] Michel's works appeared in a steady stream ending in 1542. See the bibliography in Weinberg, "Guillaume Michel," 75–76.

[78] For Michel's Vergil translations, see Hulubei, "Virgile en France au xvie siècle," 29–33. For Sallust, see Osmond, "Jacopo Corbinelli," 88, 101 n. 19.

[79] The colophon reads: "Cy finist lexposition spirituelle de Lucius Apuleius. De Lasne dore, Translate de Latin en Francoys: par Guillaume Michel: dict de Tours. Lan mil cinq cens dix et sept. Et fut acheve dimprimer en ceste ville de Paris: Le dernier iour de Juillet mil cinq cens et dixhuyt. Pour Galliot du Pre." Michel, *De Lasne dore* (1518), fol. 117r.

[80] For the date, see the previous note. For a description, see Davies, *Catalogue of a Collection*, 12–13. The 1518 edition is rare; it is not listed in *Index Aureliensis*. Except where otherwise noted, I quote from the copy of this edition at the Morgan Library (shelf mark 41001). I must express my grateful thanks to Professors Ann Moss and Philip Ford for their assistance with the French in this chapter.

[81] "Lucius Apuleius de Lasne dore; aultrement dict de la Coronne Ceres: contenant mainctes belles hystoires, delectantes fables, et subtilles invencions de divers propos Speciallement de Philosophie: Translate de Latin en langaige Francoys: Et nouvellement en sens Allegoricque expose: comme lon verra a la fin du Liure." Michel, *De Lasne dore* (1518), fol. A1r.

Figure 5. Title page of Guillaume Michel's *Lucius Apuleius de Lasne dore* (Paris, 1518). The Pierpont Morgan Library, New York. PML 41001.

Below the title appears a handsome woodcut showing an ass decked with plumes, bells, and rich saddle clothes, following a flute-playing monkey. The bookseller's address appears as usual at the foot of the page.

As a publisher and bookseller, Du Pré catered not to scholars or humanists but to vernacular readers of good education in the upper and middle classes, and he seems to have gauged their interests successfully throughout his long career.[82] His title page differs markedly from those of the Latin editions printed just a few years earlier, and especially from that published by Hornken and Hittop in 1512. Instead of a printer's mark, it presents an enticing illustration, which—like those on many modern book jackets—has little relation to the content of the work.[83] Instead of invoking "the most learned Philippo Beroaldo" or insisting on the accuracy of the edition and the care taken in its printing, it emphasizes the pleasurable aspects of the novel even as it makes a nod to serious readers with the mention of "philosophy" and promise of a new allegorical interpretation. It also awards Apuleius' novel a completely unexpected title, *The Crown of Ceres*—an interesting point that will concern us presently.

On subsequent pages Galliot Du Pré and Michel, obviously aware of the needs of their French readers, provide background, encouragement, and assistance. The background comes, not surprisingly, from Beroaldo, whose biography of Apuleius and interpretation of the work are translated with only a few small omissions and changes. (Beroaldo is credited only with the interpretation: "The intention of the author of this present book, introduced by Beroaldo.")[84] The encouragement appears in Michel's hortatory addition to Beroaldo's biography:

> Read and reread, for the more you read it the finer you will find it. If the beginning is a little tiresome, like the start of springtime, which as yet has not a single flower, have hope and trust that as your reading of this golden book proceeds, you will find pleasure and marvels in equal measure, for then the flowers will have appeared—well ornamented and painted, set close together and widespread.[85]

---

[82] For Du Pré, see Renouard, *Répertoire*, 131–32; for his career, see Tilley, "A Paris Bookseller"; for his public, see Tilley, esp. 169 and 187.

[83] It is inspired, however, by the episode in *Met.* 10.18.4 in which the Ass's master decks him out and parades him through the countryside to show off his tricks (Apuleius does not mention a monkey). The woodcut is repeated at that point in Michel's text: Michel, *De Lasne dore* (1518), fol. 108v.

[84] "Lintencion de lacteur de ce present liure. Par Beroald introduict." Ibid., fol. 1v.

[85] "Lisez et relisez, car tant plus le lirez tant plus beau le trouverez. Si le commencement vous est ung peu fascheuz comme lentree du nouveau temps qui na encore point de fleur, ayez espoir et fiance quen procedant de ce liure dore la lecture vous y trouverez si grande doulceur que merveilles, car alors les fleurs y seront apparues bien aornees, et painctes ioinctes et estandues." Ibid.

The assistance appears in a detailed table of contents, in which the *Golden Ass* is broken down into ninety-eight very short chapters, each accompanied by a brief description and the number of the folio on which it begins. The first chapter is headed "How Lucius Apuleius took the road to Thessaly to see the use of magic arts, and how as he went along he found two companions whom he accompanied."[86]

Michel is not a particularly close translator, and he does not hesitate to make both omissions and additions.[87] Not surprisingly, he omits most of the episode of the amorous matron, which had already proved a stumbling block for Wyle in his translation of "Lucian" and was carefully abridged by Sieder.[88] But he also changes passages that are not obscene, as we can see in his treatment of the speech of the priest of Isis to the newly restored Lucius in book 11. Apuleius' priest attributes Lucius' troubles to servile pleasures and curiosity.[89] Michel's priest says only that Lucius had fallen into the hands of bad fortune through harmful inprudence (*improuvence malice*).[90] The omission of "servile pleasures" and "curiosity" is significant, for it redefines Lucius' responsibility for his transformation. Michel also makes an addition to the same speech. Apuleius' priest urges the redeemed Lucius to join the procession of Isis in order to demonstrate the goddess' power to unbelievers.[91] Michel's priest wishes the unbelievers to see something more: that they are mistaken in their notion that everything happens naturally or by force of nature (*naturellement*).[92] Lucius' transformation will reveal to them

---

[86] "Comment Lucius Apuleius print le chemin de Thessalie pour veoir la maniere des ars magiques. Et comment en y allant trouva deux compaignons avecques lesquelz il sacompagna." Ibid., fol. A3r.

[87] Küenzlen surveys his treatment of several passages, including the proem (*Verwandlungen*, 225–37).

[88] He omits *Met*. 10.19.4–10.23.2, conflating the matron with the murderess of the next episode. For Wyle, see pp. 244–47. Sieder omits much of the episode (*Met* 10.20.2–22.4 (*inhaerebat*), but the sense is still clear (Berlin, Staatsbibliothek Ms. germ. fol. 1239, fols. 201v–202r, and ed. 1538, fol. 64r–v).

[89] "Nec tibi natales ac ne dignitas quidem, vel ipsa, qua flores, usquam doctrina profuit, sed lubrico virentis aetatulae ad serviles delapsus voluptates curiositatis inprosperae sinistrum praemium reportasti." *Met*. 11.15.1.

[90] "Ta dignite, ton chier et noble lignaige: pareillement et ta doctrine de laquelle tu floriz ne tont point preserve des mains de fortune qui ta pris en son pouoir des ta ieunesse, si par improuvence malice tu as trouve la main et mauvaistie de fortune la mauvaise, tu as par la bonte de nostre deesse qui est la bonne fortune trouvee la main de beatitude, doulceur, et amour." Michel, *De Lasne dore* (1518), fol. 109v.

[91] "Videant inreligiosi, videant et errorem suum recognoscant: en ecce pristinis aerumnis absolutus Isidis magnae providentia gaudens Lucius de sua Fortuna triumphat." *Met*. 11.15.4.

[92] "Viens avecq elle monstrant signe de liesse, vertu et ioieusete: si que les gens non religieux, qui de la deesse le pouoir ignorent: voient et leur erreur congnoissent, lesquels cuident et oppinent que tout se face naturellement, mais ilz errent en cella." Michel, *De Lasne dore* (1518), fol. 109v.

both the existence and the need of divine intervention: "for you have resumed your original human appearance, not by natural but by divine effort, since without divine grace one cannot help oneself, nor put oneself back into a state of glory or grace."[93] This passage has no counterpart in Apuleius. Michel has added it, just as he omitted Apuleius' reference to Lucius' curiosity and pleasures, in order to make the text support the allegorical interpretation he presents at the end of the novel.

Michel's reading of the *Golden Ass* is explicitly spiritual, created as a source of "love, solace, and comfort" for what he calls "the new people, that is, the nation of grace."[94] He interprets the story of Lucius (or, as he says, "Apuleius") as an illustration of his conviction that the devil is always on the lookout for us, and we are especially at risk when we think we are doing something good.

> By Apuleius who left his own land and country we can understand man as traveler in this world who leaves his own country, that is, his own earthly will, in order to clasp and cling to Thessaly, where the magic arts flourish, that is, to enter and continue in the state of spirituality, which is nothing else except to live spiritually, that is, according to the will of the spirit. . . . But it is not enough for the good traveler just to leave his own country, but he must take care not to be deceived in the country where he is going.[95]

"Apuleius," however, was incautious, and that was his downfall. He wanted to become a bird, "which flies in the sky, that is, in the divine and spiritual condition which is said to be accomplished by the heavenly flight of practicing good works."[96] But through the machinations of Fotis, "the temptation of the devil which one must resist,"[97] he chose the wrong box of ointment and became an ass instead. "Such is the man

---

[93] "Car tu nas pas revestu la premiere face dhomme par euvre naturelle, mais divine. Veu que sans la grace divine lon ne se peult aider ny en estat de gloire ne de grace remettre." Ibid.

[94] "Le nouvel peuple, cest assavoir la gent de grace plus damour, soulaz et consolation y treuve." Ibid., fol. 115r.

[95] "Par Apuleius qui son pays et terre propre laissa: pouons entendre lhomme viateur en ce monde, lequel laisse sa propre terre, cestassavoir sa propre vollente terrienne: pour adherer et applicquer en Thessallie, la ou florissent les ars magicques, cestassavoir venir et aller en lestat de la spiritualite, qui nest aultre chose fors vivre spirituellement et selon la vollente de lesprit. . . . Mais il ne souffeiste pas seullement au bon viateur son propre pays delaisser, mais se doibt donner garde destre deceu au pays ou il tend." Ibid.

[96] "Qui au ciel volle cestassavoir en lestat divin et spirituel, qui est dict estre faict par le vol celeste de lexcertation des bonnes euvres." Ibid.

[97] "Fotis, cestassavoir la tentation du dyable contre laquelle fault resister." Ibid.

who, believing he is placing himself in a divine state of grace, places himself in a diabolical state of sin."[98] Everyone is at risk: We can even be led astray as we go to mass or give alms—or when we choose a religious vocation.[99]

Redemption is possible through the restorative roses, which Michel identifies with the sacrament of penitence.[100] The roses are red, he says, to represent the blood of Christ by which "men who were beasts and asses without reason through mortal sin, have been reformed into their original human condition of innocence."[101] But we must still be on our guard: not all roses are real, and false penitence is as useless to us as the false roses were to "Apuleius" (cf. *Met.* 4.2). The real roses are available only with divine aid—by means of the moon, which Michel identifies with several goddesses, but most often Ceres. (He seldom calls her Isis, a name he may consider unfamiliar to his readers.) Her Christian counterpart, of course, is "the glorious Virgin Mary."[102] But "counterpart" is hardly the right word. It might be more accurate to say that Michel all but conflates Mary with Apuleius' saving goddess.

> She [Mary] sends us to the high priest, the representative of almighty God. And he will give us the hat of flowers and crown of roses which hangs on the sistrum of the image of the goddess Ceres, that is, from the cross of Jesus Christ which is so resonant. There you see the crown of roses which we must have if we want to regain our beautiful shape of innocence.[103]

In Michel's reading the saving roses of penitence provided by Ceres/Mary are the point and goal of the novel. He signals the fact by calling Apuleius' work *The Crown of Ceres*, a title that suggests not only the

---

[98] "Tel est celluy qui se cuidant en lestat divin et de grace mettre, se mect en lestat dyabolicque et de peche." Ibid.

[99] As in the case of Julian the Apostate: "Lequel luy estant seculier estoit meilleur que quant il fut moyne, car il devint apostat, ce quil neust pas faict sil eust tousiours este seculier." Ibid.

[100] "Par les roses que le viateur en lestat dasne qui est peche mortel doibt gouster et menger, jentendz le sacrement de penitence." Ibid., fol. 116r.

[101] "Les hommes qui estoient bestes par peche mortel et asnes irraisonnables, ont este refformez en leur premier estat humain, cestassavoir dinnocence." Ibid.

[102] "Nous ny pouons retourner si ce nest par le moien de la lune. Cest a entendre la glorieuse vierge Marie." Ibid., fol. 117r.

[103] "Nous envoye vers le grant prebstre vicaire de dieu tout puissant: qui nous baillera le chappeau de fleurs et couronne [*ed.* couronnes] de roses qui pend au sistre de lymaige de la deesse Ceres, cest assavoir de la Croix de Ihesucrist qui tant est sonoreuse [favoureuse, *ed.* 1522]. Voila la couronne des roses quil nous fault avoir si nous voulons reprendre nostre belle forme dinnocence." Ibid.

garland in the Latin text but also the crown of Mary, as both saint and queen of heaven.[104]

Michel's allegory is in striking contrast to the interpretation of Beroaldo printed at the beginning of his translation, for everything in it is on a metaphysical, symbolic level far from Beroaldo's commonsensical moral and ethical approach. He calls his treatment "a new interpretation,"[105] and so it might seem to an astonished modern reader. In fact, it is not new at all. Rather, it is firmly based in the tradition of medieval *allegoresis*.[106] Like Fulgentius' interpretation of Psyche and the treatment of the fourteenth-century allegorist we looked at in chapter 3, Michel's reading is essentially an independent entity, arising more from the mindset and creativity of the allegorist than from the actual words of the text.[107] We might note, too, that for Michel the allegory takes precedence over the text—hence his replacement of "curiosity" and "pleasures" with "harmful imprudence" in the speech of the priest of Isis and the addition of his homily on divine intervention. Beroaldo would no doubt have labeled Michel a "philosophaster" and disdained his violence to the text as much as his metaphysics, for Michel's method was contrary to the historical and philological approach of the humanists. Allegories like Michel's were on their way out, but in the first decades of the sixteenth century they were still popular in France—coexisting with humanist interpretations, but soon to be supplanted by them.[108] Indeed, we might suspect that interest in Michel's allegory had already begun to wane by the time his translation was reprinted in 1522, for it is no longer advertised on the title page.[109]

---

[104] In Michel's syncretistic reading Mary is also queen of earth and hell. Like Lucius' savior, she has many names, including Hecate ("Trivie"): "Cest aussi Trivie par les trois voies quelle a par sa puissance, car elle est royne du ciel, des enffers et du monde." Ibid.

[105] "Sens nouvel sur les livres de Lucius Apuleius de lasne dore." Ibid., fol. 104v.

[106] For this tradition and its manifestations in sixteenth-century France, see the important discussion of Moss, *Poetry and Fable*, 6–16. See also Moss, *Ovid in Renaissance France*, 22–27; Moss, ed., *Latin Commentaries*, 61–68.

[107] Compare Moss's comment on the *Bible des poetes*, a French paraphrase of Ovid's *Metamorphoses* printed in 1493: "Reading mythological narrative as extended metaphor or allegory, based on similitudes perceived by the reader, directs attention away from the words of the author (and in the *Bible des poetes* we in fact start from words which have already replaced Ovid's). And it encourages the reader to use his own ingenuity to create for himself a variety of reconstituted texts to superimpose on the original." *Poetry and Fable*, 12.

[108] See Moss, *Ovid in Renaissance France*, 6–7.

[109] The work was issued in 1522 by two publishers using the same impression: Philippe Le Noir and the widow of Janot Jehannot (*Index Aureliensis* *106.614). For the publishers, see Renouard, *Répertoire*, 266 and 218–19.

The *Golden Ass* in Spain: Diego López de Cortegana and *El Asno de Oro*

It is not clear when copies of Apuleius first arrived in Spain, but the *Golden Ass* was known at least by repute by the end of the fifteenth century, when it was alluded to in the novel *La Celestina* (1499).[110] The reference is slight; one character says to another, "And he ate the pickle as quickly as Apuleius ate the poison that turned him into an ass."[111] Since the author shows no secure knowledge of the story (Apuleius' hero did not *eat* the fatal mixture), it is likely that he had his information at second- or thirdhand by way of Augustine.[112] The important point, however, is not whether the author of *La Celestina* had read the *Golden Ass* but that he expected his audience to know enough about it to catch his reference.[113]

Within a few years after the publication of *La Celestina*, Spanish readers—that is, those competent in Latin—would have been able to study Apuleius' novel for themselves in Beroaldo's edition and commentary, which was available in four editions by 1510.[114] In France, as we have seen, the arrival of Beroaldo's work encouraged printers to publish and market their own Latin versions of the novel, but no such editions appeared in Spain. The first indication both of Beroaldo's influence and of serious interest in the *Golden Ass* is the earliest printed translation of the novel, the Spanish translation (*El asno de oro*) of Diego López de Cortegana, published in Seville by Jacob Cromberger around 1513.[115]

Cortegana (1455–1524) was archdeacon of Seville and an energetic inquisitor, but he also belonged to a prominent circle of humanists

---

[110] The novel was published anonymously in 1499 and subsequently edited by Fernando de Rojas. For *La Celestina* and Apuleius, see Scobie, "The Influence," 218; García-Gual, in Cortegana, *El asno de oro*, 26.

[111] "Y en tal hora comiesses el diacitron como Apuleyo el veneno, que lo convertio en asno." *La Celestina*, act 8, end.

[112] His comment is reminiscent of the descriptions of the novel by the prehumanists; see chapter 2. Augustine describes the means of Lucius' transformation in a vague ablative absolute: *accepto veneno* (*Civ.* 18.18).

[113] Another comment in the novel seems to be in the same category. A lover describes a girl's hair as beautiful enough to turn men to stone, and his interlocutor says: "into asses, rather!" ("*mas en asnos*"), *La Celestina*, act 1. The allusion is identified and discussed by Scobie, "The Influence," 218.

[114] Bologna, 1500; Venice, 1501, 1504, and 1510. See Krautter, *Philologische Methode*, 193.

[115] Until recently this edition was unknown to bibliographers. It exists in a unique copy in Paris, Bibliothèque Sainte Geneviève, OE.XVe.635 (2ème pièce). For a detailed description, see Griffin, *The Crombergers of Seville*, no. 97, *136–*139.

interested in Erasmus (the Hispalensis academia, or Seville Academy).[116] He worked closely with Cromberger on several printing projects in addition to the *Golden Ass*.[117] Cortegana and Cromberger undoubtedly wanted their edition of the *Golden Ass* to sell, but their presentation suggests that they had a different strategy from their French and German counterparts. The translations of Sieder and Michel were aimed at the vernacular general reader, and the Latin editions of Paris were printed for students and scholars. But Cromberger and Cortegana seem to have designed their work to appeal to both groups, although not always at the same time. The translation itself would suit either vernacular or humanist readers, as we shall see presently; but much of the prefatory and concluding material seems directed to one audience or the other. Most of this material is in Spanish, but some is in Latin.

The elaborately decorated title page is in Spanish and contains the name of neither printer nor translator. On the top of the page is a richly ornamented border, and below it a breathless summary of the story:

> The book of Lucius Apuleius concerning the Golden Ass. In it he treats many stories and racy tales and how his girlfriend, a maidservant, in the attempt to change him into a bird as her mistress (who was a great witch) had changed herself, mistook the box and changed him from a man into an ass. And in his travels as an ass, he saw and heard the evils and betrayals that wicked women commit against their husbands, and so he went on until at the end of a year he ate some roses and changed himself back to a man—as he tells at length in this book.[118]

This précis omits most of what happens in the novel. What about the bandits? we might ask. Or Cupid and Psyche? Or the charlatan priests?

---

[116] The facts of Cortegana's life listed by Hazañas y la Rúa (*Maese Rodrigo*, 272–78) and placed in a narration by Bataillon (*Érasme et l'Espagne*, 92) and Griffin (*The Crombergers*, 150–51) have recently been supplemented by Gil, whose study of new documents presents a darker, or at least a more nuanced, picture ("Apuleyo en la Sevilla renacentista," 297–304). Cortegana was a slave owner, and he got rich from properties confiscated by the Inquisition.

[117] Cortegana corrected the Seville missal and breviary printed by Cromberger; and Cromberger printed not only Cortegana's *Golden Ass* but also his translations of Erasmus' *Lament of Peace* and the *Tract on the Misery of Courtesans* by Aeneas Silvius Piccolomini (Pope Pius II), as well as his edition of the *Crónica del santo rey don Fernando tercero*.

[118] "Libro de lucio apuleyo del asno de oro. Enel qual trata muchas hiſtorias y fabulas alegres: y de como una moça su amiga: por lo tornar ave: como se avia tornado su señora, que era gran hechizera, erro la buxeta: y torno lo de hombre en asno. E andando hecho asno, vido y oyo las maldades y trayciones que las malas mugeres hazen a sus maridos. E aſsi anduuo haſta que acabo de un año comio de unas rosas y tornoſse hombre: segun que el largamēte lo recuēta eneſte libro." *Lucio Apuleyo del Asno de Oro* [Seville, ca. 1513], fol. a1r, quoted from Griffin, *The Crombergers*, *136.

Or the market gardener and the soldier? Or even the cook and the pastry chef and the Ass's last owner, whose plan to show him in the arena precipitates his flight and restoration? Eliminating all these as irrelevant, the title page focuses on the two points that Cromberger, and probably Cortegana as well, thought would have the widest appeal: Lucius' magic transformations and the wickedness of women.

Congratulatory verses celebrating Cortegana's achievement frame the translation.[119] These verses, in Latin, obliquely but clearly identify Cortegana. The initial verses were composed by a fellow humanist, Juan Partenio Tovar, and those at the end by Cortegana himself. Self-consciously learned and artful, the two sets of verses appeal to a smaller audience than that of the title page. They address Latin readers like Cortegana's friends in the Hispalensis academia, humanists capable not only of deciphering the words but also of appreciating their literary qualities. In a distich at the beginning Tovar touts Cortegana's translation to potential buyers: "Then the Ass was rough-rumped and rejected his load with his hooves. Now he is golden and puts up with a saddle. Buyer, appear!"[120] In another he includes a punning reference to the identity of the translator: "The Ass that the Tarpeian city could not tame for a man—Look! Seville has him make friends with a wolf."[121] (The word *wolf* (lupo) puns on López, the beginning of Cortegana's surname.) In the three closing poems, Cortegana completes the identification in a metaliterary seal or *sphragis*.[122] In the first he gives the name Cortegana in an acrostic; in the second, significantly addressed to the "learned reader" (lector docte), he identifies himself as archdeacon of Seville, gives his first name, Jacobus (that is, Diego), and provides the clue to the preceding acrostic.[123] In the third (addressed to Apuleius) he commends his translation: "Mercury himself, the messenger of the gods,

---

[119] See the important discussion of Escobar Borrego, "Textos preliminares." All the verses are quoted both by Escobar Borrego (from the first edition) and in Cortegana, *Lucio Apuleyo del Asno de Oro*, 103 (from the 1543 ed.).

[120] "Clunibus asper erat qui et onus tunc calcibus urgens, / sterni asinus patitur iam aureus. Emptor ades." *Lucio Apuleyo del Asno de Oro* [Seville, ca. 1513], fol. a3v, quoted from Escobar Borrego, "Textos preliminares," 158. Since this is Tovar's last distich, the words immediately preceding the translation are addressed to the buyer: "Emptor ades."

[121] "Quem domuisse asinum Urbs homini Tarpeia nequivit / Hispalis ecce facit gratiam in ire Lupo." Ibid.

[122] Escobar Barrego ("Textos preliminares," 162–65) discusses Cortegana's verses as presenting an *elogium* or *monumentum* and notes that Cortegana's claim of his work as a monument is modeled on Beroaldo's.

[123] The name is discovered by taking the first three letters of the first verse and the first two of the rest: "*Cor* dure tygres, hidra aut hyrcana colubris / *te*ntant huius cui fabula nulla placet. / *ga*nnit nulla quidem eius pars pietatis in aure, / *na*tus at in silvis trux garamanta fuit." *Lucio Apuleyo del Asno de Oro* [Seville, ca. 1513], fol. i8r, quoted from Escobar Borrego, "Textos preliminares," 161.

would scarcely translate your wit any better, Apuleius, by Hercules!"[124] Escobar Borrego has pointed out that Cortegana is like Mercury, "the messenger of the gods" (*interpres divum*), in two senses: as a translator and as a mediator between God and humanity in his capacity as archdeacon. (*Interpres* means both "intermediary" and "translator".) But Mercury is also *psychopomp*, conducting souls back and forth between the worlds of life and death. Cortegana can claim a similar role: that he has brought Apuleius' wit to life again in his translation.[125]

Cortegana presents his preface in both languages, first in Latin and then in Spanish—a clear indication that he is thinking of two audiences. The two versions are extremely close, although it is fair to say that the Spanish is slightly more explicit in its references to religion. He makes three points: first, that he is translating the novel to make it more accessible and better known; second, that he should not be criticized for dealing with stories that make no contribution to religion, since church fathers like Augustine, Lactantius, Jerome, and Fulgentius (called "doctores cathólicos" in the Spanish version) praised Apuleius as a philosopher and read pagan works both for relaxation and to improve their minds; and third, that the tale is applicable to everyone. It is in this last section that the Latin and Spanish versions slightly differ. Cortegana concludes his Latin preface thus:

> Indeed it [the novel] is appropriate and exactly fitted to all, since we all perpetually bear on our backs an ass not of gold but of stone, or rather mud. And no one can be divested of it except by greedily devouring the roses of prudence and reason. That is, by trampling on the vices (by which almost all men become beasts), we may come to a glorious life. Farewell. 1 August 1513.[126]

The Spanish conclusion is the same until the very end, where it substitutes "are blinded" (*se ciegan*) for "become beasts" (*brutescunt*) and revises the last sentence to read: "And so by despising such worldy deceits we can advance to life everlasting. Amen."[127] Apart from replacing the

---

[124] "Interpres divum haud melius Cyllenius umquam, / Apulleie, sales transferat, Hercle, tuos." Ibid., 162.

[125] "Compare his comment in the short note at the end of his translation. The note (which appears on the same page just above his poems) begins: "Non sin fatiga del spíritu y trabajo corporal se traduxo Apuleyo y vino a ser." Ibid., 175.

[126] Omnibus enim convenit adamussimque coaptatur. Quipe cum omnes Asinum non aureum sed lapideum immo luteum dorso iugiter feramus. Quo exui nemo potest, nisi rosis prudentie ac rationis avide devoratis. Id est viciis (quibus cuncti fere mortales brutescunt) recalcatis ad vitam lucidam veniamus. Avetote. Cal. Augusti. M. d. xiii." Ibid., fol. a1v, quoted from Escobar Borrego, "Textos preliminares y posliminares," 167.

[127] The section corresponding to the end of the Latin prologue quoted above reads as follows (changes in the Spanish version are indicated by italics): "pues que a todos conviene

notion of transformation with that of blindness, the changes do not change the meaning, but intensify it, casting the thought in explicitly religious language—including the final "Amen."[128]

The basic idea of the passage, however (whether in Latin or Spanish), is not Cortegana's but Beroaldo's, with only a few minor modifications;[129] for unlike his fellow translators in France and Germany, Cortegana is not concerned to present his own reading of the novel. In his final note to the reader he uses Beroaldo again. Here is the end of Beroaldo's concluding note: "The reading of the Ass of Apuleius is undoubtedly a mirror of human affairs, and in this wrapping one sees the depiction of our character and the portrayal of daily life, whose goal and greatest happiness is religion and the worship of divine majesty, united and joined with learning."[130] In the corresponding passage Cortegana again follows his model almost to the end, where he changes the last clause to read: "Whose goal and greatest happiness is our religion, to serve God and his divine majesty, that we might succeed in going to his glory for which we were created."[131] He replaces Beroaldo's union of religion and learning with a triumphant religious climax, but the alteration, unlike the Lutheran modifications by Sieder's editor that we noted earlier, does not change Beroaldo's theology. Here, as in the preface, Cortegana has merely intensified and amplified Beroaldo's ideas.

Cortegana does not mention Beroaldo in these passages or anywhere else in his work, but he uses him as the source for all of his ancillary material, translating and sometimes lightly reworking various sections from Beroaldo's commentary: his comparison of Apuleius' plot with that of "Lucian," his life of Apuleius and the allegorical reading in his preface,

---

y arma justamente. Porque no se puede dudar sino que todos traemos a cuestas un asno y no de oro, mas de piedra y aun (lo que peor es) de lodo. Del qual ninguno se puede despojar, sino gustadas las rosas de razón y prudencia. Conviene saber: hollando los vicios y *deleites* con los quales quasi todos los mortales *se ciegan. E assí menospreciando los tales engaños del mundo, podamos ir a la vida que dura para siempre. Amen.*" Ibid., fol. a2r, quoted from Escobar Borrego, "Textos preliminares y posliminares," 168.

[128] Cortegana's translation shows similar tendencies. For his use of Christian religious vocabulary in the Isis book, see Küenzlen, *Verwandlungen*, 291–96.

[129] Cf. Beroaldo, *Commentarii*, fol. 2v, quoted in chapter 6, n. 83.

[130] "Lectio Asini Apuleiani nimirum speculum est rerum humanarum, istoque involucro efficti nostri mores expressaque imago vitae quotidianae conspicitur, cuius finis et summa beatitas est religio cultusque divinae maiestatis una cum eruditione copulata connexaque." Beroaldo, *Commentarii*, fol. 280v.

[131] "Cuyo fin y suma bienaventuranza es nuestra religión, para servir a Dios y a su divina magestad, porque alcancemos ir a su gloria, para donde fuemos criados." *Lucio Apuleyo del Asno de Oro* [Seville, ca. 1513], i8r, quoted from Escobar Borrego, "Textos preliminares y posliminares," 175.

and the plot summaries that accompany each book.[132] This material is straightforward and informative, unlike either the enticing (and misleading) title page directed to vernacular readers or the Latin poems with their self-referential humanist learning. It would be useful to general readers and scholars alike. The translation introduced by Beroaldo's material was also designed for both audiences. It is recognized by students of Spanish literature as both faithful (and so in tune with Cortegana's talents and interests as a humanist) and of high literary quality.[133] Unlike either Sieder or Michel, Cortegana translates Apuleius' erotic passages honestly without abridging or rewriting: the episode of the amorous matron survives intact.

Cortegana's *El Asno de Oro* is one of only two sixteenth-century translations of the *Golden Ass* to enjoy lasting popularity. (The other is *The Golden Asse* by William Adlington, which I will consider in the next section.) The work was designed to reach the widest possible audience, as we have seen, but the real source of its appeal was Cortegana's scholarship and undoubted literary talent, together with intense interest in the novel in sixteenth-century Spain. In addition to its popularity in its own right, *El Asno de Oro* had some importance for Spanish literature, influencing the Spanish picaresque novel and providing the material for several Spanish works on both Cupid and Psyche and the ass story.[134] It was reprinted at least eight times in the next hundred years in various formats.[135]

---

[132] The point is amply demonstrated by several scholars, each of whom juxtaposes passages from Cortegana and Beroaldo: Scobie, "The Influence," 219–20; Miralles, "Diego López de Cortegana i Beroaldo," 370–78; Escobar Borrego, "Textos preliminares y posliminares," 166–75.

[133] Scobie calls it "faithful and elegant" ("The Influence," 219). Menéndez y Pelayo praises Cortegana's "dicción pura, sencilla, familiar y picaresca," and commends it for not reproducing Apuleius' baroque style: "en nada se parece á la violenta y atormentada latinidad de su modelo" (quoted by Bonilla y San Martin, "Advertencia," in *Orígenes de la Novela* 4:149). For a detailed analysis of Cortegana's translation of the Psyche story, see Escobar Borrego, "Diego López de Cortegna."

[134] On this large and controversial subject, see García Gual, in Cortegana, *El Asno de Oro*, 23–38, with further bibliography. See also Gil, "Apuleyo en la Sevilla renacentista," 305–6; Scobie, "The Influence," 220–25; Walsh, *The Roman Novel*, 233–38; Wilson, "Homage to Apuleius."

[135] Zamora, 1536 and 1539; Medina del Campo, 1543; Seville 1546; Amberes, 1551; Alcalá de Henares, 1584; Madrid, 1601; Valladolid, 1601. See Bonilla y San Martín, *Erasmo en España*, 26–28. For descriptions of the editions of 1543, 1551, 1584, and 1601, see Menéndez y Pelayo, *Bibliografía hispano-latina clásica*, 1:76–79. The 1546 edition is described by Escobar Borrego, "Una edición del siglo XVI." But Menéndez y Pelayo (1:72–76), Bonilla y San Martín, and Scobie all refer to yet another edition (without date or colophon), which Norton in a letter to Scobie dated ca. 1525 (Scobie, "The Dating of the Earliest Printed Spanish and French Translations," 236). For recent bibliography

The title page of the 1543 edition presents a clever depiction of Lucius' transformation in two scenes (see figure 6). On the left we see the dejected Ass facing an elegantly clothed woman holding what seems to be a riding crop. The scene on the right suggests that the artist might have seen the German translation printed five years earlier, for it shows Lucius midtransformation in a pose clearly derived from Weissenhorn's edition. The Spanish artist, surely unaware that his ultimate source was the Papstesel, wittily interprets the event. The image shows Lucius, unaware of his condition, rubbing the fatal ointment on his chest, which is rapidly becoming covered with hair. With his ass's head directed toward a nude Fotis, he gazes lasciviously down at her nether regions. The top of the page bears the pious heading "Blessed be the name of the Lord" (*sit nomen domini benedictum*). The title page of the 1546 edition slightly modifies the picture: the Ass on the left is more cheerful, the woman more imperious, and the Ass on the right—still cheeky and lewd—has raised his gaze to Fotis' breasts.[136] But the time for such witty effusions would soon come to an end. Cortegana's translation was placed on the prohibited list by the Index Expurgatorio of 1559, and the editions printed after that date not only lacked such illustrations but were also forced to omit the amorous matron and other interesting passages.[137]

Border Crossings

By 1550 the *Golden Ass* had been printed in German, French, and Spanish translations, as well as in the Italian translations of Matteo Maria Boiardo (composed in the 1470s, but first printed in 1518) and Agnolo Firenzuola (composed in the 1520s and '30s and posthumously published in 1549).[138] These several translations had one point in common: each

---

on still more editions, see Martos, in Apulyeo de Madauros, *Las Metamorfosis o El Asno de Oro* 1: lxxxv n. 399.

The edition of 1543 was reprinted in Madrid in 1890. The enduring interest of Cortegana's work is attested by its appearance nine times between 1988 and 2000 in García Gual's edition.

[136] The page is shown in Escobar Borrego, "Una edición del siglo XVI," 11.

[137] See Bonilla y San Martín, *Erasmo en España*, 27–29. (The edition of 1890 restores the expurgated passages, but in Latin.)

[138] For Boiardo, see pp. 175–80 and 185. Firenzuola (1493–1543) began his translation in the last months of 1524 and worked on it until the middle or late 1530s. See Pignati, "Agnolo Firenzuola"; Maniscalco, "Criteri e sensibilità."

Figure 6. Title page of Diego López de Cortegana's *Lucio Apuleyo del asno de oro* (Medina del Campo, 1543). Hispanic Society of America.

was a self-contained entity in its own language. All except Boiardo's had been influenced by Beroaldo, but none had drawn on a translation in a different vernacular. Such cultural isolation, however, could not last long. Books, art, and ideas were in constant movement in the sixteenth century—throughout Europe, but particularly between Italy and France—and the translators of Apuleius were about to benefit.

The movement of Apuleian interpretation from Italy to France is epitomized in the story of the engravings attributed to an anonymous artist called the Master of the Die. At some point in the middle 1530s, an artist in Rome (probably the Flemish painter Michael Coxie) produced a series of thirty-two drawings of episodes in the story of Psyche.[139] These works, which had some stylistic and iconographic affinities with Raphael's Psyche cycle in the Farnesina, were used as the basis for a set of engravings, three by Agostino Veneziano and the rest by the Master of the Die, who has given his name to the series.[140] The series was struck several times, and, from the third state on, little eight-line Italian poems were added as a narrative or explanation at the bottom of each scene. The engravings quickly achieved enormous popularity, both in their own right and as models for later artists in many media, transmitting the Psyche story in a kind of "iconographical vulgate."[141] By the early 1540s, if not before, the series had made its way to France. There, Anne de Montmorency, one of the richest and most powerful men in the kingdom, was building a great showplace for his magnificence, the Château d'Écouen. He (or his architect) used the engravings as the model for one of the chateau's most splendid features—a set of stained glass windows illustrating the story of Psyche.[142] Montmorency, not content with transplanting the images alone to French soil, brought the poems as well, commissioning three celebrated poets to translate them into French huitains.[143] The installation was completed by 1544.

Two years later, a printer in Paris, Jeanne de Marnef, capitalized on the fame of both Montmorency and the images by publishing a little

---

[139] For the history of the Psyche series, see Cavicchioli, *The Tale of Cupid and Psyche*, 154–71.

[140] The engravings are illustrated in Boorsch, *The Illustrated Bartsch 29*, 195–227. They are numbered 1–32.

[141] The phrase is Cavicchioli's (*The Tale of Cupid and Psyche*, 167). For later works modeled on the engravings, see ibid., 180 n. 21; Le Maitre, *Essai*, 42.

[142] For the windows of Château d'Écouen, see Cavicchioli, *The Tale of Cupid and Psyche*, 167–71 and plates 104–16; Le Maitre, *Essai*, 42–44.

[143] The translators were three poets popular in royal and aristocratic circles: Claude Chappuis, Antoine Héroët, and Mellin de Saint-Gelais. See Le Maitre, *Essai*, 43–45. For a modern edition of the ten huitains by Saint-Gelais, see Stone, ed., *Mellin de Saint-Gelais, Oeuvres poétiques françaises* 1:165–71.

volume entitled *L'Amour de Cupido et de Psiche*:[144] "The Love of Cupid and Psyche, mother of Pleasure, taken from the fifth and sixth books of the Metamorphosis of the philosopher Lucius Apuleius. Newly illustrated and summarized in both French and Italian verse."[145] The work was edited by Jean Maugin, who supplied some epigrams and a letter to the reader with a little interpretation of the story of Psyche: that its message is that "one should seek harmonious unions, love completely and discreetly, and, above all, pay no attention to the envious."[146] Maugin's letter and epigrams, however, are only a frame for the real meat of the book: woodcuts based on the images of the engravings, accompanied by both the Italian poems and their French translations.[147] The woodcuts and the Italian poems appear on the rectos, the French huitains on the facing versos.

If we consider the reception of Apuleius' tale of Cupid and Psyche through the engravings of the Master of the Die, we can observe a dizzying number of shifts and changes—of language, nationality, genre, and medium. We begin with Apuleius' Latin story, depicted around 1518 in the Farnesina in Rome by Raphael and his assistants (or we should say partly depicted, since only the scenes with the gods are included).[148] Then, in quick succession, the drawings of the Flemish painter Michael Coxie imitating and adding to Raphael's originals, engravings based on the drawings, Italian poems to accompany the engravings, stained glass windows in a French chateau based on the engravings, French poems to accompany the windows, and a printed book translating the engravings into woodcuts and including both the Italian and French poems. And all of this within a period of less than 30 years (only 10 or 12 if

---

[144] For Jeanne de Marnef, widow of the printer Denis Janot (d. 1544), see Renouard, *Répertoire*, 216–17. She was carrying on the publishing program of her husband, who had specialized in illustrated editions of both French works and classical texts translated into French; see Saunders, "Sixteenth-Century Book Illustration," 526. The work seems to have been issued in two different editions dated 15 September 1546; see Mortimer, *Harvard College Library . . . French 16th Century Books*, 1:41 for a description and discussion with earlier bibliography.

[145] "L'Amour de Cupido et de Psiche, mere de Volupte: prise des cinq & sixiesme liures de la Metamorphose de Lucius Apuleius Philosophe. Nouuellement historiée, & exposée tant en vers Italiens, que Françoys." *L'Amour de Cupido et de Psiche* (1546), A1r.

[146] I quote from Le Maitre's summary (*Essai*, 45): "Les recommandations de Maugin aux amoureux: rechercher les unions assorties, aimer parfaitement, secrètement et surtout ne pas écouter les envieux."

[147] The title page and the woodcuts numbered 30, 32, and 16 are illustrated in Mortimer, *Harvard College Library . . . French 16th Century Books* 1:41. Cut 7 is illustrated in Brun, *Le livre français*, planche XIb; Saunders, "Sixteenth-Century Book Illustration," 527. Many but not all of the woodcuts present the scenes of the engravings in mirror image. Their artist has been variously identified.

[148] For a discussion and color illustrations of the paintings in the Farnesina, see Cavicchioli, *The Tale of Cupid and Psyche*, 88–116, with earlier bibliography.

we begin with Coxie and his drawings) and without a single word by Apuleius himself.

The Psyche book had a fine *fortuna* of its own. It was reprinted in 1557 and 1586, and in 1586 a new version was published with the same title and images (this one with engravings by Léonard Gaultier instead of woodcuts and omitting the Italian poems).[149] Even before its first reprinting, however, it had an important influence on two French translations of the *Golden Ass: Metamorphose, autrement, L'asne d'or* by George de La Bouthière and *Luc. Apulée de l'asne doré* by Jean Louveau.[150]

The two translations were printed in Lyon in 1553 within a few months of each other. Guillaume Michel's translation had long been passé, and La Bouthière and Louveau each hoped to be the one to replace it with something more in tune with current ideas, which in practice meant something reflecting Italian influence, especially in Lyon, which for some time had been a thriving intellectual and commercial center with a cosmopolitan (and largely Italian) flavor.[151] Both writers criticized Michel's translation and disdained his religious allegory, which neither translator tried to replace with his own interpretation. Religious and moral readings were out of fashion, and they knew that their public preferred a lively and attractive work to one that was edifying. (La Bouthière presents no interpretation at all, and Louveau suggests but does not insist on an obvious allegorical reading.) The editions of both made use of *L'Amour de Cupido et de Psiche*.

La Bouthière's translation includes dozens of woodcut illustrations by the well-known artist Bernard Salomon ("Le petit Bernard").[152] Among them are fourteen from the story of Psyche, six of which are clearly

---

[149] See Brun, *Le livre français*, 112–13. For a description of the Gaultier volume, see Mortimer, *Harvard College Library . . . French 16th Century Books*, 1:41; a facsimile has been edited by Calder. At least two more versions were published in the early nineteenth century: *La fable de Psyché, figures de Raphaël* (Paris, 1802) and *Les amours de Psyché et de Cupidon, par Apulée: Traduction nouvelle, ornée des figures de Raphaël* (Paris, 1809); see Calder, *L' Amour de Cupido*, xviii–xix.

[150] Little is known about either man. George de La Bouthière of Autun was active as a translator in Lyon in the 1550s and '60s; his translations include Apuleius, his earliest work (1553); Pseudo-Aristotle, *Problems*; Polydore Virgile; and Suetonius (1566). See Chavy, *Traducteurs d'autrefois* 2:815. Jean Louveau was active in the same period, translating Apuleius, also his first work (1553), Erasmus (1559), and various Italian authors. See Chavy 2:892–93; Michaud, *Biographie universelle, ancienne et moderne* 25:340–41.

[151] For Lyon in this period, see Rigolot, "Louise Labé and the 'Climat Lyonnois'"; for the Italian influence, see Romier, "Lyons and Cosmopolitanism."

[152] La Bouthière's translation is rare; see *Index Aureliensis**106.630. For descriptions and the attribution of the woodcuts to Salomon, see Brun, *Le livre français*, 113; Cartier, *Bibliographie des Éditions des de Tournes*, 342–43; Sharratt, *Bernard Salomon*, 289–90. For a more detailed discussion of the woodcuts, see Sharratt, 88–91 and (plates) 88–94. Salomon seems to have worked exclusively for La Bouthière's printer, Jean de Tournes; see Johnson, "Books Printed at Lyons" 133.

based on the French woodcuts derived from the Italian engravings.[153] Interestingly enough, however, neither La Bouthière nor his printer, Jean de Tournes, refers to Psyche or the currently popular Psyche series in order to promote the book; in fact, neither even mentions that the work is illustrated. The omission is curious, for as we have seen in the case of every other edition in this chapter, sixteenth-century printers and authors habitually used title pages and introductions to tout the attractive features of their works. It seems even more curious when we consider both La Bouthière's efforts to appeal to fashionable readers and the "Italian" character of the work.

La Bouthière was strongly influenced by the Italian translations of Firenzuola and Boiardo. Both were old (Boiardo's was very old), but both would probably have seemed new enough to La Bouthière and his readers, since they had been printed (or in the case of Boiardo, reprinted) just a few years earlier: Firenzuola in 1550, and Boiardo in 1544 and 1549.[154] La Bouthière dedicated his translation to an aristocratic lady, a certain Madame Françoise de Mussy, "Dame de Bellegarde, et de Saint Cergue," frankly admitting that he wanted to ingratiate himself by amusing her, and piquing her interest by pointing out that Apuleius' subject was hardly worthy of her "chaste and learned ears."[155] Everything in the work is designed to please Madame de Mussy and other readers with similar fastidious tastes—aristocratic ladies, we might say, or those who would like to be. La Bouthière calls the hero Lucio, making him fashionably Italian. He criticizes Michel's translation as "heavy" and full of "long digressions stuffed with allegories and mystical meanings, as much to the point as the *Magnificat* at matins."[156] He disdains tedious word-for-word translation on the grounds that it

---

[153] The images correspond to the engravings and 1546 woodcuts numbered 17, 20, 21, 23, 25, and 30. But Salomon had recent Italian sources as well, especially one of the editions of Boiardo's translation, which had been reprinted in 1544 and 1549; see Sharratt, *Bernard Salomon*, 89–91.

[154] *Index Aureliensis* *106.623 and *106.627 (Boiardo), *106.628 (Firenzuola). The 1518 and 1549 editions of Boiardo are described in Mortimer, *Harvard College Library . . . Italian 16ᵗʰ Century Books* 1:30–32.

[155] "Ie me suis ingeré mettre en lumiere ceste mienne traduction, qui vous est auec moymesmes dediee: encores que le subiet me semblast aucunement indigne de voz doctes et chastes oreilles, volontieres tousiours occupees à ouir choses graues et serieuses. Toutefois persuadé que vostre seigneurie . . . prendra le tout en bonne part; s'arrestant plustot au bon zele et affectionné vouloir de son humble seruiteur, qui ne tend que à la faire rire, que à la matiere, en son endroit parauenture impertinente: ie nay point trop ceremonieusement craint de user de ce moyen pour m'insinuer de plus en plus en vostre bonne grace." La Bouthière, *Metamorphose*, 8. I quote from a microfilm of the copy in Munich, Bayerische Staatsbibliothek A. lat. b. 41.

[156] "Mais certeinement ie ne pense point auoir iamais leu chose plus lourde, plus confuse, ny plus mal ordonnee: . . . le traducteur, . . . laissant son propre subiet, se mettoit

"cheats our rich language of its native grace, celebrated copiousness, and delightful charm," and promises to paraphrase at will, but (as he maintains) "without diminishing or changing a thing, except what has been found completely unworthy and abhorrent to any reading."[157]

La Bouthière follows Firenzuola in trying to bring the world of the *Golden Ass* into his own time. He does not go as far as Firenzuola (who had made himself the hero of the novel and set it in fifteenth-century Tuscany), but, like Firenzuola, he re-creates Apuleius in a lively sixteenth-century idiom, embroidering and rewriting to suit contemporary taste.[158] Both translators delight in elaborating on Apuleius' already elaborate descriptions. In book 2, for example, Apuleius describes Byrrhena's dining room in an elegant paragraph (*Met.* 2.19.1–4), touching on the guests, tables and couches, goblets, and servants. Firenzuola doubles the description, adding fine bed-curtains to the couches, pearls to the goblets, and perfumes to the servants.[159] La Bouthière, inspired by but not translating Firenzuola, goes on for two and a half pages, turning Byrrhena's dining room into a ballroom, adding singers, hautboys, viols, and flutes, an embroidered silk canopy, satin and velvet coverlets embroidered with gold and silver and showing Byrrhena's coat of arms at the corners, torchères in the shape of Cupids, etc., etc.[160]

Ever mindful of his ideal reader, La Bouthière spices his style with proverbs, clichés, and contemporary references.[161] At the beginning of the story of Psyche (*Met.* 4.28.2) he says she is so beautiful that after making her, Nature "broke the mold."[162] (Neither Nature nor "the mold"

---

aux champs, faisant de *grandes digressions farcies dallegories, et sens mystiques, autant à propos que magnificat à matines.*" Ibid., 11.

[157] Italics indicate the words translated in the text: "*Defraudans en ce, nostre riche langue de sa naïve grace, celebre copiosité, et douce mignardise . . . iay usé de Phrases et circonlocutions qui m'ont semblé plus propres et conuenables: sans interrompre toutefois et discontinuer lordre et vray fil du suiet: ni en rien l'imminuer et changer, fors en ce qui sest trouué totalement indigne et aborrant de toute lecture.*" Ibid., 12.

[158] As in his treatment of Psyche: "C'est l'exemple de Firenzuola qui amena le traducteur français à parer ainsi la fable de Psyché de couleurs modernes, de traits brillants, de concetti, de préciosité pétrarquiste." Le Maitre, *Essai*, 48.

[159] Firenzuola, *L'Asino d'oro*, 231.

[160] La Bouthière, *Metamorphose*, 82–85.

[161] It is so up to date that, as Le Maitre notes, the Munich copy of the edition "est couvert de notes manuscrites qui prouvent qu'on l'a utilisé comme répertoire de fin langage français, surtout pour les proverbes et les modèles de conversation ou de lettres." *Essai*, 48 n. 1. This copy belonged to Dominus Maximilian Felix de Lesch, whose arms and ex libris appear on the flyleaf.

[162] "Mais la plus ieune de toutes, encores les surpassoit dune si rare et singuliere beauté, que iose bien dire que nature nen eust sceu former une plus excellente, et que apres la facture dicelle, elle en auoit rompu le moule." La Bouthière, *Metamorphose*, 198–99.

appears in Apuleius.) Instead of the "many citizens and foreigners" (*multi . . . civium et advenae copiosi*, Met. 4.28.3) who came to see her in Apuleius, La Bouthière tells us:

> All the princes and great lords of the realm, with an infinite number of dukes, counts, marquises, barons, all rich and powerful, arriving there from distant lands and foreign countries to see such a masterpiece of beauty, paid court to her in the hope of making her their lady and mistress, and of aquiring a share of her good grace, which in her was no less than her beauty.[163]

At the end of the story Apuleius makes Vulcan cook the wedding feast.[164] La Bouthière, with fine anachronism, says: "Vulcan, serving as their cook, had become a second Taillevant"—just as we might say "a second Escoffier or James Beard."[165]

At this point we could certainly contest La Bouthière's claim to paraphrase "without changing a thing." But he faithfully adheres to the second part of his promise: to omit or revise "what is unworthy and abhorrent." By his standards (and certainly those of his elegant readers) the category would undoubtedly include the episode of the amorous matron, which he rewrites and abridges; in his telling it is not that the matron falls in love with the Ass and contracts for his services, but that the Ass spies a woman he takes for Fotis, stands up on his hind legs, and rushes to embrace her, so amusing the bystanders that his master decides to present him in the theater as an ass who "knows how to pay court to women."[166] Perhaps more surprisingly, however, La Bouthière considers the serious as abhorrent as the obscene. He finds in book 11 "so little taste and grace that I could hardly be bothered to

---

The description caught the eye of the German reader of the Munich edition, who underlined it and wrote "rompre le moule" in the margin.

[163] "Tous les Princes et grans seigneurs du Royaume, auec un nombre infini de Ducs, Comtes, Marquis, Barons, tous riches et puissants, là venus de lointains païs et estranges contrees pour contempler un tel chef doeuure de beauté, lui faisoient la court souz esperance den faire leur dame et maistresse, et acquerir part en sa bonne grace, laquelle nestoit moindre en elle que sa beauté." Ibid., 199. (The German reader has underlined again, writing "chef doeuure de beauté" in his margin.)

[164] "Vulcanus cenam coquebat." *Met.* 6.24.2.

[165] "Vulcanus pour lors seruant de cuisinier, estoit deuenu un second Taillevant." La Bouthière, *Metamorphose*, 336. (Taillevant was a famous royal chef at the end of the fourteenth century; a cookbook attributed to him was printed at least twenty-five times in the fifteenth and sixteenth centuries.)

[166] Ibid., 606–7.

read it."¹⁶⁷ As it treats nothing but Isiac ceremonies, processions, and priests, it is "long-winded and boring," too tiresome to include with the rest.¹⁶⁸ He continues:

> All the same, not to leave the work unfinished, keeping poor Lucio forever in the miserable servitude and the vile condition of an ass, where he still was, I had recourse to the original Greek text of Lucian, from which the whole thing had been drawn in the first place and translated into Latin. And I have followed it the more boldly since another highly erudite Tuscan translator had given me the example.¹⁶⁹

La Bouthière's exemplary "Tuscan translator" is the recently reprinted Boiardo, who had substituted the ending of "Lucian's" *Onos* (the *Ass*) for Apuleius' book 11.¹⁷⁰ But no matter what La Bouthière says, he has not made much effort "to resort to the original Greek text." Instead, for the most part he has simply translated Boiardo's Italian into his own French, with some embroidery but otherwise almost word for word—except, of course, for the projected encounter with the murderess in the theater and the restored Lucio's ignominious rejection by the amorous matron at the end, both of which would have been too indecorous for his readers.¹⁷¹

---

¹⁶⁷ "Sachez donq (Lecteurs beneuoles) que paruenu à cest onzieme liure le lisant et preuoyant selon ma coutume auant y mettre la main et le traduire, *i'y trouuay si peu de gout et de grace, que à peine péuz ie prendre patience de le prelire.*" Ibid., 13.

¹⁶⁸ "Icelui ne traitant que daucunes ceremonies, pompes, processions, et sacrifices des prestres de la Deesse Isis. Le tout *tant prolixe et ennuieux*, que ie fuz grandement desgouté le mettre au rang des autres." Ibid.

¹⁶⁹ "Toutefois pour ne laisser loeuure imparfait, et detenir tousiours ce pouure Lucio en la miserable seruitude, et vile condition asinine, ou encores il estoit, ieuz recours au premier original Grec de Lucian, dont le tout auoit esté premierement tiré, et traduit en Latin: lequel iay ensuiui dautant plus hardiment, quun autre doctissime traducteur Tuscan men auoit donné lexemple." Ibid.

¹⁷⁰ See p. 176.

¹⁷¹ A full demonstration of La Bouthière's debt to Boiardo would be "long-winded and boring," but a brief comparison of their endings will suffice, since they are both similar to each other and different from the conclusion in "Lucian."

Here are the last words of Pseudo-Lucian's *Onos* in the Loeb translation: "After so very long and with such difficulty I had escaped, not from the dog's bottom of the fable, by Zeus, but from the curiosity of an ass" (*Lucius, or The Ass*, 56, trans. M. D. Macleod). Now Boiardo: "Havendo cum molta faticha e longa pena imparato de consigliare ciaschuno che per compiacere a femine non voglia uno asino diventare, se forsi non destina per dar dilecto ad altrui perder la pelle in breve tempo" (*Apulegio volgare* [Venice, 1519], fol Q4r). And La Bouthière: "apres auoir en toutes fatigues, infinies malheurtez, et dix mille hazards de mort, consumé bonne partie de ma ieunesse à conseiller un chacun, que par trop complaire aux femmes ilz ne uueillent deuenir asne, si daduenture ilz ne

The translation of Jean Louveau is less frivolous and Italianate than that of La Bouthière, but it both uses and exploits material from *L'Amour de Cupido et de Psiche*. Its wares are advertised on the title page:[172]

> Lucius Apuleius, XI books on the Golden Ass translated into French by I. Louveau of Orleans, and ordered by chapters and summaries, with a table at the end. Moreover, there are added to the fourth, fifth, and sixth books treating the love of Cupid and Psyche, xxxii huitains appropriately placed, translated from others which have been found in copper engravings in the Italian language.[173]

The huitains announced in the title duly appear in their places in the text, but without the images they were written (and translated) to accompany. A few woodcuts are scattered through the edition, but the two or three in the Psyche books bear no resemblance to those in either La Bouthière or the Psyche series.

Louveau dedicated the work to his aristocratic patron, Claude Laurencin, a royal official in Lyon whom he served as secretary.[174] He hoped to please Laurencin, to be sure, but both he and his printer, Jean Temporal, also had a wider audience in mind—not the fashionable or would-be fashionable set of La Bouthière, but rather those we might think of as "general readers." The illustrations, huitains, and references to the Psyche books cater to the current interest aroused not only by *L'Amour de Cupido et de Psiche* but also by the engravings themselves and the windows in Montmorency's chateau. But the edition is also designed for convenience and easy reference: as the title proclaims, each book is broken into several chapters with descriptive titles, and a table of contents appears at the end. Louveau provided this material at the last-minute suggestion of the printer, he says, adding that he was glad to do it to please and assist the reader, "for very often one does not have the time at his disposal to go hunting for material that he wants to see immediately."[175] The work concludes with a short book-by-book

---

uouloient (pour donner plaisir à autrui) y, laisser et perdre la peau en brief" (*Metamorphose*, 645–46).

[172] For a description of this edition (not in *Index Aureliensis*), see Brun, *Le livre français*, 113. I quote from the 1558 edition, which is a reimpression of that of 1553.

[173] "LUC. APULEE De L'Ane Dore XI Livres Traduit en François par I. Louueau d'Orleans, et mis par Chapitres et Sommaires, auec une table enfin. Plus y a sus les 4. 5. 6. liures traitans de l'amour de Cupido et de Psiches, xxxii huictains, mis en leur lieu, traduitz sus d'autres, qui ont esté trouuez, taillez en cuiure en langue Italique." Louveau, *De L'ane dore* (1558), fol. a1r.

[174] See Michaud, *Biographie universelle, ancienne et moderne* 25:340–41.

[175] "Car bien souuent chacun n'a pas le temps à commandement pour aller rechercher les matieres, que l'on desire voir sus le champ." Louveau, *De L'ane doré* (1558), fol. a4v.

listing of topics and pithy sayings that could be useful to readers looking for general information or for quotations to put in their commonplace books.[176]

Louveau and Temporal wanted their book to sell, and they were well aware of the competition—not only the old translation of Michel, but also the very new one of La Bouthière, which had come on the market just a few months earlier. Louveau criticizes both predecessors, although not by name. Michel's is "the old translation," which he calls "a new Apuleius rather than a translation" and criticizes as being full of extraneous words and content.[177] But he has harsher words for La Bouthière. Introducing his comments with a pointed reference to one of the selling points of his own work, "le beau discours de l'amour de Cupido et de Psiches," he continues:

> I have translated it from Latin into French as faithfully and carefully as I could . . . and without taking away anything from it or adding long periphrases and new subjects outside the material, or phrases at will and with no savor of their Latin author but rather of the affected trifler who created them—things that can sometimes mislead the reader and at the same time break the thread and the sense and sequence [*deduction*], or characteristic way of speaking [*phrase*], of the author.[178]

Louveau's words are clearly directed against La Bouthière's frivolous rewriting. But in case we were in doubt, he goes on in the next sentence to reject the idea of substituting "Lucian's" ending for book 11, correcting La Bouthière in almost every word. "Lucian's" work, he says in

---

[176] "Table des sentences, faits excellentes, propos, et autres choses dignes de memoire contenus aux onze Liures de Apuleius." Ibid., fols. E5v–E7r. The list includes such topics as "Oraison de Iupiter aux dieux" (book 6), "Legereté naturelle des femmes" (book 9), "Description de la montaigne Idae" (book 10), and sayings like "La fortune est aueugle, cruelle et mechante" (book 5) and "L'auarice regne encores entre les mortz" (book 6).

[177] "Amis lecteurs, il n'est ia besoing que ie vous aduertisse de l'ancienne traduction de ce present liure, laquelle i'ay trouuee estre plustost nouueau Apulee que traduction: dont ie me suis grandement esbahi, non seulement pour l'impression, mais aussi pour la correction et autres mots adiustez, qui ne sont pas au liure Latin, et mesme qui ne viennent à nulle raison, pour la matiere." Ibid., fol. a3v.

[178] "Or donc ie l'ay traduit de Latin en François le plus fidelement et songneusement qu'il ma esté possible . . . et sans y diminuer n'y adiouter grandes periphrases et nouueaux propos outre la matiere, ou dictions à plaisir, et ne sentans point son auteur Latin, mais plustost son gaudisseur et plaisanteur, choses qui peuuent quelque fois esgarer le Lecteur, et auec ce, rompre le fil, et le sens et deduction, ou phrase le l'Auteur." Ibid., fol. a4r. For a discussion of this passage in terms of sixteenth-century translation theory, see Norton, *The Ideology and Language of Translation*, 243. For the meanings of *deduction* and *phrase*, see 227–43.

passing, is "an epitome" of Apuleius'.[179] (La Bouthière, we remember, had identified "Lucian" as the original, "from which the whole thing had been drawn in the first place.") The whole goal and purpose of the novel, Louveau maintains, is contained in book 11, and he goes on to commend the very ceremonies of Isis that La Bouthière had found so tedious.[180]

Louveau could certainly have read the Italian translations of Boiardo and Firenzuola—it would be a little surprising if he had not, since he seems to have specialized in translating Italian authors. Apart from his use of the Psyche huitains, however, his work shows little sign of contemporary Italian influence. He translates the opening lines of Apuleius' prologue with verses of his own, no doubt to match the poems in the Psyche books, but perhaps also in imitation of the verse preface in Firenzuola.[181] But his nine lines have little in common with Firenzuola's ten, and he could also have seen verse prologues in Latin texts, including that of Beroaldo.[182] In general he is more indebted to Beroaldo and the Italian humanist tradition than to present vernacular models. He translates Beroaldo's *Life of Apuleius*, claims to have consulted several Latin texts, and even aspires to produce an annotated Latin edition.[183]

Louveau's translation is much more down-to-earth than those of Michel and La Bouthière. True to his word, he keeps close to the Latin text without embroidering or bowdlerizing. He adds no frills to Byrrhena's dining room or Psyche's admirers, and the episode of the amorous matron, for once, survives essentially intact. Like La Bouthière, he apologizes to his dedicatee for the slight and fictitious nature of

[179] "Quand ie suis venu à l'onzieme liure, pourceque Lucien en a fait un epitome." Louveau, *De L'ane doré* (1558), fol. a4r.

[180] "En iceluy onzieme est contenu le but ou semble que nostre Auteur Apulee ayt voulu tirer, pour y traiter le recouurement de sa premier forme: ioint qu'il est plein de belles antiquitez et plaisantes fables pour cause des cerimonies et superstitions des anciens Payons." Ibid., fol. a4r-v.

[181] "*Proeme*: Or ie te veux par maniere de rire, / En ce livret des cas nouueaux escrire, / Comptes ioyeux, et plaisans à merueilles, / Pour adoucir tes clairoyans oreilles: / Si d'escuter il te vient à plaisir, / Tu y verras sans dommage ou danger, / Les corps humains en autres corps changer: / Et puis apres, sans beaucoup seiourner, / Les mesmes corps en humains retourner." Ibid., fol. a8r. Firenzuola's more faithful ten-line poem includes "Egyptian reeds" (*calami d'Egitto*) and other Apuleian details (*Asino d'oro*, 197).

[182] For Latin verse prologues in printed editions, see Carver, "Quis ille?"; May, "The prologue," 300–308. For Beroaldo, see pp. 203–5 and figure 1.

[183] He says he has consulted both Venetian and German editions as well as commentaries (*De L' ane doré* [1558] fol. a3v), and that he hopes with the encouragement of his patron to publish his work "non seulement en François, mais aussi en Latin bien emendé, auec annotations et scholies qui pourront seruir de commentaires" (fol. a2v). The life appears on fols. a5r–a7v.

Apuleius' work, but whereas La Bouthière emphasized the novel's racy qualities the better to titillate his reader, Louveau is at pains to answer objections that fiction is worthless and keeps people from reading edifying and useful books. He is not a highly charged allegorist like Michel, but he suggests that there might be more in the novel than meets the eye. Since no intelligent person could possibly imagine that anyone could really be transformed into an ass by a magic ointment and restored by eating roses, he suggests, perhaps one should look for a deeper meaning:[184]

> Yet if we want to raise our minds a little higher and pluck the rose among the thorns, we will discover that the author (who was a great philosopher) chose such a subject not without reason, demonstrating that by our dissolute appetites and lubricious and carnal existence we become like brute beasts, and especially the ass, which is the dullest and most ignorant among all the animals, and we most often fall into many sorts of servitude and afflictions, as happened to him through his debauchery and excessive curiosity—so that his intention and true purpose seem to be directed to our instruction and the reformation of our lives.[185]

The allegory is modest enough with its simple moral and its lack of religious reference, but perhaps Louveau thought that even this much moralizing might be unpalatable to Laurencin and his other sophisticated readers, for he quickly steps back from it in the next sentence: "Nonetheless, I entrust the whole matter to your judgment and that of all good intellects."[186]

As we consider the two Lyonnaise translations of 1553 from a historical perspective, La Bouthière's edition undoubtedly appears the more interesting, for it epitomizes the fashionable taste of a particular place and moment, draws on not one but two Italian translations, and reflects

---

[184] "Ie ne pense et ne me puis aucunement persuader qu'il y ait aucun tant loing de bon iugement, et estrange de la raison, qui en lisant cest oeuure puisse croire et imaginer en son esprit un homme auoir esté mué en Asne par un si facile moyen d'un oignement: puis de rechef retourné en sa premiere forme par une simple superstition." Ibid., fols. a2v–a3r.

[185] "Toutefois si nous voulons eleuer noz espritz un peu plus hault, et entre les espines cueillir la rose, nous trouuerrons que non sans cause l'Auteur (qui estoit grand Philosophe) a prins un tel subiect: demonstrant que par noz appetiz desordonnez, vie lubrique et charnelle, sommes faictz semblables aux bestes brutes et specialement à l'Asne, qui est le plus lourd et ignorant entre tous les animaux, et le plus souuent tombons en maintes seruitudes et miseres, comme luy aduint par sa luxure et trop grande curiosite. Tant ia que son intention et vray but semble tirer à nostre doctrine et reformation de vie." Ibid., fol. a3r.

[186] "Neantmoins ie remetz le tout à vostre iugement, et de tous bons espritz." Ibid.

(at several removes) the Psyche iconography of the Master of the Die. But sixteenth-century French readers were not looking at matters from a historical perspective, and for them Louveau's usefulness and convenience trumped La Bouthière's frivolities. La Bouthière's work sank with hardly a trace.[187] Louveau's was reprinted four or five times in the next thirty years.[188] It was supplanted at the beginning of the seventeenth century by the 1602 translation of Jean de Montlyard, who was as scornful of Louveau as Louveau had been of La Bouthière, condemning his translation as not "an ass of gold" but "one of iron, one of lead."[189]

In 1566 the *Golden Ass* crossed from the continent to England, where it appeared in the English translation of William Adlington. The work was presented in a handsome quarto volume with a title page that reads as follows:

> The xi Bookes of the Golden Asse, conteininge the Metamorphosie of Lucius Apuleius, enterlaced with sondrie pleasaunt and delectable Tales, with an excellent Narration of the Mariage of Cupide and Psiches, set out in the. iiii. v. and vi. Bookes. Translated out of Latine into Englishe by William Adlington. Imprinted at London in Fleetstreate, at the signe of the Oliphante, by Henry Wykes. Anno 1566.[190]

Adlington's work is the culmination of the sixteenth-century movement of the *Golden Ass* across cultures and languages, for Adlington draws on Beroaldo, writes a verse preface in imitation of Louveau (who was perhaps inspired by Firenzuola), frequently translates Louveau, and is at least aware of Cortegana's Spanish translation.[191] By prominently mentioning on the title page the "excellent Narration of the Mariage of Cupide and Psiches, set out in the. iiii. v. and vi. Bookes," he (or his printer, Henry Wykes) even hopes to capitalize on the popularity of the

---

[187] Both Cartier (*Bibliographie . . . de Tournes*, 410) and Sharratt (*Bernard Salomon*, 288) list a reprint of 1556 by de Tournes. It does not appear in *Index Aureliensis* or WorldCat.

[188] Brun lists reprints of 1558, 1570, 1580 and 1584 (*Le livre français illustré*, 113). An edition of 1586 is listed in *Index Aureliensis* (*106.640).

[189] "Certes au lieu d'un Asne d'or il nous en avoit donné un de fer, un de plomb." Jean de Montlyard, *L'asne dor ou les Metamorphoses de Luce Apulee Philosophe Platonique* (Paris, 1602), a7r. Montlyard's translation was reprinted several times in the 1600s; the editions from 1623 on include handsome engravings.

[190] Quoted from *The xi Books of the Golden Asse*, 1566 edition. The translation is most accessible in Whibley's edition for the Tudor Translation series: *The Golden Ass of Apuleius*.

[191] He refers to it in passing: "I have not so exactly passed thorough the Author, as to point every sentence accordinge as it is in Latine, or so absolutely translated every woorde, as it lieth in the prose, (for so the French and Spanish translators have not done)." Adlington, *The Golden Asse*, fol. A3v.

French picture book *L'Amour de Cupido et de Psiche*, which La Bouthière and Louveau had tried in their different ways to exploit.[192]

Almost nothing is known about William Adlington—less in fact than about any other early translator of the *Golden Ass*.[193] No other work can be securely attributed to him, and although he dates his dedication "from Universitie College in Oxforde," there is no record that he graduated from—or even attended—the university. In his letter to the reader, he cheerfully confesses to "slender knowledge," and critics have tended to agree with him.[194] He perhaps used Beroaldo's text and certainly consulted Beroaldo's commentary, at least sporadically, for he uses Beroaldo's life of Apuleius and draws heavily on Beroaldo's allegorical reading of Lucius' transformations, which he reconciles—not very persuasively—with his own view of the novel as entertainment.

The line he will take is introduced in his dedication to Thomas Radcliffe, earl of Sussex, whom he assures that the novel is not entirely frivolous: "Although the matter therein seeme very light, and mery, yet the effect thereof tendeth to a good and vertuous morall."[195] The fables of poets, he argues, have useful lessons to teach: Tantalus "betokeneth the insatiable desire of covetous persons," Midas represents "the foule sinne of Avarice," Castor and Pollux, translated into the constellation Gemini, signify "that vertuous and godly persons shalbe rewarded after life with perpetuall blisse."[196] And so on, all leading up to the *Golden Ass*: "And in this fable or feigned jeste of Lucius Apuleius is comprehended a figure of mans life, ministringe moste sweete and delectable matter, to such as shalbe desirous to Reade the same."[197] Adlington spells out this "sweete and delectable matter" in the letter to the reader. He had been afraid, he says, that he might seem foolish in translating this work, "which seemeth a meere jest and fable. . . . But on the other side, when I had thoroughly learned the intent of the Author, and the purpose why he invented so sportfull a jest: I was verily perswaded, that my small travell should not onely be accepted of many, but the matter it selfe allowed, and praised of all."[198] After a quick summary of the story, he continues:

> Verely under the wrappe of this transformation, is taxed the life of mortall men, when as we suffer our mindes so to be drowned in the

---

[192] Henry Wykes (or Wekes) operated in London from 1557 until 1569. *The Golden Asse* seems to have been his most important book. See McKerrow, ed., *A Dictionary of Printers*, 304.
[193] See Whibley's introduction to *The Golden Ass*, xxviii–xxx.
[194] Ibid., xxi.
[195] Adlington, *The Golden Asse*, fol.*1v. For Radcliffe, see *DNB* 16.579–86.
[196] Adlington, *The Golden Asse*, fol.*2r.
[197] Ibid.
[198] Ibid., fol. A2r–v.

sensuall lustes of the fleshe, and the beastly pleasure therof (whiche aptly may be called, the violent confection of witches) that we leese wholy the use of reason and vertue . . . and play the partes of bruite and savage beastes. . . . So can we never be restored to the right figure of our selves, except we taste and eate the sweete Rose of reason and vertue, which the rather by mediation of prayer we may assuredly attaine.[199]

Although he does not say so, Adlington has taken this interpretation, or, as he says, "learned the intent of the Author," from the section in Beroaldo entitled "The Intent and Plan of the Writer" (*Scriptoris intentio atque consilium*), for it corresponds very closely to Beroaldo's reading.[200] (The "violent confection of witches" is his own idea.)

Like Beroaldo and perhaps inspired by his example, Adlington also puts forward other possible interpretations. Perhaps, he suggests, building on and simplifying Beroaldo's comments on youthful folly and mature sense, "the Metamorphosie of L. Apuleius, may be resembled to youth without discretion, and his reduction, to age possessed with wisedome and vertue."[201] Or perhaps, he proposes more implausibly, we should be reminded that a beginner at something "appeareth to him selfe an Asse without witte, without knowledge, and not much unlike a bruite beast," until he gains skill, "and tastinge the sweete floure and fruicte of his studies, doth thinke him selfe well brought to the right and very shape of a man."[202]

As we consider Adlington's comments, two points seem clear: that he genuinely likes and admires the *Golden Ass* for its "merry jests" and that he is hard pressed to see it as an allegory. He has gratefully borrowed Beroaldo's interpretation and has tried valiantly, but not very intelligently, to think up some allegories of his own; but the effort is uncongenial and the results unpersuasive. His treatment is in contrast with that of La Bouthière and Louveau a decade earlier. The French translators, operating in sophisticated (and perhaps slightly jaded) Lyon, came to terms with the novel differently: La Bouthière by ostentatiously avoiding anything he considered heavy or allegorical, Louveau by suggesting that even fiction was potentially useful and tactfully proposing a version of Beroaldo's reading. Although Adlington is obviously much closer to Louveau, his stance and intellectual milieu are by no means the same, for the morally edifying was of greater interest to Tudor London than it had been to mid-sixteenth-century Lyon. To put

---

[199] Ibid., fols. A2v–A3r.
[200] Cf. Beroaldo, *Commentarii*, fol. 2v.
[201] Adlington, *The Golden Asse*, fol. A3r. Cf. Beroaldo, *Commentarii*, fol. 2v.
[202] Adlington, *The Golden Asse*, 1566, fol. A3r.

it another way: Louveau was diffident about suggesting a serious interpretation of the *Golden Ass*; Adlington feels required to do so.

Adlington worked directly with Apuleius' Latin as he composed his translation, but he also consulted other translations, especially that of Louveau, as Carver has pointed out.[203] Louveau's translation was an obvious resource, since it was recent and no doubt easily available in either the 1553 or the 1558 edition, and Adlington used it heavily. But Louveau had a resource of his own: the despised translation of Guillaume Michel. As a result, Michel often appears indirectly in Adlington's *Golden Asse*, bobbing beneath the surface of his borrowings from Louveau.[204] We shall look at some of these cases presently, but first we must turn to the beginning of Adlington's translation of the prologue, which shows direct indebtedness to both Michel and Louveau.

> The Preface of the Authour, to his sonne Faustinus, and unto the Readers of this booke.
>
> > That I to thee some joyous jestes, may show in gentle glose:
> > And frankly feede thy bended eares, with passing pleasant prose,
> > So that thou daine in seemely sorte, this wanton booke to view
> > That is set out and garnisht fine, with writen Phrases newe.
> > I will declare how one by happe, his humaine figure lost,
> > And how in brutishe fourmed shape, his lothed life he tost:
> > And how he was in course of time, from such estate unfold.
> > Who eftsoones turnd to pristine shape, his lot unlucky told.[205]

Like Louveau and Firenzuola before him, Adlington renders the opening lines of Apuleius' prologue in verse (*Met.* 1.1.1–2).[206] But Louveau did not translate Firenzuola, and Adlington does not translate Louveau. In each case the translator has taken the idea of a verse prologue from his model but used his own words and phrasing. Firenzuola keeps but simplifies Apuleius' reference to Egypt, while Louveau and Adlington banish Egypt altogether, focusing instead on the pleasure of the book and the hero's loss and regaining of his human form. We may perhaps see a faint trace of Louveau's language in Adlington's "writen Phrases newe" (l. 4), which possibly owes its adjective to Louveau's "des cas nouveaux" (l. 2).[207] But the echo, if it exists, is very slight. In the case

---

[203] Carver, "The Rediscovery," 264.

[204] Whibley, seeing Michel's phrasing in Adlington and apparently unaware of Louveau's version, mistakenly identified Michel as Adlington's principal source. See Whibley, introduction to *The Golden Ass*, xxv–xxvii.

[205] Adlington, *The Golden Asse*, fol. Biv.

[206] For Louveau's and Firenzuola's verses, see note 181 in this chapter.

[207] The word *new* does not appear in the corresponding lines of Apuleius.

of Michel, however, Adlington's verbal indebtedness is patent. Michel does not use verse in his translation, but he entitles the prologue "Prologue de Lacteur: La proposition de lacteur a son fils Faustinus et aux lecteurs de ce present livre" (Prologue of the Author: The Statement of the Author to His Son Faustinus and to the Readers of This Present Book).[208] The resemblance to Adlington's title is close enough to guarantee that he looked at Michel's translation at least once.[209] (Louveau's title is simply "Proeme.")

Most of the time, however, Adlington bolsters his translation skills by recourse to Louveau. Four of the five passages in Adlington noted by Whibley as demonstrating his use of Michel are also found in Louveau.[210] At *Met.* 1.13.4, for example, Aristomenes comments on the appropriateness of Socrates' having called the drunken witch Meroe (from *merum*, "unmixed wine"): "Next Meroe—for then I saw that her name in fact matched Socrates' stories."[211] Michel translates: "Meroe qui estoit dicte Meroe pource quelle estoit taverniere" (Meroe, who was called Meroe because she was a taverner).[212] Louveau expands on Michel: "Meroe (ainsi nommee pource que'elle estoit vraye tavernière aymant bien à boire)" [Meroe (so called because she was a real taverner, very fond of drink)].[213] Now Adlington: "Meroe (being so named because she was a taverner, and loved well good wines)."[214] The process is clear: Adlington has translated and slightly modified Louveau, who has translated and added on to Michel, who has mistranslated Apuleius.

There are dozens of passages in *The Golden Asse* (not all of them involving mistranslation) where one can find Adlington translating Louveau, with or without an underpinning of Michel, and it is amusing to see the process at work. But that is not why Adlington's translation

---

[208] Michel, *De Lasne dore*, fol. 2v. The reference to Faustinus in Michel and Adlington goes back to Beroaldo: "Lusurus Asinum aureum exorditur ab epigrammate iambico bimembri quo faustinum filium sive lectorem alloquens." Beroaldo, *Commentarii*, fol. 3r.

[209] He may also have done so at 2.13.3, where he translates Apuleius' "Cerdo quidam nomine negotiator" as "a certayne Cobler" (*The Golden Asse*, fol. 17r). Michel has "quelque savatier" (*De Lasne dore* [1522], fol. 19r), while Louveau correctly translates as "un certain facteur appellé Cerdo" (*De L'ane dore*, 53). Beroaldo was probably Michel's source, since he also takes *Cerdo* to mean "cobbler" ("vulgo cerdonem vocitant sutorem veterum calceorum"; *Commentarii*, fol. 43r). I suspect that Adlington, perplexed by the name Cerdo, consulted all three of his predecessors and decided that Louveau, the odd man out, must be wrong.

[210] See 1.11.4, 1.13.8, 4.1.4, 8.27.4. See Whibley, introduction to *The Golden Ass*, xxvi–xxvii. The fifth passage, 2.13.3, is discussed in the previous note.

[211] "Ad haec Meroe—sic enim reapse nomen eius tunc fabulis Socratis convenire sentiebam." *Met.* 1.13.3.

[212] Michel, *De Lasne dore* (1522), fols. 7v–8r.

[213] Louveau, *De L'ane dore*, 20.

[214] Adlington, *The Golden Asse*, fol. 6r.

is important. Whatever his weaknesses as a literary critic or a Latinist, Adlington surpasses and transcends his sources, splendidly turning Apuleius' baroque Latin (whose style he terms both "darke and highe" and "franke and flourishing") into his own "large, untrammeled prose."[215] It is the language in the end by which any translation stands or falls, and Adlington's—inaccuracies and all—does not so much represent Apuleius' words as transform them into a new and wonderful shape of his own creation. Every reader will have favorite examples of Adlington's Apuleius. Mine is this passage from the opening of book 11, which—in typical fashion—gives us Apuleius, Michel, Louveau, and above all Adlington, all at once.[216]

> When midnight came, that I had slept my first sleepe, I awaked with sodein feare, and sawe the Moone shininge bright, as when she is at the full, and seeming as though she leaped out of the Sea. Then I thought with my self that, that was the moste secret time, when the Goddesse Ceres had most puisance and force, considering that all humaine thinges be governed by her providence: And not onely all beastes private and tame, but also all wilde and savage beastes be under her protection: And consideringe that all bodies in the heavens, the earth, and the seas be by her encresinge motions encreased, and by her diminishinge motions diminished: as wery of all my cruell fortune and calamitie, I founde good hope and soveraigne remedie, though it were very late, to be delivered from all my misery, by invocation and prayer to the excellent beautie of the Goddesse: whome I sawe shininge before mine eyes, wherefore shaking of mine Assy and drowsie sleepe, I arose with a joyfull face, and moved by a great affection to purifie my selfe, I plonged my head seven times into the water of the sea, which number of seven is convenable and agreeable to holy and divine thinges, as the worthy and sage philosopher Pythagoras hath declared. Then with a weeping contenance, I made this orayson to the puissant Goddesse.[217]

Adlington's *Golden Asse*, like Cortegana's *El asno de oro*, introduced Apuleius' novel in a literate, readable vernacular to readers ready to receive it and bring it into their own national literature. It was the first, and for 250 years the only, Apuleius printed in England (the first Latin text of Apuleius printed in England was the Delphin edition of 1825), and it remained the translation of choice well into the twentieth century.

---

[215] Ibid., fol. A2r. The description "large, untrammeled prose" comes from Whibley, introduction to *The Golden Ass*, xxv.

[216] For a comparison of Apuleius, Adlington, Michel, and Louveau, see appendix 5.

[217] Adlington, *The Golden Asse*, fols. 115v–116r.

• • •

In the sixteenth century the *Golden Ass* moved across Europe, crossing natural, national, religious, and linguistic boundaries. European translators turned it into their own vernaculars and interpreted it from the perspective of their own time and place. In the first half of the century the novel received what we could call local readings. In Germany Apuleius became a Lutheran, and the story of Lucius was read as exemplifying the need for inherently sinful man to be saved by God's grace. In Paris the story was seen through the distorting prism of an elaborate medieval religious allegory in which Lucius' pursuit of magic became a quest for spirituality, derailed by diabolical temptation in the form of Fotis. In Spain it was given Beroaldo's humanist reading, presented in both Latin and Spanish (where slight changes made it more explicitly Catholic). In midcentury the borders of language—as well as medium—became more permeable. The engravings of the Master of the Die moved from Italy to France, bringing with them a fascination with the story of Psyche that migrated from Italian engravings to the stained glass windows of a French aristocrat, from Italian poems to French, and into French and English translations of the novel. In urbane Lyon religious allegories were embarrassingly passé, and Apuleius was either dressed up as an Italianizing sophisticate (La Bouthière) or presented simply as the author of an interesting story whose meaning was up to the reader (Louveau). In England, by contrast, it was still important to find useful morals in one's reading, and, with Beroaldo's help, one was found—edifying, down-to-earth, and safely secular.

All the translators found Apuleius' Latin difficult, and none attempted to reproduce his baroque style in the vernacular. Instead, they smoothed out and simplified his language and either glossed or omitted potentially confusing references. No one gives us a full explanation of his method, but Adlington perhaps comes closest. He says:

> I have not so exactly passed through the Author, as to pointe every sentence accordinge as it is in Latine, or so absolutely translated every woorde, as it lieth in the prose, (for so the French and Spanish translators have not done) considering the same in our vulgar tongue would have appeared very obscure and darke, and thereby consequently, lothsome to the Reader, but nothing erringe as I trust from the given and naturall meaninge of the author, have used more common and familiar woordes (yet not so muche as I might doo) for the plainer setting foorth of the same.[218]

[218] Ibid., fol. A3v.

Adlington's unquestioned assumption is that meaning is a "given and naturall" entity that can be separated from the way in which it is expressed; it can be transferred—not only into a different language, but into a different style—safe and unchanged. Since Apuleius' style, rendered in the vernacular, would be "obscure and darke" and hence "lothsome to the Reader," he will put the author's meaning into his own "common and familiar woordes." His fellow translators of the novel seem to share both his assumption about style and meaning and his conception of the role of the translator. We can be sure which position Adlington and the rest would have taken in any theoretical debate about whether the translator should bring the reader to the author or the author to the reader. To a man they (and their printers) would have argued for the course they followed: of bringing Apuleius to the reader, no matter what he had to leave behind or what baggage he picked up on the way. The sixteenth-century translators and printers were in the business of finding an audience and selling books, which meant naturalizing Apuleius into their own cultures and packaging him as attractively as possible. By doing so, they made the *Golden Ass* available not only to individual readers but to their own national literatures, where both the novel as a whole and the stories of Lucius and Psyche enjoyed (and still enjoy) a rich afterlife. Apuleius, who knew something about packaging and presentation himself, would surely have approved.

CONCLUSION

The Fortunes of Apuleius and the *Golden Ass*

Apuleius was interested in images of all kinds—statues, reflections, appearances, descriptions—of both himself and others. He talked about how to create them, what they reveal, what they *should* reveal, and how to preserve and control them. He liked mirrors and longed to have statues of himself in public places. In his writings he went to great lengths to create his own image, confecting a persona part Platonic philosopher, part handsome celebrity orator, part scholar (and perhaps even practitioner) of magic. He projected this interesting semblance of himself on the screen of his orations and allowed it to peek through some episodes of the *Golden Ass*. But he could not project it unchanged into the future. No doubt he would have liked to, for in *Florida* 7 he speaks admiringly of Alexander the Great, who was able to ensure that his likenesses came down to posterity as he wished by allowing only the three greatest artists of his age to portray him and deterring the others with the fear of death. But Apuleius lacked Alexander's coercive power, and over time his carefully constructed image was to undergo transformations that he could never have imagined. Later literary and artistic representations of Apuleius changed with the tastes and cultural contexts of their creators, who portrayed him variously as a philosopher or magician, but—above all—identified him with Lucius, the asinine hero of the *Golden Ass*.

The survival of the *Golden Ass* and Apuleius' other works was not inevitable. We might even say that it was unlikely. Fiction, though popular, enjoyed a low reputation in late antiquity, and Apuleius' writings seem to have inspired little interest in the two centuries after his death. But Apuleius was lucky. The goddess Fortuna, so cruel to the fictional Lucius, was kindness itself both to Apuleius and to the *Golden Ass*, taking a hand at critical moments and bringing them into the best possible hands for over a millennium.

She first smiled on them at the end of the fourth century, at the point when so many books (and almost all of the ancient novels) were lost in the transition from roll to codex. In 395 Apuleius' *Apology* and *Metamorphoses* (and probably the *Florida*) came into the hands of a young Roman aristocrat named Sallustius, who corrected them with his teacher. A few years later Augustine undertook a detailed study of

De deo Socratis in order to refute the Platonic concept of *daimones* in the *City of God*, in which he blasted Apuleius' polytheism but praised other aspects of his Platonism. The encounters with Sallustius and Augustine were to be decisive. Sallustius' manuscript became the sole surviving copy of the so-called literary group and preserved it to posterity, and Augustine's commendation of Apuleius as a Latin Platonist ensured the survival of his philosophical works in northern Europe. Augustine was also important to the reception of Apuleius' novel, for in a single paragraph in the *City of God* he both transmitted the title *Golden Ass* (our oldest manuscripts call the work *Metamorphoses*) and treated the novel as a work of either real or fictitious autobiography. Both the title and the identification of Apuleius and Lucius would be taken over by scribes and prehumanists in the early fourteenth century and pass unquestioned into later interpretations.

But Augustine's influence did not stop there, for he may have been indirectly responsible for the preservation of the *Golden Ass* at another critical moment many centuries later. At some point in the Middle Ages, Sallustius' manuscript or a copy of it arrived in Monte Cassino. It was copied again in the eleventh century, when the monks embarked on a campaign of recopying their ancient manuscripts—especially those that were mutilated or damaged, and especially those associated with Augustine. Augustine, of course, would have been most interested in the philosophical works, which were out of reach in northern Europe, but the monks had their own ancient manuscript of the *Golden Ass*. The copy they made of it, Florence, Biblioteca Laurenziana 68.2, or F, is considered the archetype of all existing manuscripts of the literary works.

By the late thirteenth century at least one copy of the literary works had slipped out of Monte Cassino, and copies of the philosophical works started to percolate into Avignon and northern Italy. Within a few years scholars were beginning to mention works from both groups, always taking Augustine as their authority when they referred to the *Golden Ass*. From then on, Apuleius' survival was no longer in doubt, and his luck still held, bringing him into the hands of the two greatest humanists of the age, Petrarch and Boccaccio. Petrarch owned and annotated the earliest manuscript we have that unites the literary and philosophical groups. The manuscript contains splendid illuminations in which Apuleius is depicted in fourteenth-century conceptions of his different characters: he is shown as a philosopher, as an author, as a composite of orator, magician, and scholar, and as the hero of the *Golden Ass* in both his human and animal manifestations. Boccaccio's encounter with Apuleius was even more important—a meeting of two like minds—both with deep (if different) philosophical and religious interests, both possessed of an imagination ranging freely between realism and fantasy, and both gifted with a love of language and a talent for narrative. It was almost a lifelong association. As a young man Boccaccio studied and annotated an Apuleius manuscript in Naples; in middle age he transcribed his own manuscript of the *Golden Ass*, imitated the novel in the *Decameron* and other works, and began an allegory of Psyche in the *Genealogy of the Pagan Gods*; at the end of his life he was still revising both the *Genealogy* and his account of Psyche.

Both Petrarch and Boccaccio moved interpretation of the *Golden Ass* well beyond Augustine's jejune but influential summary in the *City of God*, but Augustine remained of great importance to the philosophical works. His commendation of Apuleius as "a famous Platonist in both Greek and Latin" had persuaded scholars in the Middle Ages to include the philosophical works in their library of Latin texts on Platonic philosophy. The collection, including Apuleius, was taken up with renewed interest by the Florentine Platonists in the fifteenth century. As a consequence, numerous manuscripts of the philosophical works were acquired or commissioned by Florentine readers, including the Medici; fifteen still remain in Florentine libraries. But Apuleius' Platonism was to have consequences more important than the production of a dozen or so Florentine manuscripts. In the 1450s a long-simmering hostility between Platonists and their conservative opponents burst into an angry controversy, and Apuleius, lucky as always, benefited from the debate, becoming only the second classical author to be printed in Italy. His complete works were printed in Rome in February 1469 by Sweynheym and Pannartz—less for their own sake than to announce and promote the publication of Cardinal Basil Bessarion's *Defense of Plato* six months later.

The first edition was a major landmark in the reception of Apuleius. Its press run of around 275 copies made Apuleius available to more readers than at any time in his history, and the editor, Giovanni Antonio Bussi, provided an introduction to each of the works for their benefit. His modest but intelligent discussion of the *Golden Ass* provides the first expository treatment of the novel, presenting a plot summary, an enthusiastic discussion of Apuleius' style, and a simple reading of the work as a cautionary depiction of human nature. But the edition was a landmark in another respect as well. Bussi and Bessarion had recognized the power of printing not only to publish and distribute the works of a classical author but also to promote ideas and agendas; and they had used Apuleius to launch what James Hankins has called "the first concerted press campaign in the history of printing."

Not all of Apuleius' readers embraced the new medium. In the 1470s Ercole d'Este, duke of Ferrara, commissioned a translation of the *Golden Ass* from Matteo Maria Boiardo, who completed it by 1479, translating from the text of Bussi's edition. Ercole claimed to like

Boiardo's *Apulegio volgare* so much that he read it every day, but he drastically limited its circulation: the only copy he is known to have authorized was given to Federico Gonzaga, duke of Mantua. (Even here, he was keeping the work in the family, since his daughter Isabella would marry Federico's son.) *Apulegio volgare* became the inspiration for several literary and artistic works on the story of Psyche at the courts of Ferrara and Mantua, but both it and the works it inspired were printed only in the sixteenth century. The artistic works have disappeared. Although Ercole would probably not have had his Apuleius without printing, aristocratic selfishness made him oppose the sharing or duplication of his books. As a result, the interpretation of Apuleius in Ferrara and Mantua in the fifteenth century took place within a closed system and had no influence elsewhere for many years.

Outside Ferrara and Mantua Apuleius' fortunes, like those of other authors, were firmly associated with printing. In 1500 Filippo Beroaldo, one of the most famous teachers in Europe, published his monumental commentary on the *Golden Ass* in a press run of at least twelve hundred copies. Beroaldo, like Boccaccio before him, had a deep, instinctive affinity with Apuleius. His affinity, like Boccaccio's, had to do with a love of language and an interest in the realistic details of daily life; but it was also professional and perhaps even temperamental. Both Beroaldo, the charismatic teacher-scholar, and Apuleius, the sophist, made their living in the lecture hall; both worked hard to create and maintain an image; and both promoted themselves to the hilt. Beroaldo used his commentary both to explicate the text of the *Golden Ass* and to immerse his students in the language, history, and culture of antiquity; but he also made it a work of literature in its own right, creating artful digressions or metatexts in which he presented himself as a modern-day counterpart of Apuleius. Beroaldo's commentary, an instant and long-lasting success, carried Apuleius all over Europe, where it was used by the German, French, Spanish, and English translators of the sixteenth century who opened the way for the reception of the *Golden Ass* in their own national literatures.

The fortunes of each classical text are unique, but each had to make the same journey: from roll to codex, into a medieval library, into the hands of humanists, into print, and finally into translation. The fickle goddess Fortuna watched over Apuleius and the *Golden Ass* at every stage, as she did for every other work of Latin literature that survives. But she has been kind to us as well, for Apuleius has obligingly left his mark at each stop, allowing us to view his progress not in isolation but in its historical and cultural context, and providing a window into each of the main points in the transmission and reception of ancient authors.

APPENDIX 1

Ancient Readers of Apuleius (ca. 350 to ca. 550 AD)

Note: The names of certain readers are shown in boldface. The names of possible readers are preceded by a question mark. Works no longer extant are indicated with a dagger. Works not by Apuleius appear in brackets.

ca. 350	?Ausonius	Gaul	*Apol., Met.,* †*De piscibus*
ca. 355–80	?St. Zeno of Verona	N. Africa?/ Verona	*Apol., Met.*[1]
395, 397	**Sallustius**	Rome/ Constantinople	*Apol., Met., Flor.*(?)
ca. 412–25	**Augustine**	N. Africa	*DDS, Mund., Plat.*(?), *Met.*(?), [*Asclep.*]
ca. 430	?Macrobius	Africa/Rome	†*Quaestiones Conviviales, Met.*(?)
ca. 470	**Claudianus Mamertus**	Gaul	*Apol.,* †*Phaedo?*
ca. 465–80	?Sidonius Apollinaris	Gaul	†*Phaedo,* †*Quaest. Conviviales*
ca. 470–80	**Martianus Capella**	N. Africa	*Met., DDS, Mund.*
ca. 500–25	**Fulgentius**	N. Africa	*Met.,* †*Hermagoras,* †*De re publ.*

[1] For echoes from the *Met.* (12) and *Apol.* (1), see Weyman, "Studien zu Apuleius," 350–59. A smaller number of parallels appears in the *apparatus* in Löfstedt and Banterle, eds., San Zenone di Verona, *I discorsi*. See also Stramaglia, "Apuleio come auctor," 155 n. 57. The suggestion that Zeno was originally from North Africa, though attractive, cannot be demonstrated.

ca. 500	Priscian	N. Africa/ Constantinople	†*Hermagoras*,[2] †*Phaedo*,[3] †*Epitome Historiarum*,[4] †*De medicinalibus*,[5] DDS
ca. 300–500?	Scholia in Lucanum	???	*Plat.*[6]

[2] Fragments 3–7 (Beaujeu).
[3] Fragments 9–10 (Beaujeu).
[4] Fragments 11–12 (Beaujeu).
[5] Fragment 14 (Beaujeu).
[6] *De Platone* 1.1 is excerpted in the *Commenta Bernensia* on Lucan (ed. Usener, 321–23). See Klibansky and Regen, *Die Handschriften*, 34. The *Commenta* were compiled in the ninth century from earlier notes whose individual dates and pedigrees are uncertain (see Werner, "On the History of the *Commenta Bernensia*"), but it is possible that the Apuleius excerpt goes back to the fourth or fifth century.

APPENDIX 2

Manuscripts of Apuleius' *Metamorphoses*

Note: Manuscripts known to Robertson ("Manuscripts of the *Metamorphoses*") are accompanied by the letters he used to designate them. Thus: Dresden, Dc 178 (= D). Editors are listed without the titles of Apuleius' works.

1. **Bergamo: Biblioteca Civica Angelo Mai (formerly Biblioteca Comunale). MA 587 (formerly Delta 8, 23).**
   Metamorphoses.
   15th century.
   Bibliog: Cremaschi, "Codice," 369; Augello 86.

2. **Dresden: Sächsische Landesbibliothek. Dc 178 (= D).**
   Metamorphoses.
   1356.
   Formerly owned by the Library of the Cloister of San Domenico in Bologna.
   Bibliog.: Robertson, "Manuscripts," 29; Schnorr von Carolsfeld and Schmidt, *Katalog der Handschriften,* 332; Hildebrand 1:lxiii–iv; Krautter, *Philologische Methode,* 132–33.

3. **Eton: Eton College Library. Eton College 147 (= E).**
   Metamorphoses and *Florida.*
   Early 15th century.
   Owned by Bernardo Bembo.
   Contains many pen and ink drawings.
   Bibliog.: Robertson, "Manuscripts," 29; Butler, xliii; James, *Descriptive Catalogue,* 76–80; Giannetto, "I codici dell'Eton College," 230; Ker, *Medieval Manuscripts in British Libraries* 2:760.

Florence: Biblioteca Medicea-Laurenziana

4. **Laur. Plut. 29.2 (= φ).**
   Apology, Metamorphoses, Florida.
   12th–13th century.
   Annotated by Giovanni Boccaccio and Zanobi da Strada.
   Bibliog.: Robertson, "Manuscripts," 29; Butler, xxxiii–xxxiv; Bandini, *Catalogus,* vol. 2, cols. 4–5; Casamassima, *Mostra* 1:132–33; Dell'Omo, *Virgilio e il chiostro,* 161–62; Lowe, "Unique Manuscript of Apuleius' *Metamorphoses.*"

5. **Laur. Plut. 54.12 (= L2).**
   De deo Socratis, Asclepius, De dogmate Platonis, De mundo, Metamorphoses, Apology, Florida.

1425.
Scribe: Antonio di Mario. Owned by Cosimo and Piero de' Medici.
Bibliog.: Robertson, "Manuscripts," 29, 38; Butler, xxxv–xxxvi; Klibansky and Regen, *Handschriften,* 68–69; Bandini, *Catalogus,* vol. 2, cols. 652–53; Ames-Lewis, *Library and Manuscripts,* 279; de la Mare, "Cosimo and His Books," item 69 in appendix; Ullman, *Origin and Development,* 99.

6. **Laur. Plut. 54.13 (= L3).**
De deo Socratis, Asclepius, De dogmate Platonis, Metamorphoses, Apology.
Ca. 1455–65.
Scribe: Ser Benedetto. Illuminator: Francesco d'Antonio del Cherico. Owner: Piero de'Medici (contains Medici impresa).
Bibliog.: Robertson, "Manuscripts," 29; Butler, xxxvi; Klibansky and Regen, *Handschriften,* 69; Bandini, *Catalogus,* vol. 2, cols. 653–4; Ames-Lewis, *Library and Manuscripts,* 279; de la Mare, "New Research on Humanistic Scribes," 433, 490.

7. **Laur. Plut. 54.14 (= L6).**
Metamorphoses.
Early 14th century.
Bibliog.: Robertson, "Manuscripts," 29; Bandini, *Catalogus,* vol. 2, col. 654.

8. **Laur. Plut. 54.24 (= L4).**
Metamorphoses, Florida, Apology (only summary of *Apology*).
1422.
Owner: Mattia Lupi.
Bibliog.: Robertson, "Manuscripts," 29; Butler, xxxvi–xxxvii; Bandini, *Catalogus,* vol. 2, col. 679.

9. **Laur. Plut. 54.32 (= L1).**
Apology, Metamorphoses, Florida (ca. 1350).
De deo Socratis (ca. 1339–40).
Ca. 1339–40; ca. 1350.
Scribe: Giovanni Boccaccio.
Bibliog.: Robertson, "Manuscripts," 29; Butler, xxxiv–xxxv; Klibansky and Regen, *Handschriften,* 69–70; Bandini, *Catalogus,* vol. 2, col. 682; Casamassima, *Mostra* 1:152–54 and plate 37; de la Mare, *Handwriting* 1:1.26–27.

10. **Laur. Plut. 68.2 (= F).**
Apology, Metamorphoses, Florida.
Ca. 1075.
Annotated by Zanobi da Strada.
Bibliog.: Robertson, "Manuscripts," 29; Butler, xxxi–xxxiii; Bandini, *Catalogus,* vol. 2, cols. 834–36; Casamassima, *Mostra* 1:129–31; Lowe, "Unique Manuscript"; Newton, *Scriptorium and Library,* 347 and plate 54.

11. **Santa Croce 24 sin. 11 (= L5).**
Metamorphoses, Florida (incomplete).
14th century.
Scribe: Tedaldo della Casa (?).

Bibliog.: Robertson, "Manuscripts," 29; Butler, xxxvii; Bandini, *Catalogus*, vol. 4, col. 177.

12. Laur. Plut. 84.24 (= L7).

Calcidius' translation and commentary on Plato's *Timaeus, De deo Socratis, Asclepius, De Platone, Metamorphoses*, Altidius *De immortalitate animae, Expositio Santi Thomae de Aquino super Boetium de Trinitate.*

Late 15th century.

Illuminator: Attavante. Owner: Lorenzo de' Medici (contains his arms).

Bibliog.: Robertson, "Manuscripts," 29; Klibansky and Regen, *Handschriften*, 72–73; Bandini, *Catalogus*, vol. 3, cols. 253–55; Dillon Bussi and Fantoni, "Biblioteca medicea"; Gentile et al., eds., *Marsilio Ficino*, 7–8; Hankins, "Study of the *Timaeus*," 117, no. 8.

13. Leyden: Bibliotheek der Rijksuniversiteit. Oudendorpianus 34 (= δ).

Metamorphoses (lacks book 1, except for last page), *Apology.*

15th century.

Bibliog.: Robertson, "Manuscripts," 29; Butler, xliii; Hildebrand 1:lxxii.

London: British Library

14. Add. ms. 24893 (= B1).

Apology, Metamorphoses, Florida.

Middle 14th century.

Annotated by Sennucio da Bene (?).

Bibliog.: Robertson, "Manuscripts," 29; Butler, xliii–xliv; Billanovich, "L'altro stil nuovo," 24–27.

15. Burney 128 (= B2).

Metamorphoses.

14th century.

Bibliog.: Robertson, "Manuscripts," 29.

16. Harley 4838 (= B3).

Metamorphoses.

14th century.

Owned and annotated by Coluccio Salutati and Zomino of Pistoia (Sozomeno).

Bibliog.: Robertson, "Manuscripts," 29; Wright, *Fontes Harleianae*, 369; de la Mare, *Handwriting* 1:42; May, "The Prologue."

Milan: Biblioteca Ambrosiana

17. A 144 sup. (= A2).

Metamorphoses, bks. 1–2.17, commentary on Terence.

15th or 16th century.

Bibliog.: Robertson, "Manuscripts," 29; Jordan and Wool, eds., *Inventory of Western Manuscripts*, 67; Van der Vliet, "Codices Apulei Italici," 359.

18. N 180 sup. (= A1).
Apology, Metamorphoses, Florida.
Late 13th century.
Bibliog.: Robertson, "Manuscripts," 29; Butler, xxxvii; Baglio, Ferrari, and Petoletti, "Montecassino e gli umanisti," 193–94.

Naples: Biblioteca Nazionale

19. IV. D. 11 (= N2).
Metamorphoses, Florida.
Late 14th century.
Owners: Giano Parrasio, Antonio Seripando.
Bibliog.: Robertson, "Manuscripts," 29; Butler, xl; Iannellius, *Catalogus*, 116–17.

20. IV. D. 12 (= N3)
Metamorphoses, Florida (incomplete).
Late 14th century.
Owner: Alexander Bonignię.
Bibliog.: Robertson, "Manuscripts," 29; Butler, xl–xli; Iannellius, *Catalogus*, 117.

21. IV. G. 55 (= N1).
De deo Socratis, De Platone, De Mundo (1377).
Florida, Apology (extracts), *Metamorphoses* (1396).
Also: *De septem liberalium artium inventoribus* (15th c.).
1377; 1396.
Scribe of literary works: Frater Ambroxius de Verona ordininis servorum Sanctę Marię. Scribe of philosophical works: Leonardus Iudex de Quinto de Verona. Owned and annotated by Giano Parrasio. Literary works copied from Vatican Library Ottob. lat. 2091.
Bibliog.: Robertson, "Manuscripts," 29; Butler, xli; Klibansky and Regen, *Handschriften*, 91–92; Iannellius, *Catalogus*, 242–43.

22. Naples: Biblioteca Oratoriana dei Girolamini. CF.3.7 (formerly Pil. XI.VIII) (= N4).
Metamorphoses, Florida, Apology, De deo Socratis, De Platone, De mundo, Asclepius.
15th century (end).
Owner: Andrea Matteo Acquaviva, duca d'Atri. Copied from *editio princeps*.
Bibliog.: Robertson, "Manuscripts," 29; Butler, xli; Klibansky and Regen, *Handschriften*, 93; Mandarini, *Codici manoscritti*, 22, no. 4.

23. Olomouc: Státní Vědecká Knihovna. M II 58 (formerly I.IV.8).[1]
Metamorphoses, Florida, De deo Socratis.

---

[1] Not known to Robertson or Butler. I think Professor G. N. Knauer for drawing my attention to this manuscript.

Also Benvenuto de Rambaldis, *Romuleon*; Leonardo Bruni, *Oratio Heliogabali*.
15th century.
Bibliog.: Beer, "Mitteilungen," 479.

24. Oxford: Bodleian Library. Laud. lat. 55 (= O).
Metamorphoses.
Late 14th or early 15th century.
Owners: John Price (Pricaeus), William Laud. Annotated by Francesco Barbaro(?).
Bibliog.: Robertson, "Manuscripts," 29; Coxe, *Bodleian Library*, 27, 539; de la Mare, unpublished note in the Bodleian Library; Purser, "Laud's Manuscript of Apuleius," 425–37.

25. Paris: Bibliothèque Nationale. Lat. 8668 (= P).
Metamorphoses.
15th century.
Bibliog.: Robertson, "Manuscripts," 29.

26. St. Gallen: Kantonsbibliothek (Vadianische Sammlung). No. 483 (= H).
Metamorphoses, *De deo Socratis*, Theophrastus, *Tractatus de Nuptiis*, Petrarch, *Rime*.
15th century (first half).
Bibliog.: Robertson, "Manuscripts," 29; Klibansky and Regen, *Handschriften*, 106; Scarpatetti et al., *Katalog der datierten Handschriften* 3:20, 46; Scherer, *Verzeichniss der Manuscripte*, 135.

27. St. Omer: Bibliothèque Publique. No. 653 (= S).
Tractatus de Solitudine; *Metamorphoses.*
15th century (first half).
Bibliog.: Robertson, "Manuscripts," 29; *Catalogue Général des Manuscrits* 3:283–84; Lehmann, *Franciscus Modius als Handschriftenforscher*, 113–14.

28. Urbana: University of Illinois Library. Ms. 7 (MCA.2) (= U).
Apology, *Metamorphoses*, *Florida*.
1389.
Scribe: Holt de Heke d'Osnabrük (written in Rome). Owner: Salvator de Achille.
Bibliog.: Robertson 1:xlviii–xlix; De Ricci, *Census of Medieval Manuscripts* 1:699–700; Finch, *Urbana Manuscript of Apuleius*.

Vatican Library

29. Pal. lat. 1574 (= V8).
Metamorphoses.
Early 15th century.

Owners: Giannozzo Manetti, Ulrich Fugger.
Bibliog.: Robertson, "Manuscripts," 29; Pellegrin, *Manuscrits classiques latin* 2.2.233.

30. Urb. lat. 199 (= V5).

Metamorphoses, Florida, De mundo, De Platone, De deo Socratis, Pseudo-Apuleius, *Asclepius, Apology.*

15th century (Butler dates between 1474 and 1482).
Owner: Federico da Montefeltro.
Bibliog.: Robertson, "Manuscripts," 29, 38; Butler, xxxix; Klibansky and Regen, *Handschriften,* 111–12; Pellegrin, *Manuscrits classiques latins* 2.2.524–25.

31. Ottob. lat. 2047 (= V3).

Apology (1–72), *Metamorphoses* (4–11), *Florida.*

Quintilian, *Declamations;* Ovid, *Metamorphoses* (extracts); Valerius Maximus, *Facta et dicta memorabilia;* Macrobius, *Saturnalia* (1–3, 6); etc.
14th century (second half).
Owners: Cardinal Sirleto, Giovanni Angelo duke d'Altemps, Cardinal P. Ottoboni.
Bibliog.: Robertson, "Manuscripts," 29; Butler, xxxix; Pellegrin, *Manuscrits classiques latins* 1:769–70.

32. Ottob. lat. 2091 (= V4).

Florida, Apology (extracts), *Metamorphoses* to 11.28.
Chronica Pontificum; De cardinalium numero et titulis; Catalogus imperatorum Romanorum.
Ca. 1316?.
Owners: Victor Giselin, Gerhard Voss, Isaac Voss, Queen Christina of Sweden, Cardinal P. Ottoboni.
Bibliog.: Robertson, "Manuscripts," 29; Butler, xxxix–xl;. Pellegrin, *Manuscrits classiques latins* 1.785–186.

33. Vat. lat. 2193 (= V1).

De deo Socratis, Asclepius, De Platone, De mundo, Florida, Apology, Metamorphoses.

Cicero, *Pro Marcello;* Frontinus, *Strategemata;* Vegetius, *Epitoma rei militaris;* Palladius, *Opus agriculturae* (1–13); Cicero, *Pro Ligario;* Petrarch (autograph), *Observationes quaedam super agricultura.*
Before 1340/43.
Owned and annotated by Petrarch.
Bibliog.: Robertson, "Manuscripts," 29; Butler, xxxvii–xxxviii; Klibansky and Regen, *Handschriften,* 115–17; Pellegrin, *Manuscrits classiques latins* 3.1.514–17; Buonocore, *Vedere i classici,* 268–74; Tristano, "Le postille del Petrarca."

34. Vat. lat. 2194 (= V6).

Metamorphoses.
1345.

Scribe: Bartolomeo de' Bartoli. Illuminator: Il Maestro del 1346 (?).
Bibliog.: Robertson, "Manuscripts," 29, 31–32; Pellegrin, *Manuscrits classiques latins* 3.1.517–18; Buonocore, *Vedere i classici*, 267–68.

35. Vat. lat. 2195 (= V7).
Metamorphoses.
1358.
Bibliog.: Robertson, "Manuscripts," 29; Pellegrin, *Manuscrits classiques latins* 3.1.518.

36. Vat. lat. 3384 (= V2).
De deo Socratis, Asclepius, De Platone, De mundo, Apology, Metamorphoses, Florida.
14th century (second half).
Owned and annotated by Benvenuto da Imola (d. 1391), Fulvio Orsini.
Bibliog.: Robertson, "Manuscripts," 29; Butler, xxxviii–xxxix; Klibansky and Regen, *Handschriften*, 118–19.

Venice: Biblioteca Nazionale Marciana

37. Cl. 14.34 (4554) (= M2).
Metamorphoses, Florida.
1409.
Bibliog.: Robertson, "Manuscripts," 29; Butler, xlii.

38. Lat. Z 468 (1967) (= M1).
Metamorphoses (1388).
Macrobius, *Saturnalia* (1389).
1388, 1389.
Owner: Iacopo Contarini.
Bibliog.: Robertson, "Manuscripts," 29.

Wolfenbüttel: Herzog August Bibliothek

39. Gud. Lat. 30 (= G).
Metamorphoses (text lacunose; begins at *Met.* 2.6.6).
Late 14th or early 15th century.
Bibliog.: Robertson, "Manuscripts," 29; Heinemann, *Handschriften der herzoglichen Bibliothek* 9:104–5; Hildebrand 1:lxiii.

40. Gud. Lat. 172 (= g).
Metamorphoses.
14th century.
Bibliog.: Robertson, "Manuscripts," 29; Heinemann, *Handschriften der herzoglichen Bibliothek* 9:178–79; Hildebrand 1:lxi–ii.

APPENDIX 3

Extant Manuscripts of the *Metamorphoses* Written before 1400

1. Manuscripts before 1300

Florence, Biblioteca Laurenziana, Laur. Plut. 68.2 (= F)
   ca. 1075
Florence, Biblioteca Laurenziana, Laur. Plut. 29.2 (= φ)
   12th–13th century
Milan, Biblioteca Ambrosiana N 180 sup. (= A1)
   13th century (late)

2. Manuscripts between 1300 and ca. 1360

Dresden, Sächsische Landesbibliothek, Dc 178
   1356
Florence, Biblioteca Laurenziana, Plut. 54.14
   14th century (early)
Florence, Biblioteca Laurenziana, Laur. Plut. 54.32
   ca. 1339–40; ca. 1350
London, British Library, Add. ms. 24893
   before ca. 1350
Vatican, Biblioteca Apostolica Vaticana, Ottob. lat. 2091
   ca. 1316
Vatican, Biblioteca Apostolica Vaticana, Vat. lat. 2193
   before 1340/43
Vatican, Biblioteca Apostolica Vaticana, Vat. lat. 2194
   1345
Vatican, Biblioteca Apostolica Vaticana, Vat. lat. 2195
   1358

3. Manuscripts between ca. 1360 and 1400

Florence, Biblioteca Laurenziana, Santa Croce 24 sin. 11
   14th century
London, British Library, Burney 128
   14th century
London, British Library, Harley 4838
   14th century (second half)

Naples, Biblioteca Nazionale IV. D. 11
    14th century (late)
Naples, Biblioteca Nazionale IV. D. 12
    14th century (late)
Naples, Biblioteca Nazionale IV. G. 55
    1377; 1396
Urbana, University of Illinois Library, ms. 7
    1389
Vatican, Biblioteca Apostolica Vaticana, Ottob. lat. 2047
    14th century (second half)
Vatican, Biblioteca Apostolica Vaticana, Vat. lat. 3384
    14th century (second half)
Venice, Biblioteca Nazionale Marciana, cod. Lat. Z 468 (= 1967)
    1388
Wolfenbüttel, Herzog August Bibliothek, Gud. Lat. 172
    14th century

APPENDIX 4

The Florentine Connection

1. Florentine Manuscripts of the *Golden Ass* in Florentine and Other Libraries

Florence, Biblioteca Laurenziana
 Laur. Plut. 29.2 (= Φ)
 Laur. Plut. 54.12
 Laur. Plut. 54.13
 Laur. Plut. 54.14
 Laur. Plut. 54.24
 Laur. Plut. 54.32
 Laur. Plut. 68.2 (= F)
 Laur. Plut. 84.24
 Santa Croce 24 sin. 11

London, British Library
 Harley 4838

Vatican Library
 Pal. lat. 1574

2. Coluccio Salutati's Verse Prologue and Notes in British Library 4838

Fol. 134v

Prohemium	Et ego tibi sermone isto milesio	1
	Varias fabulas conseram, auresque tuas	
	Benivolas, lepido susurro permulceam.	
	Modo si papirum egiptia argutia	
	Nilotici calami inscriptam non spreveris	5
	Inspicere, et figuras fortunasque hominum	
	In alias ymagines conversas, et in	
	Se rursum mutuo nexu refectas, ut	
	Mireris exordior. Quis ille? Paucis.	
	Ymetos athica, et hitmos epyrea	10
	Et thennedos spartiaca glebe felices	
	Aeternum libris felicioribus	
	Conditae mea vetus prosapia est.	
	Ibi linguam athidem primis pueritię	
	Stipendiis merui, mox in urbe latia	15

           Advena studiorum quiritium indigenum
           Sermonem erumnabili labore, nullo
           Magistro, preeunte aggressus excolui.
           Et ecce prefamur veniam siquid
           Exotici atque forensis sermonis rudis   20
           Locutor offendero, iam hec equidem ipsa
           Vocis immutatio desultorię
           Scientiae stilo quem accessimus
           Respondet. fabulam grecam incipimus
           Lector intende letaberis.   25
                          Explicit prohemium incipit tractatus

Tessaliam nam et illic originis materne nostrę fundamenta, etc. [Met. 1.2.1]

Macrobius[1]   Hic autem autor Comicus fuit. Unde Macrobius[2] in primo
                 libro commentarii super somnio scipionis inquit [1.2.8]: *vel
                 argumenta fictis casibus amatorum referta, quibus vel multum se Arbiter exercuit, vel Apuleium nonnunquam lusisse
                 miramur.* Argumentum autem comicorum fabulas esse,
                 Cicero testis est ad herennium, ubi dicit [1.13]: *Argumentum
                 est ficta res, quę tamen fieri potuit, velut argumenta comediarum.* In libro autem inventionum primo dixit idem arpinas
                 [1.27]: *Argumentum est res ficta, quę tamen fieri potuit.*
                 huius modi apud Terentium [Andr. 51]: *Nam is postquam
                 excessit ex ephebis Sosia.* Ut satis constare possit eum comicum extitisse. Fuit autem et phylosophus, imitatione et professione platonicus ut testatur pater Augustinus,
Augustinus[3]   libro viii de Civitate dei. Ubi inquit [8.12]: *Recentiores
                 tamen phylosophi nobilissimi quibus Plato sectandus placuit,
                 noluerunt se dici perhypatheticos, aut achademicos, sed platonicos. Ex quibus sunt valde nobilitati, greci Plotinus, Iamblicus, Porphyrius. In utraque autem lingua, id est et greca
                 et latina, Apuleius afer extitit, nobilis platonicus.* Et non
                 multo post inquit [8.14]: *Apuleius tamen madaurensis platonicus. De hac re sola unum scripsit librum, cuius titulum
                 esse voluit de deo socratis.* Hec inter alia a dyvo Augustino
                 sumpsisse sufficiat, ex quibus autoris, nomen Gens patria
                 atque professio declarantur, licet in re clarissima, testes adhibendi non sint. Et eo maxime, quia et ipse idem madaurensem affirmat, cognomine Lucium. Ut Lucium Apuleium

[1] In the hand of Sozomeno.
[2] *M* on the line; *acrobius* added above the line.
[3] In the hand of Sozomeno.

madaurensem afrum, hunc autorem fuisse, manifestum sit.
Fuit etiam orator eximius. cuius orationes de magia legimus,
in defensionem uxoris compositas, quae de magicę artis
ministerio fuerat accusata. Vigintiquinque autem versus
praemittit autor etc.

Fol. 135r
Viginti quinque versus praemittit autor. Genus carminis trimetrum iambicum, constans ex sex pedibus. Excipit autem poeta licentiose pedes.
Et eos etiam ubi comuniter non solent, ut in fine spondeum. Hoc autem carmen admittit iambum unde et dicitur, omnibus locis, precipue paribus, dactilum, spondeum, anapestum, tribracum, et pyrichium atque trocheum. Metra autem alia suis pedibus et sillabis constant et dicuntur achataletica. Aliquando sillaba una deficiunt et dicuntur cataletica. Aliquando duabus et dicuntur brachicataletica. Pro maiori igitur parte sunt trimetra acataletica. Ita tamen quod [added above *tamen*] prima dictio duodecimi versus per *ae* diptongum scribenda dividatur, ut illa dispertita diptongus iambum pedem efficiat. Et in sequenti versu penultima sillaba quae est *a* de metro non abiciatur. Insuper sciendum versum xviiii esse yponatium trimetrum cataleticum quia una deficit sillaba. In antepenultimo vero versu dividitur etiam diptongus in fine illius dictionis *scientię*, ut scribi debeat *scientiae*. Penultimus autem versus etiam cataleticus est una videlicet sillaba deficiens. Ultimus vero versus dimeter est iambicus ypercataleticus, constans quatuor pedibus et una sillaba qui et alchaicus dicitur.

3. Texts of the Prologue in the Florentine Manuscripts and St. Gallen 483

	Laur. 29.2 (Φ)	Laur. 54.12	Santa Croce 24 sin. 11 Verse	Santa Croce 24 sin. 11 Prose	Harley 4838 Verse	Harley 4838 Prose	St. Gallen 483
1	at	et	et or at[1]	at	et	at	at
7	imagines	ymagines	imagines	ymagines	ymagines	imagines (corr. to ymagines)	immagines
9	accipe	accipe (added)	omitted	accipe (deleted)	omitted	omitted	omitted
10	ymettos	ymetos	ymeros	ymectos (corr. to ymetos)	ymetos	ymettos (corr. to ymetos)	ymetos
	attica	athica	athica	attica (corr. to athidei)	athica	attica	athica

3. cont.

	Laur. 29.2 (Φ)	Laur. 54.12	Santa Croce 24sin. 11 Verse	Santa Croce 24sin. 11 Prose	Harley 4838 Verse	Harley 4838 Prose	St. Gallen 483
	isthomos	hitmos? (corr. to isthomos)	hitmos	hit_mos	hitmos	istomos (corr. to isthomos)	hitimos (corr. to isthmios)
	epyrea	epyrea	epyra	epyrea	epyrea	epyrea	ephirea
11	tenaros	Tenedos (corr. to Tenaros)	tenedos	tenedos	thennedos	tenedos (corr. to thennedos)	teneros
	spartiaca	spartica	spartica	spartiaca	spartiaca	spartiaca	spartica
13	vetus	vetus	omitted	vetus	vetus	vetus	vetus
14	inquam	linguam (corr. to inqua—)	linguam	linguam	linguam	linguam	linguam
	at idem	athidem	athidem	attidem	athidem	atridem	athidem
15	stipendiis	stupendus	stipendiis	stipendiis	stipendiis	stipendiis	stipendiis
19	en ecce	et ecce	en ecce	en ecce	et ecce	en ecce	en ecce
20	ac	atque	atque	ac	atque	ac	atque
24	grecanicam	gręcam (corr. to gręcanicam	grecanicam	grecaniam	grecam	grecanicam (corr. to grecam)	grecanicam

[1] Only the "t" appears. The scribe has left a space for an intial ("a" or "e"?), which has not been filled in.

APPENDIX 5

Adlington and His Sources for *Met.* 11.1

Apuleius *Met.* 11.1.
Circa primam ferme noctis vigiliam experrectus pavore subito, video praemicantis lunae candore nimio completum orbem commodum marinis emergentem fluctibus; nanctusque opacae noctis silentiosa secreta, certus etiam summatem deam praecipua maiestate pollere resque prorsus humanas ipsius regi providentia, nec tantum pecuina et ferina, verum inanima etiam divino eius luminis numinisque nutu vegetari, ipsa etiam corpora terra caelo marique nunc incrementis consequenter augeri, nunc detrimentis obsequenter imminui, fato scilicet iam meis tot tantisque cladibus satiato et spem salutis, licet tardam, subministrante augustum specimen deae praesentis statui deprecari; confestimque discussa pigra quiete <laetus et> alacer exurgo meque protinus purificandi studio marino lavacro trado septiesque summerso fluctibus capite, quod eum numerum praecipue religionibus aptissimum divinus ille Pythagoras prodidit, deam praepotentem lacrimoso vultu sic adprecabar.

Adlington (phrasing translated from Louveau is underlined, that shared with Louveau and Michel is shown in italics)
When midnight came, that *I had slept my first sleepe, I awaked* with sodein feare, and sawe the Moone shininge bright, as when she is at the full, and seeming as though she leaped out of the Sea. *Then I thought with my self that, that was the moste secret time*, when the Goddesse Ceres had most puisance and force, consideringe that all humaine things be governed by her providence: And not onely all beastes private and tame, but also all wilde and savage beastes be under her protection: And consideringe that all bodies in the heavens, the earth, and the seas be by her encresinge motions encreased, and by her diminishinge motions diminished: as wery of all my cruell fortune and calamitie, I founde good hope and soveraigne remedie, *though it were very late*, to be delivered from all my misery, by invocation and prayer to the excellent beautie of the Goddesse: whome I sawe shininge before mine eyes, wherefore shaking of mine Assy and drowsie sleepe, I arose with a joyfull face, and moved by a great affection to purifie my selfe, *I plonged my head seven times into the water of the sea*, which number of seven is convenable and agreeable to holy and divine thinges, as the

worthy and <u>sage philosopher Pythagoras hath declared</u>. Then with a weeping contenance, I made this <u>orayson to the puissant Goddesse, saiynge</u>. . . .

2. Adlington, Louveau, and Michel
<u>When midnight came</u>:
"Quand se vint sur la minuit" (Louveau, 371)
that *I had slept my first sleepe, I awaked*:
"[Quant] ieuz faict mon premier somme ie mesveillay [en soursault]" (Michel, fol. 152r)
"que i'euz fait mon premier somme, ie m'esveillay [en sursaut]" (Louveau, 371)

<u>and seeming as though she leaped out of the Sea</u>:
"et sembloit qu'elle saillit de la mer" (Louveau, 371)

Then I thought with my self that, that was the moste secret time:
"Lors ie commencay a penser que cestoit lheure la plus secrette" (Michel, fol. 152r)
"lors ie commençay à penser que c'estoit l'heure la plus secrete" (Louveau, 371)

<u>when the Goddesse Ceres had most puisance</u>:
"ou avoit plus de puissance la [sainte] deesse Ceres" (Louveau, 371)

<u>that all humaine thinges be governed by her providence: And not onely all beastes private</u> and tame, <u>but also</u> all wilde and <u>savage beastes be under her protection</u>:
"à cause que toutes choses humaines sont gouverners par sa providence, et que non seulement toutes bestes privees et sauvages sont souz sa protection" (Louveau, 371–72)

<u>wery of</u> all my cruell <u>fortune and calamitie, I founde</u> good <u>hope and soveraigne remedie</u>:
"las de [tant de] fortunes et calamitz, trouvay une esperance, et souverain remede"
(Louveau, 372)

though it were very late:
"non obstant que ce fust bien tard" (Michel, fol. 152v)
"combien que ce fut bien tard" (Louveau, 372)

and prayer to the excellent beautie of the Goddesse: whome I sawe shininge before mine eyes:
"[Ie deliberay] de prier la magnifique beauté de la [sainte] deesse, laquelle ie voyois devant mes yeux" (Louveau, 371)

wherefore shaking off mine Assie and drowsie sleepe, I arose with a joyfull face:
"Parquoy [delaissant] mon paresseux repos ie me levay [tout gay]" (Louveau, 372)

by a great affection to purifie my selfe:
"par un grande affection [que i'avois] de me purifier" (Louveau, 372)

I plonged my head seven times into the water of the sea:
"[men allay] plonger la teste sept fois dedans leaue de la mer" (Michel, fol. 152v)
"[ie m'en allay] plonger la teste dedans l'eaue de la mer par sept fois" (Louveau, 372)

which nomber of seven is convenable and agreeable to holy and divine thinges, as the worthy and sage philosopher Pythagoras hath declared:
"lequel nombre de sept est convenables aux choses saintes, et religieuses comme a demonstré [tresbien] le sage philosophe Pythagoras"

[Then with a weeping contenance, I made this] orayson to the puissant Goddess, saiynge: "Puis [en pleurant ie me mis à faire] une telle oraison à la puissante deesse, en disant" (Louveau, 372)

Bibliography

APULEIUS

A. *Editions and Commentaries*

1. COLLECTED WORKS (BY DATE)

Opera. Giovanni Andrea Bussi, ed. Rome, 1469.
Apulei Opera omnia. G. F. Hildebrand, ed. 2 vols. Leipzig, 1842.
Apulei Madaurensis opuscula quae sunt de philosophia. A. Goldbacher, ed. Vienna, 1876.

2. APOLOGY AND FLORIDA (BY DATE)

Apologia sive Pro se de magia liber. H. E. Butler and A. S. Owen, eds. Oxford, 1914.
Apologie, Florides. Paul Vallette, ed. Belles Lettres. Paris, 1971.
Apuleius of Madauros: Pro se de magia. Vincent Hunink, ed. and comm. 2 vols. Amsterdam, 1997.
Apuleius' Florida: A Commentary. Benjamin Todd Lee, ed. and comm. Berlin, 2005.
Il filosofo e la città: Commento storico ai Florida di Apuleio. Adolfo La Rocca, ed. Rome, 2005.

3. METAMORPHOSES (BY DATE)

Commentarii a Philippo Beroaldo conditi in Asinum aureum Lucii Apuleii. Filippo Beroaldo, ed. Bologna, 1 August 1500.
Lucii Apuleii de asino aureo libri XI. Robert de Keysere, ed. Paris, 1510.
Accipe candidissime lector Philippi Beroaldi . . . in asinum aureum . . . commentaria. Johann Kierher, ed. Paris, 1512.
Metamorphoseon Libri XI. Rudolf Helm, ed. Leipzig, 1908. Reprinted *cum addendis*, Leipzig, 1931.
The Golden Ass. Latin text with William Adlington's revised translation. S. Gaselee, ed. Loeb Library ed. 2 vols. Cambridge, Mass, 1915.
Metamorphoseon Libri XI. Caesar Giarratano, ed. Turin, 1929. 2nd ed. Prepared by Paolo Frassinetti. Milan, 1961.
Apulée, Les Métamorphoses. D. S. Robertson, ed. Paul Vallette, trans. 3 vols. Belles Lettres. Paris, 1940.
Metamorfosi, o Asino d'Oro di Lucio Apuleio. Giuseppe Augello, ed. 2nd ed. Turin, 1980.
Metamorphoses. J. Arthur Hanson, ed. and trans. Loeb Library ed. 2 vols. Cambridge, Mass, 1989.
Las Metamorfosis o El Asno de Oro. Juan Martos, ed. 3 vols. Madrid, 2003.

4. METAMORPHOSES, EXCERPTS (BY DATE)

Lucii Apuleii fabulosa enarratio de nuptiis Psyche non minus theologica quam poetica. [Erfurt, ca. 1515.]

The Story of Cupid and Psyche as Related by Apuleius. Louis C. Purser, ed. London, 1910.

The Isis Book (Metamorphoses, Book XI). J. Gwyn Griffiths, ed. Leiden, 1975.

Metamorphoses (Asinus Aureus) I. Alexander Scobie, ed. Meisenheim am Glan, 1975.

Cupid and Psyche. E. J. Kenney, ed. Cambridge, 1990.

Metamorphoses IX: Text, Introduction, and Commentary. B. L. Hijmans Jr., R. Th. van der Paardt, V. Schmidt, B. Wesseling, and M. Zimmerman, eds. Groningen, 1995.

Metamorphoses X: Text, Introduction, and Commentary. M. Zimmerman, ed. Groningen, 2000.

B. Translations

Adlington, William, trans. *The xi Books of the Golden Asse.* London, 1566.

———. *The Golden Ass of Apuleius.* 1639. Reprinted in the Tudor Translations IV, with an introduction by Charles Whibley. London, 1893. Reprint, New York, 1967.

Boiardo, Matteo Maria, trans. *Apulegio volgare.* Venice, 1519.

Butler, H. E., trans. *The Apology and Florida of Apuleius of Madaura.* Oxford, 1909.

Cortegana, Diego López de, trans. *Lucio Apuleyo del Asno de Oro Corregido y Añadido.* Medina del Campo, 1543. Reprinted in Marcelino Menéndez y Pelayo, ed. *Orígenes de la Novela* IV. Nueva Biblioteca de Autores Españoles 21. Madrid, 1915.

———. *Lucio Apuleyo del Asno de Oro.* Medina del Campo, 1543. Reprinted and edited by Carlos García-Gual, ed. Madrid, 1988.

Firenzuola, Agnolo, trans. *L'Asino d'oro.* In Adriano Seroni, ed. Agnolo Firenzuola, *Opere.* Florence, 1958.

Harrison, Stephen, ed. *Apuleius: Rhetorical Works.* Stephen Harrison, John Hilton, and Vincent Hunink, trans. Oxford, 2001.

La Bouthière, George de, trans. *Metamorphose, autrement l'Asne d'or de L. Apulee de Madaure Philosophe Platonique.* Lyon, 1553.

Louveau, Jean, trans. *Luc. Apulee De l'ane dore xi livres.* Lyon, 1553, 1558.

Montlyard, Jean de, trans. *L'asne dor, ou les Metamorphoses de Luce Apulee Philosophe Platonique.* Paris, 1602.

Sieder, Johann, trans. *Ain schön lieblich auch kurtzweylig gedichte Lucii Apuleii von ainem gulden Esel.* Augsburg, 1538.

———. *Sehr liebliches, kurzweiliges, kunstliches und nüßliches Gedicht Lucii Apuleii.* Frankfurt, 1605.

Walsh, P. G., trans. *The Golden Ass.* Oxford, 1994.

OTHER PRIMARY SOURCES

"Un accessus ad Apuleio e un nuovo codice del Terzo Mitografo vaticano." Gian Carlo Garfagnini, ed. *Studi medioevali* 17 (1976): 306–62.

Alcinous. *The Handbook of Platonism.* John Dillon, trans. Oxford, 1993.
Alfanus. *Vita et Passio Sanctae Christinae.* Patrologia Latina 147. Paris, 1853. Cols. 1269–82.
L'Amour de Cupido et de Psiche, mere de Volupte: Prise des cinq & sixiesme liures de la Metamorphose de Lucius Apuleius Philosophe; Nouuellement historiée, & exposée tant en vers Italiens, que Françoys. Jean Maugin, ed. Paris, 1546.
L'Amour de Cupido et de Psiché, mere de Volupté: Prise des cinq & sixiesme liures de la Metamorphose de Lucius Apuleius philosophe; Nouuellement historiée, et exposée en vers François. Claude Chappuys and Jean Maugin, eds. Léonard Gaultier, engraver. Paris, 1586. Reedited by Ruth Calder. New York, 1970.
Anastasios of Sinai. *Quaestiones.* Patrologia Graeca 89. Paris, 1888. Cols. 311–824.
Arienti, Giovanni Sabadino degli. *De triumphis religionis.* See Gundersheimer, *Art and Life at the Court of Ercole I d'Este.*
Augustine, Aurelius. *De civitate dei.* Basel, 1479. (Goff A-1241; GKW 2885.)
———. *S. Aureli Augustini De Civitate Dei.* Corpus Christianorum 47–48. Turnholt, 1955.
———. *S. Aureli Augustini Hipponiensis Episcopi Epistulae.* A. Goldbacher, ed. Corpus Scriptorum Ecclesiasticorum Latinorum 34.2. Vienna, 1898.
———. *S. Aureli Augustini Hipponiensis Episcopi Epistulae.* A. Goldbacher, ed. Corpus Scriptorum Ecclesiasticorum Latinorum 44. Vienna, 1904.
Bartoli, Bartolomeo di. *La Canzone delle Virtù e delle Scienze.* Leone Dorez, ed. Bergamo, 1904.
Bayle, Pierre. *Dictionnaire historique et critique.* Nouvelle édition. Paris, 1820.
Benvenuto da Imola. *Comentum super Dantis Aldigherii Comoediam.* G. F. Lacaita, ed. 5 vols. Florence, 1887.
Benzo of Alessandria. *Il "Chronicon" di Benzo d'Alessandria e i classici latini all'inizio del XIV secolo.* Marco Petoletti, ed. Milan, 2000.
Beroaldo, Filippo. *Annotationes centum.* Lucia A. Ciapponi, ed. Binghamton, N.Y., 1995.
———. *Commentarii a Philippo Beroaldo conditi in Asinum aureum Lucii Apuleii.* Bologna, 1 August 1500.
———. *Commentarii Questionum Tusculanarum.* Bologna, 1496.
———. "Oratio habita in narratione Lucii Apuleii." In *Orationes et poemata.* Bologna, 1500. Fols. m7v–n1v.
———. *Orationes et poemata.* Bologna, 1500.
———. *Oratio proverbiorum.* Bologna, 1499.
Bianchini, Bartolomeo. *Philippi Beroaldi vita.* In *Commentationes conditae a Philippo Beroaldo in Suetonium Tranquillum.* Bologna, 1506. Reprint, Venice, 1522.
Boccaccio, Giovanni. *Boccaccio on Poetry.* Charles G. Osgood, ed. and trans. Princeton, 1930.
———. *Decameron.* Vittore Branca, ed. Vol. 4 in Vittore Branca, ed., *Tutte le opere di Giovanni Boccaccio.* Milan, 1976.
———. *Esposizioni sopra La Comedia di Dante.* Giorgio Padoan, ed. Vol. 6 in Vittore Branca, ed., *Tutte le opere di Giovanni Boccaccio.* Milan, 1965.
———. *Genealogie deorum gentilium.* Vittorio Zaccaria, ed. Vols. 7–8 in Vittore Branca, ed., *Tutte le opere di Giovanni Boccaccio.* Milan, 1998.

———. *Genealogie deorum gentilium libri.* Vincenzo Romano, ed. 2 vols. Bari, 1951.

———. *Opere in versi: Corbaccio; Trattatello in laude di Dante. Prose latine. Epistole.* Pier Giorgio Ricci, ed. Milan, [1965].

———. *Opere latine minori.* Aldo Francesco Massèra, ed. Bari, 1928.

———. *Teseida delle nozze d'Emilia, Comedia delle ninfe fiorentine, etc.* Alberto Limentani, ed. Vol. 2 in Vittore Branca, ed., *Tutte le opere di Giovanni Boccaccio.* Milan, 1992.

Boethius. *De institutione arithmetica, De institutione musica.* G. Friedlein, ed. Leipzig, 1867.

———. *Fundamentals of Music: Anicius Manlius Severinus Boethius.* Calvin M. Bower, trans. New Haven, 1989.

Boiardo, Matteo Maria. *Apulegio volgare.* Venice, 1519.

———. *L'Inamoramento de Orlando.* Antonio Tissoni Benvenuti e Cristina Montagnani, eds. 2 vols. Milan, 1999.

———. *Opere di Matteo Maria Boiardo.* Ferruccio Ulivi, ed. Milan, 1986.

———. *Orlando Innamorato.* Charles Stanley Ross, trans. Berkeley, 1989.

———. *Tarocchi.* Simona Foà, ed. Rome, 1993.

Bracciolini, Poggio. *Lettere: Epistolarum familiarium libri.* Helene Harth, ed. 3 vols. Florence, 1984–87.

———. *Opera.* Strassburg, 1513.

———. *Opera omnia.* Basel, 1538. Reprinted in 4 vols. Riccardo Fubini, ed. Turin, 1964–69.

———. *Two Renaissance Book Hunters: The Letters of Poggius Bracciolini to Nicolaus de Niccolis.* Phyllis Goodhart Gordan, trans. New York, 1974.

Burley, Walter. *Gualteri Burlaei Liber de vita et moribus philosophorum.* Hermann Knust, ed. Bibliothek des litterarischen Vereins in Stuttgart 177. Tübingen, 1886.

Bussi, Giovanni Andrea de'. *Prefazioni alle edizioni di Sweynheym e Pannartz prototipografi romani.* Massimo Miglio, ed. Rome, 1978.

Catullus. *Carmina.* R.A.B. Mynors, ed. Oxford, 1958.

Claudian. *Claudii Claudiani Carmina.* John Barrie Hall, ed. Leipzig, 1985.

Colonna, Francesco. *Hypnerotomachia Polifili.* Giovanni Pozzi and Lucia E. Ciapponi, eds. 2 vols. Padua, 1964.

Commenta Bernensia. See Lucan.

"Conquestio uxoris Cavichioli." In Ezio Franceschini, ed., "Due testi latini inediti del basso medioevo." In *Scritti di filologia latina medievale* 1.205–29. Reprinted from *Atti e Memorie della Reale Accademia di Scienze, Lettere, ed Arte in Padova.* N.s. 54 (1937–38), 61–88.

Corpus Hermeticum. A. D. Nock and A.-J. Festugière, eds. 2 vols. Paris, 1945.

Correggio, Niccolò da. *Fabula Psiches et Cupidinis.* In Antonia Tissoni Benvenuti, ed., Niccolò da Correggio, *Opere.* (= *Scrittori d'Italia* 244.) Bari, 1969. 47–96.

Dante Alighieri. *The Divine Comedy.* Allen Mandelbaum, trans. New York, 1995.

———. *The Divine Comedy of Dante Alighieri.* Charles S. Singleton, ed. 3 vols. Princeton, 1970–75.

Degrassi, A. *Inscriptiones Italiae*. Vol. 13, *Fasti et elogia*, fasc. 2, *Fasti Anni Numani et Iuliani*. Rome, 1963.
Del Carretto, Galeotto. *Noze de Psiche e Cupidine*. In Antonia Tissoni Benvenuti and Maria Pia Mussini Sacchi, eds. *Teatro del Quattrocento: Le corti padane*. Turin, 1983. 611–725.

———. *Tempio d'amore*. Franco Magnani, intro., and Cristina Caramaschi, ed. Rome, 1997.

"The *De Monarchia* Attributed to Apuleius." Benjamin G. Kohl and Nancy G. Siraisi, eds. *Mediaevalia* 7 (1981):1–39.
Eusebius. *Contre Hiéroclès*. Marguerite Forrat, ed. Paris, 1986.
Ficino, Marsilio. *Commentaire sur le Banquet de Platon, de Amore*. Pierre Laurens, ed. and trans. Belles Lettres. Paris, 2002.

———. *Lettere*. Vol. 1, *Epistolarum familiarium liber 1*. Sebastiano Gentile, ed. Florence, 1990.

———. *Omnia divini Platonis opera tralatione Marsilii Ficini emendatione, et ad graecum codicem collatione Simonis Grynaei*. Lyon, 1548.

———. *Opera omnia*. 2 vols. in 4. Basel, 1576. Reprint, Turin, 1959.

———. *Platonic Theology*. Michael J. B. Allen and James Hankins, eds. I Tatti Renaissance Library. 6 vols. Cambridge, Mass., 2001–6.

The Fragmentary Latin Poets. Edward Courtney, ed. Oxford, 1993.
Fulgentius. *Fabii Planciadis Fulgentii V. C. Opera*. Rudolf Helm, ed. Leipzig, 1898.

———. *Fulgentius the Mythographer*. Leslie George Whitbread, trans. Columbus, Ohio, 1971.

———. *Mitologiae*. Milan, 1498.

Glossaria latina. Vol. 3. J. W. Pirie and W. M. Lindsay, eds. Paris, 1930.
Glossaria latina. Vol. 4. W. M. Lindsay and H. J. Thomson, eds. Paris, 1926.
Gsell, Stefane, ed. *Inscriptions latines de l'Algerie*. 2 vols. Paris, 1922.
Guaiferius. *S. Lucii Papae et Martyris Vita*. Patrologia latina 147:1301–10.

———. *Vita Sancti Secundini*. Patrologia latina 147. Paris, 1853. Cols. 1293–1302.

Guglielmo da Pastrengo. *De viris illustribus et De originibus*. Guglielmo Bottari, ed. Padua, 1991.
Harnack, Adolf von. "Porphyrius 'Gegen die Christen': 15 Bücher, Zeugnisse, Fragmente, und Referate." In *Abhandlungen der königlich preussischen Akademie der Wissenschaften*. Vol. 1. Berlin, 1916. 1–115.
Jerome. *Contra Rufinum*. In *S. Hieronymi Presbyteri Opera*. Part 3. Corpus Christianorum, vol. 79. Turnholt, 1982.

———. *Commentariorum in Esaiam Libri XII–XVIII*. In *S. Hieronymi Presbyteri Opera*. Part 1. Corpus Christianorum, vol. 73A. Turnholt, 1963.

———. *Tractatus de Psalmo lxxxi*. In *S. Hieronymi Presbyteri Opera*. Part 2. Corpus Christianorum, vol. 78. Turnholt, 1958.

Lactantius. *De Mortibus Persecutorum*. J. L. Creed, ed. Oxford, 1984.

———. *Divine Institutes*. Anthony Bowen and Peter Garnsey, trans. Translated Texts for Historians, vol. 40. Liverpool, 2003.

———. *Institutions divines, Livre V*. Pierre Monat, ed. Sources chrétiennes, 204–5. Paris, 1973.

Lucan, scholia to. *Scholia in Lucani Bellum Civile. Pars prior. Commenta Bernensia*. Hermann Usener, ed. Leipzig, 1869.
Pseudo-Lucian. *Asinus Aureus*. Poggio Bracciolini, trans. [Augsburg, ca. 1477].
———. *Der guldin Esel*. Niklas von Wyle, trans. [Augsburg], ca. 1477–78.
———. Facsimile of [Augsburg, 1477–78]. E. Weil, ed. Munich, 1922.
———. *Lucius, or The Ass*. M. D. Macleod, trans. In *Lucian* 8. Loeb Classical Library. Cambridge, Mass., 1967.
———. See Wyle. *Translationen*.
Lydus, John. *De mensibus*. Richard Wuensch, ed. Leipzig, 1898.
Macrobius. *Commentarii in Somnium Scipionis*. J. Willis, ed. Leipzig, 1970.
———. *Commentary on the Dream of Scipio*. William Harris Stahl, trans. New York, 1952.
Manetti, Gianozzo. *Biographical Writings*. Stefano U. Baldassarri and Rolf Bagemihl, eds. I Tatti Renaissance Library. Cambridge, Mass., 2003.
———. *Vita Socratis et Senecae*. Alfonso De Petris, ed. Florence, 1979.
Martianus Capella. *De Nuptiis Philologiae et Mercurii*. James Willis, ed. Leipzig, 1983.
———. *Martiani Capellae De Nuptiis Philologiae et Mercurii Liber Secundus*. Luciano Lenaz, ed. Padua, 1975.
Melanchthon, Philipp, and Martin Luther. *Deutung der zwo greulichen Figuren Bapstesels zu Rome und Mönchkalbs zu Freiberg in Meissen funden*. In *D. Martin Luthers Werke. Kritische Gesamtausgabe*, 70 vols. Weimar, 1883–. 11.357–85.
Petrarca, Francesco. *Le familiari* [*Familiarium rerum libri*]. Vittorio Rossi, ed. Vol. 4 edited by Rossi and Umberto Bosco. 4 vols. Florence, 1933–1942.
Opera latina. Venice, 1501.
Opera quae extant omnia. Basel, 1581.
———. *Rerum memorandarum libri*. Giuseppe Billanovich, ed. Florence, 1943.
Philip the Philosopher. Τῆς Χαρικλείας ἑρμήνευμα τῆς σώφρονος ἐκ φωνῆς Φιλίππου τοῦ φιλοσόφου. R. Hercher, ed. *Hermes* 3 (1869): 382–88.
———. *Commentatio in Charicleam*. Aristides Colonna, ed. In *Heliodori Aethiopica*. Rome, 1938. 365–70.
Philostratus. *The Life of Apollonius of Tyana*. Christopher P. Jones, trans. 2 vols. Loeb Classical Library. Cambridge, Mass., 2005.
———. *Apollonius of Tyana. Letters of Apollonius. Ancient Testimonia. Eusebius' Reply to Hierocles*. Christopher P. Jones, trans. Loeb Classical Library. Cambridge, Mass., 2006.
Pins, Jean de. *Divae Catherinae Senensis simul et clarissimi viri Philippi Beroaldi Bononiensis vita*. Bologna, 1505. *Philippi Beroaldi vita* reprinted in J. G. Meuschen, ed. *Vitae summorum dignitate et eruditione virorum*, Coburg, 1735. 1:123–51.
Porphyry. See Harnack. "Porphyrius 'Gegen die Christen.'"
Proclus. *Alcibiades I. A Translation and Commentary*. William O'Neill, trans. The Hague, 1965.
———. *Sur le premier Alcibiade de Platon*. A. Ph. Segonds, ed. and trans. 2 vols. Belles Lettres. Paris, 1986.

Psellos, Michael. *Philosophica minora*. Vol. 1. John Duffy, ed. Leipzig, 1992.
———. *Scripta minora*. Vol. 2, *Epistulae*. Eduardus Kurtz, ed. Milan, 1941.
Pseudo-Lucian. See Lucian.
Pseudo-Theodorus. *Additamenta Pseudo-Theodori ad Theodorum Priscianum*. Valentino Rose, ed. Leipzig, 1894.
PSI (Pubblicazioni della Società italiana per la ricerca dei Papiri greci e latini in Egitto). *Papiri greci e latini*. Vol. 8. Florence, 1927.
Saint-Gelais, Mellin de. *Oeuvres poétiques françaises*. Donald Stone Jr., ed. 2 vols. Paris, 1993.
Sallustius. *Concerning the Gods and the Universe*. Arthur Darby Nock, ed. Cambridge, 1926.
Salutati, Coluccio. *De fato et fortuna*. Concetta Bianca, ed. Florence, 1985.
———. *De laboribus Herculis*. B. L. Ulllman, ed. 2 vols. Zurich, 1951.
Schedel, Hartmann. *Liber chronicarum*. Nuremberg, 1493.
———. *Chronicle of the World: The Complete and Annotated Nuremberg Chronicle of 1493*. With an introduction and appendix by Stephan Füssel. Cologne, Tokyo, 2001.
Sidonius Apollinaris. *Sidoine Apollinaire, Lettres*. André Loyen, ed. Belles Lettres. Paris, 1970.
Symmachus. *Lettres*. Jean-Pierre Callu, ed. and trans. 4 vols. Belles Lettres. Paris, 1972–.
Theodorus Priscianus. *Euporiston*. Valentino Rose, ed. Leipzig, 1894.
Trebizond, Andreas. "Platonis accusatio." In F. A. Zaccaria, ed. *Iter litterarium per Italiam*. Venice, 1762. 126–34.
Trebizond, George of. *Collectanea Trapezuntiana: Texts, Documents, and Bibliographies of George of Trebizond*. John Monfasani, ed. Medieval and Renaissance Texts and Studies, vol. 25. Binghamton, N.Y., 1984.
Valla, Lorenzo. *Opera*. Basel, 1540. Reprint. E. Garin, ed. 2 vols. Turin, 1962.
Vespasiano da Bisticci. *Le vite: Edizione critica con introduzione e commento di Aulo Greco*. 2 vols. Florence, 1970–76.
Waleys, Thomas. Commentary on Augustine, *De civitate Dei*. In Augustine, *De civitate Dei*. Basel, 1479.
Wyle, Niklas von. *Translationen*. Adelbert von Keller, ed. Bibliothek des litterarischen Vereins in Stuttgart 57. Stuttgart, 1861.
Zenone di Verona, San. *I Discorsi*. Bengt Löfstedt and Gabriele Banterle, eds. Milan, 1987.

SECONDARY SOURCES

Abt, Adam. *Die Apologie des Apuleius von Madaura und die antike Zauberei*. Giessen, 1908.
Acconcia Longo, Augusta. "Filippo il filosofo a Costantinopoli." *Rivista di studi bizantini e neoellenici* 28 (1991): 3–21.
Acocella, Mariantonietta. *L'Asino d'oro nel rinascimento: Dai volgarizzamenti alle raffigurazioni pittoriche*. Ravenna, 2001.

Alexander, Jonathan. *Medieval Illuminators and Their Method of Work.* New Haven, Conn., 1992.

———, ed. *The Painted Page: Italian Renaissance Book Illumination, 1450–1550.* Munich, 1994.

Alföldi, András [Andreas]. *A Festival of Isis in Rome under the Christian Emperors of the IVth Century.* Dissertationes Pannonicae ex Instituto Numismatico et Archaeologico Universitatis de Petro Pázmány Nominatae Budapestinensis Provenientes. Ser. 2, fasc. 7. Budapest, 1937.

———. "Die alexandrinischen Götter und die *Vota Publica* am Jahresbeginn." *Jahrbuch für Antike und Christentum* 8–9 (1965–66): 53–87.

———. *Die Kontorniaten: Ein verkanntes Propagandamittel der stadtrömischen heidnischen Aristokratie in ihrem Kampfe gegen das christliche Kaisertum.* Budapest, 1943.

Alföldi, Andreas and Elisabeth. *Die Kontorniat-Medaillons.* 2 vols. in 3. Berlin, 1976.

Alimonti, Terenzio. "Apuleio e l'arcaismo in Claudiano Mamerto." In *Forma futuri: Studi in onore del cardinale Michele Pellegrino.* Turin, 1975. 189–228.

———. *Struttura, ideologia ed imitazione virgiliana nel "De mortibus boum" di Endelechio.* Turin, 1976.

Ames-Lewis, Francis. *The Library and Manuscripts of Piero di Cosimo de' Medici.* New York, 1984.

Anderson, Graham. *The Second Sophistic: A Cultural Phenomenon in the Roman Empire.* London, 1993.

Anselmi, Gian Mario. "Mito classico e allegoresi mitologica tra Beroaldo e Codro." In *Le frontiere degli umanisti.* Bologna, 1988. 13–51.

Arfé, Pasquale. "The Annotations of Nicholas Cusanus and Giovanni Andrea Bussi on the *Asclepius.*" *Journal of the Warburg and Courtauld Institute* 62 (1999): 29–59.

Armstrong, Elizabeth. "Notes on the Works of Guillaume Michel, dit de Tours." *Bibliothèque de l'Humanisme et Renaissance* 31 (1969): 257–81.

Augello, Giuseppe. See Apuleius, *Metamorfosi* in "Apuleius A.3."

Baglio, Marco, Mirella Ferrari, and Marco Petoletti. "Montecassino e gli umanisti." In G. Avarucci, R. M. Borraccini Verducci, and G. Borri, eds. *Libro, scrittura, documento della civiltà monastica e conventuale nel basso Medioevo (secoli XIII–XV): Atti del convegno di studio, Fermo (17–19 settembre 1997).* Spoleto, 1999. 183–238.

Bajoni, Maria Grazia. "La novella del *dolium* in Apuleio *Metamorfosi* IX, 5–7 e in Boccaccio, *Decameron* VII, 2." *Giornale storico della letteratura italiana* 171 (1994): 217–25.

Balsamo, L. "I primordi della tipografia in Italia e Inghilterra." *La bibliofilia* 79 (1977): 321–62.

Bandini, Angelo Maria. *Catalogus codicum latinorum Bibliotecae Mediceae Laurentianae.* 4 vols. Florence, 1777.

Barnes, Timothy D. *Constantine and Eusebius.* Cambridge, Mass., 1981.

———. "Porphyry *Against the Christians*: Date and the Attribution of Fragments." *Journal of Theological Studies* 24 (1973): 424–42.

Barnes, Timothy D. "Scholarship or Propaganda? Porphyry *Against the Christians* and Its Historical Setting." *Bulletin of the Institute of Classical Studies of the University of London* 39 (1994): 53–65.

———. "Sossianus Hierocles and the Antecedents of the 'Great Persecution.'" *Harvard Studies in Classical Philology* 80 (1976): 239–52.

———. *Tertullian: A Literary and Historical Study*. Oxford, 1971.

Bartoli, Cecilia. "Bartolomeo Cavaceppi famoso scarpellino e i restauri per il Museo Sacro di Benedetto XIV." In Maria Giulia Barberini and Carlo Gasparri, eds. *Bartolomeo Cavaceppi scultore romano (1717–1799)*. Rome, 1994. 36–50.

Baskins, Cristelle L. *Cassone Painting, Humanism, and Gender in Early Modern Italy*. Cambridge, 1998.

Bassett, Sarah. "*Historiae custos*: Sculpture and Tradition in the Baths of Zeuxippos." *American Journal of Archaeology* 100 (1996): 491–506.

———. *The Urban Image of Late Antique Constantinople*. Cambridge, 2004.

Bassi, Eleonora. "Amore e Psyche." In *Dai papiri della Società Italiana: Omaggio al XX Congresso Internazionale di Papirologia. Copenhagen, 23–29 Agosto 1992*. Florence, 1992. 93–96, plate 12.

Bataillon, Marcel. *Érasme et l'Espagne*. Nouvelle édition en trois volumes. Charles Amiel, ed. Geneva, 1991.

Baxandall, Michael, and E. H. Gombrich. "Beroaldus on Francia." *Journal of the Warburg and Courtauld Institute* 25 (1962): 113–15.

Bechtle, Gerald. "The Adultery Tales in the Ninth Book of Apuleius' *Metamorphoses*." *Hermes* 123 (1995): 106–16.

Beck, Hans-Georg. *Kirche und theologische Literatur im byzantinischen Reich*. Munich, 1959.

Beck, Roger. "Apuleius the Novelist, Apuleius the Ostian Householder and the Mithraeum of the Seven Spheres: Further Explorations of an Hypothesis of Filippo Coarelli." In Stephen G. Wilson and Michel Desjardins, eds. *Text and Artifact in the Religions of Mediterranean Antiquity: Essays in Honour of Peter Richardson*. Waterloo, Ont., 2000. 551–67.

Beer, Rudolf. "Mitteilungen über die Kaiserliche Königliche Studienbibliothek zu Olmütz." *Centralblatt für Bibliothekswesen* 7 (1890): 474–81.

Benoit, A. "Le 'Contra Christianos' de Porphyre: Où en est la collecte des fragments?" In *Paganisme, Judaïsme, Christianisme: Influences et affrontements dans le monde antique*. Mélanges offerts à Marcel Simon. Paris, 1978. 261–75.

Beroaldo, Filippo. See *Commentarii* in "Apuleius A.3."

Bianca, Concetta. "La biblioteca romana di Niccolò Cusano." In Massimo Miglio et al., eds. *Scrittura biblioteche e stampa a Roma nel Quattrocento*. Atti del 2° Seminario, 6–8 maggio 1982. Città del Vaticana, 1983. 669–708.

———. *Da Bisanzio a Roma: Studi sul Cardinale Bessarione*. Rome, 1999.

———. "Roma e l'accademia bessarionea." In Fiaccadori et al., eds. *Bessarione e l'Umanesimo*. 119–27. Reprinted in Bianca. *Da Bisanzio a Roma*. 19–41.

Bianchini, Bartolomeo. "Philippi Beroaldi vita per Bartholomeum Bianchinum Bononiensem condita ad Camillum Palaettum." In Filippo Beroaldo. *Com Bietenholz mentationes in Suetonium Tranquillum*. Venice 1522. BB4r–v.

Bietenholz, Peter G., and Thomas B. Deutscher, eds. *Contemporaries of Erasmus*. 3 vols. Toronto, 1985–87.

Bigi, E. and A. Petrucci. "Poggio Bracciolini." *Dizionario biografico degli Italiani* 13 (1971): 640–46.

Billanovich, Giuseppe. "L'altro stil nuovo: Da Dante teologo a Petrarca filologo." *Studi petrarcheschi* 11 (1994): 1–98.

———. "Petrarca e i libri della cattedrale di Verona." In Giuseppe Billanovich and Giuseppe Frasso, eds. *Petrarca, Verona e l'Europa: Atti del convegno internazionale di studi (Verona, 19–23 sett. 1991)*. Padua, 1997. 117–78.

———. *Petrarca letterato*. Rome, 1947.

———. "Petrarch and the Textual Tradition of Livy." *Journal of the Warburg and Courtauld Institute* 14 (1951): 137–208.

———. "Pietro Piccolo da Monteforte tra il Petrarca e il Boccaccio." In *Medioevo e Rinascimento: Studi in onore di Bruno Nardi*. 2 vols. Florence, 1955. 1:3–76.

———. *I primi umanisti e le tradizioni dei classici latini*. Freiburg, 1953. Reprinted in *Petrarca e il primo umanesimo*, 117–41. Padua, 1996.

———. "Quattro libri del Petrarca e la biblioteca della cattedrale di Verona." *Studi petrarcheschi* 7 (1990): 33–62.

———. "Zanobi da Strada tra i tesori di Montecassino." *Atti dell'accademia nazionale dei Lincei, Rendiconti di scienze morali, storiche, e filologiche*, s. 9.7 (1996): 653–63.

Billanovich, Guido. "Petrarca e il Catullo di Verona." In Giuseppe Billanovich and Giuseppe Frasso, eds. *Petrarca, Verona e l'Europa: Atti del convegno internazionale di studi (Verona, 19–23 sett. 1991)*. Padua, 1997. 179–220.

Binder, Gerhard, and Reinhold Merkelbach, eds. *Amor und Psyche*. Darmstadt, 1968.

Bitel, A. P. "*Quis ille Asinus aureus*? The Metamorphoses of Apuleius' Title." *Ancient Narrative* 1 (2000–2001): 209–44.

Bloch, Herbert. "Monte Cassino's Teachers and Library in the High Middle Ages." In *La scuola nell'Occidente latino dell'alto medioevo*. Settimane di studio del Centro italiano di studi sull'alto medioevo 19. Spoleto, 1972. 563–613.

———. "A New Document of the Last Pagan Revival in the West, 393–394 A.D." *Harvard Theological Review* 38 (1945): 199–244.

———. "The Pagan Revival in the West at the End of the Fourth Century." In A. Momigliano, ed. *The Conflict between Paganism and Christianity in the Fourth Century*. Oxford, 1963. 193–226.

Bode, Wilhelm von. "Zwei Cassone-Tafeln aus dem Besitz des Piero de' Medici in der Sammlung Eduard Simon zu Berlin." *Mitteilungen des kunsthistorische Institut zu Florenz* 5–6 (1917): 149–51.

Bonilla y San Martín, Adolfo. "Advertencia." In *Origenes de la Novela* 4:149–51. Nueva Biblioteca de Autores Españoles 21. Madrid, 1915.

———. *Erasmo en España*. New York, 1907. Extract from *Revue hispanique* 17.

Boorsch, Suzanne, ed. *The Illustrated Bartsch 29: Italian Masters of the Sixteenth Century*. New York, 1982.

Bottari, Guglielmo. See Guglielmo da Pastrengo in "Other Primary Sources."
Bower, Calvin. "Boethius' *De institutione musica*: A Handlist of Manuscripts." *Scriptorium* 42 (1988): 205–51.
Bowie, Ewen. "Apollonius of Tyana: Tradition and Reality." *Aufstieg und Niedergang der römischen Welt* II.16.2. Berlin, 1978. 1652–99.
———. "The Importance of Sophists." *Yale Classical Studies* 27 (1982): 29–59.
———. "The Readership of Greek Novels in the Ancient World." In James Tatum, ed. *The Search for the Ancient Novel*. Baltimore, 1994. 435–59.
Bradley, Keith. "Law, Magic, and Culture in the *Apologia* of Apuleius." *Phoenix* 51 (1997): 203–23.
———. "Apuleius and Carthage." *Ancient Narrative* 4 (2004): 1–29.
Branca, Vittore. *Giovanni Boccaccio: Profilo biografico*. Florence, 1977.
Brancaleone, Francesca. *Citazioni "apuleiane" nel Cornu copiae di Niccolò Perotti*. Genoa, 2000.
Brenk, F. E. "Demonology in the Early Imperial Period." *Aufstieg und Niedergang der römischen Welt* II.16.3. Berlin, New York, 1986. 2068–45.
Brink, C. O. *Horace on Poetry: Epistles Book II; The Letters to Augustus and Florus*. Cambridge, 1982.
Brown, Peter. "Aspects of the Christianization of the Roman Aristocracy." *Journal of Roman Studies* 51 (1961): 1–11. (= *Religion and Society in the Age of St. Augustine*, 162–82.)
Brown, Virginia. "Portraits of Julius Caesar in Latin Manuscripts of the *Commentaries*." *Viator* 12 (1981): 319–54.
Brugnoli, G. "Le statue di Apuleio." *Annali della Facoltà di lettere e filosofia della Università di Cagliari* 29 (1961–65): 11–25.
Brun, Robert. *Le livre français illustré de la Renaissance*. Paris, 1969.
Bruscagli, Riccardo. "Matteo Maria Boiardo." In Enrico Malato, ed. *Storia della letteratura italiana*. Vol. 3, *Il Quattrocento*. Rome, 1995. 635–708.
Buck, Lawrence. "The Roman Monster of 1496. Paper presented at Sixteenth Century Society Conference. October 2005.
Bühler, Curt F. *The University and the Press in Fifteenth-Century Bologna*. Notre Dame, Ind., 1958.
Buonocore, Marco, ed. *Vedere i classici: L'illustrazione libraria dei testi antichi dall'età romana al tardo medioevo*. [Rome], 1996.
Buresch, Karl. *Klaros: Untersuchungen zum Orakelwesen des späteren Altertums*. Leipzig, 1889.
Burger, Konrad. *Buchhändleranzeigen des 15. Jahrhunderts*. Leipzig, 1907.
Butler, H. E. See in "Apuleius A.2." *Apologia*.
Calder, Ruth. See *L'Amour de Cupido et de Psiché*, 1586, in "Other Primary Sources."
Callmann, Ellen. "Subjects from Boccaccio in Italian Painting." *Studi sul Boccaccio* 23 (1995): 19–78.
Calvesi, Maurizio. *La "Pugna d'Amore in Sogno" di Francesco Colonna Romano*. Rome, 1996.
Cameron, Alan. *Claudian: Poetry and Propaganda at the Court of Honorius*. Oxford, 1970.

———. "The Date and Identity of Macrobius." *Journal of Roman Studies* 56 (1966): 25–38.

———. "The Latin Revival of the Fourth Century." In W. Treadgold, ed. *Renaissances before the Renaissance: Cultural Revivals of Late Antiquity and the Middle Ages*. Stanford, Calif., 1984. 2–58.

———. "Paganism and Literature in Late Fourth Century Rome." In *Christianisme et formes littéraires de l'antiquité tardive en occident*. Entretiens Hardt 23. Geneva, 1977. 1–30.

———. "Rutilius Namatianus, St. Augustine, and the Date of the *De Reditu*." *Journal of Roman Studies* 57 (1967): 31–39.

Cartier, Alfred. *Bibliographie des editions des de Tournes, imprimeurs Lyonnais*. Marius Audin, ed. 2 vols. Paris, 1937. Slatkine Reprint. Geneva, 1970.

Carver, Robert H. F. "*Quis ille*? The Role of the Prologue in Apuleius' Nachleben." In Ahuvia Kahane and Andrew Laird, eds. *A Companion to the Prologue of Apuleius' Metamorphoses*. Oxford, 2001. 163–74.

———. "The Rediscovery of the Latin Novels." In Heinz Hofmann, ed. *Latin Fiction: The Latin Novel in Context*. London, 1999. 253–68.

———. "'True Histories' and 'Old Wives' Tales': Renaissance Humanism and the 'Rise of the Novel.'" *Ancient Narrative* 1 (2000–2001): 322–49.

Casamassima, Emanuele. "Dentro lo scrittoio del Boccaccio: I codici della tradizione." In Aldo Rossi, ed. *Il Decameron: Pratiche testuali e interpretative*. Bologna, 1982. 253–60.

———. *Mostra*. See *Mostra*.

Casciano, Paola. "Il MS. Angelicano 1097, fase preparatoria per l'edizione del Plinio di Sweynheym e Pannartz (Hain 13088)." In Concetta Bianca et al., eds. *Scrittura, biblioteche e stampa a Roma nel Quattrocento: Aspetti e problemi*. Littera antiqua 1. 2 vols. Vatican City, 1980. 1:384–94.

Casella, Maria Teresa. "Il metodo dei commentatori umanistici esemplato sul Beroaldo." *Studi medievali* 16 (1975): 627–701.

Casnati, G. "Tedaldo della Casa." *Dizionario biografico degli Italiani* 36 (1998): 723–25.

Cast, David. "Review of Werner L. Gundersheimer, *Art and Life at the Court of Ercole I d'Este*." *Art Bulletin* 57 (1975): 278–83.

Catalogue général des manuscrits des bibliothèques publiques des départements. Vol. 3. Paris 1861.

Cavallo, Guglielmo. "La circolazione libraria nell'età di Giustiniano." In G. G. Archi, ed. *L'imperatore Giustiniano: Storia e Mito, Giornate di studio a Ravenna, 14–16 ottobre 1976*. Milan, 1978. 201–36.

———. "La trasmissione dei testi nell'area beneventano-cassinese." In *La cultura antica nell'Occidente latino dal vii all' xi secolo*. Settimane di studio del centro italiano di studi sull'alto medioevo 22. Spoleto, 1975. 357–414.

Cavallo, Guglielmo, Edoardo Crisci, Gabriella Messeri, and Rosario Pintaudi, eds. *Scrivere libri e documenti nel mondo antico*. Florence, 1998.

Cavallo, Jo Ann. *Boiardo's "Orlando Innamorato": An Ethics of Desire*. Rutherford, N. J., 1993.

Cavicchioli, Sonia. "*Amore e Psiche* nella delizia estense di Belriguardo." *La Diana* 1 (1995): 125–45.

Cavicchioli, Sonia. *Le metamorfosi di Psiche: L'iconografia della favola di Apuleio*. Venice, 2002.
———. *The Tale of Cupid and Psyche: An Illustrated History*. New York, 2002.
Cesarini Martinelli, Lucia. "Sozomeno: Maestro e filologo." *Interpres* 11 (1991): 7–92.
Chastagnol, André. *Les fastes de la préfecture de Rome au Bas-Empire*. Paris, 1962.
Chavy, Paul. *Traducteurs d'autrefois: Moyen Age et Renaissance: Dictionnaire des traducteurs et de la littérature traduite en ancien et moyen français*. 2 vols. Paris, 1937–38. Slatkine Reprints. Paris, 1970, 1988.
Cherchi, P. "Mario Equicola." *Dizionario biografico degli Italiani* 43 (1993): 34–40.
Coarelli, Filippo. "Apuleio a Ostia?" *Dialoghi di Archeologia* 7 (1989): 27–42.
Cochin, Claude. "Recherches sur Stefano Colonna: Prévôt du chapitre de Saint-Omer, Cardinal d'Urbain VI, et correspondant de Pétrarque." *Revue d'histoire et de littérature religieuses* 10 (1905): 352–83.
Contemporaries of Erasmus. See Bietenholz and Deutscher.
Conti, Alessandro. *La miniatura bolognese: Scuole e botteghe, 1270–1340*. Bologna, 1981.
Coppolla, G. "PSI VIII.919." In *Papiri greci e latini*. Pubblicazioni della Società italiana per la ricerca dei papiri greci e latini in Egitto. Florence, 1927. 8:85–87.
Costanza, Salvatore. *La fortuna di L. Apuleio nell'età di mezzo*. Palermo 1937.
Coulson, Frank T. "Hitherto Unedited Medieval and Renaissance Lives of Ovid." *Mediaeval Studies* 49 (1987): 152–207.
Coulter, Cornelia C. "Boccaccio and the Cassinese Manuscripts of the Laurentian Library." *Classical Philology* 43 (1948): 217–30.
———. "The Genealogy of the Gods." In C. F. Fiske, ed. *Vassar Mediaeval Studies*. New Haven, Conn., 1923. 317–41.
Courtney, Edward. See *The Fragmentary Latin Poets* in "Other Primary Sources."
Coville, A. "Une correspondance à propos d'Apulée (1371–1375)." *Humanisme et Renaissance* 2 (1935): 203–15.
Coxe, H. O. *Bodleian Library Quarto Catalogues II: Laudian Manuscripts*. Reprinted, with an introduction, additions, and corrections, by R. W. Hunt. Oxford, 1973.
Cremaschi, Giovanni. "Un codice dei 'Metamorphoseon Libri' di Apuleio nella Biblioteca Comunale di Bergamo." *Aevum* 26 (1952): 369.
Croke, Brian. "The Era of Porphyry's Anti-Christian Polemic." *Journal of Religious History* 13 (1984): 1–14.
D'Amico, John. "The Progress of Renaissance Latin Prose: The Case of Apuleianism." *Renaissance Quarterly* 37 (1984): 351–92.
Davies, Hugh William. *Catalogue of a Collection of Early French Books in the Library of C. Fairfax Murray*. London, 1961.
Davies, Martin. "Making Sense of Pliny in the Quattrocento." *Renaissance Studies* 9 (1995): 240–57.

———. "The Senator and the Schoolmaster: Friends of Leonardo Bruni Aretino in a New Letter." *Humanistica lovaniensia* 33 (1984): 1–21.
de Filippo, J. G. "*Curiositas* and the Platonism of Apuleius' *Golden Ass.*" *American Journal of Philology* 111 (1990): 471–92.
Deichmann, Friedrich Wilhelm. *Repertorium der christlich-antiken Sarkophage.* Giuseppe Bovini and Hugo Brandenburg, eds. 2 vols. Wiesbaden, 1967.
de la Mare, A. C. "Cosimo and His Books." In Francis Ames-Lewis, ed. *Cosimo "il Vecchio" de' Medici, 1389–1464.* Oxford, 1992. 115–56.
———. *The Handwriting of Italian Humanists.* Vol. 1, fasc. 1. Oxford, 1973.
———. "Humanistic Script: The First Ten Years." In Fritz Krafft and Dieter Wuttke, eds. *Das Verhältnis der Humanisten zum Buch.* Boppard, Germany, 1977. 89–108.
———. "New Research on Humanistic Scribes in Florence." In Annarosa Garzelli, ed. *Miniatura fiorentina del Rinascimento.* 2 vols. Florence, 1985. 1:395–600.
Dell'Omo, Mariano, ed. *Virgilio e il chiostro: Manoscritti di autori classici e civiltà monastica.* Rome, 1996.
De Maria, Ugo. *La favola di Amore e Psiche nella letteratura e nell'arte italiana.* Bologna, 1899.
Demats, Paule. *Fabula: Trois études de mythographie antique et médiévale.* Geneva, 1973.
de Pins, Jean. *Clarissimi viri Philippi Beroaldi Bononiensis vita.* In J. G. Meuschen, ed. *Vitae summorum dignitate et eruditione virorum ex rarissimis monumentis literato orbi restitutae.* Coburg, 1735. 1:123–51.
De Ricci, Seymour. *Census of Medieval and Renaissance Manuscripts in the United States and Canada.* 2 vols. New York, 1935.
Die deutsche Literatur des Mittelalters Verfasserlexikon. 11 vols. to date. Berlin, 1978–.
Diller, Aubrey. "Petrarch's Greek Codex of Plato." *Classical Philology* 59 (1964): 270–72.
Dillon Bussi, Angela, and Anna Rita Fantoni. "La Biblioteca Medicea Laurenziana negli ultimi anni del Quattrocento." In Anna Lenzuni, ed. *All'ombra del lauro: Documenti librari della cultura in età laurenziana.* Florence, 1992. 137–47.
Dinkler, Erich. *Christus und Asklepios.* Sitzungsberichte der Heidelberger Akademie der Wissenschaften philosophisch-historische Klasse. Heidelberg, 1980.
Dionisotti, Carlo. "Giovan Battista Pio e Mario Equicola." In *Gli umanisti e il volgare fra Quattro e Cinquecento.* Florence, 1968. 78–130.
Dodgson, Campbell. *Catalogue of Early German and Flemish Woodcuts Preserved in the Department of Prints and Drawings in the British Museum.* 2 vols. London, 1903–11.
Dorez, Leone, ed. *La Canzone delle Virtù e delle Scienze di Bartolomeo di Bartoli di Verona.* Bergamo, 1904.
Dowden, Ken. "Cupid & Psyche: A Question of the Vision of Apuleius." In M. Zimmerman et al., eds. *Aspects of Apuleius' "Golden Ass."* Vol. 2, *Cupid and Psyche.* Groningen, 1998. 1–22.

Dowden, Ken. "Psyche and the Gnostics." In B. L. Hijmans Jr. and V. Schmidt, eds. *Symposium apuleianum groninganum*. Groningen, 1981. 157–64.
Dronke, Peter. *Fabula: Explorations into the Uses of Myth in Medieval Platonism*. Leiden, 1974.
Dugan, John. "How to Make (and Break) a Cicero: *Epideixis*, Textuality, and Self-Fashioning in the *Pro Archia* and *In Pisonem*." *Classical Antiquity* 20 (2001): 35–78.
Duranti, Alessandro. "Le novelle di Dioneo." In *Studi di filologia e critica offerti dagli allievi a Lanfranco Caretti*. 2 vols. Rome, 1985. 1:1–38.
Elsom, Helen E. "Apuleius in Erasmus' *Lingua*." *Res Publica Litterarum* 11 (1988): 125–34.
Ensoli, Serena, and Eugenio La Rocca, eds. *Aurea Roma: Dalla città pagana alla città cristiana*. Rome, 2000.
Erotica Antiqua: Acta of the International Conference on the Ancient Novel (July 1976). B. Reardon, ed. Bangor, Maine, 1977.
Escobar Borrego, Francisco Javier. "Diego López de Cortegna, traductor del *Asinus Aureus*: El cuento de Psique y Cupido." *Cuadernos de filología clásica. Estudios latinos* 22 (2002): 193–209.
———. "Textos preliminares y posliminares de la traslación del *Asinus aureus* por Diego López de Cortegana: Sobre el planteamiento de la traducción." *Cuadernos de filología clásica: Estudios latinos* 21 (2001): 151–75.
———. "Una edición del siglo XVI de hecho desconocida: La traducción del *Asinus Aureus* por Diego López de Cortegana (Sevilla, Doménico de Robertis, 1546)." *Il confronto letterario: Quaderni del Dipartimento di lingue e letterature straniere moderne dell'Università di Pavia* 20 (2003): 7–14.
Evans, Elizabeth C. "The Study of Physiognomy in the Second Century A.D." *Transactions of the American Philological Association* 72 (1941): 96–108.
Fahney, Josephus. *De Pseudo-Theodori Additamentis*. Monasterii Guestfalorum, 1913.
Fantham, R. Elaine. "Mime: The Missing Link in Roman Literary History." *Classical World* 82 (1989): 156–63
Farenga, P. "Niccolò da Correggio." *Dizionario biografico degli Italiani* 29 (1983): 466–74
Feld, M. D. "Sweynheym and Pannartz, Cardinal Bessarion, Neoplatonism: Renaissance Humanism and Two Early Printers' Choice of Texts." *Harvard Library Bulletin* 30 (1982): 282–335.
Feo, Michele, ed. *Codici latini del Petrarca nelle Biblioteche fiorentine. Mostra, 19 maggio–30 giugno 1991*. Florence, 1991.
Ferrari, Mirella. See Baglio, Ferrari, and Petoletti.
Ferraro, Vittorio. "Apuleio in Cristodoro." *Annali delle Facoltà di lettere, filosofia, e magistero della Università di Cagliari* 29 (1966): 27–36.
Fiaccadori, Gianfranco, et al., eds. *Bessarione e l'umanesimo: Catalogo della Mostra*. Naples, 1994.
Fick, Nicole. "La magie dans les Métamorphoses d'Apulée." *Revue des études latines* 63 (1985): 132–47.
———. "Magie et religion dans l'Apologie d'Apulée." *Vita latina* 124 (December 1991): 14–31.
Finch, Chauncey Edgar. *The Urbana Manuscript of Apuleius*. Urbana, 1936.

Fioravanti, Gianfranco. "Librerie e lettori a San Gimignano nel '400: Onofrio Coppi e Mattia Lupi." *Interpres* 18 (1999): 58–73.
Fiorilla, Maurizio. "La lettura apuleiana del Boccaccio e le note ai manoscritti laurenziani 29,2 e 54,32." *Aevum* 73 (1999): 635–68.
Firenzuola, Agnolo. See Firenzuola in "Apuleius B."
Foà, Simona. See Boiardo, *Tarocchi*, in "Other Primary Sources."
Foerster, Richard. "Amor und Psyche vor Raffael." *Jahrbuch der königliche preussischen Kunstsammlungen* 16 (1893): 215–33.
Forcellini, F. "Zanobi da Strada e la sua venuta nella Corte di Napoli." *Archivio storico per le provincie napolitane* 37 (1912): 243–63.
Forrat, Marguerite. See Eusebius in "Other Primary Sources."
Forti, F. "Matteo Maria Boiardo." *Dizionario biografico degli Italiani* 11 (1969): 211–23.
Fraenkel, Eduard. "A Sham Sisenna." *Eranos* 51 (1953): 151–54.
Franceschini, Ezio, ed. See "Conquestio uxoris Cavichioli" in "Other Primary Sources."
Frasso, Giuseppe. "Tre lettere di Guglielmo da Pastrengo a Francesco Petrarca." In Giuseppe Billanovich and Giuseppe Frasso, eds. *Petrarca, Verona e l'Europa*. Padua, 1997. 89–145.
Frati, Ludovico. "I due Beroaldi." *Studi e memorie per la storia dell'Università di Bologna* 2 (1911): 209–28.
Fubini, Riccardo. "Il 'Teatro del Mondo' nelle prospettive morali e storico-politiche di Poggio Bracciolini." In *Poggio Bracciolini, 1380–1980: Nel VI centenario della nascita*. Florence, 1982. 1–135.
Fumagalli, Edoardo. "Amore e Psiche in centri padani: A proposito del volgarizzamento del Boiardo." *Fontes* 3 (2000): 73–82.
———. "Francesco Colonna: lettore di Apuleio e il problema della datazione del' 'Hypnerotomachia Polifili.'" *Italia medioevale e umanistica* 27 (1984): 233–66.
———. *Matteo Maria Boiardo volgarizzatore dell' "Asino d'Oro": Contributo allo studio della fortuna di Apuleio nell'Umanesimo*. Padua, 1988.
Furno, Martine. *Le Cornu copiae de Niccolò Perotti: Culture et méthode d'un humaniste qui aimait les mots*. Geneva, 1995.
Gaide, Françoise. "Apulée de Madaure a-t-il prononcé le *De magia* devant le proconsul d'Afrique?" *Les études classiques* 61 (1993): 227–31.
Gaisser, Julia Haig. "Allegorizing Apuleius: Fulgentius, Boccaccio, Beroaldo, and the Chain of Receptions." In Rhoda Schnur et al., eds. *Acta Conventus Neo-Latini Cantabrigiensis*. Tempe, Ariz., 2003. 23–41.
———. "Apuleius in Florence: From Boccaccio to Lorenzo de' Medici." In Frank T. Coulson and Anna A. Grotans, eds. *Classica et Beneventana: Essays Presented to Virginia Brown on the Occasion of Her 65th Birthday*. Turnholt, 2007. 43–70.
——— "Catullus." In Virginia Brown, ed. *Catalogus Translationum et Commentariorum*. Washington, D.C., 1992. 7:197–292.
———. *Catullus and His Renaissance Readers*. Oxford, 1993.
———. "Filippo Beroaldo on Apuleius: Bringing Antiquity to Life." In Marianne Pade, ed. *On Renaissance Commentaries*. Noctes Neolatini 4. Hildesheim, 2005. 87–109.

Gaisser, Julia Haig. "Reading Apuleius with Filippo Beroaldo." In Philip Thibodeau and Harry Haskell, eds. *Being There Together: Essays in Honor of Michael C. J. Putnam on the Occasion of His Seventieth Birthday*. Afton, Minn., 2003. 24–42.

———. "Teaching Classics in the Renaissance: Two Case Histories." *Transactions of the American Philological Association* 131 (2001): 1–21.

García Gual, Carlos. "Sobre la version espanola de El asno de oro por Diego López de Cortegana." In *Homenaje al professor Antonio Vilanova*. Barcelona, 1989. 1: 297–307.

Garfagnini, Gian Carlo. "Un accessus ad Apuleio e un nuovo codice del Terzo Mitografo vaticano." *Studi medioevali* 17 (1976): 306–62.

Garin, Eugenio. "Note in margine all' opera di Filippo Beroaldo il vecchio." In G. B. Trezzini et al., eds. *Tra latino e volgare: Per Carlo Dionisotti*. 2 vols. Padua, 1974. 2:437–56.

———. "Note sull'insegnamento di Filippo Beroaldi il Vecchio." In *La cultura filosofica del Rinascimento italiano*. Florence, 1961. 367–87. Reprinted from *Studi e memorie per la storia dell'Università di Bologna*, n.s. 1 (1956): 357–76. Printed again in Garin's *Ritratti di umanisti*. Florence, 1967. 107–29.

———. "Noterelle sulla filosofia del rinascimento." *Rinascimento* 2 (1951): 319–36.

———. *Studi sul Platonismo medievale*. Florence, 1958.

Garzelli, Annarosa. "Le immagini, gli autori, i destinatari." In Annarosa Garzelli, ed. *Miniatura fiorentino del Rinascimento, 1440–1525*. 2 vols. Florence, 1985. 1:1–391.

Gentile, Sebastiano. "In margine all'epistola *De divino furore* di Marsilio Ficino." *Rinascimento* 23 (1983): 33–77.

Gentile, S., S. Niccoli, and P. Viti, eds. *Marsilio Ficino e il ritorno di Platone*. Mostra di manoscritti, stampe, e documenti, 17 maggio–16 giugno 1984. Florence, 1986.

Gerke, Friedrich. *Christus in der spätantiken Plastik*. Mainz, 1949.

Gersh, S. *Middle Platonism and Neoplatonism: The Latin Tradition*. 2 vols. Notre Dame, Ind., 1986.

Ghinassi, G. "Giovanni Sabadino degli Arienti." *Dizionario biografico degli Italiani* 4 (1962): 154–56.

Giannetto, Nella. *Bernardo Bembo umanista e politico veneziano*. Florence, 1985.

———. "I codici dell'Eton College provenienti dalla biblioteca di Bernardo Bembo." *Atti della Accademia nazionale dei Lincei* 378 (1981), ser. 8, *Rendiconti, Scienze morali, storiche e filologiche*. 36 (1982): 219–37.

Gil, Juan. "Apuleyo en la Sevilla renacentista." *Habis* 23 (1992): 297–308.

Gilmore, M. "Filippo Beroaldo, Senior." *Dizionario biografico degli Italiani* 9 (1967): 382–84.

Gleason, Maud W. *Making Men: Sophists and Self-Presentation in Ancient Rome*. Princeton, N. J., 1994.

Gombrich, Ernst. "*Hypnerotomachiana*." *Journal of the Warburg and Courtauld Institute* 14 (1951): 119–25.

Gordan, Phyllis Goodhart. *Two Renaissance Book Hunters: The Letters of Poggius Bracciolini to Nicolaus de Niccolis*. New York, 1974.
Grafton, Anthony. "The Scholarship of Politian and Its Context." *Journal of the Warburg and Courtauld Institute* 40 (1977): 150–88.
Grafton, Anthony, and Lisa Jardine. *From Humanism to the Humanities*. London, 1986.
Graverini, Luca. "Note di aggiornamento." In Pecere and Stramaglia, eds. *Studi apuleiani*. 179–202.
Greenblatt, Stephen. *Renaissance Self-Fashioning: From More to Shakespeare*. Chicago, 1980.
Greene, Thomas M. *The Light in Troy: Imitation and Discovery in Renaissance Poetry*. New Haven, Conn., 1980.
Griffin, Clive. *The Crombergers of Seville: The History of a Printing and Merchant Dynasty*. Oxford, 1988.
Griffiths, J. Gwyn. See Apuleius, *The Isis Book*, in "Apuleius A.4."
Griggio, Claudio. Review of *Genealogie deorum gentilium*. Vittorio Zaccaria, ed. *Studi sul Boccaccio* 28 (2000): 305–10.
Grignaschi, Mario. "Corrigenda et Addenda sulla questione dello Ps. Burleo." *Medioevo* 16 (1990): 325–54.
———. "Lo pseudo Walter Burley e il 'Liber de vita et moribus philosophorum.'" *Medioevo* 16 (1990): 131–90.
Gualandri, Isabella, and Giovanni Orlandi. "Commedia elegiaca o commedia umanistica? Il problema del *De Cavichiolo*." In *Filologia e forme letterarie: Studi offerti a Francesco della Corte*. Urbino, 1987. 5.335–56.
Guey, J. "L'*Apologie* d'Apulée et les inscriptions de Tripolitaine." *Revue des études latines* 32 (1954): 115–19.
Gundersheimer, Werner L. *Art and Life at the Court of Ercole I d'Este: The "De triumphis religionis" of Giovanni Sabadino degli Arienti*. Geneva, 1972.
———. *Ferrara: The Style of a Renaissance Despotism*. Princeton, N. J., 1973.
———. "The Patronage of Ercole I d'Este." *Journal of Medieval and Renaissance Studies* 6 (1976): 1–18.
———, ed. *French Humanism, 1470–1600*. London, 1969.
Haebler, Konrad. *The Study of Incunabula*. Lucy Eugenia Osborne, trans. New York, 1933.
Haeghen, Victor van der. *L'humaniste-imprimeur Robert de Keysere, et sa soeur Clara la miniaturiste, xve–xvie siècles*. In *Annales de la Société d'histoire et d'archéologie de Gand* 8 (1907): 325–81.
Häfner, Ralph. "*Ein schönes Confitemini:* Johann Sieders Übersetzung von Apuleius' *Goldenen Esel;* Die Berliner Handschrift Germ. Fol. 1239 aus dem Jahr 1500 und der erste Druck von 1538." *Beiträge zur Geschichte der deutschen Sprache und Literatur* 125 (2003): 94–136.
Hagendahl, Harald. *Augustine and the Latin Classics*. 2 vols. in 1. Göteborg, 1967.
Hägg, Tomas. *The Novel in Antiquity*. Berkeley, Calif., 1983.
Hahn, Johannes. *Der Philosoph und die Gesellschaft: Selbstverständnis, öffentliches Auftreten und populäre Erwartungen in der hohen Kaiserzeit*. Stuttgart, 1989.

Haight, Elizabeth Hazelton. *Apuleius and His Influence*. New York, 1927. Reprint, New York, 1963.

———. "Apuleius' Art of Story Telling." In *Essays on Ancient Fiction*. New York, 1936. Reprint, New York, 1966. 151–94.

———. "Introducing Apuleius." *Poet Lore* 26 (1915): 694–706.

———. *More Essays on Greek Romances*. New York, 1945.

———. "On Certain Uses of Apuleius' Story of Cupid and Psyche in English Literature." *Poet Lore* 26 (1915): 744–762.

Hankins, James. *Plato in the Italian Renaissance*. 2 vols. Leiden, 1990.

———. "Plato in the Middle Ages." In *Humanism and Platonism in the Italian Renaissance*. 2 vols. Rome, 2004. 1:15–25.

———. "The Study of the *Timaeus* in Renaissance Italy." In *Humanism and Platonism in the Italian Renaissance*. 2 vols. Rome, 2004. 2:113–19.

Harlfinger, Dieter, ed. *Graecogermania: Griechischstudien deutscher Humanisten*. Wolfenbüttel, 1989.

Harrison, S. J. *Apuleius: A Latin Sophist*. Oxford, 2000.

———. "The Speaking Book: The Prologue to Apuleius' *Metamorphoses*." *Classical Quarterly* 40 (1990): 507–13.

———, ed. *Apuleius: Rhetorical Works*. Stephen Harrison, John Hilton, and Vincent Hunink, trans. Oxford, 2001.

Harrison, S. J., and Michael Winterbottom. "The Prologue to Apuleius' *Metamorphoses*: Text, Translation, and Textual Commentary." In Ahuvia Kahane and Andrew Laird, eds. *A Companion to the Prologue of Apuleius' Metamorphoses*. Oxford, 2001. 9–15.

Hays, Bradford Gregory. *Fulgentius the Mythographer*. Ann Arbor, Mich.: University Microfilms, 1996.

Hazañas y la Rúa, Joaquín. *Maese Rodrigo, 1440–1509*. Seville, 1909.

Hedrick, Charles W., Jr. *History and Silence: Purge and Rehabilitation of Memory in Late Antiquity*. Austin, 2000.

Heinemann, Otto von. *Die Handschriften der herzoglichen Bibliothek zu Wolfenbüttel*. 10 vols. Wolfenbüttel, 1884–1913.

Hercher, R. See Philip the Philosopher in "Other Primary Sources."

Hijmans, B. L., Jr. "Apuleius Orator: 'Pro se de Magia' and 'Florida.'" *Aufstieg und Niedergang der römischen Welt* II.34.2. New York, 1994. 1708–84.

———. "Apuleius, Philosophus Platonicus." *Aufstieg und Niedergang der römischen Welt* II.36.1. New York, 1987. 395–475.

———. "Boccaccio's *Amor and Psyche*." In B. L. Hijmans Jr. and V. Schmidt, eds. *Symposium apuleianum groninganum*. Groningen, 1981. 30–45.

Hijmans, B. L., et al. See *Metamorphoses IX* in "Apuleius A.4."

Hildebrand, E. F. See *Apulei Opera omnia* in "Apuleius A.1."

Hirsch, Rudolf. *Printing, Selling and Reading, 1450–1550*. Wiesbaden, 1967.

———. "The Size of Editions of Books Produced by Sweynheym and Pannartz between 1465 and 1471." *Gutenberg Jahrbuch* (1957): 46–47.

Hoffmann, Adolf. *Das Psyche Märchen des Apuleius in der englischen Literatur*. Strassburg, 1908.

Hofmann, Heinz, ed. *Latin Fiction: The Latin Novel in Context*. London, 1999.

Horsfall Scotti, Mariateresa. "Apuleio tra magia e filosofia: La riscoperta di Agostino." In *Dicti Studiosus: Scritti S. Mariotti*. Urbino, 1990. 295–320.

Huet, G. "Le roman d'Apulée était-il connu au moyen-age?" *Le Moyen Age* 19 (1918): 44–52.

Hughes, Graham. *Renaissance Cassoni*. London, 1997.

Hulubei, Alice. "Virgile en France au xvie siècle: Éditions, traductions, imitations." *Revue du seizième siècle* 18 (1931): 1–77.

Hunink, Vincent. "*Apuleius, qui nobis Afris Afer est Notior*: Augustine's Polemic against Apuleius in *De Civitate Dei*." *Scholia* 12 (2003): 82–95.

———. "The Prologue of Apuleius' *De deo Socratis*." *Mnemosyne* 48 (1995): 292–312.

———. "The 'spurcum additamentum' (Apul. *Met.* 10.21) Once Again." In W. H. Keulen, R. R. Nauta, and S. Panayotakis, eds. *Lectiones Scrupulosae: Essays on the Text and Interpretation of Apuleius' Metamorphoses in Honour of Maaike Zimmerman*. Ancient Narrative. Supplementum 6. Groningen, 2006. 266–79.

———. "Two Erotic Poems in Apuleius' *Apology*." In Carl Deroux, ed. *Studies in Latin Literature and Roman History* 9 (1998): 448–61.

———. See also *Apuleius of Madauros: Pro se de magia* in "Apuleius A.2."

Hunter, Richard. "'Philip the Philosopher' on the *Aithiopika* of Heliodorus." In Stephen Harrison, Michael Paschalis, and Stavros Frangoulidis, eds. *Metaphor and the Ancient Novel*. Ancient Narrative. Supplementum 4. Groningen, 2005. 123–38.

Iannellius, Cataldus. *Catalogus bibliothecae Latinae veteris et classicae manuscriptae quae in Regio Neapolitano Museo borbonico adservatur*. Naples, 1827.

Index Aureliensis: Catalogus librorum sedecimo saeculo impressorum. 15 vols. to date. Baden-Baden, 1965–.

Jahn, Otto. "Über die Subscriptionen in den Handschriften römischer Classiker." *Berichte über die Verhandlungen der königlich sächsischen Gesellschaft der Wissenschaften zu Leipzig: Philologisch-historische Classe* 3 (1851): 327–72.

James, Carolyn. *Giovanni Sabadino degli Arienti: A Literary Career*. Quaderni di Rinascimento 32. Florence, 1996.

James, Montague Rhodes. *A Descriptive Catalogue of the Manuscripts in the Library of Eton College*. Cambridge, 1895.

Jay, Pierre. "Jérôme à Bethléem: Les *Tractatus in Psalmos*." In Yves-Marie Duval, ed. *Jérôme entre l'occident et l'orient*. Paris, 1988. 367–80.

Jöcher, Chr. G. *Allgemeines Gelehrten-Lexicon*. 11 vols. Leipzig, 1750–51, 1784–1897. Reprint, Hildesheim, 1960–61.

Johnson, A. F. "Books Printed at Lyons in the Sixteenth Century." In *Selected Essays on Books and Printing*. Percy H. Mair, ed. Amsterdam, 1970. 123–45.

Jones, A.H.M., J. R Martindale, and J. Morris. *The Prosopography of the Later Roman Empire*. 3 vols. Cambridge, 1971–.

Jones, J. W., Jr. "Allegorical Interpretation in Servius." *Classical Journal* 56 (1960–61): 217–26.

Jong, Jan L. de. "Il pittore a le volte è puro poeta: Cupid and Psyche in Italian Renaissance Painting." In M. Zimmerman et al., eds. *Aspects of Apuleius' Golden Ass.* Vol. 2, *Cupid and Psyche.* Groningen, 1998. 189–215.

———. "Renaissance Representations of Cupid and Psyche: Apuleius versus Fulgentius." *Groningen Colloquia on the Novel* 2 (1989): 75–86.

Jordan, Louis, and Susan Wool, eds. *Inventory of Western Manuscripts in the Biblioteca Ambrosiana.* Part One A-B Superior. Notre Dame, Ind., 1984.

Kahane, Ahuvia, and Andrew Laird, eds. *A Companion to the Prologue of Apuleius' Metamorphoses.* Oxford, 2001.

Kallendorf, Craig. *Virgil and the Myth of Venice: Books and Readers in the Italian Renaissance.* Oxford, 1999.

Kaster, Robert A. *Guardians of Language: The Grammarian and Society in Late Antiquity.* Berkeley, 1988.

———. "Servius and *Idonei Auctores.*" *American Journal of Philology* 99 (1978): 181–209.

Kehoe, Patrick. H. "The Adultery Mime Reconsidered." In David F. Bright and Edwin S. Ramage, eds. *Classical Texts and Their Traditions: Studies in Honor of C. R. Trahman.* Chico, Calif., 1984. 91–106.

Kenney, E. J. *The Classical Text: Aspects of Editing in the Age of the Printed Book.* Berkeley, Calif., 1974.

———. "Psyche and Her Mysterious Husband." In D. A. Russell, ed. *Antonine Literature.* Oxford, 1990. 175–98.

Ker, N. R. *Medieval Manuscripts in British Libraries.* 5 vols. Oxford, 1969–1977.

Klesczewski, Reinhard. "Erzählen als Kriegskunst: Zum Begriff 'Erzählstrategie' (mit Anwendung auf Texte von Apuleius und Boccaccio)." In Eberhard Lämmert, ed. *Erzählforschung: Ein Symposion.* Stuttgart, 1982. 384–402.

Klibansky, Raymond. *The Continuity of the Platonic Tradition during the Middle Ages.* London, 1939. Reprinted with a new preface and "Plato's Parmenides in the Middle Ages and the Renaissance." Munich, 1981.

Klibansky, Raymond, and Frank Regen. *Die Handschriften der philosophischen Werke des Apuleius: Ein Beitrag zur Überlieferungsgeschichte.* Abhandlungen der Akademie der Wissenschaften in Göttingen Philologisch-historische Klasse 3.204. Göttingen, 1993.

Knauer, Elfriede R. "Ex oriente vestimenta: Trachtgeschichtliche Beobachtungen zu Äermelmantel und Äermeljacke." *Aufstieg und Niedergang der römischen Welt* II, Principat 12,3. Berlin, 1985. 578–741.

Koch, Guntram. *Frühchristliche Sarkophage.* Munich, 2000.

Kohl, Benjamin G., and Nancy G. Siraisi. See "The *De Monarchia* Attributed to Apuleius" in "Other Primary Sources."

Kraus, H. P. *The Greek Book: An Exhibition of Greek Printing and the Book Arts from the 15th to the 20th Centuries.* New York, 1997.

Krautter, Konrad. *Philologische Methode und humanistische Existenz: Filippo Beroaldo und sein Kommentar zum "Goldenen Esel" des Apuleius.* Munich, 1971.

Krieger, Gerhard. "Studies on Walter Burley, 1989–1997." *Vivarium* 37 (1999): 94–100.

Kristeller, Paul Oskar. *Iter Italicum*. 7 vols. in 9. Leiden, 1963–97.

———. "Marsilio Ficino as a Beginning Student of Plato." *Scriptorium* 20 (1966): 41–54.

Kritzas, Haralambas. "Δύο επιγράμματα από το Πετρί Νεμέας." In (ΔΙΕΘΝΕΣ ΣΥΝΕΔΡΙΟ ΓΙΑ ΤΗΝ ΑΡΧΑΙΑ ΘΕΣΣΑΛΙΑ ΣΤΗ ΜΝΗΜΗ ΤΟΥ ΔΗΜΗΤΡΗ Ρ. ΘΕΟΧΑΡΗ) = *Acta of the International Colloquium on Ancient Thessaly in Honor of D. R. Theocharis*. Athens, 1992. 398–413.

Küenzlen, Franziska. "Cento und Kontrafaktur: Das Mariengebet Sebastian Brants nach den Worten des Apuleius." In Nine Miedema and Rudolf Suntrup, eds. *Literatur—Geschichte—Literaturgeschichte: Beiträge zur mediävistischen Literaturwissenschaft; Festschrift für Volker Honemann zum 60. Geburtstag*. Frankfurt am Main, 2003. 825–40.

———. *Verwandlungen eines Esels: Apuleius' "Metamorphoses" im frühen 16. Jahrhundert*. Heidelberg, 2005.

Labowsky, Lotte. "Bessarione." *Dizionario biografico degli Italiani* 9 (1967): 686–96.

———. *Bessarion's Library and the Biblioteca Marciana: Six Early Inventories*. Rome, 1979.

Lamberton, Robert. *Homer the Theologian: Neoplatonist Allegorical Reading and the Growth of the Epic Tradition*. Berkeley, 1986.

Lange, Konrad. *Der Papstesel: Ein Beitrag zur Kultur- und Kunstgeschichte des Reformationszeitalters*. Göttingen, 1891.

La Rocca, Adolfo. *Il filosofo e la città: Commento storico ai Florida di Apuleio*. Rome, 2005.

Lazzi, Giovanna. "L'immagine dell'autore 'classico' nei manoscritti del Quattrocento." In Marco Buonocore, ed. *Vedere i classici*. 99–110.

———. "Novità e persistenze nelle tipologie vestimentarie al tempo del Concilio: Dalla moda 'alla franciosa' a quella 'all'orientale.'" In Paolo Viti, ed. *Firenze e il Concilio del 1439: Convegno di Studi; Firenze, 29 novembre–2 dicembre 1989*. 2 vols. Florence, 1994. 1:389–407.

Leach, Eleanor Winsor. "The Politics of Self-Presentation: Pliny's *Letters* and Roman Portrait Sculpture." *Classical Antiquity* 9 (1990): 14–39.

Leccisotti, Tommaso. "Ancora a proposito del viaggio del Boccaccio a Montecassino." *Benedictina* 15 (1968): 143–45.

———. *Montecassino*. 7th ed. Montecassino, 1974.

Lee, Egmont. *Sixtus IV and Men of Letters*. Rome, 1978.

Lee Too, Yun. "Statues, Mirrors, Gods: Controlling Images in Apuleius." In J. Elsner, ed. *Art and Text in Roman Culture*. Cambridge, 1996. 133–52.

Lehmann, Paul. *Franciscus Modius als Handschriftenforscher*. Vol. 3 in Ludwig Traube, ed. *Quellen und Untersuchungen zur lateinischen Philologie des Mittelalters*. Munich, 1908.

Le Maitre, Henri. *Essai sur le mythe de Psyché dans la littérature française des origines à 1890*. Paris, 1930.

Lev Kenaan, Vered. "*Fabula anilis*: The Literal as a Feminine Sense." In Carl Deroux, ed. *Studies in Latin Literature and Roman History* 10 (2000): 370–91.

Lindsay, W. M. "The 'Abolita' Glossary (Vat. lat. 3321)." *Journal of Philology* 34 (1918): 267–82.
Lotti, Brunello. "Cultura filosofica di Bessarione: La tradizione platonica." In Fiaccadori et al., eds. *Bessarione e l'Umanesimo*. 79–102.
Lowe, E. A. "The Unique Manuscript of Apuleius' *Metamorphoses* (Laurentian. 68.2) and Its Oldest Transcript." *Classical Quarterly* 14 (1920): 150–55. Reprinted in *Palaeographical Papers*. Oxford, 1976. 1:92–98.
Lowry, Martin. *The World of Aldus Manutius: Business and Scholarship in Renaissance Venice*. Ithaca, 1979.
Lumbroso, G. "Apuleio e Psyche in Bologna." *Atti e memorie della r. deputazione di storia patria per la Romagna*, ser. 3, vol. 2 (1884): 85–89.
Lytle, Ephraim. "Apuleius' *Metamorphoses* and the *Spurcum Additamentum* (10.21)." *Classical Philology* 98 (2003): 349–65.
Magnaldi, Giuseppina, and Gian Franco Gianotti, eds. *Apuleio: Storia del testo e interpretazioni*. Alessandria, 2000.
Manca, Joseph. *The Art of Ercole de' Roberti*. Cambridge, 1992.
Mandarini, E. *I codici manoscritti della Biblioteca Oratoriana di Napoli*. Naples, 1897.
Maniscalco, Silvana. "Criteri e sensibilità di Agnolo Firenzuola, traduttore di Apuleio." *La Rassegna della letteratura italiana* 82 (1978): 88–109.
Manitius, Max. *Geschichte der lateinischen Literatur des Mittelalters*. Munich, 1923.
Maréchaux, Pierre. "Béroalde l'ancien (Philippe)." In Colette Nativel, ed. *Centuriae latinae: Cent une figures humanistes de la Renaissance aux lumières offertes à Jacques Chomarat*. Paris, 1997. 109–21.
Mariotti, S. "Lo *spurcum additamentum* ad Apul. Met. 10, 21." *Studi italiani di filologia classica* 27–28 (1956): 229–50. Reprinted in *Scritti medievali e umanistici*. Rome, 1976. 42–69. Reprint, Rome, 1994. 61–83.
Marrou, H. I. "La vie intellectuelle au Forum de Trajan et au Forum d'Auguste." *Mélanges d'archéologie et d'histoire* 49 (1932): 93–110.
Marsh, David. "Alberti and Apuleius: Comic Violence and Vehemence in the *Intercenales* and *Momus*." In Francesco Fulan, ed. *Leon Battista Alberti: Actes du Congrès International de Paris, 10–15 avril 1995*. Paris, 2000. 405–26.
——— . *Lucian and the Latins: Humor and Humanism in the Early Renaissance*. Ann Arbor, Mich., 1998.
——— . "Poggio and Alberti: Three Notes." *Rinascimento* 23 (1983): 189–215.
Marshall, P. K. "Apuleius." In L. D. Reynolds, ed. *Texts and Transmission: A Survey of the Latin Classics*. Oxford, 1983. 15–18.
Martellotti, Guido. "Le due redazioni delle *Genealogie* del Boccaccio." Rome, 1951. Reprinted in *Dante e Boccaccio e altri scrittori dall'umanesimo al romanticismo*. Florence, 1983. 137–63.
Marucchi, Adriana. "Note sul manoscritto [Vat. lat. 5991] di cui si è servito Giovanni Andrea Bussi per l'edizione di Plinio del 1470." *Bulletin de l'Institut de recherche et d'histoire des textes* 15 (1967–68): 175–82.
Mason, Hugh J. "Greek and Latin Versions of the Ass-Story." *Aufstieg und Niedergang der römischen Welt* II.34.2. New York, 1994. 1665–1707.

———. "Physiognomy in Apuleius *Metamorphoses* 2.2." *Classical Philology* 79 (1984): 307–9.
Mathews, Thomas F. *The Clash of Gods: A Reinterpretation of Early Christian Art*. Princeton, N. J., 1999.
Mattiacci, Silvia. "Apuleio in Fulgenzio." *Studi italiani di filologia classica* 4 (2003): 229–56.
Mattioli, Emilio. *Luciano e l'Umanesimo*. Naples, 1980.
May, Regine. "The Prologue to Apuleius' *Metamorphoses* and Coluccio Salutati: MS Harley 4838 (with an Appendix on Sozomeno of Pistoia and the Nonius Marginalia)." In W. H. Keulen, R. R. Nauta, and S. Panayotakis, eds. *Lectiones Scrupulosae: Essays on the Text and Interpretation of Apuleius' "Metamorphoses" in Honour of Maaike Zimmerman*. Ancient Narrative. Supplementum 6. Groningen, 2006. 280–312.
Mazza, Antonia. "L'inventario della 'parva libraria' di Santo Spirito e la biblioteca del Boccaccio." *Italia medioevale e umanistica* 9 (1966): 1–74.
Mazzarino, Antonio. *La Milesia e Apuleio*. Turin, 1950.
McCarty, Willard. "The Shape of the Mirror: Metaphorical Catoptrics in Classical Literature." *Arethusa* 22 (1989): 161–95.
McCreight, Thomas D. "Invective Techniques in Apuleius' 'Apology.'" *Groningen Colloquia on the Novel* 3 (1990): 35–62.
McKeown, J. C. "Augustan Elegy and Mime." *Proceedings of the Cambridge Philological Society* 25 (1979): 71–84.
McKerrow, R. B., ed. *A Dictionary of Printers and Booksellers in England, Scotland and Ireland, and of Foreign Printers of English Books, 1557–1640*. London, 1910.
McLaughlin, Martin L. *Literary Imitation in the Italian Renaissance: The Theory and Practice of Literary Imitation in Italy from Dante to Bembo*. Oxford, 1995.
Menéndez y Pelayo, Marcelino. *Bibliografía hispano-latina clásica*. Madrid, 1902. Reprinted in *Edición nacional de las obras completas de Menéndez Pelayo*. Vols. 44–53. Madrid, 1950.
Mercati, G. *Per la cronologia della vita e degli scritti di Niccolò Perotti arcivescovo di Siponto*. Rome, 1925.
Meredith, Anthony. "Porphyry and Julian against the Christians." *Aufstieg und Niedergang der römischen Welt* II.23.2. New York, 1980. 1119–49.
Michaud, Joseph François. *Biographie universelle, ancienne et moderne*. 45 vols. Paris, 1843–1865.
Miglio, Massimo. "Giovanni Andrea Bussi." *Dizionario biografico degli Italiani* 15 (1972): 565–72.
———, ed. *Prefazioni*. See Bussi in "Other Primary Sources."
Millar, Fergus. "The World of the Golden Ass." *Journal of Roman Studies* 71 (1981): 63–75.
Miralles, Carles. "Diego López de Cortegana i Beroaldo." In *Studia in honorem prof. M. de Riquer*. Barcelona, 1988. 363–81.
Monfasani, John. "The First Call for Press Censorship: Niccolò Perotti, Giovanni Andrea Bussi, Antonio Moreto, and the Editing of Pliny's *Natural History*." *Renaissance Quarterly* 41 (1988): 1–31.

Monfasani, John. *George of Trebizond: A Biography and a Study of His Rhetoric and Logic.* Leiden, 1976.

———. "Platina, Capranica, and Perotti: Bessarion's Latin Eulogists and His Date of Birth." In P. Medioli Masotti, ed. *Bartolomeo Sacchi Il Platina (Piadena 1421–Roma 1481): Atti del convegno internazionale di studi per il V centenario* (Cremona, 14–15 novembre 1981). Padua, 1986. Reprinted in *Byzantine Scholars in Renaissance Italy: Cardinal Bessarion and Other Emigrés.* Aldershot, UK, 1994. 97–136.

———, ed. *Collectanea Trapezuntiana.* See Trebizond, George of, in "Other Primary Sources."

Moreschini, Claudio. *Apuleio e il Platonismo.* Florence, 1978.

———. *Dall'Asclepius al Crater Hermetis: Studi sull'ermetismo latino tardoantico e rinascimentale.* Pisa, 1985.

———. "La Demonologia medio-platonica e le *Metamorfosi* di Apuleio." *Maia* 17 (1965): 30–46.

———. *Il mito di Amore e Psiche in Apuleio.* Naples, 1994.

———. "Sulla fama di Apuleio nel medioevo e nel rinascimento." In *Studi filologici letterari e storici in memoria di Guido Favati.* Medioevo e Umanesimo 29. 2 vols. Padua, 1977. 2:457–76.

———. "Towards a History of the Exegesis of Apuleius: The case of the of 'Tale of Cupid and Psyche.'" Coco Stephenson, trans. In Heinz Hofmann, ed. *Latin Fiction: The Latin Novel in Context.* London, 1999. 215–28.

———. "Una 'Piacevole storia': La novella di Amore e Psiche nelle *Metamorfosi* di Apuleio." *Humanitas* (Brescia) 50, 2 (1995). 277–96.

Morneweg, Karl. *Johann von Dalberg: Ein deutscher Humanist und Bischof.* Heidelberg, 1887.

Mortimer, Ruth. *Harvard College Library Department of Printing and Graphic Arts, Catalogue of Books and Manuscripts.* Part 1, *French 16th Century Books.* 2 vols. Cambridge, Mass., 1964.

———. *Harvard College Library Department of Printing and Graphic Arts, Catalogue of Books and Manuscripts.* Part 2, *Italian 16th Century Books.* 2 vols. Cambridge, Mass., 1974.

Moss, Ann. *Ovid in Renaissance France: A Survey of the Latin Editions of Ovid and Commentaries Printed in France before 1600.* Warburg Institute Surveys 8. London, 1982.

———. *Poetry and Fable: Studies in Mythological Narrative in Sixteenth-Century France.* Cambridge, 1984.

———. *Renaissance Truth and the Latin Language Turn.* Oxford, 2003.

———, ed. and trans. *Latin Commentaries on Ovid from the Renaissance.* Library of Renaissance Humanism. Signal Mountain, Tenn., 1998.

Mostra di manoscritti, documenti e edizioni: VI Centenario della morte di Giovanni Boccaccio. 2 vols. Certaldo, 1975.

Munk Olsen, B. *L'Étude des auteurs classiques latins aux XIe et XIIe siècles.* 2 vols. Paris, 1982.

Münstermann, Hans. *Apuleius: Metamorphosen literarischer Vorlagen.* Stuttgart, 1995.

Murano, Giovanna, Giancarlo Savino, and Stefano Zamponi. *I manoscritti medievali della provincia di Pistoia.* Florence, 1998.
Mussini Sacchi, Maria Pia. See Tissoni Benvenuti. Also see del Carretto in "Other Primary Sources."
———. "Un amico pavese di Matteo Bandello: Giorgio Beccaria." In Ugo Rozzo, ed. *Matteo Bandello, novelliere europeo: Atti del Convegno internazionale di studi, 7–8 novembre 1980.* Tortona, 1982. 411–17.
Nauert, Charles G. "Gaius Plinius Secundus." In F. Edward Cranz, ed. *Catalogus Translationum et Commentariorum.* Washington, D.C., 1980. 4:297–422.
Newton, Francis. *The Scriptorium and Library at Monte Cassino, 1058–1105.* Cambridge, 1999.
———. "Tibullus in Two Grammatical *Florilegia* of the Middle Ages." *Transactions of the American Philological Association* 93 (1962): 253–86.
Nock, A. D. *Conversion: The Old and the New in Religion from Alexander the Great to Augustine of Hippo.* Oxford, 1933.
Nolhac, Pierre de. "Boccacce et Tacite." *Mélanges d'archéologie et d'histoire* 12 (1892): 125–48.
———. "Manuscrits à miniatures de la bibliothèque de Pétrarque." *Gazette archéologique* 14 (1889): 25–32.
———. *Pétrarque et l'humanisme.* 2 vols. Paris, 1907.
Norton, Glyn P. *The Ideology and Language of Translation in Renaissance France and Their Humanist Antecedents.* Travaux d'Humanisme et Renaissance 201. Geneva, 1984.
Nützmann, Hannelore. "Verschlüsselt in Details: Hochzeitsbilder für Lorenzo de' Medici." *Jahrbuch Preussischer Kulturbesitz* 34 (1997): 223–35.
O'Donnell, James J. "Augustine's Classical Readings." *Recherches augustiniennes* 15 (1980): 144–75.
———. "The Career of Virius Nicomachus Flavianus." *Phoenix* 32 (1978): 129–43.
———. "The Demise of Paganism." *Traditio* 35 (1979): 45–88.
Ohly, Kurt. "Ein unbeachteter illustrierter Druck Eggesteins." *Gutenberg Jahrbuch* (1953): 50–61.
Oldfather, William Abbot, Howard Vernon Carter, and Ben Edwin Perry. *Index Apuleianus.* Philological Monographs published by the American Philological Association, number 3. Middletown, Conn., 1934.
Oldoni, M. "Streghe medievali e intersezioni da Apuleio." *Materiali e contributi per la storia della narrativa greco-latina* 4 (1986): 267–79.
Oliver, Revilo P. "The First Medicean MS of Tacitus and the Titulature of Ancient Books." *Transactions of the American Philological Association* 82 (1951): 232–61.
———. "'New Fragments' of Latin Authors in Perotti's *Cornucopiae.*" *Transactions of the American Philological Association* 78 (1947): 376–424.
Önnerfors, Alf. "Magische Formeln im Dienste römischer Medizin." *Aufstieg und Niedergang der römischen Welt* II.37.1. New York, 1993. 157–224.
Opeku, Fabian. "Physiognomy in Apuleius." In Carl Deroux, ed. *Studies in Latin Literature and Roman History* 1 (1979): 467–74.

Orlandelli, G., "Bartolomeo de' Bartoli." *Dizionario biografico degli Italiani* 6 (1964): 559–60.
Osgood, Charles G. *Boccaccio on Poetry*. Princeton, N.J., 1930.
Osmond, Patricia J. "Jacopo Corbinelli and the Reading of Sallust in Late Renaissance France." *Medievalia et Humanistica* 21 (1994): 85–110.
Osmond, Patricia J., and Robert W. Ulery Jr. "Sallustius Crispus, Gaius." In Virginia Brown, ed. *Catalogus Translationum et Commentariorum*. Washington, D.C., 2003. 8.183–326.
Paoletti, L. "Benvenuto da Imola." *Dizionario biografico degli Italiani* 8 (1966): 691–94.
Pastore Stocchi, Manlio. "Un antecedente latino-medievale di Pietro di Vinciolo (*Decameron*, V 10)." *Studi sul Boccaccio* 1 (1963): 349–62.
Pavis d'Escurac, Henriette. "Pour une étude sociale de l'Apologie d'Apulée." *Antiquités africaines* 8 (1974): 89–101.
Pecere, Oronzo. "Antichità tarda e trasmissione dei testi: Qualche riflessione." In Oronzo Pecere, ed. *Itinerari dei testi antichi*. Rome, 1991. 55–83.
———. "Esemplari con *subscriptiones* e tradizione dei testi latini: L'Apuleio Laur. 68,2." In C. Questa and R. Raffaelli, eds. *Il libro e il testo*. Urbino, 1984. 111–137. Reprinted in Pecere and Stramaglia, eds. *Studi apuleiani*, 7–35.
———. "I meccansimi della tradizione testuale." In Guglielmo Cavallo, Paolo Fedeli, and Andrea Giardina, eds. *La recezione del testo*. In *Lo spazio letterario di Roma antica*. Rome, 1990. 3:297–386.
———. "Qualche riflessione sulla tradizione di Apuleio a Montecassino." In Guglielmo Cavallo, ed. *Le strade del Testo*. Bari, 1987. 99–124. Reprinted in Pecere and Stramaglia, eds. *Studi apuleiani*, 37–60.
———. "La 'subscriptio' di Statilio Massimo e la tradizione delle 'Agrarie' di Cicerone." *Italia medioevale e umanistica* 25 (1982): 73–123.
———. "La tradizione dei testi latini tra IV e V secolo attraverso i libri sottoscritti." In Andrea Giardina, ed. *Società romana e impero tardoantico IV: Tradizione dei classici, trasformazioni della cultura*. Rome, 1986. 19–81 and 210–46.
———. "Una pista di attualità nelle ricerche del filologo classico." In Anna Ferrari, ed. *Filologia classica e filologia romanza: Esperienze ecdotiche a confronto*. Atti del Convegno Roma, 25–27 maggio 1995. Spoleto, 1998. 507–15.
Pecere, Oronzo, and Antonio Stramaglia, eds. *Studi apuleiani*. Cassino, 2003.
Pellegrin, Élisabeth. *La bibliothèque des Visconti et des Sforza ducs de Milan*. Paris, 1955.
———. *La bibliothèque des Visconti et des Sforza ducs de Milan. Supplément*. Florence, 1969.
Pellegrin, Élisabeth, et al. *Les manuscrits classiques latins de la Bibliothèque Vaticane*. 3 vols. in 4 to date. Paris, 1975–.
———. "Possesseurs français et italiens de manuscrits latins du fonds de la Reine à la Bibliothèque Vaticane." *Revue de l'histoire des textes* 3 (1973): 271–97.

Pertusi, Agostino. *Leonzio Pilato fra Petrarca e Boccaccio: Le sue versioni omeriche negli autografi di Venezia e la cultura greca del primo Umanesimo.* Venice, [1964].
Petoletti, Marco. "Montecassino e gli umanisti." See Baglio, Ferrari, and Petoletti.
——, ed. *Il "Chronicon" di Benzo d'Alessandria.* See Benzo in "Other Primary Sources."
Petrucci, A. *La scrittura di Francesco Petrarca.* Studi e Testi 248. Vatican, 1967.
Pezzarossa, Fulvio. "*Canon est litterarum*: I libri di Filippo Beroaldo." In Giuseppe Lombardi and Donatella Nebbiai dalla Guarda, eds. *Libri, lettori e biblioteche dell'Italia medievale (secoli IX–XV): Fonti, testi, utilizzazione del libro.* Rome, 2000. 301–48.
Pfeiffer, Rudolf. *History of Classical Scholarship, 1300–1800.* Oxford, 1976.
Piattoli, Renato. "Ricerche intorno alla biblioteca dell'umanista Sozomeno." *La Bibliofilia* 36 (1934): 261–308.
Pietri, Charles and Luce. *Prosopographie chrétienne du Bas-Empire.* 2 vols. in 4. Rome, 2000.
Pigman, G. W., III. "Versions of Imitation in the Renaissance." *Renaissance Quarterly* 33 (1980): 1–32.
Pignati, F. "Agnolo Firenzuola." *Dizionario biografico degli Italiani* 48 (1997): 216–19.
Pins, Jean de. *Divae Catherinae Senensis simul et clarissimi viri Philippi Beroaldi Bononiensis vita.* Bologna, 1505. Beroaldo's biography is reprinted in J. G. Meuschen, ed. *Vitae summorum dignitate et eruditione virorum.* Coburg, 1735. 1:125–51.
Piovesan, Francesca. "Per il testo e le fonti di Guaiferio." *Civiltà classica e cristiana* 13 (1992): 71–86.
Plank, Birgit. *Johann Sieders Übersetzung des "Goldenen Esels" und die frühe deutschsprachige "Metamorphosen"-Rezeption: Ein Beitrag zur Wirkungsgeschichte von Apuleius' Roman.* Frühe Neuzeit 92. Tübingen, 2004.
Pozzi, Giovanni, and Lucia Ciapponi. See Colonna in "Other Primary Sources."
Pratesi, A. "Pietro Balbi." *Dizionario biografico degli Italiani* 5(1963): 378–79.
Prelog, Jan. "De Pictagora phylosopho: Die Biographie des Pythagoras in den Walter Burley zugeschriebenen 'Liber de vita et moribus philosophorum.'" *Medioevo* 16 (1990): 191–251.
Prete, Sesto. "Frammenti di Apuleio e pseudo-apuleiani nel *Cornu Copiae* di Niccolò Perotti." *Nuovi studi fanesi* 2 (1987): 39–63.
Prosopography of the Later Roman Empire. See Jones, A.H.M.
Purser, L. C. "Laud's Manuscript of Apuleius." *Hermathena* 15 (1909): 425–37.
Radcliff-Umstead, Douglas. "Boccaccio's Adaptation of Some Latin Sources for the *Decameron*." *Italica* 45 (1968): 171–94.
Rafti, Patrizia. "Riflessioni sull'*usus distinguendi* del Boccaccio negli Zibaldoni." In Michelangelo Picone and Claude Cazalé Bérard, eds. *Gli Zibaldoni di Boccaccio: Memoria, scrittura, riscrittura; Atti del Seminario internazionale di Firenze-Certaldo (26–28 aprile 1996).* Florence, 1998. 283–306.
Ragni, E. "Benzo d'Alessandria." *Dizionario biografico degli Italiani* 8 (1966): 723–26.
Raimondi, Ezio. *Codro e l'umanesimo a Bologna.* Bologna, 1950.

Raimondi, Ezio. "Il primo commento umanistico a Lucrezio." In *Politica e commedia: Dal Beroaldo al Machiavelli*. Bologna, 1972. 101–40.
Rathbone, Eleanor. "Master Alberic of London, 'Mythographus Tertius Vaticanus.'" *Mediaeval and Renaissance Studies* 1 (1941–43): 35–38.
Reeve, Michael D. "The Rediscovery of Classical Texts in the Renaissance." In Oronzo Pecere, ed. *Itinerari dei testi antichi*. Rome, 1991. 115–57.
Regen, Frank. "Il *De deo Socratis* di Apuleio." *Maia* 51 (1999): 429–56.
Reichenbach, Giulio. *L' "Orlando Innamorato" di M. M. Boiardo*. Florence, 1936.
Relihan, Joel C. *Ancient Menippean Satire*. Baltimore, 1993.
Renier, R. "I Tarocchi." In *Studi su Matteo Maria Boiardo*. Bologna, 1894. 229–59.
Renouard, Philippe. *Les marques typographiques parisiennes des xve et xvie siècles*. Paris, 1926.
———. *Répertoire des imprimeurs parisiens: Libraires, fondeurs de caractères et correcteurs d'imprimerie depuis l'introduction de l'Imprimerie à Paris (1470) jusqu'à la fin du seizième siècle*. Jeanne Veyrin-Forrer and Brigitte Moreau, eds. Paris, 1965.
Reynolds, L. D., ed. *Texts and Transmission: A Survey of the Latin Classics*. Oxford, 1983.
Reynolds, R. M. "The Adultery Mime." *Classical Quarterly* 40 (1946): 77–84.
Ricci, Laura. *La redazione manoscritta del libro de natura de amore di Mario Equicola*. Rome, 1999.
Ricci, Pier Giorgio. "Contributi per un'edizione critica della 'Genealogia deorum gentilium.'" *Rinascimento* 11, no. 2 (1951): 99–144, nos. 3–4:195–208. Reprinted with some changes in *Studi sulla vita e le opere del Boccaccio*, 189–225. Milan, 1985.
Ricciardi, R. "Galeotto Del Carretto." *Dizionario biografico degli Italiani* 36 (1988): 415–19.
Richlin, Amy. *The Garden of Priapus: Sexuality and Aggression in Roman Humor*. New Haven, Conn., 1983. Rev. ed., New York, 1992.
Richter, Gisela M. A. *The Portraits of the Greeks*. 3 vols. London, 1965.
Rigolot, François. "Louise Labé and the 'Climat Lyonnois.'" *The French Review* 71 (1998): 405–13.
Rizzo, Silvia. *Il lessico filologico degli umanisti*. Rome, 1984.
———. "Note alle *Familiari* del Petrarca." In Rino Avesani et al., eds. *Vestigia: Studi in onore di Giuseppe Billanovich*. 2 vols. Rome, 1984. 2:607–11.
Robertson, D. S. "The Assisi Fragments of the *Apologia* of Apuleius." *Classical Quarterly* 6 (1956): 68–80.
———. "The Manuscripts of the *Metamorphoses* of Apuleius." *Classical Quarterly* 18 (1924): 27–42, 85–99.
Rodgers, Barbara Saylor. "Constantine's Pagan Vision." *Byzantion* 50 (1980): 259–78.
Romano, Vincenzo. See Boccaccio, *Genealogie deorum gentilium*.
Romier, Lucien. "Lyons and Cosmopolitanism at the Beginning of the French Renaissance." In Werner L. Gundersheimer, ed. *French Humanism, 1470–1600*. London, 1969. 90–109.

Rose, Anna. *Filippo Beroaldo der Ältere und sein Beitrag zur Properz-Überlieferung*. Munich, 2001.
Rosenthal, Erwin. "Die Erstausgabe von Apulejus' 'Goldenem Esel,' gedruckt durch Ludwig Hohenwang." *Zentralblatt für Bibliothekswesen* 29 (1912): 273–78.
Rossi, Aldo, ed. *"Il Decameron": Pratiche testuali e interpretative*. Bologna, 1982.
Rossi, Luca Carlo. "Benvenuto da Imola lettore di Lucano." In Pantaleo Palmieri and Carlo Paolazzi, eds. *Benvenuto da Imola lettore degli antichi e dei moderni*. Ravenna, 1991. 165–203.
Rostagno, Enrico, ed. *Tacitus: Codex laurentianus mediceus 68I[–II] phototypice editus*. Leiden, 1902.
Sabatier, J. *Description generale des médaillons contorniates*. Paris, 1860. 99. Nr. 7, taf. 15.
Sabbadini, Remigio. "Bencius Alexandrinus und der Cod. veronensis des Ausonius." *Rheinisches Museum* 63 (1908): 224–34.
———. "La biblioteca di Zomino da Pistoia." *Rivista di filologia e di istruzione classica* 45 (1917): 197–207.
———. *Le scoperte dei codici latini e greci ne' secoli XIV e XV*. 2 vols. Florence, 1905. Reprint, Florence, 1967.
Saffrey, H. D. "Pietro Balbi et la première traduction latine de la *Théologie platonicienne* de Proclus." In P. Cockshaw et al., eds. *Miscellanea codicologica F. Masai dicata MCMLXXIX*. 2 vols. Gand, 1979. 2:425–37.
Salzman, Michele Renee. *On Roman Time: The Codex-Calendar of 354 and the Rhythms of Urban Life in Late Antiquity*. Berkeley, Calif., 1993.
Sandy, Gerald N. "Apuleius' 'Metamorphoses' and the Ancient Novel." *Aufstieg und Niedergang der römischen Welt* II.34.2. New York, 1994. 1511–74.
———. *The Greek World of Apuleius: Apuleius and the Second Sophistic*. Leiden, 1997.
———. "A Neoplatonic Interpretation of Heliodorus' *Ethiopian Story*." In Alain Billault, ed. *'ΟΠΩΡΑ: La belle saison de l'hellénisme: Études de littérature antique offertes au Recteur Jacques Bompaire*. Paris, 2001. 169–78.
———. "Two Renaissance Readers of Apuleius: Filippo Beroaldo and Henri de Mesmes." In Shannon N. Byrne, Edmund P. Cueva, and Jean Alvares, eds. *Authors, Authority, and Interpreters in the Ancient Novel: Essays in Honor of Gareth L. Schmeling*. Ancient Narrative. Supplementum 5. Groningen, 2006. 239–73.
———. "West Meets East: Western Students in Athens in the Mid-Second Century A.D." *Groningen Colloquia on the Novel* 5 (1993): 163–74.
———, ed. *The Classical Heritage in France*. Leiden, 2002.
Sanguineti White, Laura. *Boccaccio e Apuleio: Caratteri differenziali nella struttura narrativa del "Decameron."* Bologna, 1977.
Saunders, Alison. "Sixteenth-Century Book Illustration: The Classical Heritage." In Gerald N. Sandy, ed. *The Classical Heritage in France*. Leiden, 2002. 503–32.
Savini, Giancarlo. "La libreria di Sozomeno da Pistoia." *Rinascimento* 16 (1976): 159–72.
Scarcia, Riccardo. *Latina Siren: Note di critica semantica*. Rome, 1964.

Scarpatetti, Beat Matthias von, Rudolf Gamper, and Marlis Stähli. *Katalog der datierten Handschriften in der Schweiz in lateinischer Schrift vom Anfang des Mittelalters bis 1550*. 3 vols. Zurich, 1977–1991.
Schefold, Karl. *Die Bildnisse der antiken Dichter, Redner und Denker*. Basel, 1997.
Scherer, Gustav. *Verzeichniss der Manuscripte und Incunabeln der vadianischen Bibliothek in St. Gallen*. St. Gallen, 1864.
Schlam, Carl. "Apuleius in the Middle Ages." In A. Bernardo, ed. *The Classics in the Middle Ages*. Binghamton, N. Y., 1990. 363–69.
———. *Cupid and Psyche: Apuleius and the Monuments*. University Park, Penn., 1976.
Schmid, Wolfgang. "Tityrus Christianus: Probleme religiöser Hirtendichtung an der Wende vom vierten zum fünften Jahrhundert." *Rheinisches Museum* 96 (1953): 101–65.
Schmidt, Victor. "Ein Trio im Bett: *Tema con variazioni* bei Catull, Martial, Babrius und Apuleius." *Groningen Colloquium on the Novel* 2 (1989): 63–72.
Schmidtchen, Volker. "Ludwig Hohenwang."*Die deutsche Literatur des Mittelalters Verfasserlexikon* 4 (1988): 101–5.
Schnorr von Carolsfeld, Franz, and L. Schmidt. *Katalog der Handschriften der königlichen öffentlichen Bibliothek zu Dresden*. 4 vols. Leipzig, 1882–1923.
Scholderer, Victor. "The Petition of Sweynheym and Pannartz to Sixtus IV." In *Fifty Essays in Fifteenth- and Sixteenth-Century Bibliography*. Amsterdam, 1966. 72–73.
———. "Printers and Readers in Italy in the Fifteenth Century." In *Fifty Essays in Fifteenth- and Sixteenth-Century Bibliography*. Amsterdam, 1966. 202–15.
Schubring, Paul. *Cassoni: Truhen und Truhenbilder der italienischen Frührenaissance*. 2 vols. Leipzig, 1923.
———. "Zwei Cassonetafeln mit Apuleius' Märchen von Amor und Psyche." *Zeitschrift für bildende Kunst* 51 (1916): 315–20.
Scobie, A. *Aspects of the Ancient Romance and Its Heritage*. Meisenheim am Glan, 1969.
———. "The Dating of the Earliest Printed European Translations of Apuleius's *Metamorphoses*." In *More Essays on the Ancient Romance and Its Heritage*. Meisenheim am Glan, 1973. 47–52.
———. "The Dating of the Earliest Printed Spanish and French Translations of Apuleius's *Metamorphoses*." *The Library* 27 (1972): 236–37.
———. "The Influence of Apuleius' *Metamorphoses* in Renaissance Italy and Spain." In B. L. Hijmans Jr. and R. Th. van der Paardt, eds. *Aspects of Apuleius' Golden Ass*. Groningen, 1978. 211–30.
Senesi, Ireneo. *La commedia*. 2nd ed. 2 vols. Milan, 1954.
Shanzer, Danuta. *A Philosophical and Literary Commentary on Martianus Capella's "De Nuptiis Philologiae et Mercurii Book 1."* Berkeley, Calif., 1986.
Sharratt, Peter. *Bernard Salomon: Illustrateur Lyonnais*. Travaux d'Humanisme et Renaissance 400. Geneva, 2005.
Shearman, John. "Die Loggia der Psyche in der Villa Farnesina und die Probleme der letzten Phase von Raffaels graphischem Stil." *Jahrbuch der kunsthistorischen Sammlungen in Wien* 60 (1964): 59–100.

Shepherd, Rupert. "Giovanni Sabadino degli Arienti, Ercole I d'Este and the Decoration of the Italian Renaissance Court." *Renaissance Studies* 9 (1995): 18–57.

Sighinolfi, Lino. "Francesco Puteolano e le origini della stampa in Bologna e in Parma." *Bibliofilia* 15 (1913): 263–467.

Simon, Erika. *Die konstantinischen Deckengemälde in Trier*. Trierer Beiträge zur Altertumskunde 3. Mainz am Rhein, 1986.

Slater, Niall W. "Passion and Petrifaction: The Gaze in Apuleius." *Classical Philology* 93 (1998): 18–48.

———. "Vision, Perception, and Phantasia in the Roman Novel," In Michelangelo Picone and Bernhard Zimmermann, eds. *Der antike Roman und seine mittelalterliche Rezeption*. Basel, 1997. 89–105.

Smalley, Beryl. *English Friars and Antiquity in the Early Fourteenth Century*. Oxford, 1960.

Smith, Warren S., Jr. "The Narrative Voice in Apuleius' *Metamorphoses*." *Transactions of the American Philological Association* 103 (1972): 514–20.

Sorbelli, Albano. *Storia della stampa in Bologna*. Bologna, 1929.

———. *Storia della Università di Bologna I: Il Medioevo*. Bologna, 1944.

Speyer, Wolfgang. "Zum Bild des Apollonius von Tyana bei Heiden und Christen." *Jahrbuch für Antike und Christentum* 17 (1974): 47–63.

Stauber, Richard. *Die Schedelsche Bibliothek*. Freiburg, 1908. Reprint, Nieuwkoop, 1969.

Stephens, Susan A. "Who Read Ancient Novels?" In James Tatum, ed. *The Search for the Ancient Novel*. Baltimore, 1994. 405–18.

———, and John J. Winkler, eds. *Ancient Greek Novels: The Fragments*. Princeton, N. J., 1995.

Stigall, John O. "The Manuscript Tradition of the *De vita et moribus philosophorum* of Walter Burley." *Medievalia et Humanistica* 11 (1957): 44–57.

Stillers, Rainer. "Erträumte Kunstwelt: Niccolò Correggios *Fabula Psiches et Cupidinis* (1491)." In József Jankovics and S. Katalin Németh, eds. *Der Mythos von Amor und Psyche in der europäischen Renaissance*. Budapest, 2002. 131–50.

Stramaglia, Antonio. "Apuleio come *auctor*: Premesse tardoantiche di un uso umanistico." *Studi umanistici piceni* 16 (1996): 137–61. Reprinted in Pecere and Stramaglia, eds. *Studi apuleiani*. 119–52.

———. "Fra 'consumo' e 'impegno': Usi didattici della narrrativa nel mondo antico." In Oronzo Pecere and Antonio Stramaglia, eds. *La letteratura di consumo nel mondo greco-latino: Atti del convegno internazionale Cassino, 14–17 settembre 1994*. Cassino, 1996. 97–166.

———. "Prisciano e l'*Epitoma historiarum* di Apuleio." *Rivista di filologia e di istruzione classica* 124 (1996): 192–98. Reprinted in Pecere and Stramaglia, eds. *Studi apuleiani*, 153–58.

Stupperich, R. "Das Statuenprogramm in den Zeuxippos-Thermen." *Istanbuler Mitteilungen* 32 (1982): 210–35.

Tarán, Leonardo. "The Authorship of an Allegorical Interpretation of Heliodorus' *Aethiopica*." In Marie-Odile Goulet-Cazé, Goulven Madec, and Denis O'Brien, eds. *Sophies Maietores "Chercheurs de sagesse": Hommage à Jean Pépin*. Paris, 1992. 204–30.

Tatum, James. *Apuleius and the Golden Ass.* Ithaca, N. Y., 1979.
———, ed. *The Search for the Ancient Novel.* Baltimore, 1994.
Thomas, P. "Remarques critiques sur les oeuvres philosophiques d'Apulée." *Bulletin de l'Académie royale de Belgique, Classe des Lettres* 37 (1900): 143-65.
Tilley, Arthur. "A Paris Bookseller—Galliot Du Pré." In *Studies in the French Renaissance.* Cambridge, 1922. 168—218.
Tissoni Benvenuti, Antonia. *Niccolò da Correggio: Opere.* See Correggio in "Other Primary Sources."
Tissoni Benvenuti, Antonia, and Maria Pia Mussini, eds. *Teatro del Quattrocento.* See Del Carreto in "Other Primary Sources."
Toynbee, J.M.C. Review of Alföldi, *Die Kontorniaten. Journal of Roman Studies* 35 (1945): 115-21.
Trecca, Monica. *La magia rinnovata.* Florence, 1995.
Tristano, Caterina. "Le postille del Petrarca nel Vaticano lat. 2193 (Apuleio, Frontino, Vegezio, Palladio)." *Italia medioevale e umanistica* 17 (1974): 365-468.
Turba, Giuseppe. "Galeotto del Carretto tra Casale e Mantova." *Rinascimento* 11 (1971): 95-169.
Uberti, Maria Luisa. "Benvenuto da Imola dantista, allievo del Boccaccio." *Studi sul Boccaccio* 12 (1980): 275-319.
Ullman, B. L. *The Humanism of Coluccio Salutati.* Padua, 1963.
———. *The Origin and Development of Humanistic Script.* Rome, 1960.
Vandelli, G. Review of N. Zingarelli, "L'Epistola di Dante a Moroello Malaspina," in *Rassegna critica della letteratura italiana* 4 (1899). *Rassegna critica degli studi danteschi* 7 (1899-1900): 59-68.
van der Paardt, Rudi Th. "The Unmasked 'I': Apuleius Met. XI. 27." *Mnemosyne* 34 (1981): 96-106.
Van der Vliet, J. "Codices Apulei Italici." *Mnemosyne* 23 (1895): 353-59.
van Mal-Maeder, Danielle. "Descriptions et descripteurs: Mais qui décrit dans les *Métamorphoses* d'Apulée?" In Michelangelo Picone and Bernhard Zimmermann, eds. *Der antike Roman und seine mittelalterliche Rezeption.* Basel, 1997. 171-201.
———. "*Lector, intende: Laetaberis*; The enigma of the Last Book of Apuleius' *Metamorphoses.*" *Groningen Colloquia on the Novel* 8 (1997): 87-118.
Vasoli, C. "Marsilo Ficino." *Dizionario biografico degli Italini* 47 (1997): 378-95.
The Vatican Collections: The Papacy and Art. New York, 1983.
Vattasso, M. *I codici petrarcheschi della Biblioteca Vaticana.* Studi e Testi 20. Rome, 1908. 161-62, 229-34, and plates 1-2.
VD17. See *Das Verzeichnis der im deutschen Sprachraum erschienenen Drucke des 17. Jahrhunderts.*
Verheyen, Egon. "Die Malereien in der Sala di Psiche." *Jahrbuch der Berliner Museen* 14 (1972): 33-68.
———. *The Palazzo Te in Mantua: Images of Love and Politics.* Baltimore, 1977.
Vertova, Luisa. "Cupid and Psyche in Renaissance Painting before Raphael." *Journal of the Warburg and Courtauld Institute* 42 (1979): 104-21.

———. "La favola di Psiche riscoperta a Firenze." *Fontes* 3 (2000): 107–31.
Das Verzeichnis der im Deutschensprachbereich erschienenen Drucke des XVI Jahrhunderts (= VD 16). Stuttgart, 1983–.
Das Verzeichnis der im deutschen Sprachraum erschienenen Drucke des 17. Jahrhunderts (= VD 17). Munich, 2006. (http://www.vd17.de.)
Vidman, Ladislav. *Isis und Sarapis bei den Griechen und Römern.* Berlin, 1970.
Vio, Gianluigi. "Chiose e riscritture apuleiane di Giovanni Boccaccio." *Studi sul Boccaccio* 20 (1992): 139–65.
Viti, Paolo. "Filippo Beroaldo traduttore del Boccaccio." *Rinascimento* 15 (1975): 111–40.
Voigt, Georg. *Die Wiederbelebung des classischen Alterthums oder das erste Jahrhundert des Humanismus.* 2 vols. Berlin, 1880–81. Reprint, Berlin, 1960.
Walser, Ernst. *Poggius Florentinus: Leben und Werke.* Leipzig, 1914.
Walsh, P. G. *The Roman Novel.* Cambridge, 1970.
———. "The Rights and Wrongs of Curiosity (Plutarch to Augustine)." *Greece and Rome* 35 (1988): 73–85.
Walter, I., and H. J Becker. "Simone da Brossano." *Dizionario biografico degli Italiani* 14 (1972): 470–74.
Walters, Jonathan. "'No More Than a Boy': The Shifting Construction of Masculinity from Ancient Greece to the Middle Ages." *Gender and History* 5, no. 1 (1993): 20–33.
Weber, Winfried. *Constantinische Deckengemälde aus dem römischen Palast unter dem Trierer Dom.* Museumsführer Nr. 1, Bischöfliches Dom- und Diözesanmuseum Trier. Trier, 1986.
Weiland-Pollerberg, Florian. *Amor und Psyche in der Renaissance: Medienspezifisches Erzählen im Bild.* Petersberg, 2004.
Weinberg, Bernard. "Guillaume Michel, dit de Tours: The Editor of the 1526 *Roman de la Rose*." *Bibliothèque de l'humanisme et renaissance* 11 (1949): 72–85.
Weir, Robert. "Apuleius Glosses in the *Abolita* Glossary." *Classical Quarterly* 15 (1921): 41–43, 107.
Werner, Shirley. "On the History of the *Commenta Bernensia* and the *Adnotationes super Lucanum*." *Harvard Studies in Classical Philology* 96 (1994): 343–68.
Wesseling, Berber. "The Audience of the Ancient Novels." *Groningen Colloquia on the Novel* 1 (1988): 67–79.
Weyman, Carl. "Studien zu Apuleius und seinen Nachahmern." *Sitzungsberichte der bayerischen Akademie der Wissenschaften, Philos. Hist. Klasse* II 2, no. 3 (1893): 321–92.
Whibley, Charles. See Adlington in "Apuleius B."
Wilson, Diana de Armas. "Homage to Apuleius: Cervantes' Avenging Psyche." In James Tatum, ed. *The Search for the Ancient Novel.* Baltimore, 1994. 88–100.
Winkler, John J. *Auctor & Actor: A Narratological Reading of the "Golden Ass."* Berkeley, Calif., 1985.
Witt, R. E. *Isis in the Greco-Roman World.* Ithaca, N.Y., 1971.
Witt, Ronald C. *Hercules at the Crossroads: The Life, Works and Thought of Coluccio Salutati.* Durham, N.C., 1983.

Worstbrock, F. J. *Deutsche Antikerezeption, 1450–1550.* Boppard am Rhein, 1976.
———. "Johann Sieder." In *Die deutsche Literatur des Mittelalters: Verfasserlexikon.* Berlin, 1992. 8: 1195–99.
———. "Niklas von Wyle." *Die deutsche Literatur des Mittelalters: Verfasserlexikon.* 6 (1987): 1016–35.
Wright, Cyril Ernest. *Fontes Harleianae: A Study of the Sources of the Harleian Collection of Manuscripts Preserved in the Department of Manuscripts in the British Museum.* London, 1972.
Zaccaria, F. A. See Trebizond, Andreas, in "Other Primary Sources."
Zaccaria, Vittorio. "Boccaccio e Tacito." In Gilbert Tournoy, ed. *Boccaccio in Europe: Proceedings of the Louvain Conference, Louvain, December 1975.* Louvain, 1977. 221–37.
———. "Per il testo delle 'Genealogie deorum gentilium.'" *Studi sul Boccaccio* 16 (1987): 179–240.
———. "Ancora per il testo delle 'Genealogie deorum gentilium.'" *Studi sul Boccaccio* 21 (1993): 243–73.
Zanichelli, Giuseppa Z. "'Non scripsit set miniavit': Turinus e i codici del Petrarca." *Studi petrarcheschi* 11 (1994): 159–81.
Zanker, Paul. *The Mask of Socrates: The Image of the Intellectual in Antiquity.* Alan Shapiro, trans. Berkeley, 1995.
Zetzel, J.E.G. *Latin Textual Criticism in Antiquity.* Salem, N.H., 1981.
———. "The Subscriptions in the Manuscripts of Livy and Fronto and the Meaning of *Emendatio.*" *Classical Philology* 75 (1980): 38–59.
Zimmerman, M. See *Metamorphoses* X in "Apuleius A.4."
Zorzi, Marino. "Cenni sulla vita e sulla figura di Bessarione." In Gianfranco Fiaccadori, ed. *Bessarione e l'Umanesimo.* 1–19.
———. "Stampatori tedeschi a Venezia." In *Venezia e la Germania: Arte, politica, commercio, due civiltà a confronto.* Milan, 1986. 115–40.

Index of Manuscripts

Assisi, Biblioteca Comunale 706, 63n107, 110n147. *See also* Zanobi da Strada (in General Index)

Berlin, Staatsbibliothek Ms. germ. fol. 1239, presentation copy of Sieder's translation, 248n20

Brussels, Bibliothèque Royale Albert Ier 3920–3923, owned by Nicolas of Cusa, 160n153

Brussels, Bibliothèque Royale Albert Ier 10054–10056: corrected by Bussi and Nicolas of Cusa, 160; oldest manuscript of the philosophical works, 6n19, 36; as a possible source for the *editio princeps*, 171

Dresden, Sächsische Landesbibliothek Dc 178, used by Pio, 201n19

Florence, Biblioteca Laurenziana 29.2: annotations by Boccaccio in, 98–99, 110, 132; annotations by Zanobi da Strada in, 65, 94, 132; copied from Florence, Biblioteca Laurenziana 68.2, 63; as an exemplar of Florence, Biblioteca Laurenziana 54.12, 133–34, 138; in Florence, 131. See also *spurcum additamentum* (in General Index)

Florence, Biblioteca Laurenziana 36.23, owned by Lupi, 139

Florence, Biblioteca Laurenziana 51.9, owned by Lupi, 138, 139n48

Florence, Biblioteca Laurenziana 54.12: annotations in, 132, 134–35; exemplars of, 133–35; Medici owners of, 132; philosophical and literary works united in, 130n6; *spurcum additamentum* in, 134; verse prologue in, 135, 137–38, 313–14. *See also* Antonio di Mario (in General Index)

Florence, Biblioteca Laurenziana 54.13: owned by Piero de' Medici, 150; philosophical and literary works united in, 130n6; portrait of Apuleius in, 150–51, plate 17. *See also* Francesco d'Antonio del Chierico (in General Index)

Florence, Biblioteca Laurenziana 54.14: as an exemplar of Florence, Biblioteca Laurenziana 54.12, 133–35; in Florence, 131

Florence, Biblioteca Laurenziana 54.24: annotations in, 132, 139–41, 142–44; owned by Lupi, 138, 139n48; *spurcum additamentum* in, 135, 139–40; verse prologue in, 144, 313–14

Florence, Biblioteca Laurenziana 54.32: annotations by Boccaccio in, 109–10, Boccaccio as scribe of, 108–9, 131–32; as a Class I manuscript, 108; diffusion of Boccaccio's annotations in, 139–41, 142–43; philosophical and literary works united in, 108, 130n4, 133n15; *spurcum additamentum* in, 110

Florence, Biblioteca Laurenziana 68.2: exemplar of, 62, 297; as an exemplar of Florence, Biblioteca Laurenziana 54.12, 134; in Florence, 93, 94, 131; at Monte Cassino, 61–63; name of Apuleius in, 6n19; subscriptions by Sallustius in, 45–48; Tacitus in, 45n20, 95. *See also* Zanobi da Strada (in General Index)

Florence, Biblioteca Laurenziana 76.36: owned and annotated by Salutati, 133n15, 147n94; as a possible source for the *editio princeps*, 171n190

Florence, Biblioteca Laurenziana 84.24: and Latin Platonic library, 151, plate 18; owned by Lorenzo de' Medici, 151; philosophical and literary works united in, 130n6. *See also* Attavante (in General Index)

Florence, Biblioteca Laurenziana San Marco 284, owned and annotated by Salutati, 133n15, 147n94

Florence, Biblioteca Laurenziana San Marco 341, 133n15

Florence, Biblioteca Laurenziana, Santa Croce 24 sin 11: as an exemplar of Florence, Biblioteca Laurenziana 54.12, 133–35, 138; in Florence, 131–32; verse prologue in, 135, 137, 313–14

Florence, Biblioteca Nazionale Centrale, ms. II. VI. 2, allegory in, 124–28

Florence, Biblioteca Nazionale Centrale, Conventi Soppressi i.IX.39, owned by Salutati, 133n15, 147n94

Florence, Biblioteca Riccardiana 709, transcribed in part by Ficino, 178

Leiden, Bibliotheek der Rijksuniversiteit, Voss. Lat. Q 10, *Cosmographia* as title of *De mundo* in, 75n156; as possible source for the first edition, 171n190

London, British Library, Add. ms. 24893: and Laur. 54.32, 108n136

London, British Library, Harley 4838: annotated by Salutati, 132, 135–36, 311–13; annotated by Sozomeno, 132, 136–37, 139, 142–44; verse prologue in, 135–37, 144, 311–14

Milan, Biblioteca Ambrosiana N 180 sup: early date of, 66n121, 93n63; title of *Metamorphoses* in, 74n154

Milan, Biblioteca Ambrosiana N 266 sup, brought to Italy from Avignon, 129n2

Milan, Biblioteca Ambrosiana S 14 sup, transcribed by Ficino, 130n7, 148

Munich, Bayerische Staatsbibliothek, Clm 621: *Cosmographia* as title of *De mundo* in, 75n156; owned by Schedel, 243n3

Naples, Biblioteca Nazionale IV.G.55, philosophical and literary works united in, 108n134, 130n4

Naples, Biblioteca Oratoriana, CF.3.7, philosophical and literary works united in, 130n6

Olomouc, Státní Vědecká Knihovna M II 58: perhaps copied outside Italy, 243n1; philosophical and literary works united in, 130n6

Paris, Bibliothèque Nationale Lat. 6634, as a possible source for the *editio princeps*, 171n190

Pistoia, Biblioteca Comunale Forteguerriana A.46, owned and annotated by Sozomeno, 142, 144, 144n81

St. Gallen, Kantonsbibliothek, Ms. 483: philosophical and literary works united in, 130n6; verse prologue in, 145, 313–14

Urbana, University of Illinois Library, ms. 7, Holt de Heke d'Osnabrük as scribe of, 243n1

Vatican Library, Ottob. lat. 2091: early date of, 93n63; Lucius as Apuleius' praenomen in, 69; Petrarch's annotations reproduced in, 77n5

Vatican Library, Pal. lat. 1574, owned by Manetti, 147

Vatican Library, Reg. lat. 1572, as a possible source for the *editio princeps*, 171

Vatican Library, Urb. lat. 199: philosophical and literary works united in, 130n6, 150n114; portrait of Apuleius in, 150n114; *spurcum additamentum* in, 135

Vatican Library, Urb. lat. 1141, as a possible source for the *editio princeps*, 171n190

Vatican Library, Vat. lat. 1520, *De monarchia* attributed to Apuleius in, 123

Vatican Library, Vat. lat. 2193: annotations by Petrarch in, 77n5, 78–79; illuminations in, 82, plates 5–8; philosophical and literary works united in, 78, 108n134, 130; title of *Metamorphoses* in, 74n154

Vatican Library, Vat. lat. 2194, illuminations and interpretation of *Golden Ass* in, 82–93, plates 9–14

Vatican Library, Vat. lat. 3082, *Apology* and philosophical works in, 130n6

Vatican Library, Vat. lat. 3384: owned and annotated by Benvenuto da Imola, 96; philosophical and literary works united in, 108n134, 130n4

Venice, Biblioteca Marciana lat. 467 (coll. 1557), owned and annotated by Bessarion, 159n144

Venice, Biblioteca Marciana lat. 469 (coll. 1856), owned by Bessarion, 159n144

General Index

Page numbers in **bold** refer to illustrations

Abolita Glossary, 60–61
Adlington, William, translation of
  Golden Ass by, 274; allegory in,
  289–91; influence of, 293; *Met*. 11.1.1
  in, 293, 315–17; title page of, 288–89;
  translation theory in, 294–95; use of
  Michel and Louveau in, 291–92,
  315–17; verse prologue in, 288,
  291–92. *See also* Beroaldo's commentary, influence of
adultery mime, 100, 105
adultery tales: in Apuleius and Boccaccio,
  100–107; in Apuleius and Boiardo,
  176–80. *See also* Mantovano
Alcinous, *Handbook of Platonism*,
  included in *editio princeps*, 161
Alexander the Great, portraits of, 12,
  14, 296
allegory: in Louveau, 279; medieval, 268;
  in Michel, 262, 268; in Philip the
  philosopher, 51–52; of possible interest
  to Sallustius and Endelechius, 49–51;
  Salutati on, 126; Stefano Colonna on,
  122–23. *See also* Lucius, allegory of;
  Psyche, allegory of
amorous matron, 63–64; in Cortegana,
  274, 275; in German editions of Poggio's
  Onos, 245–47; in La Bouthière, 282; in
  Louveau, 286; omitted by Michel, 265;
  in Sieder, 265n88
L'amour de Cupido et de Psiche: influence
  of, 279, 280, 284, 288–89; woodcuts
  based on Master of the Die in,
  277–78
Anastasios of Sinai, 37–38
Antonio di Mario: as annotator of
  Laur. 54.12, 134–35; as scribe of
  Laur. 54.12, 132–34, 137–38.
  See also *spurcum additamentum*;
  verse prologue
Apollo: Apuleius as, 28; and Marsyas,
  10–11; as Psyche's father in Boccaccio,
  113; as Psyche's father on Florentine
  cassone, 119, **plate 15**; as Psyche's
  father in Martianus Capella, 53, 113
Apollonius of Tyana: contorniate portrait
  of, 45; paired with Apuleius, 24,
  30–31, 37–38; as a wonder worker,
  22–23
Apology: allegory of in Florence,
  Biblioteca nazionale, ms II. VI. 2,
  125–26; Apuleius' self-presentation in,
  5–7, 8–10, 11–13, 15–17; beards in, 8,
  9, 10; description of by Waleys, 72–73,
  74; imitation of by Claudianus
  Mamertus, 60, 300; mirrors in, 11–13;
  physiognomy in, 8–10; quotation of
  by Ficino, 148–49; quotation of by
  Pseudo-Burley, 70; title of used by
  Pseudo-Burley, 74n154
Apulegio volgare: ending of *Onos* used in,
  176, 283; influence of in Ferrara and
  Mantua, 175, 184–86, 193, 195; influence of on La Bouthière, 280, 283. *See
  also* Ercole I d'Este
Apuleius, biography of, 1–2; Augustine as
  a source for, 13, 35–36
Apuleius, *editio princeps* of: and Bessarion's
  Defensio Platonis, 157–62; Class I
  manuscript of *Metamorphoses* used for,
  171; contents of, 161; importance of,
  172, 173; introduction to Apuleius in,
  163–69; manuscripts of philosophical
  works used in, 171. *See also* Bussi;
  Latin Platonic Library; Sweynheym
  and Pannartz
Apuleius, portraits of: on contorniate,
  28–29, 43, 45, **plate 4**; in Laur. 54.13,
  150–51, **plate 17**; in *Nuremberg
  Chronicle*, 243–44n3; in Trier, 25–27,
  plates 1 and 3; in Vatican Library,
  Urb. lat. 199, 150n114. *See also* statues
  of Apuleius
Apuleius, praenomen of unknown, 34.
  See also Lucius as praenomen of
  Apuleius

Apuleius, readers of in late antiquity, 40–43, 300–301; Augustine, 29–36, 41; Claudianus Mamertus, 60; Fulgentius, 53–59, 60; Martianus Capella, 53, 59, 60; Priscian, 60; Sallustius, 41, 43, 45–52; Sidonius Apollinaris, 59–60

Apuleius, style of: criticism of by Valla, 168; praise of by Beroaldo, 202–3; praise of by Bussi, 168–69

Apuleius and Lucius, identity of: in Augustine, 33–34; in Benzo, 67–69; in Beroaldo, 210, 219–20; in Boccaccio, 109–10; in Bussi, 165; in *Golden Ass*, 14, 17–10; in Guglielmo da Pastrengo, 81; in *La Celestina*, 269; in Louveau, 286n180; in Michel, 265, 266; in Petrarch, 80, 81–82; in Waleys, 72–73. *See also* Pseudo-Lucian's *Onos*

Apuleius and the prehumanists, 66–75, 135–36

Apuleius' works, literary and philosophical groups of, 36, 40–41; citations of in *Abolita* Glossary, 60–61, 75; knowledge of by Pseudo-Burley and Waleys, 75, 129; reuniting of in Vatican Library, Vat. lat. 2193, 78, 130; separate transmission of, 36, 61; separation of *Florida* and *De deo Socratis* in, 47; transcription of by Boccaccio, 108–9; uniting of in *editio princeps*, 161, 163; uniting of in fifteenth-century manuscripts, 130n6; works included in, 41. *See also* literary group; philosophical group

Arienti, Sabadino degli: description of Sala di Psiche at Belriguardo, 188–92. *See also Fabula Psiches et Cupidinis*

Aristippus, translation of the *Phaedo* by, in Latin Platonic library, 146

Asclepius: in Augustine, 36; in *editio princeps*, 161; in Latin Platonic library, 146; in Florence, Biblioteca Laurenziana, 84.24, 151

the Ass, illustrations of: in Pseudo-Lucian's *Onos*, 245, **246**, 247, **plate 19**; in Sieder's translation, 253, **254**, **255**, **256**; in Vatican Library, Vat. lat. 2194, 89–91, 92, **plates 13 and 14**

Attavante, as illuminator of Florence, Biblioteca Laurenziana 84.24, 151

Augustine, 29–36; Apuleian works known to, 35–36, 60; Apuleius as a magician in, 30–33; Apuleius as a Platonic philosopher in, 6n9, 34–36, 146; *Asclepius* in, 36; *De deo Socratis* criticized in, 30, 32–33, 34–35, 296–97; *De mundo* in, 73–74; on *Golden Ass*, 33–34, 41, 297; influence of on Petrarch, 81; influence of on Salutati, 136; in Latin Platonic library, 146; prehumanists influenced by, 75, 76; quotation of by Benzo of Alessandria, 67–69; quotation of by Poggio, 154; quotation of by Pseudo-Burley, 71; quotation of by Waleys, 72–74; on statue of Apuleius in Oea, 13, 31

Balbi, Pietro, Alcinous translation of in *editio princeps*, 161

Bartolomeo de' Bartoli, scribe of Vatican Library, Vat. lat. 2194, 77, 82–93, 124, 128, **plate 9**

Beccaria, Giorgio, story of Cupid and Psyche by, 195

Belriguardo, Sala di Psiche in, 185, 193; allegory in, 191–92; description of by Arienti, 188–92. *See also* de' Roberti, Ercole

Benvenuto da Imola: Boccaccio in Dante commentary of, 96–98; as owner of Vatican Library, Vat. lat. 3384, 96

Benzo of Alessandria, 66–69, 74; Lucius as Apuleius' praenomen in, 69, 71, 74

Beroaldo, Filippo: allegories in, 216–21; *Annotationes centum* of, 198–99; Apuleian vocabulary in, 202, 208n46, 211, 213n68; on *ars aemula naturae*, 225–29; on Boccaccio, 101; on Christian and pagan ritual and religious experience, 208–14; on Cupid and Psyche, 229–38; digressions as metatexts in, 222–39; on Francesco Francia, 225–26, 228, 229; on Fulgentius, 229–32; on the ideal priest, 214–16, 219–20; imitation of Apuleius by, 228–29, 233–38, 299; imitation of Pliny the younger by, 234–35; on Isis and Mary, 210–11; on Mino de' Rossi, 229, 233–36; self-presentation of in commentary, 221–23, 237–42, 299; students addressed by, 216, 219–21, 238; on style of Apuleius,

202–3; as a teacher, 197–98, 201–8, 233; and Péter Váradi, 197n4, 199, 201, 214–16, 221, 239–40; verse prologue in, 205. *See also* Beroaldo's commentary, influence of; Beroaldo's commentary, Apuleius passages discussed in

Beroaldo's commentary, influence of: on Adlington, 288, 289–90; on Cortegana, 269, 273–74; on Erasmus, 244n5; on Ernnst, 250–51; in Europe, 244, 269, 277; on de Keysere, 258; on Kierher, 259–61; on Louveau, 286; on Michel, 264; on Sieder, 248, 251–52, 254

Beroaldo's commentary, Apuleius passages discussed in: *De mundo* 20, 228–29; *Met.* 1.1.1, 203–7; *Met.* 2.4.3–10, 225–29; *Met.* 4.35.4, 207; *Met.* 5.1.3, 234; *Met.* 5.10.6, 232n138; *Met.* 5.23.3, 233; *Met.* 6.5.4, 232n137; *Met.* 6.9.2, 232n137; *Met.* 6.9.4, 232n137; *Met.* 6.23.3, 232n138; *Met.* 6.24.4, 237–38; *Met.* 8.22, 224n104; *Met.* 8.29.2, 207–8; *Met.* 9.5–7, 224n104; *Met.* 9.7.5, 102n107; *Met.* 9.7.6, 103n110; *Met.* 9.24.2, 207; *Met.* 9.27.5, 104n116; *Met.* 10.23.28, 225n105; *Met.* 11.5.1, 209–10; *Met.* 11.6.3, 210; *Met.*11.11.1, 209; *Met.* 11.13.2, 219–20; *Met.* 11.13.3, 220–21; *Met.* 11.19.3, 211; *Met.* 11.23.7, 212; *Met.* 11. 24.1, 213n70; *Met.* 11.24.5, 212–13; *Met.*11.25.1–6, 210; *Met.*11.25.6, 211; *Met.*11.25.7, 212; *Met.* 11.28.4, 213; *Met.* 11.29.5, 213; *Met.* 11.30.1, 222–23; *Met.* 11.30.5, 214

Bessarion, Basil: Bussi a client of, 160; *Defensio Platonis* of, 158–59, 162, 298; and Florentine Platonists, 152; philosophical manuscripts of Apuleius owned by, 159n144

Boccaccio, Giovanni, 77, 120–121, 124, 129, 144, 297–98; allegory of Psyche in *Genealogie deorum gentilium*, 100, 111–18, 126; allegory of Psyche in *Teseida*, 100, 110–11; annotations in Florence, Biblioteca Laurenziana 29.2, 98–99, 110; annotations in Florence, Biblioteca Laurenziana 54.32, 109–10; early borrowings from Apuleius, 98–99; on homosexuality, 106–107; imitation of Apuleius in *Comedia delle ninfe fiorentine*, 100, 111; imitations in the *Decameron*, 100–107; lectures on Dante, 96, 106n123, 113n164, 116; at Monte Cassino, 93–98, 99; notes of copied by later scholars, 132, 139–41, 142–43; as scribe of Florence, Biblioteca Laurenziana 54.32, 108–9; *spurcum additamentum* in, 110; and Tacitus, 94–95. See also *Genealogie deorum gentilium*

Boiardo, Feltrino, as possible translator of the *Golden Ass*, 173n2, 175–76

Boiardo, Matteo Maria: *Apulegio volgare* of, 175–76, 275, 277, 298; *Orlando innamorato* of, 176–80; *Tarocchi* of, 180–84

Bracciolini, Poggio. *See* Poggio on Apuleius and Lucian

Brossano, Simone da, dispute about Apuleius with Stefano Colonna, 121–24

Bussi, Giovanni Andrea: Apuleius' style praised by, 168–69, 202–3; Bessarion and Cusanus praised by, 160–62; biography of, 160, 167–68; as an editor, 170–71; influence of on Sieder, 248–49; interpretation of *Golden Ass* by, 218; introduction to Apuleius by, 163–69, 298; on *Onos* of Pseudo-Lucian, 157, 165–66; Platonist agenda of, 160–64; on printing, 160n150, 171–72. *See also* Apuleius, *editio princeps* of; Brussels, Bibliothèque Royale Albert Ier 10054–10056 (in Index of Manuscripts)

Calcidius: in Florence, Biblioteca Laurenziana 84.24, 151; in Latin Platonic library, 146; quotation of by Boccaccio, 113n164;

cassoni paintings: Boccaccio's version of Psyche story in, 118; Medici wedding commemorated by, 119, 120; Psyche's parents in, 119–20, **plate 15**; Psyche's wedding in, 120, **plate 16**

Catullus, 4–5, 76, 77

La Celestina, references to *Golden Ass* in, 269

Château d'Écouen, stained glass windows in, 277, 278

Christ, iconography of, and Apuleius' contorniate portrait, 29

Christodorus, 14, 27–28
Class I manuscripts, 108, 171
Claudianus Mamertus: *Apology* imitated by, 60, 300–301
Claudius Maximus, 5, 11
Clodius Albinus, criticism of for reading Apuleius. See *Historia Augusta*
Colonna, Francesco, *Hypnerotomachia Polifili* of, and Apuleius, 173
Colonna, Stefano: allegorical ideas of, 122–23; dispute about Apuleius with Simone da Brossano, 121–24
contorniates, 43–45. See also Apollonius of Tyana; Apuleius
Coronne Ceres: as title of *Golden Ass* in Michel, 262, 264, 267. See also Isis
Correggio, Niccolò da. See *Fabula Psiches et Cupidinis* by Niccolò da Correggio
Cortegana, Diego López de, translation of *Golden Ass* by: designed for both humanist and vernacular audiences, 270, 272–3, 274; expurgated after 1559, 275; influence of, 274, 288; Latin verses in, 271–72; title page of, 270–71, 275, **276**. See also Beroaldo's commentary, influence of
Cosmographia as title of *De mundo*, 70n137, 72, 75
Coxie, Michael, paintings of Psyche of, 277, 278
Cromberger, Jacob, printer of Cortegana's translation, 269–70
Crown of Ceres. See *Coronne Ceres*
Cupid and Psyche, illustrations of: in Ernnst, 251, **plate 20**; in frescoes at Belriguardo described by Arienti, 188–92; on papyrus leaf, 20, 27; by Raphael in Villa Farnesina, 195–96, 277, 278; on Trier ceiling, 26–27, **plate 2**. See also Psyche, illustrations of
Cupid and Psyche, story of: in Apuleius and Correggio, 185–88; in Apuleius and Del Carretto, 193–95; in Apuleius and Fulgentius, 53–57; in Beccaria, 195; in Boccaccio, 113–18; as a comedy at Carnival in Constantinople, 195; in Martianus Capella, 53. See also Psyche, allegory of

Dante: on homosexuality, 106n123; on Monte Cassino, 96; on singleness of the soul, 116n182. See also Benvenuto da Imola; Boccaccio
De deo Socratis: citation of by Priscian, 60; discussion of in Florence, Biblioteca Nazionale, ms. II. VI. 2, 125; "preface" of, 47; quotation of by Manetti, 147; quotation of by Pseudo-Burley, 75; transcription of by Boccaccio, 99n89, 108; transcription of by Ficino, 148. See also Augustine
Del Carretto, Galeotto: author of *Noze de Psiche e Cupidine*, 185, 193; author of *Tempio d'Amore*, 195. See also Gonzaga, Isabella; *Noze de Psiche e Cupidine* by Del Carretto
della Casa, Tedaldo, and Florence Biblioteca Laurenziana Santa Croce 24 sin 11, 137
De monarchia attributed to Apuleius, 122–24
De mundo: in Augustine, 73–74; quoted by Beroaldo, 228–29; in Waleys, 73–74. See also *Cosmographia*
De Platone, citation of by Manetti, 147; quotation of by Pseudo-Burley, 75
de Tournes, Jean, printer of La Bouthière's translation, 280
Du Pré, Galliot, printer of Michel's translation, 262, 264
Dilecto. See Psyche's son Dilecto

Endelechius: motives for reading Apuleius, 49, 51, 52; as teacher of Sallustius, 46, 47
Endelichia, mother of Psyche: in Boccaccio, 113; confusion of with Entelechia, 53n60, 113n164; on Florentine cassone, 119, **plate 15**; in Martianus Capella, 53, 113
Erasmus, use of Apuleius by, 244n5
Ercole I d'Este: and the *Golden Ass*, 175, 180; hoarding of books by, 185, 188, 298–99. See also Belriguardo
Ernnst, Andreas, edition of Cupid and Psyche by, 250–51, **plate 20**. See also Beroaldo's commentary, influence of

Fabula Psiches et Cupidinis by Niccolò da Correggio: emphasis on Cupid in, 187–88; influence of *Apulegio volgare* on, 186; influence of on Arienti, 190–92; influence of on Del Carretto, 193. See also Gonzaga, Isabella

Ficino, Marsilio: influence of on Florence, Biblioteca Laurenziana 84.24, 151; and Latin Platonic library, 148; on Latin Platonists, 152; quotations of *Apology* and *Metamorphoses* in, 148–49; transcription of philosophical works by, 130n7, 148; translation of Plato quoted by Beroaldo, 227–28; as translator of Plato, 147

fiction in antiquity: estimation of, 41–43; in rhetorical schools, 51

Firenzuola, Agnolo: *Golden Ass* translated by, 275; La Bouthière influenced by, 280, 281; Louveau possibly influenced by, 286, 288

first person, effect of, 4–5, 17. See also image created by Apuleius

Florence: annotations in manuscripts of *Golden Ass* in, 131–45, 311–14; Apuleius' philosophical works in, 130–31, 146–52. See also Boccacco; cassoni paintings; Latin Platonic library; Poggio; Salutati; *spurcum additamentum*; verse prologue

Flores moralium auctoritatum, 71–72, 74. See also Guglielmo da Pastrengo

Florida: Apuleius' self-presentation in, 7–8, 10–11, 13; echoes of in Guaiferius, 63, 66; quotation of by Benzo of Alessandria, 68; quotation of in *Flores moralium auctoritatum*, 71; transmission of, 47

Francesco d'Antonio del Chierico, probable illuminator of Florence, Biblioteca Laurenziana 54.13, 150n112

Francia, Francesco, celebrated by Beroaldo, 225–26, 228, 229

Fulgentius: allegory of Cupid and Psyche in, 53, 57–59; allegory rejected by Beroaldo, 229–32; corrected by Boccaccio, 112–15, 118; influence of on Ernnst, 251, **plate 20**; narrative of Cupid and Psyche in, 54–57; and Pio, 231–32; works of Apuleius known to, 59, 61, 300–301

Genealogie deorum gentilium: autograph and vulgate versions of, 112; corrections of Fulgentius in, 112–15, 118; narrative in autograph and vulgate, 117–18; parents of Pysche in, 113; Psyche and her sisters in, 113–14, 116; reference to by Sozomeno, 142; the soul in, 113, 116. See also cassoni paintings

George of Trebizond: attack on Plato by, 158; reply of to Bessarion's *Defensio Platonis*, 162

Giulio Romano and frescoes of Cupid and Psyche at Palazzo Te, 196

Golden Ass (*Metamorphoses*): description of by Benzo of Alessandria, 67–69; description and imitation of by Guglielmo da Pastrengo, 81; description of by Pseudo-Burley, 70–71; description of by Waleys, 72–74; diffusion of in Europe, 243–44, 258, 261, 269, 275, 288; editions of, 157, 172, 197, 242, 258–61, 298; in Ferrara and Mantua, 173–95, 196, 298–99; interpretation of in Vatican Library, Vat. lat. 2194, 84–93, **plates 9–14**; introduction to by Bussi, 164–67, 168–69; quotation of by Ficino, 148–49; quotation of in *Flores moralium auctoritatum*, 71; references to in *La Celestina*, 269; survival of, 43, 49–51, 61, 62, 296, 297; as title in Augustine, 33, 297. See also Beroaldo, Filippo; *Golden Ass*, translations of

Golden Ass, translations of: by Adlington, 288–95, 315–17; by Cortegana, 269–75; by Feltrino Boiardo, 173n2, 175–76; by La Bouthière, 279–83, 285–86, 288, 290; by Louveau, 284–288, 290; by Matteo Maria Boiardo, 175–76, 275, 277, 298; by Michel, 262–68, 279, 280, 285; by Montlyard, 288; by Sieder, 248–49, 251–57

Gonzaga, Isabella: correspondence of with Del Carretto, 193; dedicatee of *Fabula Psiches et Cupidinis*, 185, 188, 192

Greek novels, 42. See fiction in antiquity

Guaiferius, echoes of *Florida* in, 63, 66, 74

Guglielmo da Pastrengo: on the *Golden Ass*, 81; as possible author of *Flores moralium auctoritatum*, 72, 81

Hierocles, 22–23

Historia Augusta, on Clodius Albinus and Apuleius, 20–21, 41; quoted by Beroaldo, 206n39

Hornken and Hittorp, publishers of *Golden Ass* (Paris, 1512), 258, 260–61

image of Apuleius in antiquity and Middle Ages, 21–38; as a magician, 22–25, 29, 36–38; as magician and philosopher in Augustine, 30–34; as a philosopher, 6n19, 25–29
image created by Apuleius, 5–20, 296; as a celebrity, 7; and Lucius, 17–20; as a magician, 14, 15–16, 17; as a philosopher, 6–9, 16–17. *See also* Apollo
Isis: in *Golden Ass*, 49–50; importance of in late antiquity, 49, 50–51; Mary as counterpart of in Beroaldo, 210–11; related to Ceres and Mary in Michel, 267–68

Jerome: on the *Apology*, 25; attack on Porphyry, 24–25; on fiction, 41, 42, 43; text of corrected by Beroaldo, 206
Julian the Chaldaean, 37–38

Keysere, Robert de, bookseller of *Golden Ass* (Paris, 1510), 258–59, 261. *See also* Beroaldo's commentary, influence of
Kierher, Johann, editor of *Golden Ass* (Paris, 1512), 258, 259–61. *See also* Beroaldo's commentary, influence of

La Bouthière, George de, translation of *Golden Ass* by: criticized by Louveau, 285–86; embellishment of Apuleius in, 280–82; ending of *Onos* used in, 283; Italian influence on, 279, 280; woodcuts by Bernard Salomon in, 279–80;
Lactantius: on Apuleius, 20n78, 22, 23–24; in Trier, 25
Latin Platonic Library: Apuleius in, 146, 298; contents of, 146; in *editio princeps*, 161; in Florence, Biblioteca Laurenziana 84.24, 151, **plate 18**. *See also* Salutati
liber Alcidi: in Florence, Biblioteca Laurenziana 84.24, 151; in Latin Platonic library, 146
literary group: manuscripts of, 129–30, 302–8, 311; in north Africa, 60. *See also* Sallustius
Louveau, Jean, translation of *Golden Ass* by: allegory in, 287; criticized by Montlyard, 288; designed for easy reference 284–85; La Bouthière criticized in 285–86; verse prologue in, 286, 288. *See also* Beroaldo's commentary, influence of
L(ucius) Apuleius Marcellus of Ostia, 2n5, 34n132
Lucius, allegory of: in Adlington, 288–91; in Beroaldo, 216–21; in Florence, Biblioteca Nazionale, ms. II. VI. 2, 124–28, 218–19; in Louveau, 287; in Michel, 266–68
Lucius, illustrations of: in Vatican Library, Vat. lat. 2194, 85–6, 90–92, **plates 10 and 14**. *See also* Ass
Lucius of Patrae. *See* Pseudo-Lucian.
Lucius as praenomen of Apuleius: in Adlington, 290; in Benzo, 69, 71, 74; in Beroaldo, 202, 210; in Boccaccio's manuscript, 109; in *Flores moralium auctoritatum*, 71, 74; in Hornken and Hittop, 260; in de Keysere, 259; in Louveau, 284n173; in Michel, 262; not in oldest manuscripts, 6n19, 34; in Petrarch's manuscript, 82; in Sieder, 252; supplied in Renaissance, 34; in Vatican Library, Ottob. lat. 2091, 69
Lucius as praenomen or nomen of Pseudo-Lucian, 156–57
Lupi, Mattia, manuscripts owned by: Florence, Biblioteca Laurenziana 36.23, 139; Laur. 51.9, 138; Laur. 54.24, 132, 138, 139n48

Macrobius: on Apuleius' *fabulae*, 41–42, 43; commentary on the *Somnium Scipionis* in Latin Platonic library, 146; quotation of by Benzo of Alessandria, 67, 68; quotation of by Salutati, 136
Maestro del 1346, probable illuminator of Vatican Library, Vat. lat. 2194, 83n35
Manetti, Giannozzo, 147
Mantovano, and adultery tale of Apuleius in *Il Formicone*, 177n20
manuscripts of Apuleius, 129–30, 243; 302–10; in Florence, 130–45, 311. *See also* under shelfmarks of individual manuscripts (in Index of Manuscripts)
manuscripts of Apuleius, owners of: Augustine, 35–36; Benvenuto da Imola, 96; Bessarion, 159n144; Boccaccio, 108–110; Bruzio Visconti, 82–85

Cosimo de' Medici, 132; Ficino, 130n7, 148; Lorenzo de' Medici, 151; Lupi, 132, 138, 139n48; Manetti, 147; Nicolas of Cusa, 160, 171; Petrarch, 78–79, 82; Piero de' Medici, 132, 150; Sallustius, 41, 43, 45–48; Salutati, 135; Schedel, 243n3; Sozomeno, 138, 141;

Marnef, Jeanne de: printer of *L'Amour de Cupido et de Psiche*, 277–78

Master of the Argonauts, 119. *See also* cassoni paintings

Master of the Die, Psyche engravings by: influence of, 277–79, 288; Italian and French poems added to, 277. *See also L'Amour de Cupido et de Psiche*; Château d'Écouen; Coxie, Michael

Martianus Capella: parents of Psyche in, 53, 113; works of Apuleius known to, 59, 300

the Medici and Apuleius: Cosimo as dedicatee of Poggio's *Onos*, 153–54; Cosimo as owner of Florence, Biblioteca Laurenziana 54.12, 132; Lorenzo as owner of Laur. 84.24, 151; Piero as owner of Laur. 54.12, 132; Piero as owner of Laur. 54.13, 150. *See also* cassoni painting

Metamorphoses. *See Golden Ass*

Michel, Guillaume, translation of *Golden Ass* by: allegory in, 266–68; changes to Apuleius' text in, 265–66; criticized by La Bouthière, 280; criticized by Louveau, 285; title page of, 262, **263**, **264**. *See also* Beroaldo's commentary, influence of

Michel de Tours. *See* Michel, Guillaume, translation of *Golden Ass* by

Milesian tales, criticism of: in *Historia Augusta* 20–21, 41, 43; by Jerome, 42.

Monte Cassino, 61–62; Boccaccio at, 93–99; Dante on, 96; descendant of Sallustius' manuscript in, 61, 297; Zanobi da Strada at, 65, 94. *See also* Florence, Biblioteca Laurenziana 68.2 (in Index of Manuscripts); *spurcum additamentum*

Montlyard, Jean de, translation of *Golden Ass* by, 288

Montmorency, Anne de, owner of Château d'Écouen, 277–78

Nicolas of Cusa: Bussi secretary of, 160; and Platonism, 152, 159; praise of in *editio princeps*, 160, 161–62. *See also* Brussels, Bibliothèque Royale Albert Ier 10054–10056 (in Index of Manuscripts)

Noze de Psiche e Cupidine by Del Carretto: as a drama, 193–95; influenced by *Apulegio volgare* and Correggio, 193

Onos. *See* Pseudo-Lucian's *Onos*

Orlando innamorato, adultery tale of Apuleius in, 176–80

pagan aristocracy: and contorniates, 43–45; manuscript correction by, 44, 48

pagan magic vs. Christian miracles: in Augustine, 30–32; in Jerome, 24–25; in Lactantius, 22–24

Papstesel, influence of: on illustration of the Ass in Cortegana, 275, **276**; on illustration of the Ass in Sieder, 253, **254, 255**, 256

Peri Hermeneias, Apuleius as a philosopher in, 6n19

Perotti, Niccolò, *Cornu copiae* of, 174

Petrarch, Francesco, 77, 124; Apuleius manuscript of, 78–79, 82, 297; echoes and imitations of Apuleius in, 78–81. *See also* Vatican Library, Vat. lat. 2193 (in Index of Manuscripts)

Philip the philosopher. *See* allegory

philosophical group: *fortuna* of, 40–41, 62, 129–31, 146; oldest manuscripts of, 6n19, 36, 160; other manuscripts of, 129n2, 130, 130nn2, 6, and 7,133n15, 147n94; 159n144. *See also* Latin Platonic library

Photis: kiss of, in Florence, Biblioteca Nazionale, ms. II. VI. 2, 127; as the temptation of the devil in Michel, 266

physiognomy, 14; in *Apology*, 8–10; in *Florida* 3, 10–11

Pio, Giambattista: Dresden, Sächsische Landesbibliothek Dc 178, used by, 201n19; and Fulgentius, 231, 232;

Platonic philosophy, Latin works on. *See* Latin Platonic library

Poggio on Apuleius and Lucian, 152–56. *See also* Pseudo-Lucian's *Onos*

Porphyry, *Against the Christians*, 23, 24–25

printed editions: designed to appeal to readers, 245, 247, 256–57, 258–60, 264–65, 270–71; 280–82, 284–85, 288–89, 295; illustrations in, **246**, 251, 253, **254**, **255**, 256, **263**, 264, 264n83, 275, **276**, 277–78, 279–80, 284, 288n189

printers and booksellers: Cromberger, 269–70; de Tournes, 280; Du Pré, 262, 264; Hohenwang, 245–47; Hornken and Hittorp, 258, 260–61, 264; de Keysere, 258–59, 261; de Marnef, 277–78; Sweynheym and Pannartz, 158, 159, 160, 243; Temporal, 284; Weissenhorn, 251, 253, 256–57; Wykes, 288

Priscian, *De deo Socratis*, cited by, 60, 300–301

Psellos, Michael, 38

Pseudo-Burley, 69–71, 74–75, 129

Pseudo-Lucian's *Onos*: and Apuleius, 18; and Beroaldo, 219; confusion of with *Golden Ass*, 156–57, 247, **plate 19**; Poggio's translation of, 153–55, 155n133; and printing of Poggio's translation in Germany, 244–45, **246**, 247–48. *See also* amorous matron; Wyle, Niklas von

Pseudo-Theodorus, 37

Psyche, allegory of: in Boccaccio's *Genealogie deorum gentilium*, 111–18, 184; in Boccaccio's *Teseida*, 100, 110–11; in Boiardo's *Tarocchi*, 180–81, 184; on Florentine cassoni, 118–20; in Fulgentius, 57–59, 114–15, 184; in Martianus Capella, 53; rejection of by Beroaldo, 229–32; in Sala di Psiche at Belriguardo, 191–92; by Viti, 183–84

Psyche and her sisters: in Boccaccio's *Genealogie* (autograph), 113–115; in Boccaccio's *Genealogie* (vulgate), 116; in Del Carretto, 194–95; in Ernnst, 251, **plate 20**; in Fulgentius, 57, 251

Psyche, illustrations of: in cassoni paintings, 118–20, **plates 15 and 16**; in Château d'Écouen, 277, 278; by Coxie, 277, 278; description of in *Tarocchi*, 181–83; in La Bouthière's translation, 279–80; in Louveau's translation, 284; by Master of the Die, 277, 278; in

Vatican Library, Vat. lat. 2194, 86–89, **plates 11 and 12**. *See also* L'*Amour de Cupido et de Psiche*

Psyche, parents of: in Apuleius, 53; in Boccaccio, 113; in Del Carretto, 194; on Florentine cassone, 119, **plate 15**; in Fulgentius, 57; in Martianus Capella, 53, 113

Psyche's son Dilecto, substituted for Voluptas by Boiardo and Correggio, 192n81

Pudentilla, 2, 125

Raphael and frescoes of Cupid and Psyche at Villa Farnesina, 195–96, 277, 278

rhetorical schools: and manuscript correction, 48–49; novels used in, 51

Roberti, Ercole de', artist of Psyche frescoes at Belriguardo, 189, 191, 193

Robertus Caesaris Gandavus. *See* Keysere, Robert de

rose cure: in Beroaldo, 216, 217, 219–20; in Michel, 267; in Sieder, 253

Rossi, Mino de', praised by Beroaldo, 229, 233–36

Sallustius: archetype of *Apology*, *Metamorphoses* (and *Florida*?) owned by, 41, 43, 60, 61, 296; motives for reading *Golden Ass*, 49–52; as student in rhetorical school, 45–46; subscriptions written by, 45–48. *See also* Endelechius

Salutati, Coluccio: on allegory, 126; annotations and verse prologue in British Library, Harley 4838, 132, 135–36, 311–13; as owner of philosophical manuscripts of Apuleius, 133n15, 146–47; quotations of *De Platone* and *Metamorphoses* by, 147n95; and study of Greek, 146. *See also* verse prologue

Schedel, Hartmann, 243–44

Second Sophistic, 2–5

Self-presentation, of sophists, 3–5. *See also* Beroaldo, Filippo; image created by Apuleius

Sicinius Aemilianus, 9–10, 125

Sidonius Apollinaris: 300; Apuleius mentioned by, 59–60

Sieder, Johann, translation of *Golden Ass* by: appeal to readers in printed edition of, 256–57; Lutheranism in printed edition of, 252–53, **254**, 256; Platonism in manuscript of, 248–49; reaction to by Ernnst, 250–51; title page in printed edition of, 252–53, **254**, **255**, 256–57; two versions of, 248; woodcuts in, 251–52. *See also* Beroaldo's commentary, influence of; Pabstesel, influence of

Simon, Erika, program of Trier ceiling interpreted by, 26–27

Sozomeno: annotations of in British Library, Harley 4838, 132, 136–37, 139, 142–44; annotation system of, 141; cross references of to Pistoia, Biblioteca Comunale Forteguerriana A.46, 142, 144

spurcum additamentum: and Boccaccio, 65, 110; date of, 64–65; in Florence, Biblioteca Laurenziana 29.2, 64; *fortuna* of, 134–35, 139–40, 145; as an imitation of Apuleius, 65–66; and Zanobi da Strada, 65, 99, 134

statues of Apuleius: in Carthage, 13; in Constantinople 14, 25, 27–28; in Madauros, 6n19, 13; in Oea, 13, 31

subscriptions in manuscripts: in *Apology* and *Metamorphoses*, 45–47; in other texts, 48–49

Sweynheym and Pannartz: Bessarion's *Defensio Platonis* printed by, 159; Bussi as editor for, 160; *editio princeps* of Apuleius printed by, 158, 243, 298

Tarocchi, story of Psyche in, 180–83, 184. *See also* Viti, Pier Antonio

Temporal, Jean, printer of Louveau's translation, 284

Trier, painted ceiling in, and images of Apuleius and Cupid and Psyche, 25–27, **plates 1–3**

Váradi, Péter: as dedicatee of Beroaldo's commentary, 199, 201, 214, 239–40; praised as ideal priest, 214–16, 221,

verse prologue: in Adlington, 288, 291–92; in Beroaldo, 205; in Firenzuola, 286, 288; in Florentine manuscripts, 135–38, 144–45; in Louveau, 286, 288; in printed editions, 145, 286n182; in St. Gallen, Kantonsbibliothek, Ms. 483, 145; textual variants in, 313–14. *See also* Salutati

Visconti, Bruzio, dedicatee of Vatican Library, Vat. lat. 2194, 82–85, **plate 9**

Viti, Pier Antonio: allegory of Psyche by, 183–84; Boiardo's *Tarocchi* described by, 181–83, 190

Waleys, Thomas, 72–74, 75, 76, 129

Weissenhorn, Alexander, printer of Sieder's translation, 251, 253, 256–57

Wykes, Henry, printer of Adlington's translation, 288

Wyle, Niklas von: influence of on Sieder, 249; as translator of Pseudo-Lucian's *Onos*, 245, 247

Zanobi da Strada, 77, 129; annotations in manuscripts from Monte Cassino, 65, 94, 99, 132; role in bringing Florence, Biblioteca Laurenziana 29.2 to Florence, 99; role in bringing Laur. 68.2 to Florence, 94; and the *spurcum additamentum*, 65, 99, 134

Zomino da Pistoia. *See* Sozomeno